TRUE CRIME

TRUE CRIME

An American Anthology

Edited by Harold Schechter

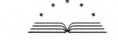

A Special Publication of
The Library of America

Some of the material in this volume is reprinted with the
permission of holders of copyright and publication rights.
Acknowledgments are on page 775 .

Cover images courtesy of Fototeka Gallery for the Los Angeles
Police Department. Copyright © City of Los Angeles.

Distributed to the trade by Penguin Putnam Inc. and in
Canada by Penguin Books Canada Ltd.

Designed by Francesca Belanger.

Library of Congress Control Number: 2008927624

ISBN 978-1-59853-031-5
First Printing

Printed in the United States of America

Contents

Introduction

In the ninth book of *The Republic*, Plato famously observed that "the virtuous man is content to dream what a wicked man really does." Elaborating on Plato, Sigmund Freud argued that violent lawbreakers make it possible for the rest of us to adapt to the demands of normality by acting out, and being punished for, our own unacknowledged impulses. In the view of the French sociologist Emile Durkheim, the criminal contributes to civic well-being not only by promoting a sense of solidarity among law-abiding citizens, united in condemnation of the malefactor, but by providing a cathartic outlet for their primal vengeful impulses.

Such theories imply that criminals can fulfill their social function only if the rest of the world knows exactly what outrages they have committed and how they have been punished. That might be one way of accounting for the genre of writing collected in this book—writing that caters to the public's need to hear the whole disturbing story. The question of how much that need is rooted in a moral imperative rather than the lure of the forbidden has often shadowed accounts of crime.

There is nothing new about this particular craving. That the strangulation of a six-year-old who competed in child pageants, or the disappearance of a vacationing co-ed, or the slaying of a pregnant California housewife can preoccupy the American news media for weeks on end—supplanting events of more obvious global significance—is often taken as a dispiriting sign of the debased sensibilities of our sensation-steeped culture. Yet the appetite for tales of real-life murder, the more horrific the better, has been a perennial feature of human society.

Long before the advent of movable type, accounts of shocking crimes were disseminated orally through Europe in the form of crime ballads, versified narratives of actual stabbings, stranglings, bludgeonings, and dismemberments. Gutenberg's invention then became a means to profit from the appetite for such narratives. Any particularly notorious killing was likely to be written up in doggerel or prose and printed on broadsheets or in cheaply made pamphlets to be sold by itinerant peddlers. Conveyed in the same tone of breathless wonderment used to report other marvelous occurrences, from the births of two-headed babies to the sightings of sea-serpents, these early crime narratives were, for the most part, crude productions, short on artistic sensibility but full of shocking detail and moralistic fervor.

America was from the beginning fertile ground for true narratives of crime. The first popular form such accounts took was the Puritan execution sermon, a genre with roots in the Old World that flourished so extraordinarily here that it can fairly be claimed as indigenous. Typically delivered right before the hanging, the execution sermon was similar in both structure and intent to other Puritan discourse; the crime itself was merely an "awful occasion" for the preaching of Calvinist doctrine. Following its initial recitation, either at church or on the scaffold itself, such sermons might be printed and sold as pamphlets and sometimes later collected in book form. A number of these, like Cotton Mather's *Pillars of Salt*, became early American best sellers.

Mirroring cultural shifts in the country at large, American true-crime writing in the early republic became increasingly commercialized and divorced from its religious origins. By the 1830s the marketplace was flooded with purely exploitive accounts of real-life horrors. A favorite subject, then as now, was lust-murder, often described in such explicit detail that, according to one contemporary critic, young men could learn more about female anatomy from these tawdry publications than from medical textbooks. Cheap crime pamphlets, trial reports, and the lurid accounts in the "penny press" were the main sources of true-crime thrills in Jacksonian America, along with such widely distributed compendiums as *The Record of Crimes in the United States* (1834).

Some of these early accounts detailed the misspent lives of pirates and frontier desperadoes, but their main focus was on the kinds of homicides that have always formed the central subject matter of the true-crime genre in its most typical form, and that in consequence make up the bulk of the present collection. The pieces collected here, with a few exceptions, do not deal with the sorts of killings committed by men for whom murder is part of a criminal way of life: bandits, hired assassins, gangsters. (The extensive literatures of outlawry and organized crime deserve volumes of their own.) The focus of this volume is on those peculiarly horrific and unsettling crimes that have from the beginning haunted the American imagination: crimes that have, in the words of pioneering newspaperman James Gordon Bennett, "some of the sublime of horror" about them, those "frightful," "horrid," "extraordinary" and "unheard-of" (to use the favorite adjectives of 19th-century sensation-mongers) acts of violence that can erupt in otherwise ordinary lives.

As the founder of America's first unabashedly sensationalistic newspaper, the New York *Herald*, Bennett was a seminal figure in the history of true-crime journalism. While earlier newspaper publishers, including Benjamin Franklin, recognized the popular appeal of grisly murder stories and offered readers the occasional account of a particularly hideous slaying, no one before Bennett was so attuned to the public's interest in tales of crime and violence. American readers, he declared, "were more ready to seek six columns of the details of a brutal murder . . . than the same amount of words poured forth by the genius of the noblest author of our times." Bennett was happy to give the public what it wanted, providing extensive and extremely graphic coverage of the most shocking crimes of the day, most famously the 1836 hatchet murder of the prostitute Helen Jewett.

Such was the success of Bennett's formula that by the 1850s Ralph Waldo Emerson was complaining in his journal that his countrymen spent their time "reading all day murders & railroad accidents." Among the most devout of these readers was Emerson's Concord neighbor Nathaniel Hawthorne. A self-confessed lover of "all sorts of good and good-for-nothing books," Hawthorne was an avid reader of murder pamphlets and trial reports throughout his life. His craving for such fare was so intense that while serving as the American consul in Liverpool he had a friend ship him the penny papers so that he could keep up with the grisly goings-on back home.

Herman Melville was likewise fascinated with accounts of real-life murders, particularly the atrocities of the Harpes, two murderous cousins who terrorized the Tennessee and Kentucky frontier during a killing spree in 1798–99. The Harpes' bloody exploits are invoked in the opening scene of *The Confidence-Man,* in which Melville describes a waterfront peddler hawking "the lives of Meason, the bandit of Ohio, Murrel, the pirate of the Mississippi, and the brothers Harpe, the Thugs of the Green River country, in Kentucky." The 1841 ax-murder of New York City printer Samuel Adams by John C. Colt (brother of the gun-maker) also made a lasting impression on Melville, who 12 years later in "Bartleby the Scrivener" accentuated the grim impersonality of the urban office by recalling that it was in "a solitary office . . . entirely unhallowed by humanizing domestic associations" that "the hapless Colt" had been driven to kill "the unfortunate Adams."

Neither Hawthorne nor Melville, however, published any true-crime writing. Hawthorne's interest in the subject is clear in a fascinating journal entry about a visit to a "Hall of Wax Statuary" included in this volume, while Melville limited his comments on true crime to a journal entry from November 1849 in which he describes how, on his first trip to London, he paid half a shilling to watch the hanging of the married murderers George and Marie Manning: "The mob was brutish. All in all, a most wonderful, horrible, & unspeakable scene." Nor, strictly speaking, did a writer even more obsessed with themes of murder, madness, and irresistible impulse, their contemporary Edgar Allan Poe. Like Melville, Poe was gripped by the Colt-Adams affair and used its most ghoulish feature—the victim's salted corpse smuggled aboard a clipper in a packing crate—as the basis for his story "The Oblong Box." Plot elements of his unfinished verse drama *Politian* are drawn from the so-called "Kentucky Tragedy" of 1825 in which a young lawyer named Jereboam Beauchamp, at the behest of his wife, killed her former lover, Colonel Solomon P. Sharp. Some scholars are also inclined to believe that Poe's pioneering mystery story "The Murders in the Rue Morgue" was at least partly inspired by a bizarre report in 1834 about an orangutan trained to burglarize apartments. In all these works, however, Poe gives free rein to his imagination, using real-life incidents as springboards into the fantastic. The closest Poe came to true-crime writing was in his detective story "The Mystery of Marie Roget," which, although presented as fiction, was in fact closely based on the 1841 slaying of the beautiful New York cigar-store salesgirl Mary Rogers, with the names changed and the setting switched to Paris.

The list of important American writers who have created fictional narratives from the stuff of actual crimes is a long one, going back to Charles Brockden Brown, the originator of American Gothic fiction, whose 1798 novel *Wieland* was modeled on a notorious case of "family annihilation" (described in this book on pages 39–44). Later examples include Frank Norris's *McTeague*, with its echoes of the case of Patrick Collins, an unemployed San Francisco ironworker who stabbed his wife to death in 1893 after she refused him money; Richard Wright's *Native Son*, which draws on the trial of Robert Nixon, an 18-year-old African-American accused of fatally assaulting a white woman with a brick during a burglary; John O'Hara's best-selling *BUtterfield 8*, suggested by the death of Starr Faithfull, a young woman whose corpse washed up on a Long Island beach in 1931; and, more recently, Joyce Carol Oates's 1995 horror novel *Zombie*, whose lobotomy-obsessed protagonist was modeled on the cannibalistic serial killer Jeffrey Dahmer. All these works, as well as Theodore Dreiser's *An American Tragedy*, based on the Chester Gillette–Grace Brown case of 1906, take major imaginative departures from the historical truth of the events that inspired them.

A milestone in American true-crime writing appeared 25 years after Poe's death, when *Atlantic Monthly* published "A Memorable Murder" by the New England writer Celia Thaxter. Like Abraham Lincoln's newspaper account of the Trailor murder mystery, Thaxter's piece was an anomaly in her career—her only foray into the realm of crime writing. It stands, however, as groundbreaking work in the genre: an explicitly nonfiction work that relies on the conventions of sentimental storytelling to build suspense and generate both horror and pathos. In her skillful manipulation of plot construction, point of view, dialogue, and other narrative devices, Thaxter foreshadows the dramatic techniques that would come to characterize the crime writings of Truman Capote and his fellow "New Journalists" a century later.

American readers were inundated with crime stories during the heyday of yellow journalism when, as A. J. Liebling recounts in his piece on a turn-of-the-century dismemberment-murder, newspapermen not only reported on crimes but conducted their own independent investigations. Though certain murder trials had generated enormous excitement since at least the time of the Jewett case, William Randolph Hearst and Joseph Pulitzer found new ways of transforming somber life-and-death proceedings into thrilling public spectacles. For example, in 1899 a dapper young New Yorker named Roland Molineux was accused of sending cyanide-laced patent medicine to two fellow members of his exclusive Manhattan athletic club. Immediately dubbed "The Great Poison Mystery" by the yellow press, the Molineux affair became the first great media circus of the 1900s, a precursor of all the other wildly ballyhooed "Trials of the Century" to follow, from that of Nathan Leopold and Richard Loeb to the O. J. Simpson extravaganza. Among the various techniques employed by Hearst to whip the public into a frenzy over Molineux's trial was the enlisting of well-known writers to cover the story, among them Nathaniel Hawthorne's son, Julian, at that time a highly successful author who had inherited his father's fascination with horror, the supernatural, and crime. In replacing the usual anonymous reporters with journalistic headliners, Hearst—along with his nemesis, Pulitzer, who assigned his own heavy-hitters to the story—planted a seed that would come to full flower during the 1920s and 30s, when celebrity authors such as Damon Runyon, Theodore Dreiser, and Edna Ferber covered high-profile stories like the Hall-Mills double murder, the Robert Edwards "American Tragedy" case, and the trial of Bruno Richard Hauptmann for the Lindbergh baby kidnapping.

Other famous writers of the interwar era, among them James Thurber and Alexander Woollcott, found an outlet for their own fascination with murder in the pages of *The New Yorker*, which began its recurrent and still-active "Annals of Crime" feature during this period. At the same time, a host of other, far less prestigious magazines were devoting themselves exclusively to the subject. The progenitor of this pulp genre, which first appeared on the newsstands in 1924, was Bernarr Macfadden's *True Detective*, whose immediate success spawned a host of even more disreputable imitators such as *Shocking Detective*, *Underworld Detective*, *Confidential Detective*, and about six dozen similar titles. Pounded out by underpaid hacks, the stories in these fact-based crime monthlies were almost always formulaic and forgettable, although, on rare occasions, pieces by writers such as Dashiell Hammett and Jim Thompson would appear in their pages.

To judge from the evidence of his novels, one of Hammett's own favorite true-crime publications was Thomas S. Duke's 1910 *Celebrated Criminal Cases of America*, which is referred to in both *The Thin Man* and *The Maltese Falcon*. Duke, a former captain of the San Francisco Police Department, was one of a long line of American law officers who produced true-crime volumes. Most, such as George S. McWatters's *Knots Untied: The Ways and By-Ways of American Detectives* (1871) and Frank Geyer's *The Holmes-Pietzel Case* (1896), were accounts of their own reallife exploits; by contrast, Duke's influential book was a compilation of criminal case histories, covering a wide range of offenders from the Colorado cannibal Alfred Packer to the Victorian serial killers Theo Durrant and H. H. Holmes.

Among true-crime aficionados—"murder fanciers," as he himself called them—the acknowledged American master of the genre in the early 20th century was Edmund Lester Pearson. Our country's answer to the revered Scottish crime historian William Roughead (who numbered Joseph Conrad and Henry James among his admirers), the Harvard-educated Pearson was a professional librarian who wrote widely on various bibliophilic subjects before devoting the last dozen years of his life to the field of true crime. His stylish, often dryly humorous examinations of historical homicides—both celebrated (the Lizzie Borden case was a particular obsession of his) and obscure (the 1897 murder-dismemberment of Willie Guldensuppe, later the subject of an article by A. J. Liebling included in this volume)—appeared in *Vanity Fair*, *Scribner's*, *Liberty*, and *The New Yorker*, and were collected in a half-dozen books, beginning with his 1924 classic *Studies in Murder*.

From Pearson's day to the 1960s, however, even the best American true-crime writers—such as Miriam Allen deFord and William Tibbetts Brannon—were, for the most part, known only to devoted fans of the genre. Despite the genuine literary gifts of authors like Pearson and his contemporary Herbert Asbury, there was still a distinctly disreputable air clinging to the form. The book-length studies published by the Gold Medal imprint of Fawcett from 1951 to 1957 are a case in point. These first-rate accounts of classic American homicides, including Harry Thaw's shooting of Stanford White, the Hall-Mills affair, and the Ruth Snyder–Judd Gray "Double Indemnity" case, were issued as cheap paperbacks whose garish covers and equally suggestive titles (*The Girl in the Red Velvet Swing*, *The Girl in Lover's Lane*, *The Girl in the Death Cell*) belied their adept, carefully researched contents. Even the crime essays of a writer as accomplished as John Bartlow Martin, an admired journalist who served as speechwriter to President Kennedy and as U.S. Ambassador to the Dominican Republic, were quickly consigned to a format that made his *Butcher's Dozen and Other Murders* indistinguishable from any other exercise in sensationalism sold at bus stations and corner drugstores.

All that changed in 1966, with the publication of *In Cold Blood*. Truman Capote's claim that his book represented a radically new literary genre, the "nonfiction novel," was widely dismissed from the moment he made it, with critics quickly pointing to Meyer Levin's 1956 best seller *Compulsion*. Constrained by legal considerations, Levin—who described his book as a "documentary novel"—altered the historical facts of the Leopold-Loeb "thrill killing" only to the extent of changing the names of the principals. (The book was so faithful to the actual facts that Leopold eventually sued the author for violating his "rights of privacy.") But while Capote's blockbuster might not have brought about a revolution in literary form, it had an enormous impact on the marketplace. True crime was instantly elevated to a major publishing category and endowed with a legitimacy it had never previously enjoyed.

To be sure, bookstores are still flooded with instant books about lurid cases whose lineage can be traced back through the anonymous pulp of *True Detective* magazine to the pamphlets and broadsides of pre-industrial times. At the same time, however, serious book-length studies of particular crimes, written by major authors and published by prestigious houses, became a staple of the best-seller lists. Works such as Norman Mailer's *The Executioner's Song*, Joseph Wambaugh's *The Onion Field*, and Joe McGinnis's *Fatal Vision* not only appealed to broad mainstream audiences but garnered often dazzling reviews, even as they fueled an increasingly heated controversy over the blurring of fact and fiction. (Because of the decision to focus on self-contained pieces in this collection, none of these lengthy books is excerpted in the present volume.)

The present volume seeks to reveal both continuities and transformations in the ways in which Americans have written about crime. The most important continuity is criminal behavior itself. The forms of transgression described in this book can arise in any place or time, their details modified only by newer weaponry or other technological changes. What differs strikingly from era to era, however, is the way such transgressions are interpreted. Acts otherwise analogous have been seen at different times as arising from sin, or irrational thinking, or mental disease, or inarticulate protest against abuse or oppression. Where a Puritan saw the mysterious workings of divine providence, a writer at the end of the 20th century might discern evidence of an absurd and random universe. The hardboiled cynicism evident in the journalism of the Roaring '20s gave way in time to a psychologically informed approach more inclined to view the criminal as a helpless victim of his own impulses. What remains the same is the sense that the most flagrant and disturbing crimes elicit from society a compulsion to find some meaning in acts that often seem meaningless. The human community, finding itself under assault from within, searches desperately for a framework or context to explain the apparently unexplainable.

For some, the true-crime genre will always retain a disreputable aura. In an essay on *In Cold Blood*, the critic Renata Adler deplored both the original book and the 1968 film adaptation for playing to the bloodlust of the audience by using "every technique of cheap fiction" to intensify the emotional impact of the killings. It is all too easy simply to turn in disgust from any close examination of the worst human acts, and to brand anyone who does not choose to look away as a voyeur or worse. On some fundamental level it is undoubtedly true that true-crime writing appeals to what William James called the "aboriginal capacity for murderous excitement," a capacity that persists even among the most decent and law-abiding citizens. The worst specimens of the genre may not rise above a quasi-pornographic level.

But blanket dismissal oversimplifies a complex question. People read about true crime for many reasons and on many levels. Some readers identify with the victims and are moved to pity and terror by their plight; some identify with those who pursue the criminal, and are either reassured by the criminal's capture and punishment and the restoration of order, or (when such a resolution is not forthcoming) are forced to confront the limits of human power in the face of unleashed malevolence. Such unsolved crimes generate the eeriest spell of all, as evidenced by the enduring public fascination with Jack the Ripper. It would be naïve to deny that an identification with the evildoer, however covert or repressed, can also be a powerful factor in the genre's hold, although deep curiosity about those who commit evil is hardly synonymous with identification. Beyond all else, true-crime writing acknowledges the disturbing persistence of the most frightening and destructive capacities of the species. Sometimes that acknowledgment results in art of a high order; sometimes merely in news reporting we find impossible to ignore. We attend to what it tells us as we would to an account of a natural disaster or a freakish anomaly—except that the disaster, the anomaly, is all too human.

—*Harold Schechter*

TRUE CRIME

WILLIAM BRADFORD

"The founders of a new colony," Nathaniel Hawthorne observes in the first chapter of *The Scarlet Letter*, "whatever Utopia of human virtue and happiness they might originally project, have invariably recognized it among their earliest practical necessities to allot a portion of the virgin soil as a cemetery, and another portion as the site of a prison." This disparity between hope and reality was confirmed by the experiences of the *Mayflower* Pilgrims who, ten years after arriving at the Promised Land of New England, found it necessary to execute one of their original members for murder.

John Billington came over on the Mayflower not as a Puritan Separatist but as a fugitive from his London creditors. Though a signatory of the Mayflower Compact—and thus a part of the hallowed band known as the Pilgrim Fathers—he was regarded by fellow-passengers as a mutinous "miscreant" and "one of the profanest men among us." A year after the landing at Plymouth, he was condemned "to have his neck and heels tied together" for making "opprobrious speeches" against Captain Miles Standish—a punishment he managed to avoid by offering an abject apology. Five years later, in a letter to Deacon Robert Cushman in England, Governor William Bradford (1590–1657) had this to say about him: "Billington still rails against you and threatens to arrest you, I know not wherefore; he is a knave, and so will live and die." The assessment proved prophetic when, in September 1630, Billington fatally shot fellow colonist John Newcomen with a fowling piece after quarreling with him over some trivial matter. The case has come down to us through this brief entry in Bradford's monumental *History of Plymouth Plantation*, completed in 1651.

The Hanging of John Billington

This year John Billinton the elder (one that came over with the first) was arrained, and both by grand & petie jurie found guilty of willfull murder, by plaine & notorious evidence. And was for the

1

same accordingly executed. This, as it was the first execution amongst them, so was it a mater of great sadnes unto them. They used all due means about his triall, and tooke the advice of Mr. Winthrop and other the ablest gentle-men in the Bay of Massachusets, that were then new-ly come over, who concured with them that he ought to dye, and the land to be purged from blood. He and some of his had been often punished for miscariags before, being one of the profanest families amongst them. They came from London, and I know not by what freinds shufled into their company. His facte was, that he way-laid a yong-man, one John New-comin, (about a former quarell,) and shote him with a gune, wherof he dyed.

History of Plymouth Plantation, 1651

COTTON MATHER

Unfairly or not, Cotton Mather (1663–1728) has come to epitomize many of the least attractive traits of the colonial Puritan, from excessive self-righteousness to persecutive zeal. Possessed of energies that in a less sanctified soul might be termed demonic, he published as many as 17 books and pamphlets a year—an estimated 4,444 bound volumes all told—while turning out five sermons a week, conducting countless fasts, devoting himself to causes ranging from penal reform to the education of slaves, and raising 15 children by three wives. Of his prodigious output, a few works have earned him an enduring place in our literary history: his magnum opus, *Magnalia Christi Americana; or The Ecclesiastical History of New-England* (1702); *Bonifacius, an Essay Upon the Good* (1710), his most popular work and a particular favorite of Benjamin Franklin's; *Wonders of the Invisible World* (1693), his disquisition on witchcraft; and *Pillars of Salt* (1699), his "History of some Criminals Executed in this Land, for Capital Crimes," presented here in its entirety.

A popular genre in colonial Massachusetts, the Puritan execution sermon—preached on the occasion of a public hanging, then quickly printed up in pamphlet form and sold for a few pence—was the earliest form of American true-crime literature. Cotton Mather's first published sermon, which appeared in 1686, concerned the crime and punishment of James Morgan, a reprobate who, in a drunken rage, impaled a man with an iron spit. Thirteen years later, following the execution of a Boston woman named Sarah Threeneedles for killing her baby, Mather issued *Pillars of Salt*. This compilation of a dozen accounts (half of which, including the case of Morgan, had been previously published) stands as a landmark work, a Puritan precursor of the true-crime miscellanies that, stripped of all religious intent, would become a staple of the genre in subsequent centuries.

Pillars of Salt

It hath been Thought, that the *Dying Speeches* of such as have been Executed among us, might be of singular Use, to Correct and Reform, the *Crimes*, wherein too many do *Live*; and it has been wish'd, that at Least, some Fragments of those *Dying Speeches*, might be preserved and published. Upon this Advice, from some *Good Persons*, I have Stollen an Hour or Two, wherein I have Collected some Accounts, of several *Ill Persons*, which have been Cut off, by the Sword of *Civil Justice* in this Land: and this Collection, I suffer to go abroad, in Hopes, that among many other *Essayes* to Suppress *growing Vice*, it may signifie something, with the Blessing of Heaven thereupon, to let the *Vicious* understand, what have been the Cries of our Miserables, when passing into another World. Behold, an *History of Criminals*, whom the Terrible Judgments of God have *Thunder struck*, into Pillars of Salt.

I

About the Year, 1646, here was one *Mary Martin*, whose Father going from hence to *England*, Left her in the House of a Married Man, who yet became so Enamoured on *her*, that he attempted her Chastity.

Such was her Weakness and Folly, that she yielded unto the Temptations of that miserable man; but yet with such horrible Regret of Mind, that begging of God, for Deliverance from her Temptations, her plea was, *That if ever she were Overtaken again, she would Leave herself unto His Justice, to be made a publick Example.*

Heaven will convince the Sinful Children of men, that the *Vowes*, which they make, Relying on the Stability and Resolution of their own Hearts, are of no Significancy. A *Chain* of *Hell* was upon her, and the forfeited *Grace* of *Heaven* was witheld from her; She fell a *Third Time*, into the Sin, against which her *Vowes* had been uttered.

Afterwards, going to Service in *Boston*, she found her self to have Conceived: But she Lived with a favourable Mistress, who would admit and allow no suspicion of her *Dishonesty*.

A Question, Like that Convincing One, of our Saviours unto the Woman of *Samaria*, was once oddly put unto her; Mary, *Where is thy Husband?* And One said also; *Did I not think, thou wer't an honest and sincere Creature, I should verily think, thou wer't with Child!* These passages, which were warnings from God, unto her guilty Soul, did serve only to strike her with *Amazement*, not with any true *Repentance*.

She concealed her Crime, till the Time of her Delivery; and then, being Delivered alone, by her self in a Dark Room, She Murdered the harmless and helpless *Infant*; hiding it in a Chest, from the Eyes of all, but the Jealous GOD.

The *Blood* of the Child Cried, when the Cry of the Child it self were thus cruelly stifled. Some circumstance quickly occurr'd, which obliged her Friends to charge her with an *Unlawful Birth*. She Denied it Impudently. A further Search confuted her Denial. She then said; *The Child was Dead Born, and she had Burnt it to Ashes*. With an Hypocritical Tear, she added, *Oh! that it were True, that the poor Babe were any where to be seen!* At Last it was found in her Chest; & when she Touch'd the *Face* of it before the Jury, the *Blood* came fresh into it. So She confessed the whole Truth concerning it.

Great Endeavours were used, That she might be brought unto a True Faith in the *Blood* of the Lord Jesus Christ, for the pardon of her *Blood guiltiness*; and it may be, none Endeavoured it more, than that Reverend man, Old Mr. *Wilson*, who Wrote several Sheets of pathetical Instructions to her, while She was in Prison. That Renowned Man, Old Mr. *Cotton* also, did his part in endeavouring that she might be Renewed by Repentance; and Preached a Sermon, on Ezek, 16. 20, 21. *Is this of thy Whoredoms a small matter, That thou hast Slain my Children?* Whereof great Notice was taken. It was hoped, that these Endeavours were not Lost: Her Carriage in her Imprisonment, and at her Execution, was very *Penitent*. But there was this Remarkable at her Execution: She acknowledged, her *Twice* Essaying to Kill her Child, before she could make an End of it; and now, through the Unskilfulness of the Executioner, she was turned off the Ladder *Twice*, before She Dyed.

II

There was a miserable man, at *Weymouth*; who fell into very ungodly practices: but would particularly Signalize his ungodliness, by flouting at those *Fools* (as he call'd 'em) who would ever *Confess* any Sins, laid unto their Charge.

This man lived in abominable *Adulteries*; but God at length smote him with a *Palsey*. His *Dead Palsey* was accompanied with a *Quick Conscience*, which compelled him to Confess his Crimes: But, he Confess'd them so Indiscreetly, that by their Divulgation, they reach'd the Ears of the Authority: And in this Confession, there was involv'd and concern'd, the Wretched Woman, who chiefly had been concern'd with him in the Transgression.

By the Law of this Country, *Adultery* was then a *Capital* Transgression, as it hath been in many other Countrys: and this poor *Adulterer*, could not escape the Punishment which the Law provided.

III

On *June* 6. 1662. At *New-haven*, there was a most Unparallel'd Wretch, One *Potter*, by Name, about Sixty years of Age, Executed for Damnable *Bestialities*; although this Wretch, had been for now Twenty years, a Member of the Church in that Place, and kept up among the Holy People of God there, a Reputation, for Serious Christianity. It seems that the *Unclean Devil*, which had the possession of this Monster, had carried all his Lusts with so much Fury into this One Channel of Wickedness, that there was no Notice taken of his being Wicked in any other. Hence t'was, that he was *Devout* in Worship, *Gifted* in Prayer, *Forward* in Edifying Discourse among the Religious, and *Zealous* in Reproving the Sins of the other People; Every one counted him, *A Saint*: And he Enjoy'd such a *Peace* in his own mind, that in several Fits of Sickness, wherein he seem'd *Nigh unto Death*, he seem'd *Willing to Dy*; Yea, *Death* (he said) *Smiled on him*. Nevertheless, this Diabolical Creature, had Lived in most infandous *Buggeries* for no less than Fifty years together; and now at the Gallows, there were killed before his Eyes, a *Cow*, Two *Heifers*, Three *Sheep*, and Two *Sowes*, with all of which he had Committed his *Brutalities*. His *Wife* had seen him Confounding himself with a *Bitch*, Ten years before; and he then Excused his Filthiness, as well as he could, unto her, but Conjured her to keep it Secret: but he afterwards Hanged that Bitch himself, and then Returned unto his former Villanies, until at last, his *Son*, saw him hideously conversing with a *Sow*. By these means, the burning *Jealousy* of the Lord Jesus Christ, at Length *made the Churches to know*, that He had all this while seen the Covered Filthiness of this Hellish Hypocrite, and Exposed him also to the Just Judgment of Death, from the Civil Court of Judicature. Very Remarkable had been the Warnings, which this *Hell-Hound*, had Received from Heaven, to Repent of his Impieties. Many years before this, he had a Daughter, who Dreamt a *Dream*, which caused her, in her Sleep, to cry out, most Bitterly; and her Father, then with much ado obtaining of her, to tell her *Dream*, She told him, she Dream't, that she was among a great Multitude of People, to see an *Execution*, and it prov'd her own *Father* that was to be hang'd, at whose Turning over, she thus cried out. This happened before the Time, that any of his Cursed Practices were known unto her! At another Time, when there was a Malefactor adjudged in those parts to Dy, for the very same Transgressions, which this Rotten Fellow was guilty of, the Governour, with some of the Magistrates, most unaccountably, without any manner of Reason, for their so doing, turn'd about unto this Fellow, and said, *What think You? Is not this man worthy to Dy?* He now Confessed, That these Warnings did so awaken his Conscience, as to make him, for a Time, Leave off his Infernal Debauches; and so, he said, *He thought all was Pardoned, all was well with him.* Nevertheless, he Return'd unto his *Vomit*, and his *Quagmire*, until the Sentence of Death, at last fell upon him; and then he acknowledged, That he had Lived in the Sin of *Bestiality*, ever since he was Ten years Old, but had sometimes Intermitted the Perpetration of it, for some years together. During his Imprisonment, he continued in a *Sottish*, and *Stupid*, frame of Spirit, and marvellously *Secure* about his Everlasting *Pardon* and *Welfare*: but the Church whereto he belonged, kept a Solemn Day of *Humiliation* on this Occasion, wherein Mr. *Davenport* Preached on Josh. 22. 20: *Did not Achan Commit a Trespass, in the Accursed Thing, and Wrath fell on all the Congregation of Israel?* And in the close of the *Fast*, that Faithful People of God, Excommunicated this *Accursed Achan*, from their own Society. But as I have seen *Bewitched Self Poisoners*, under a Singular Energy of some *Devil*, obstinately Refuse all offered Relief, until the Poisons had prevailed so far, that all Relief was too late, and then with roaring Agonies they would have given Ten Worlds for it; So this *Bewitched Beast*, that had not been afraid of Dying, till he came to the Place of Execution, when he came *There*, he was Awakened into a most Unutterable and Intolerable Anguish of Soul, and made most Lamentably Desperate Out cries; Among which Out cries, he warned men, particularly, to *Take heed of Neglecting Secret Prayer*; which he said, *had been his Bane*. He said, he never used *Secret Prayer* in his Life, and that he frequently omitted *Family Prayer* too; Yet, he said, he had *Prayed* and *Sinned*, and *Sinned* and *Prayed*; namely, by *Ejaculations*, with which he contented himself, throwing *Set Prayer* aside. But so he Perished!

IV

An English Ship, (in the year 1673) Sailing from somewhere about the Mouth of the *Streights*, was Manned, with some Cruel Miscreants, who quarrelling with the Master and some of the Officers, turn'd 'em all into the *Long-Boat*, with a Small Quantity of Provisions, about an Hundred Leagues, to the Westward of the *Spanish Coast*.

These Fellows, in the mean while, set Sail for *New England*: where, by a Surprizing providence of God, the Master, with his Afflicted Company, in the Long-boat, also arrived; all, Except one who dyed of the Barbarous Usage.

The Countenance of the *Master*, was now become Terrible to the Rebellious *Men*, who, though they had *Escaped the Sea*, yet *Vengeance would not suffer to Live a Shore*. At his Instance and Complaint, they were Apprehended; and the Ringleaders of this Murderous Pyracy, had a Sentence of Death Executed on them, in *Boston*.

Under that Sentence, there was heard among them, a grievous Lamentation for This; *Their Education had been under the means of Grace, and the faithful Preaching of the Gospel in* England; *but they had Sinned against that Education*.

And one of them sadly Cryed out, *Oh! 'Tis my Drunkenness, 'Tis my Drunkenness, that hath brought me to this Lamentable End!*

The Horrors, which attended the Chief of these Malefactors (one *Forrest*) in the last Hours of his Life, were such as Exceedingly astonished the Beholders. Though he were a very stout man; yet now his Trembling Agonies and Anguishes, were inexpressible. One Speech let fall by him, was, *I have been among drawn Swords, flying bullets, roaring Canons, amidst all which, I knew not what Fear meant; but now I have Apprehensions of the dreadful wrath of God, in the other World, which I am going into, my Soul within me, is amazed at it.*

V

On *March* 18. 1674. two men, (whose Names were *Nicholas Feavour*, and *Robert Driver*) were Executed at *Boston*. The Crime for which they were Executed, was, the Murther of their Master; whom, upon the Provocation of some Chastisement, which he had given them, they knock'd on the Head, with an Axe, in their Bloody Rage.

After they were Condemned, they bestow'd their Lamentations not only, on the *Particular Crime*, which had now brought them, to their *Untimely End*, but also on some *Others*, for which their Consciences told them, that the Righteous God, had left them unto *This*.

One of them, said, His *Pride* had been his *Bane*; For, he thought much of it, that such a one as *he*, should be a *Servant*; and he would sometimes utter such words as these, *I am Flesh and Blood, as well as my Master, and therefore I know no Reason, why my Master should not obey me, as well as I obey him*. And now, said he, *See what my Pride has brought me to!*

One of them also, said, That his *Idleness* had Ruin'd him: He would not Industriously follow his Calling, but Live an Idle, Slothful, Vagrant Life. *This*, he said, had undone him.

And one of them, said, That his *Disobedience to his Parents*, had brought this misery upon him. His *Father*, he said, gave him Good Instructions, when he was a Child: but he Regarded them not. He would not go to a *School*, when his *Father* would have sent him to it. He would not go to a *Trade*, when his *Father* would have put him to one. After his *Father* was Dead, he would not be Subject unto them that had the Charge of him; he ran away from *Them*; and after that, he ran away from several *Masters*. Thus he *Ran* into the Jaws of Death.

These things are particularized, in the Sermon Preach'd just before their Execution; and afterwards Printed under the Title of, *The Wicked mans Portion*.

VI

On *Sept.* 22. 1681. One *W. C.* was Executed at *Boston*, for a *Rape* committed by him, on a Girl, that Lived with him; though he had then a Wife with Child by him, of a Nineteenth or Twentieth Child.

This man, had been *Wicked Overmuch*. His *Parents*, were Godly Persons; but *he* was a *Child of Belial*. He began Early, to Shake off his Obedience unto *Them*; and Early had *Fornication* laid unto his Charge; after which, he fled unto a dissolute Corner of the Land, a place whereof it might be said, *Surely, the Fear of God, is not in this Place*: He being a Youth, under the Inspection of the Church at *Roxbury*, they, to win him, invited him to Return unto his Friends, with such Expressions of *Lenity* towards him, that the Reverend Old Man, their Pastor, in a Sermon, on the Day when this man was Executed, with Tears bewayled it.

After this, he Lived very Dissolutely, in the Town of *Dorchester*; where, in a Fit of Sickness, he *Vow'd*, That if God would Spare his Life, he would Live as a *New Man*: but he horribly forgot his *Vows*. The Instances of his Impiety; grew so Numerous and Prodigious, that the wrath of God could bear no longer with him: he was *Ripened* for the Gallows.

After his Condemnation, he Vehemently Protested his *Innocency,* of the Fact, for which he was Condemned; but he Confessed, *That God was Righteous, thus to bring Destruction upon him, for Secret Adulteries.*

A *Reprieve* would have been obtained for him, if his foolish and froward Refusing to hear a *Sermon* on the Day appointed for his Execution, had not hardened the Hearts of the *Judges* against him. *He,* who had been a great *Scoffer* at the *Ordinances* of God, now Expos'd himself, by being Left unto such a Sottish Action!

He had horribly slighted all calls to *Repentance,* and now through some Wretches over-perswading of him, that he should not Dy, according to Sentence & Order of the Court, he hardened himself still, in his *unrepentant* frame of mind.

When he came to the Gallowes, and saw *Death* (and a Picture of *Hell* too, in a *Negro* then *Burnt* to *Death* at the Stake, for *Burning* her Masters House, with some that were in it,) before his Face, never was a Cry, for, *Time! Time! A World for a Little Time! the Inexpressible worth of Time!* Uttered, with a more unutterable Anguish.

He then Declared, *That the greatest Burden then Lying upon his miserable Soul, was his having Lived so unprofitably under the Preaching of the Gospel.*

VII

On *March* 11. 1686. was Executed at *Boston,* one *James Morgan,* for an horrible *Murder.* A man, finding it necessary to come into his House, he Swore he would *Run a Spit into his Bowels*; and he was as bad as his word.

He was a *passionate* Fellow; and now, after his Condemnation, he much bewayl'd, his having been given to *Cursing,* in his passions.

The Reverend Person who Preached, unto a great Assembly, on the Day of this poor mans Execution, did in the midst of his Sermon take occasion, to Read a Paper, which he had Received from the Malefactor, then present in the Assembly. It was as followeth.

I *James Morgan*, being Condemned to Dye, must needs own to the glory of God, that He is righteous, and that I have by my sins, provoked Him to destroy me before my time. I have been a great Sinner, guilty of Sabbath-breaking, of Lying, and of Uncleanness; but there are especially two Sins whereby I have offended the Great God; one is that Sin of Drunkenness, which has caused me to commit many other Sins; for when in Drink, I have been often guilty of Cursing and Swearing, and quarrelling, and striking others: But the Sin which lies most heavy upon my Conscience, is, that I have despised the Word of God, and many a time refused to hear it preached. For these things, I believe God has left me to that, which has brought me to a shameful and miserable death. I do therefore beseech and warn all persons, young men especially, to take heed of these Sins, lest they provoke the Lord to do to them as He has justly done by me. And for the further peace of my own Conscience, I think my self obliged to add this unto my foregoing Confession, That I *own the Sentence* which the Honoured Court has *pass'd upon me*, to be exceeding just; inasmuch as (tho' I had no former Grudge and Malice against the man whom I have killed, yet) my Passion at the time of the Fact was so outragious, as that it hurried me on to the doing of that which makes me justly now proceeded against as a Murderer.

After the Sermon, a Minister, at his Desire, went unto the place of Execution with him. And of what passed by the way, there was a Copy taken; which here Ensueth.

The DISCOURSE of the Minister with James Morgan, on the way to his Execution.

Min. I'm come hither to answer your desires which just now you exprest to me in the Publick, that I would give you my company at your Execution.

Mor. *Dear Sir, how much am I beholden to you! you have already done a great deal for me. Oh who am I that I have been such a vile wretch, that any Servants of God should take notice of me!*

Min. I beseech you to make this use of it, I believe there is not one

Christian this day beholding you, who would not willingly be at the greatest pains they could devise to save your precious Soul: How merciful then is that *Man* who is *God* as well as man! how unspeakably ready is the Lord Christ to save the Souls of sinners that affectionately *Look* unto him! The goodness and pitifulness of the most tender-hearted man in the world is but a shadow of what is in *Him*. The compassions of any man compared with the Bowels of a merciful *JESUS* are but as the painted Sun, or the painted Fire in comparison of the real.

Mor. *Oh that I could now look unto Him as I ought to do! Lord help me.*

Min. Well, you are now a dying man, the last hour or two of your life is now running. You know your self now to stand just on the brink of Eternity; you shall presently be in a state of wonderful happiness or of horrible misery which must endure forever: which of those estates do you now count yourself stepping into?

Mor. *Oh Sir, I am afraid, but I am not without hope that God may have mercy on me.*

Min. What's your ground for that hope? O see that your confidences been't such as God will by and by reject.

Mor. *I don't know well what to say, but this I hope is a good sign, I have lived in many grievous sins, in* Lying, Drinking, Sabbath-breaking, and *evil* Company-keeping; *God has made now these so bitter to my soul, that I would not commit them again, might I have my life this afternoon by doing it.*

Min. That's a great word, God grant it may not be a word only, the good word of a good pang, without such a thro' change of heart, as you must have if you would not perish everlastingly. You are not like to have any longer time in this world to try the Sincerity of your Profession.

Mor. *I know it, and I beseech you Sir to help me what you can: I hope the means used with me since my Condemnation ha'n't been lost.*

Min. I would not have the sence of the pain and shame which your body is about to undergoe, any ways hinder your mind from being taken up about the Soul matters which I shall endeavour to set before you.

MOR. *Sir, as for the pain that my body must presently feel, I matter it not: I know what pain is; but what shall I do for my poor Soul? I'm terrify'd with the Wrath of God; This, this terrifyes me, Hell terrifyes me: I should not mind my Death, if it were not for that.*

MIN. Now the Lord help me to deal faithfully with you, and the Lord help you to receive what he shall enable me to offer unto you. Mark what I say: You were born among the enemies of God, you were born with a soul as full of enmity against God, as a Toad is full of poison. You have liv'd now, how many years?

MORG. *I think about Thirty.*

MIN. And all these thirty years have you been sinning against the Holy God. Ever since you knew how to do any thing, you have every day been guilty of innumerable sins; you deserve the dreadful wrath and curse of the infinite God. But God has brought you here, to a place where you have enjoy'd the means of Grace. And here you have added unto your old Sins, most fearful Iniquities: you have been such a matchless, prodigious Transgressor, that you are now to Dy by the stroke of civil justice; to *Dy before your time, for being wicked overmuch.* There is hardly any sort of Wickedness which you have not wallowed in. That Sin particularly which you are now to Dy for, is a most monstrous Crime. I can't possibly describe or declare the sins whereby you have made your self an astonishing Example of Impiety and punishment.

MOR. *O Sir, I have been a most hellish Sinner. I am sorry for what I have been.*

MIN. Sorry, you say: well, tell me, which of all your sins you are now most sorry for, which lies most heavy.

MOR. *I hope I am sorry for all my sins, but I must especially bewail my neglect of the means of Grace. On Sabbath dayes I us'd to lye at home, or be ill imploy'd elsewhere when I should have been at Church.* This has undone me!

MIN. And let me seriously tell you, your despising of Christ is a most dreadful sin indeed. You have for whole years together had the Call of Jesus Christ to seek an Interest in him, and you would now give all the world for that Interest, but you would take no notice of him. The Jews of Old put him to a worse death than yours will be this afternoon; and by your contempt of Christ you have said, the Jews did well to do so. How justly might he now laugh at your Calamity? And for these sins of yours, besides the direful woes and plagues that have already come upon you, you are now expos'd unto the Vengeance of eternal fire. You are in danger of being now quickly cast into those exquisite amazing Torments, in comparison of which, the anguishes which your body ever did feel, or shall feel before night, or can ever feel, are just nothing at all; and these dolorous torments are such as never had an End; as many sands as could lie between this earth and the Stars in Heaven would not be near so many as the Ages, the endless Ages of these Torments.

MOR. *But is there not Mercy for me in Christ?*

MIN. Yes, and its a wonderful thing that I have now further to tell you. Mind, I entreat you. The Son of God is become the Son of Man; the Lord Jesus Christ is both God & Man in one Person, and he is both sufficiently able & willing also, to be your Saviour. He lived a most righteous life, & this was that such as you and I might be able to say before God, *Lord, accept of me as if I had lived righteously.* He dyed at length a most cursed death, and this was that we might be able to say unto God, *Lord, let me not dye for Sin, since thy Son has dyed in my room.* This glorious Redeemer is now in the highest Heaven, pleading with God for the Salvation of His Chosen ones.—And he pours out his Spirit continually upon them that do believe on him: might you then be enabled by his Grace to carry your poor, guilty, condemned, enslaved, ignorant Soul unto Jesus Christ, and humbly put your trust in him for deliverance from the whole bad state which you are brought into. Oh then his voice is to you the same that was to the penitent Thief, *This day shalt thou be with me in Paradise.*

MOR. *Oh that I might be so! Sir, I would hear more of these things: I think, I can't better fit my self for my Death than by hearkening to these things.*

MIN. Attend then: The never-dying Spirit that lodges within you, must now within a few minutes appear before the Tribunal of the Great GOD; in what, or in whose Righteousness will you then appear? will you have this to be your Plea, *Lord, I experienced many good Motions & Desires in my Soul, and many sorrows for my sin before I dy'd*: or will you expect to have no other Plea but This, *Lord, I am vile, but thy Son is a Surety for the worst of Sinners that believe on Him; for his sake alone, have MERCY on me.*

MOR. *I thank God for what He has wrought in my Soul.*—

MIN. But be very careful about this matter: if you build on your own good Affections instead of Jesus Christ the only Rock, if you think they shall recommend you to God, *He that made you will not have mercy on you.*

MOR. *I would be clothed with the Righteousness of JESUS CHRIST.*

MIN. But you can't sincerely desire that Christ should justify you, if you don't also desire that He should sanctify you: those two always go together. Is every lust that has hitherto had possession of your heart become so loathsome to you, that it would fill your Soul with joy to hear Jesus Christ say, *I will subdue those Iniquities of thine; I will make a holy, an heavenly, a spiritually minded person of thee.*

MOR. *I would not Sin against God any more.*

MIN. But I must deal plainly with you: You have made it sadly suspicious that your repentance is not yet as it ought to be: when men truly & throughly repent of sin, they use to be in a special manner watchful against that Sin which has been their chief Sin: one of your principal sins which has indeed brought you to the Death of a *Murderer*, is *Passion*, unmortifi'd and outragious *Passionateness*: Now I have been this day informed, that no longer since than the last night, upon some Dissatisfaction about the place which the Authority hath ordered you by and by to be buried in, you did express your self with a most unruly Passionateness.

MOR. *Sir, I confess it, and I was quickly sorry for it, tho' for the pres-*

ent I was too much disturbed: 'Twas my folly to be so careful about the place where my body should be laid, when my precious Soul was in such a Condition.—

MIN. Truly you have cause to mourn for it. Secure the welfare of your soul, and this (now) pinion'd, hang'd, vile body of yours will shortly be raised unto glory, glory for evermore. And let me put you in mind of one thing more, I doubt you han't yet laid aside your unjust Grudges against the Persons concerned in your Conviction and Condemnation: You have no cause to complain of them: and you are not fit to pray, much less are you fit to dye, till you heartily wish them as well as your own soul: if you dy malicious, you die miserable.

MOR. *I heartily wish them all well, I bear Ill-will to none. What a lamentable thing is this? Ah this is that which has brought me hither!*

MIN. What do you mean?

MOR. *I over heard a man mocking and scoffing at me when I stumbled just now, he does very ill. I have done so my self. I have mock'd and scoff'd like that man, and see what it hath brought me to; he may come to the like.*

MIN. The Lord forgive that foolish hard hearted creature. But be not too much disturbed.

MOR. *Yonder! I am now come in sight of the place where I must immediately end my days. Oh what a huge Multitude of people is come together on this occasion. O Lord, O Lord, I pray thee to make my Death profitable to all this Multitude of People, that they may not sin against thee as I have done.*

MIN. Amen, Amen, ten thousand times; the Lord God Almighty say Amen to this Prayer of yours! It would indeed be an excellent thing if you would now come to receive your death with some satisfaction of soul in this thought, That much Glory is like to come to God by it: I am verily perswaded God intends to do good to many souls by means of your Execution: This a greater honour than you are worthy of.

(After the Discourse had been intermitted about a minute or two by reason of the miery way.)

MOR. *I beseech you Sir speak to me. Do me all the good you can: my time grows very short: your discourse fits me for my Death more than any thing.*

MIN. I am sorry so small a thing as a plashy Street should make me loose one minute of this more than ordinary precious time; a few paces more bring you to the place which you have now in your eye, from whence you shall not come back alive. Do you find your self afraid to dy there?

MOR. *Sir, if it were not for the Condition that my Soul must by and by be in, I should not fear my death at all; but I have a little comfort from some of Gods promises about that.*

MIN. And what shall I now say? These are among the last words that I can have liberty to leave with you. Poor man, thou art now going to knock at the door of Heaven, and to beg & cry, *Lord, Lord open to me!* The only way for thee to speed, is, to open the door of thy own soul now unto the Lord Jesus Christ. Do this, and thou shalt undoubtedly be admitted into the Glories of His Heavenly Kingdom: You shall fare as well as *Manasseh* did before you: leave this undone, and there's nothing remains for you but the *Worm which dyeth not, and the Fire which shall not be quenched.*

MOR. *Sir, shew me then again what I have to do.*

MIN. The voice, the sweet voice of the Lord Jesus Christ, (who was once hang'd on a tree, to take away the Sting and Curse of even such a Death as yours) unto all that close with him, His Heavenly voice now is, O that I and my saving work might be entertained, kindly entreated, in that poor perishing Soul of thine! Are you willing?

MOR. *I hope I am.*

MIN. His Voice further is, If I am lodged in thy Soul, I'le sprinkle my blood upon it, and on my account thou shalt find Favour with God. Do you consent to this?

MOR. *This I want.*

MIN. But this is not all that he saith, His Voice further is, If I come into thy Soul, I will change it, I will make all sin bitter to it, I will make it an holy heavenly soul. Do you value this above the proffers of all the World?

MOR. *I think I do,—and now Sir, I must go no further, Look here— what a solemn sight this is! Here lyes the Coffin which this Body of mine must presently be laid in. I thank you dear Sir, for what you have already done for me.*

MIN. When you are gone up this Ladder, my last Service for you, before you are gone off, will be to pray with you: but I would here take my leave of you. Oh that I might meet you at the Right Hand of the Lord Jesus in the Last Day. Farewell poor heart, Fare thee well. The Everlasting Arms receive thee! The Lord Jesus, the merciful Saviour of Souls take possession of thy Spirit for himself. The Great God, who is a great Forgiver, grant thee Repentance unto Life; and Glorify Himself in the Salvation of such a wounded Soul as thine for ever. With Him, and with His free, rich, marvellous, Infinite Grace, I leave you. *Farewell.*

Being Arrived unto the place of Execution, his *Last Speech* upon the Ladder, then taken in Short-Hand, was that which is here inserted.

I Pray God that I may be a warning to you all, and that I may be the last that ever shall suffer after this manner: In the fear of God I warn you to have a care of taking the Lords Name in vain. Mind and have a care of that Sin of Drunkenness, for that Sin leads to all manner of Sins and Wickedness: (mind, and have a care of breaking the sixth Commandment, where it is said, *Thou shalt not do no Murder*) for when a man is in Drink, he is ready to commit all manner of Sin, till he fills up the cup of the wrath of God, as I have done by committing that Sin of Murder. I beg of God, as I am a dying man, and to appear before the Lord within a few minutes, that you may take notice of what I say to you. Have a care of drunkenness, and ill Company, and mind all good Instruction, and don't turn your back upon the Word of God, as I have done. When I have been at meeting, I have gone out of the Meeting-house to commit sin, and to please the lust of my flesh. Don't make a mock at any poor object of pity, but bless God that he has not left you as he had justly done me, to commit that horrid Sin of

Murder. Another thing that I have to say to you is to have a care of that house where that wickedness was committed, and where I have been partly ruined by. But here I am, and know not what will become of my poor soul, which is within a few moments of eternity. I have murder'd a poor man, who had but little time to repent, and I know not what is become of his poor soul; Oh that I may make use of this Opportunity that I have! O that I may make improvement of this little little time, before I go hence and be no more. O let all mind what *I* am a saying now, I'm going out of this world. O take warning by me, and beg of God to keep you from this sin which has been my ruine. (His last words were) *O Lord, receive my Spirit, I come unto thee, O Lord, I come unto thee, O Lord, I come, I come, I come.*

VIII

One *Hugh Stone*, upon a Quarrel, between himself & his Wife, about Selling a piece of Land, having some words, as they were walking together, on a certain Evening, very barbarously reached a stroke at her Throat, with a Sharp knife; and by that *One Stroke* fetch'd away the Soul, of her, who had made him a Father of several Children, and would have brought yet another to him, if she had lived a few weeks longer in the world. The wretched man, was too soon Surprised by his Neighbours, to be capable of Denying the Fact; and so he pleaded, *Guilty,* upon his Tryal.

There was a *Minister* that walk'd with him to his *Execution*; and I shall insert the principal Passages of the Discourse between them; in which the Reader may find or make something *useful* to himself, what ever it were to the Poor man who was more immediately concerned in it.

Minister. I am come to give you what Assistance I can, in your taking of the Steps, which your eternal *Weal* or *Woe,* now depends upon the well or ill taking of.

Hugh Stone. *Sir, I Thank you, and I beg you to do what you can for me.*

Min. Within a very few Minutes your immortal Soul must appear before God *the Judge of all.* I am heartily sorry you have lost so much time since your first Imprisonment: you had need use a wonderful Husbandry of the little piece of an *Inch* which now remains. Are you now prepared to stand before the Tribunal of God?

H.S. *I hope I am.*

Min. And what *Reason* for that *Hope?*

H.S. *I find all my Sins made so bitter to me, that if I were to have my life given me this Afternoon, to Live such a Life as I have Lived heretofore, I would not accept of it; I had rather Dy.*

Min. That is *well,* if it be *True.* But suffer me a little to search into the Condition of your Soul. Are you sensible, That you were *Born* a Sinner? That the Guilt of the *First Sin* committed by *Adam,* is justly charged upon *you?* And that you have hereupon a *Wicked Nature* in you, full of Enmity against all that is *Holy, and Just, and Good?* For which you deserved to be destroyed, as soon as you first came into this world.

H.S. *I am sensible of this.*

Min. Are you further sensible, that you have lived, a very ungodly Life? That you are guilty of thousands of *Actual Sins,* every one of which *deserves the Wrath and Curse of God, both in this Life, and that which is to come?*

H.S. *I am sensible of this also.*

Min. But are you sensible, That you have broken *all* the *Laws* of God? You know the *Commandments.* Are you sensible, That you have broken every one of *Them?*

H.S. *I cannot well answer to that. My Answer may be liable to some Exceptions.—This I own, I have broken every Commandment on the Account mentioned by the Apostle* James; *that he who* breaks one is Guilty of all. *But not otherwise.*

Min. Alas, That you know your self no better than so! I do affirm to you, that you have particularly broken *every one* of the Commandments; and you *must* be sensible of it.

H.S. *I cann't see it.*

Min. But you must Remember, *That the Commandment is Exceeding Broad*; it reaches to the *Heart* as well as the *Life*: it excludes

Omissions as well as *Commissions*, and it at once both *Requires* and *Forbids*. But I pray, make an experiment upon any *one* Commandment, in which you count your self most *Innocent*: and see whether you do not presently confess your self *Guilty* thereabout. I may not leave this point slightly passed over with you.

H.S. *That Commandment,* Thou shalt not make to thy self any Graven Image; *How have I broken it?*

Min. Thus: You have had undue *Images* of God in your *Mind* a thousand times. But more than so; that Commandment not only *forbids* our using the *Inventions* of men in the worship of God, but it also *requires* our using all the *Institutions* of God. Now have not you many & many a time turned your back upon some of those glorious *Institutions?*

H.S. *Indeed, Sir, I confess it: I see my sinfulness greater than I thought it was.*

Min. You ought to see it. God help you to see it! There is a *boundless Ocean* of it. And then for that SIN, which has now brought a shameful Death upon you, 'tis impossible to Declare the Aggravations of it; hardly an Age will show the like. You have professed your self *Sorry* for it!

H.S. *I am heartily so.*

Min. But your Sorrows must be *after a Godly Sort.* Not meerly because of the miseries which it has brought on your *outward Man,* but chiefly for the *Wrongs* and *Wounds* therein given to your own Soul; and not only for the *Miseries* you have brought on your self, but chiefly for the *Injuries* which you have done to the Blessed God.

H.S. *I hope my Sorrow lies there.*

Min. But do you mourn without Hope?

H.S. *I thank God, I do not.*

Min. Where do you see a Door of Hope?

H.S. *In the Lord Jesus Christ, who has died to saved Sinners.*

Min. Truly, *There is no other Name by which we may be saved?* The Righteousness of the Lord Jesus Christ, is that alone, in which you may safely anon appear before the Judgment Seat of God. And that

Righteousness is by the marvellous and infinite Grace of God, offered unto you. But do you find, that as you have no Righteousness, so you have no Strength? that you cannot of your self *move* or *stir*, towards the Lord Jesus Christ, though you *justly* perish if you do not *Run* unto Him? that it is the Grace of God alone which must enable you to accept of Salvation from the Great Saviour?

H.S. *Sir, my Case, in short, is This, I have laid my self at the Feet of the Lord Jesus Christ for my Salvation; and had it not been for His meer Grace and Help, I had never been able to do That. But there I have laid and left my self, I have nothing to plead, why he should accept of me. If He will do it, I am happy, but if He will not, I am undone for ever; it had been good for me that I never had been Born.*

Min. And you must justifie Him if He should Reject you. You surprize me, with at once giving me so much of the Discourse, which all this while I have been labouring for. I can add but this: *The good Lord make you sincere in what you say!*—Your Crime lay in *Blood*; and your Help also, That lies in *Blood*. I am to offer you the *Blood* of the Lord Jesus Christ, as that in which you may now have the Pardon of all your sins. Now you may try the sincerity of your *Faith* in the Blood of the Lord Jesus for a Pardon, by this. Have you an *Hope* in that Blood, for all the other living effects of it? shall I explain what I mean?

H.S. *Do Sir.*

Min. The Blood of the Lord Jesus is not only *Sin Pardoning* Blood, but also *Soul purifying*, and *Heart softening* Blood. It embitters all Sin unto the Soul, that it is applied unto, and mortifies every lust in such a Soul. Are you desirous of this?

H.S. *With all my Heart?*

Min. The Lord make you so. The Lord *Seal* your *Pardon*, in that *Blood*, which is worth ten thousand Worlds! But what will you do for that God, who has given you these hopes of a *Pardon*? you must with a holy ingenuity now do something for the Honour of that God, whom you have sinned so much against.

H.S. *What shall I do?*

Min. Why, Confess and Bewail the Sins that have undone you, and publickly Advise, and Exhort, and Charge all that you can, to take heed of such evil ways.

H.S. *I will endeavor to do it as God shall help me.*

Min. I pray tell me plainly what *special Sin*, do you think it was, that laid the first Foundation of your Destruction? where did you begin to leave God, and Ruine your self?

H.S. *It was Contention in my Family. I had been used unto something of Religion: and I was once careful about the Worship of God, not only with my Family, but in secret also. But upon Contention between me and my Wife, I left off the Wayes of God and you see what I am come to.*

Min. I would pray you to Vomit up all Sin with a very hearty detestation. You are going (if I may so speak) to disgorge your Soul; if you do not first cast up your Sin, if your Soul and your Sin come away together, you cannot but know something of the dismal condition which it must pass into. O, what cause have you to fall out with Sin for ever? it has been your only Enemy. Here is the only Revenge which you may allow in your self. You must not now bear any Malice against any one man in the World, but forgive even those that have done you the greatest Injuries. Only upon Sin be as revengeful as you can; I would have you, like *Sampson*, so to Dy, taking of a just Revenge.

H.S. *I hope I shall.*

Min. Well, we are now but a very few paces from the place, where you must breathe your last. You are just going to take a most awful Step, which has this most Remarkable in it, *That it cannot be twice taken.* If you go wrong now, it cannot be Recalled throughout the Dayes of a long Eternity. I can but commit you into the Arms of a Merciful Redeemer, that he may keep you from a Miscarriage, which cannot be recall'd and redress'd throughout Eternal Ages. The Lord show unto you the *Path of Life*! Attend unto these, as the last words that I may speak before the Prayer, with which I am immediately to take a long *Farewell* of you. You are not just going to be *Confirmed* for ever. If the Great God presently find you under the power of *Prejudice* against any of His Truths and Wayes, or of *Enmity* against what has His blessed Name upon it, you shall be fixed, and settled, & confirmed in it, until the very Heavens be no more. But they are very terrible *Plagues* and *Pains*, which you may be sure will accompany this everlasting Disposition of your Soul. On the other side, if God now find your Soul, under the power of Inclinations to *Love Him, Fear Him, Serve Him*; & to esteem the Lord Jesus Christ above a thousand Worlds; you shall then be *Confirmed* in the perfection of such a Temper, and of all the *Joy*, that must Accompany it. Which of these is the Condition that I now leave you in.

H.S. *Sir, I hope the latter of them.*

Min. The Good God make it so; and grant that I may find you at the Right hand of the Lord Jesus, *in the Day of His Appearing.* May this *Ladder* prove as a *Jacobs Ladder* for you, and may you find the *Angels* of the Lord Jesus ready here to convey your departing Soul into the Presence of the Lord.

After this Discourse; ascending the Ladder, *he made the following Speech.*

Young Men and Maids; observe the Rule of Obedience to your Parents; and Servants to your Masters, according to the will of God, and to do the will of your Masters: you take up wicked ways, you set open a Gate to your *Sins*, to lead in bigger afterwards; thou can'st not do any thing but *God will see thee*, tho' thou thinkest thou shalt not be catched, thou thinkest to hide thy self in Secret, when as God in Heaven can see thee, though thou hast hid it from man. And when thou goest to *Thievery*, thy wickedness is discovered, and thou art found *Guilty*. O Young Woman, that is Married, and Young Man, look on Me here; be sure in that Solemn Engagement, you are obliged one to another; *Marriage* is an Ordinance of God, have a care of breaking that Bond of *Marriage-Union*; if the Husband provoke his Wife, and cause a Difference, he sins against God; and so does she, in such Carriage; for she is bound to be an *Obedient Wife*. O you Parents that give your Children in Marriage, remember what I have to say, you must take notice when you give them in Marriage, you give them freely to the *Lord*, and free them from that Service and Command you ought to have, yet you ought to have a tender regard to them. O thou that takest no care to lead thy life civilly and honestly, and then Committest that Abominable Sin of *Murder*, here is this *Murderer*, look upon him; and see how many are come with their eyes to behold this man, that abhors himself before God; *that* is the Sin that I abhor my self for, and desire you, take Example by *me*; there are here a great many Young People, and *O Lord, that they may be thy Servants!* Have a care, do not sin; I will tell you, that I wish I never had had the opportunity to do such a *Murder*; if you say, when a person has provoked you, *I will Kill him*: 'Tis a thousand to one, but the next time *you will do it.* Now I Commit my self into the Hands of Almighty God.

His Prayer.

O Lord our Good God; thou art a Merciful God, and a Gracious and Loving Father; Alas, that thou shouldest *Nourish up Children that have Rebelled against Thee!* O Lord, I must confess, thou gavest me opportunity to read thy *Written Word*; Thou art also my Creator and Preserver; but, Lord, I have not done according to the Offers of thy Grace; thou hast not hid from me the opportunities of the Good Things & Liberties of thy *House* and *Ordinances*; but I have waxed wanton under the Enjoyment of them. I have given thee just cause to provoke thee to Anger, and thou hast left me to *Shame*, not only on my self, but on my Relations. O Lord God I do confess that I have sinned against thee, & done all these Iniquities *against Thee*, and before thine eyes. Lord, I have sinned especially against thee; pardon my Sins of Youth; Lord, pardon this bloody Sin I stand here Guilty of. O Lord, hide not thy face from me; I humbly beg it of thee: for there is no man *can Redeem his Brothers Soul*, but only the Blood of Jesus Christ must do it. Let it be sufficient to satisfie for my poor Soul. I have not done any thing that thou shouldest be pleased to shew me thy *Love*, or that I should have any thing from thee, but only *Everlasting Misery.* I am unworthy to come to thee; yet Lord, for thy *Mercies* Sake have pity on me. Now I am coming to *Judgment*, Lord, let the Arms of thy *Mercy* Receive my Soul, and let my sin be Remitted; Good Lord, let not my sins which *Condemn* me here in this world, rise up to *Condemn* me in the World to come; though they have *Condemned* me in this world, shew mercy, Lord, when I come before thy *Judgment Seat.* If my Soul be not humbled, Lord, humble it; let my Petition be acceptable in Heaven thy Holy Mountain. I am unworthy to come into thy *Presence*, yet O let me come into thy *Kingdom*; and deliver my Soul from *Blood Guiltiness*, in the *Blood* of Jesus Christ. O let my *wounded Soul* mourn for my Sin that hath brought me here, *Sin brings* Ruine to the poor Soul; wo is unto me for mine Iniquity. *If I had gone to Prayer in the morning when I committed this Sin, Lord God, thou wouldest have kept back my hands from shedding innocent Blood.* O Gracious God, Remember thou me in *Mercy*; let me be an Object of thy pitty and not of thy wrath; the Lord hear me and pardon my sins. Take care of my poor *Children*: I have scattered them like stragling sheep flying before the Wolf; pitty the poor Children that go like so many Lambs that have lost their Keeper; that they may not come to such a *Death* as I do! Lord, for the sake of Jesus Christ, and the *Righteousness* of thy Son, accept my Soul, and receive me into the Arms of thy mercy; that I may enjoy Everlasting *Rest*. Pardon all my sins; and let the Prayers of all those that have put up their Petitions for me, be accepted for the sake of Jesus Christ. Now I am coming, now I am coming, thou mayest say, *I called to thee, and thou wouldest not come*; I must say, my sin brought me here, O the World, and the corrupt nature of man, that has proved my ruine! O Lord, Good Lord, let me enjoy Rest for my Soul. The desire of my Soul is to be with thee in thy Kingdom, let me have a share in that Kingdom. Now is the time, Lord Jesus; the Grave is opening its mouth; I am now living, though *dead in Sin*; let my prayers be heard in heaven thy holy place; thy hands hath *made* me, and I know thou canst *Save* me; hide not thy face from me; and affect the hearts of thy people with this sad Object, that they may labour to serve thee betimes, & may not give themselves up to *Profaneness* and *Wickedness*, especially that Sin of *Drunkenness*, which is an *in-let of all Abominations.*

(*When thou hast thy* head full of Drink, *the Remembrance of God is out of thy heart; and thou art unprepared to commit thy self and Family unto God; thou art unfit to come into Gods Presence. I have cause to cry out and be ashamed of it, that I am guilty of it, because I gave way to that Sin more than any other, and then God did leave me to practice* Wickedness, *& to Murder that dear Woman, whom I should have taken a great deal of contentment in, which, if I had done, I had not been here to suffer this Death.*)

Thou art Holy, Just, and Good, & therefore O Lord have mercy on me, for the sake of thy Son pitty me, now Lord, I am coming. O, that I could do thee better Service.

(*Many of you that behold me, I* [now] *wish you never had seen me here.*)

Lord, receive my Soul into a better place, if it be thy blessed will; 'tis a day of *great Trouble* with me; my Soul is greatly troubled; give me one Glimpse of Comfort in thy *Kingdom*; by and by let me have one dram of thy *Grace*. Accept of me now at this time, 'tis the last time; Good Lord, deny me not, give me, as the Woman of *Samaria*, a *Taste* of that *Living Water*, that my soul may Thirst no more. I beg it for the sake of Jesus Christ. *Amen.*

After this, he was, by the Prayers of a Minister then present, Recommended unto the Divine Mercy. Which being done, the poor man poured out a few broken Ejaculations, in the midst of which he was turned over, into that Eternity which we must leave him in.

The Speech of *Hugh Stone,* in the Prison, the morning before his Execution.

When Young People are Married, they make use of Prayer in their Families, and when they Pray, they do believe there is Sincerity and Affection in their Prayer; but when Difference between a Man and his Wife doth arise, then that doth occasion hindrance of Prayer in their Family; and when Prayer is wholly omitted, it let's in all confusion; and every evil work: He said, That he used to Pray in his Family, but when he did Pray, it was in a formal manner, but now from the Consideration of Eternity that he was going into, he was made the more Considerate in his Prayers that he made, and did hope that now he had the Spirit of Prayer in his Praying.

IX

On *June* 8. 1693[.] Two Young Women, (the one *English,* t'other *Negro*) were Executed at *Boston,* for murdering their *Bastard Children.*

The *English* Young Woman, gave to the Minister, who Preach'd that Afternoon, the following Paper of *Confessions*; which he took occasion, in the Sermon, to publish unto the Congregation, where she also was then present before the Lord.

I am a miserable Sinner; and I have justly provoked the Holy God to leave me unto that Folly of my own Heart, for which I am now Condemned to Dy. I cannot but see much of the *Anger* of God against me, in the Circumstances of my woful Death; He hath Fulfilled upon me, that Word of His, *Evil pursueth Sinners.* I therefore desire, Humbly to *Confess* my many Sins before God, and the World: but most particularly my *Blood Guiltiness.* Before the Birth of my *Twin-Infants,* I too much parlyed with the Temptations of the Devil, to smother my

Wickedness by Murthering of them: At length, when they were Born I was not unsensible, that at least, *One* of them was alive; but such a Wretch was I, as to use a *Murderous* Carriage towards them, in the place where I lay, on purpose to dispatch them out of the World. I acknowledge that I have been more Hard hearted than the *Sea Monsters*; and yet for the Pardon of these my Sins, I would Fly to the Blood of the Lord Jesus Christ, which is the only *Fountain set open for Sin and Uncleanness*. I know not how better to Glorify God, for giving me such an Opportunity as I have had to make sure of His Mercy, than by advising and entreating the *Rising Generation* here, to take Warning by my Example; and I will therefore tell the *Sins*, that have brought me to my shameful End. I do Warn all People, and especially, *Young People*, against the Sin of *Uncleanness* in particular; 'tis that Sin that hath been my Ruine; well had it been for me, if I had answered all Temptations to that Sin as *Joseph* did, *How shall I do this Wickedness, and Sin against God?* But, I see, *Bad Company* is that, which leads to that, and all other Sins; and I therefore beg all that Love their Souls to be familiar with none but such as fear God. I believe, the chief thing that hath brought me into my present Condition, is my *Disobedience to my Parents*: I despised all their Godly Counsels and Reproofs; and I was always of an Haughty and stubborn Spirit. So that now I am become a dreadful Instance of the Curse of God belonging to Disobedient Children. I must Bewayl this also, that although I was *Baptised*, yet when I grew up, I forgot the *Bonds* that were laid upon me to be the Lords. Had I given my self to God, as soon as I was capable to consider that I had been in *Baptism*, set apart for him, How happy had I been! It was my *Delay* to Repent of my former Sins, that provoked God to leave me unto the Crimes, for which I am now to Dy. Had I seriously Repented of my *Uncleanness* the *First Time* I fell into it, I do suppose, I had not been left unto what followed. Let all take it from me; they little think, what they do, when they put off turning from Sin to God, and Resist the *Strivings* of the Holy Spirit. I fear, 'tis for this, that I have been given up to such *Hardness of Heart*, not only since my long *Imprisonment*, but also since my Just *Condemnation*. I now know not what will become of my Distressed, perishing Soul. But I would humbly Commit it unto the Mercy of God in Jesus Christ; *Amen*.

X

In the Year, 1694. A miserable *Indian*, called *Zachary*, was Executed for *Murder*.

He understood so very little English, that it put the English Minister, who, after his Condemnation, visited him, unto an Inexpressible deal of trouble, to convey unto him, the *Principles* and the *Directions* of our Holy Religion. But the Lord so succeeded the endeavours used upon the wretched Salvage, that within a little while, he could give a sensible, tho' a Shattered, Account, of the *Fundamentals* in Christianity. And such an Impression, had the Doctrine of *Grace* upon him, that he professed himself, desirous rather to *Dy*, than to *Live* at his Old sinful rate. He seem'd, even to long for his Execution, that so he might be delivered from all disposition to Sin against God. But all his Hopes of Everlasting Salvation, he seem'd very Suitably to place, on the Obedience which the Lord Jesus Christ, had yeelded unto God in the room of Sinners.

Of this poor creature, nothing had been here mentioned, if it had not been to introduce the mention of this one passage.

He said, *That the Thing which undid him was This: He had begun to come, and hear the Preaching of the Gospel among the Indians: But he minded the Indian-Preacher, how he lived; and he saw plainly that the Preacher minded his Bottle, more than his Bible: he lov'd Rum too well, and when his Rum was in him, he would quarrel with other people, and with himself Particularly. This* (he said) *Prejuduced him against the Gospel. So he lived as a Pagan still; and would be Drunk too; and his Drunkenness had brought all this misery upon him.*

XI

In the Year, 1698. Was Executed at *Springfield*, one *Sara Smith*.

Her Despising the continual Counsils and Warnings of her Godly Father-in-law laid the Foundation of her Destruction. When she was married, she added unto the Crime of *Adultery*, that of *Stealing*; which latter Crime occasioned her to fly unto *New Jersey*. Afterwards coming to Reside in *Deerfield*, her (second) Husband was carried captive unto *Canada*: But the woman, in Grievous Horrour of mind, for the Breaches of the *Seventh* and *Eighth* Commandment, received many most suitable counsils, from Mr. *Williams*, the worthy Minister of that place. In conformity to his Counsils and Warnings, for a while she led a Reformed life, and seemed much affected with the word of God, in the publick Dispensations of it. But e're it was long, she lost her Seriousness, her Tenderness, her Convictions; and Relapsed into the Sin of *Adultery*. Her first Relapse into that Sin, was attended with a *Conception*, which, tho' she endeavoured for to render it an Abortive, the Holy providence of God would not suffer it to be so. She did, with much Obstinacy, Deny and Conceal her being with *Child*: and when the *Child* was Born, she smothered it: but the Neighbours found it out immediately. She then owned the matter, but made the usual pretence, *That the child was Dead Born*: and remain'd as poor Sinners undone by the Sins of *unchastity* use to be, under extream Hardness of Heart. Mr. *Williams* rarely visited her, but found her guilty of New *Lyes*; tho' sometimes violent pangs of Horror would come upon her, wherein she detected her own *Lying*, and seem'd greatly to Bewail it. The Honourable Judges, desired Mr. *Williams* to go down unto *Springfield*, (which was the place,) at the *Time* of her Execution; who then found her under an astonishing stupidity of Soul: and yet not pretending to Hopes of Happiness in another world. He found her guilty of *more Lyes!* which afterward she confessed so to be; she *slept* both at the *Prayer* and the *Sermon*: in the publick Assembly on the day of her Execution: and seem'd, the most unconcern'd of any in the Assembly: professing therewithal, *That she could not but wonder at her own unconcernedness.* At her Execution, she said but little, only, *That she desired to give Glory unto God, and to take shame unto her self, and that she would warn all others, to beware of the Sins, that had brought her unto this miserable End; especially, Stealing, Uncleanness, Lying, Neglecting to Read the Scriptures, and Neglecting to Pray unto God.* She had absented her self much from the word of God, on *Lords-Dayes*, and *Lecture Dayes*; and staid at home, till she had fallen into this capital Transgression: *Then*, she would come unto the meetings, with some seeming Devotion. She had Sinn'd away great Convictions, and Awakenings; and Satan, with *Seven more unclean Spirits*, entred into her; and God, seemed then to withhold from her, the Efficacy of the means of Grace and Good, which His Faithful Servants in the Neighbourhood, used with her.

XII

On *November* 17. 1698. There was executed in *Boston*, a miserable Young Woman, whose Extraordinary circumstances rung throughout all *New England*. On this Day of her Execution, was Preached the *Sermon*, which we have now placed, at the Beginning of this History, as an *Inscription* upon our, PILLARS OF SALT. Because the last passages of that *Sermon*, gave a summary Narrative, of what it is fit the publick should know concerning that Criminal, I have Transferr'd them, into this place. The *Sermon* Concluded in these words.

Be astonished, O Congregation of God, Stand astonished, at the Horrible *Spectacle*, that is now before You: This *House*, and perhaps this *Land*, never had in it a more Astonishing *Spectacle*.

Behold, a *Young Woman*, but an *Old Sinner*, going this Day to *Dy before her time*, for being *Wicked over-much*! Behold, One just *Nineteen* Years Old, and yet found *Ripe* for the *Vengeance* of a *Capital Execution*. Ah, Miserable Soul, *With what a swift progress of Sin and Folly, hast thou made Hast unto the Congregation of the Dead!* Behold a Person, whose Unchaste Conversation appear'd by one *Base Born* Child many months ago! *God then gave her a Space to Repent, and she repented not*: She Repeted her Whoredomes, and by an Infatuation from God upon her, She so managed the matter of her next *Base Born*, that she is found Guilty of its *Murder*: Thus the God, whose Eyes are like a Flame of Fire, is now casting her into a *Bed* of Burning *Tribulation*: And, ah, Lord, *Where wilt thou cast those that have committed Adultery with her, Except they Repent!* Since her Imprisonment, She hath Declared, That she believes, God hath Left her unto this *Undoing Wickedness*, partly for her staying so profanely at Home sometimes on *Lords-Dayes*, when she should have been Hearing the *Word of Christ*, and much more for her not minding that *Word*, when she heard it. And she has Confessed, That she was much given to *Rash Wishes*, in her *Mad Passions*, particularly using often that Ill Form of speaking, *I'll be Hang'd*, if a thing be not thus or so, and, *I'll be Hanged*, if I do not this or that; which Evil now, to see it, coming upon her, it amazes her! But the *chief Sin*, of which this *Chief of Sinners*, now cries out, is, *Her Undutiful Carriage towards her Parents*. Her *Language* and her *Carriage* towards her *Parents*, was indeed such that they hardly *Durst* speak to her; but when they *Durst*, they often told her, *It would come to This*. They indeed, with Bleeding Hearts, have now *Forgiven* thy Rebellions; Ah, *Sarah*, mayst thou Cry unto the God of Heaven to *Forgive* Thee! But under all the doleful circumstances of her *Imprisonment*, and her *Impiety*, she has been *given over*, to be a prodigy of still more *Impenitent Impiety*. A little before her *Condemnation*, she Renewed the Crimes of her *Unchastity*; she gave her self up to the *Filthy Debauches*, of a Villain, that was her Fellow-Prisoner; and after her *Condemnation*, her *Falsehoods*, and her *Furies* have been such, as to proclaim, That *under Condemnation she has not Feared God*. Was there ever seen such an *Heighth of Wickedness*! God seems to have Hanged her up in Chains, for all the *Young People* in the Countrey, to see, what prodigies of *Sin* and *Wrath* it may render them, if once they *Sell themselves* thereunto. Behold, O *Young People*, what it is to *Vex* the *Holy Spirit* of God, by *Rebelling* against Him. *This*, This 'tis to be *Given over of God*! And yet after all this *Hard-hearted Wickedness*, is it not possible for the *Grace* of Heaven to be Triumphantly Victorious, in Converting and Pardoning so *Unparallel'd* a *Criminal?* Be astonished, Miserable *Sarah*, and Let it now break that *Stony heart* of thine, to *Hear* it; *It is possible! It is possible!* But, *O thou Almighty Spirit of Grace, do thou graciously Touch, and Melt this Obstinate Soul, and once at last, mould her Heart into the Form of thy Glorious Gospel.* The *Glorious Gospel of God*, now utters unto thee, Undone *Sarah*, that Invitation, *Tho' thou hast horribly gone a Whoring, yet Return unto me, saith the Lord, and I will not cause my Anger to fall upon thee.* The *Lessons* of this *Gospel* have been both privately and publickly set before thee, with a vast variety of Inculcation. If all the Extraordinary pains that have been taken for the softening of thy *Stony Heart*, be Lost, God will dispense the more terrible Rebukes unto thee, when He anon breaks thee between the *Millstones* of His Wrath.

Oh, Give now a great Attention, to some of the *Last Words*, that can be spoken to thee, before thy passing into an astonishing Eternity.

The Blessed Lord JESUS CHRIST hath been made a *Curse* for Us; there has been a most Acceptable *Offering* and *Sacrifice*, presented by the Lord Jesus Christ unto God, for all His Chosen: there is a *Fountain set open for Sin and for Uncleanness*: and thou, O *Bloody* Sinner, art Invited unto that *Open Fountain*. Such is the Infinite *Grace* of God, that thou mayest come as freely to the *Blood* of the Lord Jesus Christ, for the Forgiveness of thy Sins, as they that never Sinn'd with a Thousandth part of so much Aggravation; *Come, and Welcome*, says the Lord, who *Receiveth Sinners*. If God Enable thee Now, to *Lay Hold* on the *Righteousness* of the Lord Jesus Christ, tho' thy Faults are Infinite, thou wilt yet before Sun-set *Stand without Fault before the Throne of God*. Thy Soul is just sinking down, into the Fiery Ocean of the Wrath of God, but the *Righteousness* of the Lord Jesus Christ, is cast forth unto thee, once more, for thee, to *Lay Hold* upon. Oh! *Lay Hold* upon it, and *Live!* If God help thee, to do so, *Then*, as it was said, *The* Mary *whose Sins are many, has them Forgiven her*, So it shall be said, *The* Sarah, *whose Sins are many, has them Forgiven her! Then*, as it was said, Rahab *the Harlot perished not*, so it shall be said, Sarah *the Harlot, perished not!* Tho' the *Blood* of thy murdered Infant, with all thy other Bloody Crimes, horribly Cry to God against thee, yet a louder and better Cry from the *Blood* of thy Saviour, shall drown that formidable Cry. Yea, *then*, There will be *Joy in Heaven* this Afternoon *among the Angels of God*; the *Angels* of Heaven will stand amazed, and say, *O the Infinite Grace, that can bring such a Sinner unto Glory!* But if ever the *Blood* of the Lord Jesus Christ, be applied unto *thy Heart*, it will immediately *Dissolve* that Heart of thine; it will cause thee to *Mourn* for every Sin, to *Turn* from every Sin, to give thy self entirely unto *God*. It will be impossible for thee, to Go on in any *Known Sin*, or to *Dy* with a *Ly* in thy mouth, no, thou wilt rather *Dy* than commit any *Known Sin* in the World. If this *Disposition*, be not *produced* in thee, before Three or Four short Hours more are Expired, thy Immortal *Spirit*, will anon pass into Eternal *Torment*: thou wilt before To morrow morning be a Companion of the *Devils* and the *Damned*; the Everlasting *Chains of Darkness* will hold thee, for the *Worm that never dies, & the Fire that never shall be Quenched*: thou shalt fall into the *Hands of the Living God*, and become as a glowing Iron, possessed by his Burning Vengeance, throughout Eternal Ages; the God that *made thee, will not have mercy on thee, and He that formed thee will show thee no Favour*. But for his Mercy, and Favour, while there is yet hope, we will yet Cry unto Him.

FINIS

Pillars of Salt, An History of Some Criminals Executed in this Land for Capital Crimes, 1699

BENJAMIN FRANKLIN

Statesman, diplomat, scientist, inventor, philosopher, publisher—
"everything but a poet," as Herman Melville remarked—Benjamin
Franklin (1706–1790) was also early in his extraordinary career a crime
reporter. As printer of *The Pennsylvania Gazette*, the most widely read newspaper of the colonial era, he was fully aware of the public's unending
appetite for sensation and scandal, making disparaging reference to "the
corrupt Taste of the Majority" in his celebrated journalistic credo, "Apology for Printers." Even while insisting that he would never pander to the
prurient interests of his readers, Franklin was not above providing them
with titillating accounts of sex and violence, a considerable number of
which involved domestic cruelty and murder: a father who, having
taken his daughter to bed when his wife refused to sleep with him, killed
the child during the night; a husband who demanded that his wife "put
her Tongue into his Mouth," then "bit off a large Piece of it"; a cuckold
named Stonecutter who attempted to decapitate the fellow he found
"napping" with his spouse; a fiddler named Piles who anticipated the
infamous "American Tragedy" murder of 1906 by taking his wife out in
a canoe and drowning her.

The horrifying story below appeared in *The Pennsylvania Gazette* on
October 24, 1734. Scholars take different views of Franklin's intention
in offering such a relentlessly grim account. Robert Bosco, for example, sees it not as a work of objective reportage but as an expression of
Franklin's "personal contempt for every horrid, coarse sign of human
depravity," while Robert D. Arner places the piece in the context of
Franklin's other writings on temperance and believes it is meant to il-
lustrate the evils of dram-drinking, the frightening potential of alcohol
to turn ordinary people "into monsters unknown to themselves and
unrecognizable by their better natures."

The Murder of a Daughter

Saturday last, at a Court of Oyer and Terminer held here, came on the Tryal of a Man and his Wife, who were indicted for the Murder of a Daughter which he had by a former Wife, (a Girl of about 14 Years of Age) by turning her out of Doors, and thereby exposing her to such Hardships, as afterwards produced grievous Sickness and Lameness; during which, instead of supplying her with Necessaries and due Attendance, they treated her with the utmost Cruelty and Barbarity, suffering her to lie and rot in her Nastiness, and when she cried for Bread giving her into her Mouth with a Iron Ladle, her own Excrements to eat, with a great Number of other Circumstances of the like Nature, so that she languished and at length died. The Evidence against them was numerous, and in many Particulars positive; but the Opinion of the Physician who had visited the Child, that whatever Usage might be given her, the Distemper she laboured under was such, as would of itself in all Probability have ended her Life about the Time she died, it is thought weighed so much with the Jury, that they brought in their Verdict only *Man-slaughter*. A Verdict which the Judge, (in a short but pathetic Speech to the Prisoners before the Sentence) told them was *extreamly favourable*; and that, as the Relation of their hitherto unheard-of Barbarity had in the highest Manner shocked all that were present; so, if they were not perfectly stupified, the inward Reflection upon their own enormous Crimes, must be more terrible and shocking to them, than the Punishment they were to undergo: For that they had not only acted contrary to the particular Laws of all Nations, but had even broken the Universal Law of Nature; since there are no Creatures known, how savage, wild, and fierce soever, that have not implanted in them a natural Love and Care of their tender Offspring, and that will not even hazard Life in its Protection and Defence.—But this is not the only Instance the present Age has afforded, of the incomprehensible Insensibility

Dram-drinking is capable of producing.—They were sentenced to be burnt in the Hand, which was accordingly executed in Court, upon them both, but first upon the Man, who offer'd to receive another Burning if so be his Wife might be excused; but was told the Law would not allow it.

The Pennsylvania Gazette, October 24, 1734

ANONYMOUS

Certain crimes draw our attention because they have inspired enduring literary works and films. Examples include the Chester Gillette–Grace Brown murder that supplied the source material for Theodore Dreiser's *An American Tragedy*; the Ruth Snyder–Judd Gray murder, the model for James M. Cain's *Double Indemnity*; the atrocities of Edward Gein that, by way of Robert Bloch's novel, inspired Alfred Hitchcock's *Psycho*; and the case of Charles Schmid, the ineffably disturbing "Pied Piper of Tucson," who lurks behind Joyce Carol Oates's famous story "Where Are You Going, Where Have You Been?" Perhaps the earliest example of such a crime in our cultural history is the domestic murder described in the newspaper article below. The subject of the story, identified in the text only by his initials, is James Yates, a farmer residing in the frontier village of Tomhanick in upstate New York. In December 1781, Yates slaughtered his wife and four children in a paroxysm of religious mania. He was declared insane and confined to a dungeon in Albany.

Fifteen years later, identical accounts of this sensational crime were reprinted in *The New-York Weekly Magazine* and the *Philadelphia Minerva*. The latter caught the attention of Charles Brockden Brown, our nation's first professional man of letters, who drew on key elements of the Yates case for *Wieland* (1798), a Gothic tale of a religious fanatic who slaughters his wife and children in obedience to a "divine voice." In the preface to his book Brown observes that "most readers will probably recollect an authentic case, remarkably similar to that of Wieland."

An Account of a Murder Committed by Mr. J—— Y——, Upon His Family, in December, A.D. 1781

The unfortunate subject of my present essay, belonged to one of the most respectable families in this state; he resided a few miles from Tomhanick, and though he was not in the most affluent circumstances, he maintained his family (which consisted of a wife and four children,) very comfortably.—From the natural gentleness of his disposition, his industry, sobriety, probity and kindness, his neighbours universally esteemed him, and until the fatal night when he perpetrated the cruel act, none saw cause of blame in him.

In the afternoon preceding that night, as it was Sunday and there was no church near, several of his neighbours with their wives came to his house for the purpose of reading the scripture and singing psalms; he received them cordially, and when they were going to return home in the evening, he pressed his sister and her husband, who came with the others, to stay longer; at his very earnest solicitation they remained until near nine o'clock, during which time his conversation was grave as usual, but interesting and affectionate: to his wife, of whom he was very fond, he made use of more than commonly endearing expressions, and caressed his little ones alternately:—he spoke much of his domestic felicity, and informed his sister, that to render his wife more happy, he intended to take her to New-Hampshire the next day; "I have just been refitting my sleigh," said he, "and we will set off by day-break."—After singing another hymn, Mr. and Mrs. J—f—n departed.

"They had no sooner left us (said he upon his examination) than taking my wife upon my lap, I opened the Bible to read to her—my two boys were in bed—one five years old, the other seven;—my daughter Rebecca, about eleven, was sitting by the fire, and my infant aged about six months, was slumbering at her mother's bosom.—Instantly a new light shone into the room, and upon looking up I beheld two Spirits, one at my right hand and the other at my left;—he at the left bade me destroy all my *idols*, and begin by casting the Bible into the fire;—the other Spirit dissuaded me, but I obeyed the first, and threw the book into the flames. My wife immediately snatched it out, and was going to expostulate, when I threw it in again and held her fast until it was entirely consumed:—then filled with the determination to persevere, I flew out of the house, and seizing an axe which lay by the door, with a few strokes demolished my sleigh, and running to the stable killed one of my horses—the other I struck, but with one spring he got clear of the stable.—My spirits now were high, and I hasted to the house to inform my wife of what I had done. She appeared terrified, and begged me to sit down; but the good angel whom I had obeyed stood by me and bade me go on. "You have more idols, (said he) look at your wife and children." I hesitated not a moment, but rushed to the bed where my boys lay, and catching the eldest in my arms, I threw him with such violence against the wall, that he expired without a groan!—his brother was still asleep—I took him by the feet, and dashed his skull in pieces against the fire-place!—Then looking round, and perceiving that my wife and daughters were fled, I left the dead where they lay, and went in pursuit of the living, taking up the axe again.—A slight snow had fallen that evening, and by its light I descried my wife running towards her father's (who lived about half a mile off) encumbered with her babe; I ran after her, calling upon her to return, but she shrieked and fled faster, I therefore doubled my pace, and when I was within thirty yards of her, threw the axe at her, which hit her upon the hip!—the moment that she felt the blow she dropped the child, which I directly caught up, and threw against a log-fence—I did not hear it cry—I only heard the lamentations of my wife, of whom I had now lost sight; but the blood gushed so copiously from her wound that it formed a distinct path along the snow. We were now within sight of her father's house, but from what cause I cannot tell, she took an opposite course, and after running across an open field several times, she again stopped at her own door; I now came up with her—my heart bled to see her distress, and all my *natural feelings* began to revive; I forgot my duty, so powerfully did her moanings and pleadings affect me, "Come then, my love (said I) we have one child left, let us be thankful for that—what is done is right—we must not repine, come let me embrace you—let me know that you do indeed love me." She encircled me in her trembling arms, and pressed her quivering lips to my cheek.—A voice behind me, said, "This is also an idol!"—I broke from her instantly, and wrenching a stake from the garden fence, with one stroke levelled her to the earth!

and lest she should only be stunned, and might, perhaps, recover again, I repeated my blows, till I could not distinguish one feature of her face! ! ! I now went to look after my last sublunary treasure, but after calling several times without receiving any answer, I returned to the house again; and in the way back picked up the babe and laid it on my wife's bosom.—I then stood musing a minute—during which interval I thought I heard the suppressed sobbings of some one near the barn, I approached it in silence, and beheld my daughter Rebecca endeavouring to conceal herself among the hay-stacks.—

At the noise of my feet upon the dry corn stalks—she turned hastily round and seeing me exclaimed, "O father, my dear father, spare me, let me live—let me live,—I will be a comfort to you and my mother—spare me to take care of my little sister Diana—do—do let me live."—She was my darling child, and her fearful cries pierced me to the soul—the tears of *natural pity* fell as plentifully down my cheeks, as those of terror did down her's, and methought that to destroy *all* my idols, was a hard task—I again relapsed at the voice of complaining; and taking her by the hand, led her to where her mother lay; then thinking that if I intended to retain her, I must make some other severe sacrifice, I bade her sing and dance—She complied, terribly situated as she was,—but I was not acting in the line of my duty—I was convinced of my error, and catching up a hatchet that stuck in a log, with one well aimed stroke cleft her forehead in twain —she fell—and no sign of retaining life appeared.

I then sat down on the threshold, to consider what I had best do— "I shall be called a murderer (said I) I shall be seized—imprisoned— executed, and for what?—for destroying my idols—for obeying the mandate of my father—no, I will put all the dead in the house together, and after setting fire to it, run to my sister's and say the Indians have done it"—I was preparing to drag my wife in, when the idea struck me that I was going to tell a *horrible lie*; "and how will that accord with my profession? (asked I.) No, let me speak the truth, and declare the good motive for my actions, be the consequences what they may."

His sister, who was the principal evidence against him, stated—that she had scarce got home, when a message came to Mr. J—n, her husband, informing him that his mother was ill and wished to see him; he accordingly set off immediately, and she not expecting him home again till the next day, went to bed—there being no other person in the house. About four in the morning she heard her brother Y—— call her, she started up and bade him come in. "I will not (returned he) for I have committed the unpardonable sin—I have burnt the Bible." She knew not what to think, but rising hastily opened the door which was only latched, and caught hold of his hand: let me go, Nelly (said he) my hands are wet with blood—the blood of my Elizabeth and her children.—She saw the blood dripping from his fingers, and her's chilled in the veins, yet with a fortitude unparalleled she begged him to enter, which—as he did, he attempted to sieze a case knife, that by the light of a bright pine-knot fire, he perceived lying on the dresser—she prevented him, however, and tearing a trammel from the chimney, bound him with it to the bed post—fastening his hands behind him—She then quitted the house in order to go to his, which as she approached she heard the voice of loud lamentation, the hope that it was some one of the family who had escaped the effects of her brother's frenzy, subdued the fears natural to such a situation and time, she quickened her steps, and when she came to the place where Mrs. Y—— lay, she perceived that the moans came from Mrs. Y——'s aged father, who expecting that his daughter would set out upon her journey by day break, had come at that early hour to bid her farewel.

They alarmed their nearest neighbours immediately, who proceeded to Mrs. J—n's, and there found Mr. Y—— in the situation she had left him; they took him from hence to Tomhanick, where he remained near two days—during which time Mr. W—tz—l (a pious old Lutheran, who occasionally acted as preacher) attended upon him, exhorting him to pray and repent; but he received the admonitions with contempt, and several times with ridicule, refusing to confess his error or *join* in prayer—I say *join* in prayer, for he would not kneel when the rest did, but when they arose he would prostrate himself and address his "father," frequently saying "my father, thou knowest that it was in obedience to thy commands, and for thy glory that I have done this deed." Mrs. Bl——r, at whose house he then was, bade some one ask him who his father was?—he made no reply —but pushing away the person who stood between her and himself, darted at her a look of such indignation as thrilled horror to her heart—his speech was connected, and he told his tale without variation; he expressed much sorrow for the loss of his dear family, but consoled himself with the idea of having performed his duty—he was taken to ALBANY and there confined as a lunatic in the goal, from which he escaped twice, once by the assistance of Aqua Fortis, with which he opened the front door.

I went in 1782 with a little girl, by whom Mr. Bl——r had sent him some fruit; he was then confined in dungeon, and had several chains on—he appeared to be much affected at her remembrance of him, and put up a pious ejaculation for her and her family—since then I have received no accounts respecting him.

The cause for his wonderfully cruel proceedings is beyond the conception of human beings—the deed so unpremeditated, so unprovoked, that we do not hesitate to pronounce it the effect of insanity —yet upon the other hand, when we reflect on the equinimity of his temper, and the comfortable situation in which he was, and no visible circumstance operating to render him frantic, we are apt to conclude, that he was under a strong delusion of Satan. But what avail our conjectures, perhaps it is best that some things are concealed from us, and the only use we can now make of our knowledge of this affair, is to be humble under a scene of human frailty to renew our petition, "Lead us not into temptation."

May, 27, 1796.

The New-York Weekly Magazine, July 20, 1796

TIMOTHY DWIGHT

The case of James Yates was far from unique. As historian Karen Halttunen has shown in her pioneering study *Murder Most Foul* (1998), domestic murder—particularly "the slaughter of an entire family by its patriarchal head"—became an increasingly common subject in late 18th-century American crime literature. One of the most sensational of these incidents was the atrocity perpetrated in December 1782 by the Connecticut shopkeeper William Beadle.

The Beadle murders became the subject of sermons, broadside ballads, and pamphlets, including a shockingly graphic account written by his friend and neighbor, Stephen Mix Mitchell, one of the first men to arrive at the murder scene. Mitchell's widely distributed narrative of the "horrid massacre" provided material for the following account by another of Beadle's intimates, Timothy Dwight (1752–1817). A pastor, educator, and prominent member of the Connecticut Wits, America's first poetic "school," Dwight owes his place in our literary history to three ambitious poems: *The Conquest of Canaan* (1785), an epic-length expansion of the biblical story of Joshua; *The Triumph of Infidelity* (1788), a lengthy defense of orthodox Calvinism; and *Greenfield Hill* (1794), a pastoral celebration of New England village life. His four-volume *Travels in New-England and New-York*, published posthumously in 1821–22, is the source of this selection.

"A crime more atrocious and horrible than any other"

Wethersfield is remarkable for having been the scene of a crime, more atrocious and horrible than any other, which has been perpetrated within the limits of New-England; and scarcely exceeded in the history of man. By the politeness of my friend, Col. Belden, I am enabled to give you an authentic account of this terrible transaction, taken from the records of the third School District in Wethersfield. I shall not, however, copy the record exactly; but will give you the substance of every thing which it contains.

William Beadle was born in a little village, near London. In the year 1755, he went out to Barbadoes, with Governor Pinfold; where he staid six years, and then returned to England. In 1762, he purchased a small quantity of goods; and brought them to New-York, and thence to Stratford in Connecticut, where he lived about two years. Thence he removed to Derby; where he continued a year, or two; and thence to Fairfield. Here he married Miss Lathrop, a lady of a respectable family, belonging to Plymouth in Massachusetts. In 1772, he removed to Wethersfield, and continued in this town about ten years; sustaining the character of a worthy, honest man, and a fair dealer.

In the great controversy, which produced the American Revolution, he adopted American principles; and characteristically, adhered with rigid exactness to whatever he had once adopted. After the continental paper currency* began to depreciate; almost every trader sold his goods at an enhanced price. Beadle, however, continued to sell his at the original prices, and to receive the depreciated currency in payment. This money he kept by him, until it had lost its value. The decay of his property rendered him melancholy; as appeared by several letters, which he left behind him, addressed to different persons of his acquaintance.

By the same letters, and other writings, it appears, that he began to entertain designs of the most desperate nature, three years before his death; but was induced to postpone them by a hope, that Providence would, in some way or other, change his circumstances for the better, so far, as to make it advisable for him to wait for death in the ordinary course of events. But every thing, which took place, whether of great or little importance, tended, he says, to convince him, that it was his duty to adopt the contrary determination. During all this time he managed his ordinary concerns just as he had heretofore done. His

---

*The paper money emitted by Congress during the Revolutionary war.

countenance wore no appearance of any change in his feelings, or views; and not one of his acquaintance seems to have suspected, that he was melancholy. The very evening before the catastrophe, to which I have alluded, took place, he was in company with several of his friends; and conversed on grave and interesting subjects; but without the least appearance of any peculiar emotion.

On the morning of Dec. 11th, 1782, he called up a female servant, who slept in the same room with his children, and was the only domestic in his family; and directed her to arise so softly, as not to disturb the children. When she came down, he gave her a note, which he had written to Dr. Farnsworth, his family-physician; and told her to carry it, and wait until the physician was ready to come with her; informing her at the same time, that Mrs. Beadle had been ill through the night.

After the servant had gone, as appeared by the deplorable scene, presented to the eyes of those who first entered the house; he took an axe, struck each of his children once, and his wife twice on the head; cut their throats quite across with a carving-knife, which he had prepared for the purpose; and then shot himself through the head with a pistol.

Dr. Farnsworth, upon opening the note, found that it announced the diabolical purpose of the writer; but supposing it impossible, that a sober man should adopt so horrible a design, concluded, that he had been suddenly seized by a delirium. Dr. Farnsworth, however, hastened with the note to the Hon. Stephen Mix Mitchell, now Chief Justice of the State. This gentleman realized the tragedy at once. The house was immediately opened, and all the family were found dead, in the manner which has been specified.

I knew this family intimately. Mrs. Beadle possessed a very pleasing person, a fine mind, and delightful manners. The children were unusually lovely and promising. Beadle in his writings, which were numerous, professed himself a Deist; and declared that man was in his opinion a mere machine; unaccountable for his actions, and incapable of either virtue or vice. The idea of a Revelation he rejected with contempt. At the same time he reprobated the *vices of others* in the strongest terms; and spoke of *duty*, in the very same writings, in language, decisively expressive of his belief in the existence of both duty and sin. The Jury of inquest pronounced him to be of sound mind; and brought in a verdict of murder, and suicide.

The inhabitants of Wethersfield, frantic with indignation and horror at a crime so unnatural and monstrous, and at the sight of a lady, and her children, for whom they had the highest regard, thus butchered by one, who ought to have protected them at the hazard of his life, took his body, as they found it, and dragged it on a small sled to the bank of the river, without any coffin, with the bloody knife tied upon it; and buried it, as they would have buried the carcase of a beast, between high and low water mark.

The corpses of the unhappy family were the next day carried, with every mark of respect, to the Church; where a sermon was preached to a very numerous concourse of sincere mourners. They were then interred in the common burying-ground, and in one grave.

Mrs. Beadle was thirty-two years of age; and the eldest child about fifteen. Beadle was fifty-two years of age; of small stature; and of an ordinary appearance. He was contemplative; possessed good sense; loved reading, and delighted in intelligent conversation. His manners were gentlemanly; and his disposition hospitable. His countenance exhibited a strong appearance of determination; yet he rarely looked the person, with whom he was conversing, in the face; but turned his eye askance, the only suspicious circumstance, which I observed in his conduct; unless a degree of reserve and mystery, which always attended him, might merit the name of suspicious. Such as he was, he was cheerfully admitted to the best society in this town: and there is no better society.

Col. Belden adds to his account the following note.

"This deed of horror seems to have been marked by the indignation of Heaven in the treatment of the body of the perpetrator."

"The ground in which he was first buried, happened to belong to the township of Glastenbury; although lying on the western side of the river. The inhabitants of Glastenbury, thinking themselves insulted by the burying of such a monster within its limits, manifested their uneasiness in such a manner, as to induce the Select-men of the town of Wethersfield to order a removal of the body. Accordingly it was removed in the night, secretly, and by a circuitous route; and buried again at some distance from the original place of sepulture. Within a few days however, the spot, where it was interred, was discovered. It was removed again in the night, and buried near the western bank of the river, in Wethersfield. The following spring it was uncovered by the freshet. The flesh was washed from the bones. At this season, a multitude of persons customarily resort to Wethersfield, to purchase fish. By these and various other persons, in the indulgence of a strange, and I think unnatural curiosity, the bones were broken off, and scattered through the country."

Pride was unquestionably the ruin of Beadle. He was, obviously, a man of a very haughty mind. This passion induced him, when he had once determined, that the paper currency would escape a depreciation, to continue selling his goods at the former prices, after the whole community had, with one voice, adopted a new rate of exchange. Under the influence of this passion he refused to lay out his money in fixed property; although prudence plainly dictated such a measure. When he saw his circumstances reduced so as to threaten him with a necessary and humiliating change in his style of living; pride prompted him, instead of making new exertions to provide for his family, to sit down in a sullen hostility against God and man, and to waste the whole energy of his mind in resentment against his lot, and in gloomy determinations to escape from it. He doated upon his wife and children. His pride could not bear the thought of leaving them behind him, without a fortune sufficient to give them undisputed distinction in the world.

A gentleman, who had long been a friend to Beadle, offered him letters of credit, to any amount, which he should wish. Of this his friend informed me personally. Pride induced Beadle to refuse the offer.

In these charges I am supported by Beadle's own writings. He alleges this very cause for his conduct; and alleges it every where; not in so many words indeed; but in terms, which, though specious, are too explicit to be misconstrued.

Beadle, as I have observed, denied the existence of a Divine Revelation. Yet he placed a strong reliance upon dreams, as conveying direct indications of the will of GOD; so strong as to make them the directories of his own moral conduct in a case of tremendous magnitude. He appears by his writings to have been long persuaded, that he had a right to take the lives of his children, because they were *his* children; and therefore, in his own view his property, and to be disposed of according to his pleasure: i.e. as I suppose, in any manner, which he should judge conducive to their good. But he thought himself unwarranted to take away the life of his wife; because, being the child of another person, she was not in the same sense his property, nor under his control. This you will call a strange current of thought: but the manner, in which he solved his scruples, was certainly not less strange. His wife, under the influence of very painful impressions from his extraordinary conduct, particularly from the fact, that he continually brought an axe, and other instruments of death, into his bedchamber, dreamed frequently, and in a very disturbed manner. One morning she told him, that in her sleep, the preceding night, she had seen her own corpse, and the corpses of her children, exposed in coffins, in the street; that the sun shone on them for a long time; and that they were ultimately frozen. This dream made a deep impression on Beadle's mind. In his writings he mentions it as having solved all his doubts; and as a direct revelation from Heaven, that it was lawful for him to put his wife, also, to death.

We have here a strong proof of the propriety, with which Infidels boast of their exemption from superstition, and credulity.

Had this man possessed even a little share of the patience, and fortitude, of a Christian; had he learned to submit to the pleasure of God with that resignation, which is so obvious a dictate even of natural religion; had that humility, which is so charming a feature of the

Christian character, formed any part of his own; he might, even now, have been alive; and might in all probability, have seen his children grow up to be the support, and the joy, of his declining years.

He died worth three hundred pounds sterling. The farmers in Connecticut were, at an average, probably not worth more, at the same period. Every one of them; at least every one of them, whose property did not overrun this sum; might, therefore, with equal propriety, have acted in the same manner. What would become of the world, if every man in it, who was worth no more than three hundred pounds sterling, were to murder himself and his family.

I think you will agree with me, that we have, here, a strong specimen, of the weakness of Infidelity; and of the wickedness, to which it conducts its votaries.

Travels in New-England and New-York, 1821–22

THE RECORD OF CRIMES IN THE UNITED STATES

One of Nathaniel Hawthorne's favorite books, *The Record of Crimes in the United States*, is an early true-crime anthology containing "A Brief Sketch of the Prominent Traits in the Character and Conduct of Many of the Most Notorious Malefactors Who Have Been Guilty of Capital Offences and Who Have Been Detected and Convicted." Among its 23 subjects are George Swearingen, a young Maryland sheriff who killed his wife so that he could run off with his prostitute-mistress; William Bevans, a marine on board the U.S. *Independence* who bayoneted a ship-mate after an exchange of words; the Harpes, a notorious pair of frontier robbers and murderers; Joel Clough, hanged for stabbing a widow who did not return his affections; and Jesse Strang, the besotted young man described below, who, at the instigation of his married paramour Elsie Whipple, shot and killed her elderly husband—an antebellum precursor of the notorious Snyder-Gray case of the 1920s. Strang's hanging in 1827 was the last public execution held in Albany, New York.

Jesse Strang

W hat we have to relate concerning the celebrated murder of Mr. Whipple, is founded on facts disclosed at Strang's trial, and on his confessions while under sentence of death.

Jesse Strang was the son of poor parents and was brought up to hard labor. When he arrived at man's estate he married, but being naturally of a restless, depraved disposition, he soon left his spouse to shift for herself, and went to Ohio. Becoming tired of the western country he returned to the east, and in July, eighteen hundred and twenty-six, arrived in Albany, whence he went to Cherry Hill, near the residence of P. P. Van Rensselaer, and hired himself to a Mr. Bates. To avoid recognition by any of his former acquaintance he took the name of Joseph Orton.

Mr. Bates kept a public house. About the beginning of August, Strang being in the bar room, saw two females enter, one of whom was young, handsome, and very giddy and playful. This person was not, as he supposed from her demeanor, a girl, but a married woman. She was the wife of Mr. John Whipple, who was much her senior. As to her character, it appears that though her husband treated her with the utmost gentleness and affection, and though she had borne him a son, she was the slave of animal passion, which influenced her conduct the more; that she was totally devoid of religion and moral principle. Such was the famous, or more properly, the infamous Elsie D. Whipple, the first sight of whom lighted the flame of lawless love in Strang's bosom.

About the end of August, Strang went to live with Mr. Van Rensselaer, who dwelt in a house in which Mr. Whipple and his wife were boarders. For a long time no particular intimacy took place between Strang and the object of his desires, nor did any part of her conduct encourage him to declare his feelings toward her, which were daily gaining strength. But near the end of October she held a conversation with him, in which she displayed so much levity, as induced him to think that she reciprocated his feelings.

Strang went by the familiar name of "The Doctor" in the family. A few hours after the conversation above mentioned, Mrs. Whipple proved herself capable of making the first advances. She accosted him with, "Doctor, I want you to write me a letter." Supposing that she could not write, he exclaimed in astonishment, "What! I write *you* a letter?" "Yes," she rejoined, "I hate to write the first one." Then desiring him to consider the matter and write that very night, she left him. For a while he doubted whether this her proposal might not be a device to entrap him, but the recollection of her manner toward him, and his own passion, gave him courage to comply. We subjoin this model of epistolary writing to show what qualifications were necessary to command the love of Mrs. Whipple. It ran thus,

Dear Elsie—I have seariesly considered on it as you requested of me yeasterday and I have concluded two compose a few lines two You and I thought that it was not my duty two right very freely not nowing Your object perhaps it is two get sum of my righting two show two your husband as you ar a marid woman, and If that is your intenshin It is my whish fore you two let me now it fore it is a thing that I skorn two make a distirbance between you and your husband but If in the outher hand It is out of pure offections I should be quite hapy for two have the information in your hand riting and I hope that you will not take any offen in my maner of riting two you as we ar pirfict strangers two each outher, but hop that thoes few lines may find free acceptan with you and after I find out your motive I can right mour freely on the subject and as for my offections thay ar quite favorable I shall expact an answer from you If that is your motive, sow I remain you well whisher.

Joseph Orton.

The morality contained in this beautiful piece of composition was suggested by the reflections of the Sabbath day, and the letter was delivered thereon. Three-quarters of an hour sufficed Mrs. Whipple to indite an answer, which began with "Dear Doctor," and assured him that she had no evil design toward him. Her motive, she said, was pure love, excited by the first sight of his beautiful eyes. Since that moment she had enjoyed neither happiness nor comfort. She had eloped to be married and could do so again. She had waited long, hoping that he would declare himself, and now desired him never to leave the place without taking her with him. She had long been of opinion that the passion of love had no real existence, but he had convinced her of her error, and she solicited a continuation of his correspondence. She subscribed herself Elsie D. Whipple, his true and affectionate lover till death.

In answer to this Strang wrote her a proposal to elope with him, promising, if she would consent, to do all in his power to support and protect her. She accepted the offer without hesitation, saying she would go to the end of the earth to get him. However, she was unwilling to start till she had obtained twelve hundred dollars for their expenses. In a subsequent conversation she explained her plans more fully by word of mouth. She had always been desirous to keep a public house and thought the sum she had mentioned would be enough to begin with. Strang objected that he knew nothing of the business, but thought that he might turn his hand to it as well as to anything else. He proposed that they should go first to Montreal, and remain there till Mr. Whipple should be reconciled to his loss, and then proceed to Sandusky in Ohio, where they might be married by fictitious names, and carry their project into execution.

The wretches had little opportunity for conversation, and therefore continued their intercourse by letter. The topics of these were the means of raising money, and being unable to hit on any feasible plan, the infatuated woman at last proposed directly that Strang should forge a check, in Mr. Whipple's name, on the bank in which his money was deposited. Strang did not want the will, but his education had not qualified him for such an act of villany. Impatient of delay, his paramour entreated him to assassinate her husband; thus proving that a woman makes more rapid strides in the path which leadeth to destruction, when she has once set her foot in it, than a man. She proposed that he should hire some laboring man to do the deed, or failing in that to do it himself. If he should conclude to take the business in his own hands she offered to procure her husband's pistols for him. This wickedness was entirely the suggestion of her own mind, for Strang had never intimated any such intention to her, and though she had often wished for Mr. Whipple's death, she had never before spoke of murdering him.

Strang was shocked at the proposal, and told her so. He said that though his affection for her was not susceptible of increase, he would rather labor all his life than be guilty of a murder. He loved her, not for her property, but for herself: if she loved him well enough to become his companion he would work himself to death to maintain her, but if the possession of her depended on the murder of an innocent man, there was an end of the affair. In writing thus he still hoped that her suggestion had not been serious.

She answered that she had thought Strang was a man as resolute as another who had offered to kill Mr. Whipple. This person she did not love, and was confident that he had no affection for her, but was actuated in his offer by the desire of obtaining her property. If Strang, she continued, really loved her as he pretended, he would have consented for the sake of her person and property, and that he might live without work: but as he had refused to do her will, she had concluded to live on the same terms with him as before, until they could otherwise obtain the means to elope.

We had forgotten to mention that while this intercourse was being carried on, Mr. Whipple was absent. In January he returned. One day in the February succeeding, his wicked wife called Strang aside, and with every appearance of indignation told him that her husband had struck her, which, probably, was false, as such an action was not in keeping with the worthy man's character. Strang asked if he should not waylay and kill the supposed offender, and Mrs. Whipple eagerly assented. He said he could not, and she then desired him, if he was so faint-hearted, at least to procure poison, which she would administer herself, being resolved to bear such abuse no longer. Strang refused to do this, too.

A few days after, as Strang was sitting in the kitchen, Mrs. Whipple passed through with a bowl of milk. She stopped and told him her husband had just called for the milk and observed that had he consented to procure the poison, it would have been an excellent opportunity to administer it unsuspected.

Matters kept on in their usual train till March, when finding it impossible to raise money, and urged by Mrs. Whipple, Strang bought a dose of arsenic, which he gave her, and she put it into her husband's tea. They then pledged themselves by the most solemn oaths, never, under any circumstances, to betray each other; as if those capable of such a crime, would regard the sanctity of an oath. But whether the druggist had suspected Strang, and given him a harmless portion, or whether Mr. Whipple's constitution was uncommonly strong, the dose had no effect on him.

Strang then bought a quantity of arsenic at another shop, divided it into three equal parts, and gave it to Mrs. Whipple. A week after, she informed Strang that she had given her husband one of the portions in sulphur, and asked if he thought it would operate taken in that manner. He replied that he thought it would, and they both impatiently waited for the result.

The next morning Mr. Whipple refused to take a second poisoned dose of sulphur proffered by his wife, the last having, as he said, cramped his stomach. She told him it had had the same effect on her, and persuaded him to persevere. He took a part, and gave the rest to his son, while the guilty mother looked on, afraid to remonstrate. By Strang's advice she gave the boy salt, by way of antidote, but the precaution was apparently needless, for the poison had no effect on father or child.

Being resolved to destroy Mr. Whipple, Strang applied to a female slave named Dinah Jackson, and asked if she would poison him for five hundred dollars. She gave him no direct reply, and on being again asked the next day if she had made up her mind to do it, replied, "No, that I wont. I wont sell my soul to hell for all the world. If I should do it, I should never have any comfort after it." What a moral contrast between this poor, miserable, degraded negro, and the young and beautiful Elsie Whipple!

In April, Mr. Whipple being about to start for Vermont, his wife requested Strang to take one of his pistols or a club, or an axe, and waylay and slay him. She even pointed out the spot where it could be done most conveniently. He replied that he would think of it, but took no measures, and Mr. Whipple departed unharmed.

Despairing of being able to work Strang to the pitch of wickedness she desired, and desperately determined on murder, Mrs. Whipple wrote, in presence of her paramour, and with his assistance, two letters to different persons, offering them five hundred dollars to kill her husband. But finding some difficulty in directing them, they were never sent.

Mr. Whipple's absence gave this abominable pair an opportunity to carry, not their adulterous intentions, but their acts, farther than they had ever done before. The injured husband's return was not suffered to interrupt their criminal enjoyment. Pretending to have business elsewhere, Strang left the house, saying he should be gone two days, and met Mrs. Whipple at a place of assignation. He took her into a wagon, and drove to a public house where they put up for the night, in the characters of man and wife. The next day they returned to Albany, and regained their house by different roads. The expenses of this excursion were defrayed by Mrs. Whipple, with her husband's money.

They now agreed to collect a hundred dollars, due Mr. Whipple from one of his tenants, and elope without farther delay; but not being able to persuade herself to leave her child, the guilty Elsie desired Strang to shoot her husband through his window, with one of his own pistols. Strang replied that he had never fired a pistol in his life, and should be as likely to kill any other of the family as the one intended: he said he could do it with nothing but a double barreled gun, and she sent him to Albany to inquire the price of the weapon. It proved too high for her means, and it was agreed between them to buy a rifle, the price of which was lower. Their course being now fixed, Strang reported that he had seen persons lurking about the house and grounds, late at night, and apparently with evil design. This he did to divert suspicion from himself when the deed should have been done.

Mrs. Whipple furnished him with money, and he bought a rifle, which he hid in the loft of the privy, after which he wrote a letter to the infatuated woman, stating that all was ready, but that if she was willing, he would go no farther. But she had gone too far in crime to stop there. She desired him to try his gun, and to shoot at the mark through a pane of glass, as she had heard of an attempt to shoot a man through a window which failed, by the glancing of the ball. This, she told him might be his case, or he might hit some other person. She furnished him with two panes of glass and powder and ball for the experiment. This done, she dressed and started for church. (It was Sunday.)

Strang took from the butt of a whip-stock a piece of lead which he cut into bullets, and then proceeded with his rifle and glass to the woods. He set a pane upon a stump, and fired through it at a mark on a pine tree, which he hit. He shot again through the glass doubled, and then at an angle with its surface, and the result was, that he satisfied himself that a bullet would not glance from a window. After this he secreted his gun and returned home.

When Mrs. Whipple returned from church she questioned him touching his experiments, and asked to see the rifle. He told her where to find the weapon, and she went and looked at it. As Strang had expended all his lead, she brought him a bullet saying, "Mr. Whipple is loading his pistol to save his own life, and I have taken the last ball he had left for you to kill him with. What a wicked creature I am!" Scarcely had this conversation ended, when Mr. Whipple entered and asked Strang what the people said to lurk about the house at night could mean, and why he did not shoot them. Strang said there was a gun hanging over the door for that express purpose. Mr. Whipple told him to be sure to hit and hurt them, so that he might be able to lay hands on them, and left him.

A short time after, Mrs. Whipple came to Strang and asked if he loaded the rifle with the ball she had given him. He said he had not, but was about to do it, and he did so. She came again, and being satisfied that preparations were thus far advanced, asked him from what place he intended to fire on her husband. He answered, from the roof of a shed, that was situated behind and close to the window of Mr. Whipple's room. She approved of the project and promised to roll up the window curtain! He asked for her over-shoes, and on being told they were so small he could not possibly get them on, said he must have a pair of socks, at any rate, and she said she would put them under his pillow. She demanded what he meant to do with the gun after firing, and he replied that he should throw it into the river, or the well. She also agreed to give him certain signals that he might know where the different members of the household should have bestowed themselves. They parted, and not having an opportunity to speak to him again, slipped a note into his hand, directing him to throw the gun as far as he possibly could, if any of the family should come out. If we had not read of the murder of Mr. White, we should say that the *sang froid* of these two criminals was never equalled.

Strang went to Albany in the afternoon and lounged away his time till the hour for the consummation of his crime had arrived. About ten o'clock he took his rifle, pulled off his boots and hose and donned the socks Mrs. Whipple had provided, according to agreement. He pulled off his upper garment, wrapped his boots and a bundle he had brought from the city in it, and deposited it under a fence about fifty yards from the house. This done he went to the shed before mentioned, and by the aid of a large box climbed upon the roof, and took his station opposite Mr. Whipple's window. The unfortunate gentleman was sitting at a table and Mr. A. Van Rensselaer was near him; not so near however, but that Strang could fire without putting his life in danger. After examining the priming, Strang put the muzzle of his rifle close to the sash, took deliberate aim under Mr. Whipple's left arm, and fired. Mr. Whipple exclaimed, "Oh Lord!" and fell from his chair.

The instant Strang discharged his piece he retreated three or four steps, slipped, threw the gun from his hand and fell from the shed to the earth. He instantly sprang to his feet, audibly thanking God he was not hurt! picked up his rifle and ran to the place where he had left his bundle. Thence he proceeded at his full speed to a wet ravine, where he buried the murderous implement in the mud, stamped it down, and strewed leaves over it. His muddy socks he disposed of in the same manner, but in another place. Having readjusted his apparel, he regained the main road from Albany, went to the house and knocked at the door. A female slave let him in, and told him Mr. Whipple had been shot. He went into the room where the body was lying and exhibited the first symptom of guilt in turning pale at the sight of it, as was afterwards specified in the trial.

Mr. Van Rensselaer desired Strang to take his gun, and go round the house, lest, peradventure, the assassin might be still lurking about it. He went accordingly, but soon returned, and was sworn as one of the coroner's jury, the sitting of which was adjourned till the next morning.

The next morning Strang averred that he suspected Mr. Whipple had been murdered by some of the laborers on the canal, and gave a minute account of the persons he said he had seen about the house. His zeal to fix the guilt on strangers aroused the suspicions of his fellow jurors, who, however, returned a verdict of "murder committed by some person or persons unknown."

In the afternoon Mrs. Whipple came to Strang as he was sitting in the kitchen, and asked if he had secured "that piece" and the socks, and he said he had. Immediately after he was summoned to the Police Office and examined, on oath, touching the persons said to have been seen about the house. Here he added perjury to the list of his crimes, and gave a plausible account of the matter.

In the afternoon of the next day Mrs. Whipple told him they were suspected, and immediately after they were apprehended. On his several examinations he stated many falsehoods, but at last admitted the facts relative to the journey to Schenectady with Mrs. Whipple, as already related. He was then fully committed on a charge of murder, and Mr. Yates to whom he applied to act as his counsel, refused to do so. He then employed Calvin Pepper, Esq. to whom he confessed his guilt. He also desired Mr. Pepper to go to the place where he had left his rifle, and remove it, lest it should be found and furnish evidence against him. But to his father and step-mother, who visited him about this time in prison, he strenuously denied his guilt, and they engaged Mr. Oakley of Poughkeepsie to assist in his defence.

He was visited by the Grand Jury, in a body, the next June, and informed by them that Mrs. Whipple herself had furnished sufficient proof of his guilt for conviction, and that his case was hopeless. Thus reduced to despair, he sent for the jailor, and confessed his crime, with all its circumstances, and told him where the rifle, socks, glass, balls, and a part of the arsenic he had procured for Mrs. Whipple might be found. The next day he was conducted to Cherry Hill by the constables, accompanied by a crowd of people, and showed them the fragments of the glass he had used in his dreadful experiment, and the marks of his bullets, which were cut out of the tree in his presence. The socks could not be found.

Mrs. Whipple was lodged in the same story in jail with Strang, and near him. By persuading the jailor to leave her door open to admit a free circulation of air, she was enabled to come to the door of Strang's apartment and converse with him. She showed no penitence or compunction, but reprimanded her wretched tool for making a confession, saying that had he been silent both might have been acquitted.

The Record of Crimes in the United States, 1834

JAMES GORDON BENNETT

Regarded—for better or worse—as one of the founders of modern American journalism, James Gordon Bennett (1795–1872) was raised on a farm in northern Scotland and educated at a Catholic seminary in Aberdeen. Immigrating to Halifax, Nova Scotia, at 24, he worked briefly as a teacher before making his way to Boston, where he scratched out a living as a proofreader in a printing house. Three years later he moved to New York City, where a chance encounter led to a job with the Charleston (South Carolina) *Courier*. In the course of the next ten years he wrote for various newspapers, honing a lively and entertaining style that—in a pattern that would characterize his entire career—attracted the public while incensing his more high-minded peers.

In 1835, after several failed ventures as a publisher, he launched the New York *Herald*, a four-page "penny paper" aimed, as Bennett proclaimed in the inaugural issue, at "the great masses of the community." Among his innovations were firsthand coverage of the financial markets and a commitment to what we now call investigative reporting. What turned his paper into a phenomenon was his unabashed exploitation of sex, scandal, and crime, beginning with the case of the beautiful 23-year-old prostitute Helen Jewett.

A former servant girl, born Dorcas Doyen, from Augusta, Maine, Jewett was killed with an axe in a stylish Manhattan brothel in the spring of 1836. One of her regular clients, a young, well-bred clerk named Richard P. Robinson was arrested, tried, and ultimately acquitted, despite overwhelming evidence of his guilt. Thanks largely to Bennett's graphic reporting, the story became a nationwide sensation, America's prototypical media circus. The case has recently been explored in depth in Patricia Cline Cohen's superb book *The Murder of Helen Jewett* (1998).

The Recent Tragedy

MOST ATROCIOUS MURDER—Our city was disgraced on Sunday by one of the most foul and premeditated murders, that ever fell to our lot to record. The following are the circumstance as ascertained on the spot.

Richard P. Robinson, the alleged perpetrator of this most horrid deed, had for some time been in the habit of keeping (as it is termed) a girl named Ellen Jewett, who has for a long period, resided at No. 41 Thomas street, in the house kept by Rosina Townsend.

Having, as he suspected, some cause for jealousy, he went to the house on Saturday night as appears with the intention of murdering her, for he carried a hatchet with him. On going up into her room, quite late at night, he mentioned his suspicions and expressed a determination to quit her, and demanded his watch and miniature together with some letters which were in her possession. She refused to give them up, and he then drew from beneath his cloak the hatchet, and inflicted upon her head three blows either of which must have proved fatal, as the bone was cleft to the extent of three inches in each place.

She died without a struggle; and the cold blooded villain deliberately threw off his cloak, cast the lifeless body upon the bed, *and set fire to that.* He then ran down stairs unperceived by any person, went out of the back door and escaped in that manner.

In a short time Mrs. Townsend was aroused by the smell of smoke— she rushed up stairs and saw the bed on fire and the mangled body of the unfortunate girl upon it. She ran down, raised the alarm, and the watchmen rushing to the spot, rescued the body and preserved the house from being consumed.

Robinson's cloak was in the room, and at once they suspected the murderer. Mr. Noble, the assistant Captain of the Watch, instantly went and aroused Mr. Brink. They received such information as the horror stricken inmates could afford them, and proceeded on their search. On Sunday morning, at seven o'clock, Robinson was arrested in bed at his boarding house, No. 42 Day street, and brought at once to the house where had been committed the foul deed.

On seeing the body he exhibited no signs of emotion, but gazed around and on his victim coolly and calmly.

The Coroner was summoned, a Jury formed, and on a patient examination of the testimony, they returned a verdict that "she came to her death by blows upon the head inflicted with a hatchet by Richard P. Robinson."

Robinson is a native of one of the Eastern States, aged 19, and remarkably handsome and intelligent, and has been for some time past in the employ of Joseph Hoxie, 101 Maiden Lane. But his conduct upon this occasion must stamp him as a villain of too black a die for mortal. Of his intentions there can be no doubt, for he took the hatchet with him, with which the murder was committed, and the deed done, he attempted to destroy all evidence of his guilt, by firing the house, and thus induce the public to believe that she had perished in the flames. He is very well and highly connected, and the sad news that must soon reach his parents ears may be fatal to them.

Ellen Jewett, was a finely formed, and most beautiful girl—a girl about twenty years of age, and endowed by nature and education, with talents and accomplishments which should have saved her from her ignoble situation.

On his examination before the Coroners Jury, Robinson denied himself and his name and asserted that he had not been in the house that night; but a woman was brought from his boarding house, who swore positively to his cloak. The fact of his having carried the hatchet with him, is substantiated, by there being a piece of twine attached to his button hole, which tallied precisely with a piece attached to the handle of the hatchet. On leaving the house yesterday, he leaped lightly into the carriage which was to carry him to Bridewell, his countenance clear, calm, and unruffled, and on being put into his cell his last request was for some segars to smoke. The remains of the poor unfortunate victim will be interred this day.

Visit to the Scene—Yesterday afternoon, about 4 o'clock, the sun broke out for a moment in splendor. I started on a visit to the scene at 41 Thomas street. In passing through Canal street, I came to the corner of Thomas street, which runs west from behind the Hospital yard to Hudson street. A large crowd of young men stood around the door, No. 41, and several groups along the street in various directions. The excitement among the young men throughout the city was beginning to spread in all directions.

The house is a large four story elegant double one, painted yellow, and on the left hand side as you go to Hudson street. It is said to be one of the most splendid establishments devoted to infamous intercourse that the city can show. I knocked at the door. A Police Officer opened it stealthily. I told him who I was. "Mr. B. you can enter," said he with great politeness. The crowds rushed from behind seeking also an entrance.

"No more comes in," said the Police Officer.

"Why do you let that man in?" asked one of the crowd.

"He is an editor—he is on public duty."

I entered—I passed forward to the sitting room or parlour. There I found another Police officer in charge of that apartment. The old lady of the house, Mrs. Townsend, was sitting on a sofa, talking to several young men, in a great state of excitement. She was describing what Ellen had said—how she discovered the fire—how she made an alarm—how she called for the watch. The room was elegantly furnished with mirrors, splendid paintings, sofas, ottomans, and every variety of costly furniture. The Police officer when he saw me said— "Mr. B. would you like to see the *place*?"

"I would," replied I.

He immediately rose—I followed him. We mounted an elegant stair case—dark and gloomy; being in the centre of a large double house.

On reaching the second story, the Police officer took a key from his pocket and opened the door. What a sight burst upon me! There stood an elegant double mahogany bed, all covered with burnt pieces of linen, blankets, pillows black as cinders. I looked around for the object of my curiosity. On the carpet I saw a piece of linen sheet covering something as if carelessly flung over it.

"Here," said the Police officer, "here is the poor creature."

He half uncovered the ghastly corpse. I could scarcely look at it for a second or two. Slowly I began to discover the lineaments of the corpse as one would the beauties of a statue of marble. It was the most remarkable sight I ever beheld—I never have, and never expect, to see such another. "My God," exclaimed I, "how like a statue. I can scarcely conceive that form to be a corpse." No vein was to be seen. The body looked as white—as full—as polished as the purest Parisian marble. The perfect figure—the exquisite limbs—the fine face—the full arms —the beautiful bust—all—all—surpassed in every respect the Venus de Medicis according to the casts generally given of her.

"See," said the Police officer, "she has assumed that appearance within an hour."

It was the first process of dust returning to dust. Not the slightest appearance of emotion was here. One arm lay over her bosom—the other was inverted and hanging over her head. The left side down to the waist, where the fire had touched, was bronzed like an antique statue. For a few moments, I was lost to admiration at the extraordinary sight—a beautiful female corpse—that surpassed the finest statue of antiquity. I was recalled to her horrid destiny by seeing the dreadful bloody gashes on the right temple, which must have caused instantaneous dissolution.

I then looked round the room. It was elegant, but wild and extravagant in ornaments. On the drawer was a small library, composed of light novels, poetry, and monthly periodicals. There hung on the wall a beautiful print of Lord Byron as the presiding genius of the place. The books were Byron, Scott, Bulwer's works, and the Knickerbocker.

A work table in a state of disorder, stood nearby. It was covered with fragments, pen, ink, paper, crayons, pamphlets &c. &c. Above the mantel piece hung several theatrical fancy sketches.

I returned to take a last look at the corpse. What a melancholy sight for beauty, wit, and talent, for it is said she possessed all, to come to such a fatal end!

I came down stairs—the house looked dark and gloomy, all the windows being half shut—but it was throughout splendidly furnished.

Such is the scene as it was seen yesterday afternoon.

This extraordinary murder has caused a sensation in this city never before felt or known. I understand that a large number of fashionable young men, clerks and others were caught in the various apartments by the Police when the cry of fire was given. *It was Saturday night.* The murdered girl was one of the most beautiful of her degraded *caste*. She was a perfect Millwood. She has seduced, by her beauty and blandishments, more young men than any known in the Police Records. She was a remarkable character, and has come to a remarkable end. The house is in danger from the mob. Let the authorities look to it. A morbid excitement pervades the city. It is said that she threatened to expose Robinson, when she lived, having discovered that he was paying attention to a respectable young lady. This threat drove him to madness. On Saturday she walked up and down Broadway half the day, nodding to her acquaintances among the dissipated young men.

In what a horrible condition is a portion of the young men of this devoted city?

New York *Herald*, April 11, 1836

NATHANIEL HAWTHORNE

Waxwork effigies of notorious killers, displayed in dime museums and traveling exhibitions, were a popular attraction in 19th-century America. That Nathaniel Hawthorne (1804–1864) would be drawn to such lurid fare is not surprising in light of his lifelong fascination with true crime. Scholar David Reynolds writes that one of Hawthorne's favorite childhood books was the 17th-century crime collection *The Triumphe of God's Revenge Against the Crying and Execrable Sin of Murther*, a volume he read so often that he damaged its binding. Later he drew inspiration for his fiction from the 1834 anthology *The Record of Crimes in the United States*. One of the last memories Hawthorne's son Julian had of his father was of the ailing man "sedulously leafing through an enormous volume of trial reports."

Of the crimes Hawthorne refers to in this journal entry, the Helen Jewett murder remains the best known. The others have faded from public memory, though they were equally infamous in Hawthorne's day. Charles Gibbs was an American pirate who prowled the Caribbean and the Gulf of Mexico in the 1820s. On one occasion, he and his cohorts captured a Dutch ship and slaughtered all its passengers and crew, except for a 17-year-old girl who, as Gibbs later recounted, "was kept on board for some time" before being killed. After a trip to North Africa to join the Barbary corsairs, Gibbs returned to the United States and, in 1830, signed on as a seaman aboard a brig bound from New Orleans to Philadelphia. Learning that the ship held a cargo of silver coins, Gibbs and other crewmembers, including the steward Thomas Wansley, staged a mutiny. After killing the captain and the mate, they steered the vessel for Long Island, scuttled it and set it ablaze, then took to the boats and made for the beach. A number of mutineers drowned in the rough sea. Gibbs and Wansley made it ashore but were eventually convicted and hanged.

Ephraim K. Avery, another figure represented in the waxworks exhibit, was a Methodist minister from Bristol, Rhode Island. A married man with several children, he was accused of hanging his pregnant mistress, a factory girl named Sarah Cornell, and staging the death to look like a suicide. Despite the mass of circumstantial evidence against him, he was acquitted at his 1833 trial.

The "Strang" mentioned by Hawthorne was Jesse Strang, the duped lover of the murderous Mrs. Elsie Whipple; their story can be found on pages 52–62 of this volume.

"A show of wax-figures"

Friday, July 13th, 1838

A show of wax-figures, consisting almost wholly of murderers and their victims,—Gibbs and Wansley, the pirates, and the Dutch girl whom Gibbs murdered. Gibbs and Wansley were admirably done, as natural as life; and many people who had known Gibbs would not, according to the showman, be convinced that this wax-figure was not his skin stuffed. The two pirates were represented with halters round their necks, just ready to be turned off; and the sheriff stood behind them, with his watch, waiting for the moment. The clothes, halter, and Gibbs's hair were authentic. E. K. Avery and Cornell,—the former a figure in black, leaning on the back of a chair, in the attitude of a clergyman about to pray; an ugly devil, said to be a good likeness. Ellen Jewett and R. P. Robinson, she dressed richly, in extreme fashion, and very pretty; he awkward and stiff, it being difficult to stuff a figure to look like a gentleman. The showman seemed very proud of Ellen Jewett, and spoke of her somewhat as if this wax-figure were a real creation. Strang and Mrs. Whipple, who together murdered the husband of the latter. Lastly the Siamese twins. The showman is careful to call his exhibition the "Statuary." He walks to and fro before the figures, talking of the history of the persons, the moral lessons to be drawn therefrom, and especially of the excellence of the wax-work. He has for sale printed histories of the personages. He is a friendly, easy-mannered sort of a half-genteel character, whose talk has been moulded by the persons who most frequent such a show; an air of superiority of information, a moral instructor, with a great deal of real knowledge of the world. He invites his departing guests to call again and bring their friends, desiring to know whether they are pleased;

telling that he had a thousand people on the 4th of July, and that they were all perfectly satisfied. He talks with the female visitors, remarking on Ellen Jewett's person and dress to them, he having "spared no expense in dressing her; and all the ladies say that a dress never set better, and he thinks he never knew a handsomer female." He goes to and fro, snuffing the candles, and now and then holding one to the face of a favorite figure. Ever and anon, hearing steps upon the staircase, he goes to admit a new visitor. The visitors,—a half bumpkin, half country-squirelike man, who has something of a knowing air, and yet looks and listens with a good deal of simplicity and faith, smiling between whiles; a mechanic of the town; several decent-looking girls and women, who eye Ellen herself with more interest than the other figures,—women having much curiosity about such ladies; a gentlemanly sort of person, who looks somewhat ashamed of himself for being there, and glances at me knowingly, as if to intimate that he was conscious of being out of place; a boy or two, and myself, who examine wax faces and faces of flesh with equal interest. A political or other satire might be made by describing a show of wax-figures of the prominent public men; and, by the remarks of the showman and the spectators, their characters and public standing might be expressed. And the incident of Judge Tyler as related by E—— might be introduced.

Notebook entry, July 13, 1838

ABRAHAM LINCOLN

Of the thousands of civil and criminal cases handled by Abraham Lincoln (1809–1865) during his 23-year legal career in Illinois, the trial of William Trailor for the murder of Archibald Fisher ranks among the most memorable.

His first account of the "curious affair"—written on July 19, 1841, the day after the trial reached its bizarre denouement—consisted of a lengthy letter to his friend Joshua Speed. Five years later, Lincoln returned to the subject in the following article, published on the front page of the April 15, 1846, issue of the *Quincy Whig*. It was preceded by this editorial note:

> The following narrative has been handed us for publication by a member of the bar. There is no doubt of the truth of every fact stated; and the whole affair is of so extraordinary a character as to entitle its publication, and commend it to the attention of those at present engaged in discussing reforms in criminal jurisprudence, and the abolition of capital punishment.

Lincoln's wide experience as a litigator stood him in good stead in his dealings with Trailor when the latter reneged on his $100 legal fee. Lincoln was obliged to file suit, and in November 1845 obtained judgment for the full amount and costs.

Remarkable Case of Arrest for Murder

In the year 1841, there resided, at different points in the State of Illinois, three brothers by the name of Trailor. Their Christian names were William, Henry and Archibald. Archibald resided at Springfield, then as now the Seat of Government of the State. He was a sober, retiring and industrious man, of about thirty years of age; a carpenter by trade, and a bachelor, boarding with his partner in business—a Mr. Myers. Henry, a year or two older, was a man of like retiring and industrious habits; had a family and resided with it on a farm at

Clary's Grove, about twenty miles distant from Springfield in a North-westerly direction. William, still older, and with similar habits, resided on a farm in Warren county, distant from Springfield something more than a hundred miles in the same North-westerly direction. He was a widower, with several children. In the neighborhood of William's residence, there was, and had been for several years, a man by the name of Fisher, who was somewhat above the age of fifty; had no family, and no settled home; but who boarded and lodged a while here, and a while there, with the persons for whom he did little jobs of work. His habits were remarkably economical, so that an impression got about that he had accumulated a considerable amount of money. In the latter part of May in the year mentioned, William formed the purpose of visiting his brothers at Clary's Grove, and Springfield; and Fisher, at the time having his temporary residence at his house, resolved to accompany him. They set out together in a buggy with a single horse. On Sunday Evening they reached Henry's residence, and staid over night. On Monday Morning, being the first Monday of June, they started on to Springfield, Henry accompanying them on horse back. They reached town about noon, met Archibald, went with him to his boarding house, and there took up their lodgings for the time they should remain. After dinner, the three Trailors and Fisher left the boarding house in company, for the avowed purpose of spending the evening together in looking about the town. At supper, the Trailors had all returned, but Fisher was missing, and some inquiry was made about him. After supper, the Trailors went out professedly in search of him. One by one they returned, the last coming in after late tea time, and each stating that he had been unable to discover any thing of Fisher. The next day, both before and after breakfast, they went professedly in search again, and returned at noon, still unsuccessful. Dinner again being had, William and Henry expressed a determination to give up the search and start for their homes. This was remonstrated against by some of the boarders about the house, on the ground that Fisher was somewhere in the vicinity, and would be left without any conveyance, as he and William had come in the same buggy. The remonstrance was disregarded, and they departed for their homes respectively. Up to this time, the knowledge of Fisher's mysterious disappearance, had spread very little beyond the few boarders at Myers', and excited no considerable interest. After the lapse of three or four days, Henry returned to Springfield, for the ostensible purpose of making further search for Fisher. Procuring some of the boarders, he, together with them and Archibald, spent another day in ineffectual search, when it was again abandoned, and he returned home. No general interest was yet excited. On the Friday, week after Fisher's disappearance, the Postmaster at Springfield received a letter from the Postmaster nearest William's residence in Warren county, stating that William had returned home without Fisher, and was saying, rather boastfully, that Fisher was dead, and had willed him his money, and that he had got about fifteen hundred dollars by it. The letter further stated that William's story and conduct seemed strange; and desired the Postmaster at Springfield to ascertain and write what was the truth in the matter. The Postmaster at Springfield made the letter public, and at once, excitement became universal and intense. Springfield, at that time had a population of about 3500, with a city organization. The Attorney General of the State resided there. A purpose was forthwith formed to ferret out the mystery, in putting which into execution, the Mayor of the city, and the Attorney General took the lead. To make search for, and, if possible, find the body of the man supposed to be murdered, was resolved on as the first step. In pursuance of this, men were formed into large parties, and marched abreast, in all directions, so as to let no inch of ground in the vicinity, remain unsearched. Examinations were made of cellars, wells, and pits of all descriptions, where it was thought possible the body might be concealed. All the fresh, or tolerably fresh graves at the grave-yard were pried into, and dead horses and dead dogs were disinterred, where, in some instances, they had been buried by their partial masters. This search, as has appeared, commenced on Friday. It continued until Saturday afternoon without success, when it was determined to dispatch officers to arrest William and Henry at their residences respectively. The officers started on Sunday Morning, meanwhile, the search for the body was continued, and rumors got afloat of the Trailors having passed, at different times and places, several gold pieces, which were readily supposed to have belonged to Fisher. On Monday, the officers sent for Henry, having arrested him, arrived with him. The Mayor and Attorney Gen'l took charge of him, and set their wits to work to elicit a discovery from him. He denied, and denied, and persisted in denying. They still plied him in every conceivable way, till Wednesday, when, protesting his own innocence, he stated that his brothers, William and Archibald had murdered Fisher; that they had killed him, without his (Henry's) knowledge at the time, and made a temporary concealment of his body; that immediately preceding his and William's departure from Springfield for home, on Tuesday, the day after Fisher's disappearance, William and Archibald communicated the fact to him, and engaged his assistance in making a permanent concealment of the body; that at the time he and William left professedly for home, they did not take the road directly, but meandering their way through the streets, entered the woods at the North West of the city, two or three hundred yards to the right of where the road where they should have travelled entered them; that penetrating the woods some few hundred yards, they halted and Archibald came a somewhat different route, on foot, and joined them; that William and Archibald then stationed him (Henry) on an old and disused road that ran near by, as a sentinel, to give warning of the approach of any intruder; that William and Archibald then removed the buggy to the edge of a dense brush thicket, about forty yards distant from his (Henry's) position, where, leaving the buggy, they entered the thicket, and in a few minutes returned with the body and placed it in the buggy; that from his station, he could and did distinctly see that the object placed in the buggy was a dead man, of the general appearance and size of Fisher; that William and Archibald then moved off with the buggy in the direction of Hickox's mill pond, and after an absence of half an hour returned, saying they had put him in a safe place; that Archibald then left for town, and he and William found their way to the road, and made for their homes. At this disclosure, all lingering credulity was broken down, and excitement rose to an almost inconceivable height. Up to this time, the well known character of Archibald had repelled and put down all suspicions as to him. Till then, those who were ready to swear that a murder had been committed, were almost as confident that Archibald had had no part in it. But now, he was seized and thrown into jail; and, indeed, his personal security rendered it by no means objectionable to him. And now came the search for the brush thicket, and the search of the mill pond. The thicket was found, and the buggy tracks at the point indicated. At a point within the thicket the signs of a struggle were discovered, and a trail from thence to the buggy track was traced. In attempting to follow the track of the buggy from the thicket, it was found to proceed in the direction of the mill pond, but could not be traced all the way. At the pond, however, it was found that a buggy had been backed down to, and partially into the water's edge. Search was now to be made in the pond; and it was made in every imaginable way. Hundreds and hundreds were engaged in raking, fishing, and draining. After much fruitless effort in this way, on Thursday Morning, the mill dam was cut down, and the water of the pond partially drawn off, and the same processes of search again gone through with. About noon of this day, the officer sent for William, returned having him in custody; and a man calling himself Dr. Gilmore, came in company with them. It seems that the officer arrested William at his own house early in the day on Tuesday, and started to Springfield with him; that after dark awhile, they reached Lewiston in Fulton county, where they stopped for the night; that late in the night this Dr. Gilmore arrived, stating that Fisher was alive at his house; and that he had followed on to give the information, so that William might be released without further trouble; that the officer, distrusting Dr. Gilmore, refused to release William, but brought him on to Springfield, and the Dr. accompanied them. On reaching Springfield, the Dr. re-asserted that Fisher was alive, and at his house. At this the multitude for a time, were utterly confounded. Gilmore's story was communicated to Henry Trailor, who, without faltering, reaffirmed his own story about Fisher's murder. Henry's adherence to his own story was communicated to the crowd, and at once the idea started, and became nearly, if not quite universal that Gilmore was a confederate of the Trailors, and had invented the tale he was telling, to secure their release and escape. Excitement was again at its zenith. About 3 o'clock, the same evening, Myers, Archibald's partner, started with a two horse carriage, for the purpose of ascertaining whether Fisher was alive, as stated by Gilmore, and if so, of bringing him back to Springfield with him. On Friday a legal examination was gone into before two Justices, on the charge of murder against William and Archibald. Henry was introduced as a witness by the prosecution, and on oath, re-affirmed his statements, as heretofore detailed; and, at the end of which, he bore a thorough and rigid cross-examination without faltering or exposure. The prosecution also proved by a respectable lady, that on the Monday evening of Fisher's disappearance, she saw Archibald whom she well knew, and another man whom she did not then know, but whom she believed at the time of testifying to be William, (then present;) and still another, answering the description of Fisher, all enter the timber at the North West of town, (the point indicated by Henry,) and after one or two hours, saw William and Archibald return without Fisher. Several other witnesses testified, that on Tuesday, at the time William and Henry professedly gave up the search for Fisher's body and started for home, they did not take the road directly, but did go into the woods as stated by Henry. By others also, it was proved, that since Fisher's disappearance, William and Archibald had passed rather an unusual number of gold pieces. The statements heretofore made about the thicket, the signs of a struggle, the buggy tracks, &c., were fully proven by numerous witnesses. At this the prosecution rested. Dr. Gilmore was then introduced by the defendants. He stated that he resided in Warren county about seven miles distant from William's residence; that on the morning of William's arrest, he was out from home and heard of the arrest, and of its being on a charge of the murder of Fisher; that on returning to his own house, he found Fisher there; that Fisher was in very feeble health, and could give no rational account as to where he had been during his absence; that he (Gilmore) then started in pursuit of the officer as before stated, and that he should have taken Fisher with him only that the state of his health did not permit. Gilmore also stated that he had known Fisher for several years, and that he had understood he was subject to temporary derangement of mind, owing to an injury about his head received in early life. There was about Dr. Gilmore so much of the air and manner of truth, that his statement prevailed in the minds of the audience and of the court, and the Trailors were discharged; although they attempted no explanation of the circumstances proven by the other witnesses. On the next Monday, Myers arrived in Springfield, bringing with him the now famed Fisher, in full life and proper person. Thus ended this strange affair; and while it is readily conceived that a writer of novels could bring a story to a more perfect climax, it may well be doubted, whether a stranger affair ever really occurred. Much of the matter remains in mystery to this day. The going into the woods with Fisher, and returning without him, by the Trailors; their going into the woods at the same place the next day, after they professed to have given up the search; the signs of a struggle in the thicket, the buggy tracks at the edge of it; and the location of the thicket and the signs about it, corresponding precisely with Henry's story, are circumstances that have never been explained.

William and Archibald have both died since—William in less than a year, and Archibald in about two years after the supposed murder. Henry is still living, but never speaks of the subject.

It is not the object of the writer of this, to enter into the many curious speculations that might be indulged upon the facts of this narrative; yet he can scarcely forbear a remark upon what would, almost certainly have been the fate of William and Archibald, had Fisher not been found alive. It seems he had wandered away in mental derangement, and, had he died in this condition, and his body been found in the vicinity, it is difficult to conceive what could have saved the Trailors from the consequence of having murdered him. Or, if he had died, and his body never found, the case against them, would have been quite as bad, for, although it is a principle of law that a conviction for murder shall not be had, unless the body of the deceased be discovered, it is to be remembered, that Henry testified he saw Fisher's dead body.

Quincy Whig, April 15, 1846

AMBROSE BIERCE

Apart from his hardscrabble upbringing as one of 13 children born to poor midwestern farmers, the Civil War was undoubtedly the single most determining influence on the outlook of Ambrose Bierce (1842–1914?). Beginning as a Union drummer in 1861, he fought in some of the war's bloodiest battles and left the army four years later with the rank of brevet major. His grim wartime experiences may not have created his dark disposition, but they could hardly fail to reinforce it, and in stories such as "Chickamauga," "An Occurrence at Owl Creek Bridge," and "A Horseman in the Sky" he offers cold-eyed confirmation of Plautus's famous proverb *homo homini lupus est*: man is a wolf to man.

The same deep-dyed pessimism pervades his journalism. Apart from a three-year stay in London and a brief, ill-fated mining venture that took him to the Dakota Territory for a few months in 1880, Bierce lived and worked in and around San Francisco from about 1867 until 1900. Publishing in various newspapers and periodicals—most importantly William Randolph Hearst's *Examiner*—he earned a reputation as a scathing satirist and fearless social critic. Though much of his output from this era never rises above the level of hackwork, even his most ephemeral pieces are characterized by the corrosive wit that made him known as "Bitter Bierce."

Crime News from California

MAKE IT A CAPITAL OFFENSE

Charles O'Neil was, it seems, temporarily insane when he threw his wife off the balcony, and broke her precious neck. Charles O'Neil, would that we had but had the sentencing of thee—there would have been another neck broken. We yearn for a law making temporary insanity a capital offense.

News Letter, December 26, 1868

THE CRIME MARKET IS ACTIVE

Our Criminal Market Review exhibits considerable activity. We may remark, generally, that under the favorable influences of the new Police, business is in a healthy condition. Since our last similar reference, moderate transactions have taken place in Burglaries, and a few operators have been cornered; Robberies are looking up; Assaults, active; Forgeries, dull; in Confidence-games there has been no movement since the late operation by the Young Men's Christian Association; Embezzlements are quiet; some improvement is looked for with continued favorable White Pine developments; Murders, neglected; Juvenile delinquencies are lively; Election frauds, out of season; Custom House, ditto, command attention; Perjuries, brisk, since the operator, Josselyn, has been booked for San Quentin; Abortions are kept strictly private; a few transactions in Black Mail are reported, by the *Alta*, p.n.t.; Drunks continue depressed; we remark a better fate of *Scan. Mag.*; Gambling tends downward; Arson is firm; Brokers, without improvement. For further details, see Sunday family papers.

News Letter, February 13, 1869

CALIFORNIANS DO HAVE A CERTAIN TALENT

We have contemplated with considerable satisfaction the various attempts to take human life during the present week. Our joy at the mutilation of old Hulton has been deeply unspeakable; our lively interest in the shooting and hacking of and by the Dudleys, Ingham and Miller, has been testified in a novel and interesting manner by a private scalp dance at our own apartments.

Within a certain limit we have a fondness for this sort of thing; the line at which it should stop being drawn quite close to our own person, but not embracing it. Within that boundary, homicide is honorable and mutilation proportionately commendable. The savor of smoking blood is peculiarly appetizing, and the dulcet note of the pistol is soothing to the senses; while the sight of reeking corpses scattered at intervals along the sidewalks, is mildly exhilarating. It pleasantly reminds us of the time when we were a soldier, with a soldier's simple taste—a warrior, with a warrior's hopes and fears—the latter in excess. Let the good work go on—within the limits aforementioned.

Give the Pacific devil his occidental due. We are liars, but we shoot and stab with inimitable skill; we are braggarts, but we know how to bring down our man. Our country is a melancholy enough affair, with no "Objects of interest to the tourist." Yosemite is a conceded fiction, and the Big Trees a screaming joke; the purely imaginary excellencies of the finest climate in the world, sir, we no longer parade; upon the subject of our agricultural greatness and commercial importance we back squarely down. But we are handy with the pistol and wield a butcher-knife as deftly as an Indian or anybody. Our proud pre-eminence in these particulars we have attested with tolerable completeness. So long as we maintain a spotless reputation as blackguards, what is the use of knowing anything?

News Letter, June 4, 1870

IT'S ALL JUST MANSLAUGHTER

Practically there is no longer such a crime as murder in the first degree; it is all manslaughter. If you brain your mother-in-law in the heat of debate with a bench-leg, that is manslaughter. If you prepare her for sepulture by the slower process of methodical poisoning, that is manslaughter, too. The punishment is the same in either case. It appears from this that there is no use in getting unduly excited and making nasty looking corpses by sudden and unskillful work. If anybody shall tweak you by the nose, don't mellow him with a mallet, mangle him with a meat-ax nor bust him with a bludgeon. Lay for him. Watch your opportunity, and while he is off his guard some night, drag him from the arms of his wife and coil him up carefully in a kettle of boiling soap. If you have previously taken the precaution to write a few incoherent letters with regard to your dishonored proboscis, that circumstance will have its effect in establishing your future pleas of temporary insanity. In any case you will not be hanged, for the jury will find you guilty of manslaughter, and recommend you to the mercy of the court, which will cost you five hundred dollars. That is the price in Chicago.

News Letter, December 3, 1870

THE POPULAR BACKGROUND

The other day the dead body of a Chinaman was found in an alley of this city, and taken to the morgue for identification. Deceased was addicted to doing odd jobs about town for what he could get, but otherwise bore a good character. The body was found partially concealed under a paving-stone which was imbedded in the head like a precious jewel in the pate of a toad. A crowbar was driven through the abdomen and one arm was riven from its socket by some great convulsion of nature. As deceased was seen by two eight-hour men enjoying his opium-pipe and his usual health just previously to the discovery of his melancholy remains, it is supposed he came to his death by heart disease.

News Letter, August 6, 1870

A MURDER IN BAD TASTE

It is difficult to regard Mr. John Beever, of St. Cloud, Minn., with feelings of respect tempered with disapprobation. This Mr. Beever is the gentleman who, the other day, went to call upon his wife, from whom he had been some time separated, and before leaving took occasion to inveigle her into a back kitchen by the chignon, and then threw off the disguise and revealed himself in his true colors with a sharp hatchet. He chopped away at the lady's head until he had made of it a basketful of unsightly chips, hanging confusedly together by tangled skeins of hair, clogged with warm brain and smoking with blood—altogether a very discouraging spectacle for the hired girl who had to clean up after him. It doesn't seem right to treat a woman in this way after having left her. When one frees himself from the obligations of matrimony he should be held to have renounced its privileges, which he has no right to resume until he shall consent to again become responsible for the household expenses. The privilege to hack and mangle the conjugal head should be very sparingly exercised anyhow, as it is one of doubtful utility, barren of satisfaction. To prevent a recurrence of such scenes as that weakly described above, we must look to a more healthy public opinion.

News Letter, January 20, 1872

HE DID IT JUST TO HELP HIS MOTHER

Senor Felipe Carillo, of Monterey county, is meanly designated by a contemporary as "the vilest wretch that walks unhanged," because he poisoned his mother with a strychniated pumpkin pie in the tenth decade of that lady's life. Some journalists appear to think a woman has the right to live forever. We do not share that opinion. Even Ninon de l'Enclos, the most beautiful, admired and elegant woman of her century—of accommodating morals withal—had the delicacy to die at ninety. If her son had had the spirit of Senor Carillo she would have perished earlier. Unfortunately he became enamored of her, and instead of performing the filial duty of assassination selfishly seized the lover's privilege of suicide. So passed from earth the sole suitor to whom this amiable lady denied the favor of her preference. Heroic, no doubt, and commendable; but in homely, substantial common sense, the act of Senor Carillo transcends it, even as the solid merits of the comestible by which it was wrought surpass the flippant virtues of an omelette souffle.

Argonaut, April 28, 1877

POINT FOR THE DEFENSE

I am sorry to observe that Mr. Lynch, of this city, a gentleman aged sixty-three, has committed the happily not very common error of killing his wife, with whom he had lived for forty years, but whom he must, of course, henceforth live without. Mrs. Lynch's offense consisted in declining to drink a glass of beer when requested; perhaps it would be more accurate to say refusing when commanded. For this the husband deemed it expedient to cut her fatally in the abdomen, though few will agree with him that such a course was either necessary or humane. On the other hand, if the beer was good there is no obvious reason why the lady should have refused it. It is to be hoped a sample has been preserved for the use of the jury.

Argonaut, July 20, 1878

A THOROUGHGOING JOB

It was a religion with Johnson—the late James Johnson, of New York—what was worth doing was worth doing well. It accordingly happened that the lady of whose society Mr. Johnson was fatigued was found, the other day, with her throat cut, her forehead broken in, and her body penetrated by sixteen knife wounds, eight of which—an impartial half—seem to have been intended for her unborn babe. This last circumstance indicates a thoroughness which even the most determined opponent of capital punishment will find it difficult to approve. Near the ruin thus wrought lay a revolver, a razor, a shoemaker's-knife, and a heavy iron stove-hook—an exposure of mechanical devices that proves Mr. Johnson to belong to the Eastlake school of Art, which scorns concealment of methods and as frankly discloses its means as its end. Altogether, it is a rather sombre "tragedy," but in simple justice to the tragedian it ought to be added that at the end of his dark performance he bowed himself off the stage with a graceful flourish of the razor that laid his head at his feet. Having been accused of annoyances of others—it seems proper that I should explain, in conclusion, that I do not entirely approve of Mr. Johnson's action in this matter, and think it would be better, on the whole, if disagreements between man and mistress could be settled by some kind of arbitration that would leave at least one of the parties alive.

Argonaut, January 26, 1878

THE ENGINE TIMED ITS HOOT

Speaking of religion, hangman's ropes, and such like moral agencies, I am reminded of an execution I once witnessed, at which a brace of miscreants assisted on the scaffold, and some thousands of not very sympathetic soldiers below it and about. It was at Murfreesboro, Tennessee, in war-time, and the fellows were hanged by the military for a murder of resulting atrocity, committed without orders. At the critical moment one of them began a self-righteous assertion that he was "going home to Jesus." As the words left his mouth a railway engine standing near by uttered a loud and unmistakably derisive *Hoot—hoot!* It may have been accident; it may have been design; at any rate it expressed the "sense of the meeting" better than a leg's length of resolutions; and when the drop fell from beneath the feet of that pious assassin and his mate, the ropes about their necks were actually kept slack for some seconds by the gusts of laughter ascending from below. They are the only persons I know in the other world who enjoyed the ghastly distinction of leaving this to the sound of inextinguishable merriment.

Argonaut, December 21, 1878

MARK TWAIN

In this selection from *Roughing It* (1872), Mark Twain (1835–1910) makes it clear that the myth of the frontier gunfight was born out of rampant real-life violence. To be sure, citizens of Wild West boomtowns like Virginia City, Nevada, were safer from certain crimes—particularly robbery, burglary, and rape—than Americans today. At the same time, as scholars such as historian Roger D. McGrath have demonstrated, murder rates were remarkably high in many frontier communities. The reasons for this phenomenon continue to be debated, but Twain puts his finger on three ingredients that undoubtedly made for a highly combustible mix: guns, alcohol, and a large population of young unmarried men who achieved respect and social status in the age-old way of males, by proving their proficiency at killing.

from Roughing It

CHAPTER XLVIII

The first twenty-six graves in the Virginia cemetery were occupied by *murdered* men. So everybody said, so everybody believed, and so they will always say and believe. The reason why there was so much slaughtering done, was, that in a new mining district the rough element predominates, and a person is not respected until he has "killed his man." That was the very expression used.

If an unknown individual arrived, they did not inquire if he was capable, honest, industrious, but—had he killed his man? If he had not, he gravitated to his natural and proper position, that of a man of small consequence; if he had, the cordiality of his reception was graduated according to the number of his dead. It was tedious work struggling up to a position of influence with bloodless hands; but when a man came with the blood of half a dozen men on his soul, his worth was recognized at once and his acquaintance sought.

In Nevada, for a time, the lawyer, the editor, the banker, the chief desperado, the chief gambler, and the saloon-keeper, occupied the same level in society, and it was the highest. The cheapest and easiest way to become an influential man and be looked up to by the community at large, was to stand behind a bar, wear a cluster-diamond pin, and sell whisky. I am not sure but that the saloon-keeper held a shade higher rank than any other member of society. His opinion had weight. It was his privilege to say how the elections should go. No great movement could succeed without the countenance and direction of the saloon-keepers. It was a high favor when the chief saloon-keeper consented to serve in the legislature or the board of aldermen. Youthful ambition hardly aspired so much to the honors of the law, or the army and navy as to the dignity of proprietorship in a saloon.

To be a saloon-keeper and kill a man was to be illustrious. Hence the reader will not be surprised to learn that more than one man was killed in Nevada under hardly the pretext of provocation, so impatient was the slayer to achieve reputation and throw off the galling sense of being held in indifferent repute by his associates. I knew two youths who tried to "kill their men" for no other reason—and got killed themselves for their pains. "There goes the man that killed Bill Adams" was higher praise and a sweeter sound in the ears of this sort of people than any other speech that admiring lips could utter.

The men who murdered Virginia's original twenty-six cemetery-occupants were never punished. Why? Because Alfred the Great, when he invented trial by jury, and knew that he had admirably framed it to secure justice in his age of the world, was not aware that in the nineteenth century the condition of things would be so entirely changed that unless he rose from the grave and altered the jury plan to meet the emergency, it would prove the most ingenious and infallible agency for *defeating* justice that human wisdom could contrive. For how could he imagine that we simpletons would go on using his jury plan after circumstances had stripped it of its usefulness, any more than he could imagine that we would go on using his candle-clock after we had invented chronometers? In his day news could not travel fast, and hence he could easily find a jury of honest, intelligent men who had not heard of the case they were called to try—but in our day of telegraphs and newspapers his plan compels us to swear in juries composed of fools and rascals, because the system rigidly excludes honest men and men of brains.

I remember one of those sorrowful farces, in Virginia, which we call a jury trial. A noted desperado killed Mr. B., a good citizen, in the most wanton and cold-blooded way. Of course the papers were full of it, and all men capable of reading, read about it. And of course all men not deaf and dumb and idiotic, talked about it. A jury-list was made out, and Mr. B. L., a prominent banker and a valued citizen, was questioned precisely as he would have been questioned in any court in America:

"Have you heard of this homicide?"

"Yes."

"Have you held conversations upon the subject?"

"Yes."

"Have you formed or expressed opinions about it?"

"Yes."

"Have you read the newspaper accounts of it?"

"Yes."

"We do not want you."

A minister, intelligent, esteemed, and greatly respected; a merchant of high character and known probity; a mining superintendent of intelligence and unblemished reputation; a quartz mill owner of excellent standing, were all questioned in the same way, and all set aside. Each said the public talk and the newspaper reports had not so biased his mind but that sworn testimony would overthrow his previously formed opinions and enable him to render a verdict without prejudice and in accordance with the facts. But of course such men could not be trusted with the case. Ignoramuses alone could mete out unsullied justice.

When the peremptory challenges were all exhausted, a jury of twelve men was impaneled—a jury who swore they had neither heard, read, talked about nor expressed an opinion concerning a murder which the very cattle in the corrals, the Indians in the sage-brush and the stones in the streets were cognizant of! It was a jury composed of two desperadoes, two low beer-house politicians, three bar-keepers, two ranchmen who could not read, and three dull, stupid, human donkeys! It actually came out afterward, that one of these latter thought that incest and arson were the same thing.

The verdict rendered by this jury was, Not Guilty. What else could one expect?

The jury system puts a ban upon intelligence and honesty, and a premium upon ignorance, stupidity and perjury. It is a shame that we must continue to use a worthless system because it *was* good a thousand years ago. In this age, when a gentleman of high social standing, intelligence and probity, swears that testimony given under solemn oath will outweigh, with him, street talk and newspaper reports based upon mere hearsay, he is worth a hundred jurymen who will swear to their own ignorance and stupidity, and justice would be far safer in his hands than in theirs. Why could not the jury law be so altered as to give men of brains and honesty an *equal chance* with fools and miscreants? Is it right to show the present favoritism to one class of men and inflict a disability on another, in a land whose boast is that all its citizens are free and equal? I am a candidate for the legislature. I desire to tamper with the jury law. I wish to so alter it as to put a premium on intelligence and character, and close the jury box against idiots, blacklegs, and people who do not read newspapers. But no doubt I shall be defeated—every effort I make to save the country "misses fire."

My idea, when I began this chapter, was to say something about desperadoism in the "flush times" of Nevada. To attempt a portrayal of that era and that land, and leave out the blood and carnage, would be like portraying Mormondom and leaving out polygamy. The desperado stalked the streets with a swagger graded according to the number of his homicides, and a nod of recognition from him was sufficient to make a humble admirer happy for the rest of the day. The deference that was paid to a desperado of wide reputation, and who "kept his private graveyard," as the phrase went, was marked, and cheerfully accorded. When he moved along the sidewalk in his excessively long-tailed frock-coat, shiny stump-toed boots, and with dainty little slouch hat tipped over left eye, the small-fry roughs made room for his majesty; when he entered the restaurant, the waiters deserted bankers and merchants to overwhelm him with obsequious service; when he shouldered his way to a bar, the shouldered parties wheeled indignantly, recognized him, and—apologized. They got a look in return that froze their marrow, and by that time a curled and breast-pinned bar keeper was beaming over the counter, proud of the established acquaintanceship that permitted such a familiar form of speech as:

"How're ye, Billy, old fel? Glad to see you. What'll you take—the old thing?"

The "old thing" meant his customary drink, of course.

The best known names in the Territory of Nevada were those belonging to these long-tailed heroes of the revolver. Orators, Governors, capitalists and leaders of the legislature enjoyed a degree of fame, but it seemed local and meagre when contrasted with the fame of such men as Sam Brown, Jack Williams, Billy Mulligan, Farmer Pease, Sugarfoot Mike, Pock-Marked Jake, El Dorado Johnny, Jack McNabb, Joe McGee, Jack Harris, Six-fingered Pete, etc., etc. There was a long list of them. They were brave, reckless men, and traveled with their lives in their hands. To give them their due, they did their killing principally among themselves, and seldom molested peaceable citizens, for they considered it small credit to add to their trophies so cheap a bauble as the death of a man who was "not on the shoot," as they phrased it. They killed each other on slight provocation, and hoped and expected to be killed themselves—for they held it almost shame to die otherwise than "with their boots on," as they expressed it.

I remember an instance of a desperado's contempt for such small game as a private citizen's life. I was taking a late supper in a restaurant one night, with two reporters and a little printer named—Brown, for instance—any name will do. Presently a stranger with a long-tailed coat on came in, and not noticing Brown's hat, which was lying in a chair, sat down on it. Little Brown sprang up and became abusive in a moment. The stranger smiled, smoothed out the hat, and offered it to Brown with profuse apologies couched in caustic sarcasm, and begged Brown not to destroy him. Brown threw off his coat and challenged the man to fight—abused him, threatened him, impeached his courage, and urged and even implored him to fight; and in the meantime the smiling stranger placed himself under our protection in mock distress. But presently he assumed a serious tone, and said:

"Very well, gentlemen, if we must fight, we must, I suppose. But don't rush into danger and then say I gave you no warning. I am more than a match for all of you when I get started. I will give you proofs, and then if my friend here still insists, I will try to accommodate him."

The table we were sitting at was about five feet long, and unusually cumbersome and heavy. He asked us to put our hands on the dishes and hold them in their places a moment—one of them was a large oval dish with a portly roast on it. Then he sat down, tilted up one end of the table, set two of the legs on his knees, took the end of the table between his teeth, took his hands away, and pulled down with his teeth till the table came up to a level position, dishes and all! He said he could lift a keg of nails with his teeth. He picked up a common glass tumbler and bit a semi-circle out of it. Then he opened his bosom and showed us a net-work of knife and bullet scars; showed us more on his arms and face, and said he believed he had bullets enough in his body to make a pig of lead. He was armed to the teeth. He closed with the remark that he was Mr. ⸺ of Cariboo—a celebrated name whereat we shook in our shoes. I would publish the name, but for the suspicion that he might come and carve me. He finally inquired if Brown still thirsted for blood. Brown turned the thing over in his mind a moment, and then—asked him to supper.

With the permission of the reader, I will group together, in the next chapter, some samples of life in our small mountain village in the old days of desperadoism. I was there at the time. The reader will observe peculiarities in our *official* society; and he will observe also, an instance of how, in new countries, murders breed murders.

CHAPTER XLIX

An extract or two from the newspapers of the day will furnish a photograph that can need no embellishment:

FATAL SHOOTING AFFRAY.—An affray occurred, last evening, in a billiard saloon on C street, between *Deputy Marshal Jack Williams* and Wm. Brown, which resulted in the immediate death of the latter. There had been some difficulty between the parties for several months.

An inquest was immediately held, and the following testimony adduced:

Officer GEO. BIRDSALL, sworn, says:—I was told Wm. Brown was drunk and was looking for Jack Williams; so soon as I heard that I started for the parties to prevent a collision; went into the billiard saloon; saw Billy Brown running around, saying if anybody had anything against him to show cause; he was talking in a boisterous manner, and officer Perry took him to the other end of the room to talk to him; Brown came back to me; remarked to me that he thought he was as good as anybody, and knew how to take care of himself; he passed by me and went to the bar; don't know whether he drank or not; Williams was at the end of the billiard-table, next to the stairway; Brown, after going to the bar, came back and said he was as good as any man in the world; he had then walked out to the end of the first billiard-table from the bar; I moved closer to them, supposing there would be a fight; as Brown drew his pistol I caught hold of it; he had fired one shot at Williams; don't know the effect of it; caught hold of him with one hand, and took hold of the pistol and turned it up; think he fired once after I caught hold of the pistol; I wrenched the pistol from him; walked to the end of the billiard-table and told a party that I had Brown's pistol, and to stop shooting; I think four shots were fired in all; after walking out, Mr. Foster remarked that Brown was shot dead.

Oh, there was no excitement about it—he merely "remarked" the small circumstance!

Four months later the following item appeared in the same paper (the *Enterprise*). In this item the name of one of the city officers above referred to (*Deputy Marshal Jack Williams*) occurs again:

ROBBERY AND DESPERATE AFFRAY.—On Tuesday night, a German named Charles Hurtzal, engineer in a mill at Silver City, came to this place, and visited the hurdy-gurdy house on B street. The music, dancing and Teutonic maidens awakened memories of Faderland until our German friend was carried away with rapture. He evidently had money, and was spending it freely. Late in the evening Jack Williams and Andy Blessington invited him down stairs to take a cup of coffee. Williams proposed a game of cards and went up stairs to procure a deck, but not finding any returned. On the stairway he met the German, and drawing his pistol knocked him down and rifled his pockets of some seventy dollars. Hurtzal dared give no alarm, as he was told, with a pistol at his head, if he made any noise or exposed them, they would blow his brains out. So effectually was he frightened that he made no complaint, until his friends forced him. Yesterday a warrant was issued, but the culprits had disappeared.

This efficient city officer, Jack Williams, had the common reputation of being a burglar, a highwayman and a desperado. It was said that he had several times drawn his revolver and levied money contributions on citizens at dead of night in the public streets of Virginia.

Five months after the above item appeared, Williams was assassinated while sitting at a card table one night; a gun was thrust through the crack of the door and Williams dropped from his chair riddled with balls. It was said, at the time, that Williams had been for some time aware that a party of his own sort (desperadoes) had sworn away his life; and it was generally believed among the people that Williams's friends and enemies would make the assassination memorable—and useful, too—by a wholesale destruction of each other.*

It did not so happen, but still, times were not dull during the next twenty-four hours, for within that time a woman was killed by a pistol shot, a man was brained with a slung shot, and a man named Reeder was also disposed of permanently. Some matters in the *Enterprise* account of the killing of Reeder are worth noting—especially the

---

*However, one prophecy was verified, at any rate. It was asserted by the desperadoes that one of their brethren (Joe McGee, *a special policeman*) was known to be the conspirator chosen by lot to assassinate Williams; and they also asserted that doom had been pronounced against McGee, and that he would be assassinated in exactly the same manner that had been adopted for the destruction of Williams—a prophecy which came true a year later. After twelve months of distress (for McGee saw a fancied assassin in every man that approached him), he made the last of many efforts to get out of the country unwatched. He

accommodating complaisance of a Virginia justice of the peace. The italics in the following narrative are mine:

MORE CUTTING AND SHOOTING.—The devil seems to have again broken loose in our town. Pistols and guns explode and knives gleam in our streets as in early times. When there has been a long season of quiet, people are slow to wet their hands in blood; but once blood is spilled, cutting and shooting come easy. Night before last Jack Williams was assassinated, and yesterday forenoon we had more bloody work, growing out of the killing of Williams, and on the same street in which he met his death. It appears that Tom Reeder, a friend of Williams, and George Gumbert were talking, at the meat market of the latter, about the killing of Williams the previous night, when Reeder said it was a most cowardly act to shoot a man in such a way, giving him "no show." Gumbert said that Williams had "as good a show as he gave Billy Brown," meaning the man killed by Williams last March. Reeder said it was a d—d lie, that Williams had no show at all. At this, Gumbert drew a knife and stabbed Reeder, cutting him in two places in the back. One stroke of the knife cut into the sleeve of Reeder's coat and passed downward in a slanting direction through his clothing, and entered his body at the small of the back; another blow struck more squarely, and made a much more dangerous wound. Gumbert gave himself up to the officers of justice, and was shortly after discharged by Justice Atwill, *on his own recognizance*, to appear for trial at six o'clock in the evening. In the meantime Reeder had been taken into the office of Dr. Owens, where his wounds were properly dressed. *One of his wounds was considered quite dangerous, and it was thought by many that it would prove fatal. But being considerably under the influence of liquor, Reeder did not feel his wounds as he otherwise would, and he got up and went into the street.* He went to the meat

---

went to Carson and sat down in a saloon to wait for the stage—it would leave at four in the morning. But as the night waned and the crowd thinned, he grew uneasy, and told the bar-keeper that assassins were on his track. The bar-keeper told him to stay in the middle of the room, then, and not go near the door, or the window by the stove. But a fatal fascination seduced him to the neighborhood of the stove every now and then, and repeatedly the bar-keeper brought him back to the middle of the room and warned him to remain there. But he could not. At three in the morning he again returned to the stove and sat down by a stranger. Before the bar-keeper could get to him with another warning whisper, some one outside fired through the window and riddled McGee's breast with slugs, killing him almost instantly. By the same discharge the stranger at McGee's side also received attentions which proved fatal in the course of two or three days.

market and renewed his quarrel with Gumbert, threatening his life. Friends tried to interfere to put a stop to the quarrel and get the parties away from each other. In the Fashion Saloon Reeder made threats against the life of Gumbert, saying he would kill him, and it is said that *he requested the officers not to arrest Gumbert, as he intended to kill him.* After these threats Gumbert went off and procured a double-barreled shot gun, loaded with buck-shot or revolver balls, and went after Reeder. Two or three persons were assisting him along the street, trying to get him home, and had him just in front of the store of Klopstock & Harris, when Gumbert came across toward him from the opposite side of the street with his gun. He came up within about ten or fifteen feet of Reeder, and called out to those with him to "look out! get out of the way!" and they had only time to heed the warning, when he fired. Reeder was at the time attempting to screen himself behind a large cask, which stood against the awning post of Klopstock & Harris's store, but some of the balls took effect in the lower part of his breast, and he reeled around forward and fell in front of the cask. Gumbert then raised his gun and fired the second barrel, which missed Reeder and entered the ground. At the time that this occurred, there were a great many persons on the street in the vicinity, and a number of them called out to Gumbert, when they saw him raise his gun, to "hold on," and "don't shoot!" The cutting took place about ten o'clock and the shooting about twelve. After the shooting the street was instantly crowded with the inhabitants of that part of the town, some appearing much excited and laughing—declaring that it looked like the "good old times of '60." Marshal Perry and officer Birdsall were near when the shooting occurred, and Gumbert was immediately arrested and his gun taken from him, when he was marched off to jail. Many persons who were attracted to the spot where this bloody work had just taken place, looked bewildered and seemed to be asking themselves what was to happen next, appearing in doubt as to whether the killing mania had reached its climax, or whether we were to turn in and have a grand killing spell, shooting whoever might have given us offence. It was whispered around that it was not all over yet—five or six more were to be killed before night. Reeder was taken to the Virginia City Hotel, and doctors called in to examine his wounds. They found that two or three balls had entered his right side; one of them appeared to have passed through the substance of the lungs, while another passed into the liver. Two balls were also found to have struck one of his legs. As some of the balls struck the cask, the wounds in Reeder's leg were probably from these, glancing downwards, though they might have been caused by the second shot fired. After being shot,

Reeder said when he got on his feet—smiling as he spoke—"It will take better shooting than that to kill me." The doctors consider it almost impossible for him to recover, but as he has an excellent constitution he may survive, notwithstanding the number and dangerous character of the wounds he has received. The town appears to be perfectly quiet at present, as though the late stormy times had cleared our moral atmosphere; but who can tell in what quarter clouds are lowering or plots ripening?

Reeder—or at least what was left of him—survived his wounds two days! Nothing was ever done with Gumbert.

Trial by jury is the palladium of our liberties. I do not know what a palladium is, having never seen a palladium, but it is a good thing no doubt at any rate. Not less than a hundred men have been murdered in Nevada—perhaps I would be within bounds if I said three hundred— and as far as I can learn, only two persons have suffered the death penalty there. However, four or five who had no money and no political influence have been punished by imprisonment—one languished in prison as much as eight months, I think. However, I do not desire to be extravagant—it may have been less.

Roughing It, 1872

ANONYMOUS

By the mid-19th century American crime pamphlets had jettisoned the religious and moral didacticism of an earlier era and evolved into an unabashedly sensationalistic form of popular entertainment. Churned out by anonymous hacks in the wake of notorious murders, these cheaply made publications, full of grisly details and overheated language, had no higher aim than sheer titillation. Typical of the genre is the following text, originally published as a 30-page booklet with a lurid cover illustration depicting a neatly dressed, blade-wielding boy attacking a terrified little girl above the caption, "With My Knife I Cut Her Throat."

Jesse Harding Pomeroy, aka "The Boston Boy-Fiend," was a juvenile sadist who, over the course of a nine-month period beginning in December 1871, lured a string of smaller boys to remote locations in South Boston, where he bound, beat, and tortured them. Arrested and sent to reform school, he was released after less than 17 months and promptly committed a pair of appalling mutilation-murders. He was only 14 when he was convicted and sentenced to death. A controversy immediately erupted over the morality of executing a minor, and his sentence was commuted to life by the governor of Massachusetts. He died in 1932, having spent just over 40 years of this nearly 60-year incarceration in solitary confinement, a record exceeded in American penal history only by the 42 years in "deep lock" endured by Robert Stroud, the famous "Bird Man of Alcatraz."

Jesse Harding Pomeroy, the Boy Fiend

The subject of this narrative, Jesse Harding Pomeroy, whose love for cruel deeds and inordinate thirst for human blood stand without precedent in history, was born in Charlestown, Mass., November 29, 1859. His father was born in Charlestown, and was a fireman in the U. S. Navy Yard at the time of Jesse's birth. His mother Ruth, was born in Maine, and was a steady industrious woman, and has maintained the family since the death of her husband. From early childhood Jesse was a very peculiar boy and acted strangely on certain occasions. When only ten months old, spots broke out on his face, and an ulcer came on his right eye which ruined its sight. When old enough he went to school and with certain peculiar traits was a good boy and a fair scholar. When Jesse was but a small boy he was seen one day with a kitten, which he had cut with his knife in three places. The kitten was badly mutilated and was taken from him, when he said he was only playing with it and that it was his little baby. Although subject to spells of despondency, with the exception of the above act, nothing happened of serious notice which exhibited his fiendish cruelty hitherto latent in his bosom, until the following acts became public which we will now narrate.

On February 21, 1872, he enticed a little boy named Tracy B. Hayden, to Powder Horn Hill in Chelsea, and there in an old out-house, Jesse tied the little one's hands and feet together, first making him take off his clothes, and then proceeded to whip him with a piece of rope.

On July 22, 1872, he treated a boy ten years old, named John Batch, in the same brutal manner; taking him to the same place that he did Hayden, he stripped him and beat him until he was black and blue.

On September 17, 1872, a seven-year-old boy, Charles A. Gould, by name, was carried away by Pomeroy to the railroad in South Boston, Pomeroy asking him to go and see the soldiers. Gould was stripped naked, his hands tied and then Pomeroy drew two knives, a large and small one, and cut Gould five times on the head and once back of each ear. A man coming along, Pomeroy was frightened away, and Gould was untied.

On August 17, 1872, George E. Pratt, another of Pomeroy's victims, was assaulted in an old boat drawn up at South Boston Point. His assaults on Pratt, consisted of beating his naked limbs with a strap, sticking pins in his face, limbs and private parts, biting and other methods of torture.

September 11, 1872, Joseph W. Kennedy, nine years old, was assaulted in Shepard's Boat House, South Boston. The first thing done by Pomeroy on this occasion, was to bump the boy's head against the timbers;

then he struck him in the face with his fist, and afterwards washed him in salt water. Afterwards Pomeroy cut the little boy three times with a knife which he had on his person. Kennedy was then made to repeat the Lord's Prayer, before Pomeroy on his knees, under threat of being killed.

Robert E. Maies, a boy eight years old, was assaulted in the fall of 1872, by Pomeroy.

He was looking into a toy shop, when Pomeroy asked him to go up to Powder Horn Hill, and after arriving there Pomeroy tied him, stripped off his clothes, put a gag in his mouth and then whipped him with a switch. While whipping the boy Pomeroy ran round him, jumped up and down and laughed. After the whipping Pomeroy drew the boy home on a sled, the latter crying most of the time. They were together three or four hours.

These repeated cruelties on these babyish victims created a tremendous excitement all over Chelsea and South Boston. The little boys went home slashed and bleeding and told their pitiful story. Of course the parents were half crazed, and search was made by the most skillful detectives for the ghoul-like monster who seemed to be preying on human blood. The little victims were so terrified that they could hardly give an intelligible description of the vampire who had tortured them; and for this reason, the police had very poor clews upon which to work. A large number of boys were suspected but the charge could be brought home to none. Pomeroy had all the cunning of a fiend and chose his time and place so well that he was never seen luring his victims to their destruction in some out of the way corner, on a remote hillside or salt marsh, where no one but some solitary sportsman was likely to wander. In some old rotten boat, or under some railroad bridge the groans and cries of the little sufferers could not be heard, and the torturer gashed and whipped and chopped them as he pleased, regardless of their tears and writhings of agony or only laughed at them in his devilish glee. Whether he ever foully murdered any other weak little victim before the final exposure of South Boston Flats will never be known, unless the chance discovery of some little bones in a retired nook, may lead to the discovery of an unrecorded tale of bloodshed. During the time he was perpetrating his cruelties, more than one child left its home in the morning to play about the neighborhood, and was never seen again. Its fate may be locked up in the heart of the boy monster, whom some are yet found to pity. His defective eye had been noticed by all his victims, and became a mark for which the police searched and he was arrested and brought before Judge Forsaith, trial justice of juvenile offenders of Boston, on the complaint of City Marshal Drury of Chelsea, charged with assault and battery with ropes and boards upon two boys in Chelsea, and with a knife upon four boys in South Boston. The boy was found guilty and committed to the Reform School. After his arrival at the school he was medically examined and pronounced sane. At the school he gave no evidence of a cruel disposition; his conduct was exceptionally good; he rose to the highest grade in the school, and had the freedom of the school, which he did not abuse.—Jan 20, 1874, sixteen months after the boy entered the school, the visiting agent was requested by one of the trustees to investigate the home of the boy, with a view to his release from the school. The investigation was carefully made by a visit to the home of the mother, by an interview with her, by inquiry of several officers and citizens in the vicinity of the home. The inquiries showed that the mother had been deserted by her husband; that she was a worthy woman, working hard for her maintenance, and was much oppressed by her domestic troubles; that she had another son, who conducted himself well and appeared to be a thrifty boy. In his business he needed the assistance of a boy of his brother's age to carry newspapers on a route, and Jesse, if released, could have regular employment in that work and in his mother's store. In a word, the condition of the home was found satisfactory. The facts of investigation were reported to the trustee who had asked for the examination, Jan. 24. After this the opinion of Capt. Dyer, in charge of Station 6, South Boston, was asked. As to the propriety of his coming home, Capt. Dyer thought it might be well to give him a trial on probation, "give him a chance to redeem himself." He expressed the opinion that "it isn't best to be down on a boy too hard or too long." On the 6th of February 1874, the trustees released the boy on probation. Pomeroy had behaved well, he had a good home, he could have steady work if released. In short, personal conduct and condition of home were satisfactory, and he was released upon probation.

After Jesse was released from the Reform School, he returned to South Boston and went to work for his brother, who kept a small periodical store and news depot at 327 Broadway. His mother also occupied dressmaking rooms in the same building. He helped his brother carry papers and was steady and industrious and showed none of his former love for cruelty and blood until the following circumstance occurred.

The horrible deed for which the young fiend is to suffer has been previously described in all its fearful details, but the general circumstances may again be repeated.

On the afternoon of the 22d of April, 1874, Officer Lyons, of the 9th Police, while patrolling his beat, was met by a deaf and dumb boy who attracted his attention by making gestures as if to indicate cutting his throat, and the infliction of stabs in the breast. The officer immediately suspected that a murder had been committed and followed the lad, who at once started off in the direction of the marsh land between Washington Village and Savin Hill, Dorchester District. On arriving at the beach at the lower end of the marsh, a circular heap of clam shells was seen. Within the hollow formed by the heap was the horribly mutilated body of a boy evidently about four years of age. The body was quite stiff, the legs and arms especially so. There were five cuts on each hand, one deep cut over the right eye and eighteen wounds in the breast. The left jugular vein was severed, and the throat was cut quite across the front. A pool of blood surrounded the head, flowing from the cut in the throat. The murdered boy's features were not distorted, and his position was that of a child lying in a calm slumber. The officer had the body immediately conveyed to the station, whence it was taken to Undertaker Waterman, on Washington street.

The news of the murder soon spread, and Coroner Allen summoned

a jury of inquest. Further examination of the body developed the facts
that the wounds were all made by a common penknife blade. Those on
the hands were doubtless received while trying to ward off the knife
from the breast. But few of the breast wounds were deep cuts. The knife
struck and glanced off the ribs several times. One wound was several
inches in depth. The throat was cut twice, once from below the right
ear to the apple, there connecting with a similar cut extending from
under the left ear. These wounds were very deep, nearly severing the
head from the body. The left jugular vein had been cut or punctured,
and this wound alone had been sufficient to cause death. There was
also a cut two inches in length in the scrotum, nearly severing the sper-
matic cord, and also cutting the femoral artery. It almost seemed that
the murderer had some knowledge of the anatomy of the human body
from the manner in which the wounds were inflicted.

The body when brought to the undertaker's was quite stiff, but the
abdominal muscles were flaccid, indicating that the boy had been dead
but a few hours. It was quite evident from the shallowness of the
wounds, the ability of the boy to resist his assailant, as shown by his
successful warding off of several blows with his hands, and other indications of a violent struggle, that the murderer could not have been a
man, and the wounds must have been inflicted by a person of little
strength either of nerve or arm. That a boy was the perpetrator of this
terrible crime, seemed almost clear. The wound over the heart indicated by its depth that it must have been made while the victim was
lying on his back. Had he been standing, the muscles would have contracted, and the coroner would have been unable to have probed the
wound to its full depth. The cut in the groin must have been made
after the boy was cold in death, for no blood flowed from it.—The
murderer was inhumanly brutal, and this unnecessary and shocking
mutilation of his victim could only have been instigated by the most
horrible motives.

About 8 o'clock on the evening of the discovery of the body, information was received which led to the identification of the murdered

boy. It appeared that during the forenoon, Horace H. Millen, a four-year-old son of Mr. H. Millen, living at No. 253 Dorchester street, had strayed from his home, and not returning at noon, information was given at the station by his parents. It further appeared that the child was last seen at 10 o'clock, playing at the corner of Dorchester and Eighth streets, and the description of the boy's dress answering to that of the murdered boy, the parents were notified and the identity of the body was established. The news spread rapidly and the excitement created is well remembered.

Shortly after 10 o'clock the same night, acting upon information in their possession, Sergt. Lucas and officer Adams of the 6th police proceeded to his parent's house on Second street, South Boston, and arrested young Pomeroy on suspicion of being the murderer. As soon as the two latter officers heard of the affair, they conjectured that no one could have performed the bloody deed but Pomeroy, and consequently, without saying a word to any one, on going to his house, they took him out of bed and to the station-house. On being searched at the station-house, blood was found upon his shirt and also upon the blade of the knife which was found in his possession.

The next day, Pomeroy was taken to the presence of the murdered boy, when he denied that he knew anything about him or had any hand in his murder. Further developments, however, tended to point to him as the guilty party, and his own admission, which follows below, corroborated the impression.

His confession was made in the presence of witnesses after he had laid in jail over four months and the discovery of the body of the Curran girl had been made.

That on the morning of April 22d, last past, he opened the store as usual; that he then went to the city proper and returned about 9 o'clock, remaining at the store until nearly noon; that he then started to come over to the city proper again, and that he went along Dorchester Avenue and there met the Millen boy, the sight of whom excited in him an unconquerable desire to gratify his fiendish propensity to shed human blood, and he resolved to torture him; that for this purpose he enticed him, under pretence of showing him a steamboat over upon the Dorchester marshes, and that upon arriving at the place where the body was afterwards found, he induced the child to lie down upon the sand; that he unhesitatingly did so, and that he, (Pomeroy) then got upon him, and, with his knife, proceeded to cut his throat; that the child fought hard, and he, (Pomeroy) getting mad at the resistance, stabbed him repeatedly in the chest and bowels, holding his left hand over the lad's mouth to prevent any outcry; that after mutilating the body (how much he does not say; even if he knows) he cleaned his knife in the sand, left the spot and went over to the city proper in accordance with his original intention when he left the store; that he visited the common, loafed about there for some time, and then returned home.

In this, as in the other case, of the Curran girl, he simply says he "could not help it." He says he had no intention of cutting any one until he saw the Millen lad; that then the feeling that he must do it took possession of him and overcame a thought he had while on the way to the marshes that he had better not. The confession is said to have been made with the same coolness that characterized his manner ever since he came into the notice of the police.

While Pomeroy was in jail, awaiting his trial for the murder of the Millen boy, and previous to his confession, a discovery came to light which again chilled the public blood, and roused a sentiment of bitter, yet just indignation in the community.

Mary Katie Curran was a little girl, ten years of age, daughter of John and Mary Curran, living at No. 377 Second street, South Boston. On the 18th of March, nearly a month before the murder of the Millen boy, her mother sent her to a neighboring store on an errand, and she never returned. It was shown subsequently that the child went to the shop, did the errand and left, and that was the last certain trace ever had of her. Her disappearance was the subject of comment in the newspapers, the police were active in the search for her, and a reward of $500 was offered for her recovery, but all to no purpose.

On Saturday, July 18th, 1874, some workmen were engaged in digging out the cellar of the building 327 Broadway, South Boston, formerly occupied by Mrs. Pomeroy and her sons, but which Mr. James Nash had then bought and was building an addition to it.

While some laborers were at work on the rear foundation wall, quite a large stone fell over upon a heap of ashes, sixteen or eighteen inches deep. In removing this stone, one of the workmen named McGinnis, struck his pick into the heap, when out rolled a human skull. This astonished the men so greatly that their labors were immediately suspended and word was sent to the 6th Station near by. Capt. Dyer sent over Officer John H. Foote, and Detective Adams immediately followed. They proceeded with their investigations and were rewarded by drawing from the ashes a piece of cloth resembling a dress, and what appeared to be the remains of the body of a child. In an instant Officer Adams said, "This is the body of Katie Curran," and subsequent disclosures proved his conjectures to be facts. A dress, skirt and scarf were also taken from the heap, but were much soiled and faded, as would be the case after lying in a heap of dirt for months.

The flesh and all the soft parts of the body were entirely decomposed, nothing but the bones remaining. John and Mary Curran, the parents of Katie, were immediately summoned, and instantly recognized the clothes as those their daughter wore when she disappeared from home exactly four months before. The poor woman was frantic with grief, and became almost crazy. It was with great difficulty she was kept from falling on her daughter's remains.

Pomeroy was interviewed by Chief of Police, Savage, and denied all knowledge of the affair, and his mother and brother were arrested on suspicion, but were soon acquitted as Jesse finally made his confession as follows:

He says that he opened his mother's store on the 18th of March, in the morning about 7 1-2 o'clock. "The girl came in for papers. I told her there was a store down stairs. She went down to about the middle of the cellar and stood facing Broadway. I followed her, put my arm about her neck, my hand over her mouth, with my knife cut her throat, holding my knife in my right hand. I then dragged her to behind the water closet, laying her head furtherest up the place, and I put some stones and some ashes on the body. Took the ashes from a box in the cellar. I sent a boy into Hoyt & Lawrence's store, near by, and bought the knife about a week before for 25 cents. The knife was taken from me when I was arrested in April last. When I was in the cellar I heard my brother at the outside door which I had locked after the girl came in. I ran up stairs and found him going towards the cellar in Mitchell's part; he came back. Two girls worked in the store for mother. They usually got there about 9 o'clock, mother came later. Brother Charles and I took turns in opening the store till about April. My mother and brother never knew of this affair. I washed my hands and the knife that were bloody at the water pipe." This water pipe was under the stairs opposite the water closet.

He said nothing about mutilating her body after he had killed her but the upper portion of the body being so badly decomposed, it was impossible to tell whether the head had been cut from the neck or whether the vertebræ of the neck had separated from natural causes. As the head was first brought to view by a pickaxe striking it, the separation might have been caused then. The clothing of the girl bore evidence that it had been literally torn to pieces, while the private parts of the body had been horribly mutilated. It is thought probable, accepting as true, Jesse's description of the manner in which he cut the little girl's throat, that after doing that and finding life still fluttering in his victim, he proceeded to cut and mutilate the body until the vital spark had fled.

The knife with which Pomeroy committed these terrible murders, is a cheap knife with one large and one small blade, both being in the same end of the handle, and it is altogether a medium sized pocket knife, the end of the little blade was bent over, as if it had been brought into forcible contact with some unyielding substance. The knife also had some partially dried blood in the crevices into which the blades shut, and there is every reason to suppose that it was the same weapon with which he so horribly butchered the poor little Millen boy, on the Dorchester Marsh, and perhaps before that tortured other victims.

Since the murder of the Joyce children in the Bussey woods, a few years since, Boston and the whole state has scarcely had a parallel excitement. Mothers clasped their little one's closer to their breasts, and fathers ground their teeth with rage and horror at the bare thought that their children might fall into the hands of a similar brutal tormenter on some unfortunate day. Happily such blood-thirsty human tigers are scarce ever found on the face of the earth among civilized people or pagans.

If the Pomeroy boy had fallen at this time into the hands of an average assembly of citizens of ever quiet Massachusetts, the chances are that he would have been torn limb from limb, like some furious beast which had fallen among those upon whom he had preyed.

The trial of the boy developed a great deal of miscellaneous testimony among which was the following cunningly prepared statement, furnished by Jesse to the Coroner at the investigation. It ran as follows:

"My name is Jesse Harding Pomeroy; was 14 years old last November, on the 29th; live with my parents at 312 Broadway; I carry newspapers as a business for my brother; commence to carry them about three o'clock in the day; began last Wednesday to carry them about three o'clock; got up at about half-past six o'clock in the morning; had breakfast at home; after I had eaten it I went over to the store, 327 Broadway; I cleared up the store, helped my brother at that time; continued that work until eight o'clock, then I went after the weekly papers to the New England News Company's store; I returned from the city about twenty minutes of nine o'clock; after I returned I fixed up the windows in the store some one else being there at the time—my mother, two girls and my brother; after I fixed up the store I went home and got some dinner, about half-past eleven o'clock; then I went back to Boston, starting for there at a little after half-past eleven o'clock; I went down Broadway, over Federal street bridge, along Federal street, up to the new post office, up Milk street to Washington street, up Bromfield street to Tremont street, and to the Common: I then walked almost all over the Common to the Public Garden; don't know how long I stayed there; I sat down on one of the benches a few minutes to rest; then went up Beacon street, then on the Common, and to Mr. Presho's dining room on Congress street, reached there at about a quarter of or two o'clock: did not get dinner there; I then went alone to my brother's and got the money for my checks at the Traveler office; I did not get my papers then but went to Quincy market; don't know how long I stopped there, but got back to the Traveler office at half-past 2 o'clock; went down to where the papers were given out and sat there until a quarter of three o'clock; got my papers and then went to the Journal office remained there until 3 o'clock, then I carried my 3 o'clock papers.

When I first left the house, and before I crossed the bridge, I spoke to no one that I knew, and until I got to the new post office and to Bromfield street, I saw not a single one that I knew. I spoke to no one from the time I left home until I reached Presho's; noticed nothing of importance on my route except people building a well with bricks on Federal street; saw nothing that excited my curiosity at the head of Bromfield street: they were laying pipes just above the Common near Winter street; saw no improvements going on in the Public Garden; there were not many people there; there was nothing particular to attract my attention from the time I left home until I reached Presho's; I was arrested Wednesday evening at ten o'clock; don't know who arrested me; have seen the officer to-day, but don't know his name; he said nothing to me, but first spoke to my mother; I was first informed of what I had been arrested for by the chief of police; this was yester-day morning when he told me about the matter; I had conversation on Wednesday night with the officer who arrested me; he wanted to know what I had been doing that day: I told him where I had been; I told him minutely what I have stated to the jury, except what I saw about the water pipes, and regarding the digging of the well; I made this state-ment to the chief of police; I stated to him almost exactly the same as I have stated to you; the chief of police told me that I was arrested for the crime of murder. He did not tell me the name of the person killed, but said I was arrested for the murder of that little boy on the marsh, yesterday morning; this was the first time I was informed of the particulars of the murder, and then I was told by the chief of police; since then no officers have told me about it; have had no access to, and have not read any newspapers. I have talked with two or three officers about the matter; don't know their names; have made no admission to any one as to my complicity in the crime. I have seen the little boy that was murdered; saw him at the undertaker's; made no remarks then to the officers; from the undertaker's I was taken to Station Six; after I was taken there I had some conversation with a gentleman who called to see me; his name was Stephen G. Deblois; the matter of that conversation was inquiry; he did not advise me what to do; there was no one else present at our conversation; have talked with the captain of Police Station Six about this affair, but he gave no advice; he did not ask me if I was guilty of the crime; I had conversation with another person, a Mr. Bragdon, who arrested me before, he gave me no advice; have talked with no one else, except the officers belonging to the station.

I was taken from Station Six to the city hall; was carried there about half-past two o'clock; was next brought to this station; have had here conversation only with the coroner and officers; there was something in our conversation I have not yet stated; you asked me if I was in my right mind and I replied I thought I was; don't remember that I was asked whether I was guilty or not guilty; the conversation between us referred mostly to matters that occurred previous to this affair; I wore last Wednesday a pair of boots, the same pants that I now have on, with the same shirt and inside coat; the outside coat I did not wear; I wore a plush cap without any visor; don't know where the boots are that I wore; they were taken from me at Station 6 Wednesday night, and I have not had possession of them since; they were common thin boots, new, or quite so; I had them tapped once and wore a hole on the right side of the right boot; had them new heeled the time they were tapped; had them re-soled three weeks ago; did not tread my boots square generally; I wore them out on the outside, and that hole came near the small toe of the right foot; I have missed, since I was at the station, my knife and pocket-book. The knife was a white-handled one with two blades, a large one and a small one; the large one was as large as my middle finger, and the small one about as large as my little finger; the small blade was about a quarter of an inch wide; have seen the knife since; the officer who arrested me had it when I saw it last; the officer did not examine it in my presence; he said nothing to me about it; I had in my pocket-book five ten cent pieces and had five cents in my vest pocket; this I collected for selling newspapers. I turned the money over to my mother or brother every evening; I never saw the little boy who was killed until I saw him at the undertaker's; am sure that I never spoke to him; was not told by the chief where the body was found, but was told by the sergeant of Station 9; he said the body was found in the cow pasture down by the Old Colony Railroad; am not acquainted with that locality; have not been there; was there two years ago this summer; when I was there were boat houses and men down there shooting; did not go over the grounds much; saw no one digging clams there; I went down there to look around; when I was there I did not go on the marsh; I stayed on the railroad track or went about it; this was two years ago, when we first moved there; don't recollect of any person speaking to me when I was there at that time; I have never been on the grounds since then at any time, but have passed by them. (At this point the knife belonging to the witness, and the boots said to have been worn by him at the time of the murder, and which fitted exactly the footmarks near where the murdered boy was found, were submitted to him, and he without any hesitancy acknowledged the articles to have been his.) Am not acquainted much on Dorchester street; have some customers on Gates street; when I went on the Old Colony road two years ago I went on E street till I struck the Old Colony road, and then I walked out as far as I went."

The confession, written by Pomeroy himself, was then read by Mr. May. It was a full and detailed statement of the crime for which he is now on trial, saying that he had no motive, nor did he know why he came to do it. It was written last July at the jail.

George E. Powers, a boy of 12 years, after first being qualified as to his knowledge of an oath and its requirements, testified: I remember the day the Millen boy was found dead, I was on the marsh with my mute brother; we went there after clams between 3 and 4 o'clock; there were some men there shooting; I found the body of the boy about half a mile out, within two feet of a creek; (witness pointed out on the map where the body was found); the body was lying about ten feet from the shore; when I found the body I called my brother and then called the men, who were fifty rods away; the dead boy had on a red dress and a jacket; I did not touch the body till I called the men; saw that it was cut and stabbed badly, and the hands bloody.

Cross-examined. The first person to touch the body was policeman Lyons; it was a long time before a policeman could be found.

Patrick Wise testified: On the 22nd of April I was gunning on the cow pasture marsh; young Powers came up to me and told me there was a dead boy on the marsh; I went to where the body was; It laid on its back with its legs expanded; there were six stabs on his left hand and his throat was cut; his drawers were drawn down, but I saw no cuts on his body; blood was issuing from his mouth and both eyes; the body was guarded by me till the officer came, who was sent for by Mr. Craw-ford, who was with me; I drove a stick into the ground at the spot where the body was found. (He showed by reference to the map where the body was found and where the Powers boy met him.) Upon the arrival of Mr. Goodspeed with the officer the body was carried to the Crescent avenue station.

Obed Goodspeed, the companion of the last witness, testified, but his evidence was simply in corroboration of Mr. Wise. The last he saw of the body it was taken away from the station by officer Lyons in a carriage.

Roswell M. Lyons, a police officer of Station 9 testified: Remember the finding of the Millen boy; my attention was called to it by a deaf and dumb boy named Powers; (witness repeated the description of the dead child's appearance;) it was evident there had been a struggle as the boy's foot had been pressed into the mud, and there were many foot prints; the body was taken to the railway station and then by me to Station 9, where Sergt. Goodwin took charge of it; the boy's clothing was cut where stabs were inflicted.

Cross examined. It was about quarter-past 5 o'clock when I arrived at the place where the body was found.

Sergeant of Police, Henry O. Goodwin of Station 9, testified: First saw the body of the Millen boy at our station; I carried it to the undertaker's; subsequently I went with several officers to the marsh where the body was found to examine foot prints found; plaster casts were made of the tracks, and a pair of boots were used to test the tracks; the boots fitted the tracks exactly; I saw several experiments made; there were two sets of tracks one much larger than the other; the two tracks, side by side were traced for a long distance; the small boots also fitted the tracks.

Dr. Ira Allen testified: Was the coroner in the case of the Millen boy; first saw the body in the evening of the 22d of April, when it was in charge of Officer Goodwin; the throat was cut by two wounds, one losing itself in the other; the artery and windpipe were severed, there were several other wounds in the neck; there was a punctured wound in the right eye, which entered the ball; there were six wounds on the left hand; on removing the clothing a large number of wounds were found (which were described); eighteen wounds were found within a circle of three inches; the little shirt worn by the boy at the time was exhibited, and the cuts and blood shown to the jury; I directed the officers to make the experiments in the tracks; the tracks were visible, and the boots fitted them as close as anything could possibly fit; the clothes worn by the Millen boy were exhibited and identified; the body was stiff in some parts when I first saw it; a knife, said to have belonged to Pomeroy, was shown to me at the inquest and there were stains upon it which were blood stains.

The fatal knife was shown to the witness and identified. It was first shown to me by Officer Adams, and I made a microscopic examination of the stain upon it; my idea is that the wounds on the deceased were all made by a small blade; the wounds in the hands were all punctured ones, as though made while attempting to ward off blows from the breast; all the wounds might have been made by the knife exhibited or one like it; (the wounds in the scrotum were described by the witness.)

Mrs. Eleanor Fosdick testified: On the 22d of April last I saw Jesse Pomeroy following another smaller boy round the corner near my house; I recognize the prisoner as the boy who was with the small boy; I noticed the little boy had on a red plaid dress, and my attention was called to him by my child wanting a hat like his.

Cross-examined: I was forty or fifty feet away, but noticed the larger boy as he looked up to my window; he acted peculiar and as though he had been doing something wrong: the little boy bought a cake and came out of the store and gave part of it to the large boy; the large boy looked so strange that I looked at him the second time with my glasses; he was evidently excited; I went to the jail two weeks ago with Officer Adams to pick out Pomeroy; I never saw the little boy before the day and time described.

Re-direct. I looked at a large number of prisoners in their cells before coming to the right one. No one gave me any information as to what cell he was in, or how he looked. When I reached his cell I knew him.

The mother of the murdered boy, Mrs. Leonora Millen testified; Am mother of the deceased, Horace Millen; last saw him alive at twenty minutes past 10 o'clock on the 22d of last April; I gave him a number of pennies before he went; (witness described the child's dress at the time he went out,) he was four years old last January. (The witness when shown the bloody clothes of her child, which she identified, was much overcome, and allowed to retire.)

Sarah Hunting testified; I live on Dorchester street; I saw the Millen boy on the day of the murder, near the lamp post on Dorchester street; he was there between 10 and 11 o'clock; I spoke with him and he showed me a cent; there were other children with him at the time, one of them a large, lop-shouldered boy; didn't notice him particularly; do not know the prisoner and never saw him before.

Elias Ashcroft testified: Remember the day the Millen boy was found; I saw him half-way between Washington Village and the marsh; he was on the railroad going out towards McKay's warf; there was some one with him, but I don't know who it was; it was near 12 o'clock when I saw him on the railroad; late in the afternoon I saw the Millen boy dead; a large boy was leading the Millen boy when I saw him at noon.

Cross-examined; Cannot describe the large boy, nor do I remember how he was dressed; he was either a man or a large boy.

Robert C. Benson testified : Am fifteen years old; remember the finding of the Millen boy's body; I was on the marsh digging clams; while washing clams I observed a boy over on the marsh running away; he was going from the direction of where the murder was committed to Carlton street and looked around often to see it he was followed. (Witness pointed out on the map the several spots referred to.)—I pointed out the places to the man who made the map; the boy had on a plush cap I think, but will not swear to it.

Cross-examined: He was running when I first saw him; how far he ran I don't know; five or eight minutes afterwards I saw him looking round; when he got to Carlton St. I lost sight of him; it was between half-past 12 and quarter to 1 when I saw him going away.

The plan of the defence was to interpose a plea of insanity. There was no chance to work upon the feelings of the jury by any allusions to the prisoner's youth or former innocence. He stood red-handed before them, with the blood of two children crying out from the ground against him. Able witnesses were brought forward who had made lunacy a study for many years, but their words fell upon dull ears. The jury returned a verdict of guilty of murder in the first degree, and the young wretch was removed to the jail, whence he was recalled and sentenced to be hung at the proper time. He heard his doom pronounced without a shiver, thinking no doubt that at the last moment his age would save him from the gallows he so richly merited. Boston has been particularly unfortunate in being the scene of dreadful human butcheries, and so many assassins have escaped after commission of crimes almost unparalleled, that public sentiment although in the main opposed to inflicting the extreme penalty of the law upon a child, would have been inexpressibly shocked if by any subterfuge, or false ideas of mercy this brutal boy should escape the doom of all murderers, and be set free after a few years of confinement in some comfortable mad-house. There was too much cool cunning and calculation in his insanity, if that it was. A remonstrance against any commutation of his punishment was prepared and signed by a score or more of the most eminent gentlemen and ladies of Boston and vicinity, and the women of East Boston alone, prepared a special appeal to Governor Gaston and his Council, which read as follows:

"We the undersigned, wives, mothers and daughters of East Boston, beg leave respectfully to represent that a horrible murder has been committed in this ward of our city in one of our most populous and frequented streets in broad daylight. That the author of this revolting crime when young was convicted of a heinous offense; but his sentence was "commuted," which if executed might have arrested him in his downward career and saved to our city a valuable and precious life. Who knows but that the delays of the law and the hope of the defeat of its just sentence may have had much to do in emboldening the fiend in his work of death on the 22d current. And if murderers are to escape the penalty due their crimes what mother knows the sight that may greet her eyes in her own cellar on her next return home? Wherefore, as the case of Jesse Pomeroy is soon to come before your honorable body for final disposition, we most earnestly pray that you will listen to no petition nor pleadings for commutation of his sentence."

The gallows is the proper doom of the wretched boy, who is as fit to roam at large, or be confined in a weak cell as the tiger who has once tasted blood.

Jesse Harding Pomeroy, the Boy Fiend, 1875

LAFCADIO HEARN

Though best known for his books about Japan, where he spent the last 14 years of his strange and peripatetic life, Lafcadio Hearn (1850–1904) began his writing career as a city newspaper reporter specializing in lurid crime stories. Born on the Greek island of Santa Maura to an Irish father and Maltese mother, Hearn was brought to Dublin at six, the first of many upheavals in his often unhappy early life. After attending a succession of Catholic schools in England and France, he set out for America at the age of 19, eventually making his way to Cincinnati. Friendless and impoverished, he struggled to subsist at a variety of menial jobs before becoming a reporter for the Cincinnati *Enquirer*, where he quickly earned a reputation for his florid accounts of sensational murders. This "period of the gruesome" ended in 1875, when Hearn created a scandal by marrying an African-American woman, Alethea Foley, and was fired from the *Enquirer*. Immediately hired by a competing daily, the Cincinnati *Commercial*, he was dispatched to New Orleans and ended up remaining there for the next ten years.

Having separated from his wife, Hearn wangled a contract from Harper and Brothers for a book about Japan and set out for East Asia, never to return. By 1896, he had wed the daughter of a poor samurai family, become a Japanese subject, and legally changed his name to Koizumi Yakumo. He remains best known for the work he produced during this last phase of his singular life, such as the retellings of traditional Japanese ghost stories collected in *Kwaidan* (1903), written in a simple, elegant style that contrasts markedly with the prose of his "gruesome" period.

Gibbeted

The execution of James Murphy, yesterday afternoon, at Dayton, for the murder of Colonel William Dawson, in that city, on the night of August 31, 1875, was an event, it must be said, which the people of Montgomery County had long looked forward to with no small degree of satisfaction. The murder was of itself peculiarly atrocious, from the fact that it was actually committed without a shadow of provocation. The victim was a worthy and popular citizen, and the feeling of the public in regard to the crime was sufficiently evinced in the fact that the city authorities, subsequent to the arrest of Murphy, were obliged to call out the militia that the claim of legal justice to deal with the criminal might be protected. Colonel Dawson, it may be remembered, was murdered apparently for no other reason than that he refused a drunken party permission to intrude upon the quiet enjoyments of a private wedding party. The Colonel was Superintendent of Champion Plow Works, at Dayton and the bridegroom being an employe of the company, the Colonel had, by request, assumed the management of the wedding ball. When Murphy was refused admittance, he induced one of his companions, Lewis Meyers, to entice the Colonel out of doors on the pretext of getting a drink, and soon after the invitation had been accepted Murphy struck Dawson, and during the subsequent scuffle, suddenly plunged a long knife up to the haft in the Colonel's left side. The victim of this cowardly assault lived but a few moments afterward, and died without being able to positively identify his assassin.

Circumstantial evidence, notwithstanding, clearly pointed to Murphy as the criminal, and to Meyers as his accomplice; the former being sentenced to death, and the latter, being convicted of manslaughter, to a term of two years in the State Penitentiary. Sentence was passed on the 28th of April, the jury having disagreed upon the first trial, in February, which necessitated a second.

The youth of the prisoner—he was only nineteen years of age—did not, strange as it may seem, excite any marked degree of sympathy for his miserable fate. He was a fair skinned, brown haired, heartless lad, with rather large features, a firm, vicious mouth; sullen, steady gray eyes, shadowed by a habitual frown; a rather bold forehead, half concealed by a mass of curly locks, brushed down,—a face, in short, that, notwithstanding its viciousness, was not devoid of a certain coarse regularity. His parents were hard-working Irish people, but his own features showed little evidence of Celtic blood.

Perhaps the dogged obstinacy of the prisoner in denying, almost to the last, his evident crime, had no little to do with the state of public feeling in regard to him. Moreover, he had long been notorious in the city as a worthless loafer and precocious ruffian, perpetually figuring in some street fight, drunken brawl or brutal act of violence. For a considerable period of time, previous to the murder of Colonel Dawson, he had been the boasted leader of a band of young roughs, from nineteen to twenty years of age, who were known in Dayton as the "chain-gang."

The boy's mother had died while he was yet young; but he did not lack a home, and the affection of an old father, and of brothers and sisters—the latter of whom he is said to have cruelly abused in fits of drunken passion. In this connection it would of course be in order, religiously, to discourse upon the results of neglecting early admonitions; and, philosophically, upon the evidence that the unfortunate lad had inherited an evil disposition, whereof the tendencies were not to be counteracted by any number of admonitions. But the facts in the case, as they appeared to the writer, were simply that a poor, ignorant, passionate boy, with a fair, coarse face, had in the heat of drunken anger taken away the life of a fellow-being, and paid the penalty of his brief crime, by a hundred days of mental torture, and a hideous death.

Perhaps there are many readers of this article, who may have perused and shuddered at the famous tale of the "Iron Shroud." You may remember that the victim, immured in the walls of a dungeon, lighted by seven windows, finds that each successive day of his imprisonment, one of the windows disappears forever. There are first seven, then six, then five, then four, then three, then two, then but one—dim and shadowy;—and then the night-black darkness that prefigures the formless gloom of the Shadow of Death. And through the thick darkness booms, hour after hour, the abysmal tones of a giant bell, announcing to the victim the incessant approach or the fearful midnight when the walls shall crush his bones to shapelessness. No one ever read that tale of the Castle of Tolfi without experiencing such horrors as make the flesh creep. Yet the agony therein depicted by a cunning writer is, after all, but a very slight exaggeration of the torture to which condemned criminals are periodically subjected in our prisons —not for seven days, forsooth, but for one hundred. This is the mercy of the law!—to compel the wretched victim to await the slow but inevitable approach of the grimmest and most ignominious of deaths for one hundred days. Fancy the ghastly mental computation of time which he must make to his own heart—"ninety-nine—ninety-eight—ninety-seven—ninety-six—ninety-five," until at last the allotment of life is reduced to a miserable seven days, as frightfully speedy as those of the Man in the Iron Shroud. And then the black scaffold with the blacker mystery below the drop, the sea of curious and unsympathetic faces, the moment of supreme suspense after his eyes are veiled from the light of the world by the sable hood. But this pyramid of agony is not absolutely complete until apexed by the vision of a fragile rope, the sudden hush of horror, and the bitterest period of agony twice endured. It is cruel folly to assert that because the criminal be ignorant, uneducated, phlegmatic, unimaginative, he is incapable of acutely feeling the torture of hideous suspense. That was asserted, nevertheless, and frequently asserted yesterday, by spectators of the execution. We did not think so. The victim was young and strong, a warm-blooded, passionate boy, with just that coarse animal vitality which makes men cling most strongly to life, as a thing to be enjoyed in the mere fact of possession—the mere ability to hear, see, feel.

The incidents of the prisoner's jail life during the last week—how he ate, drank, smoked, talked—might be very fully dwelt on as matters of strictly local interest, but may be briefly dismissed in these columns. There is, however, one story connected with that jail-life too strange and peculiar to be omitted. It seems that young Murphy learned to entertain a special affection for Tom Hellriggle, a Deputy Sheriff of Montgomery County, who had attended him kindly since his removal from the jail-room to a cell on the third floor, which opened in the rear of the scaffold. One night, recently, Murphy said to Hellriggle, confidentially: "I knew I was going to be hanged, long ago. Do you know that I knew it before I was sentenced?"

"Why, how did you know that?" curiously asked the deputy.

Then the lad told him that during the intervals of the trials, one night between 12 and 1 o'clock, he heard the voice of a woman crying weirdly and wildly in the darkness, and so loudly that the sound filled all the jail-room, and that many of the men awoke and shuddered.

"You remember that, don't you?" asked the lad.

"I do," said the deputy; "and I also remember that there was no living woman in the jail-room that night."

"So," continued the boy, "they asked me if heard it, and I said yes; but I pretended I did not know what it was. I believe I said no human being could cry so fearfully as that. But I did know what it was, Tom— *I saw the woman.*"

"Who was it?" asked Tom, earnestly.

"It was my mother. And I knew why she cried so strangely. She was crying for me."

There are few men who enter the condemned cell and leave it for the gallows without having entertained during the interval a strong desire to take their own lives, and are for the most part deterred from so doing rather by the religious dread of a dim and vague Something after death, than by any physical fear. So it appears to have been with Murphy. When all hope, except the hope of pardon from the All-forgiving Father, was dead within him, and the Governor of Ohio had refused to grant a reprieve or communication of sentence, then the prisoner listened much more calmly to the admonitions of Father Murphy, a fat, kindly, red-cheeked Irish priest, who took a heartfelt interest in the "spiritual welfare" of his namesake. He soon expressed repentance for his crime, and even agreed to confess all publicly—an act, all the circumstances properly considered, which really evinced more manhood than the act of "dying game" with the secret.

Shortly afterward he handed to Deputy Sheriff Hellriggle a small, keen knife, which he had managed to conceal, despite all the vigilance of his guards. "I would not take my own life, now," he said, "though I were to be hung twice over." Yet at that time the poor fellow probably had little idea that he would actually suffer the penalty of the law twice.

It was evident, however, that he had frequently premeditated suicide, as in a further conversation with his guard he pointed out certain ingenious and novel modes of self-destruction which he had planned. That the criminal possessed no ordinary amount of nerve and self-control under the most trying circumstances, can not for a moment be questioned; nor can it be truthfully averred that his courage was merely the result of stolid phlegm and natural insensibility. None of the family, indeed, appear to inherit oversensitive organizations, as a glance at the faces of the visitors to the condemned cell sufficiently satisfied us. When James' eldest brother, a ruddily-featured young man of twenty, visited the prisoner day before yesterday, he mounted the black scaffold erected outside the cell-door and, after a few humorous remarks, actually executed a double-shuffle dance upon the trap-door, until Sheriff Patton, hearing the noise, at once turned him out of the corridor. But James' actions in jail, his last farewell to his relations, his sensitiveness in regard to certain reports afloat concerning his past career, and lastly, the very fact that his nerve did finally yield under a fearful and wholly unexpected pressure, all tend to show that his nature was by no means so brutally unfeeling as had been alleged.

The scaffold had been erected at the rear end of the central corridor of the jail hospital ward in the third story of the building, immediately without the cell-room in which the prisoner had been confined subsequent to his removal from the gloomier jail-room below, where he had heard the loud knocking of the carpenters' hammers, and the hum of saws—sounds of which the grim significance was fully recognized by him without verbal interpretation. "Ah, they are putting up the gallows!" he said: "The noise don't frighten me much, though." To the reporter who visited the long, white corridor by lamp-light, with the tall, black-draped and ebon-armed apparition at its further end, these preparations for an execution under roof, instead of beneath the clear sky, and in the pure air, seemed somewhat strange and mysteriously horrible. It is scarcely necessary to describe the mechanism of the scaffold, further than to observe that the trap-door was closed by curved bolts, the outer ends of which were inserted into or withdrawn from shallow sockets in the framework at either side of the door, by foot-pressure upon a lever, which connected with the inner ends of the bolts, and worked them like the handles of huge pincers. The rope did, however, attract considerable attention from all who examined it previous to the execution. It seemed no thicker than a strong clothes-line, though actually three eighths of an inch, and appeared wholly unequal to the task for which it had been expressly manufactured from unbleached hemp. Yet Sheriff Gerard, of Putnam County, who had officiated at five executions, and was considered an authority upon such matters, had had it well tested with a keg of nails and other heavy weights, and believed it sufficiently strong. A bucket of water was suspended to it for some twenty-four hours, in order to remove its slight elasticity. But the bucket turned slowly around at intervals, and, under the constant pressure and motion, it seems that the rope became worn and weakened at the point of its insertion into the crossbeam. The drop-length was regulated to three feet and a half.

The unfortunate boy's mental impressions, yesterday morning, must assuredly have consisted of a strange and confused vision of solemn images and mysterious events. From the opening door of his cell he could plainly perceive every mechanical detail of the black gibbet, with its dismal hangings of sable muslin. Sisters of Charity, in dark robes; solemn-faced priests, with snowy Roman collars; Sheriffs and Deputy Sheriffs of austere countenance, which appeared momentarily to become yet more severe; policemen in full dress whispering in knots along the white corridor, a score of newspaper correspondents and reporters scattered through the crowd, writing and questioning and occasionally stealing peeps at the prisoner through the open door; calm-visaged physicians consulting together over open watches, as though eager to feel the last pulsations of the dying heart; undertakers, professional, cool and sad, gathered about a long, handsome black walnut coffin, adorned with silver crosses, which stood in the corner of one hospital room—these and other figures thronged the scene of death and disgrace while without a bright sun and a clear sky appeared for the last time to the wandering eyes of the condemned. He had early in the morning gone through the necessary formal preparations of being shaved, bathing, and putting on the neat suit of black cloth for which he had been measured a few days before. He had slept soundly all night; after having listened to the merry music of the city band, playing before the snowy-columned Court-house, but his sleep was probably consequent upon physical and mental exhaustion from haunting fear, rather than a natural and healthy slumber. He had risen at 7 o'clock, made a full confession in presence of the Sheriff, heard mass, listened to Father Murphy's admonitions, ate a light breakfast, and smoked several cigars. Father Murphy's admonitions, delivered in simple language, and a strong old-country brogue, seemed to us passive listeners somewhat peculiar, especially when he stated that the "flesh and blood of Jesus Christ, which not even the angels were worthy to eat," would give strength to the poor lad "to meet his God at half-past 1 o'clock." But if ever religious faith comforted the last moments of a young criminal, it did in this instance; and it was owing to the kindly but powerful efforts of the little priest that the youth made a full public confession of his crime. This is the confession:

MONTGOMERY COUNTY JAIL, ⎫
DAYTON, O., AUGUST 24, 1876. ⎭

To Warren Munger and Elihu Thompson, my Attorneys:

I will now say to you, and the public in general, that ever since you became my attorneys, at all times until to-day, I have denied that I struck and killed William Dawson, for which crime I am now under sentence of death. This statement I have made you in the mistaken hope and belief that it might do me some good, and I therefore put the blame on another person—Charles Tredtin. Now that all hope is gone, I have to say that you have done all you could for me as my attorneys, and that I feel satisfied with your efforts in my behalf. I am willing now to make public all I know about the murder of Colonel William Dawson, and I desire to make the statement, for I am now about to die, and do not want to die with a lie upon my lips. I do not wish Tredtin to be pointed out as long as he lives as the person who stabbed Colonel Dawson; and I desire also that justice may be done Meyers, who is entirely innocent, and was not connected in any way with the killing of Dawson. The following are the facts:

On the evening of the murder, Jim Allen, John Petty, George Petty, Charles Hooven and myself were at a dance on McClure street. From there I and Hooven and George Petty went down the street to Barlow's Hall, where there was a dance going on, but of which we did not know until we arrived there. We went in and went up to the bar, and had a drink of beer. About fifteen minutes after this, Gerdes and I started up to get into the ball-room, but before we started Kline, Petty and Tredtin had gone up. When we got within two or three steps of the top of the first stairway I met Brunner there on duty as door-keeper, and he asked me if I had a pass. I told him no, and then he said, "You'll have to go down stairs." I said, "All right." Then Dawson grabbed hold of me and said, "Get down, or I'll throw you down." I jerked away from him, laughed at him, and went down stairs. Then Gerdes and I went and saw the man who got married, and asked him if he couldn't let me up stairs. He said, "Yes, of course I can;" and I then went up with Gerdes and the man who got married, and he told Brunner to let me in. We went into the ball-room, where Kline, Tredtin and Petty were standing. Then Kline said, "Where's that big son of a bitch that was going to throw you down stairs?" I said, "What do you want to know for?" He then said, "I want to know." Then I said, "There he is; whatever you want to say to him, say it." Then Kline said, "Oh, you big son of a bitch!" After about half an hour Petty and I went down stairs to the bar-room. Gerdes, Tredtin and Kline came down there, where I saw them, but whether they came together or not I don't know. Kline, Petty and I drank beer together. We all five then went back up stairs. Dawson and Meyers went down stairs, into the bar-room; then we five followed on down, and went out at the side door on the street. We then began talking about the occurrence on the stairway between Dawson and myself, and some one said, but I don't recollect who it was, "Damn him, we'll get him before morning." I don't recollect that there was anything more said. Meyers was not with us then on the street, or at all in any way connected with us or our party that evening. All five of us then went back together up stairs, where we saw Meyers and Dawson. We staid there some five or ten minutes, when we saw Meyers and Dawson go down stairs and then we five followed after them, and saw them go out of the side door on to the street, and we followed them out. Kline said to me and Petty near the corner of the side street and Fifth street, "You go down this side of the street and we'll go down the other." Petty and I followed after Meyers and Dawson, some distance behind them, while Kline, Gerdes and Tredtin went across to the north side of the street, and went down west on that side of Fifth street. We saw Meyers and Dawson try to get in at the big gate at Weidner's, and then they turned and came east toward Petty and myself. We met them between Weidner's and Pearl street. When we came together Dawson sort of turned around, and I struck him with both fists in the breast; Petty struck Meyers, and Meyers caught hold of a post and prevented himself from falling into the gutter, and then straightened himself up and ran away eastward, and Petty started across the street as soon as Meyers ran. My strokes in Dawson's breast staggered him, and he didn't recover himself until after Meyers and Petty had left. About the time Dawson recovered himself, Kline and Tredtin run in and struck Dawson too. My passions were now aroused. I drew my knife out of my inside breast coat pocket and stabbed Colonel Dawson. I did it on the instant, and took no second thought about it. I do not remember of hearing Dawson say anything before or after I cut him. He may have said something, but I did not hear him. The purpose of our party of five in following Meyers and Dawson out was to lick them both. I saw Gerdes about the middle of the street coming towards us, but he didn't get up to us. Which way Kline and Tredtin went I do not know. Dawson started east on Fifth street on a run. I was facing the east when I cut Dawson. After Dawson run I was alone on the sidewalk, when Funk came up and struck at me with his club. I dodged him and struck at him with my knife, but don't know whether I cut his clothes or not. I then wheeled and started to run west. As I run he threw his club at me, and as I started to run across the street, I fell over the hitching-post in front of Weidner's, and there I dropped my cap and knife. Funk fired at me with a pistol, and shot at me just as I fell. I got up and started to run across the street, and Funk fired a second time at me as I was about to enter the alley on the north side of Fifth street. I stood in the alley awhile, and then I went home to my father's house where I was afterward arrested by the police. Whisky and bad company have been the ruination of me, and the cause of all my bad luck. I had drank a good deal that night of beer and whisky.

This is a true and correct statement about the murder, and is all I wish to say about the matter.

JAMES MURPHY.

He also dictated a letter of thanks to Sheriff Patton, his deputies, and all who had been kind to him during his confinement. Sheriff Patton himself paid for the prisoner's coffin, a very neat one.

At half-past 1 o'clock, Deputy Sheriff Freeman appeared at the door of the cell-room, which opened directly upon the ladder leading to the scaffold, and observed in a low, steady voice: "Time's up, Jim; the Sheriff wants you." The prisoner immediately responded, "All right; I am ready," and walked steadily up the steps of the ladder, accompanied by Fathers Murphy and Carey. His arms had been pinioned at the elbows by a strong bandage of black calico. Probably he looked at that moment younger and handsomer than he had ever appeared before; and a hum of audible surprise at his appearance passed through the spectators. Accompanied by his confessor and Father Carey he walked steadily to the front of the platform; and after looking quietly and calmly upon the faces below, spoke in a deep, clear, bold voice, pausing between each sentence to receive some suggestion from the priest at his left side.

"Gentlemen, I told a lie in the Court-house by saying Tredtin was guilty."

"I think I am guilty"—with a determined nod of the head.

"I return thanks to Sheriff Patton, his deputies and all my friends.

"I forgive all my enemies and ask their forgiveness.

"If there is any one here who has any hard feelings toward me, I ask their forgiveness.

"This is my last request.

"Gentlemen, I want all young men to take warning by me. Drink and bad company brought me here to-day.

"And I ask the forgiveness of Mrs. Dawson and her children, whom I injured in passion, when I did not know what I was doing.

"I believe Jesus Christ will save me."

Sheriff Patton then read in a quiet, steady voice, the death-warrant. It was heavily bordered in black, and bore a great sable seal. "It is my solemn duty," said the Sheriff, "to execute the sentence passed upon you by the Court:

"State of Ohio, Montgomery County—To William Patton, Sheriff: Whereas, at the January Term, 1876, of the Court of Common Pleas, within and for the County of Montgomery and State of Ohio, to-wit, on the 28th day of April, 1876, upon a full and impartial trial, one James Murphy, now in your custody, was found guilty of deliberate and premeditated murder of one William Dawson, in manner and form as found in a true bill of indictment by the grand jury on the 30th day of October, 1875; and whereas the Court aforesaid, at the term aforesaid, to wit: on the 12th day of May, 1876, upon the conviction aforesaid, ordered, adjudged and sentenced the said James Murphy to be imprisoned in the County jail until the 25th of August, 1876, and that on that day, between the hours of 10 A.M. and 4 P.M., he be taken from said jail, and hanged by the neck until he be dead, this is therefore to command that you keep the said James Murphy in safe and secure custody until said day, August 25, 1876; and that on said day, between said hours, you take said James Murphy, and in the place and manner provided by law, hang him by the neck until he be dead. Of this warrant, and all your proceedings thereon, you shall make due return forthwith thereafter.

"Witness: JOHN S. ROBERTSON, Clerk of said Court.

"And the seal thereof of the city of Dayton, in said county, this 20th day of June, 1876.

"[Seal Court of Common Pleas.]

"JOHN S. ROBERTSON, Clerk."

In the meantime Deputy Sheriff Freeman adjusted the thin noose about the prisoner's neck, and pinioned his lower limbs. "James Murphy, good-bye, and may God bless you!" observed Patton in a whisper, handing the black cap to a deputy. At this moment the representative of the Commercial succeeded in obtaining admittance to the little audience of physicians in rear of the scaffold; and took up his position immediately to the left of the trap-door. The next instant the Sheriff pressed the lever with his foot, the drop opened as though in electric response, the thin rope gave way at the crossbeam above, and the body of the prisoner fell downward and backward on the floor of the corridor, behind the scaffold screen. "My God, my God!" cried Freeman, with a subdued scream; "give me that other rope, quick." It had been laid away for use "in case the first rope should break," we were told.

The poor young criminal had fallen on his back, apparently unconscious, with the broken rope about his neck, and the black cap vailing his eyes. The reporter knelt beside him and felt his pulse. It was beating slowly and regularly. Probably the miserable boy thought then, if he could think at all, that he was really dead—dead in darkness, for his eyes were vailed—dead and blind to this world, but about to open his eyes upon another. The awful hush immediately following his fall might have strengthened this dim idea. But then came gasps, and choked sobs from the spectators; the hurrying of feet, and the horrified voice of Deputy Freeman calling, "For God's sake, get me that other rope, quick!" Then a pitiful groan came from beneath the black cap.

"My God! Oh, my God!"

"Why, I ain't dead—I ain't dead!"

"Are you hurt, my child?" inquired Father Murphy.

"No, father, I'm not dead; I'm not hurt. What are they going to do with me?"

No one had the heart to tell him, lying there blind and helpless and ignorant even of what had occurred. The reporter, who still kept his hand on the boy's wrist, suddenly felt the pulsation quicken horribly, the rapid beating of intense fear; the youth's whole body trembled violently. "His pulse is one hundred and twenty," whispered a physician.

"What's the good of leaving me here in this misery?" cried the lad. "Take me out of this, I tell you."

In the meantime they had procured the other rope—a double thin rope with two nooses—and fastened it strongly over the crossbeam. The prisoner had fallen through the drop precisely at 1:44½ P.M.; the second noose was ready within four minutes later. Then the deputies descended from the platform and lifted the prostrate body up.

"Don't carry me," groaned the poor fellow. "I can walk—let me walk."

But they carried him up again, Father Murphy supporting his head. The unfortunate wanted to see the light once more, to get one little glimpse at the sun, the narrow world within the corridor, and the faces before the scaffold. They took off his ghastly mask while the noose was being readjusted. His face was livid, his limbs shook with terror, and he suddenly seized Deputy Freeman desperately by the coat, saying in a husky whisper, "What are you going to do with me?" They tried to unfasten his hand, but it was the clutch of death-fear. Then the little

Irish priest whispered firmly in his ear, "Let go, my son; let go, like a man —be a man; die like a man." And he let go. But they had to support him at arm's length while the Sheriff pressed the trap-lever—six and one-half minutes after the first fall. It was humanely rapid work then.

The body fell heavily, with a jerk, turned about once, rocked backward and forward, and became almost still. From the corridor only the head was visible—turned from the audience. Father Murphy sprinkled holy water upon the victim. The jugular veins became enlarged, and the neck visibly swelled below the black cap. At this time the pulse was beating steadily at 100; the wrist felt hot and moist, and we noticed the hand below it tightly clutched a little brass crucifix, placed there by the priest at the last moment. Gradually the pulse became fainter. Five minutes later, Dr. Crum, the jail physician, holding the right wrist, announced it at eighty-four. In ten minutes from the moment of the drop it sunk to sixty. In sixteen minutes the heart only fluttered, and the pulse became imperceptible. In seventeen minutes Dr. Crum, after a stethoscope examination, made the official announcement of death.

The body was at once cut down by Sheriff Patton, and deposited in the handsome coffin designed for it. Half an hour later we returned to the jail, and examined the dead face. It was perfectly still; as the face of a sleeper, calm and undisfigured. It was perhaps slightly swollen, but quite natural, and betrayed no evidence of pain. The rope had cut deeply into the flesh of the neck, and the very texture of the hemp was redly imprinted on the skin. A medical examination showed the neck to have been broken.

Cincinnati Commercial, August 26, 1876

CELIA THAXTER

Until Lizzie Borden's father and stepmother received their famous whacks on the sweltering afternoon of August 4, 1892, the most notorious axe-murder case in the annals of New England crime was the atrocity committed in 1873 on Smutty Nose, one of the small, barren Isles of Shoals, a rugged archipelago of small islands ten miles off the coast of New Hampshire. Sensational as it was at the time, however, the crime would have fallen into obscurity had it not been for the New England writer Celia Laighton Thaxter (1835–1894). Thaxter grew up on the Isles of Shoals, where her family eventually opened a summer hotel that became a popular resort for New England writers and artists, among them Nathaniel Hawthorne, Childe Hassam, James Russell Lowell, and Richard Henry Dana. Married at 16 to her father's business partner, Levi Thaxter, Celia accompanied him to Newtonville, Massachusetts, where she found herself trapped in what she described as a "household jail." Longing for the stark beauties of her childhood home, she wrote a poem called "Land-locked" that was published by Lowell in the March 1861 *Atlantic Monthly*, launching a literary career that would include such books as *Among the Isles of Shoals* (1873) and *An Island Garden* (1894). Increasingly estranged from her husband, she took to spending extended stretches on the Isles. She was residing there when the double murder occurred, and was among the first to arrive at the lone survivor's side the morning after the tragedy. Her powerful account of the case, published in the May 1875 *Atlantic Monthly*, stands as a milestone of American true-crime writing, one of the first pieces to apply a sophisticated literary sensibility to the narrative re-creation of a horrifying murder. It should be noted that Louis Wagner was hanged for the murders on June 25, 1875. In recent years the case inspired Anita Shreve's novel *The Weight of Water* (1997).

A Memorable Murder

At the Isles of Shoals, on the 5th of March in the year 1873, occurred one of the most monstrous tragedies ever enacted on this planet. The sickening details of the double murder are well known; the newspapers teemed with them for months: but the pathos of the story is not realized; the world does not know how gentle a life these poor people led, how innocently happy were their quiet days. They were all Norwegians. The more I see of the natives of this far-off land, the more I admire the fine qualities which seem to characterize them as a race. Gentle, faithful, intelligent, God-fearing human beings, they daily use such courtesy toward each other and all who come in contact with them, as puts our ruder Yankee manners to shame. The men and women living on this lonely island were like the sweet, honest, simple folk we read of in Björnson's charming Norwegian stories, full of kindly thoughts and ways. The murdered Anethe might have been the Eli of Björnson's beautiful Arne or the Ragnhild of Boyesen's lovely romance. They rejoiced to find a home just such as they desired in this peaceful place; the women took such pleasure in the little house which they kept so neat and bright, in their flock of hens, their little dog Ringe, and all their humble belongings! The Norwegians are an exceptionally affectionate people; family ties are very strong and precious among them. Let me tell the story of their sorrow as simply as may be.

Louis Wagner murdered Anethe and Karen Christensen at midnight on the 5th of March, two years ago this spring. The whole affair shows the calmness of a practiced hand; *there was no malice in the deed*, no heat; it was one of the coolest instances of deliberation ever chronicled in the annals of crime. He admits that these people had shown him nothing but kindness. He says in so many words, "They were my best friends." They looked upon him as a brother. Yet he did not hesitate to murder them. The island called Smutty-Nose by human perversity (since in old times it bore the pleasanter title of Haley's Island) was selected to be the scene of this disaster. Long ago I lived two years upon it, and know well its whitened ledges and grassy slopes, its low thickets of wild-rose and bayberry, its sea-wall still intact, connecting it with the small island Malaga, opposite Appledore, and the ruined break-water which links it with Cedar Island on the other side. A lonely cairn, erected by some long ago forgotten fishermen or sailors, stands upon the highest rock at the southeastern extremity; at its western end a few houses are scattered, small, rude dwellings, with the square old Haley house near; two or three fish-houses are falling into decay about the water-side, and the ancient wharf drops stone by stone into the little cove, where every day the tide ebbs and flows and ebbs again with pleasant sound and freshness. Near the houses is a small grave-yard, where a few of the natives sleep, and not far, the graves of the fourteen Spaniards lost in the wreck of the ship Sagunto in the year 1813. I used to think it was a pleasant place, that low, rocky, and grassy island, though so wild and lonely.

From the little town of Laurvig, near Christiania, in Norway, came John and Maren Hontvet to this country, and five years ago took up their abode in this desolate spot, in one of the cottages facing the cove and Appledore. And there they lived through the long winters and the lovely summers, John making a comfortable living by fishing, Maren, his wife, keeping as bright and tidy and sweet a little home for him as man could desire. The bit of garden they cultivated in the summer was a pleasure to them; they made their house as pretty as they could with paint and gay pictures, and Maren had a shelf for her plants at the window; and John was always so good to her, so kind and thoughtful of her comfort and of what would please her, she was entirely happy. Sometimes she was a little lonely, perhaps, when he was tossing afar off on the sea, setting or hauling his trawls, or had sailed to Portsmouth to sell his fish. So that she was doubly glad when the news came that some of her people were coming over from Norway to live with her. And first, in the month of May, 1871, came her sister Karen, who stayed only a short time with Maren, and then came to Appledore, where she lived at service two years, till within a fortnight of her death. The first time I saw Maren, she brought her sister to us, and I was charmed with the little woman's beautiful behavior; she was so gentle, courteous, decorous, she left on my mind a most delightful impression. Her face struck me as remarkably good and intelligent, and her gray eyes were full of light.

Karen was a rather sad-looking woman, about twenty-nine years old; she had lost a lover in Norway long since, and in her heart she fretted and mourned for this continually: she could not speak a word of English at first, but went patiently about her work and soon learned enough, and proved herself an excellent servant, doing faithfully and thoroughly everything she undertook, as is the way of her people generally. Her personal neatness was most attractive. She wore gowns made of cloth woven by herself in Norway, a coarse blue stuff, always neat and clean, and often I used to watch her as she sat by the fire spinning at a spinning-wheel brought from her own country; she made such a pretty picture, with her blue gown and fresh white apron, and the nice, clear white muslin bow with which she was in the habit of fastening her linen collar, that she was very agreeable to look upon. She had a pensive way of letting her head droop a little sideways as she spun, and while the low wheel hummed monotonously, she would sit crooning sweet, sad old Norwegian airs by the hour together, perfectly unconscious that she was affording such pleasure to a pair of appreciative eyes. On the 12th of October, 1872, in the second year of her stay with us, her brother, Ivan Christensen, and his wife, Anethe Mathea, came over from their Norseland in an evil day, and joined Maren and John at their island, living in the same house with them.

Ivan and Anethe had been married only since Christmas of the preceding year. Ivan was tall, light-haired, rather quiet and grave. Anethe was young, fair, and merry, with thick, bright sunny hair, which was so long it reached, when unbraided, nearly to her knees; blue-eyed, with brilliant teeth and clear, fresh complexion, beautiful, and beloved beyond expression by her young husband, Ivan. Mathew Hontvet, John's brother, had also joined the little circle a year before, and now Maren's happiness was complete. Delighted to welcome them all, she made all things pleasant for them, and she told me only a few days ago,

"I never was so happy in my life as when we were all living there together." So they abode in peace and quiet, with not an evil thought in their minds, kind and considerate toward each other, the men devoted to their women and the women repaying them with interest, till out of the perfectly cloudless sky one day a bolt descended, without a whisper of warning, and brought ruin and desolation into that peaceful home.

Louis Wagner, who had been in this country seven years, appeared at the Shoals two years before the date of the murder. He lived about the islands during that time. He was born in Ueckermünde, a small town of lower Pomerania, in Northern Prussia. Very little is known about him, though there were vague rumors that his past life had not been without difficulties, and he had boasted foolishly among his mates that "not many had done what he had done and got off in safety;" but people did not trouble themselves about him or his past, all having enough to do to earn their bread and keep the wolf from the door. Maren describes him as tall, powerful, dark, with a peculiarly quiet manner. She says she never saw him drunk—he seemed always anxious to keep his wits about him: he would linger on the outskirts of a drunken brawl, listening to and absorbing everything, but never mixing himself up in any disturbance. He was always lurking in corners, lingering, looking, listening, and he would look no man straight in the eyes. She spoke, however, of having once heard him disputing with some sailors, at table, about some point of navigation; she did not understand it, but all were against Louis, and, waxing warm, all strove to show him he was in the wrong. As he rose and left the table she heard him mutter to himself with an oath, "I know I'm wrong, but I'll never give in!" During the winter preceding the one in which his hideous deed was committed, he lived at Star Island and fished alone, in a wherry; but he made very little money, and came often over to the Hontvets, where Maren gave him food when he was suffering from want, and where he received always a welcome and the utmost kindness. In the following June he joined Hontvet in his business of fishing, and took up his abode as one of the family at Smutty-Nose. During the summer he was "crippled," as he said, by the rheumatism, and they were all very good to him, and sheltered, fed, nursed, and waited upon him the greater part of the season. He remained with them five weeks after Ivan and Anethe arrived, so that he grew to know Anethe as well as Maren, and was looked upon as a brother by all of them, as I have said before. Nothing occurred to show his true character, and in November he left the island and the kind people whose hospitality he was to repay so fearfully, and going to Portsmouth he took passage in another fishing schooner, the Addison Gilbert, which was presently wrecked off the coast, and he was again thrown out of employment. Very recklessly he said to Waldemar Ingebertsen, to Charles Jonsen and even to John Hontvet himself, at different times, that "he must have money if he murdered for it." He loafed about Portsmouth eight weeks, doing nothing. Meanwhile Karen left our service in February, intending to go to Boston and work at a sewing machine, for she was not strong and thought she should like it better than housework, but before going she lingered awhile with her sister Maren—fatal delay for her! Maren told me that during this time Karen went to Portsmouth and had her teeth removed, meaning to provide herself with a new set. At the Jonsens', where Louis was staying, one day she spoke to Mrs. Jonsen of her mouth, that it was so sensitive since the teeth had been taken out; and Mrs. Jonsen asked her how long she must wait before the new set could be put in. Karen replied that it would be three months. Louis Wagner was walking up and down at the other end of the room with his arms folded, his favorite attitude. Mrs. Jonsen's daughter passed near him and heard him mutter, "Three months! What is the use! In three months you will be dead!" He did not know the girl was so near, and turning, he confronted her. He knew she must have heard what he said, and he glared at her like a wild man.

On the fifth day of March, 1873, John Hontvet, his brother Mathew, and Ivan Christensen set sail in John's little schooner, the Clara Bella, to draw their trawls. At that time four of the islands were inhabited: one family on White Island, at the light-house; the workmen who were building the new hotel on Star Island, and one or two households beside; the Hontvet family at Smutty-Nose; and on Appledore, the household at the large house, and on the southern side, opposite Smutty-Nose, a little cottage, where lived Jörge Edvardt Ingebertsen, his wife and children, and several men who fished with him. Smutty-Nose is not in sight of the large house at Appledore, so we were in ignorance of all that happened on that dreadful night, longer than the other inhabitants of the Shoals.

John, Ivan, and Mathew went to draw their trawls, which had been set some miles to the eastward of the islands. They intended to be back to dinner, and then to go on to Portsmouth with their fish, and bait the trawls afresh, ready to bring back to set again next day. But the wind was strong and fair for Portsmouth and ahead for the islands; it would have been a long beat home against it; so they went on to Portsmouth, without touching at the island to leave one man to guard the women, as had been their custom. This was the first night in all the years Maren had lived there that the house was without a man to protect it. But John, always thoughtful for her, asked Emil Ingebertsen, whom he met on the fishing-grounds, to go over from Appledore and tell her that they had gone on to Portsmouth with the favoring wind, but that they hoped to be back that night. And he would have been back had the bait he expected from Boston arrived on the train in which it was due. How curiously everything adjusted itself to favor the bringing about of this horrible catastrophe! The bait did not arrive till the half past twelve train, and they were obliged to work the whole night getting their trawls ready, thus leaving the way perfectly clear for Louis Wagner's awful work.

The three women left alone watched and waited in vain for the schooner to return, and kept the dinner hot for the men, and patiently wondered why they did not come. In vain they searched the wide horizon for that returning sail. Ah me, what pathos is in that longing look of women's eyes for far-off sails! that gaze so eager, so steadfast, that it would almost seem as if it must conjure up the ghostly shape of glimmering canvas from the mysterious distances of sea and sky, and draw it unerringly home by the mere force of intense wistfulness! And those gentle eyes, that were never to see the light of another sun, looked anxiously across the heaving sea till twilight fell, and then John's messenger, Emil, arrived—Emil Ingebertsen, courteous and gentle as a youthful knight—and reassured them with his explanation, which having given, he departed, leaving them in a much more cheerful state of mind. So the three sisters, with only the little dog Ringe for a protector, sat by the fire chatting together cheerfully. They fully expected the schooner back again that night from Portsmouth, but they were not ill at ease while they waited. Of what should they be afraid? They had not an enemy in the world! No shadow crept to the fireside to warn them what was at hand, no portent of death chilled the air as they talked their pleasant talk and made their little plans in utter unconsciousness. Karen was to have gone to Portsmouth with the fishermen that day; she was all ready dressed to go. Various little commissions were given her, errands to do for the two sisters she was to leave behind. Maren wanted some buttons, and "I'll give you one for a pattern; I'll put it in your purse," she said to Karen, "and then when you open your purse you'll be sure to remember it." (That little button, of a peculiar pattern, was found in Wagner's possession afterward.) They sat up till ten o'clock, talking together. The night was bright and calm; it was a comfort to miss the bitter winds that had raved about the little dwelling all the long, rough winter. Already it was spring; this calm was the first token of its coming. It was the 5th of March; in a few weeks the weather would soften, the grass grow green, and Anethe would see the first flowers in this strange country, so far from her home where she had left father and mother, and kith and kin, for love of Ivan. The delicious days of summer at hand would transform the work of the toiling fishermen to pleasure, and all things would bloom and smile about the poor people on the lonely rock! Alas, it was not to be.

At ten o'clock they went to bed. It was cold and "lonesome" upstairs, so Maren put some chairs by the side of the lounge, laid a mattress upon it, and made up a bed for Karen in the kitchen, where she presently fell asleep. Maren and Anethe slept in the next room. So safe they felt themselves, they did not pull down a curtain, nor even try to fasten the house-door. They went to their rest in absolute security and perfect trust. It was the first still night of the new year; a young moon stole softly down toward the west, a gentle wind breathed through the quiet dark, and the waves whispered gently about the island, helping to lull those innocent souls to yet more peaceful slumber. Ah, where were the gales of March that might have plowed that tranquil sea to foam, and cut off the fatal path of Louis Wagner to that happy home! But nature seemed to pause and wait for him. I remember looking abroad over the waves that night and rejoicing over "the first calm night of the year!" It was so still, so bright! The hope of all the light and beauty a few weeks would bring forth stirred me to sudden joy. There should be spring again after the long winter-weariness.

> "Can trouble live in April days,
> Or sadness in the summer moons?"

I thought, as I watched the clear sky, grown less hard than it had been for weeks, and sparkling with stars. But before another sunset it seemed to me that beauty had fled out of the world, and that goodness, innocence, mercy, gentleness, were a mere mockery of empty words.

Here let us leave the poor women, asleep on the lonely rock, with no help near them in heaven or upon earth, and follow the fishermen to Portsmouth, where they arrived about four o'clock that afternoon. One of the first men whom they saw as they neared the town was Louis Wagner; to him they threw the rope from the schooner, and he helped draw her in to the wharf. Greetings passed between them; he spoke to Mathew Hontvet, and as he looked at Ivan Christensen, the men noticed a flush pass over Louis's face. He asked were they going out again that night? Three times before they parted he asked that question; he saw that all the three men belonging to the island had come away together; he began to realize his opportunity. They answered him that if their bait came by the train in which they expected it, they hoped to get back that night, but if it was late they should be obliged to stay till morning, baiting their trawls; and they asked him to come and help them. It is a long and tedious business, the baiting of trawls; often more than a thousand hooks are to be manipulated, and lines and hooks coiled, clear of tangles, into tubs, all ready for throwing over-board when the fishing-grounds are reached. Louis gave them a half promise that he would help them, but they did not see him again after leaving the wharf. The three fishermen were hungry, not having touched at their island, where Maren always provided them with a supply of food to take with them; they asked each other if either had brought any money with which to buy bread, and it came out that every one had left his pocketbook at home. Louis, standing by, heard all this. He asked John, then, if he had made fishing pay. John answered that he had cleared about six hundred dollars.

The men parted, the honest three about their business; but Louis, what became of him with his evil thoughts? At about half past seven he went into a liquor shop and had a glass of something; not enough to make him unsteady,—he was too wise for that. He was not seen again in Portsmouth by any human creature that night. He must have gone, after that, directly down to the river, that beautiful, broad river, the Piscataqua, upon whose southern bank the quaint old city of Ports-mouth dreams its quiet days away; and there he found a boat ready to his hand, a dory belonging to a man by the name of David Burke, who had that day furnished it with new thole-pins. When it was picked up afterward off the mouth of the river, Louis's anxious oars had eaten half-way through the substance of these pins, which are always made of the hardest, toughest wood that can be found. A terrible piece of rowing must that have been, in one night! Twelve miles from the city to the Shoals,—three to the light-houses, where the river meets the open sea, nine more to the islands; nine back again to Newcastle next morning! He took that boat, and with the favoring tide dropped down the rapid river where the swift current is so strong that oars are scarcely needed, except to keep the boat steady. Truly all nature seemed to play into his hands; this first relenting night of earliest spring favored him with its stillness, the tide was fair, the wind was fair, the little moon gave him just enough light, without betraying him to any curious eyes, as he glided down the three miles between the river banks, in haste to reach the sea. Doubtless the light west wind played about him as delicately as if he had been the most human of God's creatures; nothing breathed remonstrance in his ear, nothing whispered in the whispering water that rippled about his inexorable keel, steering straight for the Shoals through the quiet darkness. The snow lay thick and white upon the land in the moonlight; lamps twinkled here and there from dwellings on either side; in Eliot and Newcastle, in Portsmouth and Kittery, roofs, chimneys, and gables showed faintly in the vague light; the leafless trees clustered dark in hollows or lifted their tracery of bare boughs in higher spaces against the wintry sky. His eyes must have looked on it all, whether he saw the peaceful picture or not. Beneath many a humble roof honest folk were settling into their untroubled rest, as "this planned piece of deliberate wickedness" was stealing silently by with his heart full of darkness, blacker than the black tide that swirled beneath his boat and bore him fiercely on. At the river's mouth stood the sentinel lighthouses, sending their great spokes of light afar into the night, like the arms of a wide humanity stretching into the darkness helping hands to bring all who needed succor safely home. He passed them, first the tower at Fort Point, then the taller one at Whale's Back, steadfastly holding aloft their warning fires. There was no signal from the warning bell as he rowed by, though a danger more subtle, more deadly, than fog, or hurricane, or pelting storm was passing swift beneath it. Unchallenged by anything in earth or heaven, he kept on his way and gained the great outer ocean, doubtless pulling strong and steadily, for he had not time to lose, and the longest night was all too short for an undertaking such as this. Nine miles from the light-houses to the islands! Slowly he makes his way; it seems to take an eternity of time. And now he is midway between the islands and the coast. That little toy of a boat with its one occupant in the midst of the awful, black, heaving sea! The vast dim ocean whispers with a thousand waves; against the boat's side the ripples lightly tap; and pass and are lost; the air is full of fine, mysterious voices of winds and waters. Has he no fear, alone there on the midnight sea with such a purpose in his heart? The moonlight sends a long, golden track across the waves; it touches his dark face and figure, it glitters on his dripping oars. On his right hand Boone Island light shows like a setting star on the horizon, low on his left the two beacons twinkle off Newburyport, at the mouth of the Merrimack River; all the light-houses stand watching along the coast, wheeling their long, slender shafts of radiance as if pointing at this black atom creeping over the face of the planet with such colossal evil in his heart. Before him glitter the Shoals' light at White Island, and helps to guide him to his prey. Alas, my friendly light-house, that you should serve so terrible a purpose! Steadily the oars click in the rowlocks; stroke after stroke of the broad blades draws him away from the lessening line of land, over the wavering floor of the ocean, nearer the lonely rocks. Slowly the coast lights fade, and now the rote of the sea among the lonely ledges of the Shoals salutes his attentive ear. A little longer and he nears Appledore, the first island, and now he passes by the snow-covered, ice-bound rock, with the long buildings slowing clear in the moonlight. He must have looked at them as he went past. I wonder we who slept beneath the roofs that glimmered to his eyes in the uncertain light did not feel, through the thick veil of sleep, what fearful thing passed by! But we slumbered peacefully as the unhappy women whose doom every click of those oars in the rowlocks, like the ticking of some dreadful clock, was bringing nearer and nearer. Between the islands he passes; they are full of chilly gleams and glooms. There is no scene more weird than these snow-covered rocks in winter, more shudderful and strange: the moonlight touching them with mystic glimmer, the black water breaking about them and the vast shadowy spaces of the sea stretching to the horizon on every side, full of vague sounds, of half lights and shadows, of fear, and of mystery. The island he seeks lies before him, lone and still; there is no gleam in any window, there is no help near, nothing upon which the women can call for succor. He does not land in the cove where all boats put in, he rows round to the south side and draws his boat up on the rocks. His red returning footsteps are found here next day, staining the snow. He makes his way to the house he knows so well.

All is silent: nothing moves, nothing sounds but the hushed voices of the sea. His hand is on the latch, he enters stealthily, there is nothing to resist him. The little dog, Ringe, begins to bark sharp and loud, and Karen rouses, crying, "John, is that you?" thinking the expected fishermen had returned. Louis seizes a chair and strikes at her in the dark; the clock on a shelf above her head falls down with the jarring of the blow, and stops at exactly seven minutes to one. Maren in the next room, waked suddenly from her sound sleep, trying in vain to make out the meaning of it all, cries, "What's the matter?" Karen answers, "John scared me!" Maren springs from her bed and tries to open her chamber door; Louis has fastened it on the other side by pushing a stick through over the latch. With her heart leaping with terror the poor child shakes the door with all her might, in vain. Utterly confounded and bewildered, she hears Karen screaming, "John kills me! John kills me!" She hears the sound of repeated blows and shrieks, till at last her sister falls heavily against the door, which gives way, and Maren rushes out. She catches dimly a glimpse of a tall figure outlined against the southern window; she seizes poor Karen and drags her with the strength of frenzy within the bedroom. This unknown terror, this fierce, dumb monster who never utters a sound to betray himself through the whole, pursues her with blows, strikes her three times with a chair, either blow with fury sufficient to kill her, had it been light enough for him to see how to direct it; but she gets her sister inside and the door shut, and holds it against him with all her might and Karen's failing strength. What a little heroine was this poor child, struggling with the force of desperation to save herself and her sisters!

All this time Anethe lay dumb, not daring to move or breathe, roused from deep sleep of youth and health by this nameless, formless terror. Maren, while she strives to hold the door at which Louis rattles again and again, calls to her in anguish, "Anethe, Anethe! Get out of the window! run! hide!" The poor girl, almost paralyzed with fear, tries to obey, puts her bare feet out of the low window, and stands outside in the freezing snow, with one light garment over her cowering figure, shrinking in the cold winter wind, the clear moonlight touching her white face and bright hair and fair young shoulders. "Scream! scream!" shouts frantic Maren. "Somebody at Star Island may hear!"

but Anethe answers with the calmness of despair, "I cannot make a sound." Maren screams, herself, but the feeble sound avails nothing. "Run! run!" she cries to Anethe; but again Anethe answers, "I cannot move."

Louis has left off trying to force the door; he listens. Are the women trying to escape? He goes out-of-doors. Maren flies to the window; he comes round the corner of the house and confronts Anethe where she stands in the snow. The moonlight shines full in his face; she shrieks loudly and distinctly, "Louis, Louis!" Ah, he is discovered, he is recognized! Quick as thought he goes back to the front door, at the side of which stands an ax, left there by Maren, who had used it the day before to cut the ice from the well. He returns to Anethe standing shuddering there. It is no matter that she is beautiful, young, and helpless to resist, that she has been kind to him, that she never did a human creature harm, that she stretches her gentle hands out to him in agonized entreaty, crying piteously, "Oh, Louis, Louis, Louis!" He raises the ax and brings it down on her bright head in one tremendous blow, and she sinks without a sound and lies in a heap, with her warm blood reddening the snow. Then he deals her blow after blow, almost within reach of Maren's hands, as she stands at the window. Distracted, Maren strives to rouse poor Karen, who kneels with her head on the side of the bed; with desperate entreaty she tries to get her up and away, but Karen moans, "I cannot, I cannot." She is too far gone; and then Maren knows she cannot save her, and that she must flee herself or die. So, while Louis again enters the house, she seizes a skirt and wraps round her shoulders, and makes her way out of the open window, over Anethe's murdered body, barefooted, flying away, anywhere, breathless, shaking with terror.

Where can she go? Her little dog, frightened into silence, follows her,—pressing so close to her feet that she falls over him more than once. Looking back she sees Louis has lit a lamp and is seeking for her. She flies to the cove; if she can but find his boat and row away in it and get help! It is not there; there is no boat in which she can get away. She hears Karen's wild screams,—he is killing her! Oh where can she go? Is there any place on that little island where he will not find her? She thinks she will creep into one of the empty old houses by the water; but no, she reflects, if I hide there, Ringe will bark and betray me the moment Louis comes to look for me. And Ringe saved her life, for next day Louis's bloody tracks were found all about those old buildings where he had sought her. She flies, with Karen's awful cries in her ears, away over rocks and snow to the farthest limit she can gain. The moon has set; it is about two o'clock in the morning, and oh, so cold! She shivers and shudders from head to feet, but her agony of terror is so great she is hardly conscious of bodily sensation. And welcome is the freezing snow, the jagged ice and iron rocks that tear her unprotected feet, the bitter brine that beats against the shore, the winter winds that make her shrink and tremble; "they are not so unkind as man's ingratitude!" Falling often, rising, struggling on with feverish haste, she makes her way to the very edge of the water; down almost into the sea she creeps, between two rocks, upon her hands and knees, and crouches, face downward, with Ringe nestled close beneath her breast, not daring to move through the long hours that must pass before the sun will rise again. She is so near the ocean she can almost reach the water with her hand. Had the wind breathed the least roughly the waves must have washed over her. There let us leave her and go back to Louis Wagner. Maren heard her sister Karen's shrieks as she fled. The poor girl had crept into an unoccupied room in a distant part of the house, striving to hide herself. He could not kill her with blows, blundering in the darkness, so he wound a handkerchief about her throat and strangled her. But now he seeks anxiously for Maren. *Has* she escaped? What terror is in the thought! Escaped, to tell the tale, accuse him as the murderer of her sister. Hurriedly, with desperate anxiety, he seeks for her. His time was growing short; it was not in his programme that this brave little creature should give him so much trouble; he had not calculated on resistance from these weak and helpless women. Already it was morning, soon it would be daylight. He could not find her in or near the house; he went down to the empty and dilapidated houses about the cove, and sought her everywhere.

What a picture! That blood-stained butcher, with his dark face, crawling about those cellars, peering for that woman! He dared not spend any more time; he must go back for the money he hoped to find, his reward for this! All about the house he searches, in bureau drawers, in trunks and boxes: he finds fifteen dollars for his night's work! Several hundreds were lying between some sheets folded at the bottom of a drawer in which he looked. But he cannot stop for more thorough investigation; a dreadful haste pursues him like a thousand fiends. He drags Anethe's stiffening body into the house, and leaves it on the kitchen floor. If the thought crosses his mind to set fire to the house and burn up his two victims, he dares not do it: it will make a fatal bonfire to light his homeward way; besides, it is useless, for Maren has escaped to accuse him, and the time presses so horribly! But how cool a monster is he! After all this hard work he must have refreshment to support him in the long row back to the land; knife and fork, cup and plate, were found next morning on the table near where Anethe lay; fragments of food which was not cooked in the house, but brought from Portsmouth, were scattered about. Tidy Maren had left neither dishes nor food when they went to bed. The handle of the tea-pot which she had left on the stove was stained and smeared with blood. Can the human mind conceive of such hideous *nonchalance*? Wagner sat down in that room and ate and drank! It is almost beyond belief! Then he went to the well with a basin and towels, tried to wash off the blood, and left towels and basin in the well. He knows he must be gone! It is certain death to linger. He takes his boat and rows away toward the dark coast and the twinkling lights; it is for dear life, now! What powerful strokes send the small skiff rushing over the water!

There is no longer any moon, the night is far spent; already the east changes, the stars fade; he rows like a madman to reach the land, but a blush of morning is stealing up the sky and sunrise is rosy over shore and sea, when panting, trembling, weary, a creature accursed, a blot on the face of the day, he lands at Newcastle—too late! Too late! In vain he casts the dory adrift; she will not float away; the flood tide bears her back to give her testimony against him, and afterward she is found at

Jaffrey's Point, near the "Devil's Den," and the fact of her worn thole-pins noted. Wet, covered with ice from the spray which has flown from his eager oars, utterly exhausted, he creeps to a knoll and reconnoitres; he thinks he is unobserved, and crawls on towards Portsmouth. But he is seen and recognized by many persons, and his identity established beyond a doubt. He goes to the house of Mathew Jonsen, where he has been living, steals up-stairs, changes his clothes, and appears before the family, anxious, frightened, agitated, telling Jonsen he never felt so badly in his life; that he has got into trouble and is afraid he shall be taken. He cannot eat at breakfast, says "farewell forever," goes away and is shaved, and takes the train to Boston, where he provides himself with new clothes, shoes, a complete outfit, but lingering, held by fate, he cannot fly, and before night the officer's hand is on his shoulder and he is arrested.

Meanwhile poor shuddering Maren on the lonely island, by the water-side, waits till the sun is high in heaven before she dares come forth. She thinks he may be still on the island. She said to me, "I thought he must be there, dead or alive. I thought he might go crazy and kill himself after having done all that." At last she steals out. The little dog frisks before her; it is so cold her feet cling to the rocks and snow at every step, till the skin is fairly torn off. Still and frosty is the bright morning, the water lies smiling and sparkling, the hammers of the workmen building the new hotel on Star Island sound through the quiet air. Being on the side of Smutty-Nose opposite Star, she waves her skirt, and screams to attract their attention; they hear her, turn and look, see a woman waving a signal of distress, and, surprising to relate, turn tranquilly to their work again. She realizes at last there is no hope in that direction; she must go round toward Appledore in sight of the dreadful house. Passing it afar off she gives one swift glance toward it, terrified lest in the broad sunshine she may see some horrid token of last night's work; but all is still and peaceful. She notices the curtains the three had left up when they went to bed; they are now drawn down; she knows whose hand has done this, and what it hides from the light of day. Sick at heart, she makes her painful way to the northern edge of

Malaga, which is connected with Smutty-Nose by the old sea-wall. She is directly opposite Appledore and the little cottage where abide her friend and countryman, Jörge Edvardt Ingebertsen, and his wife and children. Only a quarter of a mile of the still ocean separates her from safety and comfort. She sees the children playing about the door; she calls and calls. Will no one ever hear her? Her torn feet torment her, she is sore with blows and perishing with cold. At last her voice reaches the ears of the children, who run and tell their father that some one is crying and calling; looking across, he sees the poor little figure waving her arms, takes his dory and paddles over, and with amazement recognizes Maren in her night-dress, with bare feet and streaming hair, with a cruel bruise upon her face, with wild eyes, distracted, half senseless with cold and terror. He cries, "Maren, Maren, who has done this? what is it? who is it?" and her only answer is "Louis, Louis, Louis!" as he takes her on board his boat and rows home with her as fast as he can. From her incoherent statement he learns what has happened. Leaving her in the care of his family, he comes over across the hill to the great house on Appledore. As I sit at my desk I see him pass the window, and wonder why the old man comes so fast and anxiously through the heavy snow.

Presently I see him going back again, accompanied by several of his own countrymen and others of our workmen, carrying guns. They are going to Smutty-Nose, and take arms, thinking it possible Wagner may yet be there. I call down-stairs, "What has happened?" and am answered, "Some trouble at Smutty-Nose; we hardly understand." "Probably a drunken brawl of the reckless fishermen who may have landed there," I say to myself, and go on with my work. In another half-hour I see the men returning, reinforced by others, coming fast, confusedly; and suddenly a wail of anguish comes up from the women below. I cannot believe it when I hear them crying, "Karen is dead! Anethe is dead! Louis Wagner has murdered them both!" I run out into the servants' quarters; there are all the men assembled, an awe-stricken crowd. Old Ingebertsen comes forward and tells me the bare facts, and how Maren lies at his house, half crazy, suffering with her torn and frozen feet.

Then the men are dispatched to search Appledore, to find if by any chance the murderer might be concealed about the place, and I go over to Maren to see if I can do anything for her. I find the women and children with frightened faces at the little cottage; as I go into the room where Maren lies, she catches my hands, crying, "Oh, I so glad to see you! I so glad I save my life!" and with her dry lips she tells me all the story as I have told it here. Poor little creature, holding me with those wild, glittering, dilated eyes, she cannot tell me rapidly enough the whole horrible tale. Upon her cheek is yet the blood-stain from the blow he struck her with a chair, and she shows me two more upon her shoulder, and her torn feet. I go back for arnica with which to bathe them. What a mockery seems to me the "jocund day" as I emerge into the sunshine, and looking across the space of blue, sparkling water, see the house wherein all that horror lies!

Oh brightly shines the morning sun and glitters on the white sails of the little vessel that comes dancing back from Portsmouth before the favoring wind, with the two husbands on board! How glad they are for the sweet morning and the fair wind that brings them home again! And Ivan sees in fancy Anethe's face all beautiful with welcoming smiles, and John knows how happy his good and faithful Maren will be to see him back again. Alas, how little they dream what lies before them! From Appledore they are signaled to come ashore, and Ivan and Mathew, landing, hear a confused rumor of trouble from tongues that hardly can frame the words that must tell the dreadful truth. Ivan only understands that something is wrong. His one thought is for Anethe; he flies to Ingebertsen's cottage, she may be there; he rushes in like a maniac, crying, "Anethe, Anethe! Where is Anethe?" and broken-hearted Maren answers her brother, "Anethe is—at home." He does not wait for another word, but seizes the little boat and lands at the same time with John on Smutty-Nose; with headlong haste they reach the house, other men accompanying them; ah, there are blood-stains all about the snow! Ivan is the first to burst open the door and enter. What words can tell it! There upon the floor, naked, stiff, and stark, is the woman he idolizes, for whose dear feet he could not make life's ways smooth and pleasant enough—stone dead! Dead—horribly butchered! her bright hair stiff with blood, the fair head that had so often rested on his breast crushed, cloven, mangled with the brutal ax! Their eyes are blasted by the intolerable sight: both John and Ivan stagger out and fall, senseless, in the snow. Poor Ivan! his wife a thousand times adored, the dear girl he had brought from Norway, the good, sweet girl who loved him so, whom he could not cherish tenderly enough! And he was not there to protect her! There was no one there to save her!

> "Did Heaven look on
> And would not take their part!"

Poor fellow, what had he done that fate should deal him such a blow as this! Dumb, blind with anguish, he made no sign.

> "What says the body when they spring
> Some monstrous torture-engine's whole
> Strength on it? No more says the soul."

Some of his pitying comrades lead him away, like one stupefied, and take him back to Appledore. John knows his wife is safe. Though stricken with horror and consumed with wrath, he is not paralyzed like poor Ivan, who has been smitten with worse than death. They find Karen's body in another part of the house, covered with blows and black in the face, strangled. They find Louis's tracks,—all the tokens of his disastrous presence,—the contents of trunks and drawers scattered about in his hasty search for the money, and, all within the house and without, blood, blood everywhere.

When I reach the cottage with the arnica for Maren, they have returned from Smutty-Nose. John, her husband, is there. He is a young man of the true Norse type, blue-eyed, fair-haired, tall and well-made, with handsome teeth and bronzed beard. Perhaps he is a little quiet and undemonstrative generally, but at this moment he is superb, kindled from head to feet, a fire-brand of woe and wrath, with eyes that flash and cheeks that burn. I speak a few words to him,—what words can meet such an occasion as this!—and having given directions about the use of the arnica, for Maren, I go away, for nothing more can be done for her, and every comfort she needs is hers. The outer room is full of men; they make way for me, and as I pass through I catch a glimpse of Ivan crouched with his arms thrown round his knees and his head bowed down between them, motionless, his attitude expressing such abandonment of despair as cannot be described. His whole person seems to shrink, as if deprecating the blow that has fallen upon him.

All day the slaughtered women lie as they were found, for nothing can be touched till the officers of the law have seen the whole. And John goes back to Portsmouth to tell his tale to the proper authorities. What a different voyage from the one he had just taken, when happy and careless he was returning to the home he had left so full of peace and comfort! What a load he bears back with him, as he makes his tedious way across the miles that separate him from the means of vengeance he burns to reach! But at last he arrives, tells his story, the police at other cities are at once telegraphed, and the city marshal follows Wagner to Boston. At eight o'clock that evening comes the steamer Mayflower to the Shoals, with all the officers on board. They land and make investigations at Smutty-Nose, then come here to Appledore and examine Maren, and, when everything is done, steam back to Portsmouth, which they reach at three o'clock in the morning. After all are gone and his awful day's work is finished at last, poor John comes back to Maren, and kneeling by the side of her bed, he is utterly overpowered with what he has passed through; he is shaken with sobs as he cries, "Oh, Maren, Maren, it is too much, too much! I cannot bear it!" And Maren throws her arms about his neck, crying, "Oh, John, John, don't! I shall be crazy, I shall die, if you go on like that." Poor innocent, unhappy people, who never wronged a fellow-creature in their lives!

But Ivan—what is their anguish to his! They dare not leave him alone lest he do himself an injury. He is perfectly mute and listless; he cannot weep, he can neither eat nor sleep. He sits like one in a horrid dream. "Oh, my poor, poor brother!" Maren cries in tones of deepest grief, when I speak his name to her next day. She herself cannot rest a moment till she hears that Louis is taken; at every sound her crazed imagination fancies he is coming back for her; she is fairly beside herself with terror and anxiety; but the night following that of the catastrophe brings us news that he is arrested, and there is stern rejoicing at the Shoals; but no vengeance taken on him can bring back those unoffending lives, or restore that gentle home. The dead are properly cared for; the blood is washed from Anethe's beautiful bright hair; she is clothed in her wedding-dress, the blue dress in which she was married, poor child, that happy Christmas time in Norway, a little more than a year ago. They are carried across the sea to Portsmouth, the burial service is read over them, and they are hidden in the earth. After poor Ivan has seen the faces of his wife and sister still and pale in their coffins, their ghastly wounds concealed as much as possible, flowers upon them and the priest praying over them, his trance of misery is broken, the grasp of despair is loosened a little about his heart. Yet hardly does he notice whether the sun shines or no, or care whether he lives or dies. Slowly his senses steady themselves from the effects of a shock that nearly destroyed him, and merciful time, with imperceptible touch, softens day by day the outlines of that picture at the memory of which he will never cease to shudder while he lives.

Louis Wagner was captured in Boston on the evening of the next day after his atrocious deed, and Friday morning, followed by a hooting mob, he was taken to the Eastern depot. At every station along the route crowds were assembled, and there were fierce cries for vengeance. At the depot in Portsmouth a dense crowd of thousands of both sexes had gathered, who assailed him with yells and curses and cries of "Tear him to pieces!" It was with difficulty he was at last safely imprisoned. Poor Maren was taken to Portsmouth from Appledore on that day. The story of Wagner's day in Boston, like every other detail of the affair, has been told by every newspaper in the country: his agitation and restlessness, noted by all who saw him; his curious, reckless talk. To one he says, "I have just killed two sailors;" to another, Jacob Toldtman, into whose shop he goes to buy shoes, "I have seen a woman lie as still as that boot," and so on. When he is caught he puts on a bold face and determines to brave it out; denies everything with tears and virtuous indignation. The men whom he has so fearfully wronged are confronted with him; his attitude is one of injured innocence; he surveys them more in sorrow than in anger, while John is on fire with wrath and indignation, and hurls maledictions at him; but Ivan, poor Ivan, hurt beyond all hope or help, is utterly mute; he does not utter one word. Of what use is it to curse the murderer of his wife? It will not bring her back; he has no heart for cursing, he is too completely broken. Maren told me the first time she was brought into Louis's presence, her heart leaped so fast she could hardly breathe. She entered the room softly with her husband and Mathew Jonsen's daughter. Louis was whittling a stick. He looked up and saw her face, and the color ebbed out of his, and rushed back and stood in one burning spot in his cheek, as he looked at her and she looked at him for a space, in silence. Then he drew about his evil mind the detestable garment of sanctimoniousness, and in sentimental accents he murmured, "I'm glad Jesus loves me!" "The devil loves you!" cried John; with uncompromising veracity. "I know it wasn't nice," said decorous Maren, "but John couldn't help it; it was too much to bear!"

The next Saturday afternoon, when he was to be taken to Saco, hundreds of fishermen came to Portsmouth from all parts of the coast, determined on his destruction, and there was a fearful scene in the quiet streets of that peaceful city when he was being escorted to the train by the police and various officers of justice. Two thousand people had assembled, and such a furious, yelling crowd was never seen or heard in Portsmouth. The air was rent with cries for vengeance; showers of bricks and stones were thrown from all directions, and wounded several of the officers who surrounded Wagner. His knees trembled under him, he shook like an aspen, and the officers found it necessary to drag him along, telling him he must keep up if he would save his life. Except that they feared to injure the innocent as well as the guilty, those men would have literally torn him to pieces. But at last he was put on board the cars in safety, and carried away to prison. His demeanor throughout the term of his confinement, and during his trial and subsequent imprisonment, was a wonderful piece of acting. He really inspired people with doubt as to his guilt. I make an extract from The Portsmouth Chronicle, dated March 13, 1873: "Wagner still retains his amazing *sang froid*, which is wonderful, even in a strong-nerved German. The sympathy of most of the visitors at his jail has certainly been won by his calmness and his general appearance, which is quite prepossessing." This little instance of his method of proceeding I must subjoin: A lady who had come to converse with him on the subject of his eternal salvation said, as she left him, "I hope you put your trust in the Lord," to which he sweetly answered, "I always did, ma'am, and I always shall."

A few weeks after all this had happened, I sat by the window one afternoon, and, looking up from my work, I saw some one passing slowly,—a young man who seemed so thin, so pale, bent and ill, that I said, "Here is some stranger who is so very sick, he is probably come to try the effect of the air, even thus early." It was Ivan Christensen. I did not recognize him. He dragged one foot after the other wearily, and walked with the feeble motion of an old man. He entered the house; his errand was to ask for work. He could not bear to go away from the neighborhood of the place where Anethe had lived and where they had been so happy and he could not bear to work at fishing on the south side of the island, within sight of that house. There was work enough for him here; a kind voice told him so, a kind hand was laid on his shoulder, and he was bidden come and welcome. The tears rushed into the poor fellow's eyes, he went hastily away, and that night sent over his chest of tools,—he was a carpenter by trade. Next day he took up his abode here and worked all summer. Every day I carefully observed him as I passed him by, regarding him with an inexpressible pity, of which he was perfectly unconscious, as he seemed to be of everything and everybody. He never raised his head when he answered my "Good morning," or "Good evening, Ivan." Though I often wished to speak, I never said more to him, for he seemed to me to be hurt too sorely to be touched by human hand. With his head sunk on his breast, and wearily dragging his limbs, he pushed the plane or drove the saw to and fro with a kind of dogged persistence, looking neither to the left nor right. Well might the weight of woe he carried bow him to the earth! By and by he spoke, himself, to other members of the household, saying, with a patient sorrow, he believed it was to have been, it had so been ordered, else why did all things so play into Louis's hands? All things were furnished him: the knowledge of the unprotected state of the women, a perfectly clear field in which to carry out his plans, just the right boat he wanted in which to make his voyage, fair tide, fair wind, calm sea, just moonlight enough; even the ax with which to kill Anethe stood ready to his hand at the house door. Alas, it was to have been! Last summer Ivan went back again to Norway—alone. Hardly is it probable that he will ever return to a land whose welcome to him fate made so horrible. His sister Maren and her husband still live blameless lives, with the little dog Ringe, in a new home they have made for themselves in Portsmouth, not far from the river-side; the merciful lapse of days and years takes them gently but surely away from the thought of that season of anguish; and though they can never forget it all, they have grown resigned and quiet again. And on the island other Norwegians have settled, voices of charming children sound sweetly in the solitude that echoed so awfully to the shrieks of Karen and Maren. But to the weirdness of the winter midnight something is added, a vision of two dim, reproachful shades who watch while an agonized ghost prowls eternally about the dilapidated houses at the beach's edge, close by the black, whispering water, seeking for the woman who has escaped him—escaped to bring upon him the death he deserves, whom he never, never, never can find, though his distracted spirit may search till man shall vanish from off the face of the earth, and time shall be no more.

Atlantic Monthly, May 1875

JOSÉ MARTÍ

Charles Julius Guiteau failed spectacularly in a variety of pursuits—law, theology, lecturing—before turning his highly disordered mind to politics. Apparently convinced that an obscure speech he delivered in support of Republican presidential candidate James Garfield had been instrumental in Garfield's election in 1880, he bombarded the new administration with increasingly strident requests for a diplomatic appointment. Consistently rebuffed, he resolved to assassinate Garfield and shot him twice on July 2, 1881, as the President waited for a train in the Washington railroad station. When he was arrested Guiteau proclaimed his allegiance to the "Stalwarts," a Republican faction that was feuding with the administration over the distribution of patronage appointments, but as Martí's account records, Guiteau's politics were as puzzling as his religious views. Subjected to the inadequate medical ministrations of the day—his wounds were probed by unsterilized hands and instruments—Garfield lingered in agony for two and a half months before dying on September 19. After a protracted trial, a legal milestone in the development of the modern insanity defense, Guiteau was convicted in January 1882 and executed the following June.

José Martí (1853–1895), a poet, journalist, orator, and leader of the Cuban independence movement, covered the proceedings for the Caracas newspaper *La Opinión National*, whose readership, as scholar Esther Allen (the translator of this piece) points out, had a particular interest in the case "because the Venezuelan ambassador, Simon Camacho, had been standing at Garfield's side when he was shot, and took the witness stand during the trial." Exiled to Spain in 1871 for his subversive activities, the Havana-born Martí earned degrees in philosophy and law before embarking on a peripatetic life that took him to France, Mexico, Guatemala, the United States, and Venezuela, with a few brief returns to his homeland. Throughout these peregrinations, he produced poems, plays, articles, translations, and political essays that made him a revered figure throughout Latin America. He lived in New York City for much of the last 14 years of his life, writing for the *New York Sun* and contributing regularly to several Spanish-American newspapers. Shortly after returning to Cuba to fight in the war for independence, he was shot and killed in a Spanish ambush on May 19, 1895.

The Trial of Guiteau

Interest in the trial of Garfield's killer has not waned or tapered off. It's as if a wild beast were on exhibit and the entire nation were gathering to have a look at it. Guiteau is a cold, demonic, livid figure. He resembles nothing so much as a wild pig: he has the gleaming eyes, full of hatred, the thick, bristling hair, the same way of charging to the attack, taking fright, running away. It would be impossible to imagine him any uglier than he is—he is a fantastical creature out of the tales of Hoffmann. The moral gamut that runs from the wild beast to man has its degrees, like the zoological gamut. Victory consists in subduing the wild beast. In this criminal—for the court of human opinion holds him to be a criminal—the wild beast has gnawed away the man and seated itself in the hollow space that was left in his spirit. And little by little, shining in his eyes, speaking through his lips, working through his hands, it gave the external creature its own appearance. He does not arouse pity; he does not arouse forgiveness; he arouses no desire to excuse him. There is no place for him in men's hearts, only in their hatred. Reason demands that his life be spared, because of the futility of his horrendous act and because killing the monster is an inadequate way of ending nature's power to grow monsters—for, in the end, moved by prolonged solitude and fear and watered by tears, the gnawed-away man may revive deep within his body, and in these days of wrath justice might appear to be vengeance. One should not kill a wild beast at a time when one feels oneself to be a wild beast: that is to be the same as he is, and not his judge. Man must always keep a tight hold on his own reins and not release them or let the tempest carry them away. Tremendous winds can blow from within, as from a deep cavern. One must be very sure of one's own path before accusing others of having gone astray. For what greater punishment could be dealt this man than that of seeing all his calculations go up in smoke, and his misery revealed, and his desires unfulfillable, and his final effort frustrated, and his decaying mind revealed to itself, and all the advantages that he hoped to gain by his act irrevocably gone? In truth, there was never a greater villain! The indictment shows it, the trial reveals it. The man does not even have the dignity of his crime. He toys with it, makes it a matter for laughter and sophistries. Neither the image of the death he caused nor the image of himself as a skeleton that now taps him on the shoulder and threatens him has settled in beside him or is reflected in any sadness in his eyes. He seems already a creature of the nether-worlds where the judges of his crime may hurl him. He loves life with abominable adhesion. He remains a source of confusion to the mind, but he will always be a source of displeasure to the eyes. He is like a sea of ice floes that drift apart at the slightest push from the wind.

Good Scoville has called on a retinue of favorable witnesses: the sister of the accused has on his behalf told the story of his downfalls, extravagances, and miseries; his brother, who once believed he was guilty, has come to prove, in his honorable and forthright testimony, that he no longer believes him to be master of himself, but mentally deranged. The defense has turned up a host of experts who proclaim him to be demented. But he himself, though he took a seat in the witness box with jocose tone and friendly smile to testify on his own behalf, arose from it haggard and rattled, as if he could still feel his able prosecutor's iron hand on his skull.

And the prosecution has brought on its witnesses, who contradict and combat the defense's affirmations; it has lined up its experts and readied them for the fight.

Guiteau's very brother—infuriated because in the quest to excuse the killer, a good, kind sister of theirs, just starting out in life, was made out to be mad—has come to vigorously stamp out the belief in some permanent family madness on which good Scoville is basing his defense of the killer, and on which the experts based their declarations.

What a singular spectacle this courtroom presents! To one side, where they have been from the beginning, are the jurors who are forbidden to have any contact with anything unrelated to the trial: they are mute as oracles, and later they will break into oracular speech. There is the judge who is enhancing his own and his nation's reputation with his exceptionally benevolent treatment of the prisoner, which the courtroom and the whole world beholds so that it cannot later be said that he was put to death without a defense, or was deprived of any chance of saving himself, or was unjustly condemned. There is the defense counsel, with his weary, benevolent face and anxious eyes. There is the accused's sister, sad and shaken. The prosecutors are in their place. Protecting the prisoner's back is a wall of policemen. And the public section is full of magnificent ladies and suffocating old men who call for help as they struggle out of the throng—the public: curious, laughing, profane, which, as if watching the convulsions of a drunken animal, rejoices in the spasms, outbursts, jeers, cynical jokes, and brutal gestures of the accused. The onlookers rock with gales of laughter; the prisoner shares in the laughter he provokes; the ushers call for silence; and the judge scolds in vain. The mournful ghost of the venerated victim does not come to trouble the merriment of the room.

One of the prosecutors, the grave and solemn Judge Porter, placed his implacable hand on the prisoner's entrails and felt him convulse, and wrested from him his only honorable cry, his only moan of remorse, his only sign of deference to human nature. Another of them—Davidge, who cross-examined the experts—makes a show of his refined language and dexterity, his ability to arouse fear and his mischievousness: and he squeezes the witnesses, exasperates, shakes and wounds them, provoking taunts from Guiteau and shooting back his own witticisms, squabbling with the defense, and bragging that his jokes are always met with choruses of laughter. His services are high-priced and valuable; his laugh is chilling, his perspicacity great, and his conduct in the courtroom puerile and reprehensible. The widow of a cousin of Guiteau who died in an insane asylum states that Guiteau took a fancy to her daughter and wanted to bring her up himself so as later to make her his wife.

"Oh!" Davidge exclaims. "That's a very common form of madness!"

He then repeats the words of another witness, saying of the prisoner, "A blabbermouth and swaggerer who's a little shaky in the upper storey? Well, there are a lot of madmen like that walking around!"

One of the experts estimates that among every five men who appear to be sane, one is actually mad, and Davidge says, "That means there are two and a half madmen on the jury!"

"Careful, Judge, that's close to home," says Guiteau.

"Perhaps certain of the lawyers could stand in for the jurors," Scoville snorts angrily.

Scenes like this one send the public into raptures, and they happen every day. Now Guiteau, like a wilful child, turns his back on the prosecutor who is questioning him and silently starts reading a newspaper; now he hurls insults at him in a frenzy of rage, pounding the table in front of him, threatening the prosecutors with a fulminating gaze, his arm held high, pushing away the guards who try to calm him with his elbows and his irreverent words; now, like a schoolboy, he recites part of a speech in a dramatic tone, announcing it and commenting on it afterward in a vulgar tone; now he reads a newspaper extracted from the bundle of newspapers he carries to the courtroom each morning in his shackled hands, and hands a page from it to the guards who form a wall behind him; now, affecting gentility, he speaks with senatorial tongue and manner to his highly cultured prosecutor, and all is honeyed words, delight, and dandified charm; now, as if he knows he is clutching at the last plank of his life, pale, threatening, wrathful, anguished, terrible, both hands gripping the table, he disputes, shouts, pushes at the table as if he were seeking to escape from himself and from his prison, and snarlingly defends the fragile fabric that his defense has woven: he acted on God's orders, not out of rage at seeing himself passed over or in the hope of gaining something by his crime;

the division within the Republican party was not a pretext, concealing the real reason for his act, it was the real reason for it; from his mother's breast and his father's thoughts of love he came away a madman, and men must deem insanity that which for him was a spontaneous and irresponsible fulfillment of a divine command.

Meanwhile, the prosecution maintains that he acted out of a despicable hope of extracting some advantage from his act; that he planned to commit for his own benefit the act by which, at the same time, he gratified his vengeful instincts; that he prepared the crime carefully so that it would appear to be the work of a political hothead to whom those borne to triumph by his act would then be indebted, and not the work of a religious fanatic, because if that were what he was, he would not have thought, as he did, that those men should repay him; that in the Republican dissensions he saw, with his fatal perspicacity, a pretext to excuse him and a thing to be taken advantage of, but that those dissensions were not the cause of his crime, which he began to conceive of as soon as he began to see that his ambition was being rebuffed.

Listen to his sister, who tells the prisoner's strange story very quickly, as if she wanted to have done with it, and in a very low voice that seems to emerge from an exhausted soul. The prisoner contradicts, interrupts, insults her. What a strange case! The lawyer questioning her is her husband; the man on whose behalf she is testifying is her brother. She is at once the person on trial and the witness. In a more energetic tone she checks the prosecutor who is trying to fluster her. Her voice is supplicating; her unhappiness makes the room fall silent; her narration is clear.

"My poor mother was always ill; she was dying when he was born, and died not long after. He was a strange boy; he still wasn't talking at the age of six; but later he was very loving. When he was sixteen I visited him at his school and found him already possessed by his strange mania for redemption and reformation; he was full of extravagant lectures and wanted to go off with the Christian Socialists of Oneida, and did. When I went to see him in the Oneida community, I thought they had destroyed him, given him a hard blow to the head, or jarred his mind. Then came all the misfortunes: his mad ambitions, his marriage, his impoverishment, his absurd, audacious enterprises, and his constant mishaps. He came back to my house, where he had lived as a child. His every action was that of a madman: he wouldn't obey any direct order; he looked askance at my children; the Bible was always in his hands and he did not conceal his loathing or his wrath. Finally one day he raised the ax he was using to chop wood against me: I held my daughter close: 'Get him away from here! Get him away from here!' and what terrified me most was not the ax but his eyes. I've never been able to forget those eyes! He disappeared and then came back to the house. He learned that we believed he was insane and that if we could have persuaded his father and brothers to agree to it we would have put him in an asylum, and then he ran away. Who doesn't know the rest of his sad story?"

Now listen to his brother. His brother is an unusual, fierce, exalted, truthful man. He tells how, after a bitter quarrel with the prisoner, he went to see him in his cell, afraid of him. At first, he spoke to him from a distance, like one fearing an assault. Then he approached him, reassured. "I want to honor our name!" the prisoner was saying loudly. "I want to be called 'Guiteau the patriot'; I want it understood that no one must say 'Guiteau the assassin.'"

His brother went closer to him and told him in a low voice, "I believe you are honorable in what you say."

"I acted on God's orders; it doesn't matter to me if I die or suffer for it."

"But you are honorable?"

"I am honorable."

"And you wish to die for this principle, as Christ died?"

"Yes, I do."

"But you know that the jury that is to pass judgment on you will not accept your concept of divine inspiration."

"I know."

"And you will suffer the penalty that the jury gives you if it does not accept it?"

"Yes, I will suffer it."

"They say you're afraid of dying."

"I'm not afraid; my life doesn't matter to me in the least."

And all of that in the dank air of the dark cell, in rapid voices.

"And would you rather be hung by the law or killed by a lynch mob?"

"'Aaagh!' shouted the prisoner, running to a corner of the cell and hiding behind a table, 'neither lynched nor hung!'"

"And immediately he burst out laughing at his own cowardly behavior, and we all laughed. Since then I believe he is telling the truth: I believe he is insane. Before then, I had thought him responsible for his actions, for I judged that in his prior life he had always voluntarily chosen the path of evil over the path of good. In Boston, he came to pick a quarrel with me because he'd been told I was spreading information that was prejudicial to him and accusing him of not paying his debts, and in Boston I told him what I've just said. And when we were talking about how he did not pay his rent on time, he answered that he wanted to live like Christ. Christ went to a house and if people took him in he blessed them. He was working for God, and it was up to God to pay his landlords. I spoke approvingly of the Oneida community, and he, who hated them by then, flew into a rage. In his rage he wanted me to leave my own office. As I was pushing him toward the door, he called me a thief and a scoundrel: I hit him on the nape of the neck with the back of my hand, and he hit me back in the face, so hard it gave me new respect for him. And I thought he was demon-possessed. Religious theory holds that there are two forces in the Universe: one led by Satan, or the devil, the other by God or Jesus Christ: my father maintained that some people were possessed by the devil or Satan and others by Christ or God: he believed that the two powers were at war with each other and that after the fall of man Satan came to captivate as many men as he could, those who were not good believers in the Savior and had not saved themselves from the power of sin by a complete union with Jesus. He believed that all evil, all sickness, all deformity, was a defect caused by sin or by the power of the devil who is the spirit of evil, the wicked side of nature. And my brother and I held the same beliefs as my father. And I believe that my brother, out of wickedness, willfulness, and pride, allowed Satan to dominate him to such a degree that he was left in Satan's power. And therefore I believed that my brother was responsible before God for having chosen Satan as his master, but not responsible before the law for the deeds that Satan had inspired him to commit, given that he was already in one sense deprived of his reason. But that must not be said of my father, who followed God and was not mad. That was why I said, when I took out a life insurance policy, that there had been no cases of dementia in my family."

"No one would have had the slightest doubt that he was deranged," said the widow of the cousin of Guiteau who died insane, in an asylum, "if they had seen him constantly watching, pursuing, courting, importuning my daughter, who was still just a child then and became terrified of him."

But it was the prisoner himself who really had to be heard.

"Listen to him," Scoville had said, as if the prisoner's dementia were so clear that it was proven just by hearing him. He toys with his judges; he feigns resistance; he must not be forced to speak when he doesn't feel like it; he will acknowledge a few letters, but he will not speak.

Watch him as—fearful that if he turns to face the public some attempt on his life will be made—he looks to the right and the left with ceremonious and self-satisfied gestures, and a fleeting smile, like an orator certain of his own prowess who is about to address an enthusiastic public. But then fear overcomes him and he asks for a seat so as to make less of a target for murderous hands: it is good that God watches over his life but he does not think it improper for the wooden boxes of the courtroom to protect him as well. He pushes his stylish glasses up his straight nose, and with the air of a satisfied author reads some letters that he identifies one by one. He has many talents as a writer and as a penman. He seems to overflow with gloating enjoyment. "Oh, what script!" "Beautiful script!" "This one is even better." "And this letter looks as if it were a steel engraving." "Magnificent script." He looks like a boy warming to a new toy. Then the letters he identifies are read aloud, and he adds to them, refutes them, clarifies them, delights in them. In one he writes, "My eternal marriage to Jesus and his followers in this world takes precedence within me over all other attractions." And in another, "I have forgotten everything for Christ: reputation, my manly honor, wealth, fame, and worldly renown. For me, the pursuit of the world's goods is over and may God grant that it be so forever. This community of Oneida is the seed of the kingdom of God, and we hope that through the calm and vigorous progress of the association the whole world will soon be his kingdom." But now he has begun to testify, and you have to see the way he starts out serenely but soon gives a shudder and then explodes, pounding the table, grasping the wooden bar that separates him from the jury box in sudden flashes of wrath, with grotesque words and a loud, violent tone, and you have to see the way that—as if unaware of it—he comes out with all the statements or versions of events that concur with the defense's theory, while staying away from anything that could strengthen the prosecution's case. And you have to hear his flowing, self-assured, vaulting, lashing words.

Like a fox, he sidesteps the dangers of his narration. And like a hungry dog he sinks his teeth into the episodes he can base his hopes on. As if he were fighting a rival dog for them, he shakes them, chews them, holds them high. He makes the public laugh; he is applauded. And after wounding the wooden railing with his closed fist and abandoning himself to scandalous transports, after disturbing the judge, who demands that he be silent, and his lawyer, who tries to soothe him, and the public, which is moved, and his guards, who try to restrain him, he stares at the public and at his judges, as if he were peering out from beneath his own gaze. And this was the story of his life that he told:

"I always felt motherless. I saw her when she was dying and then never again. Already at the age of twelve I was living in Scoville's house and going to school. My father then remarried without my consent, which was a very strange way of doing things. Oh, my father! I wanted to get an education and he wanted to save my soul. I wanted to study history, law, languages, and he wanted me, as the only way of preparing me for divine glory, to enter the Oneida community. He made me go to that stinking den of iniquity! And he told me that even were I the greatest man on earth it would be worth nothing if I did not save my soul! He sent me the *Bereano*, which is the Bible of the community, and their magazines. All of it poisoned me: as I read it I lost my eyes, my will, my zeal for science. At last I went to the community; there I beheld the theory of inspiration of which Noyes, the Christ of that communion, said he was the repository. Noyes said that his community was the beginning of the kingdom of God on earth and that he was God's partner and that only through him would men be saved because he was greater and more divine than the Lord Jesus Christ. And I have to say that as a boy I once received a great blow to the head: I can still fit half an inch of my little finger into the wound. My father was fanatical about such things and believed that the devil entered human bodies, and therefore I myself, when my head was hurting in Oneida, didn't try any cure but said to the devil, 'Get out of me, old devil!' But my father was very sincere, very intense, very vehement, very impetuous in his beliefs! And I left Oneida and went to New York to found a newspaper—*The Theocrat*—which I wasn't able to found, but which was a royal idea. Then I studied law for three or four months in a lawyer's office and went to see the district attorney who asked me three or four questions, of which I answered one wrong, and he gave me a certificate that said: 'This certifies that Charles J. Guiteau has been examined by us and we consider him fit for the practice of law in the Supreme Court of the State of Illinois.' And that was how I became a lawyer. And because of my appearance I was given very good cases. I went to the wealthy businesses and asked for cases, and I didn't stop going until they gave them to me, and so I earned thousands of dollars in Chicago and New York. But the *Herald* called me a swindler, and ruined all of it for me. Then I went to hotels, and one day they threw me into a cell in the Tombs. Horrible cell! Scoville got me out of there and I rushed to soak my body in hot water. Oh, I would have made good money if it hadn't been for the *Herald*."

The accused went on to recount an extraordinary undertaking of his, a plan to buy the *Inter-Ocean*, a famous Chicago newspaper, for $75,000—for which purpose he asked one of the people he considered his friends for $200,000. And it was interesting to see how he didn't leave a thing undone that might have been advantageous to the deal. He didn't see underlings—he went right to the top. It was his plan to bring together upon the colossal page the ad-selling genius of the *Tribune* (a well-known Chicago paper), the enterprising spirit of the founder of the *Herald*, and the brilliant Republicanism of the greatly celebrated journalist Horace Greeley. He sought out the best editors. He agreed on a splendid building. He left nothing undone. He tried to establish an excellent wire service; he looked over and chose printing presses; and he wrote to the *Herald*, which of course did not reply, demanding the right to publish at the same time as the *Herald* all the highly detailed news cables which at great cost that New York newspaper receives from all parts of the earth. And what did he offer the famous paper in exchange for this tremendous benefit? Since the *Herald* had called him a swindler, he had filed suit against the *Herald* for $100,000 in damages—a dead lawsuit!—the quarrel of a desperate man. And he promised the *Herald*, in exchange for its wire service, that he would abandon his strange lawsuit! He had already grown scornful of his own lawsuit because he was of the opinion, and still is, that "though it no longer matters to me, and I would give up the position," he was destined to become president of the United States, and he doesn't believe a president should have the *Herald* against him!

At that juncture of his life there arrived in Chicago a pair of grotesque, frenzied preachers who attracted an enormous public to their revival meetings there, just as they are now doing in London where equally large crowds gather for their "Hosannah Testimonies" and their "invitations to Paradise." Predictably enough, Guiteau became an usher for Moody and Shaddey.

"And that was when, after a sermon I heard a pastor give, I began to study the second coming of Christ. Oh, great researches! I never left the Chicago Public Library. I wrote my lecture, the subject of which I had been pondering for years, and which did no less than prove that the second coming of Christ occurred at the time of the destruction of Jerusalem, up in the clouds, directly over the city, and that the destruction of Jerusalem was nothing less than the visible sign of the coming of Christ. Because that is the truth, and not, as they believe in the churches, that Christ will come in the future. And then I set off like Saint Peter, falling and getting back on my feet, thrown out of a house today and out of a train tomorrow, to publish my religious discovery and read my speech. For the same thing happened to Peter: neither he nor I had the money to pay for a room, and neither of us had any success because we had discovered new ideas in theology. And wasn't I working for the Lord? Well, the Lord would take care of me, as he has said he would do for whoever works for him. I went on my way, always thinking of Saint Peter and running from conductors. I still laugh and enjoy myself when I remember those good times. And the Lord always protected me. One day he did it so well that when I was forced to leave one car of a train, I changed seats and went on traveling to Washington and the Lord sat me next to a man who asked me if I wanted a good place to stay in the city. And that was precisely what I was praying to the Lord for—a good house I could stay in."

Good Scoville, eager to prove how the extravagant ideas of fanatics were embedded in the prisoner's fragile mind as if in wax, possessing him utterly, stripping him of all self-control, and making him capable of his future crime, then had him describe the belief of the Oneida Community that any man who enters the community is a man of God, and inspired by God; and that the Leader is in direct communication with the heavens and a prophet of the Lord among men, whom the members of the community obey and in whose hands they place their goods, their thoughts, their wills, and every possession of their bodies and souls.

"And I went on lecturing without any luck; in Boston that great heretic Ingersoll was going to give his speech denying the existence of hell, and he had a full, overflowing house: and I, who wanted to prove that there is a hell, had no more than a dozen people. They paid fifty cents to hear that there was no infernal torment, but they didn't want to pay a cent to hear that there was one. I set up a law practice and that went badly. I went on another lecture tour and that went badly. I published my 'Truth, or the Bible Companion' and no one took any notice. And then came the presidential election and I decided to become a politician. I fashioned my speech, the one titled 'Garfield against Hancock,' which I had to rewrite so that it would support Garfield, because I first wrote it in the belief that Grant would be the Republican candidate. That speech"—said Guiteau in a grave tone, the tone of one telling the centuries to come about the work of a colossus—"was written in the Boston State Library!"

In such insolent, naked, shameless, shifting, restless terms as these, he recounted his futile visits to leading figures—"those friends," as he calls them—such as Arthur, Logan, who is an Olympian personage, and others of no less stature. He told of his forays into the campaign offices that sent his speech out in every direction, of how he delivered part of it to a meeting of men of color and "those friends treated me very well and were glad to see me and all of that." He said that as soon as Garfield was elected he wrote to him demanding the ambassadorship to Austria, because there was a possibility that he was going to marry a rich woman, and the ambassadorship would be most welcome; he said he saw Blaine in Washington when he was seeking the position of consul in Paris, and was finally rejected, and that he watched his party boil over and break apart and read about the dispute in the newspapers, and wrote pacifying letters to Garfield—in which, of course, his advice was followed by questions about the position of consul he now desired—that went unanswered. He said that on the night when the rift within the party came to a head with the resignation of the two senators who were offended by Garfield, he received from God the inspiration for his act.

He spoke in lugubrious, sad, or dramatic tones like one who hears and sees marvels and is the cause of them. "I went to sleep that night tormented by somber ideas about those dissensions, and like a bolt of lightning the thought came to my mind that if Garfield was no longer in the way all problems would be resolved. In the morning, the thought returned. And after that the idea of removing the president did not leave me; it worked on me, tortured me, oppressed me for two weeks. I was filled with horror and shook it, strangled it, cast it far from me, but it went on growing and growing until after two weeks my mind was certain of the necessity of removing the president. As for the divinity of the inspiration—I say to all of you that it was divine!" he exclaimed in a tremendous voice. "I then believed and I still believe now that it was divine. I prayed, prayed, prayed, because I wanted the Lord to reveal himself to me in some way and tell me if it was not his will that I remove the president. And the Lord did not reveal himself to me, because this act was inspired by him for the good of the great American people."

"How was it for the good of the American people?" asked Scoville, who was extracting these answers and clarifications from him.

"To unite the factions within the Republican party, which was then in bitter and deplorable schism, and to prevent war from breaking out anew in this nation because of the destruction of the Republican party. Yes, God inspired me when I entered Oneida; when I tried to found the *Theocrat*, when I went out to preach like Saint Peter, and when I had the idea of removing the president! God is taking care of me. See how he has kept me safe from murderers! God is protecting me, God and the government: these soldiers, these jurors, these experts, this court, all are here to serve God and to protect me!" Like fiery lava the words flow from his lips. "I wished no harm to the president. I was in great spiritual agitation, distraught and drowning: I had no relief until it was all done: then I felt happy, and gave thanks to God."

La Opinión National (Caracas), December 26, 1881

THOMAS BYRNES

Though publicized in his day as the world's greatest "thinking detective," Thomas Byrnes (1842–1910) was no Sherlock Holmes. His much-vaunted success as a crime-fighter stemmed less from his analytical skills than from his extensive use of "stool pigeons"—generally petty criminals who were allowed to keep plying their trade as long as they fed information to the police—and his fondness for the "third degree," a term he is credited with coining.

Byrnes joined the New York City Metropolitan Police Department in 1863 after serving with the Union Army and made a rapid ascent through the ranks, rising from patrolman to captain in seven years. He shot to fame in 1878 for breaking the Manhattan Savings Institution robbery case, one of the biggest heists in the city's history. Two years later, he became head of the Detective Bureau with the rank of inspector and quickly transformed it into one of the most efficient of its kind in the world. Typical of his methods was the famous "Dead Line" he established to cordon off the financial district: any known criminal who ventured south of Fulton Street was arrested on sight and summarily shipped off to Blackwell's Island.

To connoisseurs of true crime, Byrnes remains best known for *Professional Criminals of America* (1886), a book compiled, as he explains in the preface, "with the view to thwarting thieves" by "circulating their pictures, together with accurate descriptions of them and interesting information regarding their crimes and methods." Though the bulk of the work consists of a rogues' gallery of "burglars, forgers, sneak thieves, and robbers of lesser degree," it also contains a section on "Mysterious Murders," from which the following selection—a suggestive snapshot of the miseries of gaslight New York—is taken.

The Murder of Annie Downey,
Alias "Curly Tom"

As a flower girl Annie Downey started out in life, and the acquaintances which she formed while peddling bouquets along the Bowery doubtless led to her ruin. Small in stature and possessed of a shapely form and a handsome face, she soon made hosts of friends. In time she became a degraded creature, and was entered upon the books of the filthy dens in which she lived as "Curly Tom" and "Blonde Annie." She was naturally a brunette, but was in the habit of dyeing her hair to a light blonde. All her relatives were respectable people, and to save them from the shame of her disgrace she passed under the name of Annie Martin. She was found dead in the house kept by a woman named Smidt, at No. 111 Prince Street, on January 17, 1880, under circumstances so mysterious as not to give the faintest clue to her murderer.

During the day preceding the night of her murder she remained in the house and received a number of visitors, none of whom were known to the proprietress. The young woman seemed to be in unusually gay spirits. On retiring to her room, the second floor front, at eleven o'clock, she called out over the banisters to Mrs. Smidt, saying that she expected a visit from an old friend before midnight, and asked to be called as soon as he arrived. She was never seen alive again.

Up to half-past twelve o'clock no one entered the house, and at that hour Mrs. Smidt's husband locked the front door and went to bed, taking the keys with him, according to custom. The back door was always left unlocked.

The Smidt bedroom was on the first floor in the rear. Rosa Schneider, the cook, and a colored chambermaid, whose rooms were in the attic, were the only other persons who slept in the house that night.

Bertha Levy, a hair-dresser, called at ten o'clock next morning to dress Annie Downey's hair. She attempted to open the door to the girl's room, but found it locked. Being unable to get any response to her repeated knocks she called Mrs. Smidt, who, becoming alarmed, called a policeman.

There were three doors leading into the room, one from the hall, one from the adjoining hall bedroom, and the third from the rear room. The two former were locked. The bed was placed against the latter.

Going into the rear room the policeman forced open the door, pushing the bed back with it, and entered the room. Lying on the bed, face upward and drenched in blood that had flowed from several ghastly wounds in the head, he found the body of Annie Downey. It was cold and stiff.

Tied so tightly around the neck as to blacken the face and force the eyeballs from their sockets, was a thin pillow-slip taken from the bed. The fingers of the left hand clutched one end of the slip with a death grip. The limbs were extended straight along the bed, and the attitude of the body did not suggest that a struggle for life had taken place. The only other marks were two small cuts over the left eye that looked as if they had been inflicted with a blow of a fist.

Everything about the apartment was in perfect order. The girl's clothing was neatly arranged over a chair by the bedside. In the ears of the corpse were a pair of handsome amethyst earrings and a diamond ring flashed on her finger. Evidently the murderer's motive had not been robbery.

The only thing missing was a watch and chain of little value, but it was soon remembered that the girl had disposed of them a few days before.

Search was made for the key of the door, but it could not be found. All the inmates of the house were strictly interrogated, but no information that could throw a ray of light on the mystery could be elicited. No unusual sounds had been heard during the night.

Smidt was positive that no man was in the house when he locked the door for the night. Annie's last visitor had gone away long before eleven o'clock, the hour at which she went to her room. The only theory of the case was that the murderer had entered the house during the evening without attracting attention, and secreted himself in the room until the girl entered, when he surprised and killed her before she could make any outcry.

This view was supported by the condition of the body, which indicated that the murder took place at least ten hours before it was discovered.

By way of the back door the assassin could easily have made his way to an alley running along the eastern side of the house to the street. The padlock which fastened the door of this alley was found to have been twisted off.

The coroner's examination showed that death had been caused by strangulation, and that the wounds on the head were merely superficial and had been inflicted after the pillow-slip had been knotted round the throat, evidently in an effort to still the girl's struggles for life.

Professional Criminals of America, 1886

FRANK NORRIS

Frank Norris (1870–1902) was still an undergraduate at Berkeley when he began publishing short stories in the San Francisco weekly *The Wave*. He joined the paper in 1896, after postgraduate work at Harvard and a trip to South Africa, where he covered the Jameson Raid as a newspaper correspondent.

That the future author of *The Octopus*, a devastating depiction of the stranglehold of railroad companies on western farmers, should serve his literary apprenticeship on this particular periodical is not without irony, since *The Wave* was started by a publicist for the Southern Pacific Railroad to promote travel to Monterey. It soon evolved into a lively weekly, covering all aspects of San Francisco society, culture, and politics. In the course of his 22-month career as assistant editor, Norris contributed approximately 120 pieces of short fiction, character sketches, book reviews, editorials, theater criticism, and sports columns, along with colorful accounts of the bustling life of the city.

This article, from the January 23, 1897, number, describes a dockside stakeout by a team of Australian and American lawmen awaiting the arrival of a ship carrying a fugitive multiple murderer and reflects Norris's keen interest in crime, an interest that would bear literary fruit in his naturalistic masterpiece *McTeague*, published the year after he left *The Wave* and partly based on a sensational real-life case of domestic murder.

Hunting Human Game

On the 21st of November in the year 1896 there appeared in one of the newspapers of Sydney, Australia, an advertisement to the effect that one Frank Butler—mining prospector, was in search of a partner with whom to engage in a certain mining venture. It was stipulated that applicants should possess at least ten pounds and come well recommended.

Captain Lee Weller answered the advertisement and accompanied

Butler to the Blue Mountains mining region, in what is known as the Glenbrook district. There Butler shot him in the back of the head and buried the body in such a way that a stream of trickling water would help in its decomposition. But Captain Weller had friends; he was missed; a search was made and it was not long before the detectives discovered the grave and identified the remains.

Meanwhile, news had been brought to the Australian police that another man named Preston had gone into the mountains and never returned. Next the body of this Preston was discovered. Then it was found that another man had disappeared under the same circumstances as those surrounding the vanishing of Weller. Then another and another, and still another. The news of these disappearances ran from end to end of Australia, and the whole police system of the country was brought to bear upon the case. Finally it was found that a man named Lee Weller had applied to the Sailor's Home at Newcastle for a berth on a ship. Seven days later this Lee Weller shipped out of Newcastle before the mast on the British tramp ship Swanhilda, bound for San Francisco in coal. This was all the detectives wanted to know. The man calling himself Weller was Butler beyond any doubt, suddenly grown suspicious and resolved upon a bolt. Butler's photograph was identified at once by the Superintendent of the Sailor's Home as the supposed Lee Weller. It was out of the question to overhaul Butler now, but two Australian detectives, McHattie and Conroy, took passage on a steamer for San Francisco, where they arrived some three weeks ago. They outstripped Butler and are now waiting for him to catch up with them. That is the story in brief of this extraordinary criminal who, Mr. McHattie says, has killed—no, assassinated is the word—fourteen men.

I saw the "death watch" the other day—the watch for the tramp collier ship Swanhilda—that is being maintained at Meiggs' wharf by seven men, whose business it is to hunt criminals down. There is but little of that secrecy and dark mystery about this famous "death watch" that sensational story-writers would have you believe. The detectives live upstairs in a little two-story house at the end of Meiggs' wharf, close to the customs offices. I had imagined that I would be met at the door with all sorts of difficulties, that permits and passes would be demanded and explanations and the like; that the detectives would be austere and distant and preoccupied, preoccupied as men are who are watching for a sign or listening for a signal. Nothing of the sort. I tramped in at the open door and up the stairs to the room and sat me down on Mr. McHattie's bed—it's a lounge, but it does for a bed—as unchallenged as if the place had been my own; nor was I armed with so much as a letter of introduction. I was not even asked to show a business card.

The room is a little room, whose front windows give out upon the bay and the Golden Gate. Not a row-boat could pass the Gate without being noted from this vantage point. There were four beds made up on the floor of the room, and Conroy was dozing in one, pretending to read "Phra the Phoenician," the whiles. The other detectives sat about a gas stove, smoking. They were for the most part big, burly men, with red faces, very jovial and not at all like the sleuths you expected to see. They are, however, heavily muscled fellows, with the exception of Conroy, who singularly enough is slighter than any of them, though a trained athlete. I remember that the room was warm. That there were pictures of barks and brigs about the walls, that a pair of handcuffs were in a glass dish on the top of a dresser, and that, lying in a cubby hole of a desk, was Detective Egan's revolver in a very worn case. The detectives impressed one as positively jolly. They told me many funny yarns about the crowd of visitors on the wharf, of the "Branch office of the Chronicle," a room ten feet square, just back of the Customs building, and once when "The Examiner" reporter cried out that a girl was waving a handkerchief from a window on the hill back of the wharf, they made a rush for the rear window of the room, crowding about it like so many boys.

And at that very moment somewhere out there beyond the Farallones a certain great four-masted ship, 58 days out of Newcastle, was rolling and lifting on the swell of the Pacific, drawing nearer to these men with every puff of the snoring trades. Some time within the next few days the signal from the Merchants' Exchange will be rung in that room, there on Meiggs' wharf, the signal which some of these men have come around half of the world to hear. It will be rung on the telephone bell, and it may come at each instant—it may be ringing now as I write these lines, or now as you read them. It may come in the morning, or while the "watch" is at supper, or in the very dead of night, or the early dawn. May I be there to hear it and to see as well. The scene cannot be otherwise than dramatic—melodramatic even. I want to hear that exclamation "Here she is" that some one is bound to utter. I want to see Egan reach for the revolver in the worn leather case, and Conroy take the handcuffs from the glass dish. I want to see the sudden rousing of these seven men, these same men who waved their hands to the girl in the window, and I want to hear the clatter of those seven pairs of boots going down the stair and out upon the wharf. I fancy there will not be much talking.

The Wave, January 23, 1897

SUSAN GLASPELL

Sometime around midnight on December 1, 1900, John Hossack, a well-to-do, 59-year-old Iowa farmer, was attacked in bed by an axe-wielding assailant who literally beat out his brains as he slept. His wife became the prime suspect after neighbors testified to her long-simmering hatred of her abusive spouse. Covering the sensational case was 24-year-old Susan Glaspell (1876–1948), at that time the legislative reporter for the *Des Moines Daily News*, the largest daily in the state.

Shortly after Mrs. Hossack was convicted and shipped off to Anamosa State Penitentiary, Glaspell—who had been publishing short stories in *Harper's Monthly* and *American Magazine*—quit journalism to devote herself full-time to fiction. She and her new husband, the writer George Cram Cook, moved east in 1913, joining the Bohemian community of artists and intellectuals who wintered in Greenwich Village and summered in Provincetown on Cape Cod. In 1915 they founded the Provincetown Players, a company that would nurture dozens of playwrights—most notably Eugene O'Neill—and for which Glaspell created her one-act play *Trifles*, a thinly veiled take on the Hossack case with a decidedly feminist slant. The following year, she reworked the material into a short story, "A Jury of Her Peers."

In August 1916, less than three weeks after the premiere of *Trifles*, Margaret Hossack died at home in Indianola, Iowa, a free woman. One year after her incarceration in Anamosa, her conviction was overturned on appeal, and a second trial in 1903 ended with a hung jury. The state declined to retry her, and the murder of her husband remains officially unsolved.

The Hossack Murder

INDIANOLA, Dec. 3.—(Special.)—A foul murder was committed Saturday night near Medford, fifteen miles southwest of Indianola. A farmer named Hossack was struck over the head and killed by unknown parties, at his home a few miles out from Medford.

The assault was probably committed by burglars, though of this the officers are not yet sure. Sheriff Lew Hodson and Dr. Harry Dale, coroner, went to the place Sunday, and subpoenaed a jury which was called to meet this morning for an inquest. Mr. Hossack was an early settler, a prominent farmer, highly respected. He was about 60 years of age and leaves a wife and large family.

INDIANOLA, Dec. 4.—(Special.)—Persons who went to the home of John Hossack Monday and saw the murdered man in his bed, and heard portions of the testimony before the coroner's jury, are all at sea as to who killed Hossack or for what reason. There is no evidence of burglary. The murderer came through a porch and front room to the bed room where Mr. and Mrs. Hossack slept. He evidently reached across the bed with an ax and struck two blows. One crushed in the skull and the other made a deep cut, yet Hossack lived from Saturday night until 10 a.m. Sunday, though he did not regain consciousness, and no one has yet been found who can give a clue to the murder. The ax was found under a shed about fifty feet from the house. Mrs. Hossack swore before the jury that she was awakened about midnight by the slamming of a door, saw a flash of light and then all was dark. She called to her husband but as he did not respond, she got up and lighted a lamp. Then she discovered him on the bed, with blood all over the clothing. She said she did not hear the blows nor see any one. The officers are investigating.

It is rumored that trouble had arisen in the Hossack household and that possibly some relative committed the murder.

The funeral of Mr. Hossack was set for Wednesday at 1 p.m. from the First M.E. church at New Virginia. The family consisted of wife, and four children, who were at home.

Bert Osborn and Harry Hartman of Indianola went to the Hossack home Sunday afternoon and took flash light photographs of the remains of Hossack as they lay on the bed. The left temple is crushed in, probably by the butt end of the ax, while the upper part of the head is deeply gashed.

The ax, which was found under a shed and covered with blood, has been sent to a chemist, who is to report whether or not the blood is human or from chickens, as stated by some members of the family.

The report that Hossack did not regain consciousness is contradicted. One of his sons testified before the coroner's jury that he said to his father, "Well, pa, you are badly hurt," and that he replied:

"No, I'm not hurt, but I'm not feeling well."

It is said that Hossack did not make any statement as to whom he suspected of the crime.

INDIANOLA, Dec. 5.—(Special.)—The Hossack murder case took a sensational turn today when the sheriff went to Medora for the avowed purpose of arresting Mrs. Hossack, wife of the murdered man. The departure of the sheriff was kept a profound secret for a time, but eventually some of the county officials were induced to reveal to your correspondent that the object of the trip was the arrest of Mrs. Hossack.

The evidence is by no means conclusive of Mrs. Hossack's guilt, but the testimony before the coroner's jury was such as to raise a suspicion of guilt and her arrest was decided upon as a matter of precaution.

Members of the Hossack family are understood to have testified before the coroner's jury that the blood on the ax found under the corn crib was caused by chopping off the head of a turkey the day before the murder. It is now reported that a child admitted on cross-examination that he himself placed the ax in the corn crib the evening before the murder and that at that time there was no blood on it.

Friends of Mrs. Hossack are beginning to suggest that she is insane and that she has been in this condition for a year and a half under the constant surveillance of members of the family.

The robbery theory has been wholly abandoned, as absolutely nothing was taken and no suspicious characters were seen in the neighborhood prior or subsequent to the murder.

The most suspicious circumstance in connection with the crime is the testimony of Mrs. Hossack that she lay in bed by the side of her husband while his skull was crushed in two places, and was not awakened in time to see anyone leave the house.

The developments since the murder that the members of the Hossack family were not on pleasant relations with each other is a complete surprise, as Hossack was not supposed to have an enemy in the world.

The verdict of the coroner's jury found this morning was as follows:

"We do find said deceased came to his death by two blows upon the head; one with a sharp instrument and one with a blunt instrument. (Signed) C. D. Johnson, Fred Johnston, T. W. Passwater."

The wife of John Hossack, arrested on the charge of having beaten out his brains with an ax, has employed Henderson and Berry as her attorneys and is preparing to fight the case to the end.

She was locked up in the county jail here last night at 8:30. She manifested no emotion, took her arrest calmly and absolutely declined to make any statement concerning her guilt or innocence.

Members of the Hossack family are standing by her solidly, but public sentiment is overwhelmingly against her.

Though past 50 years of age, she is tall and powerful and looks like she would be dangerous if aroused to a point of hatred. It is claimed by the prosecution that she and her husband quarreled violently over their second son, John Hossack, Jr., because the father was unwilling to overlook his son's shortcomings.

An effort was made at the coroner's inquest to bring out that Mrs. Hossack had threatened her husband's life and had intimated to William Haines that she would like to get her husband out of the way. Haines only partially corroborated this story.

Hossack owned 300 acres of fine land and was considered well-off. It is claimed now, however, that the farm was in his wife's name and that possession of it could have furnished no incentive to the crime. Deceased, however, carried $2,000 in life insurance, made payable to his wife.

INDIANOLA, April 2. —(Special.)— Selection of jurors in the Hossack murder trial is completed. The panel is as follows: D. Agard, J. P. Anderson, J. B. Bitting, J. W. Bruce, J. W. Hadley, Geo. W. Lewis, F. E. Miller, John Niles, W. C. Pitman, J. W. Poland, Wm. Powers and S. R. Richards. At 11 o'clock Judge Gamble swore in the jury. Reading of the indictment by County Attorney Clammer followed.

During the recital of counts contained in the indictment, the defendant, Mrs. Hossack, was visibly affected, her eyes frequently filled with tears and her frame shook with emotion.

It is expected the balance of the day will be taken up by the prosecution in submitting facts they expect to prove.

A large diagram of the arrangement of the Hossack homestead mounted upon a frame and easel has been introduced by the prosecution. The purpose of the prosecution is to show by use of the diagram that Mrs. Hossack alone could have committed the crime.

The defense made objection to the introduction of this exhibit, claiming that the scale upon which the house was drawn was not the same as used in locating out buildings. The court ordered its admission on the statement of the prosecuting attorney that a uniform scale was used in preparing the diagram.

INDIANOLA, April 3.—(Special.)—Fully 1,200 people flocked out of the court house when court adjourned yesterday at the close of the second day of the Hossack murder trial. During the afternoon session, which began sharply at 1:30 o'clock, the seating capacity of the court room proved inadequate to the demand and scores of people crowded into the aisles and stood packed in about the railing separating the attorneys, witnesses and defendant from the promiscuous multitude.

Tomorrow morning's session will commence at 9 o'clock with cross examination of Dr. Dean, the third witness for the prosecution.

When Attorney Berry yesterday afternoon addressed the jury for the defense and took up the events of the day preceding the night of the murder and detailed them in their proper sequence, the stillness in the court room became oppressive. Carefully he went over the actions of each member of the family. He told how on the night of the killing five of the children were asleep in the house; how that at the side of the death bed eight of the nine children gathered while the mother, stunned by what had happened, attended to the wants of the sufferer, frequently administering water to the parched lips and bathing the wounded head.

During the description of this scene Mrs. Hossack, who occupied a seat by the sheriff's wife, surrounded by three of her daughters and all but one of her sons, broke completely down and wept bitterly. Grief was not confined to her alone, it spread until the weeping group embraced the family and the sympathetic wife of Sheriff Hodson, who frequently applied her handkerchief to her eyes.

The first witness to be called by the prosecution was William Hossack.

After describing preliminary incidents and being called by his mother, he said he was the first to enter the room in which his father lay.

"What did you see?" he was asked.

"I saw my father in bed."

"How was he lying?"

"With his head turned slightly to the left."

"Who spoke first?"

"I did."

"What did you say?"

"I asked him who hit him."

"What did he say?"

"He said he wasn't hit."

"Did you hear your mother say anything?"

"Do not think she did."

"You may state what she said to you."

"She said she heard a noise like two boards being slapped together. That she got up and ran out of the room. That as she went out she saw a light on the wall. That the blinds were shut but she saw a light shining through a crack."

"Did you look for any money in the house?"

"I did. I found some in the secretary."

"Do you remember of any fowls being killed on the place about Thanksgiving time?"

"Yes. I killed a turkey."

"What did you kill it with?"

"With an ax."

"Did your mother and father quarrel any?"

"Not within a year."

An objection was taken to this question by the defense but the court held it to be pertinent. Efforts to have the witness determine and say when he last heard them quarreling, resulted in his maintaining the former statement. He was certain that, while during former years there had been frequent differences between them, nothing like a serious misunderstanding had transpired since a year from last Thanksgiving. When questioned about the proposed division of the property at the time a separation was talked of, he stated that it was intended his father should take the east eighty acres and his mother the rest.

He described finding the axe under the granary and said there were blood stains on the handle but none on the blade; that when he examined it he found several hairs sticking to one side of the cutting edge which he picked off and turned over to the sheriff.

Mrs. Haines was next called to the stand. She is a small woman, who looks to be suffering from some nervous ailment. In answer to the county attorney's questions she described a scene which occurred in her house when the defendant called one afternoon.

"What did the defendant say to you on the occasion you refer to?" asked Clammer.

"She said 'it would be a Godsend if Mr. Hossack was gone.'"

She also stated that she and her husband had often called at the Hossack house and that they had sometimes been called upon to talk to Mr. Hossack. That she knew the Hossacks frequently quarreled. That on one occasion Mrs. Hossack had asked her and her husband to come down to her home and bring with them several of the neighbors as she was afraid that her husband would kill the family before morning.

The last witness of the day was Dr. W. F. Dean. He testified to being the family physician and to being called to the Hossack homestead on the night of December 1. That he reached the house about 4:30 o'clock in the morning and he found Mr. Hossack in bed and unconscious. He described the wounds on the head, going into minute detail. He testified to having remained at the house until after the death of Mr. Hossack, which occurred a little after 9 o'clock and that the latter did not regain conciousness while he was there.

He repeated in substance the talk he had with Mrs. Hossack which did not differ from her statement to her son William.

He then described having assisted at the examination of Mrs. Hossack's wearing apparel the following day. He described the undervest as being covered with blood at a point between the shoulders in the back and showing a few bloody spots on the right shoulder and about the upper portion of the neck in front.

"In your opinion was Mr. Hossack ever conscious after being struck?"

"I don't know whether he could return to consciousness or not after those blows."

The purpose of the prosecution in these questions was to show that the reported conversations between the dead man and members of his family could not have taken place.

INDIANOLA, April 5.—(Special.)—Slowly but surely the prosecution in the Hossack murder case is weaving a web of circumstantial evidence about the defendant that will be hard to counteract. The examination of each additional witness leaves a perceptible effect on the jury and their faces become more and more set and stern. Mrs. Hossack is bearing up well under her trying ordeal, but day by day her countenance becomes more haggard and drawn. She may come out of the trial a victor, but the terrible strain cannot but have the effect of permanently undermining her health and bringing her to an early grave. To many it seems her hair is turning perceptibly lighter, and the gray is gradually giving away to silver.

The damaging admissions of Mrs. Hossack's favorite son, John Hossack, Jr., yesterday, while fairly wrung from him by the county attorney and being in many cases directly contradictory to his evidence given before the grand jury, were so palpably an effort to shield his mother as much as possible as to have just that much greater effect on the jury.

To the expert testimony of physicians yesterday tending to show that the murder was committed with the axe and that the statements of Mrs. Hossack and her children to the effect that the murdered man had addressed them after the crime was committed were physically impossible, was added that of Drs. Porterfield and Surber today, both men of learning and great influence. The testimony of Mrs. Lou Hinstreet was likewise damaging to the defendant.

When court convened at 9 o'clock this morning, Dr. E. Porterfield took the stand. He stated that he was a graduate of the Bellevue hospital in New York; that he was present and assisted in the autopsy upon the remains of the dead man on Monday following the murder. He minutely described the nature of the wound and stated that the incisive wound was made first; that in his opinion, from the nature of the wound it would have been impossible for the man to have regained consciousness at any time within thirty minutes after the assault; and that he thought it probable that he did not recover consciousness for an hour. He described the location of the sense of speech as being on both sides of the brain, although more largely developed on the left side; and that from the nature of the wound he believed the power of speech to have been seriously injured. On cross examination the defense was unable to elicit contradictory statement. When asked about the celebrated "crowbar" case he said that there was considerable difference between that case and the Hossack case.

The next witness sworn was Dr. L. H. Surber. On direct examination, he said that the time required to produce the discoloration about the eyes would be about twenty minutes. He also stated on cross examination that the dead man suffered from a chronic abdominal trouble, the inference being that his vitality would have been greatly lessened, although he stated the dead man to be in normal condition and equal to the average man in the power of physical endurance. In reply to inquiry as to how long, in his opinion, it was before the dead man spoke after being assaulted, he said he did not believe it would have been possible to have articulated within thirty minutes.

The next witness was Mrs. Sue Hinstreet. She described the scene in the second story of the back room when Mrs. Hossack was examined by County Attorney Clammer on Monday. She stated that Mrs. Hossack had told her she was awakened during the night by hearing a sound like the clapping together of two boards; that she got up and went to the stairs and called her daughters; that Cassie answered and inquired what was the matter; that she told Cassie she thought someone was in the house, and that Cassie told her to go back to bed, as she must be mistaken; that she heard her husband groaning and went back and called the girls again; that in a few minutes Will came down and that he was followed by the girls; that together they lit a lamp and went into the bedroom.

When asked if Mrs. Hossack had said anything about the axe the witness replied that Mrs. Hossack said that one of the older boys had told the young boy to put it in the granary but that she did not think he had done so, as he was gone so short a time and that he must have put it under the granary.

The witness also described the appearance of the undervest as she saw Mrs. Hossack at the examination Monday. She stated that she did not see any blood on the front, but that she saw blood on the right shoulder and on the sleeve, and a spot on the back between the shoulders.

When court adjourned at noon she was on the stand on cross examination.

Yesterday afternoon, James Hossack, the 16-year-old son of the defendant, testified that he had not told the truth before the grand jury, that he had been intimidated by the county attorney. He denied everything that he said to the grand jury relative to the quarreling on the night of the murder, prior to the aged couple's retiring. He declared yesterday that he had heard no quarrel or angry words. The introduction of the evidence as given before the grand jury by this witness is thought to be a great point in favor of the prosecution as it is generally thought the boy on more mature deliberation is making an endeavor to shield his mother.

Several witnesses were examined who testified to having heard Mrs. Hossack say repeatedly that it would be a God's blessing if Mr. Hossack was dead.

During the day the bed in which the murdered man had been killed was introduced for the purpose of showing it impossible for two people to have slept in it without one being awakened if the other was hit. The bed was of three-quarter size, constructed of wood and contained all the bedding upon it at the time of the murder. This was badly stained with blood and presents a most repulsive sight.

INDIANOLA, April 9.—(Special.)—Seldom, if ever, have the people of Indianola seen such an Easter sabbath as Sunday. It was not so much the beauty of the day, for, although it began and finished with ideal Easter conditions, there has been many another as balmy, as full of the freshening vigor of spring. There were other elements at work than those of external nature; other influences beside those arising from the deep significance of the day. Blended with it was the spirit of tragedy, and it penetrated and permeated all classes and found vent in the intensity with which the questions: "Is she guilty?" "Will they convict her?" were asked.

It was the atmosphere of tragedy surrounding Mrs. Hossack who, shut in from the world in a narrow, padded cell in the gloomy interior of the county jail, listening throughout the day to the inspiring clanging of church bells or catching the half lost strains of chanting choirs, which even heavy walls and iron-gated windows could not entirely exclude.

Spring had come and with it, as if by magic within a day, many an emerald spot, fresh and vigorous with the new life of summer, shown brilliantly against the sober brown, where winter yet reigns. But they were not for the eye of Mrs. Hossack.

In churches great banks of delicately colored flowers buried pulpits and adjacent aisles and exhaled upon the air a perfume that will linger in the vaulted roofs and shadowy pews until another Easter shall come. But they were not there for Mrs. Hossack to enjoy.

On the streets, especially those most remote from the jail, a throng of gaily dressed people enjoyed the warmth of an ideal Easter. Then they were merry; they laughed and chatted and walked; they talked and jested, but less as they approached the jail, until, when parading beneath its grated windows, a hush would fall upon them.

Was there something fascinating in those walls that they could so suddenly silence the gay interchanges of the day, or was it for the woman within, for Mrs. Hossack, invisible to the multitude, that they felt a sympathy, which no evidence could entirely destroy?

But about and beyond the jail, far enough away that it might not be heard within there was that buzzing of human voices which always accompanies public excitement, and in it could be heard that question which lingers on the lips of everybody here: "Is she guilty?" and the answer is lost in the discord, but the discord has an ugly sound.

Mrs. Hossack spent the day quietly. Other members of the family attended one of the churches during the morning and some of them visited the jail in the afternoon. They are remaining in town during the trial, perhaps they will never go back to the farm again. Wherever they went yesterday they were pointed out; they had become curiosities; they awaken speculation, and following each came those questions: "Is she guilty?" and "Will they convict her?"

Were it possible to obtain a consensus of opinion representing the entire community it might present Mrs. Hossack as an innocent woman, but that which can be gathered does not do so. That she has the sympathy of many people is certain; why, unless it be because she is a woman? When asked to express an opinion as to her guilt they refuse.

It is possible the general condemnation of the woman is due to the few who talk it so incessantly. Perhaps it is these thirteenth jurors who are responsible for the public verdict.

When the first week of the trial ended Saturday at noon it was difficult to understand how the defense had strengthened its case by the evidence introduced during the day. The impression was general the case of the prosecution had not been materially weakened by the testimony of the witnesses for the defense, although it was not thought the former had made out a case strong enough to relieve the minds of the jurors of reasonable doubt. That it had accomplished more than at first anticipated was generally conceded.

INDIANOLA, April 10.—(Special.)—All day long Margaret Hossack and her children have sat in the court room listening to the terrible arraignment of the defendant by Attorney McNeal, who is closing the argument for the prosecution.

His repeated declaration that the gray haired mother, sitting there with bowed head in the midst of her children, is a murderess, must constitute a fearful ordeal but through it all, neither the defendant nor her children have betrayed the least sign of emotion.

Attorney McNeal stated at 3 o'clock this afternoon that he would probably not complete his argument until tomorrow morning. Judge Gamble will then instruct the jury and Mrs. Hossack's fate will be determined by twelve good men. A verdict is scarcely expected short of twenty-four hours, and if none is reached by that time, a disagreement is probable. The chances of conviction appear stronger, since the argument of Attorney McNeal than at any time before.

He then spoke of the attempt of the defense to throw suspicion upon William Haines and wondered why it was the man had not been in court. He thought their failure to produce him significant. He failed to understand how the dog could have been drugged unless it was done by a member of the household.

He next took up the evidence of the doctors and showed conclusively that in all material matters they agreed; that where, as McCrary and Parr had testified, a man would speak at once after being hurt, they also stated that in their opinion he had never spoken. He wanted to know why it was if the murdered man spoke immediately after being hurt he did not answer Mrs. Hossack's question after she returned to the bedroom from calling the girls the first time.

He then took up the condition of the axe showing that both of the experts testified it had been washed and one of them testified that it had been washed twice before it came into his possession.

He asked how it was that Mrs. Hossack knew that the axe had been placed under the granary when Ivan told her he was going to put it in the granary late the night before. He took up the question of Hossack having been struck by a left-handed person and showed that by the position of the head on the pillow the contused blow must have been struck by a right-handed person. In support of this he argued that the incision would have filled with blood and that the deepest portion of the contused wound was below the former, accounting in this way for the large quantity of blood on the north wall, which he said had been thrown out by the contused wound and passed over the foot of the bed.

He humorously pointed to the hair which had been found by Johnson in March under the granary. He said he pitied Johnson and wondered why it was he came to mix up in it anyway, the crime having been committed in December. He stated that from the testimony of experts there was reason to believe that the hair was human hair and that it came from the head of John Hossack. He asked whether or not the conduct of Mrs. Hossack on the night of the murder when her husband lay in bed mortally wounded had been that of a woman who loved the man. He recalled that she said she had taken hold of the dead man's hand and the attorney asked if in the opinion of the jury a woman under those circumstances would not have manifested greater concern.

When court opened this morning at 9 o'clock, Attorney J. W. McNeal, who is assisting County Attorney Clammer in the prosecution, opened the closing address to the jury. He first called the attention of the jury to the barking of the dog. He stated that on the testimony given by the various witnesses, somebody had lied; that the dog, according to one story had been heard to bark after the murder had been committed and that the defendant admitted in her own statement that the dog had barked in the early evening.

INDIANOLA, April 11.— (Special.)— Mrs. Margaret Hossack must pay the penalty for the murder of her husband. The jury has just now returned a verdict of guilty as charged in the indictment. Judge Gamble has sentenced her to the penitentiary for life. The court room was packed when it was reported the jury had reached a conclusion and was ready to make known the fate of Margaret Hossack. The latter sat calmly in her seat, the rigid expression which she had carried all through the trial, changing to that of earnest expectation of either good or evil news. Slowly the twelve men filed to their seats in the jury box. The foreman delivered the verdict to the bailiff, who handed it to the clerk. The latter stood erect. A death-like silence pervaded the room.

"We, the jury, find the defendant, Mrs. Margaret Hossack, guilty as charged in the indictment," he read.

The silence continued several seconds giving way to a low murmur plainly audible around the court room.

The aged prisoner sat looking helpless and in a sort of dazed condition at the clerk. Then, suddenly seeming to realize the meaning of the verdict, she sank back in her chair and for the first time during the long and trying ordeal, gave completely away to her feelings.

She was surrounded by her friends whose sobbing could be heard through the hall and into the open court yard, continuing until Sheriff

Hodson led the prisoner back to the jail awaiting final judgment. Senator Berry announced that he would move for a new trial.

The case went to the jury unexpectedly last night at 6 o'clock. Attorney McNeil had intended to continue his address until 10 o'clock today but suddenly, shortly before 5 o'clock last evening, he collapsed from the continued exertion and rested the case. The effect of his appeal for a conviction was great.

Judge Gamble's instructions were read at 5:30 and the jury retired to deliberate at 6 o'clock. The instructions were generally regarded as favorable to a conviction. Judge Gamble's instructions to the jury follow:

In no case is it necessary, in order to establish a criminal charge against defendant, that there should be direct proof of her guilt by witnesses who were present and saw her commit the crime. In criminal, as well as in civil cases, the evidence may be, and frequently is, not direct, but circumstantial. In fact in criminal cases the guilt of the defendant if shown at all, is most generally shown by the latter kind of evidence; that is to say, but the proof of such facts and circumstances as establish her guilt, and when evidence in a case consists of a chain of well authenticated circumstances, it is often more convincing and satisfactory and gives a stronger ground of assurance of the defendant's guilt than the direct testimony of witness unconfirmed by circumstances.

To justify the inference of guilt on circumstantial evidence show the facts proven from which it is asked that the guilt of the defendant be inferred, must be consistent with each other, and such circumstances must not only clearly point to her guilt, but they must be incompatible with her innocence; that is to say they must be incapable of explanation on any other reasonable supposition than that of her guilt. But as against consistent and well authenticated circumstances plainly indicating the guilt of a defendant, the supposition which would entitle her to an acquittal must be reasonable, and arise out of and be founded on the evidence in the case, and it must not arise out of or be founded on any fact or state of facts which by probability might have existed, but of which there is no proof.

When conviction by a jury is sought on circumstantial evidence alone, before a verdict of guilty can be reached, the jury must be satisfied beyond a reasonable doubt that the crime charged has been committed by some one in the manner and form as charged in the indictment. It is further incumbent upon the prosecution to establish that the facts and circumstances relied upon are true and that such facts and circumstances are not only consistent with the defendant's guilt, but also that they are inconsistent with any other reasonable hypothesis or supposition than guilt. It is not sufficient that such circumstances are consistent with and point to her guilt, but to warrant a conviction upon such evidence alone. The facts and circumstances proven must not only be in harmony with the guilt of the accused, but they must be of such a character that they cannot reasonably be true in the ordinary nature of things and the person accused be innocent.

You should bring into consideration the evidence your every day common sense and judgment as reasonable men, and make those just and reasonable inferences from circumstances proven, which the guarded judgment of a reasonable man would ordinarily make under like circumstances; and those just and reasonable inferences and deductions which you, as reasonable men, would ordinarily draw from facts and circumstances proven in the case you should draw and act on as jurors; and if, on a consideration of the whole evidence before you, you then have no reasonable doubt, as in these instructions defined, as to the guilt of the defendant, you should convict her; but if you then entertain such a doubt, you should acquit her.

"Sheriff Hodson, tell my children not to weep for me. I am innocent of the horrible murder of my husband. Some day people will know I am not guilty of that terrible crime."

Those were the parting words of Margaret Hossack, the Indianola murderess, to Sheriff Hodson when she was turned over to the prison warden at Anamosa penitentiary last night. All along she has proclaimed her innocence of the murder and hopes the time is near at hand when the real murderess or murderer will be found out and punished.

It is universally believed at Indianola that if Mrs. Hossack did not murder her husband she knows who did.

Des Moines Daily News, December 3, 1900–April 19, 1901

MURDER BALLADS

As far back as the Middle Ages, the sung or recited murder ballad served to disseminate news about sensational crimes to a largely illiterate populace. By Shakespeare's time, unusually ghastly slayings were quickly translated into broadside, page-long sheets of doggerel that sold for a pittance—the forerunners of modern tabloid newspapers.

Imported to America, the traditional murder ballad, both in its sung and printed forms, flourished well into the 20th century. Many of these "bloody versicles" (as the great Scottish crime historian William Roughead called them) described killings of strictly local interest. The popular ballad "Poor Naomi," for example, is based on the 1807 murder of one Naomi Wise by her lover, John Lewis, in Randolph County, North Carolina. Archival evidence indicates that the real-life Naomi was a young woman who bore three children by three different men before meeting her untimely end. Through a process typical of folk narratives, the untidy facts of the case were assimilated to the sentimental plot pattern that scholars call the "murdered-girl" formula: a tear-jerking tale of a trusting young woman's death at the hands of her cold-hearted seducer.

Though its origins remain a matter of debate, evidence suggests that "Stackalee" sprang from an equally obscure crime. According to scholar Cecil Brown, this famous American murder ballad—a favorite of bluesmen and folksingers who have recorded countless versions, often under the title "Stagolee"—was inspired by the slaying of one William Lyons, shot dead in a St. Louis tavern on Christmas night 1895 by a local pimp named Lee Shelton (aka "Stack Lee") after the two men got into an altercation involving Shelton's milk-white Stetson hat.

By contrast, "The Murder at Fall River" is a singsong synopsis of one of the most notorious homicides in American history, the savage slaying of Andrew and Abby Borden in Fall River, Massachusetts, on April 4, 1892, a crime attributed to Abby's 32-year-old spinster stepdaughter Lizzie, who, despite her acquittal at trial, has entered into popular mythology as a legendary ax-killer. Unlike the anonymous creators of most murder ballads, the author, Alexander B. Beard, not only adorned his broadside with a pen-and-ink portrait of himself but included his home address in West Manchester, New Hampshire.

Though he never attained the mythic status of Lizzie Borden, Chester Gillette achieved perhaps an even greater distinction, supplying the raw material for one of the masterpieces of 20th-century American fiction. During a trip to an Adirondacks resort in July 1906, Gillette took his pregnant girlfriend, Grace Brown, out in a rowboat which mysteriously overturned. Brown's body was found the next day at the bottom of the lake. His trial for murder became an international sensation and the basis for Theodore Dreiser's 1925 classic, *An American Tragedy*. Gillette, who was electrocuted in March 1908, went to his death asserting his innocence and, as the "The Murder of Grace Brown" suggests, the ultimate truth will always be shrouded in uncertainty.

A different sort of mystery surrounds Belle Gunness, Indiana's infamous "Lady Bluebeard" and one of the few American serial killers of either gender to be immortalized in a murder ballad, although this anonymous production is admittedly more humorous than the starker products of the early folk tradition. After dispatching her first husband with strychnine and collecting on his life insurance policy, the Norwegian-born Gunness used the proceeds to purchase a farm in LaPorte. She promptly remarried but was soon widowed again when her new husband was killed, supposedly by accident, leaving her with another hefty insurance payment. Over the next six years, a string of well-to-do bachelors were lured to her home by matrimonial ads placed in various midwestern newspapers and then vanished without a trace. After a mysterious fire destroyed her farmhouse in 1908 searchers found a dozen butchered male corpses buried around the property, along with the charred remains of Belle's three youngest children and a decapitated female who may or may not have been Gunness herself. For years rumors persisted that she had faked her own death and was still alive and well and engaged in her "favorite occupation," the "butchering of men."

Another ballad with a readily identifiable author is "Trail's End," composed by one of its self-mythologizing subjects, Bonnie Parker, the distaff half of the notorious outlaw couple Bonnie and Clyde. Between 1932 and 1934, Parker and her sociopathic lover Clyde Chestnut Barrow, along with several cohorts, conducted a violent interstate crime spree of bank robbery, burglary, car theft, and murder. Romanticized as Robin Hood–style bandits, the two were shot to death in an ambush set by

Texas Rangers. Their legend would be revived by Arthur Penn's 1967 film *Bonnie and Clyde*.

Poor Naomi

Come all good people, I'd have you draw near,
A sorrowful story you quickly shall hear;
A story I'll tell you about N'omi Wise,
How she was deluded by Lewis's lies.

He promised to marry and use me quite well;
But conduct contrary I sadly must tell,
He promised to meet me at Adams's spring;
He promised me marriage and many fine things.

Still nothing he gave, but yet flattered the case.
He says we'll be married and have no disgrace,
Come get up behind me, we'll go up to town,
And there we'll be married, in union be bound.

I got up behind him and straightway did go
To the banks of Deep river where the water did flow;
He says now Naomi, I'll tell you my mind,
Intend here to drown you and leave you behind.

O pity your infant and spare me my life;
Let me go rejected and be not your wife;
No pity, no pity, this monster did cry;
In Deep river's bottom your body shall lie.

The wretch then did choke her, as we understand,
And threw her in the river below the milldam;
Be it murder or treason, O! what a great crime,
To drown poor Naomi and leave her behind.

Naomi was missing they all did well know,
And hunting for her to the river did go;
And there found her floating on the water so deep,
Which caused all the people to sigh and to weep.

The neighbors were sent for to see the great sight,
While she lay floating all that long night;
So early next morning the inquest was held;
The jury correctly the murder did tell.

Stackalee

Come all you sporty fellows,
And listen unto me,
I will tell to you the awful tale
Of that bad man Stackalee,
     That bad, that bad man Stackalee.

The night was dark and stormy,
And the rain came pouring down;
There was nary a police
In that part of town.
     That bad, that bad man Stackalee.

It was on this dark and
Cold stormy night
That Billy Lyons and Stackalee
They had that awful fight.
     That bad, that bad man Stackalee.

Billy Lyons on the sidewalk
Dropped his razor from his hand;
In front of him a-shootin'
Old Stackalee did stand,
     That bad, that bad man Stackalee.

"O Stackalee, O Stackalee,
Please spare my life,
For I have got two babies
And a darling little wife."
    That bad, that bad man Stackalee.

"I care not for your babies
Nor your darling little wife;
You dun ruint my Stetson hat,
And I am bound to have your life."
    That bad, that bad man Stackalee.

Then he leaned down right close
And put that gun agin Billy's breast,
And fired two shots so close to him
They sot fire to his vest,
    That bad, that bad man Stackalee.

Down Walker Street
Old Stackalee did run,
Holding in his right hand
That smoking forty-one,
    That bad, that bad man Stackalee.

He run into Ben Scott's saloon
And before the bar did stand,
Saying, "Take my pistol, bar boy,
I dun killed another man."
    That bad, that bad man Stackalee.

Ben Scott sent for the police
And they came on the run;
The bar boy up and told them
What old Stackalee dun done,
    That bad, that bad man Stackalee.

Says a police to the Sergeant,
"Now what do you think of that!
Old Stackalee shot Billy Lyons
About a damned old hat,
That bad, that bad man Stackalee."

Says the Captain to the police,
"Just keep still as any mouse,
And we will sure catch old Stackalee
At his woman's house,
That bad, that bad man Stackalee."

Two police in the alley
Hiding behind a tree;
Two more out in the front yard
For to catch old Stackalee,
That bad, that bad man Stackalee.

A man run up the alley,
Splashing through the mud;
He run right up against that tree
Where them two police stood—
That bad, that bad man Stackalee.

"Your name is Henry Wells,
But they call you Stackalee;
You are my prisoner;
Come and go with me."
That bad, that bad man Stackalee.

"My name's not Stackalee,
Nor is it Henry Wells;
I am not your prisoner
You go get someone else."
That bad, that bad man Stackalee.

They put the handcuffs on him
And took him to the jail,
And there they put him in a cell
And wouldn't take no bail,
    That bad, that bad man Stackalee.

Mrs. Stackalee,
When she heard the awful news,
Was sitting in the bedroom
A-taking off her shoes.
    That bad, that bad man Stackalee.

She rushed down to the jailhouse
And fell upon her knees,
"I'll give ten thousand dollars
Just to get the jailor's keys."
    That bad, that bad man Stackalee.

Next morning in the jailhouse,
Old Stackalee in bed,
A turnkey came and told him
That Billy Lyons was dead.
    That bad, that bad man Stackalee.

Then they took him into court
To have him make his plea,
The judge says, "Are you guilty?"
"I is," says Stackalee,
    That bad, that bad man Stackalee.

"I cannot sleep,
Neither can I eat,
Since I shot poor Billy Lyons
Down in Walker Street."
    That bad, that bad man Stackalee.

The judge put on the black cap,
His voice was stern and cold;
"I sentences you to be hanged—
The Lord have mercy on your soul."
    That bad, that bad man Stackalee.

Now all you sporty fellows
That have listened to my tale,
Do not shoot another man
Or they'll hang you in the jail,
    Like they did that bad man Stackalee.

The Murder of Grace Brown

The dream of the happy is finished,
The scores are brought in at last.
A jury has brought in its verdict,
The sentence on Gillette is passed.

Two mothers are weeping and praying;
One praying that justice be done;
The other is asking for mercy,
Asking God to save her dear son.

All eyes are turned on the drama,
A-watching the press night and day,
A-reading the sweet pleading letters,
Wondering what Gillette would say.

He is now in State's Auburn dark prison,
Where he soon will give up his young life,
Which might have been filled with sweet sunshine
Had he taken Grace Brown for his wife.

But Cupid was too strong for Gillette,
It was playing too strong with his heart,
For the one that loved him so dearly,
Yet from her he wanted to part.

'Twas on a hot sultry day in the summer,
When the flowers were all aglow,
They started out on their vacation,
For the lakes and the mountains to roam.

Did she think as she gathered those flowers
That grew on the shores of the lake,
That the hand that plucked those sweet lilies
Her own sweet life they would take?

They were seen on the clear crystal waters
Of the beautiful Big Moose lake,
And nobody thought he'd be guilty,
Of the life of that poor girl to take.

It happened along in the evening,
Just at the close of the day,
With the one that had loved him so dearly
They drifted along on South Bay.

They were out of the view of the people,
Where no one could hear her last call.
And nobody knows how it happened,
But Gillette and God knows it all.

Belle Gunness

Belle Gunness was a lady fair,
In Indiana State.
She weighed about three hundred pounds,
And that is quite some weight.

That she was stronger than a man
Her neighbors all did own;
She butchered hogs right easily,
And did it all alone.

But hogs were just a side line,
She indulged in now and then;
Her favorite occupation
Was a-butchering of men.

To keep her cleaver busy
Belle would run an ad,
And men would come a-scurrying
With all the cash they had.

Now some say Belle killed only ten,
And some say forty-two;
It was hard to tell exactly,
But there were quite a few.

The bones were dug up in her yard,
Some parts never came to light,
And Belle, herself, could not be found
To set the tally right.

And where Belle is now no one knows,
But my advice is fair:
If a widow advertises
For a man with cash, beware!

The Murder at Fall River

The crimes we read of every day
  Cause many hearts to shiver;
But few surpass in magnitude
  The murder at Fall River.

Now Andrew Borden was a man
   Of wealth and great renown.
Quite unexpectedly did fall
   The blow that struck him down.

Upon the morn of August fourth,
   In eighteen ninety two
The neighbors heard three piercing screams
   That thrilled them through and through.

They hastened to the Borden home,
   Oh! what did they find there?
Cries of affright and deep alarm
   Broke on the morning air.

The sight they saw on entering in
   Filled each with wild dismay.
There weltering in his own life blood,
   Poor Mr. Borden lay.

His head was by a hatchet hacked
   Which took away his life,
And in her room in the same plight
   They also found his wife.

Investigations soon began
   To probe that awful crime.
It still remains a mystery
   Up to the present time.

Suspicion fell on different ones
   Amidst excitement wild;
Till they arrested Lizzie B.
   The victims' youngest child.

They placed her in the prison walls
   To let the court decide
If she was guilty of that act
   The crime of parricide.

No evidence could her convict
   The jury did agree
That it was all by far too weak
   So Lizzie was set free.

Now I have briefly told this tale
   Some points I have left out;
Up to this day in many minds
   The matter is in doubt.

This much I'll say to one and all
   Let's pray with all our might;
Whoever did that awful deed
   That God will bring to light.

Trail's End

You've read the story of Jesse James,
Of how he lived and died;
If you still are in need of something to read,
Here's the story of Bonnie and Clyde.

Now Bonnie and Clyde are the Barrow gang,
I'm sure you all have read
How they rob and steal and how those who squeal
Are usually found dying or dead.

There are lots of untruths to their write-ups,
They are not so merciless as that;
And they fight because they hate all the laws,
The stool pigeons, spotters and rats.

They class them as cold-blooded killers,
They say they are heartless and mean;
But I say this with pride that I once knew Clyde
When he was honest and upright and clean.

But the law pestered them, fooled around
And kept locking him up in a cell;
Till he said to me, 'I will never be free,
So I'll meet a few of them in hell.'

This road was so dimly lighted,
There was no highway signs for to guide,
But they made up their minds if the roads were all blind,
They wouldn't give up till they died.

The road it gets dimmer and dimmer,
Sometimes you can hardly see;
Still it's fight, man to man, and do all that you can,
For they know they can never be free.

If they try to act like citizens,
And rent them a nice little flat,
About a third of the night they're invited to fight
By a sub-machine gun's rat-a-tat.

If a policeman is killed down in Dallas,
And they have no clues for a guide,
If they can't find a friend they just wipe the slate clean
And hang it on Bonnie and Clyde.

Two crimes have been done in America,
Not accredited to the Barrow mob,
For they had no hand in the kidnapping demand
Or the Kansas City depot job.

A newsboy once said to his buddy,
'I wish that old Clyde would get jumped;
In this awful hard times we might make a few dimes,
If five or six outlaws got bumped.'

The police haven't got the report yet,
Clyde sent out a wireless today,
Saying, 'We have a peace flag of white we stretch out at night,
We have joined the NRA.'

They don't think they are too tough and desperate,
They know that the law always wins;
They've been shot at before, but they do not ignore
That death is the wages of sin.

From heartbreaks some people have suffered,
From weariness some people have died,
But take it all in all, our troubles are small,
Till we get like Bonnie and Clyde.

Some day they will go down together,
And they will bury them side by side.
For a few it means grief, for the law it's relief,
But it's death to Bonnie and Clyde.

THOMAS S. DUKE

In much the same way that serial killers obsess the contemporary imagination, Gilded Age America was haunted by the specter of the poisoner. Arsenic-wielding murderers plied their insidious trade in countless sensational novels and detective stories, while the yellow press convinced the public that the country was in the midst of a "poison epidemic." The number of such crimes was in fact statistically negligible, amounting to less than one percent of all recorded homicides committed in late-19th-century America. In light of this disparity between fact and fantasy, it may be that in an unregulated era when everything from medicine to milk to canned meat posed an active danger to consumers, the cultural fixation on the poisoner stemmed from the public's deep-seated anxiety about the substances it was ingesting.

Thanks largely to the sensationalizing efforts of William Randolph Hearst, the Cordelia Botkin case became one of the most widely publicized crimes of the 1890s. The following account is taken from *Celebrated Criminal Cases of America* by San Francisco police captain Thomas S. Duke (1871–1919). A collection of brief, straightforward narratives, Duke's book was a particular favorite of Dashiell Hammett, who mentions it in his two most famous novels. Describing Sam Spade's home in the second chapter of *The Maltese Falcon*, Hammett refers to "Duke's *Celebrated Criminal Cases of America*—face down on the table" beside the hero's bed. Later in the novel, while waiting in Spade's apartment, the "fat man," Casper Gutman, "smoked a cigar and read *Celebrated Criminal Cases of America*, now and then chuckling over or commenting on the parts of its contents that amused him." Duke's anthology makes an even more prominent appearance in *The Thin Man*, where an entire entry on the Colorado "man-eater" Alfred G. Packer is reprinted verbatim.

Mrs. Cordelia Botkin, Murderess

On February 12, 1891, John P. Dunning, who became famous as a war correspondent, married Miss Mary Pennington, daughter of ex-Congressman John Pennington, in Dover, Delaware, and the couple came to San Francisco to reside.

The next year a little daughter was born. The family then moved to 2529 California street, and while living at this address, Dunning took a stroll in Golden Gate Park one afternoon and flirted with a woman sitting on a bench. They entered into a conversation, during which the woman said her name was "Curtis," and that her husband was in England. After they became more familiar the woman admitted that she was the wife of Welcome A. Botkin, whom she married in Kansas City on September 26, 1872, and that she had a grown son named Beverly. Her maiden name was Cordelia Brown, and the town of Brownsville, Neb., was named after her father. Botkin was for many years connected with the Missouri Valley Bank in Kansas City, but lived in Stockton, Cal., with his son, Beverly, at the time his wife met Dunning. While his wife remained in San Francisco Dunning met Mrs. Botkin clandestinely, but Mrs. Dunning took her baby to her father's home in Dover, Delaware, and thereafter her husband and Mrs. Botkin were constant companions at the races and cafes.

Mrs. Botkin moved to 927 Geary street and Dunning took a room in the same building. In the course of conversation he told Mrs. Botkin that his wife was passionately fond of candy and that she had a very dear friend in San Francisco named Mrs. Corbaley.

On March 8, 1898, Dunning accepted a position as war correspondent with the Associated Press, which made it necessary for him to depart immediately for Porto Rico. When he told Mrs. Botkin his plans, she pleaded with him to remain with her. He turned a deaf ear to her pleadings and told her bluntly that he would never return to San Francisco. She accompanied him across the bay and wept bitterly when they parted.

On August 9, 1898, a small package arrived in Dover, Delaware, addressed to Mrs. John P. Dunning. That package was placed in the mail box belonging to her father, and was called for by Mr. Pennington's little grandson and taken home.

The family consisted of Mr. and Mrs. Pennington, their two

daughters, Mrs. Dunning and Mrs. Joshua Deane; their son-in-law, Mr. Deane, and the two little children of Mr. and Mrs. Deane.

After supper the family repaired to the veranda, and Mrs. Dunning opened the package, which proved to be a fancy candy box containing a handkerchief, chocolate creams and a small slip of paper on which were the following words:

"With love to yourself and baby.—Mrs. C."

Mrs. Dunning could not imagine who had sent the package, but being a noble woman, with friends galore, she did not suspect that she had an enemy in the world, and therefore her suspicion was not aroused.

Mrs. Dunning and Mrs. Deane and the latter's two children partook of the candy, as did also two young ladies, Miss Millington and Miss Bateman, who chanced to pass the Pennington residence while the family were seated on the veranda. During that night all who partook of the candy were taken with retching pains in the stomach and vomited freely.

All recovered with the exception of Mrs. Dunning, who died on August 12, and Mrs. Deane, who died on August 11. Autopsies disclosed the fact that these ladies died from arsenic poisoning.

Mr. Pennington examined the handwriting on the box and on the slip of paper and discovered that it corresponded with the handwriting of an unknown person who had written an anonymous communication from San Francisco to Mrs. Dunning many months previously, in which it was alleged that Mr. Dunning was on intimate terms with a woman in San Francisco. Dr. Wood, a chemist, examined the candy which had not been eaten, and discovered a large amount of arsenic present.

John P. Dunning was advised by telegraph of what had transpired and he proceeded at once to Dover. He immediately recognized the handwriting as that of Mrs. Botkin and recalled his remark to her regarding his wife's fondness for candy, and also that his wife had a friend in San Francisco named Mrs. Corbaley, which accounted for the initial "C." signed to the note.

Detective B. J. McVey was sent to San Francisco with the candy, handkerchief, candy box and the note found in the box. Chief of Police I. W. Lees took charge of the case. Mrs. Botkin was located in Stockton, Cal., where she was living with her husband and son. Detective Ed. Gibson brought her to San Francisco, and in a few days an overwhelming amount of circumstantial evidence was piled up against her.

She was positively identified by Miss Sylvia Heney and Miss Kittie Dittmer as the woman who, on July 31, bought candy in the candy store of George Haas under the Phelan block on Market street. Miss Heney furthermore swore that this woman requested that the candy be placed in a fancy box which did not have the firm's name on it, and also instructed that the box be not filled completely as she had another article to place in the box.

John P. Dunning produced love letters written to him by Mrs. Botkin, and handwriting expert Theodore Kytka testified to what was obvious to all, namely, that the person who wrote the love letters wrote the address on the candy box and the note therein.

Mrs. Botkin even neglected to remove the store tag from the handkerchief which she purchased in the "City of Paris" store from Mrs. Grace Harris, who even recalled the conversation she held with Mrs. Botkin. When asked why she recalled this so clearly, she stated that Mrs. Botkin's resemblance to her dead mother startled her. She subsequently produced a photograph of her mother to show the striking resemblance.

Frank Grey, a druggist employed at the "Owl" drug store, positively identified Mrs. Botkin as the woman who had purchased two ounces of arsenic for the alleged purpose of bleaching a straw hat, and insisted upon getting this drug even when the druggist informed her that there were other preparations better adapted for the purpose.

On August 4 the package of candy was mailed at the Ferry Post-office and was particularly noticed by a postal clerk named John

Dunnigan because the address, "Mrs. John Dunning," reminded him of his own name. On this same day Mrs. Botkin left San Francisco for St. Helena.

Mrs. Almura Ruoff related a conversation she had with Mrs. Botkin in Stockton on July 27, 1898, in which the latter made inquiries as to the effect of different poisons on the human system, and asked if it was necessary to sign one's name when sending a registered package through the mail.

After Mrs. Botkin left the Hotel Victoria at Hyde and California streets, where she had been stopping some months, W. P. Rossello, a porter, and W. W. Barnes, a clerk, found a torn piece of a gilded seal, similar to those pasted on candy boxes, on the floor of room 26, which Mrs. Botkin vacated. It was proved that the seal came from Haas' store and the wrapping on the candy box clearly showed where it had been removed.

Extradition papers were forwarded from Delaware as it was planned to take her there for trial, but her attorney, George Knight, attempted to procure her release on the grounds that the evidence was insufficient, and furthermore, that the jurisdiction for the trial was in California and not Delaware.

Superior Judges Cook, Borden, Wallace, Troutt and Seawell, sitting *en banc*, rendered a decision on October 23 to the effect that the jurisdiction for the trial was in California, as Mrs. Botkin's flight from Delaware was not actual but constructive. This decision was upheld by the Supreme Court.

The evidence was presented to the Grand Jury and on October 28, 1898, Mrs. Botkin was indicted. On December 9, 1898, the trial for the murder of Mrs. Dunning began.

On December 19, while testifying in the case, John P. Dunning refused to mention the names of other women he had been intimate with, and he was adjudged guilty of contempt and sent to jail, where he remained for several days until the question was withdrawn.

On December 30, 1898, Mrs. Botkin was found guilty and on February 4, 1899, she was sentenced to life imprisonment.

On March 9 Mrs. Botkin's husband, Welcome A. Botkin, sued her for a divorce on the grounds that she had been convicted of a felony.

Before Mrs. Botkin could be sent to State prison, a decision was rendered by the State Supreme Court in the case of "Hoff," who murdered Mrs. Clute on Guerrero street, wherein it was decided that the trial Judge erred when, in his charge to the jury, he stated that "circumstantial evidence has the advantage over direct evidence, because it is not likely to be fabricated." It was held that by so doing he expressed to the jury his opinion upon the force and effect of the testimony and intimated his views of its sufficiency. As the same form of charge was delivered in the Botkin and numerous other cases, she experienced no difficulty in obtaining a new trial.

This necessitated the bringing of all the Delaware witnesses back to San Francisco. The second trial also resulted in a verdict of guilty and on August 2, 1904, she was again sentenced to life imprisonment, which judgment was affirmed by the State Supreme Court on October 29, 1908.

After the conviction of Mrs. Botkin she was confined in the Branch County jail, pending the decision from the higher court.

About this time Superior Judge Cook lost his wife and each Sunday he visited her grave, riding out on a car which passed the jail. On one Sunday he was astonished at seeing Cordelia Botkin in the same car and apparently unguarded. The murderess signaled the car to stop at the county jail and she proceeded in the direction of that institution, but was lost to the Judge's view, as he remained on the car.

The next day he instituted an investigation. It was charged that the voluptuous woman was on intimate terms with one or more of the guards, which accounted for the fact that she was surrounded with every comfort at the jail. It was also charged that she was probably accompanied on the pleasure trip by a friendly guard who was on another part of the car.

Judge Cook failed to find any one connected with the jail who would admit that the prisoner had been away from the building on Sunday, and the woman attempted to take advantage of the situation by claiming that the person who resembled her so much that the trial judge was mistaken, was probably the person who purchased the arsenic, candy and handkerchief, but the claim was not seriously considered.

After the great earthquake and fire the branch county jail, where Mrs. Botkin was confined, became crowded because of the destruction of the main jail, and as a result this woman lost the comfortable quarters she had enjoyed for years.

Although the Supreme Court had not yet reached a decision in her case, she made application to be transferred to San Quentin State Prison, and the request was complied with on May 16, 1906.

After her conviction her erstwhile lover, her mother, sister, son, and also her former husband, died within a short time.

The prisoner became a victim of nervous prostration and was soon a physical wreck. During the latter part of 1909 she began to suffer from melancholy. In February, 1910, she applied for parole because of her health, but it was decided that she was not eligible.

On March 7, 1910, she became unconscious and died. The death certificate shows that she died from "softening of the brain, due to melancholy."

She was 56 years old at the time of her death.

Celebrated Criminal Cases of America, 1910

EDMUND PEARSON

Among connoisseurs of American true-crime writing, Edmund Pearson (1880–1937) is esteemed as the dean of the genre, our national counterpart to the great Scottish crime historian William Roughead, with whom Pearson conducted extensive correspondence on "matters criminous." A librarian by training and profession, the Harvard-educated Pearson published a number of bibliographic volumes before turning his scholarly attentions to crime. His first and best-known book, *Studies in Murder* (1924), contained his now-classic essay on the Lizzie Borden affair, a case that would command his interest for the rest of his life. The book's commercial and critical success earned Pearson widespread praise as a "master storyteller of true stories of murder" (*The New York Times Book Review*) and an "artful social historian" (*Time*).

Four more crime books followed, collecting essays originally published in *The New Yorker*, *Vanity Fair*, and other national magazines: *Murder at Smutty Nose* (1926), *Five Murders* (1928), *Instigation of the Devil* (1930), and *More Studies in Murder* (1936). Though long out-of-print and little known to the general public, they are highly prized by true-crime devotees for their urbane style, dry wit, and wide-ranging erudition.

Hell Benders
or
The Story of a Wayside Tavern

The wholesale murderer is often the grimmest and most disagreeable character in all the list. He has, however, the power to provoke myth and legend; to fire the imagination; and to set the human mind at work constructing tales of giants and goblins. Rather prosaic persons become ecstatic in thinking about him; soon they have him enlarged to the proportions of a monster of heroic size; a werewolf; something with which to scare generations of children.

This was perfectly illustrated in Mr. C. K. Munro's play, "At Mrs. Beam's." Two or three elderly gossips sit in a London boarding house, chilling their blood with talk about Landru, the French "Bluebeard," then supposed to be at large in Paris. It pleases them to fancy that he may have escaped and have come into their very midst, in the person of a mysterious boarder—who happens to have a Paris label on his luggage. Their conversation is something like this:

"They say that he has killed *dozens* and *dozens* of women!"

"And *eaten* them!"

"No, no; I hardly believe that; I doubt that."

"I understand that he *always* eats them."

"Well, at all events, he has killed *hundreds* of women!"

"No, my dear. Let us be just. We *must* agree to be just. Not hundreds. *Thirty-nine.* That is a better figure. Yes; we can agree, I think, on thirty-nine."

By what reasoning this lady has arrived at the figure thirty-nine, she does not say. She has, as a matter of fact, no more basis for her opinion than has the lady who prefers to deal in hundreds; but she makes her assertion with as much quiet assurance as if she had been in direct communication with the Ministry of Justice.

The wholesale murderer is of two kinds: the wandering and the stationary. Of the wanderers, Landru is the famous example of our own time; so, in a lesser degree, is the Englishman, G. J. Smith, of the "brides in the bath" case. He is far more interesting than the Frenchman, to my mind, since he invented a new way to commit murder. There is also H. H. Holmes, the American. Still living (until recently, at all events), in San Quentin prison, California, is one of the strangest and least-known of them all: J. P. Watson,* a mild-looking little man, who was believed by some persons to have married twenty-one women

---

*His great predecessor, Mr. Holmes, perished, at the hands of the law, in 1896. The Californian came too late to remark: "Really, my dear Holmes!"

within a space of three years, and to have slain nine of them. These figures, especially the marriages, are open to question; but the facts seem to have been bizarre enough.

Of the wholesale murderers who remain stationary and carry on their trade at home, the Edinburgh firm of Burke and Hare will suggest itself. In the neighbourhood of Laporte, Indiana, the memory will not soon perish of Mrs. Gunness and her establishment, which the newspapers invariably called the "murder farm." The lonely farm, or better still the wayside tavern, where the solitary traveller comes but never departs—this has been a favourite subject for stories, true or fictitious, ever since stories have been told. In how many secluded places in Europe must there have existed these inns of evil repute; some of them furnished with beds which slowly sank into the cellar, where the inn keeper and his assistants, armed with "stout" cudgels, awaited the sleeping traveller. Others relied upon the bottle of drugged wine, and still others upon the midnight visit to the bedside of the hapless stranger, with the gleaming dagger, or other familiar properties. It is really a part of the folklore of every nation.

Except America. Attempts have been made to domesticate it here, but we have usually preferred brisker and less gloomy methods of assassination. Frequently they have been emigrants from the older countries who have tried to inaugurate this business on our soil; Mrs. Gunness originated, I think, in Norway, while the remarkable family whose history is the subject of this chapter, seem to have brought the idea with them from one of the other countries of northern Europe. This is a pleasant subject for patriotic reflection, and in this field rather a rare one, for when we discuss the virtuous superiority of Americans over the other nations of the earth, we are wise if we slide discreetly over those branches of sin which include murder and all forms of the taking of human life.

Late in the year 1870, there appeared in Labette County, Kansas, a family of four persons: John Bender and his wife; their son, or reputed son, John, and his sister, Kate. Almost everything about them is in dispute, and it is often said that the younger man was really John Geb-hardt, the son of Mrs. Bender by a former husband. It is also asserted that Kate Bender was not the sister, but the mistress of the younger man. Many imaginary but no authentic portraits of the quartette are in existence, and these differ as widely as do the written descriptions of them. One portrait of old Bender shows him as a stolid peasant, not remarkable in any way; another makes him a shaggy-looking monster from a nightmare. The young John is depicted as a commonplace-looking man, under thirty; but, elsewhere, it is said that his face "had the fierce malice of the hyena." Concerning the appearance of Kate Bender, the writers have done their best, with the result that you may read that she was "a large, masculine, red-faced woman"; that she was a rather good-looking red-haired girl; or that she was a siren of such extraordinary charms that one has to call on every famous beauty, from Cleopatra to Mrs. Langtry, for suitable comparisons. She was the most interesting of the family; her father was a poor second; while the elder Mrs. Bender and young John were tied for third place.

From some official descriptions of them, issued by Governor Osborn of Kansas at a time when he was dealing in facts, rather than impressionism, these details are selected: John Bender was about sixty years old, and of medium height. He was a German, and spoke little English. He was dark, spare, and wore no beard. His wife was ten years younger; heavy in frame; had blue eyes and brown hair. There was nothing distinctive about John Bender, Jr.; he was twenty-seven, of slight build, wore a light brown moustache, and spoke English with German pronunciation. Kate was "about twenty-four years of age, dark hair and eyes, good-looking, well formed, rather bold in appear-ance, fluent talker, speaks English with very little German accent."

Everybody agrees on two matters: old Bender was a disagreeable, surly fellow; and Kate was notably attractive to the men of that region, who found her pleasant, vivacious, and a desirable partner at the occa-sional country dance. She danced well, was a good horsewoman, and went to Sunday school and to "meetin's" in the schoolhouse. For a few weeks, in 1871, she condescended to act as waitress in the hotel at

Cherryvale. There was about her, however, a more marked peculiarity: she believed in spiritualism, lectured on the subject, and claimed to be a medium, with the power to call up spirits of the dead. Her lectures, in the various towns of the county, caused a mild sensation. This was the decade when lecturing women aroused great curiosity and antagonism; often they were accused, not only of the offence of seeking to vote, but also, like the Claflins, of advocating various degrees of laxity of morals. How much these lecturers actually risked by putting themselves too far in advance of their time, and how far the reports about them were the exaggerations of horrified men, determined to put down the pestiferous creatures, by foul means or fair, it is always hard to discover. The stories about Kate Bender's lectures soon pass over, I think, into legend as fantastic as the accompanying picture. The alleged fragment of one of her manuscripts, found in the house, in which she gravely advocates one or two crimes, including murder, may safely be attributed to some imaginative journalist.

A curious light is thrown upon Kate Bender's character by an advertisement which she seems to have had published in some of the newspapers in neighbouring towns, about a year before she became nationally famous. This was it:

> Professor Miss Kate Bender can heal disease, cure blindness, fits and deafness. Residence, 14 miles east of Independence, on the road to Osage Mission. June 18, 1872.

Nothing at all is really known about the antecedents of the Benders. The older man described himself to a neighbour, one of the township trustees, as "a Hollander, who had lived in Germany, near the French line, where he had been a baker." The younger man said that he had been born in the United States. A neighbour, by the way, at this date, and in this part of Kansas, might mean a man whose house was not more than ten miles distant.

As in the contemporary accounts of the murder of Captain White in Salem, the aspect of Essex County, Massachusetts, becomes wildly romantic, with caves, fastnesses, and gloomy forest glades, so the section of Kansas over which the Benders cast their spell has been described as one of dismal swamps, rugged cliffs, and other awe-inspiring bits of scenery. It was, in fact, cheerful and pleasant country: high, rolling prairie. For a short time, the Benders lived on the claim of a German named Rudolph Brockmann—a disastrous acquaintance-ship for this harmless citizen. At last, however, after one move, they built a frame house on the main road from Parsons to Cherryvale, about seven miles northeast of the latter town. This road was used by travellers from Fort Scott and the Osage Mission to the town of Inde-pendence, and southwest to the Indian Territory, now Oklahoma.

Travellers were mounted as a rule, or driving a team—a pair of horses with a wagon or carriage. Men often went armed; the traditions of frontier days were not past, although there was seldom any use for weapons. The inhabitants were, ordinarily, peaceable, kindly folk; the horror which was aroused by subsequent events shows how shocking to them were lawlessness and bloodshed. Nevertheless, there were, still living, men of the pioneer times, and men who had been through both the wars—the lesser war and the great Civil War—which had racked Kansas. These men knew how to handle a horse and a rifle, and in the face of certain crimes did not always care to wait for the slow proce-dure of courts, nor for the aid of the public executioner.

The Bender family moved into their new house in the spring of 1871. It was built in a small hollow at the end of a long vale in the prairie. Near by was a stream, Drum Creek, bordered with thickets of wild plum and of cottonwood trees. The house seems to have had but two rooms, divided by a heavy curtain. The Benders professed to offer entertainment for man and beast: there was a small stock of tinned food and other supplies for sale in the front room; somewhere or other in the house sleeping space was found for travellers who cared to stay all night; while their horses could be sheltered in a stable in the rear. Back of the stable and house were a garden and orchard.

For a year and a half, the Benders seem to have lived the usual life of a family in that region, and to have attracted no especial notice, favour-able or otherwise. Many of their neighbours, men and women who were living recently, remember meeting and talking with them. The two younger members of the family were often absent from their wayside tavern for days at a time; John Bender, Jr., on business unexplained, and Professor Miss Kate on her lecturing tours in Parsons, Oswego, Labette, or Chetopa, holding séances for the purpose of calling spirits from the grave; or perhaps exercising her remarkable curative powers upon persons afflicted with blindness, fits, or deafness. It is believed, however, that her most remarkable and permanent cures were effected, not during these visits, but upon patients who came for office consultation and treatment at her residence on the road to the Osage Mission.

It is impossible to determine exactly when it began to be rumoured in the country round about that there was something queer in the Bender ménage. Nearly everything about them and their performances depends upon statements never tested in a court of law; never sifted by cross-examination. Reputable persons can be found making assertions of an exactly opposite nature, and with perfect sincerity. With many people, no form of belief is held so tenaciously as that founded upon nothing more certain than local tradition and impressions acquired in childhood. They simply *know* that certain things are true because they have always been told that they were true. A number of the early adventures of travellers at the Bender house, and a number of fortunate escapes therefrom, sound much like things remembered—with additions—after the event. It is said, probably with truth, that the Benders did not begin their peculiar operations until the autumn of 1872, and that their entire career in the business which made them famous was during a period of about six months. Whatever they did during the autumn and winter of 1872 to 1873 caused no public outcry or investigation. It was not until the disappearance of Doctor York that any general suspicions were aroused.

Early in March, 1873, Dr. William H. York, who lived at Independence, was visiting his brother, Colonel A. M. York, at Fort Scott. On the ninth of the month, he left his brother, intending to ride to his own home. He was well mounted; had a good saddle; and carried a large sum of money and a fine watch. He spent the first night at Osage Mission, and left there on the morning of March 10th. Some of his friends met him, riding alone, on the road near the Bender house. He told them that he intended to stop for his midday dinner at the Benders'. And that was the last seen of Doctor York.

A considerable time, perhaps as much as two or three weeks, elapsed, and Colonel York was making a determined search for his brother. He traced him to a point on the road a few miles east of the Benders', but could get no farther in his investigations. At Independence he heard rumours of a strange adventure which two other travellers had experienced while dining with the Benders. These men had become convinced that they were about to be attacked; they left the house hurriedly; one of them went to the stable and brought out their carriage, while the other stood with a drawn revolver to cover the retreat. They believed that they were fired at, as they drove away toward the town of Parsons.

Colonel York prevailed upon twelve men from Cherryvale and elsewhere to visit the Bender house with him. They made the call on April 24th and had interviews with all that engaging group. Old Mrs. Bender, it was true, muttered something about a crowd of men disturbing a peaceable family, but the others were affable enough. Young John, who had been sitting by the side of the road with a Bible in his hand, searching the Scriptures, said that he had often been shot at by outlaws near Drum Creek. Doctor York had had dinner with them, Miss Kate had served it; on his departure, he had been foully slain, so the young Mr. Bender believed, by these same audacious bandits. One of the party, believing in spectral aid, asked Professor Miss Kate to consult the spirits, but she replied that there were too many unbelievers present; the spirits would be reluctant to assist. She made an appointment with him for a séance, alone, five days later. The men of the family helped Colonel York and his friends drag Drum Creek and search elsewhere. Altogether, they convinced Colonel York of their desire to aid him and of their ignorance of the fate of his brother. So the Colonel and his followers departed, and came not there again for eleven days.

On May 5th, with a larger number of men, who were still of the opinion that the Benders were somewhat maculate, he returned, to find the neighbours already on the premises. On the day before, May 4th, two brothers named Toles, who lived near by, were passing the Benders' house at eight in the morning. The agonized lowing of a calf attracted them; they found the animal nearly starved in its pen, while its mother was standing outside in as great distress to nourish her child as the calf was to be fed. They turned the two together, and then knocked on the door to see if the folk inside were ill and in need of help. There was no response; they looked in at the windows—the house was empty and in confusion, as if after a hurried departure of the family. This, in fact, had taken place. The Benders left, it is believed, on the night of April 29th, five days after Colonel York's first visit. The house had therefore been abandoned for four or five days.

On Monday, May 5th, when Colonel York and his men arrived, the door had already been broken open and the place was under examination. Aside from the clothing on the floor, household utensils, and "manuscripts" of the lecturer, there was, at first, nothing remarkable to be seen. A trapdoor in the floor of the rear room was opened, and some of the men entered the cellar. This led by a tunnel toward the garden and orchard. On the floor of the cellar were damp spots which seemed to be human blood.

The search had been in progress for some length of time when Colonel York, standing in the rear of the house, and looking toward the orchard, suddenly remarked:

"Boys, I see graves yonder in the orchard!"

They laughed at him, and suggested that he had graves on the brain. Presently others were convinced that there were a number of long, narrow depressions, like graves, in the ground which old Bender had always kept freshly ploughed and harrowed. Soundings were made, with disquieting results, and presently spades were procured and one of the hollows was opened. At a depth of five feet, they discovered the naked body of a man, lying face downward. It was lifted out, and Colonel York's search for his brother was at an end.

Amid great excitement, everybody set to work, and other graves were opened, until the orchard was thoroughly excavated. They found eleven bodies: nine men, a young woman, and a little girl. The skulls of all, except that of the child, had been crushed in one or more places from a blow with some blunt instrument like a sledge hammer. The girl was found lying under the body of her father, and from the absence of any wounds and from other indications, it appeared that she had died by suffocation; had, in fact, been buried alive.

Except for the young woman and one of the men, all the victims were identified, then or later. Three of the men, at least, had been known to be carrying large sums of money. These were a man named McKigzie, and two others, William F. McCrotty and Benjamin M. Brown. The two latter had three thousand dollars between them, so the Benders carried an unknown but considerable amount of loot when they fled. The number of bodies varies in different accounts: to the eleven buried in the orchard are added, by one writer, two or three skeletons afterward discovered in or near Drum Creek and attributed to the work of the Benders. Other authorities set the figure at from seven to ten. The histories of Kansas set the number, conservatively, at seven. The names of the nine in the orchard who were identified are given, however, in more than one published account, so I think that, bearing in mind the counsel of the lady in the play to "be just," we can credit the Bender family with the murders of from ten to twelve persons.

The exact figures did not matter to the men who had carried on the search. When the body was exhumed of Doctor York—a man well liked and respected—and when the pitiful spectacle was revealed of the little girl, evidently put still living into the ground, and buried beneath the dead body of her father, there was an immediate desire for vengeance upon somebody, and the spirit of a lynching mob swept over the group.

Rudolph Brockmann, fellow countryman and neighbour of the Benders, had been helping in the search. He had worked as hard as any of the others; there was no reason to suppose that he did not share their horror at the murders. Nothing has been alleged against his character, but the mere fact told against him that he had talked with old Bender in a foreign language. He was questioned closely as to his knowledge of the crimes, and while the group of excited men stood around him, some one—the usual fool—shouted:

"Get a rope!"

This was done: a noose was put around Brockmann's neck, and he was pulled aloft from a tree branch or whatever was the nearest support. After a moment or two he was let down and given a chance to confess. He protested his innocence—and he probably spoke the truth. He was again hauled up and let down, until he was nearly choked to death. At last the mob were satisfied; the cooler and more reasonable men prevailed upon the others to cease; Brockmann was liberated and allowed to go home.

The process of the murders became apparent from an examination of the arrangement of the house, together with what could be learned from some of the surviving travellers who had taken a meal there. The diner sat on a bench or chair, with his back to the curtain which separated the two apartments. Sometimes he was entertained with pleasant conversation by whichever of the ladies was serving the meal. This was generally the younger one. One or two of the men of the family, attending behind the curtain with a sledge hammer, could await the moment when the guest, taking his ease, leaned back and showed the outline of his head. Or the curtain was perhaps moved cautiously forward to meet him. The first blow, sufficient to stun him, if not to kill, was then delivered through the curtain. After that, the Benders worked rapidly. The body was dragged to the rear room, robbed and stripped. The trapdoor being opened, one of the family cut the victim's throat and tumbled him into the cellar. If this happened by day, all was then secure, until night, when the dead man could be carried to the orchard and buried. Great precautions had been taken to keep the graves from becoming noticeable; these were successful at the time of Colonel York's first visit and nearly successful the second time.

Many stories are told of the part which Professor Miss Kate took, as the meal was served to a traveller. Sometimes she merely charmed him with her good looks, agreeable manners, and light table-talk. If he were docile, and took his chair as she set it, closely snuggled up against the curtain, she became an especially gracious hostess. But if he disliked the arrangement of things, became captious—as we all of us do at times—about the method of seating the guests, she would begin to sulk. Her conversation lost its sparkling qualities, and the dinner was practically a failure, from the point of view of both guest and hostess. One or two suspicious persons had moved to the other side of the table, so as to face the curtain; and two especially nervous gentlemen, who perhaps heard the sound of shuffling feet, and of heavy breathing behind the arras, insisted upon eating their meal standing up—which annoyed the Benders almost to the verge of incivility.

The romantic school, among the Benders' historians, have it that Kate dealt in mesmerism and other psychic methods of allaying suspicion and putting the traveller at his ease. There seems to be little doubt that she conversed with many of them upon spiritualism, and found willing listeners. The eagerness with which these hardy pioneers listened to her revelations upon the subject, suggests the facility with which all kinds of mediums, clairvoyants, crystal gazers, and soothsayers find their clients to-day, not among poets, artists, and the so-called impractical classes, but among "hardheaded" business men.

The Benders had four or five days' start; they vanished into darkness. Vigilance committees, mounted posses of men, soon started in pursuit, but the result of their efforts is a disputed theme in Kansas. Here are some of the beliefs—all of which are stated with much assurance:

First—they got away and were never seen again.

Second—they went by wagon to Chanute, and bought tickets to some point in Texas. Leaving the train, however, at Chetopa, they started on foot through the Indian Nation (Oklahoma). They were overtaken, as they were about to cross the Grand (?) River, and all hanged. This is related by Colonel Triplett; he was present at the search of the Bender house. He discredits it, however, as probably "a mere sensational story."

Various persons, as he points out, were being arrested for months afterward, and taken to Oswego, Kansas, for identification. This would not have happened if the Benders were really dead. At Chanute (then called New Chicago) a pair of horses with a wagon were left hitched to a post, and without food or water for two days, before any one realized that they had been abandoned. This wagon was thought either to have been left by the Benders, or else by confederates, as a false clue to mislead pursuers.

Third—Captain Duke, in compiling his " Celebrated Cases," wrote to the chiefs of police of Cherryvale and Independence, Kansas. The replies are dated 1910. Chief Kramer of Cherryvale wrote that his father-in-law lived on a farm adjoining the Bender place and helped find the bodies. When he was asked what became of the family, he would give a knowing look, and reply that they would never bother any one else. After the Vigilance Committee had gone in pursuit, old man Bender's wagon was found by the roadside riddled with bullets. Chief Kramer adds: "You will have to guess the rest." Chief Van Cleve of Cherryvale wrote that he had lived in that town for forty years, and it was his opinion that the Benders never escaped. Some of the Vigilance Committee were still living, in 1910; they would not talk, but would look wise when the subject was mentioned. They smiled at reports of recent discoveries of the Benders.

Fourth—the Benders were members of a large and well-organized gang of desperadoes and horse thieves, operating on the southern border of Kansas, in the Indian Territory, and in Texas. This accounts for the disappearance of all the horses and wagons which were stolen from their victims. Some of the gang helped the Benders to escape.

Fifth—still another theory is that they went by railway from Thayer to Humboldt, Kansas, a small town on a railroad which ran to Vinita, Indian Territory, and thence to Denison, Texas. They travelled on that train to the south and disappeared for ever. This theory is arrived at by the process of eliminating other possible routes. It is given, apparently as the opinion of the author, in the book by Mr. J. T. James—the most complete and rational work on this subject which I have seen.

There are undoubtedly many other theories. The chief problem is not the route by which they escaped, but the question whether they escaped at all. The posse which started in pursuit divided into four parties; many of these men were veterans of the Civil War; they were skilful, brave, and determined. One party went south toward the Indian Territory: they were seven in number, under command of a former captain in the Union Army. Another party went toward Thayer, Kansas; a third toward Cherryvale and Independence; and a fourth toward Parsons and thence to Oswego. Three of these groups returned in a few days, in the belief that the Benders had escaped. The Captain and his seven men came back from the Indian Territory saying that they had given up the chase. They instantly dropped the subject and would never talk about the Benders again. To some persons, this fact was indication that they had caught and lynched the whole family.

In favour of the theory that they were caught are the character and skill of the men who went in pursuit, the fact that no satisfactory trace of the Benders was ever found again, and the statements of the police chiefs of Cherryvale and Independence. To account for the singular and unnecessary silence about their success, it has been said that when the Benders were captured they were carrying seven thousand dollars. Their captors decided that this was prize money, and after the Benders were "laid under the ground," divided it amongst themselves. To avoid any further discussion about the ownership of this money, they agreed upon complete silence and kept their agreement.

Against the theory of the capture and in favour of the belief that the Benders got away, it may be urged, first, that they had a long start. Second, there was no reason for reticence if anybody did catch the fugitives—lynching the Benders would not have imperilled anybody's popularity. Next, in 1880, the Commissioners of Labette County offered a reward of $500 for proof that they were taken and put to death. The reward was not claimed. Finally, there were found, as late as 1889, a number of reputable citizens, willing to take oath that they recognized two living women as Mrs. Bender and Kate. It is true that they were quite mistaken in this identification, but the fact shows that these persons, who had known the Benders, did not believe that the whole family had been exterminated.

The Benders are, in a sense, deathless. Certainly they are immortals in Kansas, and even elsewhere. Two years ago it was surprising to note that a South African, Mr. William Bolitho*, writing in London, included in his book of essays, "Leviathan," a few pages entitled "Old Man Bender's Orchard." The account is founded on Captain Duke's narrative of the case. But the Benders made their first and only appearance in Court, by proxy, in the years 1889–90. This was at Oswego, Kansas, when, for a while, Kate and old Mrs. Bender were resurrected to the satisfaction of a certain number of people.

About 1886, there was living in McPherson, Kansas, a washerwoman named Sarah Eliza Davis, who had come thither from Michigan. One of her employers was a lady named Mrs. Frances McCann, a dreamer of dreams and a seer of visions. Mrs. McCann, in the dead vast and middle of the night, dreamed of the murder of an old man by an old woman and her daughter. Much perturbed, she laid the matter before the nearest expert, her washerwoman, Mrs. Davis. This lady expounded the dream as follows: the murder was at Windsor, Canada. The murdered man was John W. Sanford, while the murderesses were the mother and elder sister of Mrs. Davis, the gifted washerwoman. It happened when she—Mrs. Davis—was a little girl. Mrs. McCann was the daughter of the murdered man. And, to make it trebly interesting, the wife of the murdered Mr. Sanford afterward married Edward Stokes of New York, the man who shot Jim Fisk.

Mrs. McCann had long been curious about her parentage, which was mysterious. An enthusiastic traveller, she set out for Kentucky, and for the orphan asylum in which she had spent her childhood. There she learned as she had expected—that her name was Sanford. Next to Windsor, Canada, where she verified the murder of old Mr. Sanford. Then back to her home in McPherson, to dog the footsteps and

---

*Author, recently, of "Murder for Profit," an interesting study of wholesale murderers.

penetrate the most secret recesses of the mind of the sinister washer-woman. Mrs. McCann, not less gifted than Professor Miss Kate Bender, practised mesmeric and hypnotic rites upon Mrs. Davis; visited her while sick; played tricks on her with a magnet, and generally bedev-illed her for months. One day, it came over Mrs. McCann, "like a flash," that Mrs. Davis and her mother were really the Bender women.

Now there is only one infallible way to get information, and that is to have it come over you like a flash. Once that happens, you need fear neither powers nor principalities; your knowledge is founded on a rock. She set traps, and one day, when Mrs. Davis's hands were deep in the suds, asked her suddenly how many there were in the Bender fam-ily. Said Mrs. Davis:

"Well, let me see. There was Mother——"

Then she stopped, and throwing up her hands, cried out:

"Now you have my secret! I have told you all."

Not long afterward, Mrs. Davis, with her two little children, moved back to Michigan. Here she was speedily followed by the sleuth hound, Mrs. McCann, bent on bringing the whole detestable gang to justice. She found Mrs. Davis's mother, Mrs. Almira Griffith, living at Niles, Michigan. Mrs. McCann shadowed them by day, and often spent the whole night in outbuildings upon the premises to keep watch upon them, and prevent their escape. Consultations with the local police, who said these women had a bad reputation; correspondence with the authorities in Labette County, Kansas; communications between the Kansas and the Michigan officials; an investigation by an agent; legal formalities and delays; and, in November, 1889, sixteen years after the flight of the Benders, Mrs. Davis and Mrs. Griffith were brought into Court at Oswego, charged with the murder of Doctor York. The only question upon which the Court had to pass was the identification of these women with the Benders. Mrs. Davis was charged with being Kate Bender. A number of the county officials were really convinced that they had the two female Benders in custody.

The State called eleven and the defence called six witnesses. Some of the State witnesses positively asserted that these were Mrs. Bender and Kate; others showed great hesitation about it. One of the witnesses for the State was Mr. Rudolph Brockmann, who must have had unpleasant recollections of the family. His career, since the day he had been half hanged, had been respectable, and his testimony sounds like that of a truthful man. He made a bad witness for the State, as he was fairly certain that these were not his former neighbours. Mrs. Davis and Mrs. Griffith both testified, and disclosed some incidents in careers which were checkered with matrimonial and extramatrimonial adventures and not free from collisions with the law. There must, however, have been some resemblance between these wretched women and the Benders, for after hearing arguments on both sides, the three justices decided that there was sufficient cause to hold them for trial before the higher Court.

They had been defended by Mr. J. T. James, and by a Judge Webb, who would appear to be one of the travelers who left their dinners uneaten and departed in haste from the Bender house at about the time of the murder of Doctor York. These attorneys had great difficulty in getting any help from their clients, as the past which they could disclose was sufficiently dubious to make the ladies very reticent. During the interval after the first hearing, Mr. James secured, in Michigan, such convincing affidavits as to the identity of Mrs. Griffith that the County Attorney abandoned the prosecution against both women and obtained their discharge. The reason set forth in these affidavits why Mrs. Griffith could not have engaged, as Mrs. Bender, in the slaughter of travelers in Labette County, in 1873, was that she was occupied at that time, to the exclusion of everything else, in serving a term in a prison in Detroit, on a charge of manslaughter.

Her daughter, Mrs. Davis, was described as a "colossal liar," a notoriety seeker, with a strange taste for involving her family and herself in false accusations of crime—as if they did not have a sufficient number of real ones to answer. Probably she was determined to amuse her employer, Mrs. McCann, at all costs.

That lady, the dreamer and resolute detective, is easily the most important personage in this epilogue to the Bender story. I wish that I could reproduce her picture here, as well as the fanciful one of Miss Bender; it deserves a place no less. While the hearing went on, and the two women from Michigan sat in the shadow of the rope, Mrs. McCann occupied a seat inside the bar, near the prosecuting attorney. She took careful notes. She was of slight figure, weighing only about ninety-five pounds. She had large, penetrating gray eyes, and a prominent chin. Her features were passive, no matter what turn the evidence was taking.

No doubt that her chin was prominent; she had more determination than a whole community of other women. She said that she was guided by intuitions, by impressions made on her mind by some mysterious influence. She had not seen her family for six months, so busy had she been in tracking down the imaginary murderesses of her imaginary father. She was sure that she was right, and would have stuck by her guns, even if every old resident and neighbour of the Benders had sworn that these women were other than what she accused them of being.

A heroic figure in a good cause, but a dreadful enemy. I am not sure that any man in Kansas would not have been safer in the clutches of Professor Miss Kate Bender. If he could not fight, or run, that person might have taken his money and his life, but he could have kept, in the grave, his good name. If, however, Mrs. McCann should have it come over her, like a flash, that he was guilty of anything whatever—of piracy on the high seas, committed within the borders of Kansas—the destruction she would visit upon him might be dreadful. She would blast his reputation and set him on the gallows—and do it all in the name of righteousness.

Murder at Smutty Nose and Other Murders, 1926

DAMON RUNYON

The murder of Albert Snyder by his wife, Ruth, and her mousy "lover-boy" Judd Gray was one of the most sensational crimes in a decade that, having already produced the Hall-Mills and Leopold and Loeb cases, seemed to witness another "Trial of the Century" every few years. Edmund Wilson, seeking an explanation for the case's peculiar horror, observed at the time: "Judd Gray and Mrs. Snyder were 'respectable': they seemed to have been living exactly like three quarters of the people in America . . . They had dared to go all the way with a gamble that others must have dreamed of, must have tried on a smaller scale; and their deaths have been a purge for frustration, a petrifying warning to guilt, a substitute for baffled vengeance." The story would later inspire James M. Cain's classic noir novella *Double Indemnity* (1938), filmed in 1944 by Billy Wilder. Of the countless accounts of the Snyder-Gray trial, an event attended by such Jazz Age celebrities as David Belasco, D. W. Griffith, Sister Aimee Semple McPherson, the Reverend Billy Sunday, and best-selling philosopher Will Durant, the most detailed and memorable coverage was provided by Damon Runyon (1884–1946).

The son of an itinerant newspaper publisher, the Kansas-born, Colorado-raised Runyon misspent much of his youth as a street tough, underage barfly, and whorehouse messenger boy before becoming a full-time reporter at the age of 15. After service in the Philippines during the Spanish-American War, he returned to Colorado, working sporadically in various small-town dailies when he wasn't on drinking binges or bumming around the Midwest. In 1911 he moved East to become a sports reporter for William Randolph Hearst's *New York American* and quickly earned attention for snappy, anecdotal baseball coverage. By the 1920s his lively city reporting, freely embellished with colorful "human interest" details, had made him one of the country's most popular and highly paid journalists. Though the first of his famous Broadway tales did not appear until 1929, the year after Ruth Snyder and Judd Gray were electrocuted at Sing Sing, the storytelling skill that would make him rich as the creator of Nathan Detroit, Harry the Horse, Benny Southstreet, and other delightfully shady denizens of the urban demimonde is on full display in this firsthand account that has all the wit and drama of his streetwise fiction.

The Eternal Blonde

Long Island City, New York, April 19, 1927

A chilly looking blonde with frosty eyes and one of those marble, you-bet-you-will chins, and an inert, scare-drunk fellow that you couldn't miss among any hundred men as a dead set-up for a blonde, or the shell game, or maybe a gold brick.

Mrs. Ruth Snyder and Henry Judd Gray are on trial in the huge weatherbeaten old court house of Queens County in Long Island City, just across the river from the roar of New York, for what might be called for want of a better name, The Dumbbell Murder. It was so dumb.

They are charged with the slaughter four weeks ago of Albert Snyder, art editor of the magazine, *Motor Boating*, the blonde's husband and father of her nine-year-old daughter, under circumstances that for sheer stupidity and brutality have seldom been equalled in the history of crime.

It was stupid beyond imagination, and so brutal that the thought of it probably makes many a peaceful, home-loving Long Islander of the Albert Snyder type shiver in his pajamas as he prepares for bed.

They killed Snyder as he slumbered, so they both admitted in confessions—Mrs. Snyder has since repudiated hers—first whacking him on the head with a sash weight, then giving him a few whiffs of chloroform, and finally tightened a strand of picture wire around his throat so he wouldn't revive.

This matter disposed of, they went into an adjoining room and had a few drinks of whiskey used by some Long Islanders, which is very bad, and talked things over. They thought they had committed "the perfect crime," whatever that may be. It was probably the most imperfect crime on record. It was cruel, atrocious and unspeakably dumb.

They were red-hot lovers then, these two, but they are strangers now. They never exchanged a glance yesterday as they sat in the cavernous old court room while the citizenry of Long Island tramped in and out of the jury box, and the attorneys tried to get a jury of twelve men together without success.

Plumbers, clerks, electricians, merchants, bakers, butchers, barbers, painters, salesmen, machinists, delicatessen dealers, garage employers, realtors and gardeners from the cities and the hamlets of the County of Queens were in the procession that marched through the jury box answering questions as to their views on the death penalty, and their sympathies toward women, and other things.

Out of fifty men, old and young, married and single, bald and hairy, not one was found acceptable to both sides. Forty-three were excused, the State challenged one peremptorily, the attorneys for Mrs. Snyder five, and the attorneys for Gray one. Each defendant is allowed thirty peremptory challenges, the State thirty against each defendant.

At this rate they may be able to get a jury before the Long Island corn is ripe. The State is asking that Mrs. Snyder and her meek looking Lothario be given the well-known "hot seat" in Sing Sing, more generally known as the electric chair, and a lot of the talesmen interrogated today seemed to have a prejudice against that form of punishment.

Others had opinions as to the guilt or innocence that they said they couldn't possibly change. A few citizens seemed kindly disposed toward jury service, possibly because they haven't anything at hand for the next few weeks, but they got short shrift from the lawyers. The jury box was quite empty at the close of the day's work.

Mrs. Snyder, the woman who has been called a Jezebel, a lineal descendant of the Borgia outfit, and a lot of other names, came in for the morning session of court stepping along briskly in her patent-leather pumps, with little short steps.

She is not bad looking. I have seen much worse. She is thirty-three and looks just about that, though you cannot tell much about blondes. She has a good figure, slim and trim, with narrow shoulders. She is of medium height and I thought she carried her clothes off rather smartly. She wore a black dress and a black silk coat with a collar of black fur.

Some of the girl reporters said it was dyed ermine; others pronounced it rabbit.

They made derogatory remarks about her hat. It was a tight-fitting thing called, I believe, a beret. Wisps of her straw-colored hair straggled out from under it. Mrs. Snyder wears her hair bobbed, the back of the bobbing rather ragged. She is of the Scandinavian type. Her parents are Norwegian and Swedish.

Her eyes are blue-green, and as chilly looking as an ice cream cone. If all that Henry Judd Gray says of her actions the night of the murder is true, her veins carry ice water. Gray says he dropped the sash weight after slugging the sleeping Snyder with it once and that Mrs. Snyder picked it up and finished the job.

Gray's mother and sister, Mrs. Margaret Gray, and Mrs. Harold Logan, took seats in the court room just behind Mrs. Snyder. At the afternoon session, Mrs. Gray, a small, determined-looking woman of middle age, hitched her chair over so she was looking right into Mrs. Snyder's face.

There was a rather grim expression in Mrs. Gray's eyes. She wore a black hat and a black coat with a fur collar, a spray of artificial flowers was pinned to the collar. Her eyelids were red as if she had been weeping.

The sister, Mrs. Logan, is plump and pleasant looking. Gray's wife has left him flat, in the midst of his troubles and gone to Norwalk, Conn., with their nine-year-old daughter. She never knew her husband was playing that Don Juan business when she thought he was out peddling corsets. That is she never knew it until the murder.

Gray, a spindly fellow in physical build, entered the court room with quick, jerky little steps behind an officer, and sat down between his attorneys, Samuel L. Miller and William L. Millard. His back was to Mrs. Snyder who sat about ten feet distant. Her eyes were on a level with the back of his narrow head.

Gray was neatly dressed in a dark suit, with a white starched collar and subdued tie. He has always been a bit to the dressy side, it is said. He wears big, horn-rimmed spectacles and his eyes have a startled expression. You couldn't find a meeker, milder looking fellow in seven states, this man who is charged with one of the most horrible crimes in history.

He occasionally conferred with his attorneys as the examination of the talesmen was going forward, but not often. He sat in one position almost the entire day, half slumped down in his chair, a melancholy looking figure for a fellow who once thought of "the perfect crime."

Mrs. Snyder and Gray have been "hollering copper" on each other lately, as the boys say. That is, they have been telling. Gray's defense goes back to old Mr. Adam, that the woman beguiled him, while Mrs. Snyder says he is a "jackal," and a lot of other things besides that, and claims that he is hiding behind her skirts.

She will claim, it is said, that while she at first entered into the conspiracy to kill her husband, she later tried to dissuade Gray from going through with it, and tried to prevent the crime. The attorneys will undoubtedly try to picture their respective clients as the victims of each other.

Mrs. Snyder didn't want to be tried with Gray, but Gray was very anxious to be tried with Mrs. Snyder. It is said that no Queens County jury ever sent a woman to death, which is what the State will ask of this jury, if it ever gets one. The relations among the attorneys for the two defendants are evidently not on the theory of "one for all and all for one." Probably the attorneys for Gray do not care what happens to Mrs. Snyder, and probably the attorneys for Mrs. Snyder feel the same way about Gray.

Edgar Hazelton, a close-trimmed dapper looking man, with a jutting chin and with a pince-nez balanced on a hawk beak, who represents Mrs. Snyder, did most of the questioning of the talesmen for the defense. His associate, Dana Wallace, is a former district attorney of Queens County, and the pair are said to be among the ablest lawyers on Long Island. It is related that they have defended eleven murder cases without a conviction going against them.

Supreme Court Justice Townsend Scudder is presiding over the court room, which has a towering ceiling with a stained glass skylight,

and heavy dark oak furniture with high-backed pews for the spectators. Only no spectators were admitted today because the room was
needed for the talesmen.

The court room is so huge it was difficult to hear what was going on
at any distance from the bench. I believe it is the largest court room
in the country. It was there that the trial scene in the picture *Manslaughter* was filmed.

In the court room on the floor below was held the trial of Mrs.
Nack in the famous Guldensuppe murder thirty years ago, when the
reporters used carrier pigeons to take their copy across the river to
Park Row.

Microphones have been posted on the tables, and amplifiers have
been rigged up on the walls, probably the first time this was ever done
in a murder trial, but the apparatus wasn't working any too well today,
and one hundred and twenty newspaper writers scattered around the
tables listened with their hands cupped behind their ears.

Here is another record, the number of writers covering the trial. We
have novelists, preachers, playwrights, fiction writers, sports writers
and journalists at the press benches. Also we have nobility in the persons of the Marquis of Queensbury and Mrs. Marquis. The Marquis is
a grandson of the gent whose name is attached to the rules governing
the manly art of scrambling ears, but the young man wore a pair of
fancy-topped shoes yesterday that surprised me. It isn't done you
know, really!

The Reverend John Roach Straton was present wearing a Buster
Brown necktie that was almost unclerical. A Catholic priest was on
hand, but he carried no pad or pencil to deceive us. Some of the writers
came attended by their secretaries, which shows you how far we have
gone since the days of the carrier pigeons at the Guldensuppe trial.

There were quite a number of philosophers. I have been requested by
my Broadway constituency to ascertain if possible what, if anything,
philosophy suggests when a hotsy-totsy blonde with whom a guy is
enamoured tells him to do thus and so. But then a philosopher probably
never gets tangled up with blondes, or he wouldn't be a philosopher.

Mrs. Snyder showed signs that might have been either nervousness or just sheer impatience during the day. Her fingers constantly toyed with a string of black beads at her throat. Her entire set-up suggested mourning. She has nice white hands, but they are not so small as Gray's. His hands are quite effeminate.

In fact, the alienists who examined Gray and pronounced him quite sane say he is effeminate in many ways. Gray showed no signs of nervousness or any particular animation whatever. He just sat there. It must be a strain on a man to sit for hours knowing the eyes of a woman who is trying to get him all burned up are beating against the back of his neck and not turn around and give her at least one good hot glare.

April 27, 1927

Some say Mrs. Ruth Snyder "wept silently" in court yesterday. It may be so. I could detect no sparkle of tears against the white marble mask, but it is conceivable that even the very gods were weeping silently as a gruff voice slowly recited the blond woman's own story of the murder of her husband by herself and Henry Judd Gray.

Let no one infer she is altogether without tenderness of heart, for when they were jotting down the confession that was read in the court room in Long Island City, Peter M. Daly, an assistant district attorney, asked her:

"*Mrs. Snyder, why did you kill your husband?*"

He wanted to know.

"Don't put it that way," she said, according to his testimony yesterday. "It sounds so cruel."

"Well, that is what you did, isn't it?" he asked, in some surprise.

"Yes," he claims she answered, "but I don't like that term."

A not astonishing distaste, you must admit.

"Well, why did you kill him?" persisted the curious Daly.

"To get rid of him," she answered, simply, according to Daly's testimony; and indeed that seems to have been her main idea throughout, if all the evidence the State has so far developed is true.

She afterward repudiated the confession that was presented yesterday, with her attorneys trying to bring out from the State's witnesses that she was sick and confused when she told her bloody yarn five weeks ago.

The woman, in her incongruous widow's weeds sat listening intently to the reading of her original confession to the jury, possibly the most horrible tale that ever fell from human lips, the tale of a crime unutterably brutal and cold-blooded and unspeakably dumb.

Her mouth opened occasionally as if framing words, and once she said no quite distinctly, an unconscious utterance, which may have been a denial of some utterance by the lawyer or perhaps an assurance to her soul that she was not alive and awake.

This is a strange woman, this Mrs. Ruth Brown Snyder, a different woman to different men.

To the inert Henry Judd Gray, her partner in crime, sitting at the table just in front of her, as soggy looking as a dummy in his loose hanging clothes, she was a "woman of great charm," as he said in his confession which was outlined in court by a police officer yesterday.

To big, hale and hearty George P. McLaughlin, former police commissioner of New York City, who heard her original statement of the butchery, she was a "woman of great calm," as he said on the witness stand yesterday.

To the male reporters who have been following the trial she is all that, anyway, though they construe her calm as more the chill of the icy Northland, whence came her parents.

The attorneys for Mrs. Snyder, the nimble Dana Wallace and Edgar Hazelton, indicated yesterday clearly that part of their line of defense, in this devil-take-the-hindmost scramble between Ruth and Henry Judd is to be an attempted impeachment of the confession, and Gray's attorneys showed the same thought.

Samuel L. Miller, representing Gray, charged that the confession of the corset salesman was secured while he was under duress and by intimidation and threats.

Gray sat with his chin in his hands, his eyes on the floor, scarcely moving a muscle as Mrs. Snyder's confession, damning him in almost every word, was read. I have never seen him show much animation at best, but yesterday he seemed completely sunk. He occasionally conferred in whispers through his fingers with one of his attorneys, but with not the slightest show of interest.

It was Gray who slugged poor Albert Snyder with the five-pound sash weight as the art editor lay asleep in his bed, so Mrs. Snyder's confession relates, while Mrs. Snyder stood outside in the hall, seeing, by the dim light thrown into the chamber of horror by an arc in the street, the rise and fall of the paper-wrapped weight in Gray's hand.

What a scene that must have been!

Twice she heard her husband groan. Roused from an alcoholic stupor by the first thump on his head, he groaned. Then groaned again. Silence. Out came Henry Judd Gray, saying: "Well, I guess that's it."

But the confessions do not jibe here. The outline of Gray's confession, which will be read today, indicates Gray says he dropped the weight after whacking Snyder once, and that Ruth picked it up "and belabored him."

"Those were Gray's words—'belabored him,'" ex-Commissioner McLaughlin said yesterday.

District Attorney Newcombe overlooked an opportunity for the dramatic yesterday that old David Belasco, sitting back in the crowd, probably envied, in the reading of Ruth's confession. This was first identified by Peter M. Daly, the assistant mentioned above, after Ruth's attorneys had failed in a hot battle against its admission.

Newcombe stood before the jury with the typewritten sheets in one hand and talked off the words without elocutionary effort, the microphone carrying his voice out over the silent court room. The place was jammed. Women again. At the afternoon session they almost tore the buttons off the uniforms of the coppers on guard at the doors, trying to shove past them. The cops gallantly repulsed the charge.

The first paragraphs of the confession, made to Daly soon after the murder and under circumstances that the defense is attacking, were given over to a recital of Ruth's early life—born on Manhattan Island thirty-three years ago, a schoolgirl, an employee in the same magazine office with Snyder, then an artist when she married him.

The thing has been told so often before that I here go over it sketchily. Soon she was unhappy with her husband, fourteen years older than herself. He constantly belittled her. He threatened to blow out her brains. He was a good provider for herself and their nine-year-old daughter, but wouldn't take her out—so she took to stepping out, as they say. An old, old yarn—Friend Husband a non-stepper, Friend Wife full of go.

She met Henry Judd Gray, the corset salesman, in Henry's restaurant in the once-throbbing Thirties in New York, and the first thing anybody knew she and Henry were thicker than is meet and proper. She told Henry of her matrimonial woes, and Henry, himself a married man, with a young daughter, was duly sympathetic.

But let's get down to the murder.

She wrote Henry and told him how Albert Snyder had threatened her life. She wrote in a code they had rigged up for their own private use, and Henry answered, saying the only thing to do was to get rid of Albert. They had talked of ways and means, and Gray gave her the famous sash weight and went out to Queens Village one night to wipe Albert Snyder out.

They got cold feet that night and Albert lived. Then Snyder again threatened her, the confession said, and told her to get out of his house, so she wrote to Henry once more, and Henry wrote back, saying, "We will deliver the goods Saturday." That meant Saturday, March 19. They arranged all the details by correspondence.

Henry arranged his alibi in Syracuse and came to New York the night she and her husband and child were at the Fidgeons' party. She left a door unlocked so Henry could get in the room of her mother, Mrs. Josephine Brown, who was away for the night. Ruth saw him there and talked with him a moment when she came back from the party with her husband and child.

Henry had the sash weight which she had left under the pillow in

Mrs. Brown's room for him. He had chloroform, some cheesecloth and a blue cotton handkerchief. Also, she had hospitably left a quart of liquor for him of which he drank about half. She put her child to bed, then went into her husband's room and waited until he was asleep, then returned to the waiting Henry.

They talked briefly, and Henry kissed her and went into Albert Snyder's room. She stood in the hallway and saw Gray pummel the sleeping man with the sash weight as related. Then Gray tied Snyder's hands and feet, put the handkerchief, saturated with chloroform, over his face, besides stuffing his mouth and nostrils with the gauze, also soaked with chloroform. Then Henry turned Snyder over so the art editor's face would be buried in a pillow and rejoined Ruth.

Henry Judd wore rubber gloves at his sanguinary task, the confession said, and he went to the bathroom to wash his hands. He found blood on his shirt, so Ruth went into the room where the dead man lay, got one of Albert Snyder's shirts and gave it to Henry Judd. Then they went into the cellar and burned the bloody shirt and put the sash weight into a tool box after rubbing it with ashes.

Now, they returned to the sitting room, this pair, and Henry Judd suddenly thought of some picture wire he had brought along, presumably to tie Snyder's hands and feet. At least, he had two pieces, Ruth said. One he had lost, so he took the other and went into the death chamber and wrapped the wire around Albert Snyder's throat tightening it with his fingers.

Then he went around and upset the premises generally, to bear out the robbery idea, then sat and gossiped, talking of this and that until daybreak, when Henry Judd tied his sweetheart's hands and feet and left to return to Syracuse. She first went out and got a wallet out of Albert Snyder's pocket and gave it to Henry Judd. She does not know how much it contained.

After Henry's departure, she rolled out of her mother's bed, whereon he had placed her, and aroused her little daughter, telling her to get a neighbor.

Such, in substance and briefly, was the story of that night in Queens Village.

There was a supplemental statement with reference to some letters, including one from Gray, sent from Syracuse after he had departed from New York to join hands with her in the slaughter. Peter M. Daly asked her, at a time when Gray had not yet been definitely hooked with the crime, how she reconciled the postmark with her statement of the murder and she said it was part of Henry's alibi.

Thus Ruth was "hollering copper" on Henry, even before she knew Henry was "hollering copper" on her. They didn't stand hitched a minute after the showdown came.

Wallace wanted to know if Mrs. Snyder hadn't said she was confused and sick while making the statement, but Daly said no. He admitted Mrs. Snyder had a crying spell and that a physician was called in. Wallace mentioned it as a fainting spell, but Daly wouldn't concede it was such. It seemed to be agreed it was some kind of a spell, however.

Daly said she asked if she could see Gray when he got to town. He said she seemed to know that Gray was on his way to New York. The defense devoted more time to Daly than to any other witness so far, Millard of Gray's counsel joining in the cross-examination.

Gray's attorneys had objected to some questions asked by Wallace and now Mrs. Snyder's lawyers objected to Millard's questions.

This case has been presented from the beginning in rather a disordered manner, it seems to me, like one of those new-fangled plays that violate all the established rules from the theatre.

For instance, at the morning session, Millard started out cross-examining Lieutenant Dorschell, of the New York Police Department, relative to a drawing made by Gray of the hardware store in Kingston, where he bought the sash weight and the picture wire. This drawing was made at three o'clock in the morning of Gray's arrival in New York after his ride from Syracuse, where he was arrested. Millard inquired into the physical condition of Gray at the time he made the drawing and Dorschell said he seemed to be all right.

Millard then explained to Justice Scudder that he wanted to show under what conditions the drawing was made. He said he desired to present testimony showing that the drawing came after a long examination of Gray by the police, and to that end Justice Scudder gave him permission to call and cross-examine a witness who had not appeared before.

It is certainly somewhat unusual to bring in for cross-examination by the defense a witness who would ordinarily be one of the State's most important witnesses.

The witness was Michael S. McDermott, another lieutenant of New York Police, who brought Gray from Syracuse, and who told with infinite detail of Gray's confession. He said Gray took the thing as a joke at first, maintaining his complete innocence.

McDermott said Gray seemed to find the company he was in "congenial" most of the journey, a statement that produced a light giggle in the court. He said that Gray at no time seemed to become serious until they told him they had the contents of his wastepaper basket, which included the Pullman stub.

"'Do you know, Judd, we have the Pullman ticket you used from Syracuse to New York?' Then he said, 'Well, gentlemen, I was at the Snyder home that night.'"

McDermott said Gray voluntarily launched into a narrative of the bloody night in Queens Village. He told how Gray had subsequently given this same narrative to a stenographer and identified and initialed the various articles used in the commission of the crime.

Now the State proceeded to establish the purchase of the sash weight and picture wire by Gray in Kingston, March 4, last.

Margaret Hamilton, a buyer for a Kingston store, who knows Henry Judd, said she saw him there on that date. She is a stout lady, and wore a startlingly red hat and red scarf.

Arthur R. Bailey, a thin, gray, studious looking man, wearing glasses, a clerk in a Kingston hardware store, didn't seem to remember selling a five-pound sash weight on March 4, although he identified what you might call a bill of sale in his handwriting, taken from the records of the store. He said his store sold any number of sash weights, but he never recalled any transaction involving one sash weight. Mr. Bailey obviously didn't care about being mixed up in this trial business, anyway.

John Sanford, a young Negro, testified most briefly to getting this sash weight from the warehouse.

It seemed a lot of bother about a sash weight that has lost some of its importance since the doctors testified that the wallops with it alone did not cause Snyder's death.

Reginald Rose, youthful, black-haired, black-browed and a bit to the sheikish side, a ticket seller for the New York Central, told of selling Gray a railroad ticket to Syracuse and a Pullman seat reservation to Albany on the night of March 19 for the following day, which was the day after the murder. Gray made the return reservation immediately upon his arrival in New York the night he ran down for the killing.

Millard became a bit curious over Rose's clear recollection of this particular sale of a ticket out of the many a ticket seller makes every day and it developed that Rose even remembered how Gray was dressed. He wore a fedora hat and an overcoat.

Rose said he remembered the sale because it wasn't commonplace to sell a railroad ticket to Syracuse and a seat to Albany.

Now came testimony about the party which Mr. and Mrs. Snyder and their small daughter, Lorraine, attended the night of the murder. It was at the home of Milton C. Fidgeon, and Mr. Fidgeon himself took the stand, stout, smooth of face and prosperous-looking.

There had been liquor at the party said Mr. Fidgeon. He served one drink, then someone asked if it was not time for another, so he went into the kitchen to produce the second shot.

Mrs. Snyder came to him there and said she wasn't drinking, but to give her portion to her husband. The Snyders went home about two o'clock in a pleasant frame of mind, as Mr. Fidgeon said on cross-examination by Wallace.

April 28, 1927

Right back to old Father Adam, the original, and perhaps the loudest "squawker" among mankind against women, went Henry Judd Gray in telling how and why he lent his hand to the butchery of Albert Snyder.

She—she—she—she—she—she—she—she. That was the burden of the bloody song of the little corset salesman as read out in the packed court room in Long Island City yesterday.

She—she—she—she—she—she. 'Twas an echo from across the ages and an old familiar echo, at that. It was the same old "squawk" of Brother Man whenever and wherever he is in a jam, that was first framed in the words:

"She gave me of the tree, and I did eat."

It has been put in various forms since then, as Henry Judd Gray, for one notable instance close at hand, put it in the form of eleven long typewritten pages that were read yesterday, but in any form and in any language it remains a "squawk."

"She played me pretty hard." . . . "She said, 'You're going to do it, aren't you?'" . . . "She kissed me." . . . She did this . . . She did that . . . Always she—she—she—she—she ran the confession of Henry Judd.

And "she"—the woman-accused, how did she take this most gruesome squawk?

Well, on the whole, better than you might expect.

You must remember it was the first time she had ever heard the confession of the man who once called her "Momsie." She probably had an inkling of it, but not its exact terms.

For a few minutes her greenish blue eyes roared with such fury that I would not have been surprised to see her leap up, grab the window sash weight that lay among the exhibits on the district attorney's table and perform the same offices on the shrinking Gray that he says she performed on her sleeping husband.

She "belabored him," Gray's confession reads, and I half expected her to belabor Gray.

Her thin lips curled to a distinct snarl at some passages in the statement. I thought of a wildcat and a female cat, at that, on a leash. Once or twice she smiled, but it was a smile of insensate rage, not amusement. She once emitted a push of breath in a loud "phew," as you have perhaps done yourself over some tall tale.

The marble mask was contorted by her emotions for a time, she often shook her head in silent denial of the astounding charges of Gray, then finally she settled back calmly, watchful, attentive, and with an expression of unutterable contempt as the story of she—she—she—she ran along.

Contempt for Henry Judd, no doubt. True, she herself squawked on Henry Judd, at about the same time Henry Judd was squawking on her, but it is a woman's inalienable right to squawk.

As for Henry Judd, I still doubt he will last it out. He reminds me of a slowly collapsing lump of tallow. He sat huddled up in his baggy clothes, his eyes on the floor, his chin in hand, while the confession was being read. He seems to be folding up inch by inch every day.

He acts as if he is only semi-conscious. If he was a fighter and came back to his corner in his present condition, they would give him smelling salts.

The man is a wreck, a strange contrast to the alert blonde at the table behind him.

The room was packed with women yesterday, well-dressed, richly-befurred women from Park Avenue, and Broadway, and others not so well dressed from Long Island City, and the small towns farther down the Island. There were giggling young schoolgirls and staid-looking matrons, and my friends, what do you think? Their sympathy is for Henry Judd Gray!

I made a point of listening to their opinions as they packed the hallways and jammed the elevators of the old court house yesterday and canvassed some of them personally, and they are all sorry for Gray. Perhaps it is his forlorn looking aspect as he sits inert, numb, never raising his head, a sad spectacle of a man who admits he took part in one of the most atrocious murders in history.

There is no sympathy for Mrs. Snyder among the women and very little among the men. They all say something drastic ought to be done to her.

How do you account for that—

But while Henry Judd's confession puts most of the blame on the woman, Mrs. Snyder's attorneys, the pugnacious Edgar Hazelton and the sharp Dana Wallace, who remind me for all the world of a brace of restless terriers with their brisk maneuvers, began making an effort yesterday that shows they intend trying to make Henry Judd the goat.

When District Attorney Newcombe stood up to read Gray's confession, a deep silence fell over the room, packed from wall to wall. Many of the spectators were standing. Mrs. Snyder leaned forward on the table in front of her, but Gray never raised his eyes from the floor, then or thereafter.

You could hear little gasps as of horror or unbelief from some of the women spectators as Newcombe read on in a cold, passionless voice, especially when the confession got down to the actual murder.

It began with the story of their meeting in Henry's restaurant about two years ago. They were introduced by Harry Folsom of New Canaan, Conn., who had picked Mrs. Snyder and another up in the restaurant, so ran the confession, rather giving the impression that the blonde was one of those women who can be "picked up." Gray said:

"She is a woman of great charm. I probably don't have to tell you that. I did like her very much, and she was good company and apparently a good pal to spend an evening with."

I looked over at Mrs. Snyder as this paragraph was read, and there was a shadow of a smile on the marble mask. The expression altered when the story began to tell an instant later of them starting intimate relations in August. Gray added:

"Prior to that she was just a woman I respected."

Perhaps I should here explain that most of this confession was made by Gray on the train when he was being brought from Syracuse to New York after the murder and later elaborated in its details by him.

Well, they got very friendly, and soon she was calling him up and writing him. "She played me pretty hard," he said. He went out to her house for luncheon, and met her mother, although he did not think the mother knew anything of their relations.

Presently Mrs. Snyder got to telling of her unhappiness with Albert. Gray told her, he says, that he himself was married and had a fine wife and was very happy at home, so there could never be anything between him and Mrs. Snyder.

She told him of several attempts she had made on Albert Snyder's life, once giving him sleeping powders, and again bichloride of mercury, but Albert kept on living.

Finally, said Gray, "She started to hound me on this plan to assist her."

The plan for killing Snyder, presumably. But the little corset salesman added quite naively, "I have always been a gentleman and I have always been on the level with everybody. I have a good many friends. If I ever have any after this I don't know."

He said he absolutely refused to listen to the charmer's sanguinary wiles at first, then "with some veiled threats and intents of love-making, she reached the point where she got me in such a whirl that I didn't know where I was at."

Clarence A. Stewart, superintendent of the safety deposit vault of the Queens-Bellaire Bank of Queens Village, testified that Mrs. Snyder rented two boxes, one under the name of Ruth M. Brown, the other under the name of Ruth M. Snyder. Stewart is a mild-looking man who kept his overcoat on while testifying. He stood up when asked to identify Mrs. Snyder and peered at her through his specs.

Edward C. Kern, cashier of the same bank, heavy-set and bland, testified to the contents of these boxes. In the box taken in the name of Ruth M. Brown was $53,000 worth of insurance policies on Albert Snyder and receipts for the payment of the premiums. In the box under the name of Ruth M. Snyder were papers mainly of a family nature relating to the affairs of Ruth and her dead husband, such as fire and burglary insurance policies, receipts and the like.

There seemed to be plenty of fire insurance on the Snyder home. There was some Roxy Theatre stock among other things and papers representing small investments by the dead art editor.

Samuel Willis, a tall, spare, elderly resident of Queens Village, told of seeing Henry Judd Gray waiting for a bus at 5:50 on the morning of March 20, hard by a police booth at Hillside Avenue and Springfield Boulevard, in Queens Village. Police Officer Smith, on duty there, was indulging in a little pistol practice at bottles and Willis said Gray remarked after the officer finished:

"I'd hate to stand in front of him and have him shoot at me."

The bailiffs had to rap for order. Cross-examined by Samuel L. Miller, the witness said his attention was attracted to Gray "by that little dimple in his chin." He said Gray took the bus with him and he saw no more of Henry Judd. This was just after Gray had left the Snyder home to hurry back to Syracuse, you understand.

April 29, 1927

There was little breathing space left in the yellowish-walled old court room when the morning session opened.

In the jam I observed many ladies and gents with dark circles around their eyes which indicated loss of sleep, or bad livers. I identified them as of the great American stage, playwrights, producers, actors, and even actresses.

They were present, as I gathered, to acquire local color for their current, or future contributions to the thespian art, and the hour was a trifle early for them to be abroad in the land. They sat yesterday writing through the proceedings and perhaps inwardly criticizing the stage setting and thinking how unrealistic the trial is as compared to their own productions.

Among the other spectators comfortably chaired, or standing on tired feet, were ladies running from a couple of inches to three yards wide. They were from all parts of Long Island, and the other boroughs of the large and thriving City of New York, the inmates of which are supposed to be so very blasé but who certainly dearly love their murder cases.

A big crowd waited in the hallways and outside the court house. Tearful females implored the obdurate cops guarding the stairs and the court room doors, to ease them through somehow.

It was a strange gathering. Solid-looking citizens found a morning to waste. They would probably have felt greatly inconvenienced had they been requested to spend the same amount of time on a mission of mercy. Several preachers and some of our best known public "pests" were scattered around the premises. What a fine commentary, my friends, on what someone has mentioned as our vaunted intelligence.

Peggy Hopkins, Countess Morner and what not, Joyce, the famous grass-widow, came again to dazzle all the beholders with the magnificence of her display. It was Peggy's second visit. Probably she didn't believe her eyes and ears on her first visit that a lady had seemed to have some difficulty in getting rid of her husband. Peggy never did, you can bet on that. She wore a suit of a distressing green and a red fox collar and arrived at the court house in a little old last year's Rolls-Royce.

Paul Mathis, a thin, dark youth, was the first witness. He remembered carting Henry Judd from the Jamaica Station on the subway on Fifty-eighth Street, March 20, the morning of the murder.

The fare was $8.55. Gray gave him a five cent tip. It is not likely Mathis will ever forget Henry Judd if the young man is like the average taxi jockey.

William L. Millard of Gray's counsel, verbally belted away at Mathis rather snappishly, trying to find out if the young man's memory of Henry Judd hadn't been encouraged by the district attorney's office. Millard has a cutting voice when he is cross-examining and is given to sharp asides. The Court has generally admonished him on several occasions.

Justice Scudder does not allow the lawyers to get far out of conversational bounds. My friend, Senator Alexander Simpson, of Hall-Mills fame, would probably feel his style was quite cramped in Justice Scudder's court.

Van Voorhees, a thin, middle-aged man, conductor of the train that carried Gray back to Syracuse from his murder errand, identified Gray. So did George Fullerton, a dusky porter.

"We concede the defendant was on the train," said Millard, closing that line of testimony.

Now came Haddon Gray, of 207 Clark Street, Syracuse, the insurance man who unwittingly helped Judd Gray with his famous alibi. Haddon and Judd had been friends twenty years, but are not related. Gray is a young man of brisk manner and appearance, of medium height, with black hair parted in the middle and slicked down. He was neatly dressed and displayed a lodge emblem on his watch chain and another on his lapel. He spoke very distinctly.

Haddon Gray said Judd had enlisted his support in Syracuse in the keeping of a date in Albany with a woman Judd referred to as "Momsie." Judd had once shown him a photo of "Momsie." Haddon Gray said he now knew her as Mrs. Snyder.

This obliging Haddon, thinking he was merely assisting an old pal in a little clandestine affair, hung a sign, "Don't Disturb," on Judd's door at the Onondaga Hotel, rumpled the bed, called the desk downstairs and left word he was ill and was not to be aroused before a certain hour, and finally mailed some letters that Judd had written. All this after Judd had left Syracuse for New York.

Judd told Haddon he was afraid his firm might check up on him, wherefore the arrangements set forth above. Haddon did not hear from Judd again until Sunday afternoon, March 20, when Judd, just back from his bloody errand to Queens Village, called him on the telephone. Haddon Gray and a friend named Harry Platt went to see Judd at the Onondaga and Judd said he had not kept the "date" in Albany as a telegram from Momsie had reached him there summoning him on to New York. Then the witness said Judd told him a startling story.

He—Judd—said he had gone to the home of Momsie while she and her husband were out and entered by a side door. He was waiting in a bedroom when he heard Momsie and her husband returning. Then he heard a great commotion and looking out through the door of the room he saw Momsie slugged by a dark man.

Henry Judd told Haddon he hid in a closet, and two men came in and rummaged around in the closet over his head, looking for something. Then they went out and Henry Judd bolstered up his courage and looked about. He went into a bedroom and found Momsie's husband on the floor. He lifted the man onto the bed, and said in doing so he must have gotten blood on his vest and shirt as he bent over the man and listened if his heart was beating.

He showed Haddon Gray the shirt and said it was Snyder's shirt but the witness wasn't clear as to how Judd explained having it. Also Judd had a suitcase containing the suit of clothes he had worn to New York, also the bloody shirt and a briefcase, which Harry Platt took to get rid of at Judd's request. Platt took the suitcase to his office.

After relating this tale Judd went to Haddon's home and spent the evening playing with Haddon's children. Haddon came to New York after Judd's arrest, saw his old pal in jail and said:

"Judd, did you do this?"

"Yes, Haddon; I did."

Henry Judd, inert, head down as usual, never glanced up as he heard his boyhood friend testify, and Haddon Gray proved in his testimony that he was about as good a friend as a man could hope to have.

Harry Platt, an insurance adjuster of Syracuse, very bald, rather florid, and with glasses, was next. There was a touch of the old beau to Harry's appearance. He repeated the tale of slugging told him and Haddon by Judd. He said he gave the suitcase to his stenographer to be destroyed.

Mrs. Anna Boehm, of Syracuse, stenographer for Platt, a plump lady wearing glasses and obviously a bit nervous, told of receiving a package from Platt containing a suitcase. In the suitcase was a suit of clothes and a hat. She gave it to her husband. The husband, Anthony Boehm, corroborated that statement. He burned the package in a furnace.

At 12:27, Newcombe stood up and said:

"*The People Rest.*"

There was a sudden stir and the bailiffs rapped for order. All the attorneys gathered about Justice Scudder's bench in a conference with the Court.

When the State rested rather sooner than was generally expected, the attorneys for the defendants asked for time to prepare certain motions They were given until four o'clock in the afternoon. These motions, all for dismissal on one ground or another, were probably presented more on the broad premise that they can't rule you off for trying, rather than the expectation they would be granted. Millard wanted the motions made in the absence of the jury, but Justice Scudder saw no necessity for that.

If the jurors didn't understand the motions any better than most of the laymen collected in the court room, Justice Scudder was quite right. The language was quite technical.

Now the woman and the crumpled little corset salesman, their once piping-hot passion colder than a dead man's toes, begin trying to save their respective skins from the singeing at Sing Sing, each trying to shove the other into the room with the little green door.

"What did Mrs. Snyder say about the confession of Gray's—that squawk?" I asked her attorneys yesterday.

"Well, let's see, she said he—" began Dana Wallace, the buzzing, bustling little man who sits at Mrs. Snyder's side in the court room when he isn't on his feet, which is seldom.

"She said—Well, wait now until I recall what she said," put in Edgar Hazelton, the other attorney for the woman.

They seemed at a loss for words. I suggested: "Did she say he is a rat?"

"Well I suppose it would amount to that in your language," replied Wallace. (What did he mean "my" language?) "Only she didn't use that term."

"No, no," chimed in Hazelton, "not rat."

"She said, in substance, 'and to think I once loved that—that—' Well, I think she used a word that means something like coward," Wallace concluded.

"Do you think she will keep her nerve on the stand?" I asked.

"Yes," they both answered in unison.

I am inclined to think so, too.

Whatever else she may lack, which seems to be plenty, the woman appears to have nerve. Or maybe she hasn't any nerves. It is about the same thing.

In any event, she has never for a moment cowered like her once little pal of those loving days before the black early morning of March 20. She has been cold, calm, contemptuous, gutsy, angry, but never shrinking, save perhaps in that little walk to and from the court between the recesses. She then passes before the hungry eyes of the spectators.

That seems to be her most severe ordeal. She grips her black corded-silk coat in front with both hands, and seems to hasten, her eyes straight ahead. However, we shall see about that nerve now.

April 30, 1927

We were, in a manner of speaking, in the chamber of horrors with Mrs. Ruth Brown Snyder yesterday afternoon, mentally tip-toeing along, goggle-eyed and scared, behind her, when the blond woman suddenly gulped, and began weeping.

She had taken us, just before the tears came, step by step to a bedroom in her little home in Queens Village. We were standing there, you might say, all goose-pimply with the awfulness of the situation as we watched, through the medium of the story she told on the witness stand, the butchery of her husband by Henry Judd Gray.

Maybe the ghost of the dead art editor suddenly popped out on her as she got us into that room and was showing us the picture of the little corset salesman at his bloody work while she was trying to stay his murderous hand. Anyway, the tears came, welling up into the frosty eyes of the blonde and trickling down over that marble mask of a face.

Plump Mrs. Irene Wolfe, the gray-haired matron of the Queens County jail, hurried to Mrs. Snyder's side and put her arms around the weeping woman. A few sips from a glass of water, and Mrs. Snyder was again composed sufficiently to go on with the fearful tale of the killing of her husband that she started early in the afternoon and by which she hopes to save herself from the electric chair.

She blamed it all on Gray, even as he will blame it all on her. The baggy little man sitting inertly, as always, in the chair just a few feet from her listened to the woman with only an occasional glance at her.

Yet it would be interesting to know his thoughts. This was his old Momsie. This was the woman he once thought he loved with a great consuming love—this woman who was trying to consign him to the electric juices. He seemed to stagger slightly as he walked out of the court room at the close of the session, whereas before he had tried to put a little snap into his tread.

This woman broke down twice while she was on the witness stand, once when she had us in that death chamber, with Henry Judd Gray pounding the life out of her husband, as she claims, and again when she mentioned the name of her nine-year-old daughter, Lorraine.

But in the main she was as cold and calm sitting there with a thousand people staring at her as if she were at her dinner table discoursing to some guests. She kept her hands folded in her lap. She occasionally glanced at the jury, but mostly kept her eyes on Edgar Hazelton, one of her lawyers who examined her on direct-examination.

This examination was not concluded when Court took a recess at 4:30 until Monday morning. It is the custom of Queens County courts to skip Saturday.

Mrs. Snyder wore the same black dress and black coat that has been her attire since the trial started. She made one change in hats since then, discarding a tight-fitting thing that made her chilly chin jut out like an iceberg. Someone probably told her that the hat was most unbecoming, so now she wears one with a brim that takes some of the ice out of the chin.

Her dress and coat are neither fashionable nor well cut, so I am informed by ladies who may be taken as authorities on the subject. Still, they make her look smaller than her weight of around 150 pounds would indicate. She wears black silk stockings and black pumps.

Her face was flushed a bit today, probably from excitement, but she uses no make-up. Slap a little rouge and powder on Mrs. Snyder, give her a session with a hairdresser, and put some of Peggy Joyce's clothes on her, and she would be a snappy-looking young matron.

When her name was called by her attorney, Hazelton, soon after court opened this afternoon, she stood up quickly and advanced to the witness chair with a firm step. She had been twisting her hands and biting her nails just before that, however, indicating she felt nervous, which is not surprising, in view of the eyes turned on her.

It seems a great pity that old man Hogarth isn't living to depict the crowd scene in the court room yesterday. Tad* might do it, but Tad has too much sense to risk his life and limbs in any such jams.

Some strange-looking characters almost fought for a chance to leer at the principals in the trial. Apparently respectable men and women showed the court attendants cards, letters, badges, birth certificates and automobile licenses in an effort to impress the guardians of the portals with their importance and the necessity of their getting into the court room.

Dizzy-looking dolls said to represent the social strata of Park Avenue—the upper crust, as I understand—were there, not a little proud of their heroism in getting out so early. Some were escorted by silly-looking "muggs" wearing canes and spats.

But also there were men who might be business men and women with something better to do, standing chin deep in the bloody scandal of this bloody trial and giving some offense to high heaven, it seems to me, by their very presence.

The aisles were jammed so tightly that even the smallest copy boys, carrying copy of the day as it ran red-hot from the fingers of the scribbling writers of the newspaper delegations, could scarcely wiggle through. The women outnumbered the men about three to one. They stood for hours on their tired feet, their eyes and mouths agape.

---

*Tad was the penname of T. A. Dorgan, satiric artist whose drawings were a popular syndicated newspaper feature in the Twenties.

Justice Scudder peered over his glasses at a jammed court room and warned the crowd that at the first disturbance he would order the premises cleared.

Then he bowed slightly to the attorneys for the defense and Hazelton arose and stepped up to the table in front of the jury box.

He is a short, serious-looking man, with a hawk nose, and a harsh voice. A pince-nez straddled his beak. He wore a gray suit, and a white starched turned-down collar and a black tie yesterday morning. The collar flew loose from its neck and moorings early in Hazelton's discourse and one end scraped his ear.

He at first stood with his hands behind him, but presently he was gesticulating with his right, waggling a prehensile index-finger most forcibly. He perspired. He stood on his tiptoes. He was so close to Henry Judd that he almost stuck the index-finger in the defendant's eye when he pointed at Judd.

Occasionally a titter ran over the crowded court room at some remark made by Hazelton, who has an idiomatic manner of expression. That's what most of the crowd came for, apparently—to laugh at something, even though it might be human misery! The bailiffs would bawl "Silence!" and glare around furiously.

The purport of Hazelton's opening was about what had been anticipated. He said he expected to show that Henry Judd Gray was the arch criminal of the whole affair, and he depicted him in the light of a crafty, designing fellow—

"Not the man you see sitting here," yelled Hazelton, pointing at the cowering Henry Judd, while the eyes of the jurors turned and followed the finger. It was quite possible to believe that the villain described by Hazelton was not the man sitting there. Henry Judd looked anything but villainous.

Hazelton spoke about an hour, then Samuel L. Miller, of Gray's counsel, stepped forward, dark, stout, well-groomed and slick-haired —a New York type of professional young man who is doing all right.

He laid a batch of manuscript on the table in front of the jury and began to read his opening, rather an unusual proceeding. His opening addresses partook more of the nature of closing appeals. Miller had evidently given no little time and thought to his address and had dug up a lot of resounding phrases, but he was comparatively brief.

Harry Hyde, manager of the Jamaica branch of the Prudential Life Insurance Company, was the first witness called for Mrs. Snyder. He is a thin man with a Woodrow Wilson face and glasses, and he kept his new spring topcoat on as he sat in the witness chair. His testimony was what you might call vague.

Hazelton tried to show by him that Mrs. Snyder had called at his office relative to cancelling the insurance on her late husband's life, but he didn't recognize Mrs. Snyder as the woman and didn't remember much of the conversation.

He did faintly recall some woman calling at his office, however, and speaking of the Snyder policies. District Attorney Newcombe moved to strike out the testimony, but the motion was denied.

John Kaiser, Jr., another insurance man of Jamaica, a heavy-set rotund man with a moustache and horn-rimmed specs, testified on the subject of the insurance policies that are said by the State to have been reasons for the murder of Albert Snyder.

He said he recalled Mrs. Snyder coming to his offices and discussing the policies, but he couldn't recall the exact nature of the conversation.

Hazelton made a point of a clause in the policy that bore Snyder's signature, reserving the right to change the beneficiary.

Mrs. Josephine Brown, mother of Mrs. Snyder, was called.

Mrs. Brown is a woman who must be around sixty. She speaks with a very slight accent. Mrs. Brown is a Scandinavian. Her face is wrinkled and she wears gold-rimmed glasses. She was dressed in black but her black hat had a bright ornament. She gave her answers clearly and quickly.

She said her daughter had been operated on for appendicitis when she was a child and that the wound had to be reopened when she was eighteen. She lived with her daughter and son-in-law for six years and told of the visits to the Snyder home by Gray. On the third visit she told her daughter not to let Gray call again as "it didn't look right." Gray came no more.

On the occasions of his visit Mrs. Brown said Gray talked mainly about the stock market.

Newcombe examined her closely as to her knowledge of Gray's relations with her daughter. She admitted she called him Judd and had never told Albert Snyder of his visits to the Snyder home. She was away on a professional visit the night Henry Judd hid in her room on murder bent.

So many daffy women and rattle-headed men outside, eager to see whatever they might see, rushed the court house corridors at one o'clock on a rumor that Mrs. Snyder was on the stand, that the confusion took on the proportion of a riot. The halls and stairways were packed with struggling females. They pushed and shoved and pulled and hauled, and squealed and squawked. It was a sorry spectacle. The cops on duty at the court house were well nigh helpless against the onrush for a time.

Justice Scudder heard the tumult from his chambers and went out to take a look. Then he ordered the hallways cleared. In the meantime, the court room was jammed, and the spectators piled into the press section, grabbing all unoccupied seats. For half an hour the cops outside the court room would not recognize credentials of any kind until they could stem the human tide to some extent.

I doubt if there has ever been anything quite like it in connection with these trials, and I speak as a survivor of the Hall-Mills trial, and of the Browning trial, which wasn't a murder trial, except with relation to the King's English. The court room is said to be one of the largest in the country, but it could have been three times as large today and there wouldn't have been room for the crush.

A big crowd stood in the street outside all morning and afternoon, though they can see nothing there except the photographers at their sprinting exercises when a witness walks out of the court house.

When Mrs. Snyder was sworn as a witness, Justice Scudder told her in a quiet voice that she was not required to testify as the law protected her but that on the stand she is subject to the same cross-examination as any other witness.

She turned in her chair and looked the judge in the face as he talked, and bowed slightly.

Her voice is a soprano, and very clear. It came out through the amplifiers much harsher than its natural tone, of course. The microphone on the desk in front of the witness stand was in the line of vision between Mrs. Snyder and Hazelton, and she cocked her head to one side to get a clearer view of the lawyer.

She often emphasized some of her words, for instance, "We were *not* happy," when answering Hazelton's question about her married life with Albert Snyder. She never glanced at the staring crowd, though she often looked at the jury. As for the members of that solemn body, most of them watched her closely as she talked for a time, then their attention seemed to wander. Juror No. 11 never looked at her at all, but then Juror No. 11 never seems to be looking at anyone on the witness stand.

He has a faraway expression. Possibly he is wondering how business is going while he is away listening to all this murder stuff.

Mrs. Snyder's first attack of tears came early in the examination, but was very short. The second time court suspended operations for several minutes while she wept. A dead silence reigned. It is well for men to remain silent when women weep, whatever the circumstances.

I asked a lot of men how she impressed them. They said they thought she made a good witness for herself. Then I asked some of the girls, who have been none too strong for Mrs. Snyder, just as a general proposition. They, too, thought she had done very well.

You must bear in mind that this woman is talking for her life. If she is the cruel and cunning blond fury that Gray's story would cause you to believe, you would expect her to be calm. But if she is the wronged, home-loving, horror-stricken woman that her own tale would imply, her poise is most surprising.

She always referred to Albert Snyder as "my husband," and to her former paramour as "Mr. Gray"—"I tried to stop Mr. Gray from hitting my husband and he pushed me to the floor. I fainted and when I came to I pulled the blanket off. . . ."—It was here that she was overcome by tears the second time.

She pictured Gray as the aggressor in the love-making of their early meetings. She wasn't happy at home, and she accepted the advances of the little corset salesman to intimacy. She said Gray was her only love adventure.

He borrowed her money and didn't pay it back, she said. He first suggested the idea of getting rid of her husband, and mentioned poisoning to her. Wherever Gray said "she" in his confession, Mrs. Snyder said "he" in her testimony today. They have turned on each other with a vengeance, these two once-fervid lovers. There is no doubt they hate each other thoroughly.

It was difficult to tell just what effect Mrs. Snyder's tale had on the jury, of course. In fact it would be unfair to make a guess until her tale is finished. It certainly had some elements of plausibility, despite the confession she now says was obtained under duress, and despite the motive of Albert Snyder's life insurance that is advanced by the prosecution.

Mrs. Snyder's attorneys attempted to show today that she had tried to have the insurance reduced to cut down the premium, but their evidence on that point did not seem particularly strong. She insisted in her testimony that this had been the purpose.

She smiled just once with any semblance of joy, which was when Justice Scudder admitted, over the objections of the State, the bank books showing that Albert Snyder and Ruth had a joint account. It is by this account that the defense expects to show that Albert Snyder had full cognizance of his wife's payment of the premiums on the policies.

She says Gray always referred to Albert Snyder as "the governor." Once she accidentally tripped over a rubber gas tube in the house and pulled it off the jet. She went out and when she came back her husband was out of doors and said he had nearly been asphyxiated. She wrote Gray of the incident, and he wrote back:

"It was too damn bad the hose wasn't long enough to shove in his nose."

When she testified in just that language there was something in her manner and way of speaking out the word that caused a distinct stiffening among the women in the court room.

"Brazen!" some of them whispered.

This gas jet incident, by the way, was alleged by the State to have been one of the times when Mrs. Snyder tried to murder her husband.

She says Gray threatened to kill himself and her if she didn't do what he told her. She was afraid of Gray, she said, although the drooping little man in front of her didn't seem to be anything to be afraid of. She tried to break off with him, she said, and he threatened to expose her.

She said Gray sent her sleeping powders to give "the governor" on the night of the party at Fidgeons', which was Albert Snyder's last night on earth. Moreover, Gray announced in the letter accompanying the powders, according to her testimony, that he was coming down Saturday to finish "the governor."

He came down all right.

"My husband was asleep. I went to my mother's room, where I met Mr. Gray. We talked several minutes. He kissed me and I felt the rubber gloves on his hands. He was mad. He said, 'If you don't let me go through with this I'll kill us both.' He had taken my husband's revolver. I grabbed him by the hand and took him down to the living-room.

"I pleaded with him to stop when we got downstairs, then I went to the bathroom. I said to Mr. Gray, 'I'll bring your hat and coat down to you.' I heard a terrific thud. I rushed to my husband's room. I found Gray straddling my husband. I pulled the blankets down, grabbing him and then I fainted. I don't remember anything more."

That's her story and I presume she will stick to it.

May 3, 1927

For five hours and a half yesterday questions went whistling past that marble chin of Mrs. Ruth Brown Snyder's, but she kept on sticking it out defiantly from under the little brim of her black hat, like a fighter that can't be hurt.

At a pause just before recess in the old court room with the sickly yellow walls in Long Island City she reached out a steady hand, picked up a glass of water from the table in front of her, took a big swig, and looked at Charles F. Froessel, the assistant district attorney, who had been cross-examining her, as much as to say "Well, come on."

But Froessel seemed a bit fagged out, and mopped a steaming brow with a handkerchief as Justice Townsend Scudder granted a motion by one of Mrs. Snyder's attorneys for a recess until tomorrow morning.

The dialogue between Froessel and Mrs. Snyder toward the close of the day was taking on something of the aspect of a breakfast table argument between a husband and the little woman, who can't exactly explain certain matters that the old boy wants to know.

She is a magnificent liar, if she is lying. You must give her that. She stands out 'mid keen competition these days, if she is lying. And if a liar she is a game liar, one of those "that's my story and I'll stick to it" liars, which is the mark of the able liar.

And I regret to report that she seems to impress many of her listeners in the light of a wonderful liar rather than as a poor widowed soul falsely accused. The men were rather softening up toward the blond woman at the close yesterday in sheer admiration of her as a possible liar, and even the women who leer at her all day long had stopped hating her. They seemed to be commencing to think that she was reflecting credit to femininity just as a prodigious liar.

Even Henry Judd Gray, the baggy-looking little corset salesman who was on trial with her for the murder, and who has been sitting inert and completely befogged since the case began, sat up yesterday as if they had suddenly puffed air into him.

He had a fresh haircut and clean linen and looked all sharpened up. He half started when she fairly shrilled "no" at Froessel when he was asking her about the life insurance on Albert Snyder. Perhaps Gray had heard her say 'no' in that same voice before.

It was about the life insurance for $53,000 on Snyder's life that the assistant district attorney was most curious in his cross-examination, and about which Mrs. Ruth Brown Snyder was the least convincing. It was to double in the event of her husband's death by accident, and the State claims that Albert Snyder didn't know his wife had taken it out.

It was a very bad session for her on that particular point. Her answers were at times vague and evasive, but her voice never lost its snap. She said the only motive Gray could have had for killing her husband was to get the life insurance money, and when it was suggested to her that she was the beneficiary, she argued: "Well, he knew he would get it away from me just as he got money from me before."

"Isn't it a fact, that you and Gray planned to spend that insurance money together?" she was asked.

"No," she said quickly.

Most of her answers were sharp yesses, or noes. In fact, Froessel insisted on yes-or-no answers, though sometimes she whipped in a few additional remarks to his great annoyance.

He hectored and badgered the blonde at times until her counsel objected and the Court admonished him. Froessel, a plump-built man of medium height, in the early forties, has a harsh voice and a nagging manner in cross-examination. He wears spectacles and is smooth-shaven and persistent, and there is no doubt that Mrs. Snyder at times wished she had a sash weight handy.

She broke down once—that was when she was again leading the way into the room where her husband was butchered, and where she claimed she saw Judd Gray astraddle of Albert Snyder in the bed. She repeated the story she told on her direct-examination.

"I grabbed Judd Gray and he pushed me to the floor and I fainted. When I came to I pulled the blankets off my husband and—"

Then the tears came. There was a microphone on the witness stand, and her sniffles came out through the amplifiers quite audibly. Mrs. Irene Wolfe, the plump matron of the county jail, moved to her rescue with water, and presently Mrs. Snyder went on.

"Watch her hands," a woman advised me. "You can always tell if a lady is nervous by her hands. If she presses them together she is under a strain. If they are relaxed, she isn't nervous."

So I watched Mrs. Snyder's hands as they lay together in her lap. They were limp, inert. Once or twice she raised one to adjust a strand of yellow hair that drifted out under the little black hat, or to apply a small handkerchief to her well-shaped nose.

Under a dim light, backgrounded by the old brown plush hangings behind the judge's bench, and seated on an elevated platform, the black-gowned figure stood out distinctly. Occasionally she fingered the black jet beads at her throat, and she always leaned forward slightly, the white chin pushed out belligerently. Her feet were still. She sometimes shook her head to emphasize a "no." Her voice, a little raspy through the "mike," has a musical quality.

Her speech is the speech of your average next door neighbor in the matter of grammar. I mean to say she is no better and no worse than millions of the rest of us. She says "ain't" but I just read a long dissertation by some learned fellow who says "ain't" will eventually be considered good grammar.

She displayed more boldness than adroitness in her denials when it was patent that she didn't care to go into details.

But she showed no disposition to hide anything about her affair with Henry Judd Gray.

May 4, 1927

That scared-rabbit looking little man, Henry Judd Gray, the corset salesman, is now engaged in what the cops would describe as "putting the finger" on Mrs. Ruth Brown Snyder, only such a short time back his ever-loving, red-hot Momsie.

He seems to be a fairly expert "finger man," so far. Perhaps his proficiency goes back to his early youth and much practice pointing the accusatory digit and saying, "Teacher, he done it."

He lugged us through many a rendezvous in many a different spot with Mrs. Snyder yesterday afternoon, while the lady, who had done a little "fingering" herself for three days, sat looking daggers at Henry Judd, and probably thinking arsenic, mercury tablets, chloroform, picture wire and sash weights.

This was after she had come out of a spell of weeping when her little daughter, Lorraine, was on the stand. That was a spectacle, my friends —the child in the court room—to make the angels shed tears, and men hide their faces in shame, that such things can be.

Henry Judd had scarcely gotten us out of the hotels which he and Mrs. Ruth Brown Snyder infested in the days—ah, yes, and the nights— when their heat for each other was up around 102 Fahrenheit, when a recess was taken until this morning.

Everybody was weary of traipsing up and down hotel corridors and in and out of hotel rooms, but Henry Judd kept making a long story longer under the direct examination of Samuel L. Miller, the stout, sleek-looking young lawyer who is associated with William L. Millard in defending Gray.

Henry Judd hadn't gotten right down to brass tacks, which is after all the story of the butchery of Mrs. Snyder's husband, Albert, and which Henry Judd will undoubtedly blame on the blond woman who has made him out the arch-sashweighter of the bloody business.

He had gone over his own early life before he met Mrs. Snyder and was a happy little corset salesman, with a wife and child down in New Jersey. He wept when he spoke of that, but composed himself with a stiff jolt of water from the same glass that had but recently been pressed by the lips of his former sweetie.

It was a dull, dry recital, especially those numerous little excursions to hotel rooms. A trip to one hotel room might be made exciting, but when you start going through one of these modern hotels, room by room, the thing lacks zest.

Gray stepped to the stand with a quick tread, and an almost soldierly bearing, which was most surprising in view of the fact he has looked all folded-up like an old accordion since the trial started. He did not commence straightening up until Friday, when he found Mrs. Snyder nudging him toward that warm chair at Sing Sing.

He raised his right hand with great gravity as the clerk of the court administered the usual oath. He did not sit down until told to do so by Justice Townsend Scudder, and he listened gravely while Justice Scudder told him he did not have to testify unless he wished. Gray bowed to the Court.

Sitting there was a scholarly-looking young fellow, such a chap as would cause you to remark, "There's some rising young author," or maybe a college professor. He wore a dark, double-breasted suit of clothes with a white linen collar and a tie that had an almost indecorous stripe. A white handkerchief peeped out of the breast pocket of the coat.

His dark hair, slightly kinky, made a tall pompadour. His horn-rimmed spectacles have yellowish lenses, which, added to the old jail-house tan he has acquired, gave him a sickly complexion under the stand lamp by the witness stand with its three lights like a pawnbroker's sign.

His hands rested quietly in his lap, but occasionally he raised one to his probably throbbing forehead. His voice is slow and steady, and rather deep-throated. A cleft in the middle of his chin is wide and deep. The psychologists and philosophers have noted it without knowing just what to make of it. He has a strange trick of talking without moving his upper lip. Or maybe there isn't anything strange about it.

He answered Miller's questions without hesitation and with great politeness. You might say with suavity, in fact.

"I did, sir," he would say. Always the "sir." He would impress you as a well-educated, well-bred, well-mannered young chap. You can't see inside 'em, you know. He has a remarkably bad memory that will probably get him in trouble when the abrupt Froessel, of the district attorney's office, takes hold of him.

"My memory does not serve me well as to conversation," he remarked on one occasion. He did not seem to be abashed by any of the very personal questions asked him, or rather read by Miller, who has a stack of typewritten notes in front of him. He is obviously frightened, however, which is not surprising when you consider he is facing the electric chair.

He invariably referred to the blond woman, who he says got him in all this mess, as "Mrs. Snyder," his tale of their introduction in Henry's restaurant by one Harry Folsom not varying from hers. He said he did plenty of drinking when he was with her on those hotel trips, and on jaunts through the night life of New York. She told him of her domestic troubles and he said she talked of leaving her husband and putting their child in a convent. He told her, so he said, that he hated to see a home broken up, which sounded almost ironical coming from a gent with a wife and child himself.

They exchanged Christmas presents, and he bought one for her mother.

Gray's own mother cried bitterly when her son took the stand. Mrs. Snyder talked much to him on insurance, Henry Judd said, and once he had induced her to pour out some arsenic which she had in the house to poison rodents, and one thing and another, as she explained to him.

But he hadn't reached sash weights and such matters when Justice Scudder declared the recess. It was a long day in court, with much happening before the defense for Mrs. Snyder rested and the defense of Gray began with the immediate production of Henry Judd.

Out of the dark tangles of this bloody morass there stepped for a brief moment a wraith-like little figure all in black—Lorraine Snyder, the nine-year-old daughter of the blond woman and the dead art editor. She was, please God, such a fleeting little shadow that one had scarcely stopped gulping over her appearance before she was gone.

She was asked just three questions by Hazelton as she sat in the big witness chair, a wide-brimmed black hat shading her tiny face, her presence there, it seemed to me, a reproach to civilization.

Justice Scudder called the little girl to his side, and she stood looking bravely into his eyes, the saddest, the most tragic little figure, my friends, ever viewed by gods or men.

"You understand, don't you, that you have to tell the truth?" asked Justice Scudder kindly. I thought he was going to seize the child in his arms.

"Yes," she said faintly.

"Then sit right down there and listen carefully," said Justice Scudder. 'If you do not understand the question just say, "I do not understand." Lean back in the chair and be comfortable. The Court rules the child shall not be sworn.'

So she sat down and the jurors gazed at her and everybody in the room felt like bawling. Mrs. Snyder gasped and shed tears when her child appeared—tears that probably came from her heart.

She hasn't seen Lorraine since her arrest. I doubt if Lorraine saw her mother across the big room or that the child fully comprehended where she was. Surely she could not know that all these strange-looking men gathered there were trying to kill her mother. It was a relief when Lorraine left the stand. Two minutes more and they would have been short one reporter in the press section.

"Lorraine," said Hazelton, "do you remember the morning your mother called you?"

"Yes, sir."

"Was it daylight or dark?"

"Light."

"And how long after she called you did you call the Mulhausers?"

"Right away," piped the child.

"That's all," said Hazelton.

"Not one question by the district attorney, Your Honor," said Newcombe.

"No questions," said Miller of Gray's counsel.

Thereafter while Gray was being examined, Mrs. Snyder sat with her elbows on the table, her head bowed, a picture of dejection as great as that presented by Gray for some days. The child seemed to have touched her heart, and the defiant pride with which she has faced her accusers disappeared.

Finally the head came up again and the greenish blue eyes, a bit watery, were leveled on Gray, but it soon drooped once more. The woman seemed a picture of remorse. One-tenth the thoughts she was giving to Lorraine at that moment applied three months ago would have kept her out of that court room.

Mrs. Snyder was on the stand three hours and a half yesterday. She quit the witness chair at 2:05 at the afternoon session and walked with slow step back to her seat at her attorneys' table followed by plump Mrs. Wolfe, the jail matron.

She was "all in." She kept her head down as she passed in review before the leering eyes of the spectators. Her face was a dead, dull white. Her dearest girl friends, as Mrs. Snyder calls them, couldn't have called her pretty without being arrested for perjury. She looked very badly indeed. She had no pep left but still I defy any other woman to produce any pep after so many hours of dodging.

The conclusions of some of the more nervous listeners at the close of Mrs. Snyder's examination were that hereafter no blonde shall be permitted to purchase a window sash weight without a prescription and that all male suburbanites should cancel their life insurance forthwith and try all the doors before going to bed.

She left not one but two doors open for Henry Judd Gray, so Froessel dug out of her. I think the fact of these unlocked doors will weigh heavily against Mrs. Snyder when the jury commences tossing the evidence into the scales of consideration. That, and the insurance that "the governor" didn't know was loaded on his life. He was carrying plenty of weight along with this mortal coil, was "the governor." That was Henry Judd Gray's name for him. Imagine the gall of the little whippet who sneaked into Albert Snyder's home and had a jocular title for him!

Not much jocularity to Henry Judd Gray now as he shrinks in and out of the court room in Long Island City while the ponderous machinery of the law grinds the sausage of circumstance into links of evidence.

It is likely that the case will go to the jury by Friday. It has taken two weeks to try a mother that the citizens of Pueblo County, Colorado, could have settled in two minutes under any cottonwood tree on the banks of the Arkansas, if all the State of New York has developed is true. But the citizens of Pueblo County are forehanded and forthright gents.

*

Spectators were permitted to remain in the court room during the noon recess and the ladies brought their ham sandwiches and tatting right along with them to while away the hour. They gossiped jovially about the troubles of their sister, Ruth, and a lovely time was apparently had by all. Strange it is, my friends, that morbid impulses move the gals to bite and kick for a place on the premises where a sad, distorted version of life is being aired.

The reader may recall that yesterday I drew attention to the blonde's magnificence as a liar, if she were lying, and today she stepped right out and admitted her qualifications as a prevaricator. She claimed the belt, you might say, when the following tête-à-tête came off between her and Assistant District Attorney Charles F. Froessel when the cross-examination was in progress this morning. "You lied to the neighbors?" "Yes." . . . "You lied to the policemen?" "Yes." . . . "You lied to the detectives?" "Yes." . . . "You lied to Commissioner McLaughlin?" "Yes." . . . "You lied to the Assistant District Attorneys?" "Yes." . . . "You lied to your mother?" "Yes." . . . "You lied to your daughter?" "Yes." . . . "You lied to everybody that spoke to you or with you?" "Yes."

If that isn't lying it will do until some lying comes along.

Mrs. Snyder came in for the morning session looking a bit more marbley than usual. She seemed somewhat listless as Froessel began "madaming" her again. Her voice was tired. Still, nearly six hours on a witness stand is not calculated to enliven anyone.

Froessel started off in soft accents as if he wished to be a gentleman no matter how painful, possibly in view of the fact that some folks thought he was a little harsh with her Monday. By about the third question, however, he was lifting his voice at the witness. He desired brevity, yes or no, in her answers, since she had a penchant for elucidation. Froessel didn't seem to realize that a blonde loves to talk.

She sat all morning with her hands in her lap; listless, loose hands they were. The familiar black jet beads were missing from the throat in the morning, but she came back with them in the afternoon and toyed with them constantly. Nerves at last!

The greenish blue eyes looked at Froessel so coldly that once he shivered and glanced around to see whence came that draft.

The blond woman wasn't as self-possessed as she had been the day before and she got somewhat tangled up right off the reel as to what she had testified with reference to her knowledge of Gray's murderous intentions against "the governor." The poor old "governor"! There were two strikes on him any time he walked under his own rooftree.

The ice in the blonde cracked up as Froessel kept picking at her, and her voice was petulant as she answered one question with: "I tell you I don't remember what I did."

She was sore at Froessel, that was apparent. It takes a bold man to deliberately make a blonde sore, even though she be a prisoner of old John Law. Froessel yelled at her with great violence, especially when she tried to go beyond his questions, and she gave him some very disquieting glares.

"May I explain that?" she asked a couple of times.

"You may not!" he said acidly, and the greenish blue eyes sizzled.

"Just answer questions, madam, and do not attempt to explain matters," said Justice Scudder from the bench, peering down at her over his glasses.

"Well, yes or no covers so much, Judge, I can't answer," she replied sulkily.

Froessel escorted the woman back to her home in Queens Village and to that bloody early morning of March 20. He went over her story on that occasion with her, word by word. He got a bit excited at her answers and hammered the table with great violence.

"No buts—no buts!" he yelled.

"I object to the attitude of the district attorney," interposed Hazelton, and Justice Scudder chided Froessel, but requested Mrs. Snyder to be more direct in her answers.

"And when you went into the room of your mother you saw Henry Judd Gray was there again. . . . And the first thing he did was to kiss you?"

"Yes."

"And you kissed him?"

"Yes."

"Knowing, or believing, whatever you want to say, that he was there to kill your husband?"

"Yes."

Just like that.

Three gentlemen contemplating marriage to blondes hastened to the telephone booths to cancel their troth, shivering in their boots as they went.

She said that the thud she heard while she was in the bathroom was the impact of the sash weight landing on the sleeping Albert Snyder. It must have sounded like Babe Ruth hitting a home run, judging from her description, though the doctors found no fracture of the skull.

Anyway, that was when she rushed to her husband's room to find Gray on the bed astraddle of Albert Snyder, where she grabbed at Gray, when he pushed her away, and when she fainted—as she told it.

Froessel was very curious about her actions after she came out of the faint. He wanted to know if she had tried to do anything for her husband in the way of kindly ministration. Any wifely aid? Any tender care?

"No," she said, just like that. She hadn't done a thing, merely pulled back the blankets and took a quick look at him. She said she didn't see the wire around his throat or anything like that. She didn't even touch the body to see if it was cold.

Jim Conroy, another assistant district attorney, got out the suitcase that was checked at the Waldorf by Gray and which was recovered by the police after the murder.

"Whose pink pajamas are these?" asked Froessel, as Conroy, a young man, blushingly held up some filmy robes de nuit, as we say at the club.

"Mine," she said.

"Whose blue pajamas are these?" asked Froessel, and Conroy gingerly exhibited more slumber suitings.

"Gray's," she answered, grimly. No "Mr. Gray," not even "Judd Gray," today. Just Gray-like.

"Whose toilet articles are in this box?" inquired Froessel.

"Both," she said, laconically.

Hazelton objected to the district attorney "parading for the forty-ninth time adultery before this jury—we are not trying that." The spectators glared at Hazelton for interference with their just due for all the effort it cost to get into the court room.

Froessel picked up a copy of the confession she made immediately after the murder and read it line by line, asking after each line, "Is that the truth?"

He finally got tired of asking that and requested her to say "yes" or "no" at proper intervals and save his breath.

She denied most of the statements attributed to her in the confession, especially with any reference to her part in the actual slaughter of her husband. She had more lingual vigor left at the finish than he did.

May 5, 1927

Bloody apparitions rising out of his memory of that dreadful night in Queens Village probably gibbered at the window of Henry Judd Gray's soul yesterday afternoon.

His voice kept lifting, and hurrying, as he sat on the witness stand, telling his version of the murder, until finally as he reached the climax of the tale, it came pouring out of the amplifiers with a rush, hard driven by a note of terror.

You wouldn't have been much surprised to see the little corset salesman suddenly leap up and go tearing out of the crowded court room with his hair on end. The red fingers of fear were clutching his heart as he said:

"I struck him on the head, as nearly as I could see, one blow. I think I hit him another blow, I think I hit him another blow because with the first blow he raised up in bed and started to holler. I went over on the bed on top of him, and tried to get the bedclothes over his mouth, so as to suppress his cries." A distinct thud was heard and a commotion stirred the men and women packed like sardines in one part of the court. A couple of court attendants quickly picked up the limp form of

Warren Schneider,* brother of the dead man, and carried him from the court room, beating the air with his hands and crying aloud, "Albert, Albert."

Few eyes turned to see. They were all watching the man on the witness stand, up to this moment more like a baggy dummy, popping out, through a mechanical mouth, words thrown in by the ventriloquist's voice.

"He was apparently full of fight. He got me by the necktie. I was getting the worst of it because I was being choked. I hollered, 'Momsie, Momsie, for God's sake help me.' I had dropped the sash weight. She came over and took the weight and hit him on the head, and throwing the bottle of chloroform and the handkerchief and the wire and everything onto the pillow."

Necks craned for a look at the woman who has been called "The Bloody Blonde," as she sat almost hidden from view among her attorneys and guards, and the spectators crowded in close around her on every side. The blond head, covered with a little black hat was bent low. You could not see the marble white face at that moment. It was between her hands. She was crying. Her mother, Mrs. Josephine Brown, was crying. So, too, was the mother of Henry Judd Gray, a small woman in black. She was sitting so close to Mrs. Snyder she could have reached out and snatched the black hat off the blond head.

The spectators gasped. For one brief moment, at least, Henry Judd Gray, most of the days of his life a dull, drab sort of a fellow, busied with a corset clientele, attained the proportions of a dramatic figure.

He was gulping as he turned on the high light of his tale, and frequently swigged water from the glass on the table in front of him. His attorney, Samuel L. Miller, stepped to the bench at 4:30, the usual hour of the afternoon recess, and suggested the recess to Justice Scudder.

"Oh, I can go on all night," Gray spoke up, addressing his remarks to the Court. "There are some points that I want to clear up."

Justice Scudder nodded.

---

*Albert Snyder had modified the family name.

The little corset salesman started to backtrack in his story and Justice Scudder said, "You told us that a moment ago."

"Well, I'd like to go back if possible, Your Honor, because we went down into the cellar."

"Very good, but don't repeat."

"I see," said Gray, picking up the crimson trend of his story, on down to where he said, his voice now lifting even above any previous note:

"I tied her feet. I tied her hands. I told her it might be two months, it might be a year, and it might be never, before she would see me again —and I left her lying on her mother's bed, and I went out."

His voice broke. The eyes that show much white, like the eyes of a mean mule, glistened behind the yellowish glasses in the vague light of the old court room. Henry Judd Gray, but a few minutes before the stark figure of a dreadful tale of blood, was close to blubbering.

As the Court announced the recess, a babble of voices broke out in the court room, and men and women stared at one another and argued noisily.

"I say to you that if ever human lips uttered the truth, this was the time!" bawled Willard Mack, the playwright, one fist clutching a wad of paper, the other his hat, as he stared about him wild-eyed and excited. "They'll never shake that fellow!"

"The man told a good story," ruminated David Belasco, the famous dramatist and producer, who hasn't missed a day of the trial. "I thought he would. A good story, indeed—indeed—but," and he shook his gray head, "weak in spots, weak in spots."

Thus the opinions differed among the celebrities, and we had a fresh batch of them, including Olga Petrova, and Irving Berlin, and Ruth Hale, the Lucy Stoner, who would officially be Mrs. Heywood Broun if her conscience permitted. Also Frankie Farnum, the hoofer, as well as all our good old standbys like the Marquis of Queensbury.

One thing is certain, Henry Judd Gray made a far stronger impression on the side of veracity than did the lady who is popularly referred to as his paramour. At times I thought Henry Judd was undergoing all the keen pleasure of a small boy telling a swell ghost story to his play-mates such was his apparent joy, but along toward the finish my flesh was creeping, like everybody else's.

At first he seemed to have a certain air of bravado, perhaps a rem-nant of the same curious spirit that may have sent him into the mur-der in the first place—the desire of a weakling fellow to show off, you might say.

But gradually it became rather apparent it seemed to me, that here was a man who had something on his chest that he greatly desired to unload. He was making public confession, perhaps by way of ease-ment to a sorely harassed conscience.

That is, if he was indeed telling the truth, the whole truth, and nothing but the truth, so help him God. He put all the blame on the woman, to be sure.

He said she egged him on to the murder, steadily, insistently, until he found himself sprawling on top of poor Albert Snyder that night in Queens Village. He said she plied him with liquor at all times. He made himself out pretty much of an "A-No. 1" fathead right from taw, a vic-tim of an insidious blonde, though at no time yesterday did he men-tion any of his feelings for her, if any.

That will perhaps come today. He babbled all their indiscretions, though it was expected he would tell even more—and worse. In fact, it was rumored during the afternoon that Gray's counsel intended asking the court to bar the ladies from the court room, a canard that had several hundred females prepared to go to law for their rights as listeners.

If anyone retains an impression that Prohibition still prevails in the land, they should read Henry Judd Gray's testimony, although they may get a vicarious snootfull before they have gone very far, if they are susceptible to suggestion.

Henry Judd was quite a rumpot to hear him tell it, especially when he was with Mrs. Snyder. He said she cared for gin, while he went in for Scotch. He inhaled all of a small bottle of whiskey left for him by Mrs.

Snyder and most of a quart that he found himself in the room the night he waited in the Snyder home on murder bent.

In fact, one gathered the murder was conceived in whiskey and executed in whiskey, as is not uncommon with many other forms of crime these days. They were in bed together in the Waldorf, and she had come in "so plastered up" that he had a lot of trouble getting her into the feathers, when she first suggested the murder to him.

It was born in that bed in the Waldorf, he said, about the third week in February of 1927. "The plan that was later carried out," as Henry Judd put it.

One way and another, Henry Judd gave Mrs. Ruth Brown Snyder quite a bad reputation with the jurors, who sat listening open-mouthed to his tale, though it must be admitted he didn't spare himself. He pictured himself more as an able two-handed drinker than as a murderer, however. He gave the palm to Mrs. Snyder in this respect.

"I had two or three drinks," or "I had four or five drinks," or "I drank plenty."

This was the tenor of the early part of his discourse, tending to show no doubt that he was generally well tanked-up when he was with Mrs. Snyder. In fact, he said he was usually in a fog. He must have been if he drank all he says, what with the quality of liquor these days.

Mrs. Snyder's favorite pastime was trying to knock her husband off, as one gathered from Henry Judd's tale. She told Gray she had tried sleeping powders, gas, auto accidents, and bichloride of mercury, but had no luck. She put it just that way to Gray, he testified—"no luck."

She gave him four mercury tablets when he had an attack of hiccoughs, so she informed Gray, and the corset salesman says he remarked, "My God, don't you know that's deadly poison?"

"I thought so, too, but it only made him vomit."

"It is a wonder it didn't kill him."

"It is a wonder," she agreed, "but it only made him vomit fifteen or sixteen times that night."

"What were the aftereffects of this?" Gray asked her, he said.

"It apparently cured the hiccoughs," she replied.

"Well, that's a hell of a way to cure hiccoughs," Gray said was his comment. There were no titters from the crowded court room. Somehow, the situation in which poor Albert Snyder moved, was commencing to dawn on the spectators. They gazed in wonder and awe at the blond woman who is all the Borgias rolled into one, if what Gray says is true.

She was despondent most of the day. The defiance with which she faced the world at first has faded. Only once or twice she sat up yesterday and glared at Gray. His recital of the ten-day trip that they took through New York State, told without the omission of any of the details, was probably shameful even to this woman who must be shameless, if what the man says is the truth.

He admitted he borrowed money from her, but he claimed he had paid it all back a little at a time, except $25, which he still owes her. Mrs. Snyder will probably always have something coming to her. The impression you got from Gray's early recital was of a most despicable little tattle-tale, but you must bear in mind the man is fighting for his life, and men stoop to anything when life is at stake.

Gray's testimony, as drawn from him by Attorney Miller, was really not much different from the story set forth in his original confession made to the police and already read into the records of this case, save in detail, until he came to the murder.

You may remember Mrs. Snyder says she was in the bathroom when she heard a thud, and looked into her husband's room to find Gray astride her husband on the bed. She said she tried to pull Gray away, that he pushed her, and that she fainted, and recalls nothing else.

It is for the twelve good men and true to say who is telling the truth. For the first week of the trial, the blond woman appeared to be the stronger character of the two, and with the little corset salesman an inert heap in his chair, she was apt to impress the casual observer.

Now the situation is just reversed. The woman seems to be completely sunk, and while I wouldn't say that Gray stands out as any

Gibraltar, he at least shows some signs of life. But where she seemed defiant, he appears repentant in his attitude. He did not hate Albert Snyder—he had never met the man, he testified yesterday, though he may have seen him on one occasion with Mrs. Snyder, whereas he claims the woman often expressed to him her dislike of her husband. Gray said:

"She asked me once if I would please help her out by shooting her husband. I said absolutely no. I had never shot a man in my life, and I wasn't going to start in by murder. She asked me if I knew of any other plan, and I said absolutely no, I could not help her out, and she must see the thing through alone."

But she kept at him, he said. Blondes are persistent, as well as insidious. She kept at him. Drunk, or sober, he was always hearing the suggestion that he step out to Queens Village and slaughter Albert Snyder. You couldn't have seen the average man for heeldust after the first crack from the lady, but Henry Judd held on.

He suggested something of Mrs. Snyder's regard for him by testifying she said she would rather have him at home at all times instead of traveling around with those corsets, though he were only a truck driver.

"I told her that was impossible, that I had a family and a home to maintain and that they must be taken care of—that I would not break up my home," Henry Judd so declared, though it was quite apparent he didn't have any qualms about breaking up Albert Snyder's home.

He often cleared his throat as he talked, probably stalling a bit for time before his answers, though in the main he answered only too readily to suit attorneys for Mrs. Snyder. Both Dana Wallace and Edgar Hazelton were on their feet several times objecting to the testimony.

Henry Judd said he didn't know much about life insurance, but testified Mrs. Snyder had shown him one of her husband's policies and wanted to know how much she would get from it in case of his death. It would appear Mrs. Snyder went to work on that murder thought with Henry Judd soon after they met in the often-mentioned Henry's restaurant.

He at first told her that she was crazy and advised her to have a doctor look at a bump on her blond head. But she kept at him.

She wrote him every day and bought him silk pajamas. She even bought a Christmas present for his little daughter, who is about the same age as Lorraine. This was when there was a general exchange of presents between Henry Judd and Mrs. Snyder. She told him she enjoyed spending money on him.

The story of their ten-day trip to Kingston, Albany, Schenectady, Amsterdam, Gloversville, Booneville, Watertown and Syracuse was interesting only in its disclosures of the fact that you can get plenty of liquor in those spots. At least, Henry Judd did. He took a few drinks about everywhere they stopped, and they both got loaded in Scranton, Pa. when the trip was coming to an end.

It was when they got back from that journey that Henry Judd commenced to be more reasonable when she talked of making a murderer of him. He finally told her he would buy some chloroform for her but wouldn't help her use it. In the end he fell for it.

She had spoken about some heavy instrument, such as a hammer as a good thing to use in tapping Albert Snyder while he slept before the chloroform was applied.

"I think I suggested the window weight," remarked Gray, quietly. He bought one on a trip to Kingston, a little later, bought the chloroform, the colored handkerchief, and all else.

"I went to Albany and had a lot of drinks, and I got to thinking this thing over, and I thought how terrible it was and I—"

"One moment," bawled Hazelton, and the Court said never mind what he thought, to Gray.

He said Mrs. Snyder wrote him outlining what he should do, just as he related in the original confession, and he obeyed her instructions, he said. He didn't say why. That remains the most interesting thing that he has to tell—Why?

He told of going down to Mrs. Snyder's March 7 with the idea of disposing of the murder matter then, but Mrs. Snyder met him at the kitchen door and said the time wasn't ripe. He walked around Queens

Village quite a bit before he went to the house, Gray said; the mention of his wanderings telling more of his mental trepidations than anything else could have done.

Then came the plans for the second attempt, which proved only too successful.

"My God," Mrs. Snyder said to him at a meeting before the murder, "you're certainly nervous, aren't you?"

"I certainly am. I hardly know what I am doing."

Henry Judd shed what we might accept as a sort of sidelight on the Mrs. Snyder that was before she bogged down under the strain of the past two weeks, when he testified about the letters she wrote to him when he was on the road, and the murder plot was well afloat.

She asked about his health. About his business. She mentioned little Lorraine. Then she told him to drop down by her home Saturday night and bring the things he carried, which were the murder things. She concluded:

"I hope you aren't as nervous as you were."

May 6, 1927

Mankind at last has a clue, developed by the Snyder-Gray trial, as to the approximate moment when a blonde becomes very, very dangerous.

Gentlemen, if she asks you to try out a few sleeping powders, that is the instant you are to snatch up the old chapeau and take the air.

Henry Judd Gray gave this valuable tip to his fellow citizens from the witness stand yesterday, when he was under cross-examination.

He said that not until Mrs. Ruth Brown Snyder induced him to serve as a sort of guinea pig of experimentation with sleeping powders, which she purposed using on her husband, did he realize he was completely under the spell of her magnetism that caused him to later join hands with her in the slaughter of her husband, Albert Snyder.

It was in May a year ago, that he inhaled the powders for her so she might see how they would work. He had knocked around with her quite a bit up to that time, but it seemed the old spell hadn't got down to business. After that, he said, he knew he would do anything she wanted.

He was in her power. Narrowly did I escape writing it powder. It wasn't fear, he said; no, not fear. She had never threatened him. It was more magnetism than anything else.

"And this magnetic force drew you on even without her presence and was so great it overcame all thoughts of your family—of your wife and child?"

So asked Dana Wallace, one of Mrs. Snyder's attorneys, who was cross-examining for her side. There was a note of curiosity in the lawyer's voice.

"Yes," said Henry Judd Gray, and the spectators turned from him to peer at Mrs. Snyder, the blond magnet. She looked about as magnetical as a potato yesterday. She sat crouched at her attorney's table with her black hat between her hands most of the time, though now and then she lifted her face to glare at Henry Judd.

One side of the marble mask is now red from the pressure of her hand against it as she listens to the man who claims she magnetized him into a murderer. He was surprisingly steady under Wallace's hammering at his story of the crime.

Someone remarked it may be because he is telling the truth. It is always rather difficult to rattle a man who sticks to the truth, a bright and highly original thought for the editorial writers.

Wallace is trying in his cross-examination to make it appear that Henry Judd's was the master mind of the murder, and, while Henry Judd is not dodging a lot of activity in the matter, he is harking back to the original defense of man, the same being woman. I wonder if Eve was a blonde?

Early in cross-examination, Wallace had Henry Judd standing up in the witness chair with the sash weight that figured to such an extent in the butchery held in his hands, showing the pop-eyed jurors just how he slugged the sleeping art editor on the early morning of March 20.

Henry Judd has a sash-weight stance much like the batting form of

Waner, of the Pittsburgh Pirates. He first removed his big horn-rimmed glasses at Wallace's request.

"Show us how you struck."

"I used both hands, like this."

So explained the corset salesman, lifting the sash weight, which weighs five pounds, and looks like an old-fashioned coupling pin over his right shoulder. He "cocked it," as the ball players would say, pretty well back of his right ear. He is a right-hand hitter.

The tags tied to the sash weight to identify it as evidence dangled from the heavy bar below Gray's hands. The jurors and the spectators stared at the weird presentation. Gray did not seem at all abashed or nervous. Wallace asked, "How hard did you strike?"

"Well, I could not strike very hard."

He said Mrs. Snyder had done a little practicing with the sash weight first—perhaps a bit of fungo hitting—and found that the weight was too heavy for her, and asked him to pinch hit for her when the time came.

"Did you practice with her?" demanded Wallace.

"Well—ultimately," remarked Gray.

It was a gruesomely humorous reply, though I doubt if Henry Judd intended it that way.

You may recall that he said on direct examination that after he whacked Snyder one or two blows—he is not sure of the number—he dropped the sash weight to pile on top of the struggling art editor, and that Mrs. Snyder picked up the weight and beaned her husband.

Wallace picked on Gray on that point no little and in the course of the dialogue the corset salesman uttered one tremendous truism.

"You testified you thought you hit him another blow because at the first blow he raised up in bed and started to holler," said Wallace. "Didn't you hear Dr. Neail testify here that any of the three blows that struck Snyder would by itself have rendered him unconscious?"

Gray gazed owlishly at the lawyer through his thick yellowish lenses, and said, "I was there, Mr. Wallace, and Dr. Neail wasn't."

One thing Wallace did manage to do was to make it rather clear in his cross-examination that Gray did a lot of able, if murderous thinking, in going about the crime, especially for a man who was as soaked with booze as Gray claims he was. He had already drunk enough in his story to sink the battleship *Mississippi*.

He started out with the inevitable "I had a few drinks" with which he prefaces most of his answers, and Wallace interrupted.

"Is there any day you know of in connection with this case that you didn't take a lot of drinks?" he demanded.

"Not since I've known Mrs. Snyder," replied Gray with surprising promptness.

When closely pressed, he was almost defiant, and sometimes a trifle stubborn. Wallace kept asking him about the chloroform—whose thought was that?

"Wasn't it your idea?" Wallace asked.

"Well, let it be my idea," replied Gray.

He admitted he picked up a piece of Italian newspaper on the train en route to New York to kill Snyder and that it was after the murder he had suggested the mention of two foreigners by Mrs. Snyder, whereas in the original plan for the crime, a colored man had been in their minds as the fictitious object of suspicion.

It developed, too, from his cross-examination that the murder was finally planned in a chop suey place in Jamaica. He admitted he took the wire from his office with which Snyder's throat was bound. He said she had told him to get rope, but he didn't get the rope because "his mind was on his work" and he didn't think of it until he was leaving his office.

"Well, was Mrs. Snyder's presence or spirit around you in the atmosphere dominating and controlling you when you picked up the wire?" demanded Wallace.

"It might have been," said Gray.

"Do you believe in such things?" queried Wallace, eyeing the man carefully.

"I might," answered Gray.

It seems that Henry Judd has some sense of shame left anyway, and probably a lot of remorse. Wallace got to questioning him on his testimony that he and Mrs. Snyder occupied Lorraine Snyder's room for their intimacies whenever he went to the Snyder home.

"In spite of the fact that you had a little girl of your own, you did that?" asked Wallace.

"I'm ashamed to say I did," replied Gray.

"You forgot your own flesh and blood?"

"I'm ashamed to say I did."

Mrs. Snyder raised her head and looked at him. Then she shook her head and dropped her face in her hands again. Gray said that, with only one or two exceptions, they always used the child's room as their trysting place, if that is what you call it.

Wallace referred to the plot for the murder formulated in the chop suey joint as "the Chinese plan," and Millard asked, "Is that facetious, Your Honor?"

"The Court is quite ignorant," replied Justice Scudder, wearily. "The Court could not say. Proceed, gentlemen."

Gray said, rather surprisingly, that he was not thinking of murder when he prepared his Syracuse alibi. He didn't know why he had picked up the waste in the street in Rochester that was used to give Albert Snyder chloroform. At times he didn't remember, too.

Hazelton darted to Wallace's side at intervals and coached his partner on some questions. Gray held himself in such a collected manner that both Miller and Millard, his counsel, were grinning gleefully.

He admitted he had felt the hands of the dead man, Snyder, though later he said it might have been the foot, and "announced to the widow," as Wallace casually put it, he thought the art editor was defunct. He said Mrs. Snyder was standing at his side at the moment.

But he claimed he never saw the wire around Snyder's neck. He pressed a pistol into Snyder's hand though he couldn't exactly explain why. He denied Wallace's suggestion it was to show Snyder's fingerprints on the gun.

He admitted removing his glasses before entering the bedroom, and said the reason he took them off, he thought, was in case of anything in the way of a fight.

"So your mind was so attuned to the situation, that although you were drinking, you were preparing yourself for a combat?" asked Wallace. "Not necessarily—no," replied Gray.

That was where he was weak—on his explanation of his apparently well-planned actions leading up to them.

"And you remember that occasion very well when you struck Snyder, don't you?" asked Wallace.

"I do not remember very well now," answered Gray.

He claimed he was in a haze from the time of the murder until he had passed Albany on his way back to Syracuse, yet he admitted sweeping up the cellar to hide his footprints and arranging to have the sash weight covered with ashes to make it appear it hadn't been touched. He said he did these things "automatically."

"You mean your mind was working to protect yourself?"

"Not necessarily—no."

"Well, what did you do it for?"

"I don't know."

Court then recessed until ten o'clock this morning.

Our line-up of celebrities was fairly strong again yesterday taking the field as follows:

Marquis of Queensbury, L. F.

Dave Belasco, R. F.

Olga Petrova, 1 b.

Francine Larrimore, 2 b.

Thurston, 3 b.

Willard Mack, ss.

Clare Briggs, c. f.

Lois Meredith, c.

One-eyed Connolly, p.

Mr. Brick Terrett, one of the gentlemanly inmates of the press section, circulated a petition among his brethren that Thurston, the magician, be requested to conjure up a few additional seats from his hat for the newspaper folks.

It was a swell idea.

This remains the best show in town, if I do say so, as I shouldn't. Business couldn't be better. In fact, there is some talk of sending out a No. 2 company and 8,000,000 different blondes are being considered for the leading female role. No one has yet been picked for Henry Judd Gray's part but that will be easy. Almost any citizen will do with a little rehearsal.

May 7, 1927

The Snyder-Gray murder trial—you instinctively put the woman first in this instance—is about over, and the twelve good men and true, who have been stolidly listening to the horrible tale for two weeks will decide soon what shall be done with this precious pair, the cheaters who tried to cheat the laws of God and man and wound up trying to cheat each other.

At about three o'clock yesterday afternoon, all hands rested as they say when they have dug up all the testimony they think will do any good, or any harm, either. If the Sabbath peace and quiet of any neighborhood is offended by loud stentorian voices, that will be the lawyers warming up for a lot of hollering Monday.

Court has taken a recess until then. Dana Wallace will open in defense of Mrs. Snyder. William L. Millard will follow Wallace, in an effort to talk Gray out of the chair.

Richard S. Newcombe, the grave district attorney of Queens County, will do most of the arguing for the State of New York.

And what, think you, do the blond woman and the little corset salesman expect from the twelve good men and true?

Gray—nothing. Gray's attorneys say he now has a clean conscience, since relieving it of the details of the butchery of Albert Snyder, and he thinks the jury will believe his story of how the woman wound her insidious blond coils about his life until he couldn't help doing anything she desired.

I gather from the statement that he expects no clemency. Blessed be he who expects nothing, for mayhap he will not be disappointed. I suppose that deep down Gray is hoping for mercy.

And the blonde? You can always look for a blonde to say something unique. Mrs. Ruth Brown Snyder says, through her attorneys, Dana Wallace and Edgar Hazelton, that she doesn't see how "any red-blooded men" can believe Gray's story—that hers was the heavy hand in the hammering and chloroforming and wiring to death of her husband.

He seemed to be red-blooded himself, this Albert Snyder, whose ghostly figure has stalked in the background of this horrible screen presentation of human life and death for two weeks. Much of that red blood is still on a pillow on which his head rested when Gray first beat down upon it with the sash weight, and which was still lying on the district attorney's table along with the other horrible exhibits of the crime after Court took a recess yesterday afternoon.

Two hundred men and women gathered about the table, pushing and struggling with each other for a mere peek at the exhibits. Several hundred others had gone into the street outside to pull and haul for a view of Olga Petrova, as she stood beside her Rolls-Royce, being photographed, and of Leon Errol, the comedian, and other celebrities who honored us with their presence yesterday.

That scene in the court was one that should give the philosophers and psychologists pause. The women were far more interested in the bloody pillow than they would have been in a baby buggy. It was the last thrill left to them after Gray and Mrs. Snyder walked out of the court, the woman passing rows of the leering eyes of her sisters with her head down, but with a dangerous gleam in the greenish blue eyes.

Henry Judd started off the day with a good big jolt of water from the glass on the table in front of the witness stand. He imbibed water while he was on the stand at the same rate at which he used to drink whiskey, if he was the two-handed whiskey-wrestler that his story would indicate.

Wallace touched briefly on Gray's whiskey drinking again as he went into the corset salesman's finances. He wanted to know if Henry

Judd always paid for the drinks. Henry said he did, a statement which interested all the bootleggers present. They wondered how he could do so much elbow-bending on his income.

That was about $5500 a year, out of which Gray gave his family $3500 a year. He had around $2000 left for himself. Wallace asked:

"And you visited night clubs and went to parties and did your drinking and clothed yourself on $2000 a year?"

"That is correct."

And then the philosophers and psychologists really had something to think about. Also the domestic economists then and there present.

Wallace seemed to be trying to connect Gray's purchase of some shares of stock in the corset concern for which he worked with some possible interest in the death of Albert Snyder, for financial reasons.

Q. May I ask you, with your mind in the condition it was under Mrs. Snyder's dominance, and being fully aware of your own home conditions and business affairs, what did you expect to gain by aiding and bringing about the death of Albert Snyder? What was your idea, your personal idea, of what you would gain?

A. That is what I would like to know.

Q. What's that?

A. That is what I would like to know.

Q. And without any reason for it that you know of, a man of your intelligence, you struck a man over the head with a sash weight and did the things you say you did?

A. I did.

Q. And you want to tell this jury you do not know why you did it?

A. I am telling.

Q. What did you intend to do after it was all over?

A. I didn't intend to do anything. I was through.

Henry Judd fell into a slightly philosophical strain as he proceeded. He may have been qualifying to cover the next murder case for some newspaper. Also his attitude toward Wallace became gently chiding. He remarked, "One sometimes does things under the influence of liquor that one does automatically."

It sounds quite true.

Wallace whipped many a question at Gray and then shouted, "I withdraw it" before Gray could answer. He could not keep the little corset salesman from going beyond the question at times. Henry Judd was inclined to be verbose while Wallace tried to keep him pinned down to yes and no.

"Are you answering my questions that way because in one form it involves her and in another form it involves you?"

"I am already involved."

May 9, 1927

If you are asking a medium-boiled reporter of murder trials, I couldn't condemn a woman to death no matter what she had done, and I say this with all due consideration of the future hazards to long-suffering man from sash weights that any lesser verdict than murder in the first degree in the Snyder-Gray case may produce.

It is all very well for the rest of us to say what *ought* to be done to the blond throwback to the jungle cat that they call Mrs. Ruth Brown Snyder, but when you get in the jury room and start thinking about going home to tell the neighbors that you have voted to burn a woman— even a blond woman—I imagine the situation has a different aspect. The most astonishing verdict that could be rendered in this case, of course, would be first degree for the woman and something else for the man. I doubt that result. I am inclined to think that the verdict, whatever it may be, will run against both alike—death or life imprisonment.

Henry Judd Gray said he expects to go to the chair, and adds that he is not afraid of death, an enviable frame of mind, indeed. He says that since he told his story to the world from the witness stand he has found tranquility, though his tale may have also condemned his blond partner in blood. But perhaps that's the very reason Henry Judd finds tranquility.

He sat in his cell in the county jail over in Long Island yesterday, and read from one of the epistles of John.

"Marvel not, my brethren, if the world hates you. We know that we have passed from death unto life, because we love the brethren. He that loveth not his brother abideth in death. Whosoever hateth his brother is a murderer: and ye know that no murderer hath eternal life abiding in him."

A thought for the second Sunday after Pentecost.

In another cell, the blond woman was very mad at everybody because she couldn't get a marcel for her bobbed locks, one hair of which was once stronger with Henry Judd Gray than the Atlantic Cable.

Also she desired a manicure, but the cruel authorities would not permit the selected one to attend the lady.

Thus Mrs. Snyder will have to go into court today with hangnails, and just those offices that she can give her bobbed bean herself. I fear that this injustice will prove another argument of sinister persecution when the folks start declaiming against burning the lady, if such should chance to be the verdict of the jury.

However, with all her troubles about her fingernails and the marcel, Mrs. Snyder did not forget Mother's Day. She is herself a mother as you may remember, though the fact seemed to skip her mind at times when she was all agog over Henry Judd. Also she has a mother, who spent the Sabbath very quietly in that house of horror in Queens Village with Mrs. Snyder's little daughter, Lorraine.

From the old jail Mrs. Snyder sent her mother this:

> Mother's Day Greeting—I have many blessings and I want you to know how thankful I am for all that you have done for me. Love to you and kiss Lorraine for me.
>
> RUTH

Henry Judd Gray, although calm yesterday, declined his breakfast. Moreover, he scarcely touched his lunch. Mrs. Snyder, on the other hand, is reported to have breakfasted well and was longing for some of the good Signor Roberto Minotti's spaghetti and roasted chicken at noon.

They both attended divine services at the jail in the afternoon. Mrs. Snyder seems quite calm, though at similar services last week she was all broken up. As between the two, the blonde seems to be rallying for the last round better than her former sweet daddy of the days before the murder.

Judge Scudder, the tall, courtly, dignified man, who has impressed all beholders of this proceeding as one of the ablest jurists that ever wrapped a black robe around himself, will charge the jury at some length because he must outline what consists of four different degrees of homicide. He will undoubtedly devote much time to the conspiracy charge in the indictment.

The jurors are men of what you might call average intelligence, I mean to say there are no intellectual giants in the box. They are fellows you might meet in any club or cigar store, or speakeasy. A good jury, I call it. I doubt if they will be influenced by any psychological or philosophical twists that the lawyers may attempt to offer them, if any.

May 10, 1927

Mighty short shrift was made of Mrs. Ruth Brown Snyder and Henry Judd Gray by that jury of Long Islanders—the verdict being murder in the first degree for both, the penalty death in the electric chair.

The twelve men went out at 5:20 yesterday afternoon and were back in the box ready to deliver their verdict at 6:57, an hour and thirty-seven minutes. They took off their coats as they entered the jury room, hoisted the windows for a breath of air, and took two ballots.

The first was ten to two for first degree murder, so I understand, the second was unanimous. Justice moved on the gallop against the murderers once the jury got hold of the case.

Mrs. Snyder, standing up to hear the verdict, dropped in her chair and covered her face with her hands. Henry Judd Gray, standing not far from her, held himself stiffly erect for a moment, but more like a man who had been shot and was swaying ever so slightly for a fall. Then he sat down, pulled a prayer book out of his pocket and began reading it.

He kept on reading even while the lawyers were up at Justice Scudder's bench arguing with the Court against immediate sentence. Mrs. Snyder sat with her face buried between her hands. Justice Scudder finally fixed the time of sentence for Monday morning at ten o'clock.

Gray finally put the prayer book back in his pocket and sat looking straight ahead of him, as if he had found some comforting passage in the word of the Lord. He said to his guard on his way to his cell, "I told the truth and my conscience is clear. My mother is glad I told the truth and God Almighty knows I told the truth."

"Oh, I thought they'd believe me—I thought they'd believe me," moaned Mrs. Snyder to Father Patrick Murphy when she met him in the hallway going back to the jail. But before she left the court room there was a flash of the old defiance that marked her demeanor until the late stages of the trial.

"I haven't lost my nerve. My attorneys know that I have not had a fair trial, and we will fight this verdict with every ounce of strength."

They have a curious custom in New York State of taking the prisoners before the clerk of the court after a verdict is returned and setting down their "pedigree"—age, occupation, habits and the like. John Moran, the clerk of the Queens County Court, sits in a little enclosed booth like a bank teller's cage, just in front of the judge's bench, and Mrs. Snyder was asked to step up there. Mrs. Irene Wolfe, the matron of the county jail, and a guard supported her, the man putting his arm around the blond woman as if he was afraid the black-gowned figure would crumble and fall.

The law is a harsh institution. It would have seemed more merciful to take the woman away at once to some quiet place, where she could allow the tears she was choking back with difficulty to fall as they might.

But they stood her up there and asked her a lot of questions that seemed fatuous in view of what is already known of her, and she answered in a low voice—Ruth Brown Snyder, thirty-two years old, born in New York and all that sort of thing. Married? A widow. The tears began trickling down the marble-white cheeks.

Then they finally took her out of the court room by the same path she had trod so often the last couple of weeks. She was pretty thoroughly licked at that moment, and small wonder, for she had just heard twelve men tell her she must die.

Gray stood up before Moran, still holding himself stiffly, but did not weep. In answer to one of the set questions as to whether he is temperate or otherwise he said temperate, which sounded somewhat ironical in view of Gray's testimony during the trial as to the prodigious amounts of liquor he consumed.

He, too, was finally taken away, still walking as if he had put a ramrod down the back of his coat to hold himself so. Henry Judd Gray had said he expected such a sentence, and he was not disappointed.

The pair probably knew they were gone when they received word to make ready to return to the court room in such a short time after the jury retired. Rumor had tossed the verdict pretty well around Long Island City and the court room when the announcement came that the jury was ready to report, and the verdict was a foregone conclusion.

A few hours' delay might have produced hope for one or the other of the man and woman that fate tossed together with such horrible results. It was still daylight over Long Island City, although the yellowish-walled old court room was vaguely lighted by electric lamps, which shed less illumination than any lights I ever saw.

There was a painful stage wait, and in came Mrs. Snyder and Gray, the former between two matrons, Mrs. Wolfe and another, and Gray between two guards. Attorney Edgar Hazelton came in with her. He had evidently gone out to steel her for the verdict. He knew what it was, no doubt of that. She walked in with her little quick, short steps, but her face was gray—not white-gray, a dull, sickening gray.

The man walked firmly, too, but you could see by the expression in his eyes he felt what was coming. He seemed to be holding himself together with a strong effort.

Now a stir told of the coming of Justice Scudder, a lean, stooping figure in his black robe, bobbing his head to the right and left with little short bows like an archbishop. The crowd always rises at the entrance of the judge, then sits down again in some confusion, but this time everyone seemed to adjust himself in his seat again noiselessly.

Justice Scudder peered around from under the green-shaded stand lamp on his desk with an inquiring expression, and, as the roll of the jurors was called, they answered in very low voices. Only one said "here" rather loudly, almost defiantly, it seemed.

The clerk of the court motioned the jurors to stand and then Mrs. Snyder and Henry Judd Gray were also told to rise. They stood there, Mrs. Snyder just behind Gray, leaning against the table. Gray had no support. They could not see each other.

Ten women fainted in the court room in the course of the day, such was the pulling and hauling and the general excitement of the occasion, but Mrs. Ruth Brown Snyder remained as cool as the well-known old cucumber, even when she heard herself termed enough different kinds of animals to populate the zoo.

She was mentioned as a serpent by William L. Millard. Also as a tigress. Still, Millard gave her a back-handed boost, at that, when he called her a sinister, fascinating woman. Perhaps Mrs. Snyder would have been just as well pleased if he had left off the sinister.

Cruel, calculating and cunning, he said she was. She kept her eyes closed while Millard was berating her, supporting her head on her right hand, an elbow leaned on the table. Her left hand was across her breast. Once she dabbed her eyes with a little kerchief, as if she might be mopping away a few tears.

But all that Millard said about Mrs. Snyder was just a few sweet nothings compared to what Dana Wallace said about Gray. He was "human filth," "diabolical fiend," "weak-minded," "despicable creature," "falsifier," and finally a "human anaconda," which is interesting if true, and ought to get Harry Judd a job in any side show.

The little corset salesman just stared straight ahead while Wallace was blasting him. However, he was upright and alert and heard everything Wallace said, probably figuring it sounded libelous. His mother and his sister sat near by and comforted him.

There was much talk of the Deity on all sides. Both Millard and

Wallace appealed to Him, and so, too, did the district attorney, when he came to summing up for the State. Newcombe was brief, and omitted brickbats for the defendants. He did compare Mrs. Snyder with a jungle cat, possibly just to make sure that no animals had been left out.

The district attorney was in what you may call a soft spot, anyway, with the defendants at loggerheads, and each trying to push the other into the electric chair. However, from the beginning Newcombe has conducted this case with singular simplicity of method, and without any attempt at red fire.

Millard's argument for Gray was as expected, that Henry Judd was a poor fool, a dupe, and a lot of other things that mean a chump, who was beguiled by the woman.

However, he astonished the populace by advancing the theory that Mrs. Snyder slipped Henry Judd a dose of poison the night of the murder, expecting her little playmate in blood would fold up and die also after he had assisted in dispatching Snyder. The poison didn't work, Millard said.

Furthermore, Millard made the first open suggestion of abnormality in Mrs. Snyder. I heard hints that Gray's attorneys intended trying to show that the lady wasn't altogether normal, during the trial, but all that junk was kept out—by agreement, as I understand it—and only in his argument yesterday did Millard mention the abnormality.

For Mrs. Snyder, the defense was she was the victim of Henry Judd, "the human anaconda," and he was but "hiding behind the woman's skirts." This caused Lieutenant McDermott, of the Police Department, to suggest mildly to me that it was a great phrase and true, in the old days, but now a woman's skirts are nothing to hide behind if a gent wishes to be really concealed.

Both Millard and Wallace were in favor of their clients being acquitted. Millard's was something of an appeal for pity, but Wallace said, in the spirit of Mrs. Snyder's defiance throughout this trial, that she was not asking for pity, she was asking for justice.

*

In some ways it was a disheartening spectacle, if one happened to think how many spectators would have been attracted to Long Island City to hear a few pleas for the Mississippi Flood sufferers. In another, it was something of a tribute to the power of good old publicity. It pays to advertise. We have been three-sheeting Henry Judd and Ruth to good purpose.

Trials and Other Tribulations, 1947

HERBERT ASBURY

Unlike other chroniclers of crime, Herbert Asbury (1889–1963) displayed little interest in the marquee names of American homicide, leaving the cases of Lizzie Borden, Dr. John Webster, Harry Thaw, et al. to historians such as his contemporary Edmund Pearson. Asbury's subjects were the gang members and gamblers, con men and crooks, whores and pimps, and other miscreants who made up the teeming underworld of 19th-century urban America. After a decade as a newspaper reporter, interrupted by army service during World War I, Asbury gained notice with an excerpt from his 1926 memoir, *Up From Methodism*: a sketch, set in his hometown of Farmington, Missouri, about a prostitute nicknamed "Hatrack," whose efforts to find redemption are cruelly rebuffed by the Pecksniffs of the local church. When H. L. Mencken published the piece in the April 1926 issue of *The American Mercury*, the magazine was banned in Boston, leading to a landmark court ruling that proved a victory for the anti-censorship cause.

Two years later, Asbury published his most famous and enduringly popular book, *The Gangs of New York* (1928), an engaging if not always reliable miscellany of anecdotes about Gotham's colorful lowlife past that long afterward provided the inspiration for Martin Scorsese's 2002 epic film. The book's success spawned a series of other "informal histories" of big-city sin and corruption, including *The Barbary Coast* (1933), *All Around the Town* (1934), *The French Quarter* (1936), and *Gem of the Prairie* (1940). Though Asbury's books sprang from a genuine debunking impulse—a cynic's desire to expose the tawdry underside of the American dream—paradoxically they are now read as highly romanticized accounts, loving evocations, even celebrations of a gaudy bygone age.

from The Gangs of New York

1

The moving pictures and the stage have always portrayed the gangster as a low, coarse person with an evilly glinting eye, a chin adorned with a rank stubble of unkempt beard, a plaid cap drawn down over beetling brows, and a swagger which in itself was sufficient to inform the world that here was a man bent on devilment. It is true that there were many such, and in the lore of the gangs there are numerous tales of their mighty exploits, but in the main the really dangerous gangster, the killer, was more apt to be something of a dandy. He dressed well, he shaved daily, he kept his nails manicured and his hair oiled and plastered to his skull, and when his gang gave a racket he generally contrived to grace the festivities in all the glory of a dress suit. In the days of the Dead Rabbits and the Bowery Boys, and later when Dandy Johnny Dolan of the Whyos was the fashion plate of gangland, the gangster was a big man; but in the course of years the misery and congestion of tenement life took their toll, and police and prison records show that the average gang member of the time of the Gophers, the Eastmans and the Five Pointers was not more than five feet and three inches tall, and weighed between 120 and 135 pounds.

Such noted followers of Paul Kelly as Eat 'Em Up Jack McManus and Louis Pioggi, better known as Louie the Lump, who was but a slim and beardless boy when he acquired a reputation as a murderer, followed the fashions with great care; and even Biff Ellison, for all his hugeness and great strength, was a fop in matters of dress. Ellison dearly loved to sprinkle himself with scent, of which he had his own private blend especially compounded by a druggist sworn to secrecy. Johnny Spanish was always arrayed like a lily of the field, as were Kid Twist and Richie Fitzpatrick, the most famous of Eastman's lieutenants; and Razor Riley, a noted Gopher who weighed less than a hundred pounds, but made up for his lack of heft by an amazing proficiency in the use of revolver, blackjack, and a huge razor which gave him his nickname. And Paul Kelly, who is now reformed and honorably occupied as a real estate broker and business agent for labor unions, was a perfect example of this type of gangster. Throughout his long career as chief of the Five Pointers Kelly exercised power second only to that of Monk Eastman, yet he was a dapper, soft-spoken chap who seldom engaged in rough-and-tumble fighting, although in his early youth he had been a bantam-weight pugilist of more than local renown. He resembled a bank clerk or a theological student more than a gang chieftain, and his dive, the New Brighton, was one of the flashiest palaces of sin in the city. Unlike most of his fellows, Kelly was fairly well educated. He spoke French, Spanish, and Italian, and with his well-bred manner could have moved at ease in relatively cultured society.

The story is told of a woman who went to New Brighton in Great Jones street, under the protection of a Headquarters detective, for the express purpose of seeing Paul Kelly, who had been mentioned in the newspapers in connection with some particularly sensational gang affray. For some time they sat in the midst of thieves and gangsters, literally surrounded by the current of miserable humanity which boiled up in the Bowery and Chatham Square and swirled through Chinatown and the East Side. Meanwhile they chatted with a dark, quiet little man who had been sitting at a table when they entered. He entertained them for half an hour with a dissertation on art, and then the woman and her escort departed. As they stepped out of the place the woman said:

"I am sorry we did not get to see Paul Kelly."

"Why," said the detective, "that was Paul Kelly you were talking to."

"Good gracious!" she exclaimed. "I thought he was slumming, too!"

But no one would ever have mistaken Monk Eastman, a worthy successor to Mose the Bowery Boy and as brave a thug as ever shot an enemy in the back or blackjacked a voter at the polls, for a bank clerk or a theological student. So far as looks were concerned, and actions, too, for that matter, Eastman was a true moving picture gangster. He began life with a bullet-shaped head, and during his turbulent career acquired a broken nose and a pair of cauliflower ears, which were not calculated to increase his beauty. He had heavily veined, sagging jowls, and a short, bull neck, plentifully scarred with battle marks, as were his cheeks. He seemed always to need a hair cut, and he accentuated his ferocious and unusual appearance by affecting a derby hat several sizes too small, which perched precariously atop his shock of bristly, unruly hair. He could generally be found strutting about his kingdom very indifferently dressed, or lounging at his ease in the Chrystie street rendezvous without shirt, collar, or coat. His hobby was cats and pigeons—animals have always seemed to possess a fascination for gangsters; many of them, after they reformed, or had been compelled by the police to abandon the active practice of thuggery, opened bird and animal stores and prospered. Monk Eastman is said to have owned, at one time, more than a hundred cats and five hundred pigeons, and although they were offered for sale in his bird and animal store in Broome street, it was seldom that he could be induced to part with any of them. He sometimes went abroad, on peaceful missions, with a cat under each arm, while several others trailed along in his wake. He also had a great blue pigeon which he had tamed, and which perched on his shoulder as he walked.

"I like de kits and boids," Eastman used to say. "I'll beat up any guy dat gets gay wit' a kit or a boid in my neck of de woods. "

When a reporter once asked Eastman, a few months before his death, how many times he had been arrested, the gang leader replied that he would be damned if he knew; and at Headquarters the police said that they had lost count of the number. "What difference does it make?" asked a detective who had often performed the thankless task. "The politicians always sprung him. He was the best man they ever had at the polls." Nor could Eastman number his marks of battle. He had at least a dozen scars from knife wounds on his neck and face, and as many more on other parts of his body. He boasted that he had been shot so often that when he climbed on the scales he had to make allowance for the bullets imbedded in his body. When he enlisted in the New York National Guard at the outbreak of the World War and stripped for examination, the physicians thought they had to do with a veteran of every battle since Gettysburg. They asked him what wars he had been in.

"Oh!" replied Eastman, grinning, "a lot of little wars around New York!"

During his career as a gang chieftain Monk employed a score of aliases, among them Joseph Morris, Joseph Marvin, Edward Delaney, and William Delaney, but it was as Edward Eastman that he was best known. His real name appears to have been Edward Osterman. He was born about 1873 in the Williamsburg section of Brooklyn, the son of a respectable Jewish restaurant owner. His father set him up in business before he was twenty years old with a bird and animal store in Penn street, near the family establishment, but the boy was restless, and dissatisfied with the monetary rewards of honest toil. He soon abandoned the store and came to New York, where he assumed the name of Edward Eastman and quickly sank to his natural social level. In the middle nineties he began to come into prominence as Sheriff of New Irving Hall, and is said to have been even more ferocious than Eat 'Em Up Jack McManus, who was making history in a similar office at Suicide Hall and the New Brighton. Eastman went about his duties carrying a huge club, while a blackjack nestled in his hip pocket, and each of his hands was adorned with a set of brass knuckles. In the use of these weapons he was amazingly proficient, and in an emergency could wield a beer bottle or a piece of lead pipe with an aptitude that was little short of genius. He was also a skillful boxer, and was a formidable adversary at rough-and-tumble, although he was not more than five feet and five inches tall, and his weight never exceeded one hundred and fifty pounds.

Within a year after his career began Eastman had cracked scores of heads, and he boasted that during his first six months as Sheriff of the New Irving fifty men whom he honored with his attentions had required the services of surgeons; his clubbings became so frequent, indeed, that the jocose drivers of Bellevue Hospital ambulances referred to the accident ward as the Eastman Pavilion. But Monk was always a gentleman; he was proud of the fact that he had never struck a woman with his club, no matter how much she annoyed him. When it became necessary to discipline a lady for a lapse in manners, he simply blackened her eyes with his fist.

"I only give her a little poke," he exclaimed. "Just enough to put a shanty on her glimmer. But I always takes off me knucks first."

Naturally, Eastman became one of the most celebrated citizens of the East Side, and innumerable young men began to imitate him in speech and manner, so that there came into existence a Monk Eastman school of hoodlums and brawlers. They expressed their admiration for the great bouncer by their slovenly appearance, their clipped, slangy speech, and a willingness to fight anybody, any time, and anywhere. Practically all of them enlisted under Eastman's banner when he surrendered his post at the New Irving and embarked upon a career as a practicing gang leader, and by 1900 he felt powerful enough to claim sovereignty over the domain which later became his by right of might. Then began his feud with Paul Kelly of the Five Pointers over the strip of territory between the Bowery and Nigger Mike's place in Pell street. Scarcely a week passed in which the gang chieftains did not send patrols into this No Man's Land, armed with blackjacks and revolvers and with instructions to kill or maim every opposing gangster found within the disputed territory.

The merciless warfare between the great captains kept the Chatham Square, Bowery and Chinatown districts in an uproar of excitement and terror, for not all of the gangsters were good shots, and their wild bullets frequently injured non-combatants and smashed windows. Occasionally the police appeared in force and made spectacular pretence of clubbing both sides, but in general these were meaningless gestures, for both Eastman and Kelly had strong political connections and were in high favor with the Tammany Hall statesmen. Eastman, in particular, became an especial pet of the Wigwam; for years he served the Tammany organization in many ways, and was especially useful around election times, when he voted his gangsters in droves and employed them to blackjack honest citizens who thought to cast their ballots according to their convictions. Whenever Eastman got into trouble Tammany Hall lawyers appeared in court for him and Tammany bondsmen furnished his bail, which was promptly forfeited and the case expunged from the records. In the intervals between his political engagements Eastman did what may best be described as a general gang business. He became interested in houses of prostitution and stuss games, he shared in the earnings of prostitutes who walked the streets under his protection, he directed the operations of his pickpockets, loft burglars and footpads, and provided thugs for men who wished to rid themselves of enemies, graduating his fees according to the degree of disability desired. Eastman himself sometimes led selected members of his gang in raids upon the stuss games which flourished throughout the East Side, and also, on occasion, personally accepted a blackjacking commission.

"I like to beat up a guy once in a while," he used to say. "It keeps me hand in."

Eastman had frequently felt the thud of a fist against his flesh while officiating as Sheriff of the New Irving, but it was not until the summer of 1901 that he experienced his first contact with a bullet. Then, having ventured abroad without his body guard, he was assailed in the Bowery, near Chatham Square, by half a dozen Five Pointers who fell upon him with blackjack and revolver. Unarmed except for his brass knuckles and his slung-shot, Eastman defended himself valiantly, and had knocked down three of the attacking force when a fourth shot him twice in the stomach. They fled, leaving him for dead upon the sidewalk, but he scrambled to his feet and staggered to Gouverneur Hospital, closing a gaping wound with his fingers. For several weeks the gang leader lay at the point of death, but in conformity with the code of the underworld he refused to divulge to the police the name of the man who had shot him. Meanwhile the war with the Five Pointers proceeded with redoubled ferocity, and a week after Eastman had been discharged from the hospital the police found a dead Five Pointer lying in the gutter at Grand and Chrystie streets; he had been decoyed from his accustomed haunt by a woman and shot to death.

For more than two years the conflict between the Eastmans and the Five Pointers raged almost without cessation, and the darkened streets of the East Side and the old Paradise Square section were filled night after night with scurrying figures who shot at each other from carriages, or from that strange new invention, the automobile, or pounced one upon the other from the shelter of doorways, with no warning save the vicious swish of a blackjack or section of lead pipe. Stuss games owned by members of the Eastman clan were held up and robbed by the Five Pointers, and Kelly's sources of revenue were similarly interfered with by the redoubtable Monk and his henchmen. Balls and other social functions in New Irving and Walhalla Halls were frequently interrupted while the gangsters shot out their mutual hatred without regard for the safety and convenience of the merry-makers; and the owners of dives and dance halls lived in constant fear that their resorts would be the scene of bloody combat, and so subject them to unwelcome notoriety. But it was not until the middle of August, 1903, that the crisis of the war was reached and the gangs met in the battle which marked the end of the feud, for it aroused the politicians to a realization of the needless slaughter of their most valuable assets, and awakened the general public to a knowledge of the power of the gangs.

There had been desultory fighting throughout the hot days of summer, and at eleven o'clock on a sultry August night half a dozen prowling Eastmans came upon a like number of Five Pointers preparing to raid a stuss game in Rivington street, under the Allen street arch of the Second avenue elevated railroad. The game was in Eastman territory and was known to be under Monk's personal protection, for it was operated by one of his friends who faithfully gave him a large percentage of the take. The indignant Eastmans promptly killed one of the invading Five Pointers, and after a flurry of shots the adherents of Paul Kelly sought refuge behind the pillars of the elevated structure, whence they emerged cautiously from time to time to take pot shots at the Eastmans, who had availed themselves of similar protection. After half an hour of ineffectual firing, during which two policemen who attempted to interfere fled down Rivington street with their uniforms full of bullet holes, messengers were dispatched to the headquarters of both gangs, and within a short time reinforcements began to arrive.

Eastman himself led a detachment of his thugs on the run from the Chrystie street dive, and from the shelter of an elevated pillar in the fore front of the battle directed the fire of his gangsters. The police were never able to learn whether Paul Kelly himself took part in the fight, but it is quite likely that he did, for he was never one to shirk danger, and whenever there was trouble he was generally to be found in the midst of it. At any rate, more than a hundred gangsters, about evenly divided between Eastmans and Five Pointers, had arrived by midnight, and were blazing away at each other with every elevated pillar sheltering a gunman. Half a dozen Gophers, wandering out of Hell's Kitchen into the East Side in quest of profitable adventure and honorable advancement, came upon the scene, and stayed not to learn the point at issue or even who was fighting, but unlimbered their artillery and went joyfully into action, firing indiscriminately at both Eastmans and Five Pointers. As one of the Gophers later explained:

"A lot of guys was poppin' at each other, so why shouldn't we do a little poppin' ourselves?"

While the battle raged storekeepers of the district barricaded their doors and windows, and dwellers in the tenements locked themselves in their rooms. Half a dozen policemen arrived after the fighting had been in progress about half an hour, but retired in disorder when the gangsters greeted them with a hail of bullets. It was not until the reserves from several stations charged down Rivington street with roaring revolvers that the thugs left the protection of the elevated railroad structure and fled into their dens. They left three dead and seven wounded upon the field, and a score were arrested before they could get away. One of the prisoners was Monk Eastman, who gave the name of Joseph Morris and said that he had just happened to be passing and heard the shooting. Naturally, he stopped to see what was going on. He was arraigned before a magistrate next morning and promptly discharged.

The politicians suffered excruciating pain when they opened their newspapers and read the accounts of the fighting under the elevated structure. Having provided burial for the dead and proper hospital care for the wounded, they called upon Eastman and Paul Kelly and impressed upon them the obvious fact that such wholesale combat jeopardized their usefulness. The gang chieftains were told that no one objected to an occasional murder or blackjacking if they were strictly in line of business, and that even a little fancy sniping now and then might be overlooked, for everyone knew that gangsters would be gangsters; but that engagements in force terrorized the East Side and must stop. A meeting between Eastman and Kelly was arranged, and a few days later the gang leaders came face to face in the Palm, an unsavory dive in Chrystie street near Grand, Kelly having been guaranteed safe conduct at the request of the Tammany politicians. Tom Foley, a notable figure in the councils of the Wigwam, who had employed Eastman to good advantage during a hot campaign in the Second Assembly district, acted as mediator, and after he had presented the case for peace, with covert threats that both gangs would be smashed if they continued their private feud, Kelly and Eastman agreed to stop the shooting and stabbing. It was further agreed that the disputed strip between the Bowery and Nigger Mike's should be neutral territory, subject to the operations of either gang. Foley then gave a ball to celebrate the truce, and just before the grand march Eastman and Kelly met in the center of the dance floor and ceremoniously shook hands. Thereafter they viewed the revels of their followers from a box, while the Eastmans and the Five Pointers danced with each others' girls under the benign eye of Tom Foley; and there was peace on earth and good will toward men.

So far as the actual number of men engaged was concerned, the battle of Rivington street was not to be compared with some of the earlier conflicts between the great gangs of the Bowery and Five Points. But it probably marked the heaviest concentration of firearms in gang history, for the old-timers were inclined to settle their differences with clubs, teeth, fists, and brickbats, and only an occasional gangster sported a pistol. But during the Eastman period there were few thugs who did not carry at least two revolvers; some lugged as many as four, besides the standard equipment of blackjacks and brass knuckles. Before the passage of the Sullivan law early in 1911, which made the possession of a firearm a prison offense, one or more guns was carried openly at the hip or thrust into the belt, while another could generally be found slung by a special harness under the gangster's armpit. This was a favorite device of the killers; a revolver so carried was easier to draw than if borne in any other position, and there was scant likelihood that it would be snatched by an adversary. Occasionally, when the police were on their infrequent rampages, a gang leader who was temporarily in bad odor with the authorities went about with his pockets sewed up, attended by a henchman who supplied him with cigarettes, matches and other articles which he might require. Prying detectives then not only failed to find a revolver on his person, but could not put one there and so send him to prison on manufactured evidence.

But such a gangster was by no means unprotected. Behind and before him marched his thugs with their pockets literally crammed with knives, blackjacks, and revolvers, and if trouble developed the chieftain found the proper weapon immediately ready to his hand. These gun-carriers were frequently arrested but they took the chance gladly in order that they might serve the Master and win favor in his eyes. Often a woman bore the revolver; she carried it in her muff, or in the huge hat of the period, or in a pocket of her jacket. The enormous coiffures called Mikado tuck-ups, which were popular in the nineties, offered excellent places for the concealment of a weapon; and when the pompadour came into vogue, the wire contrivance called a rat, upon which the hair was built up over the forehead, was replaced by a revolver. And sometimes the gangster's sweetheart carried his pistol smuggled against the bare skin of her upper arm, where it was held in place by elastic bands and was instantly available through a slit in her leg-of-mutton sleeve. Many of the gangsters kept reserve revolvers and blackjacks, which they called Bessies, in cigar and stationery stores throughout their districts.

2

Debarred by the terms of his agreement with Tom Foley from battling the Five Pointers, Monk Eastman sought an outlet for his restless spirits by increasing the frequency with which he attended in person to the various sluggings and blackjackings which had hitherto been largely carried out by his henchmen. Less than three weeks after the battle in Rivington street Eastman and two of his gangsters went to Freehold,

N.J., where they assaulted James McMahon, a coachman employed by David Lamar, whose financial operations had earned him much fame as the Wolf of Wall street. McMahon was to have appeared in court against Lamar, but as he and his lawyers walked up the courthouse steps Eastman and his thugs fell upon them, and beat and stabbed McMahon so savagely that he was unable to testify, and the case was dismissed. The gangsters escaped in a cab, but were captured a few hours later and lodged in the Freehold jail, where Eastman gave his name as William Delaney.

The gang chieftain sent word of his plight to Kid Twist, his principal lieutenant, who promptly mustered fifty heavily armed gangsters and loaded them into a string of carriages, intending to storm the New Jersey prison. But before the vehicles could leave the Chrystie street rendezvous Inspector McCluskey swooped down upon them with a large force of patrolmen, and after a fierce fight forced the thugs back into their den. Kid Twist then notified Tammany Hall, and the next morning two of the Wigwam's most brilliant legal luminaries proceeded post haste to Freehold. There political wires were pulled and witnesses obtained, and when Eastman and his followers were arraigned on a charge of felonious assault they were discharged and returned to Manhattan in triumph. That night Monk held a levee in his headquarters to celebrate his escape from Jersey justice.

The truce between the Eastmans and the Five Pointers was scrupulously observed by both sides for several months, but in the winter of 1903 an Eastman named Hurst wandered into a Bowery dive and became involved in a weighty argument with a disciple of Paul Kelly, one Ford, the issue being the bravery of their respective chieftains. The dispute ended in a fight, and Hurst was badly mauled; it is related that his nose was broken in two places and one of his ears twisted off. Monk Eastman immediately sent word to Kelly that Ford's life was forfeit, and that if Kelly did not care to attend to the matter of putting him out of the way, the Eastmans would invade the domain of the Five Pointers and take summary vengeance. As Monk expressed it, "We'll wipe up de earth wit' youse guys." Kelly replied tartly that the Eastmans were welcome to Ford if they could take him, and both sides prepared for war. But again the anxious politicians interfered, and once more a meeting was arranged between Eastman and Kelly, who made no promises but agreed to talk the matter over in the presence of neutral persons. Accompanied by armed body-guards, the gang leaders again met in the Palm. They shook hands with great formality and then, each with a huge cigar between his teeth and a hand on his revolver, sat at a table and proceeded to discuss ways and means to retain their honor and at the same time keep their thugs from each other's throats. They recognized that something must be done, for the politicians had informed them that if another outbreak occurred protection would be withdrawn and the police permitted to wreak their will upon them. And there were many policemen who yearned for just such an opportunity, for the honest members of the force had long suffered at the hands of the gangsters.

After much discussion it was agreed that the issue of supremacy should be decided by a prize fight between Kelly and Eastman, the loser to accept the overlordship of the victor and be content to remain strictly within his own domain. On the appointed night the gang chieftains, each accompanied by fifty of his best fighters, repaired to an old barn in the farthest reaches of The Bronx. Because of his early experience in the professional prize ring, Kelly possessed superior science, but it was offset by Eastman's weight and greater ferocity. They fought for two hours without either gaining an advantage, and at length, after they had collapsed and lay one across the other still trying feebly to strike, their followers loaded them into carriages and hauled them to the East Side and the Five Points. The bout was pronounced a draw, and as soon as they had recovered from their wounds the gang chieftains marshalled their resources and prepared for war to the finish, despite the protests of the politicians.

There were a few unimportant skirmishes, but the end of Monk Eastman's rule was in sight, and great trouble was also brewing in the pot for Paul Kelly. Eastman's downfall came first. At three o'clock in the morning of February 2, 1904, he and Chris Wallace, having gone far afield to Sixth avenue and Forty-second street to blackjack a man who had annoyed one of the gang leader's clients, saw a well-dressed young man staggering uncertainly down the street. Behind him, at a distance of some few yards, was a roughly dressed man who the gangsters thought was a lush worker waiting for his victim to fall. Eastman and Wallace promptly held up the young man, but it developed that he was a member of a rich family, and that the rough-looking man was a Pinkerton detective hired to protect him while he sowed his wild oats. The Pinkerton method has always been to shoot first and then ask questions of criminals, and as soon as Eastman and Wallace had poked their revolvers under the young man's nose and begun to slip their nimble fingers into his pockets, the detective promptly shot at them. The surprised gangsters returned the fire, and then fled down Forty-second street, turning occasionally to send a warning bullet in the direction of the pursuing Pinkerton. But at Broadway and Forty-second street, in front of the Hotel Knickerbocker, they ran into the arms of a policeman. Wallace escaped, but the patrolman knocked Eastman down with his nightstick, and when the gang leader regained consciousness he was in a cell in the West Thirtieth street station, and had been booked on charges of highway robbery and felonious assault. Indictments were promptly procured, and although at first Eastman laughed at the efforts of the District Attorney to bring him to trial, he became frantic when Tammany Hall ignored his appeals for aid. He was abandoned by his erstwhile friends, and almost before he knew what had happened to him he had been tried, convicted and was on his way to Sing Sing Prison under a ten-year sentence. Paul Kelly professed profound grief when he heard of his rival's misfortune. "Monk was a soft, easy-going fellow," said Kelly. "He had a gang of cowards behind him, second story men, yeggs, flat robbers and moll-buzzers. But he was a game fellow. He fought everyone's battles. I'd give ten thousand dollars to see him out of prison." The politicians, however, would not give ten cents, and so Eastman donned the stripes, and was never more a power in the underworld.

The Gangs of New York, 1928

ALEXANDER WOOLLCOTT

The Nan Patterson case, one of the most widely covered New York crimes of the early 20th century, epitomizes the type of sensational murder that many people, for better or worse, find more titillating than horrifying. A 19-year-old vaudeville dancer, Patterson was accused of shooting her married lover during a carriage ride down Broadway to the Fulton Street pier, where he and his wife were scheduled to board a steamship for Europe. Set free after two highly publicized trials that ended with hung juries, Nan was widely believed to have gotten away with murder, a belief reinforced by reliable reports that, on the night of her acquittal, she attended a banquet at which her lawyer toasted her as "the guilty girl who beat the case." Unlike other perceived miscarriages of justices, such as the O. J. Simpson case, this outcome provoked little outrage, since the public largely viewed the crime not as a tragedy but as an irresistibly lurid potboiler.

Given the flamboyantly theatrical personality he cultivated throughout his career, it seems natural that Alexander Woollcott (1887–1943)— actor, drama critic, writer for *The New Yorker*, leading Algonquin wit, literary arbiter for the American book-buying public—would be drawn to a character as histrionic as Nan Peterson. The exuberant tone of this piece nicely conveys the atmosphere surrounding the case in 1905, the heyday of yellow journalism, when (not for the first or last time) cold-blooded murder was routinely transformed into tabloid entertainment.

The Mystery of the Hansom Cab

It was in 1905 on May third, my dears, that, for the second and last time, the case of the People of the State of New York (ever a naïve litigant) against Nan Randolph Patterson was entrusted to the deliberations of an infatuated jury. After being locked up all night, they tottered from the juryroom to report that they, like the susceptible twelve who had meditated on the same case six months before, were unable to decide whether or not this handsome wench was guilty of having murdered Cæsar Young. At that report the exhausted People of the State of New York threw up their hands and, to the cheers of a multitude which choked the streets for blocks, Nan Patterson walked out of the Criminal Courts Building into American legend.

It was in the preceding June that the killing had been done. Cæsar Young, that was a *nom de guerre*, his real name was Frank Thomas Young—was a gay blade of the racetracks, a bookmaker, gambler, and horseman, personable, rich, generous, jovial, English. For some two years he was enchained by the loveliness of this Nan Patterson, a brunette, pompadoured, well-rounded show-girl from the sextette of a *Florodora* road company. He had picked her up on a train bound for California where, according to testimony which later put all manner of ideas into Eastern heads, they spent several days together in what must have been a singularly liberal minded Turkish Bath. But by the spring of 1904 he had returned penitent to the bosom of his wife and, for a healing voyage of reconciliation, the Youngs booked passage on the *Germanic*, due to sail from her pier at the foot of West Fulton Street at 9:30 on the morning of June 4.

On the night before, they had come in from Sheepshead Bay after the fifth race and taken lodging for the night with Mrs. Young's sister in West 140th Street. Indeed that last evening, Young's life was fairly swarming with in-laws, all bent, I suspect, on seeing that this, their Cæsar, should not change his mind at the last moment and run back to that dreadful Patterson woman. At seven next morning Young jumped out of bed, dressed, and sallied forth, explaining to his wife that he needed a shave and a new hat and would meet her on the pier not later than nine o'clock. He never kept that appointment and, too late to get her heavy luggage off the boat, poor Mrs. Young decided to let it go on without her.

Young never reached the pier because, at ten minutes before nine, just as the hansom he had picked up in Columbus Circle was rattling along West Broadway near Franklin Street, he was shot through the chest. The cabman, although subsequently disinclined to recall having noticed anything at all that morning, was at the time sufficiently alert to draw up in front of a drug store. Passersby who hurried forward found within the cab a dying man. Oddly enough the pistol which had killed him lay hot in the pocket of his own coat and he had fallen forward across the knees of the fair creature who was sharing the cab with him. Nan, for it was she, was extremely emotional and clasping her hands in supplication to the Deity, exclaimed (with admirable presence of mind, the State afterwards contended), "Cæsar, Cæsar, why did you do this?"

In the following November, the American people settled back to enjoy a real good murder trial, with Nan's face pale in the shade of a vast black picture hat, with her aged father, a patriarch superbly caparisoned with white mutton-chop whiskers, sitting beside her and kissing her in benediction at the end of every session. For the State appeared the late William Rand, who looked rather like Richard Harding Davis in those days. He was a brilliant advocate, although in talking to a jury, the tobacco-chewing members of the bar would tell you, he did rather suggest an English squire addressing the tenantry. For the defense the humbler Abraham Levy had been retained—the mighty Abe Levy who looked like a happy blend of cherub and pawnbroker and who, as the most adroit and zestful practitioner of the criminal law in this country, was called for the defense in more than three hundred homicide cases. The foreman of the first jury was the late Elwood Hendrick, eventually Professor Hendrick of Columbia, if you please, but— marvelous in this restless city—still living in 1930 in the East Fortieth Street house which he gave as his address on that day when Nan, after looking him sternly in the eye, nodded to her counsel as a sign that he would do as a juror for her.

The aforesaid American people, fairly pop-eyed with excitement, were at first defrauded. On the tenth day of the proceedings, one of the jurors succumbed to apoplexy and the whole verbose, complicated trial had to be started all over again. This form of mishap occurs so often in our courts that there is considerable backing now for a proposed law to provide a thirteenth juror who should hear all the testimony but be called on for a vote only in such an emergency. Roughly the idea is that every jury ought to carry a spare.

In the testimony it was brought out that Nan, aided by her sister and her sister's husband, had in that last spring worked desperately to regain a hold over her once lavish lover, trying every trick from hysterics to a quite fictitious pregnancy. On the night before the murder they had spent some clandestine time together in what was supposed to be a farewell colloquy. It was begun late in the evening at Flannery's saloon in West 125th Street, with one of Mrs. Young's plethora of watchful brothers-in-law sitting carefully within earshot. Nan had reached the morbid stage of predicting darkly that Cæsar would never, never sail next day. Profanely, he taunted her with not even knowing on what boat his passage was booked. Indeed he tossed a hundred-dollar bill on the beer-stained table and offered to lay it against fifty cents that she could not name the ship.

"Cæsar Young, Cæsar Young," she made answer, while abstractedly pocketing the stakes, "Cæsar Young, there isn't a boat that sails the seas with a hold big enough or dark enough for you to hide in it from me tomorrow morning."

Between two and three on the morning of the fourth, they parted—unamicably. Indeed there was testimony to the effect that at the end he called her by an accurate but nasty name, slapped her in the mouth, and threatened to knock her damned block off. It was the more difficult for the State to surmise how a few hours later they ever came together in that hurrying and fatal hansom. It was 7:20 when he left his wife in West 140th Street. It was not yet nine when he was shot at the other end of the city. Nor was all of that brief time at Nan's disposal. For the new hat was on his head when he was killed. And somewhere, somehow he had also paused for that shave.

There were sundry such *lacunæ* in the State's case. The pistol had been sold the day before in a pawnshop on Sixth Avenue but the proof that it had been bought by Nan's sister and her husband was far from watertight. Anyway the jury must have been left wondering why, if these people had all been battening on Cæsar Young, they should have wished so golden a goose slain. Another weakness was Young's general rakishness. But the State's chief weakness, of course, was Nan herself. She was such a pretty thing.

The strength of the State's case lay in the fact that it seemed physically impossible for anyone else to have fired the pistol. The direction of the bullet, the powder marks, the very variety of the trigger-action all pointed only to her. To the ill-concealed rapture of the reporters, a skeleton was trundled into court as a model whereby to convince the jury that Cæsar Young would have had to be a contortionist to have pulled the trigger himself, as Nan implied he did. Of course she was not sure of it. It seems she was looking dreamily out of the window at the time and was inexpressibly shocked at his having been driven so desperate by the thought of a parting from her.

It is needless to say that Mr. Levy, who managed to suggest that he was just a shabby neighbor of the jurors, seeking to rescue a fluttering butterfly from the juggernaut of the State, made the most of that "Cæsar, Cæsar, why did you do this?" At such a time, could this cry from the heart have been studied?

"Is there a possibility," Mr. Levy agrued, "that within two seconds after the shot, she could have been so consummate an actress as to have been able deliberately to pretend the horror which showed itself in her face at that moment? Do you believe that this empty—frivolous, if you like—pleasure-loving girl could conceive the plot that would permit her at one second to kill, and in the next second to cover the act by a subtle invention? Why, it passes your understanding as it does mine. My learned and rhetorical and oratorical and brilliant friend will tell you that this was assumed. My God, you are all men of the world. You are men of experience. Why, you would have to pretend that this girl possessed ability such as has never been possessed by any artist that ever trod the boards, not even by the emotional Clara Morris, not even by the great Rachel, not even by Ristori, not even by Mrs. Leslie Carter!"

Reader, if you are faintly surprised to find the name of Mrs. Carter in that climactic spot, consider that it may have been a delicate tribute to her manager, Mr. Belasco, who was attending the trial as a gentleman (*pro tem*) of the press. Then, as always, the Wizard's interest in the human heart and his warm compassion for people in distress took him often to murder trials, especially those likely to be attended by a good many reporters.

Mr. Levy's "learned and rhetorical friend" was not impressed. Indeed, he could not resist pointing out that Levy himself, while no Edwin Booth precisely, nor any Salvini either, had just read that very line with considerable emotional conviction.

"It does not require the greatness of histrionic talent," Mr. Rand said dryly, "to pretend that something has happened which has not."

Mr. Levy referred a good deal to Nan's dear old dad sitting there in court and, to play perfectly safe, he also read aloud from Holy Writ the episode of the woman taken in adultery. The jury disagreed.

The State tried again in the following April, moving the case for trial this time before Justice Goff, perhaps in the knowledge that, despite his saintly aspect, that robèd terror to evil-doers could be counted on to suggest to the jury, by the very tone of his voice, that hanging was too good for Nan. In his final argument, Colonel Rand was magnificent. In after years at the civil bar he argued in many cases of far greater importance and it was always one of the minor irritations of his distinguished life that laymen everywhere always tagged him as the man who prosecuted Nan Patterson. This gaudy prestige even followed him overseas when he was a high-ranking member of the Judge Advocate's staff stationed at Chaumont for the prosecution of those of us in the A.E.F. who were charged with cowardice, rape, insubordination, and other infractions of the military code.

"Oh, gentlemen, gentlemen," cried Mr. Rand in his peroration, reaching at last his guess at the scene in the hansom cab. "We are near the end, we are near the end now. Going back to revisit his early home and his old friends, a richer, stronger, heartier man than Cæsar Young that morning you shall not find. But the harvest of the seed he had sown was still to be reaped and the name of the reaper was Nan Patterson. And his companion, what were her thoughts? What were her reflections as she sat there by his side? One call, you may be sure, was insistent in her thoughts. One call she heard again and again. 'You have lost, Nan, you have lost. The end has come, your rival has triumphed, the wife has won. The mistress has lost, lost her handsome, generous lover. No more riots, no more love with him. He is going back, he is going back. Cæsar is going back, Nan. Back, back, to his first love. Back to his true love. Cæsar is going back, Nan. Back, back to the woman who had shared his poverty, who had saved his money, who has adorned his wealth. Back. Cæsar is going back to the wife he had sworn before God to love, honor and cherish.' Oh, if she had doubts, they vanished then; then she saw red; then the murder in her heart flamed into action, and she shot and killed. A little crack, a puff of smoke, a dead man prostrate on a woman's knee, the wages of sin were paid!"

Thus the District Attorney. But again the jury disagreed and after a few days he moved for a quashing of the indictment. It was immediately announced that Nan would be starred in a musical show called *The Lulu Girls*. It opened a fortnight later in Scranton, Pennsylvania, and got as far as Altoona, where, although billed by that time as *A Romance of Panama*, it quietly expired. Shortly thereafter Nan was remarried, after a lively vacation, to an early husband from whom she had been obscurely divorced. She then vanished from the newspapers, although there occasionally finds its way into print a legend that she is living in Seattle a life given over to good deeds and horticulture.

Ten years ago an elderly and indignant washerwoman living in a shanty in White Plains found herself surrounded one morning by a cordon of reporters and photographers all conjured up by a fanciful and self-sprung rumor that she was Nan Patterson. The White Plains *blanchisseuse* was furious, as it seems she was not Nan Patterson at all. Why, she had never been in a hansom cab or a Turkish Bath in all her life. She had never even been in *Florodora*.

While Rome Burns, 1934

JOSEPH MITCHELL

For every sensational homicide that transfixes the nation and earns a place in the annals of crime, there are countless murders that barely register on the public awareness and matter only to those immediately affected: the victims, perpetrators, and their relatives and friends. The case recounted here is just such a sad affair, and thus a perfect subject for Joseph Mitchell (1908–1996), the great chronicler of New York City's obscure, outcast, and often eccentric denizens.

A native of North Carolina, Mitchell arrived in Manhattan the day after the 1929 stock market crash. He worked as a newspaper reporter for eight years before joining the staff of *The New Yorker*, where he became a revered figure among his journalistic peers for his spare, elegantly crafted essays on characters such as Cockeye Johnny, self-declared "King of the Gypsies," Arthur Samuel Colborne, one-man crusader against barroom profanity, and Joe Gould, master of sea-gull language and author of the (nonexistent) nine-million-word "Oral History of Our Times." In this piece Mitchell's sympathy for the socially marginal is evident even in his treatment of the hapless killers, whose execution seems as sordid and pointless as the death of their victim.

Execution

A bleak throng of relatives of three murderers who were to die in the electric chair huddled on the steps of Sing Sing Prison last night and waited. They passed around a quart bottle and whispered hoarsely. They still were sitting there when Robert Elliott, the State's thin, bent little executioner, trudged up the steps and entered the barred lobby.

"That's Elliott," whispered a taxicab driver, sitting with the relatives. "That's the man that pulls the switch."

The relatives turned and stared. Elliott shook the gate and a keeper let him in. The executioner carried a little black traveling bag. He nodded to the keeper and went upstairs to prepare the utensils with which he would destroy the three men who succeeded, after a fantastic amount of trouble, in murdering Michael Malloy, the "durable barfly."

Elliott did not do as well as was expected last night because only three of the four men scheduled for death by electrocution reached the chair. Two hours before the time appointed for his death, the fourth man was given a respite of two weeks because someone believes he is a mental defective. So the State paid the executioner $450 for his night's work, instead of $600.

The three momentarily awaiting what is still referred to at Sing Sing as "the hot squat" were the principal members of the Bronx insurance-murder trust, the men who killed the barfly to get the $1,290 for which they had insured his life. That was back in February 1933. The matter was arranged in a grimy little speakeasy at 3804 Third Avenue, now a vacant store.

Anthony Marino, 28, the proprietor, needed some cash and one night he said, "Business is lousy." Frank Pasqua, 25, a Bronx undertaker, who was standing at the bar, thought the remark over. "Why don't we insure Malloy's life and bump him off?" he asked.

Joseph Murphy, 29, whose real name is Archie R. Mott, a bartender in Marino's speak, and Daniel Kriesberg, 30, a fruit dealer, who passed a lot of time in the speak, were selected to help with the murder.

Malloy, a former stationary engineer, who had been a drunken derelict for many years, was insured. Then the murderers started treating him to poisonous whiskey. Malloy enjoyed it.

They gave him oysters pickled in wood alcohol. Malloy enjoyed them.

Then they gave him a plate of poisoned sardines into which bits of ground tin had been thrown. Malloy liked the sardines.

The barfly was stubborn. They kept feeding him wood alcohol, and one night they took him, dead drunk, to a park, stripped him to the waist, threw several buckets of water on him, and left him to die. Next morning Malloy came into the speakeasy and said, "Give me some of that good whiskey. I'm about to freeze."

Twice he was purposely run over by a taxicab. That did no good.

So, on the night of February 22, 1933, the gentle band took the barfly to a furnished room in the Bronx, rented especially for the event, and held a gas tube in his mouth.

That killed him. Pasqua, the undertaker, got a doctor to sign a death certificate signifying that pneumonia killed the barfly. Then Malloy was buried in one of Pasqua's cheapest coffins.

But the insurance companies had the barfly's body exhumed, and so last night four men waited in the pre-execution cells. They were to be executed at 11 P.M. At 9 o'clock a telephone call came from Acting Governor M. William Bray giving Murphy two weeks' respite on the strength of his lawyer's assertion that he had new evidence that Murphy was subnormal mentally.

But no telegrams came for Pasqua, or Marino, or Kriesberg. Consequently, at a few minutes before 11 o'clock two prison vans backed up to the rear door of the prison's administration building, within the walls.

Into the vans climbed the thirty-odd men selected by the State to witness the execution of three of its citizens. The relatives, stubborn, still waited on the stone steps.

The van rolled slowly through the prison's yard and paused at the lane leading to the death house. The witnesses got out and stood under the bright lamp. They were ordered to walk single file down the lane. At the end of the lane two guards grabbed each witness and expertly frisked him. Then the witnesses, jostling one another to reach the front seats first, entered the electrocution chamber.

It is a little room. On the right, as you enter, are five benches for witnesses. The electric chair is in the middle of the room. It rests on three sheets of rubber carpet.

There is a sign above the door through which the doomed are escorted. It reads "Silence." At this door stood Principal Keeper John J. Sheehy. He stood there, red-faced, solemn, fingering the bunch of keys at his belt. On one side of the chair was a white operating table. On the other was a wooden pail.

Frank Pasqua, the Bronx undertaker, was the first to go. He wore carpet slippers, a gray sweater and an unpressed pair of flannel trousers. Father John McCaffery, the prison's Catholic chaplain, walked beside him.

The witnesses stirred in their seats when the pale, staring human shuffled into the room, and a keeper said, "Silence, please." Pasqua sat down in the chair. He did not say anything. He stared.

The priest held a cross in front of Pasqua's gray face. Pasqua leaned slightly and kissed it.

Elliott, the executioner, came into the room. He went to work methodically. He pulled the headpiece, the mask, over Pasqua's face. Then he began strapping him into the chair. A keeper kneeled and adjusted the electrode to Pasqua's leg.

Elliott left the room. The switches are in another room. The witnesses could see Pasqua's fingers clutching the wooden arms of the electric chair. He clutched so fiercely that his knuckles were white.

The witnesses could hear Elliott pull the switch.

It did not last long—only three minutes.

They placed the pale little man, still staring, on the white operating table and wheeled him into the autopsy room.

Then they brought in Anthony Marino, the speakeasy proprietor who needed cash. Elliott dipped the headgear into the brine pail. He brought it out dripping. He rubbed some of the water out of it. Then he placed it on Marino's head.

Marino smIled faintly. He kissed the ivory cross proffered by the priest. He kept on smiling. He crossed his legs, but a keeper nudged him and he uncrossed them so the electrode could be fastened to his right leg.

Elliott, the precise little executioner, hurried off and threw the switch that sent 2,200 volts of electricity through Marino's body. It took three minutes.

It took only two minutes to kill Daniel Kriesberg, the wry-faced fruit dealer. He came in, not as pale as his comrades, and sat down. He was escorted by Rabbi Jacob Katz, the Jewish chaplain.

As soon as the electricity whirred into the man in the chair the rabbi left the room, holding the Old Testament firmly against his breast.

"All out," said a keeper. "Walk quietly."

The relatives still were huddled on the prison steps. They got up and stood in the shadows, aloof, as the witnesses departed. A woman among them was moaning.

One of the men drank the last whiskey in the bottle and threw it away.

The relatives were waiting to claim the bodies of the three men who helped kill a barfly for $1,290. It took them a long time to kill Malloy. It took the State only sixteen minutes to kill them.

New York World-Telegram, June 8, 1934

H, L, MENCKEN

There was a period, from around 1910 to the early 1930s, when Henry Louis Mencken (1880–1956) exerted an enormous influence on American culture as a journalist, author, editor, book reviewer, and social critic. A relentless enemy of the American "booboisie" and gleeful slayer of sacred cows (he was known as "The Great Iconoclast"), he prided himself on his fiercely libertarian politics, radical freethinking opinions, and frankly held prejudices. "The plain fact is that I am not a fair man and don't want to hear both sides," he once wrote. "On all subjects, from aviation to xylophone playing, I have fixed and invariable ideas."

Mencken's intemperate style is fully displayed in the following piece from the December 3, 1934, issue of the Baltimore *Evening Sun*, his primary workplace and forum for more than 30 years. In his sneering assault on the "New Penology"—the emerging emphasis on the psychological and social roots of crime—the author sounds a note that, in subsequent decades, would be struck far more crudely by everyone from Mickey Spillane to the hosts of right-wing radio talk shows. Mencken's satirical use of honorific titles ("Baby Face Nelson LL.D.," "Dr. Pretty Boy Floyd") underscores his contempt not only for these lowlife outlaws but for anyone inclined to romanticize them.

More and Better Psychopaths

I

The criminal career of the late Baby Face Nelson, LL.D., covered twelve years. During that time he is known to have had a hand in the murder of three officers of the law, and in the intervals between these crimes he engaged in general practice as a thug and bully. The diligent cops first took him when he was only fourteen years old, but he was quickly rescued by the New Penology, which turned him loose on parole to perfect himself in his art. Taken again, he was paroled again, and thereafter he showed such rapid progress in technique that he was presently pushing Dr. John Dillinger and Dr. Pretty Boy Floyd for first honors. When they fell, he became undisputed cock of the walk.

The astounding thing about such scoundrels is that they survive so long. Nelson was a notorious thief and black-leg from 1922 to 1933, but he was behind the bars barely three years of that time. The cops arrested him over and over again, but always he managed to get out. Twice, as I have said, he was paroled, and once he managed to procure a pistol while in custody, and with it overcame a prison guard. How he escaped punishment the other times I don't know, but always he escaped. Finally, growing impatient with the cops who so constantly retook him, he decided to shoot them at sight, and during the last six months of his life he and his friends disposed of three of them.

Of such sort are the abysmal brutes that the New Penology tells us ought to be handled more tenderly. They are not responsible, it appears, for their wanton and incessant felonies; the blame lies upon society. And the way to deal with them is not to butcher them, nor even to jug them, but to turn them over to "trained experts," that they may be rehabilitated. Simply stating such imbecilities is sufficient refutation of them. Society is actually no more to blame for a gorilla of that kidney than it is for a mad dog, and the bogus "experts" can no more cure him than a madstone can cure the dog. There is only one way to deal with him, and that is to put him to death as soon as possible.

II

This the cops now do with great industry, to the applause of all sensible people. It is a hazardous business and the mortality is not all on one side, but there is plenty of courage in the constabulary camp, and it seems likely to suffice for the job. The cops, in fact, are the only agents of justice who show any competence and resolution. They almost always bring in their man, but once he is brought in he is in the hands of his friends, and if he doesn't escape by one trick he is pretty certain to escape by some other. Either he fools a jury or his lawyer fools a judge. And if both devices fail, then he buys a jail guard, or breaks out with firearms, or convinces a parole board that he deserves another chance.

An example of what all this amounts to was lately under our very eyes. Some time ago a professional criminal named Mais, wanted for various murders and robberies, went into hiding in Baltimore. The cops, getting his scent, tracked him down promptly, and took him into custody. He was heavily armed, and they risked their lives, but nevertheless they took him. Sent to Richmond to answer for a peculiarly brutal murder, he was convicted and sentenced to death. But in a few weeks he had broken out of jail, and on the way he had killed a policeman. Now he is at large again, and robbing and killing again, and other cops will have to risk death to take him again.

Dr. Mais' escape was a monument to the sentimentality with which such swine are now treated. Though he was known to be an incorrigible criminal, and all his friends were known to be of the same sort, he was permitted to receive visits from them in jail. Presently one of them slipped him a pistol, and the next day he was on his way, leaving one man dead and two wounded behind him. Suppose you were a cop, and met this Mais tomorrow? Would you approach him politely, tap him on the shoulder, and invite him to return to the deathhouse? Or would you shoot him at sight, at the same time giving thanks to God that he didn't see you first?

III

How many such men have been executed during the past year? I can recall but one—the Hon. John Pierpont, lately put to death in Indiana after two escapes. But the case of Dr. Pierpont was so exceptional that he must have been a victim of witchcraft rather than of justice. To his last moment he expected his lawyer to save him with some sort of preposterous writ or other, or his colleagues to break into the jail and deliver him by force. He went to the chair a much surprised and disappointed man, and he well may have been, for he was the first public enemy to face Jack Ketch since the memory of man runneth not to the contrary.

All sorts of lesser felons are hanged or electrocuted—women who poison bad husbands for the insurance, drunkards who shoot their mistresses, country Aframericans who run amok, and so on—, but it is almost unheard-of for a genuine professional to be dispatched in due form of law. Always he and his friends can raise money enough to hire a sharp lawyer, and always the lawyer is able to delay proeedings long enough for psychiatry and sentimentality to save him. Two years ago, in Missouri, such a scoundrel was convicted of kidnapping and promptly sentenced to death. But he is still very much alive and very busy with writs, petitions and psychoanalysis, and he will still be alive long after most of us are no more.

Here in Baltimore we once hanged a Whittemore, but Whittemore, like Pierpont, ran in such extraordinarily bad luck that one can only suspect the intervention of magic. On form, he should have escaped not only the noose, but also the penitentiary. Jack Hart was better served by the powers and principalities of the air, for he made two separate escapes, once through the door and once through the roof. And Duker and the Norris murderers also ran more true to normalcy, for all of them save Dr. Allers, who succumbed to the stiletto of a colleague, are still alive, fat and full of hope, with the taxpayers of Maryland providing them with free board and lodging, and the procession of the seasons ripening them for their inevitable parole.

IV

But the real masterpiece of the New Penology is not to be found among such lowly brutes, but in the person of the Hon. Thomas H. Robinson, Jr., LL.D., who as I write is still being sought by the cops for the kidnapping and cruel bludgeoning of Mrs. Berry V. Stoll, of Louisville. The Hon. Mr. Robinson, if he is ever shot by Department of Justice agents or taken alive and hanged, should be stuffed by the psychiatrists and given the place of honor in their museum, for he is an alumnus of two of their plants for reconditioning the erring, and seems to have been a prize pupil. Not even Duker throws a more effulgent beam upon their art and mystery.

Like all other such rogues, Dr. Robinson was a bad boy, and got into trouble early. His natural destination was the hoosegow, with the gallows to follow, but he was lucky enough to encounter a judge who was also a fool, and so he was turned over to "trained experts." Two separate gangs of them had at him. One (I quote from Dr. E. W. Cocke, State Commissioner of Institutions of Tennessee) diagnosed his malady as "dementia præcox (insanity)," and the other decided that he was a "psychopathic personality (not insane)." Between the two he wriggled out of custody, and was soon engaged in crime again, with literary endeavor as a sideline. His demand for ransom in the Stoll case was an eloquent argument for a literal carrying out of the New Deal.

If such deliberate and incorrigible criminals as Robinson are "psychopathic personalities," then what is a criminal? Obviously, the answer is that no such thing as a criminal exists, and that is the answer made by the more advanced wing of New Penologists. The felonious, they say, are simply sick, and the cause of their sickness is the faulty organization of society. Let wealth be better distributed, and the Robinsons will stop writing hold-up letters to the Stolls. And even though wealth continue to be distributed badly, the mysterious arcana of the "trained expert" can cure them.

How many sane people actually believe in this nonsense? Probably not many. Of one class I am pretty sure: the cops. I have never encountered or heard of one who thought of the Dillingers and Floyds, the Nelsons and Robinsons, as psychopaths, or as any other kind of paths. Nay, they think of these brethren as criminals, and when they go out to rope one of them they take their sidearms along. Certainly it is lucky for the rest of us that they do.

Baltimore *Evening Sun*, December 3, 1934

THEODORE DREISER

As early as 1892, while working as a reporter in Chicago, Theodore Dreiser (1871–1945) began to notice a recurrent type of crime that he regarded as symptomatic of America's obsession with "money success." This was a murder committed by a poor, ambitious young man who, having fallen in love with a well-off young woman he saw as his ticket to fortune, committed murder as a way of ridding himself of a once-desirable but now inconvenient girlfriend. With an eye to treating this topic in fiction, Dreiser began collecting newspaper clippings on a number of these crimes, finally settling on the 1906 case of Chester Gillette, who was executed for drowning Grace Brown, his pregnant factory-worker girlfriend, in an Adirondacks lake. The result was Dreiser's 1925 masterpiece, *An American Tragedy*.

Nine years after the novel's publication, a crime occurred that so closely mirrored the events in Dreiser's best seller that it was immediately dubbed the "American Tragedy" murder. The perpetrator was 23-year-old Robert Allen Edwards, who drowned his pregnant girlfriend, Freda McKechnie, in a Pennsylvania lake so that he could be free to marry Margaret Crain, a young music teacher with whom he was conducting a torrid affair. Because of its startling resemblance to Dreiser's story, the case became a nationwide sensation. More than 50 journalists, representing publications from *The New York Times* to the *Polish Everybody's Record*, flocked to Wilkes-Barre for the trial. (Among the reporters was Dorothy Kilgallen, whose vivid account follows the present selection.) Dreiser, fascinated by the parallels between the Edwards case and his novel, leapt at an offer to cover the story for the *New York Post*. His accounts appeared over five days, October 2–6, 1934, and were later expanded into a serialized series of articles, "I Find the Real American Tragedy," for *Mystery Magazine*. The following piece, the penultimate in Dreiser's reports for the *Post*, sets forth his view that the killer was ultimately less to blame for the crime than the societal and sexual forces that drove him.

Dreiser Sees Error in Edwards Defense

Opening Address to Jury a Mistake, Says
Author—Analyzes Letters, Finds
Swain "Insanely in Love"

WILKES-BARRE, Oct., 5.

Personally, in such a case as this, I consider it a tactical error for the defense to make any opening address whatsoever.

I know it is the customary thing so to do, but it is a stupid one. The jury does not need to know in advance what the defense is to be. I should think it would be a great advantage just to begin where the State left off, call your own witnesses and the State's also, and when you were through with them and had made your real defense, which in the main can only be made by testimony anyhow, then make an appeal to the jury clarifying all that you thought was wrong with what the State offered and showing why your story was the correct one.

However, in this case, Mr. McGuigan, brilliant lawyer that he is, permitted a very tame and commonplace outline of the defense story to be presented by Phillips. Why I wish to speak of this here is this:

The first witness he put on was Edwards himself, and obviously he had decided that the story as Edwards told it was about correct and that he would let him repeat it, trusting to later explanations and clarifications of alleged facts and denial of others, to make it effective.

It would have been more effective than the way it was.

You can see what I mean because of one thing. In Phillip's opening address he said that Edwards threw the blackjack into the water. When Edwards came on the stand and was telling his story, he said he noticed the blackjack was gone and couldn't find it.

Here is a conflict which, as you see, is ridiculous and could have been avoided by beginning with Edwards first.

But once more I feel it to be absolutely the wrong and unjust way to go about adjudicating these love tragedies. To begin with, I personally assume that Edwards committed the crime. Naturally the law, not knowing the circumstances, wishes him punished for something that it sees but does not understand.

The proper procedure under a more civilized state of society might well begin with an examination of the defendant's explanation, and then the duty of the court would be to examine not only what the defendant thought of his acts and why he did them, and what people who were merely observers of his acts, but I would have the officers of such a court examine into all of the facts of his life; all of the social pressures and all of the lacks of social pressures which might have influenced him to the course which he took.

In a trial like this, under the conditions not only provided but insisted upon, so much that should come into the picture never comes into the picture, and so much that is of no real exculpatory or explanatory character is kept out.

Take this particular boy. How is the effect of a very limited financial life to a very proud, very sensitive and very ambitious temperament to be shown? It is perfectly plain from this story that this boy was seeking not only a presentable but a gay and interesting life. The money with which he had to do was almost nothing. He could not continue in school because there was no money. He could not travel any or really go and do the many things which a better organized social system would have made possible.

Humdrum work, begun at the age of sixteen, brought him into contact with Freda MacKechnie and because of the closeness of their homes kept him more or less in constant contact with her.

It was the easier because it was the more convenient way to a pleasant relationship. The relationship which he would have liked to have maintained with Margaret Crain, whom he met at Mansfield, was made for a time impossible and even later very difficult for the want of money. That that will be shown I doubt. That it should be shown is to me only obvious and just.

Instead, the State insists on presenting a blood thirsty, calculating sensualist, who not satisfied with one attractive girl, goes to another. Not only that, but according to a number of letters read to the jury before the defense began, the state seeks to make him a brutal, soulless sensualist seeking to make capital of the lives of two women at once.

As I see it, this is not true. A little money in the possession of this boy before he established relations with Freda MacKechnie would have permitted him to indulge in his desire to be with Margaret Crain. And he would have been with her, that is, he would have returned to Mansfield, and from Mansfield very likely would have followed her to wherever she was, and not only that, but married her. And that, I submit, can be proved to the average reader if he will only examine the letters which were read to the jury.

Last night, before these letters were read, the general impression given out to the public was that they were too terrible for words and would destroy Edwards and his defense once and for all. And today, as Mr. Flannery began to read them, I thought I would hear just how irredeemable this defendant is.

Well I hope that a large number of these letters are quoted verbatim in the newspapers so that you can judge for yourself. In case they are not so quoted, I will say to you in their entirety they are nothing more than the excited, emotional, erratic blather of a boy of twenty-one, bewitched by the physical and emotional charms of the girl of his choice.

"I love you! I love you! I love you! I love you!"

I think there were perhaps six or seven hundred such remarks.

"I want to see you. I want to see you. I want to see you."

I think I might count up three or four hundred of those.

"Oh darling, darling, darling! I miss you! I miss you! I miss you!"

Take an adding machine and multiply that. Here and there in each letter, since they were intimate, he begins to recite the physical charms that are recited, for instance, in the song of songs that is Solomon's.

The letters prove the boy was almost insane about her. He wrote like either a damn fool or a boy of twenty-one.

If you want to know, when I was eighteen and nineteen and twenty and twenty-one I wrote such letters myself, and I was blissfully happy in doing so and so was the girl who received them. And the thought of crime never entered my mind at all. It seemed I loved a girl and a girl loved me. As a matter of fact, I couldn't think of anything else to talk about.

In the court room, as the letters were being read, I noticed that by the way they craned forward and glued their eyes on Mr. Flannery and put their hands to their ears every one thought that it was pretty swell to be loved like that.

In the case of the older ones it probably refreshed their memory as to their own youthful enthusiasm, and it is entirely possible that a number of them said to themselves: "Well, it is just too bad. The good old days are over."

I don't doubt that in the audience there were a number of people dominated by an abnormal, unreal conventionality, by the theory of some church, or the fear of the opinion of some of their friends, or this or that; who maybe felt that it was all wrong and that they were listening to something unbelievably bad.

If they felt so I noticed that they did nothing about it. They hung to their chairs for fear that five or six hundred outside might get one of them.

Now please don't imagine that I am an ogre descended on the world to destroy its conceptions of right, truth, beauty, fair-mindedness and fair play. I am not.

If this boy really cold-bloodedly and with malice aforethought killed this girl and killed her without being terribly swayed or bewildered by some other influence which he did not individually bring upon himself but which came upon him as life comes upon all of us, I would say, sure, execute this monster, because in that case he would be a monster.

But I cannot get out of my mind—and these letters that I heard help to keep it there—that he was influenced by the very chemical and physical influences which betray all of us at certain times in our life, and particularly in our youth.

New York Post, October 5, 1934

DOROTHY KILGALLEN

Though best known to people of a certain age as a panelist on the popular 1950s television quiz show "What's My Line?"—on which participants tried to uncover the offbeat occupations of weekly guests—Dorothy Kilgallen (1913–1965) first gained prominence as a news reporter and columnist. The daughter of James Kilgallen, a star journalist for the Hearst syndicate, she began her own writing career after her freshman year in college and, at a time when most female reporters were relegated to the society and women's pages, was soon earning bylines for her stories on disasters, murders, trials, and executions. A publicity stunt devised by her newspaper—an around-the-world race by commercial airline against a competing team of reporters—brought her international attention and she soon found herself in Hollywood, where she reported show-business gossip, collaborated on a film (*Fly Away Baby*) inspired by her globe-spanning exploits, and even appeared as a reporter in *Sinner Take All* (1936). She returned to New York City in 1937 and became a popular Broadway columnist and eventually a radio and television personality.

This account of the Robert Allen Edwards case, based on her firsthand reporting, appeared in a posthumously published collection of her work, *Murder One: Six On the Spot Murder Stories.*

Sex and the All-American Boy

In Court

The Defendant:	ROBERT ALLEN EDWARDS
For the Defense:	LEONARD MORGAN
	FRANK McGUIGAN
	JOHN C. PHILLIPS
For the Prosecution:	DISTRICT ATTORNEY
	THOMAS M. LEWIS
	ASSISTANT DISTRICT ATTORNEY
	HAROLD FLANNERY
Presiding:	JUDGE WILLIAM A. VALENTINE

It was the consensus among my male colleagues, who either saw Margaret Crain in the flesh or studied her photographs, that she had about as much sex appeal as a pound of chopped liver. At twenty-three she was thin, dark-haired, shapeless, with a hawklike nose that seemed always to be sniffing something unpleasant. Her pale blue eyes looked coldly out through large silver-rimmed spectacles. Her demeanor was decorous, demure, and virginal. If ever a truck driver had whistled at Margaret, his license would have been revoked immediately because of defective vision.

Margaret lived in the upstate New York town of East Aurora. She taught music in the school system of nearby Endicott, and she was known as an excellent teacher. Her parents were highly respected citizens, devout churchgoers. Her brother was an ordained minister and Margaret sang in the church choir. In all, the Crains were an exemplary family.

Robert Allen Edwards, the older of two brothers, came from a family that generations ago had given its name to the town in which they lived, Edwardsville, Pennsylvania, a hundred miles from East Aurora, New York. At twenty-one Robert was a handsome young man with bright black eyes, dark wavy hair, and the perfectly regular features we used to associate with Arrow Collar ads. In behavior he was quiet, polite to his elders, unfailing in his attendance at church on Sundays. Indeed, he frequently mentioned a desire to become a minister. Robert had the kind of clean-cut appearance and generally trustworthy manner that made people believe he would go far one day.

At the time Robert was twenty-one and Margaret twenty-three, Freda McKechnie was twenty-six (or possibly twenty-seven, her age was in dispute). Freda was a little meatier than Margaret Crain, but even the newspapers hadn't the courage to call her a beauty. Freda lived with her parents and a younger brother next door to the Edwards home, and as is only natural, the two families were well acquainted. Both Mr. Edwards and Mr. McKechnie worked for the Kingston Coal Company. McKechnie had a somewhat better job, but Edwards, because of the family's historic connection with the town, had a bit more status. The

McKechnies were pleased when Robert Edwards took Freda to church picnics or parties, although they may have wondered what incredibly handsome Robert saw in their plain-Jane daughter, who was, besides, more than a little older than the boy.

Margaret, Robert, Freda—I don't believe a more unlikely trio has ever played a sex-saturated love game that ended in tragedy so terrible, so unexpected.

Margaret and Robert had met while both were students at Mansfield State Teachers College in Mansfield, Pennsylvania, in the fall of 1931. Margaret was a senior, president of the college Y.W.C.A., a member of the vested choir and the campus orchestra. Robert was a freshman and president of his class. Margaret and he were first attracted by their mutual interest in music and dancing. Not long after, they discovered a mutual interest in more earthy things. The would-be minister and the teacher-to-be made a perfect pair: he ministered to her insatiable needs; she taught him a thing or two he hadn't known before.

In the spring of 1932 Margaret was graduated and returned to her home in East Aurora. A year later Robert left school when the financial burden became too great on his family and went to work for the same company that employed his father. Only distance separated him from Margaret, distance easily conquered when she helped him to buy and maintain the auto he needed to wipe out the intervening miles. Robert became a frequent weekend visitor at the Crain home, where his good looks, good manners, and unfailing consideration for others made him welcome in that house of virtue and godliness. The Crains liked him. He wasn't wealthy but he was steady. When he was out with their daughter, the Crains slept well.

Back in Edwardsville, Mr. and Mrs. George McKechnie felt much the same way. They had known Robert for years—he was the boy next door. Of course, he far outshone Freda in physical attractiveness, but Robert spent so much time around the McKechnie house, and took Freda out so often, that everyone assumed the two young people eventually would marry.

If Robert knew of this assumption, he certainly didn't share it. But Freda, approaching spinsterhood, was infatuated with him, and in his gentlemanly way, always ready to help out a friend, he availed himself of her favors from time to time. The cemetery in Edwardsville was one of their favorite resting places. There, during the intermissions, so to speak, our All-American Boy read detective stories to his partner in passion, scoffing at the endings, which always found the culprit in custody. He also gave her a copy of James Joyce's *Ulysses*, the "shocking" novel that had been allowed free entry into the United States only a few months before. At night, lying on her bed and gazing dreamily across at "Bobby's" house, Freda would invoke some of the more memorable passages in the book, the few she could understand.

Thus Robert, in modern parlance, had it made. Weekends in East Aurora with Margaret, the rest of the week in Edwardsville with Freda—his young life was filled with thrills. The girls knew of each other's existence, of course, but Robert kept the true nature of their relationships well concealed.

By mid-June of 1934, Freda discovered that she and Robert had gone to the cemetery once too often. The knowledge made her uncharacteristically nervous and depressed. She refused to eat, complained of sleeplessness, and began to look decidedly run-down. Her normally cheerful disposition left her. Always quick to laugh, she now didn't laugh at all. At last she let her sister Mary Ellen persuade her to see a doctor.

Early in the afternoon of July 23, 1934, accompanied by her mother, she entered the offices of Dr. Meyers. She left her mother in the reception room and talked to the physician in his private office, well aware of what he was going to tell her.

After the doctor had examined her and asked the usual questions, he said gently: "How did this happen? You know who the boy is?"

Freda bowed her head. "Yes. I know when and who."

"You ought to get married," the doctor advised.

"Yes," Freda said, "I want to."

"Will he marry you?"

Freda hesitated. "I don't know," she said.

As he scrawled a prescription for a sedative the doctor urged her to talk to the young man—he tactfully didn't ask for his name—about getting married as soon as possible. Then he said: "I suppose you want to tell your mother about this now, don't you?"

Freda jumped up in alarm. "No, no. I won't tell Mother. Please, Doctor, don't tell her!"

Dr. Meyers agreed. Freda joined her mother, and the two women left in silence. Mrs. McKechnie maintained later that she thought her daughter was suffering from nothing more serious than a nervous complaint.

As soon as she safely could, Freda telephoned "the boy" at the office to give him the news. They agreed to meet that night. Robert's voice over the phone had lulled Freda's fears and she dressed carefully for the rendezvous, more eager to be with her lover than worried about the thing they must discuss.

They drove around aimlessly in Robert's family car (his own was in East Aurora being repaired) while she told him what the doctor had said. Robert had no doubt that he was the father of the baby because, as he was to say later, "I knew it wasn't any other fellow."

When Freda had finished, Robert thought for a while. Then he said: "You can do one of two things. We can get married or you can go to a doctor about it. I'll give you your choice." Freda chose without an instant's hesitation. "I'd rather get married. I would rather have the baby."

Robert made no protest. He accepted her decision, but suggested that they wait until his next payday, August 1, when they could elope to Eunice, West Virginia. He knew a man there, Robert said, who would probably give him a job. They could begin a new life.

Freda went home, bursting with happiness. Robert went home to brood.

Freda's parents and friends were overcome with joy when she told them she was a bride-to-be. In the week that followed she laughed and joked like her old self. She bought material and started to make a wedding dress. To her best friend, Rosetta Culver, she confided that she was going to embroider all her underwear with lover's knots, and as they laughed and giggled, even drew the pattern with a fork on a tablecloth.

Robert had other ideas for tooling up for the wedding. On Saturday, July 28, he traveled to East Aurora to pick up his repaired car—and to repair his relationship with Margaret Crain. She had, of course, received his "Dear Margaret" letter. But he discovered that she had lost none of her desire for him, nor he for her. It must have been a spectacular weekend, for, as he admitted later, he began to think about a plan to unravel his now hopelessly tangled love life.

On Monday night, July 30, Bobby was back home, dutifully dining with his fiancée, her family, and Rosetta Culver. He was rather quiet that evening, but Freda, giddy with wedding preparations, was lively enough for both of them. Her jokes and antics left everyone but Bobby convulsed with laughter.

After dinner Robert and Freda drove Rosetta Culver to her home in nearby Wilkes-Barre. On the way back Freda suggested that they drive to Harvey's Lake—a favorite resort—for a swim. It was raining, and rather cold, but Freda insisted. So Robert drove to the lake and parked near one of the docks.

A cottage not far off was occupied by Mrs. William Patton, mother-in-law of Freda's sister Elizabeth. Freda visited with Mrs. Patton for half an hour before returning to Robert in the car.

As Robert said later: "She undressed first and then I did. It was when I was undressing, the thought struck me that I should do away with her because of her condition and my other girl."

So Robert Edwards, that nice boy, that model of Christian upbringing, that young man who one day hoped to minister to the souls of his fellow men, took a leather-covered blackjack from the glove compartment of his car and slipped it into the waistband of his bathing trunks. Then he and Freda walked slowly toward the water's edge.

A few minutes after ten o'clock he emerged from the water alone. He dressed, dumped Freda's clothes under a tree a short way off, and drove home. On the way he bought some chocolate bars for his mother. Before going into the house he hung his wet trunks on a clothesline behind it.

Next morning, the thirty-first, Freda's mother telephoned Rosetta Culver. She was frantic with worry, she said, because Freda hadn't come home the night before. Rosetta said she had no idea where Freda might be: Freda and Bobby had driven her home and then left. She hadn't heard from Freda since.

Mrs. McKechnie waited until noon before phoning Robert, who was home from the mines for lunch. He walked next door to the McKechnies', and seemed unconcerned that his fiancée had been out all night.

"Bobby," Mrs. McKechnie pleaded, "where is Freda?"

"Why, I don't know."

"Wasn't she with you last night?"

"Yes, but I drove her back home and left her on Main Street near the house."

"Oh, Bobby," Mrs. McKechnie wailed, "something terrible has happened to Freda. I know it."

He smiled. "Why, Mrs. McKechnie, nothing has happened to her. What could happen to her?"

"I don't know, Bobby, but that girl didn't call me last night. She never did that before—stayed out all night and didn't let me know where she was. Bobby, is there anything wrong with Freda?"

Bobby's face shifted expression. He looked deeply sincere. "No, Mrs. McKechnie," he answered. "Freda and I were never intimate. We were good pals, that's all."

Mrs. McKechnie then said in despair: "Bobby, don't stand there. Do something. Get your car and look. See if she has wandered off somewhere."

Robert Edwards left, but not to look for Freda. He went back to work.

As the afternoon hours dragged by, the McKechnie family huddled in the parlor, sick with apprehension, waiting for some word from

Freda. White-haired George McKechnie was home, and his elder son, and his married daughter, Elizabeth Patton, and Freda's uncle, Shadrich Dodd.

Five o'clock passed with still no word, and they sent for Bobby Edwards again. He reappeared, as nonchalant as he had been in the morning, and went into the kitchen and sat down to talk with Mr. Dodd. As Mrs. McKechnie had, Mr. Dodd questioned Robert closely.

"Robert," he began, "I'm deeply concerned over Freda. Now tell me the truth—what happened between you and Freda last night?"

"Well . . ." Robert started to reply.

But the ringing of the telephone cut him short.

John McKechnie, Freda's brother, answered. It was a policeman. Freda's body had been found in Harvey's Lake. John walked back into the parlor. "They've found Freda," he said. "She's dead. She's met with foul play."

Old George McKechnie leaped from his chair and shouted: "Our Freda's been murdered."

Elizabeth Patton walked into the kitchen and broke the news to her sister's fiancé. He paled, and looked surprised. All he could say was "What?"

Elizabeth heard her father stumbling toward the kitchen. She pushed Robert toward the door. "Bobby," she cried, "get out of here before my father kills you."

With Freda's body in the hands of the police, bits and pieces of the tragedy fell swiftly into place. Newspaper reporters streamed into Edwardsville and Wilkes-Barre. They observed, and concluded the obvious: the death of Freda McKechnie had all the appearance of a second *American Tragedy*. The first had been the drowning of pretty "Billy" Brown by Chester Gillette in the waters of New York's Moose Lake in 1906, the case on which Theodore Dreiser had based his celebrated novel.

Freda McKechnie, her belly already beginning to swell with the murderer's seed, had been found in shallow water at the edge of Harvey's Lake by a frightened teen-ager who saw her white bathing cap bobbing at the shoreline. When the body, clad in an orange bathing suit, was taken from the water, it became apparent that this was no ordinary summer drowning. The back of Freda's skull had been crushed by a blow of terrific force.

A few minutes later bathers passing a clump of trees near the lake came upon the clothes Freda had been wearing when she left the house the night before. With them was the red pocketbook Robert Edwards had given her for Easter. In the meantime, detectives had found a blackjack lying a few feet from the water's edge.

An autopsy, mandatory in the case of violent or mysterious death, revealed no water in the dead girl's lungs, proof that she was dead before she sank into the lake. The coroner decided she had died as the result of a blow by a blunt instrument. The autopsy also disclosed that Freda was pregnant.

That was enough for Chief County Detective Richard Powell. He ordered the arrest of Robert Allen Edwards on suspicion of murder.

Edwards was picked up at his home at ten o'clock on the night of July 31 and taken to the nearest state police barracks. His father, stunned but protesting his son's innocence, went along.

An hour later Detective Powell began the first of his interrogations.

"Bobby, give me the truth about what happened to Freda that night."

"Well," Robert began, "I had eaten supper and started down the street in my car. I met Freda and a girl friend and drove the girl friend to her home in Wilkes-Barre. I let the girl friend off and returned to Edwardsville. I let Freda off at Plymouth and Main streets between eight-fifteen and eight-thirty."

"Why did you let Freda off nearly a mile from her home?"

"I didn't want her parents to see us together. I saw her walk away toward the brewery. I was tired and wanted some sleep. I had driven from Buffalo on Sunday and didn't get home until three o'clock Monday morning. But actually I didn't go home anyway. I met some of my friends."

"Okay," said Powell, "give me their names."

Edwards grinned sheepishly. "It's funny, Mr. Powell, but I can't remember their names."

But he did remember that before going home he had stopped off at a drugstore to pick up some chocolate bars for his mother. And the drugstore clock, he recollected, was running slow. But the names of those friends: he just couldn't remember.

"Bobby," Powell said, "we found tire tracks near where Freda was killed. They match the tires on your car. We found your bathing suit hanging on the line in back of your house."

Edwards shrugged his shoulders.

Powell walked outside, went back five minutes later to ask: "Bobby, are you telling me the truth?"

Bobby raised his right hand. "Mr. Powell, I'm telling God's truth."

Suspect and detective fell silent. On the wall above their heads an old clock hammered out the seconds, and only its sound broke the heavy silence.

"Look," Edwards said at last, "I want to tell you what really happened. Freda and I were at the lake. She telephoned me in the morning and made a date to see me. We met that night and went to Sandy Beach. The bathhouses were locked. We changed our clothes in the car. We went into the water and waded to the float. I got a notion to dive. I dove. When I came up, my hand struck her under the chin; she fell backward and hit her head against the float."

"Go on," said Powell.

"We swam to the float and got up on it. She got cold and went back into the water. I saw her white bathing cap disappear. I went out for her but couldn't find her. I went back and got in my car and drove away. When I realized I had her clothing, I hid it at the foot of the tree."

There were no further questions that night. Robert Edwards was detained, however, and spent the first of what were to be many nights behind bars, the last place on earth anyone who knew Bobby Edwards ever expected him to be.

Tuesday night they took the suspect out to Harvey's Lake. When they returned to the state police barracks, Bobby called Powell aside. "I want to tell the truth," he said.

Powell led him into the interrogation room and they sat down facing each other. "Bobby," Powell asked, "when were you intimate with Freda?"

"I never was intimate with her."

A note of pleading crept into Powell's voice. He had known Bobby and Freda since they were children. "Robert, she's dead, and her child is dead. Don't blacken her any more than what she is."

The young man considered this for a few seconds. "I'm going to tell the truth, but when I tell you it was an accident you won't believe me."

Powell told him to continue.

"While we were getting from the float into a boat she slipped and fell. I felt her and there was no pulse and no heartbeat. I was afraid. I went back and got my blackjack and let her have it so it would look like an accident."

Would he dictate a statement to that effect? Robert said he would, and did—ten typewritten pages of it. Then he went back to his cell. He had told three stories. He would tell a fourth.

The next morning Robert was questioned by the Wilkes-Barre police chief, Ira C. Stevenson. They went back over the conflicting stories. Stevenson pointed out the wealth of circumstantial evidence against him—the fact that Freda was pregnant, his romance with Margaret Crain, the blackjack. Finally the chief said: "There's two lives gone, Bobby, hers and the baby's. You better tell the whole truth."

And this time he did.

"We swam for a while," he said. "We talked about getting married and about her having a baby. The water was a little over four feet deep, and when she ducked down once, she came up with her back to me.

"I pulled out the blackjack quick and hit her on the back of the head. I hit her with the blackjack and then I left her in the water. I could see her white cap go under. I got out and dressed as fast as I could, but I threw the blackjack in the water. Freda's clothes were in the car. After I'd put mine on, I drove back a way and left them under a tree. Then I drove on home after stopping to get a couple of chocolate bars for my mother, and went to bed."

When he had finished, Robert buried his face in his hands and wept.

On Friday, August 3, Robert Allen Edwards was charged with the murder of Freda McKechnie and remanded to the Luzerne County Jail. The next day Margaret Crain rushed down from East Aurora to be at his side. Her mother and her brother the minister came with her. Margaret and Bobby spent a half-hour alone. Then she talked to reporters.

Bobby, she said, could not possibly be guilty. Was she engaged to him? Engaged? Well, there was an understanding between them. "It had not been officially announced," her brother interposed, "but it was definitely understood by the families." At this point Leonard Morgan, Robert's chief counsel, stepped forward and remarked: "At the request of the family I want to take this opportunity to deny certain rumors that have been reported to us concerning the relations of Miss Crain and Edwards. They are absolutely untrue."

"Absolutely," Margaret added. "And I'll stick to him no matter what happens. Bobby's in trouble. My place is with him." For the time being, Margaret explained, she was returning to East Aurora. But she would be back to see her Bobby.

After Margaret's whirlwind arrival and departure, reporters went to see the McKechnies. Had they known about Miss Crain and Mr. Edwards?

They most certainly had, Mrs. McKechnie answered, biting off each word. "Freda and Bobby had quarreled about Margaret Crain. She had come down from East Aurora to stay with Bobby's folks, but Bobby had promised Freda that Margaret was going home the next day and that he would never see her again."

George McKechnie didn't much want to talk about Margaret Crain. He preferred to talk about Robert. "It's a good thing I didn't get my hands on him, that's all," he declared. "Bobby wouldn't be in Luzerne

County Jail. He would be in a place where his only judge would be the Lord. If justice is done he will be sent to the electric chair."

On August 21 a Luzerne County grand jury indicted Robert Allen Edwards for first-degree murder. The panel had needed only thirty minutes to arrive at its decision. Yet the speed with which the grand jury moved did not allay the fears of the prosecution that something might go wrong at Robert's trial. He had repudiated that confession he spilled out to Chief Stevenson. It was just possible, the prosecution reasoned, that the trial judge might refuse to admit the confession as evidence. Without Robert's incriminating statements, with only his admission to Detective Powell that he had blackjacked Freda after she died accidentally, the state's case against the defendant was far from airtight. And it might collapse altogether unless motive could be proved beyond a shadow of reasonable doubt. Margaret Crain had already sown the seed of doubt by stating publicly that her relationship with the handsome defendant had never gone beyond the hand-holding stage.

But a few days later a couple of detectives entered Robert's bedroom for a methodical search of his belongings. Hidden in one of his bureau drawers they found a packet of letters from Margaret. They proved that she and Robert had indeed been intimate, that she was extremely passionate and very much in love.

District Attorney Thomas M. Lewis read the letters, noted their fervent tone, and assumed that if Margaret had written love letters to Robert, then Robert might have reciprocated in kind. He also decided that if letters from Robert to his music-teaching sweetheart could be produced in court, they might establish a motive for Freda's murder that could be made perfectly clear to any jury of level-headed citizens. A few hours later Harold Flannery, Lewis' assistant, was on a train bound for East Aurora, fully aware of two important points of the law: Pennsylvania could not extradite Margaret from New York as a witness; she could not be forced to part with the letters, if such there were.

Margaret's father came to the door, and when the assistant prosecutor explained something of his reason for being there, Mr. Crain invited him inside to meet Margaret and Mrs. Crain. For the next hour or so Flannery, Mr. Crain, and his wife talked about the weather, the crops, the depression, anything but the murder of Freda McKechnie. Margaret sat on a rose-colored love seat with her legs curled beneath her and said nothing. Finally Mr. Crain asked his visitor if it was true Freda was carrying Bobby's child at the time of her death. Flannery nodded.

"About what they say Bobby has done," Mr. Crain said hesitantly. "Couldn't there be some mistake?"

"No," said Flannery, "there couldn't. The prosecution has the black-jack—the blackjack that Robert had in his car when he drove home from East Aurora the weekend before the murder."

He then turned to Margaret. "We have your letters to Bobby," he said.

For the first time since Flannery's arrival, Margaret showed some sign of emotion. She blushed. "Well," she sighed, "they should make interesting reading."

"Now, now," Flannery said soothingly, "they're just the letters of a girl in love. What we would like," he added smoothly, "are Bobby's letters to you."

She looked down at her hands, wound tightly together. "Tell me," she said. "If I gave you Bobby's letters, would they be read aloud in court?"

"Only those parts which are offered in evidence," Flannery replied.

"How much would that be?"

"I don't know. I'd have to read the letters."

"All right," she said slowly, "I'll get them for you. Do you want them all?"

"No, only the ones he sent you during the past few months."

Margaret walked upstairs to her room. She was back in a few minutes. "Do you want them wrapped?"

"I'd appreciate it," Flannery replied.

The following morning District Attorney Lewis and his assistant, Flannery, began reading Bobby's letters to Margaret. They expected to find the usual avowals of undying love and affection expressed strongly enough to provide a motive for Freda's murder. They found the avowals, all right, but "usual" is hardly the word. What they uncovered was a cesspool of erotic, profane, and obscene writings that made *The Memoirs of Fanny Hill* look like a toned-down version of *Little Women*. And threaded through these steaming passages, most of them apparently tactical reconstructions of some of their sexual activities of the recent past, was the sought-after motive—as plain as Margaret Crain's face: Bobby and Margaret were dead set on marriage.

Flannery returned to East Aurora the next day. He made it perfectly clear how much Margaret might be hurt if those letters were read in court. It would be better for her simply to testify that she expected Bobby to marry her; that it had been understood between them; that they were in love with each other.

While Margaret hesitated, Mr. Crain asked Flannery to leave so that Margaret could have time to think things over before coming to a decision. Flannery checked into a local hotel to await the girl's call. It never came. Instead, Thomas Mangan, a Binghamton, N.Y., attorney telephoned to say that he was representing Miss Crain and that he thought it unnecessary for her to go through the ordeal of testifying against Mr. Edwards.

Flannery went to see Mangan and patiently outlined the damning contents of the letters. But Mangan refused to try to persuade his client to change her mind. "It is unnecessary," he said, "for my client to go to Wilkes-Barre."

At precisely ten o'clock on the morning of October 1, Judge Valentine hurried into his third-floor courtroom, mounted the bench, and looked toward the clerk of the court. The clerk arose and cried out: "The Commonwealth of Pennsylvania versus Robert Allen Edwards."

Thirty newspaper reporters and a battery of special writers, including Theodore Dreiser (representing the New York *Post*), whose novel *An American Tragedy*, as I've mentioned, so closely resembled the Edwards case, opened their notebooks and awaited the questioning of prospective jurors. Two hundred spectators, who had maneuvered their way into the musty courtroom, leaned forward. In the corridors on the first, second, and third floors of the courthouse, policemen struggled to control five hundred others who hadn't the special passes that would have admitted them to the courtroom itself. Outside, the line of would-be spectators extended a half-block to River Street and down River Street to the banks of the Susquehanna River. For Wilkes-Barre it was quite a spectacle.

Only the defendant appeared bored by it all: he showed no trace of emotion. He was impeccably dressed—freshly pressed blue serge suit, white shirt, dark blue tie, and highly polished black shoes. He was closely shaven; his black hair was slicked back and down. The legend beneath his high school yearbook graduation picture had read: "Smiles for the ladies, never tears; Bobby's conquests will last for years." I could see why.

By late afternoon the panel was complete: twelve "blue-collar" workers, all male.

When darkness came, lights winked on in the courtroom. A light breeze blew from the Susquehanna River, bending the trees outside like performers bowing at curtain call. Assistant District Attorney Flannery rose, stepped to within a few feet of the jurors, and began the prosecution's opening statement.

He ran through the early moments of Bobby and Freda's "court-ship," his voice gay, his face alight with Freda's joy. "Freda was happy as a girl can be," Flannery said. "She had made a dress—she was going to be married. Last Christmas, Edwards gave her jeweled clasps. And at Easter he gave her a red purse—the one that was found in the lake when her body was lifted to the surface!"

The defendant leaned forward. He was no longer bored. He glowered at the prosecutor. But Flannery, ignoring him, dragged the image of Margaret Crain on stage, told of her torrid relationship with Bobby, then dismissed her in one curt sentence: "She made the down payment on the car in which Bobby Edwards drove Freda McKechnie to her death."

The prosecutor shifted the scene to Harvey's Lake on the night of July 30: "They undressed in the car near the icehouse. It was raining heavily. They put on their bathing suits for a swim, although the weather was so unfavorable. Freda skipped light-heartedly down to the water. Edwards closed the car door and followed her. In his hand he carried the blackjack with which he planned to kill her. Two other couples were on the beach. Two lights showed. That could not be the place. He led her further on into the pitch-darkness. She ran into the water—he lagged on the beach.

"Freda started swimming. He stepped into the water after her. Freda's back was turned. Her hour had come. And he was ready! He drew the blackjack from his bathing suit and struck her a frightful blow on the head. She stopped swimming, swayed—and he seized her hips and forced her down under the water until she sank. He flung the blackjack into the lake."

Flannery stopped. The deed had been done. There was little left to tell, but the prosecutor told it well. He recounted Bobby's various stories, each one more fantastic than the last. And finally the confession.

"'Is it too late to tell the truth now?'" Flannery quoted the defendant. "'Well, I've prayed and read my Testament and my parents tell me to tell the truth. Here it is. Freda didn't faint, she didn't fall and hurt herself. I had been thinking of doing this ever since she told me she was to become a mother—because I wanted to marry Margaret Crain.'"

When the trial resumed Tuesday morning, October 2, District Attorney Lewis called Freda's mother as his first witness. She walked briskly to the witness chair: a study in black—black dress, black coat, black slightly brimmed hat.

"Freda and Robert went to the same church," she said in reply to Lewis' first question. "Freda had a boy friend, George Thomas, but she gave him up for Bobby. Bobby used to visit Freda four or five nights a week. They didn't do much. Bobby would just come in and sit with Freda. They went for walks and to the movies sometimes. They were very friendly. When Bobby went away to Mansfield College, they corresponded. Bobby gave Freda a pair of lingerie clasps for Christmas. For Easter he gave her a pocketbook. Freda carried that pocketbook the night she went out."

Mrs. McKechnie's voice grew husky and her words stumbled a bit as she told how the romance between Bobby and Freda cooled with the intrusion of Margaret Crain.

"I saw Margaret Crain one night in the backyard of the Edwards home during one of her visits. I heard a voice say, 'Honey, it's too hot. Please don't kiss me.' I looked out and there was Margaret Crain with her hand on Bobby's shoulder. I was surprised. Freda was away from the house at the time."

She told how Freda had become ill a few weeks before her death. "She seemed depressed. She lost her appetite, was very nervous and worrying. I took her to see Dr. Meyers. She began taking medicine." The medicine, said Mrs. McKechnie, her voice barely above a whisper, was for Freda's "nervousness."

District Attorney Lewis picked up the thread of his interrogation.

Q. I want you to tell me what occurred on the Sunday before your daughter's death.

A. She had bought some clothes. She tried on a dress and stood around looking at herself in the mirror.

Q. What was her demeanor on that occasion?

A. She was as happy as a lark. I never saw her so gay. She asked me how she looked and I said fine. The dress fitted her real well.

Q. Did she try on anything else?

A. Yes, a skirt.

Q. Do you recall Monday night—the last night Freda was home?

A. Yes.

Q. She had dinner at home that evening?

A. Yes. I never saw her so happy. She had us all in stitches at the table, imitating Joe Penner and all the funny radio stars, and she had us hilarious.

Q. Tell us when you saw her after dinner, what happened?

A. I saw her last walking down the street with Rosetta Culver. They were laughing. I don't know about what.

Q. That was the last time you saw her alive?

A. Yes.

Lewis was finished. Defense Counsel McGuigan moved in to cross-examine. He asked her to remember the time she and Freda visited Bobby at Mansfield College.

Q. You say Margaret Crain was there at the time?

A. Yes.

Q. You saw her and you knew Edwards was paying quite a bit of attention to her, didn't you?

A. Yes.

Next on the stand for the prosecution was Rosetta Culver. She was everything Freda was not—blond, attractive, poised. I wondered if handsome Bobby had ever tried to lead her down the cemetery path. Apparently not. Because on the Wednesday before he went to East Aurora for the last time, Bobby had provided Rosetta with a date and the two couples went driving in the Poconos.

"Did you stop at some point?" Lewis asked.

"Yes."

Q. Was it on a lonely country road?

A. Yes.

Q. Was it dark?

A. Yes.

Q. Did anyone get out of the car after you parked?

A. Yes, Freda and Robert got out.

Q. Where did they go?

A. Down the road.

Q. Did they take anything with them?

A. Yes, a blanket.

Q. How long were they gone?

A. About fifteen or twenty minutes.

Q. You stayed in the car?

A. Yes.

Q. When they came back, what did you do?

A. They took me home.

Lewis then asked Miss Culver to describe Freda's manner and appearance prior to that nighttime excursion to the Poconos.

"Very melancholy and down-hearted," the girl replied.

And after the Poconos jaunt?

"Lively and joking," Miss Culver recalled. "She seemed happier than I'd ever seen her."

Mr. McGuigan, in cross-examining Rosetta, wrung from her the admission that her blind date on that Wednesday night was in fact a married man. "I didn't know that until afterward," she explained primly.

Lewis then called three more important witnesses during the morning session: Dr. Meyers, the physician who told Freda she was pregnant; the dead girl's married sister, Elizabeth; and Elizabeth's mother-in-law, Mrs. William Patton, Sr.

Dr. Meyers recounted Freda's visit to his office. Mrs. Patton described the dead girl's short visit to her cottage at Harvey's Lake just before she and Robert went swimming that fateful night. Elizabeth, tense and on the verge of tears, admitted that Freda had undergone a drastic change in the week before her death. But Elizabeth thought her sister's gaiety was "synthetic." Mr. McGuigan objected, and Lewis cautioned Elizabeth against "giving your opinion." The dramatic moment of her testimony came when she described her conversation with Robert Edwards on the day after the murder.

"I asked Bobby where Freda was," Elizabeth said. "He said he had no idea. I said, 'Bobby, Freda isn't in trouble, is she? Is there anything wrong with her?'"

Q. What did he say?

A. He said: "Why, no. Freda is too big for anything like that. We were never intimate that way; Freda was too big for that."

During the afternoon session the district attorney summoned Reverend Elson Ruff, minister of the Lutheran Church at Harvey's Lake. The clergyman explained that he had been chaperoning a party of young people at the lake and happened to be standing at a window in the skating-rink pavilion at about nine-thirty on the night of July 30.

"It was raining," he testified. "I watched two young people—a young man and young woman—going down into the water almost directly below me. I saw them go out about a hundred and fifty feet along the edge of the water until they got beyond the float and out of sight. They were wading, not swimming."

Back in his cell that night, Bobby learned that Margaret Crain had talked to reporters in East Aurora. "No matter what happens," she told them, "I'm through with Bobby Edwards." This could hardly be classified as one of the great renunciations of history. Since her appearance in Wilkes-Barre a few days after Freda's death, Margaret had communicated with her pornographic pen pal but once. She sent him a Bible and a brief plea to read from the Good Book. "Do it," she implored, "for the good of your soul."

Detective Powell, frequently in tears because "I knew Robert all my life," was the third day's first witness. He told the jury how the defendant gave conflicting versions of Freda's death before finally blurting out: "I want to tell the real truth." Then Robert's ten-page typewritten statement, describing how he cracked Freda's skull with the blackjack, but only after he found she had died in a fall from the lake's float, was admitted into evidence.

Freda's father followed Powell to the stand. Difficult to understand at times, because his speech was laced with a heavy Scotch burr, Mr. McKechnie described his daughter's relationship with Robert Edwards, and told how he tried to assault Bobby when he learned that Freda's body had been fished out of Harvey's Lake. "I went toward him," Mr. McKechnie said. "But they grabbed me and guzzled me and put me to the floor."

McKechnie's testimony drew a wisp of a smile from Theodore Dreiser. Judge Valentine noticed the smile, glared at the novelist, and snapped: "Mr. Dreiser, I cannot tolerate this facial expression in the presence of the jury." For the remainder of the day Dreiser kept his features locked in solemnity, but I wondered what had amused him. Could he have been wondering, somewhat sardonically perhaps, whether Bobby Edwards had ever read *An American Tragedy*? Had Bobby, like Dreiser's Clyde Griffith, pulled back at the last critical minute, only to have an accident complete the job for him?

There was little to interest Dreiser, the reporters, or even the spectators, until late in the trial day. Then District Attorney Lewis very methodically began submitting for handwriting identification the 172 love letters written by Edwards to Margaret Crain.

Assistant District Attorney Flannery's hobby was amateur theatrics. He had appeared in a number of theater group productions in and around Wilkes-Barre and was regarded as quite accomplished for a non-professional. Logically, then, he should have welcomed—even relished—the opportunity to read in court Robert's letters to Margaret Crain. But he didn't welcome it at all. He was to say later that reading publicly what the defendant had written privately was "one of the hardest jobs of my life." Fortunately for Mr. Flannery, but unfortunately for the spectators, whose ears were flapping in anticipation, the defense and the prosecution had agreed privately that only as many of the letters need be read as were necessary to demonstrate that Robert had a flaming passion for the outwardly chaste music teacher. Even so, the "selected" correspondence boosted the courtroom temperature quite a few degrees.

When court convened for the fourth trial day, the letters lay in a neat pile on the prosecution table. A few minutes after ten o'clock on the morning of October 4, Flannery reached down, picked up the top letter and began to read:

"November 24, 1933

Sweetest Darling:

Well, after last night I feel more in love than ever. I swear I love you more than ever. We have our sweet honeymoon dreams, haven't we? I guess I didn't tell you last night, but I want you to know.

I love you. I love your letters. I was so happy to get them. Let's do our tryst, kissing on paper when we are apart, but the originals are better. Beloved, I love you more than life. I'll love you forever."

Flannery took up another letter:

"Momet Perfect: ["Momet," French-Canadian for "my kid," was Robert's pet name for Margaret.]

I love you, dearest, I love you much more than any of my letters begin to say. The only way I can ever show you a bit of my love is by actions. I am worshipping you, my Momet. And I pray the day is not long when I can take you into my arms and keep you there for all time to come. I truly adore you, dearest. Our souls are one, one forever."

Flannery read on:

"I'm sorry you didn't get my letter. I love you, my sweetheart. Do forgive your boy. I love you, blessed, truly I do. I love your long happy letters. Of course I remember that night with you—in the car. How could I forget?

A week from tonight you come to me. I can hardly wait. I want you—all of you. Let's make it next year—our marriage. I can't wait. Keep your lips warm and wet for me. I love to give you a massage. You know I love to do everything for you."

The defendant looked miserable, almost sick. His face was a ghastly white, and his hands when they ruffled the sheets of paper (he had been given typewritten copies of the letters) were shaking. Sometimes he followed the words with his eyes. Sometimes he merely looked up and listened.

Flannery read on:

"My Goddess:

Hello, dear wife. How much do you love me now? Oh, I love you. I will surely have a lump of love to show you this weekend. We are really man and wife now. Don't you feel that? I'm coming to you on Saturday. Your loving and devoted husband."

(At this point Freda's father rose from his seat and left the courtroom.)

"Momet Blessed:
I am dying to see you and be with you so we could be one in body again. I love you more and more. I can't hardly wait for summer to come so I can take you swimming."

The defendant buried his face in his hands, and those sitting near heard him cry out: "Oh, God, I wish I had a gun."

Relentlessly Flannery picked up still another:

"I saw the blast furnaces roaring last night and I thought how cool they were compared to my ever-glowing love. I can't stop loving you. It would kill me. I love every cell in your body. It is our blessed trysting time and I am lying on my bed and thinking of you and I know you are thinking of me. You have showed me an abundance of love I didn't know could exist. I love you with all of me. Do you recall our actions the last time? How I wish we were together doing them again."

The letters were filled with promises of marriage. "I'll get you drunk and marry you someday, okay?" he wrote in one message.

And in the confusion of his sex-tormented mind, he wrote often to her of prayer, and of church, and even of his hope of one day becoming a minister.

"I was offered a job in a brewery, Momet, but I refused. After all, I am going to be a minister someday and it might not look right to work in a brewery."

Flannery reached for a letter dated July 26—just four days before Freda's death:

"It is our trysting time, Momet, I am going to go to bed in a few minutes and hold you close. Our love is growing with every breath I take. I love you to the deepest depths of my soul. I love you in a divine way, my blessed sweet wife."

And, finally, on July 27:

"I love you. I will love you always. I cannot wait until Sunday when I will see you."

Flannery was finished. Robert sat with his head bowed. The prosecutor turned toward the judge. "The state rests," he said.

*

John Phillips launched Robert's defense with an eloquent opening statement in which he depicted the defendant as a young man ensnared by a woman five—or was it six?—years his senior.

"He went to Mansfield College and there he met Margaret Crain," Phillips told the jury. "A love and affection grew out of their companionship. His friendship for Freda McKechnie did not grow cold—it was interrupted. And his companionship with the other girl grew into love. When he returned home he had to have love and companionship—so he turned to Freda. Their love was a mutual desire. He was twenty-one, she was twenty-seven. There was no ring, no letters, no promises. There was no concealment of his love for Margaret Crain. But a physical desire arose between Robert and Freda."

Phillips then told of Freda's telephone call to the defendant, telling him that she was pregnant. He retraced their steps to Harvey's Lake on the night of July 30.

"They rested on the dock," Phillips said. "Freda was cold. She said: 'I think I'll have one more dip.' Robert said: 'My bathing suit is dry. I'll wait here.' To the left of the dock a rowboat was tied. Freda stepped to the prow of the boat. She threw her right leg over the side. She fell back, her left shoulder against the side of the boat, her head striking the other side. Robert got up. He went to her. He felt her pulse. There was none. He felt her heart. There was no beat.

"He thought to himself: 'Freda's dead. She's pregnant. I've been with her. I'm to blame.' He had a stampede of judgment. His mind was a turmoil. Reason had fled him. He didn't know what had happened."

Phillips paused. "You have waited this long, gentlemen of the jury, to hear the real story of this boy's life. We call to the stand the defendant, Robert Allen Edwards."

Bobby was calm as he raised his right hand to take the oath. Then he sat in the witness chair, crossing his left leg over his right. Phillips asked how old he was.

He told his age, his residence, his school, his meeting with Freda.

Q. Then when you went to Mansfield, did you correspond with her?

A. Yes, in the first part of the school year. About three letters apiece. We never wrote after that.

Q. And when you came home, were you on friendly terms with her?

A. Yes.

Q. In 1932 did any members of the McKechnie family visit you at Mansfield?

A. Yes, Freda's mother and brother.

Q. You had met Margaret Crain by this time? You were friendly with her?

A. Yes.

Q. Now, when you left school, did you correspond with Miss Crain?

A. Yes.

Q. Were you friendly with Freda McKechnie?

A. Yes, casually.

Phillips then asked his client to explain why he had given Freda a set of lingerie clasps the previous Christmas.

"Well," Bobby replied smoothly, "I went over to Freda's home because she had sent me a card and I wanted to thank her for it. I asked her what she had received, and it seems she had not been particularly blessed. I felt sorry for her. My mother had some clasps she was giving to her Sunday school girls. I wrapped up a pair and brought them to Freda."

Phillips swung suddenly to the question of Freda's pregnancy.

Q. Did you discuss it?

A. Yes.

Q. Did she say you were the father of the child?

A. Yes.

Q. When you learned you were the father of her unborn child, what did you tell her?

A. That we would be married.

Deftly, then, Phillips led Robert, the jury, and the spectators back once again to Harvey's Lake on the rainy night of July 30. Yes, the defendant said, they swam out to the float. And Freda fell and struck her head. He found no pulse, no heartbeat. He panicked, pure and simple.

"What did you do next?" Phillips asked.

Robert leaned forward in his chair. "I hit her over the head with a blackjack to make it look like an accident," he whispered. "She was already dead. She had fallen into a rowboat and I felt her pulse and knew she was dead."

Phillips turned toward the prosecution table. "Your witness."

But the prosecutor would have to wait. Judge Valentine rapped his gavel twice, and court was adjourned for the day.

On October 5, 1934, in Wilkes-Barre, two enterprising youths stood outside the Luzerne County Courthouse, hawking mimeographed copies of Bobby Edwards' love letters to Margaret Crain. Inside the courthouse the young man who had been dubbed the "coal-town sheik" settled himself in the witness chair and awaited cross-examination by District Attorney Lewis.

"Isn't it true," the prosecutor began, "that to carry out your pledge to be true to eternity to Margaret Crain, you intended to tap Freda on the head and slide her body into the water to make it look like a drowning?"

"No, sir," Robert replied respectfully, "I had no such intention."

Q. You struck her to make it appear like an accident, you say?

A. Yes.

Q. And then you placed her clothes hundreds of feet away—to make it look like more of an accident, I suppose?

A. I put them there. I don't know why.

Q. You didn't just throw her in the water? You eased her in?

A. Yes.

Q. Can you show how you hit her with the blackjack?

Robert recoiled slightly as Lewis pushed the blackjack toward him. "I don't know," he replied. "It doesn't look natural."

Q. But you did hit her a terrific blow?

A. I don't know.

Q. But you heard the medical examiner testify it was a blow that would fell an ox, didn't you?

A. Yes, I heard him say that. I remember he said it was a terrific blow.

Q. Isn't it true that while striking her on the head—"letting her have it," as you told the police—you broke the strap on the blackjack?

A. No, that isn't true, so far as I know.

Lewis turned toward the jury and held up the weapon, dangling it by the broken thong. Then he turned back to the defendant. "Isn't it true," he inquired, "that to carry out your pledge to be true to eternity to Margaret Crain you intended to hit Freda on the head and slide her into the water to make it look like a drowning?"

"No," Robert retorted sharply.

"You hit her harder than you intended to," the prosecutor shouted. "Isn't that true?"

Bobby slumped back in the chair. "I don't know," he whispered.

"What! Speak up! The jury can't hear you."

"I said I don't know."

The prosecutor then picked from previous testimony a series of lies the defendant admitted telling in the past—to Margaret, to Freda, to her parents, to the police.

Q. You told those lies, didn't you?

A. Yes.

Q. But you want this jury to believe you are now telling the truth?

A. Yes.

Without trying to mask his disgust, Lewis snapped, "That's all," and strode back to his chair. Robert rose slowly. His eyes swept the courtroom. Then, with head down, he walked rapidly back to the defense table.

Mr. McGuigan had two more witnesses—the defendant's mother and father. Mrs. Edwards came to the stand, dressed entirely in black as if she were already mourning her dead son.

The defense lawyer started by asking her if she was at home on the night of July 30. "Yes," she replied.

Q. Did he bring you anything?

A. Yes, he brought me some candy bars.

Q. Did he then go to his room?

A. Yes, at about midnight.

Q. Do you know whether or not he slept?

A. I don't think so. I could hear him tossing and moving about, and I said to his father: "Robert is restless. He can't seem to sleep."

Mr. Edwards followed his wife to the stand. It was his fiftieth birthday that day. He was asked only one question—how did his son behave on the morning of July 31?

"He was unusually quiet," Mr. Edwards answered. "He was pale and not as talkative as usual."

That was it. Five days of sensational testimony and suddenly it was over.

After a brief recess District Attorney Lewis began his closing statement. It was a scathing denunciation of the defendant and his mistress from East Aurora.

He described Robert as "the cruelest, coldest defendant who ever walked into a courtroom." Margaret he termed "a red-hot mama" and "a filthy hag."

"If you acquit this boy," the prosecutor rumbled at the jurors, "then let's get blackjacks by the thousands and give them to all our boys and say to them: 'If you get a good girl in trouble, take her to the lake some night and give it to her.'

"He said he loved that creature—you can't call her a lady—as a wife. But he didn't love that pure, clean creature who was about to bear his child. Freda has gone to her reward. Gentlemen, it is your duty to send him to meet her, the mother of his unwelcome child. Gentlemen, I ask you to send him to eternity."

Lewis' comparatively short address packed quite a wallop. McGuigan could never hope to match it. So instead of breathing fire, he invoked cool logic in pleading with the jurors to find Robert innocent.

"The Commonwealth has no case," McGuigan said. "Its case is built on suspicion and circumstantial evidence so weak it is afflicted with pernicious anemia. Robert's amateurish way of thinking drove him to blackjack the girl to make it look like an accident. He was bewildered, he was confused. If he committed this crime, this boy is the dumbest criminal agency I ever observed. How can you say all these preparations —these dumbbell preparations—were part of a plan to kill this girl?

"You can't," the defense attorney concluded. "The arrows of logic point to his innocence. The case the Commonwealth built is an empty shell. Unless you find the victim died a violent death at the hands of the defendant, your verdict must be not guilty."

The twelve jurors retired at 8:54 on the night of October 5, 1934, to start their deliberations. Robert sat in his cell, writing a letter to Margaret Crain. At midnight Judge Valentine notified the jurors that they could break off deliberations—or continue them. They sent back word that they would continue. And so, as Wilkes-Barre and Edwardsville slept, and as a light rain fell, twelve stolid men weighed the fate of Robert Allen Edwards.

It was still raining at seven-thirty the following morning when the jury sent word to judge Valentine that a verdict had been reached. A half-hour later Robert walked into the near-empty courtroom and took his seat at the defense table. Phillips wasn't there. Neither was McGuigan. He had sent his son, a young attorney who appeared slightly bewildered and highly nervous. The defendant seemed calm. But the twitching of a muscle below his right eye betrayed him.

At 8:10 A.M. the jurors filed into the courtroom. They had to walk past Robert Edwards. He looked up at each, searching their faces for a clue, an answer, a sign. None would meet his eyes.

They shuffled into the jury box and remained on their feet. They shifted their bodies nervously, ducked their hands into their pockets, or kept them behind their backs. The foreman handed an envelope to

Clerk William Henderson. Judge Valentine asked if they had reached a verdict. Yes, they had. Judge Valentine nodded toward Henderson, and the clerk took the envelope to the bench. Then, at another nod from the judge, Henderson tore open the sealed document. His hands shook slightly as he did so. His voice quavered, as he read:

"We find the defendant, Robert Allen Edwards, guilty of murder in the first degree with the death penalty."

In Edwardsville, George McKechnie sat on the front porch of his cottage. Reporters stood around him, asking what he thought of the verdict. "Well," he answered slowly, "I'm sorry for Dan Edwards and his wife and that other boy of theirs, too. But Robert Edwards took my little girl's life, and justice has been done—as far as it can be done."

In East Aurora, Margaret Crain's father met reporters at the door of his home. Margaret, he said, was in seclusion. She would see no one. A newsman asked Mr. Crain: "What do you think of the verdict?" "We have always felt the ends of justice would be met," Mr. Crain answered, then he shut the door.

Robert Allen Edwards was twenty-two years old when it came time for him to die. Early on the morning of May 6, 1935, he walked without assistance to the electric chair at Rockview Penitentiary in Bellefonte, Pennsylvania. He was murmuring a prayer as the black hood fell over his head.

I've sometimes wondered who—or perhaps "what" is more appropriate—was really responsible for the death of Freda McKechnie and the execution of Bobby Edwards. Bobby murdered Freda, of that there is no question. And the sovereign State of Pennsylvania exacted payment from Bobby for his crime. But what overpowering fear inspired Bobby's desperate act? It was a premeditated but not a reasoned act. There were alternatives. Bobby rejected them. Why? Out of love for Margaret Crain? In spite of the letters, I say: Impossible! (I'd like to have a dollar for every salacious love letter, complete with proposals of marriage, that has passed between young people who never wound up within a mile of an altar!) Was marriage to Freda so certain to be a *permanent* disaster? He could not know, he could not even guess.

Bobby felt a responsibility toward Freda, a responsibility that derived from his understanding, *and abject fear*, of the moral code in which he had been brought up. He had been born into a society that encouraged the kind of cowardice that to him made murder, a dark and forbidden avenue of escape, seem more acceptable than the simpler risk of marriage—a risk that, in time, might have been no risk at all.

He was afraid. He was afraid to talk to any of those who might have helped him. That was what has struck me so forcibly about Bobby's puny, misspent young life. He was afraid to confide in anyone whose mature advice and counsel might have shown him a bit of daylight on the road ahead. He was afraid of society—afraid and ashamed. And out of his fear and his shame and his cowardice, he gambled away Freda's life and his own. You might almost say it was society who handed him the dice and urged him to throw.

Murder One, 1967

EDNA FERBER

For Depression-era Americans, no crime in living memory was as heinous as the abduction of the 20-month-old son of the revered "Lone Eagle," Charles Lindbergh. On the evening of March 1, 1932, Charles Jr. was spirited from his second-floor nursery in the Lindberghs' home in Hopewell, New Jersey; a note left on a radiator grill demanded $50,000 in cash for his safe return. The crime set off a worldwide paroxysm of outrage and grief (H. L. Mencken deemed it "the biggest story since the Resurrection"). After weeks of false leads, dashed hopes, and cruel hoaxes, the mystery of the baby's whereabouts came to a terrible resolution when his decomposed corpse was discovered in the woods four miles from the Lindbergh home. More than two years passed before a suspect—a German-born carpenter named Bruno Richard Hauptmann —was arrested for the crime. His sensational 1935 trial ended with his conviction, and on April 3, 1936, Hauptmann went to the electric chair protesting his innocence.

Among the writers sent to cover the trial was Edna Ferber (1885–1968), one of the most popular authors of her time, best known for her novels *So Big* (1924), winner of the Pulitzer Prize; *Show Boat* (1926), the basis for the perennial musical classic by Jerome Kern and Oscar Hammerstein; and *Giant* (1952), one of seven of her books that were turned into successful films. The sharp social conscience that infuses Ferber's books is equally evident in this scathing firsthand portrait of the media circus surrounding the Hauptmann trial.

Miss Ferber Views 'Vultures' At Trial

Writer Is Shocked by Chatter of the 'Chic' Who Gather for Flemington Holiday.

FLEMINGTON, N.J., Jan. 27.—It is considered chic to go to the Hauptmann trial. Though I myself am not chic, and have never been invited to an Elsa Maxwell party, I hope I know what is being done. A mink coat, one of those Cossack hats, the word "divine" in your vocabulary, and there you are, if a woman, equipped complete for a day at Flemington. It's as easy as that.

I know, because, stepping out of the motor car in front of the Union Hotel on the snowy main street of the little Jersey town, I found all the Maxwell party countersigns and passwords were being cooed back and forth. All the mink coats were saying to the Saville Row topcoats and burgundy mufflers, "Hel-lo, dar-ling! How are you! Isn't this divine? Isn't it wonderful!"

Well, it was wonderful. It was wonderful. It was horrible and sickening and depressing and wonderful, and it made you want to resign as a member of the human race and cable Hitler saying, Well Butch, you win.

The little town of Flemington at noon looked like a frosted picture postcard gone mad. Mobs churning the prim little courthouse steps. Crowds milling in and out of the quaint Union Hotel. A constant stream pouring toward the lunch room in the basement of the church just across from the courthouse. Flemington townspeople. New Jersey politicians. Actors. Theatrical producers. Society. Reporters. Lawyers. Novelists. Playwrights. Hel-lo dar-ling? Isn't it divine! Have you had lunch?

If some one is to make money on the Hauptmann trial it may as well be the ladies of the church, and it most emphatically is. The church lunch room is the swank place to eat and don't make a mistake. For the duration of the Hauptmann trial that church lunch room is the Algonquin, the Colony Restaurant, the Rainbow Room of Flemington. Seventy-five cents and a very decent meal—clam chowder, roast beef, boiled potatoes, stewed tomatoes, cole slaw, apple pie and coffee—with all the visiting celebrities thrown in. Real apple pie, too. Flaky, juicy, hot.

You are served by the ladies of the church, and no nonsense. Neat, dowdy, no lipstick, no rouge; black dresses with a collar of home-made tatting fashioned with a round brooch. Did you taste the pie? It's divine! Oh, well, diet tomorrow. Darling, is that Wilentz? Is that Reilly? Is that Winchell? Is that stomach-turning?

The court room. Through the side entrance, brushing past the fenders of the faded green-gray car which belongs to Bruno Hauptmann. You fight for your seat to which your newspaper card entitles you, only to be thrown out later, but you manage to sneak in again for a two-hour session with Hauptmann in the witness chair.

I was astonished to see that this Bruno Hauptmann is a distinguished-looking man—distinguished and graceful. The line his body makes from shoulder to ankle as he sits there is fluid, graceful. A painter or a sculptor would be pleased with it. The face. Now, I've seen that before. I've seen a thing like that before. It is no color. It is, for that matter, no face. That is, it is no living face. It is not white, or gray or yellow. It is wax. That's it. It is the face of a corpse.

Curiously enough, it has a sort of dignity which is the dignity of the dead. It has the deadness of the face in the glass box of that marble sepulchre in Red Square in Moscow. As dead as that, except for two small sunken eyes, like dark coals that smoulder dully in the caverns under the brows.

So there we sit and look and look, hundreds and hundreds of us who have no business there, who should be turned away from there. We sit and stare hungrily like vultures perched on a tree, watching a living thing writhe yet a while. We are like the sans-culottes, like the knitting women watching the heads fall at the foot of the guillotine. We have got into the room through cajolery and bribery and trickery and lies and high up and low downs.

A good show. Most of them had been there day after day, day after day. I felt like a frosh at a senior brawl. Darling, were you here this morning. What did they do? Are you coming tomorrow? I'm lunching with Reilly. I'm lunching with Fisher. Do you want to meet the Sheriff? Oh, he's sweet.

I should like to say, as a taxpayer and a human being, and an old busybody, that that court room in Flemington, N.J., should be emptied and kept emptied of all except the judge, the jury, the lawyers, witnesses, reporters, special writers and such people as are definitely connected with the trial of Bruno Richard Hauptmann. For the jammed aisles, the crowded corridors, the noise, the buzz, the idiot laughter, the revolting faces of those of us who are watching this trial are an affront to civilization.

This man Hauptmann, when he speaks, does so in a hollow voice— a voice without a tinge of warmth or life. A voice as dead as his face. I fought, he says, in his lifeless voice, I fought in the war when I was 17.

Guilty or innocent, this man, when he was 17, his bones not yet a man's bones, his mind not yet a man's mind, saw and knew fear, agony, ruthlessness, murder, hunger, cold. He was a German soldier in the war and a product of war. And perhaps this man with the face of the dead and the hollow cold voice like a voice from the grave is the complete and triumphant product of war.

The New York Times, January 28, 1935

JIM THOMPSON

At the end of his life, not one of the two dozen books written by Jim Thompson (1906–1977) remained in print, but his prediction to his wife that he would be famous "about ten years" after his death turned out to be quite accurate. Starting in the 1980s, his novels were rediscovered by a new generation of readers who found the hardboiled nihilism of his paperback crime novels irresistible, and many (including *The Grifters*, *Pop. 1280*, and *After Dark, My Sweet*) were adapted for the screen. Thompson was born in the Oklahoma Territory, the son of a frontier sheriff who eventually hightailed it to Mexico on horseback in the wake of an embezzlement scandal. Thompson's own early resumé included a stint as an all-night bellboy-cum-procurer at a Fort Worth hotel, an appropriate initiation into the kind of seamy, small-time underworld that would figure so prominently in his best-known fiction. Following his graduation from high school, he spent a few years tramping around the West Texas oil fields before enrolling at the University of Nebraska College of Agriculture to study journalism.

During the 1930s, he turned out dozens of articles for oil trade magazines and regional farm journals before becoming a regular contributor to true-crime pulps such as *Master Detective*, where the following piece appeared in the April 1936 issue. Thompson typically published his crime stories under an "as-told-to" byline, narrating in the voice of the investigating lawman; on occasion he would also pose as the detective, killer, or murder victim in the accompanying photo-illustrations. According to his sister—who served as his researcher, scouring the newspapers for potential subjects—Thompson was squeamish about real-life gore. His articles, however, didn't hold back on the grisly violence expected by the readership of the true-crime pulps of the era.

Ditch of Doom

The Crimson Horror of Keechi Hills
By Deputy Sheriff C. C. Ruff
Caddo County, Oklahoma
As told to Jim Thompson

Vague wisps of moonlight filtered through the dust-grimed windows. Shadows fell upon the bed, the shabby sticks of ancient furniture—crept through the dingy rooms in quiet terror, and vanished. In the black-jacks, the wind soughed miserably; and from the ghostly hills an owl hooted his eternal question.

"Uncle Billy" Royce threw back the covers of his bed, which had protected him from the January cold, and swung his bare feet to the floor. He felt for, and found, his boots. Habitually, he wore his shirt and trousers while sleeping. So, with the addition of the boots, he was dressed.

He shot the rusted bolt of the door, and pulled it open. Again, standing on the little porch, he listened. Again, he heard the owl's echoing cry.

That, and other sounds.

The soft shuffle of a spade. Digging. The quiet click of a pick, striking its way through the rocky shale. And. . . .

The grisly crunching of an axe; the terrified pleading of a woman—choking, groaning.

Then—silence!

Uncle Billy shivered in the January wind. He couldn't stand the cold, the hardships, the loneliness, as he once had. He was very old. Eighty or ninety. He didn't rightly know which, himself. Still, in spite of his years, he made an arresting figure. He was thin to the point of emaciation; but he was six feet, four inches tall, and stood straight like the Indians who had once roamed these rocky hills.

He grew calmer as the sounds he had heard were not repeated.

Finally, he chuckled, his parchment-like jaws shaking silently. Those digging noises were probably the echo of his own day's work; they'd got in his ears that way before, and stayed with him. As for the others—well, the wind had a way of teasing and frightening a lonely old man.

A man had to be careful, though; no doubt about that. There was gold on the farm: the buried treasure of the James and Dalton gangs. Jesse and Frank, both, had told him it was there; and they wouldn't lie to a member of their own gang. And, if any further proof were needed, the woman he had called his wife had furnished it.

She had found five thousand dollars. She had left with it, laughing; refusing him any part. Gone away with another man.

Thus Uncle Billy ruminated and his thoughts were bitter. His old eyes strayed out over the barnyard, and came to rest upon the shambling chicken-house. Then, shaking his head in the manner of a man whose memory is not of the best, he went back inside and locked the door. . . .

Morning came to the Keechis.

It was Saturday; but Saturday and every other day was the same to William Royce. He had to dig for his treasure as he had dug daily for the past thirty years. In the aggregate, a good fifth of his hundred and sixty acres were one shovel-scarred battlefield. There were holes in the barn, the chicken-house, the pigpen, along the creek—in every place that a person might look. And still his digging continued.

He ate breakfast hurriedly and stepped out to the porch. A voice hailed him. He stiffened, peered near-sightedly.

A neighboring farmer, one Thomas Taylor, came up the path from the lane.

"Oh, it's you," grunted Uncle Billy. "How are you, Tommy?"

"First rate." Taylor sat down out of the wind and rolled a cigarette. "See all your in-laws out here yesterday evening," he remarked conversationally.

"Yes, the whole durn gang was out," swore the old man. "Clifford, and those two Meads."

Clifford was his sixteen-year-old stepson. The Meads were his wife's daughter and son-in-law. Taylor laughed. He had known Uncle Billy for years, and took a good-natured interest in the old man's affairs.

"Where is your wife this morning?" he inquired carelessly. "Inside?"

As he spoke he tried to peer through the window which fronted on the porch. But flour sacks had been hung up there to dry, and he could obtain no hint of the interior.

"No, she ain't inside," said the veteran sourly. "She's gone."

"Yes? Where to?"

"None of your——." Uncle Billy halted in the middle of his rude speech. After all, Taylor was his friend even if he was a trifle tactless. "She went away," he said grimly. "Went to New Mexico with a Dutchman, in a big seven-passenger car."

Taylor laughed again, and settled down for a morning's conversation. "You have a pretty hard time with housekeepers, don't you, Uncle Billy? That makes about six that came and went."

"None of them are any good," declared Royce. "Now, you run along, Tommy; I ain't got any more time to talk. I've got work to do."

When Taylor had gone, the old man went about the work of watering and feeding his scanty stocks of chickens and pigs. Then taking pick and shovel he set out for the field.

On his way, he encountered the rusting and dilapidated remains of an ancient touring car. For a moment, although he had passed the car a thousand times, he had difficulty in remembering how it had got there; and he studied its drab lines carefully. Then memory returned. The ancient vehicle had belonged to two young men—tourists—who had camped on the farm one night a few years before.

What had happened to them? Why had they gone away and left their car?

Uncle Billy chuckled.

Every door on the Royce farm bore a sturdy padlock, and only Uncle Billy carried the keys. So, when the tall old man returned to the house for lunch after a fruitless morning of digging, he found the Meads, husband and wife, waiting for him in the yard.

"Where's mother?" asked Mrs. Mead, anxiously.

Uncle Billy told her, briefly and lucidly.

"Why, she didn't tell us she was going," said Mead. "We planned on taking her in town with us. What time did she leave?"

"Long about dark. Little while after you left."

"But I can't understand why she would do it," frowned the daughter. "You say she left with a Dutchman? What was his name?"

"Don't know, and don't care!" snapped the old man. "All I know is she's gone, and he had a big seven-passenger car."

"Sure about that, are you?" inquired Mead.

Mrs. Mead put a hand on her husband's arm. The two were not on the friendliest terms with Royce. There had been an argument about some livestock.

Besides this, the daughter knew that her mother was accustomed to taking care of herself. Uncle Billy was past eighty. Her mother was strong, able-bodied, and only a little more than forty years of age.

"Well, Uncle Billy," she smiled, "if you say she's gone we'll take your word for it. But what does she intend to do about Clifford?"

Royce nodded vehemently. "Now, don't you worry about Clifford. Ethel's going to send back for him. This Dutchman's got a big ranch, and he's going to give Clifford a job. Ethel made him agree to that before she'd go. You tell Clifford to come out here and stay with me. His mother will be ready for him in a few days."

No mention of the five thousand dollars in gold she had found. No need to tell them about that.

The Meads drove away, returning to their home in Chickasha.

Clifford Alexander, Mrs. Royce's son by a former marriage, was waiting for them eagerly. When told that he was about to be reunited with his mother, he lost no time in setting out for Uncle Billy's farm. His mother wouldn't leave him there long, he knew. She'd send back after him or come herself, and he'd have to be on hand when she did.

Meanwhile, there were still other persons interested in the unorthodox departure of Lela Ethel Royce.

Uncle Billy had been married first in 1902, and had four daughters by this marriage. About five years before his second marriage, he and his first wife had separated, and she had taken the children. One of the girls died, one was still single, and two of them were married. The first Mrs. Royce made her home with one of these married daughters, Mrs. Reed Norris and her husband, of Norge, Oklahoma—a little town a few miles northeast of Uncle Billy's farm.

The second Mrs. Royce, Lela Ethel Alexander, had kept house for Uncle Billy several months before she married him. And to induce her to marry him the old man had agreed to will her his farm upon his death. And it was well worth inheriting—one hundred and sixty acres of land, with an oil well which produced a royalty of from thirty to sixty dollars per month. Even at a forced sale the farm would bring thousands of dollars.

Sunday afternoon, January 6th, 1935, Clifford Alexander arrived at the farm, and entered the gate. Uncle Billy was seated on the porch, and he displayed more cordiality to his stepson than was his usual wont. Clifford went inside to get a bite to eat, and lie down.

He did neither.

He walked into the kitchen, and found himself looking squarely into the bedroom. He stopped dead in his tracks, transfixed.

"Oh, Uncle Billy," he called. "Ma hasn't come back yet, has she?"

"No, she hasn't, son. Don't worry, though. She'll send for you."

Cold terror wormed through the boy's veins. Like a man in a trance he continued to stare into the bedroom, at something which lay there on the bed. Then, slowly, he began to back toward the door. He reached the porch, and stepped off.

Uncle Billy peered at him curiously.

"What's the matter, son? You look kind of peaked."

"N-nothing. Nothing's the matter." Still watching the old man, the boy backed away.

"Where are you going, then?" demanded Royce.

"Over to the rock-crusher. I—I want to see Mr. Swanson a minute."

Swanson worked as watchman for a sand and gravel company, which had holdings on an adjoining farm.

Uncle Billy arose. He looked dreadfully tall to the boy.

"Now, see here, Clifford," he began. "You better stay right here. When your mother comes you don't want her chasing all over the country looking for you."

He took a step forward.

Clifford whirled and ran.

At the rock quarry, the frightened boy found his friend Swanson, and told what he had seen in the bedroom. Swanson was alarmed, but he had his job to take care of; so it was not until Monday evening that he came to town to advise me of his suspicions. And since I am regularly employed by the town of Cement, as night watchman, it was Tuesday before I got out to the Royce farm.

The doors were all locked, and no one was there. I sat down to wait.

Dusk came early, and with it, walking wearily through the trees, came Uncle Billy. He walked toward me silently.

"Hello, Uncle Billy," I called.

He said nothing. He acted as if he intended to walk over me or through me. Then, suddenly, when we were almost face to face, he threw his hand out and gripped my shoulder.

"Why—it's Curry!" he exclaimed.

Things like that get a man's nerves. "Yes, it's Curry, all right," I said. "But where's your wife?"

"She's gone."

"Where?"

"New Mexico, I think. She left Friday night with a Dutchman."

I was speaking rapidly; if he had no lies made up, I was not going to give him time to think and create them.

"Listen, Uncle Billy," I said. "Clifford saw your wife's hat and coat on the bed, when he was here Sunday. Why didn't she take them with her?"

"How should I know? I wasn't asking her any questions when she left. More than likely she figured on getting some new things when she got to town. This Dutchman had plenty of money."

He spoke without the slightest hesitation, and his eyes met mine, unblinking. I had known him for almost thirty years, and in all that time his word had been as good as his bond. He had had trouble with housekeepers before. They were always getting mad and quitting. I found myself believing the man; I couldn't help but believe him.

"Where did this Dutchman live?" I asked.

"Just a little north of Chickasha. I don't know his name, Curry. Wish I did. I'd like to help you out."

"All right, Uncle Billy," I said. "I've got to get back to town now, but I'll be out again tomorrow. You stay right here on the place, will you?"

"I sure will," he promised.

I got in my car and stepped on the starter. Once, before turning out into the highway, I looked back. Uncle Billy stood silhouetted against the sky, gazing out over the ghostly Keechis. And I saw that the last rays of the winter sun had left those rocky crags dripping with scarlet. . . .

Returning to Cement, I worked through the night on my regular job as watchman. Wednesday, I started out to check on Uncle Billy's story.

I inquired all around Chickasha, where he had said the Dutchman lived. I went to Tuttle, Amber, Minco—towns northeast of the Royce farm.

But I found no Dutchman; no sign of the missing Mrs. Royce. My way led back by the farm. I drove in. Uncle Billy was gone. Believing that there was nothing to be gained by searching through those hills in the dark, I drove on to Cement. I did not think the old man was hiding out on me; but if he was it would be foolhardy to look for him at night.

At noon of the next day—Thursday—I visited the farm again. Uncle Billy was still gone; but from a passing truck driver I learned that he had driven the old man into Chickasha, Wednesday afternoon. I went back to town, got a search warrant, and returned to the farm, taking two residents of Cement—Sam Kuykendall and C. B. Cook—with me.

The house was still dark, and every door was padlocked.

The shack faced the north, two small rooms setting east and west.

On the south, a small combination dining-room and kitchen had been built on. We broke the lock on the north door and entered, tearing the obscuring flour sacks from the windows to let in the light.

At first glance, nothing seemed to be out of the way. Cabinet, stove, and table were in their usual places. I looked into one of the front rooms; as usual it was piled with the accumulated junk and worn out bric-a-brac of thirty years.

From there we examined the bedroom with its two beds. There was nothing to point to the fact that Mrs. Royce had met with foul play.

Turning to enter the kitchen, my gaze was arrested by something I saw on the north wall of that room. Startled, I leaned closer. It was a few tiny clumps of fuzz, glued to the siding by a thin dark streak of what was unmistakably blood. A few feet further along the wall was another of those curious stains; and following them around the room I counted eight, in all.

Eight streaks of splattered blood. Eight murderous strokes of an axe or knife. But here was a curious thing. While the blood on the wall was obvious to anyone, the floor was spotless.

I got down on my hands and knees. Tiny grains of grit bit into my palms. That was it. *Sand!* One of the best cleaning agents known. The floor had been scoured with it.

We retraced the spots on the walls; and through them the details of the tragic drama that had been played in that lonesome shack became almost as clear as if we had witnessed it.

The murder victim had backed away, terror-stricken eyes on the grisly weapon glittering there in the moonlight. But matching each footstep with his own, the murderer had advanced. One step, two steps, *slash!* Three steps, four steps, *slash!* . . . Backing away, slowly; gasping out unheeded pleas. Six steps, seven steps, nine, ten . . . Every two steps, like the measured rhythm of a pendulum, the dreadful instrument had swung, and found its mark . . . Fifteen, sixteen . . . then, eternity.

At the south door, the stains ended.

We broke it down.

Just below the doorstep was a slight depression, and the earth was loose. But looking along the path which led to the outbuildings, we saw more blood-stains, and we followed them. A few feet from the chicken-house there was a large splotch of blood-stained sand. The body had lain there, temporarily, while the murderer rested. Undoubtedly, the body was near by, for there were no other such large pools.

Tearing the lock from the rotting door of the chicken-house, we entered. In front of us, the ground was swelling ever so slightly; I would not have noticed it at all, except for one thing: cotton hulls had been scattered over the dirt floor in an attempt to conceal the loose earth. I called Clifford over from Swanson's, and asked him if that was the way the floor should look. He replied that it was not.

I began to dig.

A few turns of my shovel, and the steel struck something that was not earth. I scraped the soil carefully, and uncovered a woman's shoe, a stocking, a leg . . . And in a minute more I had uncovered the nearly nude body of a woman, lying face down. Her fair head grimed now by the dust of days, was horribly mutilated.

Slowly, for the body was beginning to decompose, we turned it over, into a blanket. Clifford began to sob, softly.

There before us was all that remained of Lela Ethel Royce, second wife of Uncle Billy.

I had the body sent to a funeral home in Anadarko, and notified Jim Bond, Sheriff of Grady County at Chickasha, to pick up Uncle Billy. Meanwhile, I learned from some men who were working on the road in front of the house that Reed Norris, Uncle Billy's son-in-law, had visited the place the day before. He had driven into the yard and was seen to walk down to the chicken-house, remaining there for several minutes.

Norris, and his mother-in-law, the first Mrs. Royce, were placed under arrest and taken to Anadarko for questioning. One was placed in the city jail, the other in the county jail.

At this juncture, we received word from Chickasha that Uncle Billy had been apprehended. He was picked up in the center of town, on Chickasha Avenue. But while he was armed he offered no resistance. I went to Chickasha and questioned the old man in the private office of Sheriff Bond.

"What became of your wife, Uncle Billy?" I demanded.

"She went away with that Dutchman."

"Now, Uncle Billy," I said. "You're in a bad jam, here. We've found your wife buried in the chicken-house. She was killed with an axe. Did you do it? Come, now, tell me the truth."

"No, no, Curry," he replied. "I didn't do it. I don't know a thing about it."

"Tell me the truth, Uncle Billy."

"I already have."

He answered me very steadily, and rationally. Again, if we had not discovered the body, I would have believed him. And, in spite of the discovery, I still could not definitely connect him with the crime. Mrs. Royce had been in her prime; a fine, healthy, vigorous figure of a woman. As for Uncle Billy—well, to look at him you'd think the first puff of wind would blow him over. He was past eighty, too, remember. Supposing that he had the necessary strength to overpower the woman, how could he have managed to carry her body to the grave in the chicken-house? That was a job for a strong man.

"You don't know anything about it, then?" I repeated.

"No, I don't. All I know is that she went away with the Dutchman."

That was his story, and he stuck to it. So, in company with Elmer Finley, Sheriff of Caddo County, Deputy Steve Steverson, and Assistant County Attorney Haskell Pugh, I loaded Uncle Billy into a car and started back to the farm. I figured that if anything would loosen his tongue the sight of his wife's grave would.

The yard of the place was thronged with the curious when we arrived. We drove through the gate, passed the house, and stopped in front of the chicken-house. Steverson went in first, followed by Uncle Billy who walked between us. The old man started forward quickly.

"Curry—there is my shovel! Where did you find it?"

I caught hold of him, to prevent him from hurting himself or anyone else, if he were so minded.

"Uncle Billy," I said softly, "why in the world did you do this?"

He made no reply.

I led him out, toward the house, showed him the dried blood. He looked at it like a man in a trance, but remained silent. I allowed him to stand there a minute, then continued the slow march to the house. We passed more traces of blood, and started around to the front door where the lock had been broken. About five feet from the door, he spoke.

"Wait, Curry."

I stopped. "All right, Uncle Billy, I'm waiting."

He sniffled; started to cry.

"I didn't kill her, Curry. I struck her twice with a piece of pipe; once in the house, and once in the yard. We had quarreled. She got a butcher knife and ran me around the table. I hit her with this pipe, and knocked her down, and jumped in the bedroom and shut the door.

"She tried to get in. I opened the door quickly and she fell down. She had got the axe and still had the knife. I ran out over her and she ran me down to the chicken-house. I hit her again, and she didn't get up any more. There was a man standing by me when I looked around and I told him I would give him five dollars to take care of her, and he said he would. I paid him, and that is all I know."

I studied the old man carefully, an inkling of the real solution to the mystery creeping into my mind. Steverson and Pugh had come up and listened to the story.

"Who was this man who helped you?" I said.

"The Dutchman."

"That won't do, Uncle Billy. You've told part of the truth, but I'll have to have all of it: Who was the man?"

He hesitated. "All right. I'll tell you. It was Reed Norris, my son-in-law."

"Who else?"

"My first wife. She planned the job, and Reed and I did it."

You will note that he contradicted his first story here, wherein he stated that he was the attacked instead of the attacker. I made no comment on it.

"Why did you do it?" I asked.

"So Reed could move back on the place and take care of me."

"You're still holding out on me, Uncle Billy," I said. "Which one of you used the axe?"

"Well, Reed was in the room with me when I knocked her down with the pipe."

"Where was Reed standing when you knocked her down?"

"Standing right by me with the axe in his hand, but I didn't see him hit her."

Still another story! And all within the space of a few minutes.

We took Uncle Billy into Anadarko and placed him in jail.

As I have said before, Reed Norris and the first Mrs. Royce had been put in separate jails; they had been given no opportunity to get together and arrange concurring stories. But when Pugh, fortified by his talk with Uncle Billy, confronted them with their supposed misdeeds they promptly denied them. Furthermore, while their accounts of their doings on the fatal Friday of the murder disagreed on minor points, they told substantially identical and satisfactory stories.

When questioned as to whether he had been on the farm the Wednesday the body was found, Norris at first asserted that he had not been. Then, he changed his mind and declared that he had been there for a few minutes, intending to take Uncle Billy a belated Christmas present. Not finding the old man at home, he went out to let the stock in to water, Uncle Billy having forgotten to do so.

His first hesitation on this point could probably be laid to the fact that he was nervous and excited. A man suddenly put into jail, is often too upset to say definitely just where he has been and what he has done on given days.

Special detectives from the State Department of Investigation furnished further proof of the pair's innocence. They went to Norge and made a thorough investigation of Norris' and Mrs. Royce's stories and found them to be absolutely true. They could have had nothing to do with the murder for they were in Norge at the time it happened.

Were they accessories to the act? No, neither before nor after. And they had absolutely no motive. One half of the farm—eighty acres—had been deeded to one of the Royce girls, several years before; the other half to Mrs. Royce. They had simply permitted the old man to stay on there, splitting the royalty from the oil well with him.

Uncle Billy had had no right to will the land to his second wife. The first Mrs. Royce furnished deeds to show that the farm did not belong to him.

Mrs. Royce and Norris were promptly released with an official apology, which, like good citizens, they accepted.

Had Uncle Billy committed the crime alone, then?

He was capable of it. Remember, this was not an ordinary old man, used to an easy chair and house slippers. Uncle Billy had worked hard all his life. For thirty years, without missing a day, he had gone out into the Keechis and dug. Hard, manual labor, that. His appearance was deceiving. He was thin, but wiry. And having handled him, I can testify that this man who might have been eighty or ninety was unusually strong

The motive?

Insane people do not need motives for their actions.

And Uncle Billy was insane. Waiting there in the Anadarko jail, he told still another story of the tragedy. But no longer did he talk mildly, with a bold eye. His eyes rolled, and his voice rose to a screech.

"She found money! She found $5,000 buried on the farm, down in the valley just below the barn. When I asked her for part of it she told me that it was hers—that I should have none of it. She wouldn't give me my share, and we fought. I hit her, and she fell down. Then I dragged her into the hole in the hen house and covered her up."

Then he began to babble about the mythical Dutchman.

But was this the only murder the grim Keechis had witnessed? Did the little farm, on whose rocky acres Jesse James had camped, hold further grisly mysteries?

With the discovery of the body in the chicken-house grave, rumors that had lain somnolent for years sprang to life once more. What had become of the two young men who had stopped at the farm overnight; whose car now stood rusting in the barnyard? Where had they gone to? *If they were alive, why was the car still there?*

And what of those two women—two of a long series of house-keepers—who had worked for Uncle Billy a few days each, and disappeared. Women, friendless and homeless, without relatives to make inquiry.

Where were they?

Uncle Billy's arrest had received national attention. Few could escape reading of it. Yet days passed, and none of the missing four came forward.

Questioned, the old man declared that each of the four had been back to visit him since their departure. And he was vehement in his denial that he had harmed any of them. But neighbors contradicted his statement.

Not one of the four had ever been back. Or, if they had been, Uncle Billy was the only person who could testify to the fact. No one else had seen them.

Why had the boys left their car? He couldn't say: that had been a long time ago. It was an old car. Maybe they hadn't wanted it any longer. As for the two housekeepers—well, they were fine women. He had liked both of them, and they had liked him.

He wouldn't hurt anyone.

But an oil company scout testified that the old man had shot him in the arm with a rifle. Another man had climbed the fence one day in search of a stout pole to pry his car out of the ditch—and had been marched back to the road at the point of Royce's gun.

How about those two? Uncle Billy scowled. They had been trying to steal his gold. He had given them what they deserved.

The Sunday following the discovery of the chicken-house grave, a large body of volunteers congregated at the farm to search for the bodies of the missing people. But it was an impossible task which they had set for themselves; a fact which I realized from the outset. Let me explain.

Uncle Billy had been digging on that farm for thirty years, and more. You could scarcely go half a dozen steps without stumbling into some depression he had dug in his search for treasure. Sometimes he had thrown the dirt back into the barren holes; sometimes he had not. But in every place that a person might look—in the sheds, the fields, the pigpen—were the marks of his pick and shovel. There were thousands of possible graves on that farm—figuring each excavation a grave; thousands of places where he had dug for a day, two days, or an hour.

Which of these thousand holes should be investigated? Where should the digging start?

There was only one answer. Unless Uncle Billy admitted the crimes of which he was suspected, and pointed out the unmarked graves, finding them would be practically impossible. True, the searchers did start digging, but when they gradually realized the enormity of their task, they loaded up their tools and departed one by one, until only a few remained.

Then, once again it was dusk; once more the looming Keechis grinned with scarlet.

The scattered picks rattled slowly against the rocks, and spades, suddenly gone lazy, clung to the soil as if unseen hands reached up and gripped them. An aching, whining little wind rose out of the south, whispering weird and terrible things. . . .

Terror struck into the limbs of the stragglers. Across the serried and darkening fields they ran, toward the comforting safety of the highway.

If the hills had any secrets they kept them.

And so did Uncle Billy.

At his hearing, he was represented by Attorney H. W. Morgan, of Anadarko, who entered a plea of not guilty for the old man. At the same time, Mr. Morgan entered a plea to the Court for an insanity hearing. This was granted. On January 21st, 1935, a little over two weeks after the murder, he was brought before an insanity board of two Anadarko doctors, presided over by County Judge Oris L. Barney.

There followed one of the most unique court procedures in the history of the State.

Under the law, if Uncle Billy was guilty of murder he could not be insane. Likewise, if he was insane, he could not be guilty of murder, since the State does not hold the insane responsible for their acts.

But here was a contradiction. The old man's guilt was established; and it was also true, beyond a doubt, that he was insane. What could be done in a case of this kind? Would Royce escape the penalty of his crime?

Not at all. Judge Barney, who is one of the youngest judges in Oklahoma, ordered the murder charges withdrawn. The board then declared the old man insane, and he was duly committed to the State insane asylum at Fort Supply, Oklahoma.

Two weeks after he arrived there, he died.

He was a very old man, Uncle Billy Royce. Eighty or ninety. He couldn't rightly say which himself.

Master Detective, April 1936

JAMES THURBER

Like Mark Twain, to whom he has often been compared, James Thurber (1894–1961) endured a series of tribulations in his later years that left him increasingly bitter. "People are not funny," he remarked near the end. "They are vicious and horrible—and so is life." Even in his younger days, long before he descended into blindness, depression, and outright misanthropy, there was a dark streak in his work. For all their gentle offbeat humor, his tales are rife with violent fantasy, particularly his celebrated stories of "little men" and their domineering mates whose marital warfare sometimes culminates in actual homicide. That a writer with such a worldview had a lifelong fascination with famous American murder cases is no surprise.

In 1927 Thurber, until then a struggling freelancer, went to work for the recently launched *New Yorker* magazine, where his short humorous "casuals" and surreal cartoons helped establish the magazine's sophisticated tone. The article included here, a follow-up story on the notorious Hall-Mills case of 1922, was part of the magazine's regular "Where Are They Now?" series and credited to "Jared L. Manley," one of the pseudonyms Thurber employed at *The New Yorker*. It later appeared in his 1942 collection *My World—and Welcome to It*.

A Sort of Genius

On the morning of Saturday the 16th of September, 1922, a boy named Raymond Schneider and a girl named Pearl Bahmer, walking down a lonely lane on the outskirts of New Brunswick, New Jersey, came upon something that made them rush to the nearest house in Easton Avenue, around the corner, shouting. In that house an excited woman named Grace Edwards listened to them wide-eyed and then telephoned the police. The police came on the run and examined the young people's discovery: the bodies of a man and a woman. They had been shot to death and the woman's throat was cut. Leaning against one of the man's shoes was his calling card, not as if it had fallen there but as if it had been placed there. It bore the name Rev. Edward W. Hall. He had been the rector of the Protestant Episcopal Church of St. John the Evangelist in New Brunswick. The woman was identified as Mrs. Eleanor R. Mills, wife of the sexton of that church. Raymond Schneider and Pearl Bahmer had stumbled upon what was to go down finally in the annals of our crime as perhaps the country's most remarkable mystery. Nobody was ever found guilty of the murders. Before the case was officially closed, a hundred and fifty persons had had their day in court and on the front pages of the newspapers. The names of two must already have sprung to your mind: Mrs. Jane Gibson, called by the avid press "the pig woman," and William Carpender Stevens, once known to a hundred million people simply as "Willie." The pig woman died eleven years ago, but Willie Stevens is alive. He still lives in the house that he lived in fourteen years ago with Mr. and Mrs. Hall, at 23 Nichol Avenue, New Brunswick.

It was from that house that the Rev. Mr. Hall walked at around 7:30 o'clock on the night of Thursday the 14th of September, 1922, to his peculiar doom. With the activities in that house after Mr. Hall's departure the State of New Jersey was to be vitally concerned. No. 23 Nichol Avenue was to share with De Russey's Lane, in which the bodies were found, the morbid interest of a whole nation four years later, when the case was finally brought to trial. What actually happened in De Russey's Lane on the night of September 14th? What actually happened at 23 Nichol Avenue the same night? For the researcher, it is a matter of an involved and voluminous court record, colorful and exciting in places, confused and repetitious in others. Two things, however, stand out as sharply now as they did on the day of their telling: the pig woman's story of the people she saw in De Russey's Lane that night, and Willie Stevens' story of what went on in the house in Nichol Avenue. Willie's story, brought out in cross-examination by a prosecutor whose name you may have forgotten (it was Alexander Simpson), lacked all the gaudy melodrama of the pig woman's tale, but in it, and in the way he told it on the stand, was the real drama of the Hall-Mills trial. When the State failed miserably in its confident purpose of breaking Willie

Stevens down, the verdict was already written on the wall. The rest of the trial was anticlimax. The jury that acquitted Willie, and his sister, Mrs. Frances Stevens Hall, and his brother, Henry Stevens, was out only five hours.

A detailed recital of all the fantastic events and circumstances of the Hall-Mills case would fill a large volume. If the story is vague in your mind, it is partly because its edges, even under the harsh glare of investigation, remained curiously obscure and fuzzy. Everyone remembers, of course, that the minister was deeply involved with Mrs. Mills, who sang in his choir; their affair had been for some time the gossip of their circle. He was forty-one, she was in her early thirties; Mrs. Hall was past fifty. On the 14th of September, Mr. Hall had dinner at home with his wife, Willie Stevens, and a little niece of Mrs. Hall's. After dinner, he said, according to his wife and his brother-in-law, that he was going to call on Mrs. Mills. There was something about a payment on a doctor's bill. Mrs. Mills had had an operation and the Halls had paid for it (Mrs. Hall had inherited considerable wealth from her parents). He left the house at about the same time, it came out later, that Mrs. Mills left her house, and the two were found murdered, under a crab apple tree in De Russey's Lane, on the edge of town, some forty hours later. Around the bodies were scattered love letters which the choir singer had written to the minister. No weapons were found, but there were several cartridge shells from an automatic pistol.

The investigation that followed—marked, said one New Jersey lawyer, by "bungling stupidity"—resulted in the failure of the Grand Jury to indict anyone. Willie Stevens was questioned for hours, and so was Mrs. Hall. The pig woman told her extraordinary story of what she saw and heard in the lane that night, but she failed to impress the Grand Jurors. Four years went by, and the Hall-Mills case was almost forgotten by people outside of New Brunswick when, in a New Jersey court, one Arthur Riehl brought suit against his wife, the former Louise Geist, for annulment of their marriage. Louise Geist had been, at the time of the murders, a maid in the Hall household. Riehl said in the course of his testimony that his wife had told him "she knew all about the case but had been given $5,000 to hold her tongue." This was all that Mr. Philip Payne, managing editor of the *Daily Mirror*, nosing around for a big scandal of some sort, needed. His newspaper "played up" the story until finally, under its goading, Governor Moore of New Jersey appointed Alexander Simpson special prosecutor with orders to reopen the case. Mrs. Hall and Willie Stevens were arrested and so was their brother, Henry Stevens, and a cousin, Henry de la Bruyere Carpender.

At a preliminary hearing in Somerville the pig woman, with eager stridency, told her story again. About 9 o'clock on the night of September 14th, she heard a wagon going along Hamilton Road near the farm on which she raised her pigs. Thieves had been stealing her corn and she thought maybe they were at it again. So she saddled her mule, Jenny (soon to become the most famous quadruped in the country), and set off in grotesque pursuit. In the glare of an automobile's headlights in De Russey's Lane, she saw a woman with white hair who was wearing a tan coat, and a man with a heavy mustache, who looked like a colored man. These figures she identified as Mrs. Hall and Willie Stevens. Tying her mule to a cedar tree, she started toward the scene on foot and heard voices raised in quarrel: "Somebody said something about letters." She now saw three persons (later on she increased this to four), and a flashlight held by one of them illumined the face of a man she identified first as Henry Carpender, later as Henry Stevens, and it "glittered on something" in the man's hand. Suddenly there was a shot, and as she turned and ran for her mule, there were three more shots; a woman's voice screamed, "Oh, my! Oh, my! Oh, my!" and the voice of another woman moaned, "Oh, Henry!" The pig woman rode wildly home on her mule, without investigating further. But she had lost one of her moccasins in her flight, and some three hours later, at 1 o'clock, she rode her mule back again to see if she could find it. This time, by the light of the moon, she saw Mrs. Hall, she said, kneeling in the lane, weeping. There was no one else there. The pig woman did not see any bodies.

Mrs. Jane Gibson became, because of her remarkable story, the chief witness for the State, as Willie Stevens was to become the chief witness for the defense. If he and his sister were not in De Russey's Lane, as the pig woman had shrilly insisted, it remained for them to tell the detailed story of their whereabouts and their actions that night after Mr. Hall left the house. The Grand Jury this time indicted all four persons implicated by the pig woman, and the trial began on November 3rd, 1926.

The first persons Alexander Simpson called to the stand were "surprise witnesses." They were a Mr. and Mrs. John S. Dixon, who lived in North Plainfield, New Jersey, about twelve miles from New Brunswick. It soon became apparent that they were to form part of a net that Simpson was preparing to draw around Willie Stevens. They testified that at about 8:30 on the night of the murders Willie had appeared at their house, wearing a loose-fitting suit, a derby, a wing collar with bow tie, and, across his vest, a heavy gold chain to which was attached a gold watch. He had said that his sister had let him out there from her automobile and that he was trying to find the Parker Home for the Aged, which was at Bound Brook. He stuttered and he told them that he was an epileptic. They directed him to a trolley car and he went stumbling away. When Mrs. Dixon identified Willie as her visitor, she walked over to him and took his right hand and shook it vigorously, as if to wring recognition out of him. Willie stared at her, said nothing. When she returned to the stand, he grinned widely. That was one of many bizarre incidents which marked the progress of the famous murder trial. It deepened the mystery that hung about the strange figure of Willie Stevens. People could hardly wait for him to take the stand.

William Carpender Stevens had sat in court for sixteen days before he was called to the witness chair, on the 23rd of November, 1926. On that day the trial of Albert B. Fall and Edward L. Doheny, defendants in the notorious Teapot Dome scandal, opened in Washington, but the nation had eyes only for a small, crowded courtroom in Somerville, New Jersey. Willie Stevens, after all these weeks, after all these years, was to speak out in public for the first time. As the New York *Times* said, "He had been pictured as 'Crazy Willie,' as a town character, as an oddity, as a butt for all manner of jokes. He had been compared inferentially to an animal, and the hint of an alien racial strain in his parentage had been thrown at him." Moreover, it had been prophesied that Willie would "blow up" on the stand, that he would be trapped into contradictions by the "wily" and "crafty" Alexander Simpson, that he would be tricked finally into blurting out his guilt. No wonder there was no sound in the courtroom except the heavy tread of Willie Stevens' feet as he walked briskly to the witness stand.

Willie Stevens was an ungainly, rather lumpish man, about five feet ten inches tall. Although he looked flabby, this was only because of his loose-fitting clothes and the way he wore them; despite his fifty-four years, he was a man of great physical strength. He had a large head and a face that would be hard to forget. His head was covered with a thatch of thick, bushy hair, and his heavy black eyebrows seemed always to be arched, giving him an expression of perpetual surprise. This expression was strikingly accentuated by large, prominent eyes which, seen through the thick lenses of the spectacles he always wore, seemed to bulge unnaturally. He had a heavy, drooping, walrus mustache, and his complexion was dark. His glare was sudden and fierce; his smile, which came just as quickly, lighted up his whole face and gave him the wide, beaming look of an enormously pleased child. Born in Aiken, South Carolina, Willie Stevens had been brought to New Brunswick when he was two years old. When his wealthy parents died, a comfortable trust fund was left to Willie. The other children, Frances and Henry, had inherited their money directly. Once, when Mrs. Hall was asked if it was not true that Willie was "regarded as essential to be taken care of in certain things," she replied, "In certain aspects." The quality of Willie's mentality, the extent of his eccentricity, were matters the prosecution strove to establish on several occasions. Dr. Laurence Runyon, called by the defense to testify that Willie was not an epileptic and had never stuttered, was cross-examined by Simpson. Said the Doctor, "He may not be absolutely normal mentally, but he is able to take care of himself perfectly well. He is brighter than the average person, although he has never advanced as far in school learning as some others. He reads books that are above the average and makes a good many people look like fools." "A sort of genius, in a way, I suppose?" said Simpson. To which the Doctor quietly replied, "Yes, that is just what I mean."

There were all sorts of stories about Willie. One of them was that he had once started a fire in his back yard and then, putting on a fireman's helmet, had doused it gleefully with a pail of water. It was known that for years he had spent most of every day at the firehouse of Engine Company No. 3 in Dennis Street, New Brunswick. He played cards with the firemen, ran errands for them, argued and joked with them, and was a general favorite. Sometimes he went out and bought a steak, or a chicken, and it was prepared and eaten in the firehouse by the firemen and Willie. In the days when the engine company had been a volunteer organization, Willie was an honorary member and always carried, in the firemen's parades, a flag he had bought and presented to the firehouse, an elaborate banner costing sixty or seventy dollars. He had also bought the black-and-white bunting with which the front of the firehouse was draped whenever a member of the company died.

After his arrest, he had whiled away the time in his cell reading books on metallurgy. There was a story that when his sister-in-law, Mrs. Henry Stevens, once twitted him on his heavy reading, he said, "Oh, that is merely the bread and butter of my literary repast." The night before the trial opened, Willie's chief concern was about a new blue suit that had been ordered for him and that did not fit him to his satisfaction. He had also lost a collar button, and that worried him; Mrs. Henry Stevens hurried to the jail before the court convened and brought him another one, and he was happy. At the preliminary hearing weeks before, Simpson had declared with brutal directness that Willie Stevens did indeed look like a colored man, as the pig woman had said. At this Willie had half risen from his chair and bared his teeth, as if about to leap on the prosecutor. But he had quickly subsided. All through the trial he had sat quietly, staring. He had been enormously interested when the pig woman, attended by a doctor and a nurse, was brought in on a stretcher to give her testimony. This was the man who now, on trial for his life, climbed into the witness chair in the court-room at Somerville.

There was an immense stir. Justice Charles W. Parker rapped with his gavel. Mrs. Hall's face was strained and white; this was an ordeal she and her family had been dreading for weeks. Willie's left hand gripped his chair tightly, his right hand held a yellow pencil with which he had fiddled all during the trial. He faced the roomful of eyes tensely. His own lawyer, Senator Clarence E. Case, took the witness first. Willie started badly by understating his age ten years. He said he was forty-four. "Isn't it fifty-four?" asked Case. Willie gave the room his great, beaming smile. "Yes," he chortled, boyishly, as if amused by his slip. The spectators smiled. It didn't take Willie long to dispose of the Dixons, the couple who had sworn he stumbled into their house the night of the murder. He answered half a dozen questions on this point with strong emphasis, speaking slowly and clearly: he had never worn a derby, he had never had epilepsy, he had never stuttered, he had never had a gold watch and chain. Mr. Case held up Willie's old silver watch and chain for the jury to see. When he handed them back, Willie, with fine nonchalance, compared his watch with the clock on the courtroom wall, gave his sister a large, reassuring smile, and turned to his questioner with respectful attention. He described, with techni-cal accuracy, an old revolver of his (the murders had been done with an automatic pistol, not a revolver, but a weapon of the same caliber as Willie's). He said he used to fire off the gun on the Fourth of July; remembering these old holidays, his eyes lighted up with childish glee. From this mood he veered suddenly into indignation and anger. "When was the last time you saw the revolver?" was what set him off. "The last time I saw it was in this courthouse!" Willie almost shouted. "I think it was in October, 1922, when I was taken and put through a very severe grilling by—I cannot mention every person's name, but I remember Mr. Toolan, Mr. Lamb, and Detective David, and they did everything but strike me. They cursed me frightfully." The officers had got him into an automobile "by a subterfuge," he charged. "Mr. David said he simply wanted me to go out in the country, to ask me a very few questions, that I would not be very long." It transpired later that on this trip Willie himself had had a question to ask Detective David: would the detective, if they passed De Russey's Lane, be kind enough to point it out to him? Willie had never seen the place, he told the detective, in his life. He said that Mr. David showed him where it was.

When Willie got to the night of September 14th, 1922, in his testimony his anger and indignation were gone; he was placid, attentive, and courteous. He explained quietly that he had come home for supper that night, had gone to his room afterward, and "remained in the house, leaving it at 2:30 in the morning with my sister." Before he went to bed, he said, he had closed his door to confine to his own room the odor of tobacco smoke from his pipe. "Who objected to that?" asked Mr. Case. Willie gave his sudden, beaming grin. "Everybody," he said, and won the first of several general laughs from the courtroom. Then he told the story of what happened at 2:30 in the morning. It is necessary, for a well-rounded picture of Willie Stevens, to give it here at some length. "I was awakened by my sister knocking at my door," said Willie, "and I immediately rose and went to the door and she said, 'I want you to come down to the church, as Edward has not come home; I am very much worried'—or words to that effect. I immediately got dressed and accompanied her down to the church. I went through the front door, followed a small path that led directly to the back of the house past the cellar door. We went directly down Redmond Street to Jones Avenue, from Jones Avenue we went to George Street; turning into George Street we went directly down to Commercial Avenue. There our movements were blocked by an immense big freight automobile. We had to wait there maybe half a minute until it went by, going toward New York.

"I am not at all sure whether we crossed right there at Commercial Avenue or went a little further down George Street and went diagonally across to the church. Then we stopped there and looked at the church to see whether there were any lights. There were no lights burning. Then Mrs. Hall said, 'We might as well go down and see if it could not be possible that he was at the Mills' house.' We went down there, down George Street until we came to Carman Street, turned down Carman Street, and got in front of the Mills' house and stood there two or three minutes to see if there were any lights in the Mills' apartment. There were none." Willie then described, street by street, the return home, and ended with "I opened the front door with my latchkey. If you wish me, I will show it to you. My sister said, 'You might as well go to bed. You can do no more good.' With that I went upstairs to bed." This was the story that Alexander Simpson had to shake. But before Willie was turned over to him, the witness told how he heard that his brother-in-law had been killed. "I remember I was in the parlor," said Willie, "reading a copy of the New York *Times*. I heard someone coming up the steps and I glanced up and I heard my aunt, Mrs. Charles J. Carpender, say, 'Well, you might as well know it— Edward has been shot.'" Willie's voice was thick with emotion. He was asked what happened then. "Well," he said, "I simply let the paper go— that way" (he let his left hand fall slowly and limply to his side) "and I put my head down, and I cried." Mr. Case asked him if he was present at, or had anything to do with, the murder of Mr. Hall and Mrs. Mills. "Absolutely nothing at all!" boomed Willie, coming out of his posture of sorrow, belligerently erect. The attorney for the defense turned, with a confident little bow, to Alexander Simpson. The special prosecutor sauntered over and stood in front of the witness. Willie took in his breath sharply.

Alexander Simpson, a lawyer, a state senator, slight, perky, capable of harsh tongue-lashings, given to sarcasm and innuendo, had intimated that he would "tie Willie Stevens into knots." Word had gone around that he intended to "flay" the eccentric fellow. Hence his manner now came as a surprise. He spoke in a gentle, almost inaudible voice, and his attitude was one of solicitous friendliness. Willie, quite unexpectedly, drew first blood. Simpson asked him if he had ever earned his livelihood. "For about four or five years," said Willie, "I was employed by Mr. Siebold, a contractor." Not having anticipated an affirmative reply, Simpson paused. Willie leaned forward and said, politely, "Do you wish his address?" He did this in good faith, but the spectators took it for what the *Times* called a "sally," because Simpson had been in the habit of letting loose a swarm of investigators on anyone whose name was brought into the case. "No thank you," muttered Simpson, above a roar of laughter. The prosecutor now set about picking at Willie's story of the night of September 14th: he tried to find out why the witness and his sister had not knocked on the Mills' door to see if Mr. Hall were there. Unfortunately for the steady drumming of questions, Willie soon broke the prosecutor up with another laugh. Simpson had occasion to mention a New Brunswick boarding house called The Bayard, and he pronounced "Bay" as it is spelled. With easy politeness, Willie corrected him. "*Bi*yard," said Willie. "Biyard?" repeated Simpson. Willie smiled, as at an apt pupil. Simpson bowed slightly. The spectators laughed again.

Presently the witness made a slip, and Simpson pounced on it like a stooping falcon. Asked if he had not, at the scene of the murder, stood "in the light of an automobile while a woman on a mule went by," Willie replied, "I never remember that occurrence." Let us take up the court record from there. "Q.—You would remember if it occurred, wouldn't you? A.—I certainly would, but I don't remember of ever being in an automobile and the light from the automobile shone on a woman on a mule. Q.—Do you say you were not there, or you don't remember? A.—I say positively I was not there. Q.—Why did you say you don't *remember*? A.—Does not that cover the same thing? Q.—No, it don't, because you might be there and not remember it. A.—Well, I will withdraw that, if I may, and say I was not there positively." Willie assumed an air of judicial authority as he "withdrew" his previous answer, and he spoke his positive denial with sharp decision. Mr. Simpson abruptly tried a new tack. "You have had a great deal of experience in life, Mr. Stevens," he said, "and have read a great deal, they say, and know a lot about human affairs. Don't you think it sounds rather fishy when you say you got up in the middle of the night to go and look for Dr. Hall and went to the house and never even knocked on the door—with your experience of human affairs and people that you met and all that sort of thing—don't that seem rather fishy to you?" There was a loud bickering of attorneys before Willie could say anything to this. Finally Judge Parker turned to the witness and said, "Can you answer that, Mr. Stevens?" "The only way I can answer it, Your Honor," said Willie, scornfully, "is that I don't see that it is at all 'fishy.'" The prosecutor jumped to something else: "Dr. Hall's church was not your church, was it?" he asked. "He was not a *Doctor*, sir," said Willie, once more the instructor. "He was the Reverend *Mister* Hall." Simpson paused, nettled. "I am glad you corrected me on that," he said. The courtroom laughed again.

The prosecutor now demanded that Willie repeat his story of what happened at 2:30 A.M. He hoped to establish, he intimated, that the witness had learned it "by rote." Willie calmly went over the whole thing again, in complete detail, but no one of his sentences was the same as it had been. The prosecutor asked him to tell it a third time. The defense objected vehemently. Simpson vehemently objected to the defense's objection. The Court: "We will let him tell it once more." At this point Willie said, "May I say a word?" "Certainly," said Simpson. "Say all you want." Weighing his words carefully, speaking with slow emphasis, Willie said, "All I have to say is I was never taught, as you insinuate, by any person whatsoever. That is my best recollection from the time I started out with my sister to this present minute." Simpson did not insist further on a third recital. He wanted to know now how Willie could establish the truth of his statement that he was in his room from 8 or 9 o'clock until his sister knocked on the door at 2:30 A.M. "Why," said Willie, "if a person sees me go upstairs and does not see me come downstairs, isn't that a conclusion that I was in my room?" The court record shows that Mr. Simpson replied, "Absolutely." "Well," said Willie expansively, "that is all there was to it." Nobody but the pig woman had testified to seeing Willie after he went up to his room that night. Barbara Tough, a servant who had been off during the day, testified that she got back to the Hall home about 10 o'clock and noticed that Willie's door was closed (Willie had testified that it wouldn't stay closed unless he locked it). Louise Geist, of the annulment suit, had testified that she had not seen Willie that night after dinner. It was

Willie's story against the pig woman's. That day in court he overshadowed her. When he stepped down from the witness chair, his shoulders were back and he was smiling broadly. Headlines in the *Times* the next day said, "Willie Stevens Remains Calm Under Cross-Examination. Witness a Great Surprise." There was a touch of admiration, almost of partisanship, in most of the reporters' stories. The final verdict could be read between the lines. The trial dragged on for another ten days, but on the 3rd of December, Willie Stevens was a free man.

He was glad to get home. He stood on the porch of 23 Nichol Avenue, beaming at the house. Reporters had followed him there. He turned to them and said, solemnly, "It is one hundred and four days since I've been here. And I want to get in." They let him go. But two days later, on a Sunday, they came back and Mrs. Hall received them in the drawing room. They could hear Willie in an adjoining room, talking spiritedly. He was, it came out, discussing metallurgy with the Rev. J. Mervin Pettit, who had succeeded Mr. Hall as rector of the Church of St. John the Evangelist.

Willie Stevens, going on seventy, no longer visits the firehouse of No. 3 Engine Company. His old friends have caught only glimpses of him in the past few years, for he has been in feeble health, and spends most of his time in his room, going for a short ride now and then in his chauffeur-driven car. The passerby, glancing casually into the car, would not recognize the famous figure of the middle 1920's. Willie has lost a great deal of weight, and the familiar beaming light no longer comes easily to his eyes.

After Willie had been acquitted and sent home, he tried to pick up the old routine of life where he had left it, but people turned to stare after him in the street, and boys were forever at his heels, shouting, "Look out, Willie, Simpson is after you!" The younger children were fond of him and did not tease him, and once in a while Willie could be seen playing with them, as boisterously and whimsically as ever. The firemen say that if he encountered a ragged child he would find out where it lived, and then give one of his friends the money to buy new clothes for it. But Willie's adventures in the streets of the town became fewer and farther apart. Sometimes months would elapse between his visits to the firehouse. When he did show up in his old haunts, he complained of headaches, and while he was still in his fifties, he spent a month in bed with a heart ailment. After that, he stayed close to home, and the firemen rarely saw him. If you should drop by the firehouse, and your interest in Willie seems friendly, they will tell you some fond stories about him.

One winter Willie took a Cook's tour to Hawaii. When he came back, he told the firemen he had joined an organization which, for five dollars, gave its subscribers a closer view of the volcanoes than the ordinary tourist could get. Willie was crazy about the volcanoes. His trip, however, was spoiled, it came out, because someone recognized and pointed him out as the famous Willie Stevens of the Hall-Mills case. He had the Cook's agent cancel a month's reservation at a hotel and rearrange his schedule so that he could leave on the next ship. He is infuriated by any reference to the murders or to the trial. Some years ago a newspaper printed a paragraph about a man out West who was "a perfect double for Willie Stevens." Someone in the firehouse showed it to Willie and he tore the paper to shreds in a rage.

Willie still spends a great deal of time reading "heavy books"—on engineering, on entomology, on botany. Those who have seen his famous room at 23 Nichol Avenue—he has a friend in to visit him once in a while—say that it is filled with books. He has no use for detective stories or the Western and adventure magazines his friends the firemen read. When he is not reading scientific tomes, he dips into the classics or what he calls the "worth-while poets." He used to astound the firemen with his wide range of knowledge. There was the day a salesman of shaving materials dropped in at the enginehouse. Finding that Willie had visited St. Augustine, Florida, he mentioned an old Spanish chapel there. Willie described it and gave its history, replete with dates, and greatly impressed the caller. Another time someone mentioned a certain kind of insect which he said was found in this country. "You mean they used to be," said Willie. "That type of insect has been extinct in this country for forty years." It turned out that it had been, too. On still another occasion Willie fell to discussing flowers with some visitor at the firehouse and reeled off a Latin designation—*crassinae carduaceae*, or something of the sort. Then he turned, grinning, to the listening firemen. "Zinnias to you," he said.

Willie Stevens' income from the trust fund established for him is said to be around forty dollars a week. His expenditures are few, now that he is no longer able to go on long trips. The firemen like especially to tell about the time that Willie went to Wyoming, and attended a rodeo. He told the ticket-seller he wanted to sit in a box and the man gave him a single ticket. Willie explained that he wanted the whole box to himself, and he planked down a ten-dollar bill for it. Then he went in and sat in the box all alone. "I had a hell of a time!" he told the firemen gleefully when he came back home.

De Russey's Lane, which Detective David once pointed out to Willie Stevens, is now, you may have heard, entirely changed. Several years ago it was renamed Franklin Boulevard, and where the Rev. Mr. Edward W. Hall and Mrs. Eleanor Mills lay murdered there is now a row of neat brick and stucco houses. The famous crab apple tree under which the bodies were found disappeared the first weekend after the murders. It was hacked to pieces, roots and all, by souvenir-hunters.

The New Yorker, January 23, 1937

MEYER BERGER

Little known to the public at large but highly esteemed by his colleagues, Meyer "Mike" Berger (1898–1959) ended his formal education at age 12 when he dropped out of high school to take a $1.50-a-week job at *The New York World*. After working his way up from messenger to copy boy to reporter, Berger moved to *The New York Times* in 1928, and—apart from a yearlong interlude at *The New Yorker*—remained there for the rest of his life.

Between 1939 and 1940, and again from 1953 to 1958, he turned out daily "About New York" pieces for the *Times*, beautifully detailed vignettes that captured the color and spirit of his beloved metropolis and the infinitely variegated characters who inhabited it. It was not, however, these widely admired human-interest stories that won him his highest journalistic honor but a classic piece of front-page crime reporting.

On the morning of September 6, 1949, Howard Unruh, a 28-year-old World War II veteran armed with a 9-mm Luger pistol, went on a murderous rampage in his hometown of Camden, New Jersey. By the time he was done, he had killed or wounded 16 of his neighbors and earned a place in the annals of American crime as our country's first modern mass murderer.

Arriving on the scene shortly after the shootings, Berger spent six hours retracing Unruh's path and interviewing 50 witnesses. He then raced back to the office and, in the space of two and a half hours, typed out a 4,000-word story that was published the following day without a single alteration by the rewrite desk. The article brought him a much-deserved Pulitzer Prize in 1950.

Veteran Kills 12 in Mad
Rampage on Camden Street

Shoots 4 Others in Revenge for 'Derogatory Remarks' About His Character

CAMDEN, N.J., Sept. 6—Howard B. Unruh, 28 years old, a mild, soft-spoken veteran of many armored artillery battles in Italy, France, Austria, Belgium and Germany, killed twelve persons with a war souvenir Luger pistol in his home block in East Camden this morning. He wounded four others.

Unruh, a slender, hollow-cheeked six-footer paradoxically devoted to scripture reading and to constant practice with firearms, had no previous history of mental illness but specialists indicated tonight that there was no doubt that he was a psychiatric case, and that he had secretly nursed a persecution complex for two years or more.

The veteran was shot in the left thigh by a local tavern keeper but he kept that fact secret, too, while policemen and Mitchell Cohen, Camden County prosecutor, questioned him at police headquarters for more than two hours immediately after tear gas bombs had forced him out of his bedroom to surrender.

The blood stain he left on the seat he occupied during the questioning betrayed his wound. When it was discovered he was taken to Cooper Hospital in Camden, a prisoner charged with murder.

He was as calm under questioning as he was during the twenty minutes that he was shooting men, women and children. Only occasionally excessive brightness of his dark eyes indicated that he was anything other than normal.

He told the prosecutor that he had been building up resentment against neighbors and neighborhood shopkeepers for a long time. "They have been making derogatory remarks about my character," he said. His resentment seemed most strongly concentrated against Mr.

and Mrs. Maurice Cohen, who lived next door to him. They are among the dead.

Mr. Cohen was a druggist with a shop at 3202 River Road in East Camden. He and his wife had had frequent sharp exchanges over the Unruhs' use of a gate that separates their back yard from the Cohens'. Mrs. Cohen had also complained of young Unruh's keeping his bedroom radio tuned high into the late night hours. None of the other victims had ever had trouble with him.

Unruh, a graduate of Woodrow Wilson High School here, had started a GI course in pharmacy at Temple University in Philadelphia some time after he was honorably discharged from the service in 1945, but had stayed with it only three months. In recent months he had been unemployed, and apparently was not even looking for work.

His mother, Mrs. Rita Unruh, 50, is separated from her husband. She works as a packer in the Evanson Soap Company in Camden and hers was virtually the only family income. James Unruh, 25 years old, her younger son, is married and lives in Haddon Heights, N.J. He works for the Curtis Publishing Company.

On Monday night, Howard Unruh left the house alone. He spent the night at the Family Theatre on Market Street in Philadelphia to sit through several showings of the double feature motion picture there—"I Cheated the Law" and "The Lady Gambles." It was past 3 o'clock this morning when he got home.

Prosecutor Cohen said that Unruh told him later that before he fell asleep this morning he had made up his mind to shoot the persons who had "talked about me," that he had even figured out that 9:30 A.M. would be the time to begin because most of the stores in his block would be open at that hour.

His mother, leaving her ironing when he got up, prepared his breakfast in their drab little three-room apartment in the shabby gray two-story stucco house at the corner of River Road and Thirty-Second Street. After breakfast he loaded one clip of bullets into his Luger, slipped another clip into his pocket, and carried sixteen loose cartridges in addition. He also carried a tear-gas pen with six shells and a sharp six-inch knife.

He took one last look around his bedroom before he left the house. On the peeling walls he had crossed pistols, crossed German bayonets, pictures of armored artillery in action. Scattered about the chamber were machetes, a Roy Rogers pistol, ash trays made of German shells, clips of 30-30 cartridges for rifle use and a host of varied war souvenirs.

Mrs. Unruh had left the house some minutes before, to call on Mrs. Caroline Pinner, a friend in the next block. Mrs. Unruh had sensed, apparently, that her son's smoldering resentments were coming to a head. She had pleaded with Elias Pinner, her friend's husband, to cut a little gate in the Unruhs' backyard so that Howard need not use the Cohen gate again. Mr. Pinner finished the gate early Monday evening after Howard had gone to Philadelphia.

At the Pinners' house at 9 o'clock this morning, Mrs. Unruh had murmured something about Howard's eyes; how strange they looked and how worried she was about him.

A few minutes later River Road echoed and re-echoed to pistol fire. Howard Unruh was on the rampage. His mother, who had left the Pinners' little white house only a few seconds before, turned back. She hurried through the door.

She cried, "Oh, Howard, oh, Howard, they're to blame for this." She rushed past Mrs. Pinner, a kindly gray-haired woman of 70. She said, "I've got to use the phone; may I use the phone?"

But before she had crossed the living room to reach for it she fell on the faded carpet in a dead faint. The Pinners lifted her onto a couch in the next room. Mrs. Pinner applied aromatic spirits to revive her.

While his mother writhed on the sofa in her house dress and worn old sweater, coming back to consciousness, Howard Unruh was walking from shop to shop in the "3200 block" with deadly calm, spurting Luger in hand. Children screamed as they tumbled over one another to get out of his way. Men and women dodged into open shops, the women shrill with panic, men hoarse with fear. No one could quite understand for a time what had been loosed in the block.

Unruh first walked into John Pilarchik's shoe repair shop near the north end of his own side of the street. The cobbler, a 27-year-old man who lives in Pennsauken Township, looked up open-mouthed as Unruh came to within a yard of him. The cobbler started up from his bench but went down with a bullet in his stomach. A little boy who was in the shop ran behind the counter and crouched there in terror. Unruh walked out into the sunlit street.

"I shot them in the chest first," he told the prosecutor later, in meticulous detail, "and then I aimed for the head." His aim was devastating—and with reason. He had won marksmanship and sharpshooters' ratings in the service, and he practiced with his Luger all the time on a target set up in the cellar of his home.

Unruh told the prosecutor afterward that he had Cohen the druggist, the neighborhood barber, the neighborhood cobbler and the neighborhood tailor on his mental list of persons who had "talked about him." He went methodically about wiping them out. Oddly enough, he did not start with the druggist, against whom he seemed to have the sharpest feelings, but left him almost for the last.

From the cobbler's he went into the little tailor shop at 3214 River Road. The tailor was out. Helga Zegrino, 28 years old, the tailor's wife, was there alone. The couple, incidentally, had been married only one month. She screamed when Unruh walked in with his Luger in hand. Some people across the street heard her. Then the gun blasted again and Mrs. Zegrino pitched over, dead. Unruh walked into the sunlight again.

All this was only a matter of seconds and still only a few persons had begun to understand what was afoot. Down the street at 3210 River Road is Clark Hoover's little country barber shop. In the center was a white-painted carousel-type horse for children customers. Orris Smith, a blonde boy only 6 years old, was in it, with a bib around his neck, submitting to a shearing. His mother, Mrs. Catherine Smith, 42, sat on a chair against the wall and watched.

She looked up. Clark Hoover turned from his work, to see the six-footer, gaunt and tense, but silent, standing in the doorway with the

Luger. Unruh's brown tropical worsted suit was barred with morning shadow. The sun lay bright in his crew-cut brown hair. He wore no hat. Mrs. Smith could not understand what was about to happen.

Unruh walked to "Brux"—that is Mrs. Smith's nickname for her little boy—and put the Luger to the child's chest. The shot echoed and reverberated in the little 12 by 12 shop. The little boy's head pitched toward the wound, his hair, half-cut, stained with red. Unruh said never a word. He put the Luger close to the shaking barber's hand. Before the horrified mother, Unruh leaned over and fired another shot into Hoover.

The veteran made no attempt to kill Mrs. Smith. He did not seem to hear her screams. He turned his back and stalked out, unhurried. A few doors north, Dominick Latela, who runs a little restaurant, had come to his shop window to learn what the shooting was about. He saw Unruh cross the street toward Frank Engel's tavern. Then he saw Mrs. Smith stagger out with her pitiful burden. Her son's head lolled over the crook of her right arm.

Mrs. Smith screamed "My boy is dead. I know he's dead." She stared about her, looking in vain for aid. No one but Howard Unruh was in sight, and he was concentrating on the tavern. Latela dashed out, but first he shouted to his wife, Dora, who was in the restaurant with their daughter Eleanor, 6 years old. He hollered "I'm going out. Lock the door behind me." He ran for his car, and drove it down toward Mrs. Smith as she stood on the pavement with her son.

Latela took the child from her arms and placed him on the car's front seat. He pushed the mother into the rear seat, slammed the doors and headed for Cooper Hospital. Howard Unruh had not turned. Engel, the tavern keeper, had locked his own door. His customers, the bartender, and a porter made a concerted rush for the rear of the saloon. The bullets tore through the tavern door panelling. Engel rushed upstairs and got out his .38 caliber pistol, then rushed to the street window of his apartment.

Unruh was back in the center of the street. He fired a shot at an apartment window at 3208 River Road. Tommy Hamilton, 2 years old, fell back with a bullet in his head. Unruh went north again to Latela's place. He fired a shot at the door, and kicked in the lower glass panel. Mrs. Latela crouched behind the counter with her daughter. She heard the bullets, but neither she nor her child was touched. Unruh walked back toward Thirty-second Street, reloading the Luger.

Now the little street—a small block with only five buildings on one side, three one-story stores on the other—was shrill with women's and children's panicky outcries. A group of six or seven little boys or girls fled past Unruh. They screamed, "Crazy man!" and unintelligible sentences. Unruh did not seem to hear, or see, them.

Alvin Day, a television repair man who lives in near-by Mantua, had heard the shooting, but driving into the street he was not aware of what had happened. Unruh walked up to the car window as Day rolled by, and fired once through the window, with deadly aim. The repair man fell against the steering wheel. The car seemed to wabble. The front wheels hit the opposite curb and stalled. Day was dead.

Frank Engel had thrown open his second-floor apartment window. He saw Unruh pause for a moment in a narrow alley between the cobbler's shop and a little two-story house. He aimed and fired. Unruh stopped for just a second. The bullet had hit, but he did not seem to mind, after the initial brief shock. He headed toward the corner drug stores, and Engel did not fire again.

"I wish I had," he said, later. "I could have killed him then. I could have put a half-dozen shots into him. I don't know why I didn't do it."

Cohen, the druggist, a heavy man of 40, had run into the street shouting "What's going on here? what's going on here?" but at sight of Unruh hurried back into his shop. James J. Hutton, 45, an insurance agent from Westmont, N.J., started out of the drug shop to see what the shooting was about. Like so many others he had figured at first that it was some car backfiring. He came face to face with Unruh.

Unruh said quietly, "Excuse me, sir," and started to push past him. Later Unruh told the police: "That man didn't act fast enough. He didn't get out of my way." He fired into Hutton's head and body. The insurance man pitched onto the sidewalk and lay still.

Cohen had run to his upstairs apartment and had tried to warn

Minnie Cohen, 63, his mother, and Rose, his wife, 38, to hide. His son Charles, 14, was in the apartment, too. Mrs. Cohen shoved the boy into a clothes closet, and leaped into another closet herself. She pulled the door to. The druggist, meanwhile had leaped from the window onto a porch roof. Unruh, a gaunt figure at the window behind him, fired into the druggist's back. The druggist, still running, bounded off the roof and lay dead in Thirty-second Street.

Unruh fired into the closet where Mrs. Cohen was hidden. She fell dead behind the closed door, and he did not bother to open it. Mrs. Minnie Cohen tried to get to the telephone in an adjoining bedroom to call the police. Unruh fired shots into her head and body and she sprawled dead on the bed. Unruh walked down the stairs with his Luger reloaded and came out into the street again.

A coupe had stopped at River Road, obeying a red light. The passengers obviously had no idea of what was loose in East Camden and no one had a chance to tell them. Unruh walked up to the car, and though it was filled with total strangers, fired deliberately at them, one by one, through the windshield. He killed the two women passengers, Mrs. Helen Matlack Wilson, 43, of Pennsauken, who was driving, and her mother, Mrs. Emma Matlack, 66. Mrs. Wilson's son John, 12, was badly wounded. A bullet pierced his neck, just below the jawbone.

Earl Horner, clerk in the American Stores Company, a grocery opposite the drug store, had locked his front door after several passing men, women and children had tumbled breathlessly into the shop panting "crazy man * * * killing people. * * * " Unruh came up to the door and fired two shots through the wood panelling. Horner, his customers, the refugees from the veteran's merciless gunfire, crouched, trembling, behind the counter. None there was hurt.

"He tried the door before he shot in here," Homer related afterward. "He just stood there, stony-faced and grim, and rattled the knob, before he started to fire. Then he turned away."

Charlie Petersen, 18, son of a Camden fireman, came driving down the street with two friends when Unruh turned from the grocery. The three boys got out to stare at Hutton's body lying unattended on the sidewalk. They did not know who had shot the insurance man, or why and, like the women in the car, had no warning that Howard Unruh was on the loose. The veteran brought his Luger to sight and fired several times. Young Petersen fell with bullets in his legs. His friends tore pell-mell down the street to safety.

Mrs. Helen Harris of 1250 North Twenty-eighth Street with her daughter, Helen, a 6-year-old blonde child, and a Mrs. Horowitz with her daughter, Linda, 5, turned into Thirty-second Street. They had heard the shooting from a distance but thought it was auto backfire.

Unruh passed them in Thirty-second Street and walked up the sagging four steps of a little yellow dwelling back of his own house. Mrs. Madeline Harrie, a woman in her late thirties, and two sons, Armand, 16, and Leroy, 15, were in the house. A third son, Wilson, 14, was barricaded in the grocery with other customers.

Unruh threw open the front door and, gun in hand, walked into the dark little parlor. He fired two shots at Mrs. Harrie. They went wild and entered the wall. A third shot caught her in the left arm. She screamed. Armand leaped at Unruh, to tackle him. The veteran used the Luger butt to drop the boy, then fired two shots into his arms. Upstairs Leroy heard the shooting and the screams. He hid under a bed.

By this time, answering a flood of hysterical telephone calls from various parts of East Camden, police radio cars swarmed into River Road with sirens wide open. Emergency crews brought machine guns, shotguns and tear gas bombs.

Sergeant Earl Wright, one of the first to leap to the sidewalk, saw Charles Cohen, the druggist's son. The boy was half out the second-floor apartment window, just above where his father lay dead. He was screaming "He's going to kill me. He's killing everybody." The boy was hysterical.

Wright bounded up the stairs to the druggist's apartment. He saw the dead woman on the bed, and tried to soothe the druggist's son. He brought him downstairs and turned him over to other policemen, then joined the men who had surrounded the two-story stucco house where Unruh lived. Unruh, meanwhile, had fired about thirty shots. He was out of ammunition. Leaving the Harrie house, he had also heard the police sirens. He had run through the back gate to his own rear bedroom.

Edward Joslin, a motorcycle policeman, scrambled to the porch roof under Unruh's window. He tossed a tear-gas grenade through a pane of glass. Other policemen, hoarsely calling on Unruh to surrender, took positions with their machine guns and shotguns. They trained them on Unruh's window.

Meanwhile, a curious interlude had taken place. Philip W. Buxton, an assistant city editor on The Camden Evening Courier had looked Unruh's name up in the telephone book. He called the number, Camden 4-2490W. It was just after 10 A.M. and Unruh had just returned to his room. To Mr. Buxton's astonishment Unruh answered. He said hello in a calm, clear voice.

"This Howard?" Mr. Buxton asked.

"Yes, this is Howard. What's the last name of the party you want?"

"Unruh."

The veteran asked what Mr. Buxton wanted.

"I'm a friend," the newspaper man said. "I want to know what they're doing to you down there."

Unruh thought a moment. He said, "They haven't done anything to me—yet. I'm doing plenty to them." His voice was still steady without a trace of hysteria.

Mr. Buxton asked how many persons Unruh had killed.

The veteran answered. "I don't know. I haven't counted. Looks like a pretty good score."

"Why are you killing people?"

"I don't know," came the frank answer. "I can't answer that yet. I'll have to talk to you later. I'm too busy now."

The telephone banged down.

Unruh was busy. The tear gas was taking effect and police bullets were thudding at the walls around him. During a lull in the firing the police saw the white curtains move and the gaunt killer came into plain view.

"Okay," he shouted. "I give up. I'm coming down."

"Where's that gun?" a sergeant yelled.

"It's on my desk, up here in the room," Unruh called down quietly. "I'm coming down."

Thirty guns were trained on the shabby little back door. A few seconds later the door opened and Unruh stepped into the light, his hands up. Sergeant Wright came across the morning-glory and aster beds in the yard and snapped handcuffs on Unruh's wrists.

"What's the matter with you," a policeman demanded hotly. "You a psycho?"

Unruh stared into the policeman's eyes—a level, steady stare. He said, "I'm no psycho. I have a good mind."

Word of the capture brought the whole East Camden populace pouring into the streets. Men and women screamed at Unruh, and cursed him in shrill accents and in hoarse anger. Someone cried "lynch him" but there was no movement. Sergeant Wright's men walked Unruh to a police car and started for headquarters.

Shouting and pushing men and women started after the car, but dropped back after a few paces. They stood in excited little groups discussing the shootings, and the character of Howard Unruh. Little by little the original anger, born of fear, that had moved the crowd, began to die.

Men conceded that he probably was not in his right mind. Those who knew Unruh kept repeating how close-mouthed he was, and how soft spoken. How he took his mother to church, and how he marked scripture passages, especially the prophecies.

"He was a quiet one, that guy," a man told a crowd in front of the tavern. "He was all the time figuring to do this thing. You gotta watch them quiet ones."

But all day River Road and the side streets talked of nothing else. The shock was great. Men and women kept saying: "We can't understand it. Just don't get it."

The New York Times, September 7, 1949

JOHN BARTLOW MARTIN

Why certain homicides become media sensations while other equally heinous ones fail to grip the public's attention is a complex question, though in many cases the answer clearly has to do with the victims: their social status, race, and other factors that make their murders either resonate or not with a mostly white, middle-class audience. It is unsurprising that the hideous murder and dismemberment of the Los Angeles party girl Elizabeth Short—the so-called "Black Dahlia"—has become the stuff of legend, while the appalling butchery of at least a dozen midwestern hoboes, drifters, and other "drab unfortunates" in roughly the same period has largely faded into obscurity.

This novelistic account of the atrocities committed by the "Mad Butcher of Kingsbury Run" (aka the "Cleveland Torso Killer") comes from the pen of author and diplomat John Bartlow Martin (1915–1987). An enormously prolific contributor to the mass-circulation magazines of the 1940s and 1950s whose powerful stories on labor racketeering, poor working conditions, crime, the abuse of mental patients, and other muckraking subjects led, in a number of cases, to major public policy changes, Martin became a political speechwriter, first for Adlai Stevenson and then for John Kennedy. Following Kennedy's election, he was appointed ambassador to the Dominican Republic and has the distinction of being the only important American true-crime writer whose bibliography includes such diverse works as *Why Did They Kill?*, *U.S. Policy in the Caribbean*, and a two-volume biography of Adlai Stevenson.

One intriguing aspect of the "Mad Butcher" case that Martin fails to highlight is the fact that Eliot Ness, the legendary lawman of "Untouchables" fame, was actively involved in the investigation, having become Cleveland's Director of Public Safety in 1935 following his successful investigation of Al Capone in Chicago. It is also worth noting that Martin consistently describes the "Mad Butcher" as a "mass murderer," a catchall phrase back then for all perpetrators of multiple homicide. Nowadays, the term is reserved for the kind of rampage killer who slaughters a number of victims in a single burst of devastating gun violence before (in most instances) ending his own life. In current terminology, the "Mad Butcher" was a serial killer, a phrase not yet coined at the time Martin's article was written.

Butcher's Dozen

A ll night, mastiffs prowl the cobbled street on guard by the darkened brewery. At the riverfront an ore boat squats by a dock. High above, the steel towers of the drawbridge rear black and naked against the sky. Looking up is like looking from the bottom of a well— up sixty feet to the street level of Cleveland (bright-lit Public Square is only two blocks away). Down here, in a ditch alongside a crumbling wall of masonry, is a hobo campground—blackened embers, chicken feathers, dirty wet excelsior, empty tin cans labeled "Do Not Take Internally Will Cause Blindness" (but the hobos drink it anyway— "smoke," they call it, not torch fuel). Streets here are short passageways between factory walls and boxcars. On a broken curb, in the glow of a single feeble street lamp, a human figure totters uncertain, a hobo, drunk. Railroad tracks glisten damp and dull. High on the clay bank in the bridge abutment are cavities maybe two feet deep and five feet long, and in each is a clutter of lousy brown boxcar paper and rags: a hobo's nest. The concrete abutment drips, the sound of a running sewer is everywhere in the dark.

Up the tracks in the southeast distance, a long freight on the Nickel Plate trestle runs across the fiery sky; they are tapping a heat in the steel-mill furnace; and above an oil refinery a tremendous flame lashes to and fro, waste gas burning, a column of roaring fire. A little beyond, up Kingsbury Run, factories end and blackness closes in. Kingsbury Run is a wide gully debouching into the river valley, its floor laced with thirty-odd pairs of rails, green and red switch lights winking dimly. Here in the East 55th Street yards switch engines work all night, cutting the strings of boxcars and coal cars, marshalling the trains bound for Youngstown and Pittsburgh and Buffalo, Sandusky and Toledo and Chicago. Atop the crumbling cliffs perch the homes of working men, all still now and dark, back fences sagging over the rubbish-strewn slopes. About 49th Street the tracks split, the Erie going up a narrow side gully, the rest following the sweeping curve of Kingsbury Run; and the eminence of land between is called Jackass Hill. At its base a narrow ravine slashes briefly into it, then ends. Even the head-light of the rushing Rapid Transit does not penetrate the weed-choked mouth of this ravine.

And here, on the afternoon of September 23, 1935, some boys found the bodies of two men, both headless. The boys told a Nickel Plate railroad detective and he called the Cleveland police. The bodies were male, white, and naked (except that one, the younger, had socks on his feet). One detective remembers, "They had been laid out," that is, neatly positioned as though by an undertaker, arms along their sides, heels together. There was no blood on the ground or the bodies; one detec-tive, pointing out that "the jugular vein is a snaky thing, it splatters blood everywhere when you cut it," has argued that the murderer be-headed the men elsewhere (probably indoors), drained and washed the bodies, then brought them here. They lay only a few feet apart. The younger was about twenty-eight, five feet eleven, 150 pounds, light, complexioned. He had been dead only two or three days. The older man, about forty-five, short and squat and heavy-set, had been killed about five days earlier. His skin was reddish-yellow and tough, and a laboratory technician thought "some unknown chemical had been applied," perhaps as a preservative.

Some distance away were a railroad engineer's torch, a dipper and a tin bucket. In the bucket was a heavy black oily fluid—automobile crankcase drainings, analysis showed, containing partially decom-posed blood and straight black hair, probably human. Like most of the evidence in this case, the bucket is still of controversial import: some detectives believe it proves that the murderer had attempted to burn the body; others think it was not connected with the case. Detectives spotted some hair sticking out of the opposite bank of the ravine about fifty feet away. They carefully tunneled under it and two heads rolled out. They fitted the bodies. Near by lay several pieces of rope, a shirt, and a cap, as well as a blue coat labeled "Baker Co." which seemed to fit the older man. None of these could be traced. The bodies were taken to the Cuyahoga County Morgue.

These were the first bodies found in Kingsbury Run belonging to Cleveland's series of torso murders, one of America's greatest criminal mysteries. Over a period of three or four years the unknown whom the newspapers called the Mad Butcher of Kingsbury Run murdered no less than twelve persons and he may have made off with as many as thirty-four; and yet, although the Cleveland police questioned upward of five thousand persons in their search for him, to this day almost nothing is known of him. And most of his victims remain as anonymous as he himself. Let us explore this murder cycle, rummaging among the unanswered questions. Who were his victims? Why were they killed? What kind of man was their murderer? How did he kill them? Where was his abattoir? Is he still alive and at large? If so, why did he cease operations? Our journey will take us into the lower depths of American life, indeed, into the very lowest depths, inhabited by prostitutes, pimps, hobos, dwellers of caves and shanties, homosexuals, and the kind of twisted persons that interested Krafft-Ebing. Though we shall get no final answers to our questions, we shall at least learn as much (consonant with the public weal and delicacy) as anybody knows about one of the world's greatest mass murderers, except the murderer himself.

The autopsy on the younger man revealed that he had eaten a vegetable meal shortly before dying. His wrists—but not those of the older man—were abraded, as though by ropes, suggesting he had been tied up. His head was cut off "in mid-cervical region," that is, at about the level of a man's coat-collar in the back, and the mid-cervical vertebrae were fractured. The skin was cleanly cut. The muscles were retracted, that is, drawn back from the skin edges, indicating the man's head was cut off while he was alive or immediately after death. For this reason, and also since the body showed no other marks of violence (except the rope burns) and since the heart was almost bloodless, the autopsy surgeon concluded that death was caused by the decapitation itself, plus shock and hemorrhage, a most unusual circumstance. (Most murderers who decapitate their victims do so only after having already stabbed or beaten them to death.) The dead man's fingerprints were on file in the police records. His name was Edward Andrassy.

Immediately the police concentrated on backtracking his life in the hope of finding his murderer, piecing together information from scores of sources—his relatives and friends, and police informers. They found that Andrassy was twenty-nine years old and had lived with his parents in a big old frame house in a rooming-house section of the near West Side of Cleveland. In his early twenties he had been an orderly in the psychopathic ward of a hospital. There he had met a young nurse. She had married Andrassy November 12, 1928, and left him after about three weeks; a baby was born later. Andrassy had left the hospital about 1931. He sold magazines for a time. But from then until he was found dead in 1935 his means of livelihood and the identities of his associates were a mystery. His parents knew little about them. Once he was sent to the Workhouse for thirty days for carrying concealed weapons. He was picked up several times for intoxication. He hung out near his home with some cheap sports who shot craps in a gully and slept off liquor in a graveyard alongside the railroad right-of-way. A railroad detective remembers, "Andrassy was the type fellow gives a cop a lot of lip when he's questioned. Once I had to knock him down."

Andrassy also hung out on West 25th Street, since nicknamed Rowdy Row. But he appears to have spent most of his time across the river, in the Roaring Third Police Precinct back of Public Square in downtown Cleveland. The Roaring Third was a region of peeling billboards and sagging tenements, warehouses and flophouses and gambling joints. On Bolivar Road near the ancient Central Markethouse aged Greeks sit, hats squarely on their heads, at a table in the window of a coffeehouse, and a fat butcher comes out of a saloon carrying a bottle of beer, his apron bloody. Factories are encroaching on the district, and Negroes have moved into many tenements, and the police are called mostly to deal with family cutting scrapes. But in the early 1930's this was a region of Italian and Greek vendettas, of speakeasies and secret distilleries, of narcotics dens and houses of prostitution; and more than one man went to the electric chair from the Roaring Third.

Apparently Andrassy got in trouble several times here during the summer before he was killed. His mother said that one night he had been brought home in a taxicab, his head cut; he didn't know how he'd been hurt, only that the cab driver had picked him up at East 9th Street and Bolivar Road. His mother recalled that about two weeks before he was murdered a stranger had come to her home and, accusing her son of sleeping with his wife, threatened to "take care of" him. She told Andrassy about it and he said the man "must of been crazy." Andrassy told his sister that he had stabbed an Italian in a fight at East 9th Street and Bolivar "and that the gang was after him." He stayed close to home. There was no police report on such a fight. An informer said he had concealed Andrassy for three days, until an Italian drove up in a Dodge touring car, invited the informer to go for a ride (he declined), and took Andrassy away. A little earlier Andrassy had told a friend that he was begging, that he had been drinking heavily, that he intended to quit, that while panhandling in Detroit he had knocked down a Chinaman and been obliged to leave town.

Now, the murderer had emasculated the bodies of both Andrassy and the unidentified man (the genitalia were found near the bodies). The police believed this indicated that the murderer was a sexual pervert and they wondered if Andrassy was one himself. The evidence was contradictory. During the summer Andrassy visited a nightclub several times, each time with a different woman, including a Chinese. On the other hand, a woman recalled that her son said Andrassy had tried to sell him some Spanish Fly (an aphrodisiac), and Andrassy had picked up another boy in a park and had taken him to a speakeasy. A married couple told the queerest story of all. The man, who had known Andrassy most of his life, said that early in the summer Andrassy had remarked "how bad" the man's wife looked. "She had female trouble," the police reported. "Andrassy then spoke up and told them that he was a 'female' doctor and that he would like to examine her." In doing so Andrassy committed sodomy upon her (it isn't clear whether her husband did not protest because he didn't understand or because Andrassy was bigger than he). "He then told Mr. and Mrs. —— that if he would go home and get his instruments he could fix her within a month, so that she could have children." But they "told Andrassy not to bother." Searching Andrassy's room later, detectives reported finding "two doctor books and five physical magazines." A while later the couple moved, and one night the man found Andrassy and a stranger standing in the dark outside the door of his new home. Andrassy said they were considering sleeping in the adjoining apartment, which was empty. Andrassy introduced his friend as "Eddie," a chauffeur for a wealthy woman in suburban Lakewood whom Andrassy "was doctoring . . . for the same trouble." The host invited them to have coffee, but "Eddie seemed very nervous" and they left in a large new touring car, a Lincoln or a Buick. "Eddie" was described as "28-30-5-6-150 good looking very good set of teeth appeared to have had a broken nose and wore a dark trousers blue shirt, checkered gray cap, and dark brown hair." The detectives never could find "Eddie." The couple said he was not the unidentified man found dead a month later with Andrassy. But, oddly, they said a cap found near the bodies was his.

Andrassy left home for the last time at 8 P.M. on September 19th, 1935, not saying where he was going. Nobody ever admitted having seen him thereafter. This was a Thursday. The coroner thought he probably was killed Friday. On Monday his body was found below Jackass Hill, a spot he was never known to have frequented. On Friday morning a neighbor had seen two young shabbily dressed Italians park an old Ford coupe at the top of Jackass Hill and walk down toward the spot where the bodies were later found. For three weeks railroad detectives had noticed an Italian sitting in a green coupe atop Jackass Hill, studying the terrain through binoculars; the police found him but could not connect him with the crime. How the murderer dumped the bodies without being seen either from the signal tower at the bottom of Jackass Hill or the houses atop it remains a puzzle. Captain J. C. Van Buren of the Nickel Plate police believes he carried them along the lee of an embankment a quarter of a mile from East 37th Street; others argue he would have deposited them in a safer jungle of bushes closer to 37th Street and, moreover, that they were too heavy to be carried so far. Van Buren replies that perhaps there were two murderers. But no other evidence supports the theory.

Once the detectives spent weeks tracing a man from one flophouse to another until they reached his last known residence—only to discover it had been condemned and wrecked. Once they reported: "Went to the home of ———, learned from his wife that he is out on a drunk and his whereabouts are unknown." Time and again they reported: "Canvassed cheap hotels, rooming houses, poolrooms . . . beer parlors . . . near the Market, where he was known to hang around," but the reports always ended inconclusively. It was not even learned whether Andrassy had been acquainted with the man found dead beside him. Decomposition prevented the police from obtaining fingerprints of the older man and he never was identified.

A year earlier, on September 5, 1934, a man picking up driftwood on the Lake Erie shore near Euclid Beach, an amusement park some eight miles east of downtown Cleveland, had found a piece of a woman's naked body partly buried in the sand. It was the lower half of the torso plus the thighs. The torso had been severed between the second and third lumbar vertebrae, that is, at about the small of the back. The legs had been cut off at the knees. The section of torso was seventeen inches long, the thigh fourteen inches, and the whole weighed thirty pounds, leading the autopsy surgeon to estimate that the woman in life had been about five feet, six inches tall and had weighed about 115 pounds. The uterus had been removed by legitimate surgery. The body had been in the water three or four months, had been dead longer. Discoloration of the skin led the police to believe the body had been scorched, but the city chemist said a preservative had been applied, probably calcium hypochloride. Two days later the upper section of the torso was found on the beach thirty miles farther east. (A man had found it two weeks earlier, but when he had reported it a deputy sheriff had told him to bury it, explaining later he'd thought it probably was some meat left by a beach party—"There's always something like that laying around.") Coroner A. J. Pearse said the murderer had operated clumsily upon the arms, sawing through the shoulder blade to get the right arm off. But the neck, like the torso, was cut cleanly. The police never found the lower legs, the arms (except for an upper left arm-bone), or the head. Nor was the body ever identified. It was not that of any of the thirty-one women listed that year in the Cleveland Missing Persons files. The coroner marked the file "Unknown causes; probable murder."

The official records of the coroner and the police Homicide Unit agree that this body did not belong to the torso murder cycle, because they found it long before they realized they had a case of mass murder on their hands and because it was not found in or near Kingsbury Run. Cleveland is a big city, but from all its territory the Butcher chose for his favorite graveyard Kingsbury Run and the adjacent Third Precinct, and the clues to his identity led always straight back there. A body as far away as Euclid Beach is an embarrassment. But there it was. How did it get there? All evidence indicates it was cast up onto the beach by the waters of the lake. It is not at all unlikely that it reached the lake via the mouth of the Cuyahoga River and then drifted up the shore (as did portions of another body which the authorities include in the murder cycle, as we shall see). So, since the police designate Andrassy and his companion No. 1 and No. 2 of the torso murders, we shall refer to this female torso as No. 0, and consider it the first of the murder cycle.

Four months after Andrassy and his companion were found, No. 3 turned up in the Roaring Third Precinct that Andrassy had frequented. The police were called at 11:23 A.M. on January 26, 1936, a bitter cold Sunday. A butcher, Charles Paige, said that a Negro woman had told him "some meat was in a basket" in an alley. He had found parts of a white woman's mutilated body—two thighs, a right arm, and the lower half of a torso. They had been wrapped in newspapers, placed in two half-bushel baskets, covered with two burlap bags, and deposited on the cinders against the back wall of a factory. The coroner thought the woman had been dead two to four days. A neighbor, however, said a barking dog had awakened her at 2 A.M. this same Sunday, and one of the newspaper wrappings was dated the day before, the *News* of January 25. The others were several months old. Near by was a suit of man's underwear. Embedded in the torso were pieces of coal (no coal was found near by) and chicken feathers. Chicken feathers also were found inside the burlap bags.

On one of the bags was printed in red "Wills W-W-C-B. J.2" and on the other "A.O.Drawback Reserve A.H.N.Co." To one bag was wired a tag labeled "Danches Co." and dated January 17. A poultry dealer several miles away named William Danches said the tag evidently was affixed to the bag on January 17 by John Willis, a driver for the Cleveland Feather Company, which bought all his chicken feathers. The Cleveland Feather Company was at 1838 Central Avenue, just a few blocks from the spot where the body was found. The Feather Company owner said only Willis collected feathers for him. The detectives searched the Feather Company premises, paying particular attention to the boiler room and ash pit, but found nothing. They picked up Willis, searched his home, questioned him, and released him, satisfied he knew nothing of the murder. That was that—until a year and a half later different detectives, rechecking this same clue, found a man who said that on January 17 he had bought some burlap bags from the Cleveland Feather Company and sold them the next day to a nearby junk shop, Dave Cohn's. This reopened the bag clue, since it meant the bag may have been removed from the Cleveland Feather Company several days before the murder. But careful investigation at Cohn's and the shop of another dealer, Oshi Tally, who had bought some bags from Cohn, failed to produce any useful evidence. This was only one of scores of promising clues that evaporated during the discouraging investigation of the murder cycle.

At the morgue the autopsy surgeon estimated (with laudable accuracy, it turned out, considering how little of the dead woman he had at his disposal) that she had been about forty-two, five feet four, 160 pounds, light complexioned, with dark brown hair. The torso had been severed between the second and third lumbar vertebrae (just as had the lady in the lake, No. 0). The abdominal wall was cut open and the pubic region partly cut. Some detectives thought this indicated that the murderer was a pervert, but probably it simply meant that his knife had slipped. The uterus, Fallopian tubes, and ovaries had been removed long before by legitimate surgery. The legs had been cleanly disarticulated at the hip joints and at the knee joints, an operation requiring considerable skill. All the skin edges were sharply cut. The only instrument employed was a sharp knife. There were no wounds other than those made by dismemberment.

Even though one hand was missing, identification from fingerprints was accomplished. This was the dead woman's police record:

Florence Martin, alias Clara Dunn, age 36 on December 6 1930, height 5 ft-7 with shoes on, 160 lbs, medium stout build, light complexion dark chestnut hair (dyed red) dark chestnut eyes—All the upper and lower teeth are false, claimed to have been born in Ashtabula, O. Irish-American descent. Not married. Florence Martin 1628 East 78 St, waitress by occupation arrested June 14 1931 charge investigation. Suspected of occupying rooms for immoral purposes. . . . Released on June 15 1931. Also as Clara Dunn No 48123 arrested at Washington D.C. May 2 1934 charge Street Soliciting.

Her police picture showed her to have been a big woman, fat, squat, with dark stringy hair, tiny eyes, and almost no neck.

This was the kind of person the police could work on—a woman arrested as a prostitute. They went to the Roaring Third, where dwelt their stool pigeons. Their first reports said: "We also visited a house of ill fame located at . . . operated by. . . . She had white girls working for her until recently, but stated that she had seen all of them since the torso was found," and "Jean. . . . Prostitute. All her girls O.K." But before long the detectives had traced the dead woman to her last address, a rooming house on Carnegie Avenue. In a trunk they found letters useful in backtracking her. Her true name was Florence Polillo.

Her landlady, Mrs. Mary Ford, said Flo Polillo had been living there alone about nine months, was on relief, "never had company," drank heavily, argued when drunk. Nonetheless, the roomers and Mrs. Ford liked her. In her room were a dozen dolls neatly arranged; each had a name. She had played with Mrs. Ford's children and lent them her dolls.

She was married to a respectable man named Andrew Polillo, a post-office worker in Buffalo, New York. Polillo said he had met her about 1921 when she was visiting in Buffalo. She took him home to meet her mother, then went back to Buffalo and got a job as a maid. Polillo wasn't sure whether they were married in 1922 or 1923. She had been married previously, Polillo didn't know to whom. After six years she left Polillo. ". . . she said that she was going to visit her mother for two weeks at Ashtabula, Ohio, as she wanted to get straightened out. As she had been drinking quite hard. . . . While she was gone I lived in the flat. She had been gone for about fifteen days. And I went to one of the fights at Buffalo and coming home I went to get something to eat. At Charles Restaurant as I came out of this place about 11:45 P.M. I met her on the street. She was with a man and she had a hold of him by the arm, I looked at her and she looked at me, and after she passed I turned and looked at her and she turned and looked at me. The next night I was out and while I was out she went to the flat and took all of her clothes and went away." He saw her alive once again, in his lawyer's office. She only wrote to him once. He didn't know where she'd been or what she'd been doing since.

She must have spent most of her time after 1930 in Cleveland, for she was well known among saloon keepers, bootleggers, prostitutes, whorehouse madames, and shady Italians of the Roaring Third Precinct. One police report said: ". . . inteviewed the following named [63] persons and most of them knowed her by seeing her walking around in that vicinity, but were unable to tell us anything of value." About 1934 she had lived for a time at a cheap hotel on Walnut Street with a man she claimed was her husband, "Harry Martin," a truck driver. The hotel manager told Detectives Orley May and Emil Music that Martin often beat her up. They moved away. Six months later

Martin returned alone briefly. He was described as forty, five feet eleven, or six feet, 185 pounds, blond, light complexion, "nice looking," but the police never found him. About six weeks before she was murdered, Flo Polillo had returned to the hotel, this time with "an unknown Italian," described as twenty-seven years old, five eight or nine, 135 pounds, dark complexioned, wearing a dark suit and dark cap, a description that nearly matched the description of Andrassy's friend, "Eddie." Sometimes the case seemed almost to make sense. The manager sent the detectives to a woman who ran a rooming house near the central Police Station. This woman knew the deceased as Flo Davis, but hadn't seen her for a year. She sent them to a restaurant to look for an Italian bartender who "may be able to furnish us with further information." He knew her as Flo Gallagher—two years before she had come into his speakeasy with Martin who, he thought, had come from Washington, and was "an Army man"—"he sold Army buttons on the street." When the bartender had last seen her, about three months before her death, she had been on crutches. The speakeasy where he had worked had been next door to an old taxicab garage. Another informant told the detectives that Florence Polillo had dated a taxi-driver who hung out around that same garage.

A beat patrolman reported learning that only two weeks before her death Flo Polillo had been living with an Italian of this unsavory description: "35–40 years, 5 ft-9-10-150 very dark comp and bushy hair large flat nose, heavy black eye brows, ugly looking. Generally poorly dressed . . . on Relief. . . . Hangs out in a bootleg joint. . . . Also is known in a butcher shop." A woman said she had seen Flo Polillo walking past her house all summer, meeting "a very dirty looking" Italian at East 22nd Street and Scovill Avenue. And there was "an Italian named Al" who "is a Drug addict and also furnished Florence Martin with Drugs."

The police crossed the trails of several other of her paramours, including a number of Negroes, a seaman on the lake boats, a man with two fingers off one hand, a peddler whom she had lived with and who, two weeks before her body was found, reportedly had told a friend that "he was looking for Florence and when he could catch up with her 'he would cut her all up.'" For a time she had worked in a speakeasy; its proprietor was in the Workhouse when she was killed. Her former pimp, a gambler, could not be found. Neither could several prostitutes who were her confidantes. (People who cannot stand police investigation vanish when one impends.) But nothing came of all this.

The last person who admitted seeing her alive was her landlady, Mrs. Mary Ford. Florence Polillo had left the house at eight o'clock Friday evening. She was wearing a black cloth coat with a gray fur collar, brown oxfords, brown stockings, and, probably, a small black hat. (None of these ever was found.) Flo Polillo usually ironed on Saturday, Mrs. Ford recalled; so when she didn't do so, Mrs. Ford told her handyman to notify the police. They told him to call back later if she didn't show up. Next day, Sunday, the parts of her body were found. All this fixes the time of death pretty well, sometime between 8 P.M. Friday and 11:30 A.M. Sunday. Friday night seems most likely, though this would mean she was killed Friday, then wrapped up and dumped the next night. A detective, however, later heard that a Negro called One Armed Willie, who at one time had lived with Flo Polillo, had had a fight with her on Saturday. Willie (or possibly another Negro—the reports are not clear) had worked for an Italian bootlegger, and two days before her death Flo Polillo had tried to sell a revolver to a bootlegger on Scovill Avenue, very likely this same one. But when the police found Willie he convinced them he was innocent. Mrs. Ford recalled that Flo Polillo had told her shortly before she was killed that she had encountered a young Negro woman whom she originally had met in jail and who now was singing on the radio. This encounter had taken place in a tavern or speakeasy near East 19th and Central, not far from where the parts of Flo Polillo's body were found. From jail records detectives identified this woman. They looked for her, hard, for, as Detective Ralph Kennedy wrote, "it may have been from [this tavern] that Florence Polillo went to her death." But they never found her.

On February 7, twelve days after the first portions of Flo Polillo's body were found, all the rest except the head—the upper torso, the two lower legs and feet, and the left arm—was found behind a vacant house several blocks away, scattered carelessly against a back fence as though in haste. Both deposits could have been made the same night. The head had been expertly disarticulated with few hesitation marks between the fourth and fifth cervical vertebrae. Oddly, although the muscles of the neck were retracted, indicating decapitation was accomplished before or immediately after death, the muscles of the shoulder joints were not retracted, indicating that the butcher waited a while before he removed her arms. The head was never found.

The police learned more about Edward Andrassy and Flo Polillo than about any of the other drab unfortunates murdered by the Butcher. For this reason, as we now know, never again did the police have so good a chance of catching the Butcher. But they did not know it then. Who would have believed that one of history's most remarkable mass murderers had begun to perform in Cleveland and that he would kill nine times more? A connection among these early crimes was not even suspected. Not until much later did the police reopen these cases, trying to link them. One detective has said, "At first we thought it was a 'nationality case'—it's not unusual for a Hungarian or Bohemian to cut up people, they learn to butcher in the old country. So we figured what the hell, we'll send a couple detectives up on Jackass Hill that can speak the language, ask a few questions, and that's it." But as the cases piled up the files grew thicker and thicker, until in the end nearly every policeman in Cleveland, as well as scores of amateurs, were hunting the Butcher.

On the morning of June 5, 1936, two boys playing hooky to go fishing were walking down Kingsbury Run when they saw a pair of pants rolled up beneath a willow tree. One of them recalled, "So we take a fishpole and poke the bundle and out pops a head." They ran home and hid all day. The head was that of a handsome young man, twenty to twenty-five years old, with reddish brown hair, brown eyes, a thin face, sharp and fine, even sensitive, features, probably a Pole or Slav. It lay near the Kinsman Road Bridge over Kingsbury Run less than a mile up the railroad yards from Jackass Hill. No body lay near the head. The trousers were brown tweed, fitted with a black and white thirty-two-inch belt and a zipper. Wrapped with the head were a pair of blue-striped shorts laundry-marked "JDX," a brown-striped shirt labeled "Desmond," a green-striped shirt, a dirty white handkerchief, and a white knit polo shirt labeled "Park Royal Broadcloth" torn and blood-stained at the shoulder. About twenty feet from the head was a pair of worn tan shoes, size 7½, tied together, and in them a pair of striped gray and brown socks with orange tops. About fifty feet from the shoes lay a dirty, oily brown cap.

The next day two railroad men found the body that belonged to the head. It was intact. It lay in a thicket between two sets of tracks near the 55th Street Bridge over Kingsbury Run, about halfway between Jackass Hill and the Kinsman Road Bridge, only a couple of hundred feet from the office of the Nickel Plate Railroad Police. The head had been expertly disarticulated by cutting through the soft disc between the first and second cervical vertebrae. The skin edges were sharply cut with a heavy sharp knife; there were few hesitation marks. The autopsy surgeon estimated that the man had been dead two or three days. It would have been easy for the Butcher to drive down a roadway through the yards from Kinsman Road. He probably had deposited the head and body June 4, the night before the head was found—a railroad detective was certain the head had not been there at 3 o'clock that afternoon, and another railroader had seen an old dark Cadillac sedan parked under the Kinsman Road Bridge about 11 o'clock that night.

Although this victim's fingerprints were not on file nor had anyone of his description been reported missing, the chances of identification seemed good. On his body were six tattoos, as follows: left shoulder, a butterfly; calf of left leg, the cartoon figure "Jiggs"; left arm, the initials "W.C.G.," an arrow through a heart, and a standard of flags; right calf, a cupid superimposed upon an anchor; right arm, a dove below "Helen-Paul." Moreover, a lower left molar, an upper right molar, and three lower right molars were missing. Both head and body were in excellent condition. Some two thousand people crowded the morgue the first night. Detectives showed the dead man's photograph to hundreds of informers and tramps, it was widely published and the description broadcast. A plaster death mask of the face was viewed by thousands at the Cleveland Exposition during the summers of 1936 and 1937. Detectives checked the Transient Bureau and police and factory files, looking for W.C.G. or W.G. (from the tattoo) or J.D. (from the laundry mark JDX—X is appended by a laundry that has more than one customer with the same initials). They found several W.G.'s and J.D.'s, all alive. They traced one of the shirt labels to a California manufacturer. But the tattooed young man remains to this day nameless, known only as No. 4.

For the first time, the police began to connect all the crimes. They searched Kingsbury Run, scarcely knowing what they were looking for, afraid if they didn't find the murderer there they'd find another body.

But the next body was found some miles away—on the southwest side of Cleveland, across town from Kingsbury Run and the Roaring Third. It lay along side Big Creek in a desolate area near some railroad tracks. Nearby were the embers of hobos' campfires. The head and body were about fifteen feet apart. The man had been dead two or three months, which meant he had been killed before the Tattooed Man, though discovered six weeks later. Like the other bodies, this one was nude. The clothes were close by—a single-breasted, dark gray suit, a dark brown leather belt with a nickel buckle, black worn-out shoes, size 8, a black gray-striped cap, a light blue polo shirt trademarked "Sport (Loomknit) Wear," light blue cotton socks, white shorts. The sleeves of the coat were turned inside out. On the right sleeve was a cleaner's mark, "217"; on an inside coat pocket was an NRA label, "A A B 5382878." The head had been expertly disarticulated by cutting through the disc between the third and fourth cervical vertebrae. This was the only wound, and apparently the cause of death. The man was about forty years old, five feet five, 145 pounds, and his hair was unusually long. Decomposition prevented fingerprinting, and the body never was identified.

No other body ever was found near the spot where his was. And he alone had been killed where he lay. But why here? Two theories have been advanced: that the Butcher, wandering aimlessly along the railroad tracks, came upon him by chance at the hobo jungle; or that the Butcher once had lived on the southwest side and this one time returned to it, bringing his victim with him.

And very soon the investigation moved back to Kingsbury Run. For there, about six weeks later, the body of No. 6 was found, and in a peculiarly grisly manner. A half mile from Jackass Hill, where 37th Street crosses Kingsbury Run, was a big hobo jungle. Beside it the sewers which flow underground down Kingsbury Run emerged to form a deep, wide, open, stagnant pool, and it was floating on this fetid water that the parts of No. 6 began to turn up. On September 10, a hobo from St. Louis, waiting by a water tower for an eastbound freight, saw them—the two halves of a man's torso. Police with grappling hooks brought up the lower legs and the thighs; but though a diver was sent to the bottom of the murky pool and, finally, the pool was flushed dry, the head and arms were never found. Neither were the genitalia; this body, like the first two (but no others), had been emasculated. All the dismemberment was skillful; the skin was sharply cut and there were few hesitation marks. Since the neck showed no muscle retraction, decapitation had not caused death, as in most of these cases; yet no other cause could be assigned; perhaps the secret was with the missing head. Coroner S. R. Gerber (who by this time had succeeded Pearse in office) thought the man had been dead only a day or two. It seemed likely that the parts had been dropped into sewers farther back in Kingsbury Run and had floated out. On the other hand, a Nickel Plate switchman had seen a green Model T Ford truck parked beside the pool at about 10:15 the night before—though dumping the body thus would have been extremely hazardous—and some clothing was found near by: a bloody blue denim shirt with two knife cuts on the collar, a pair of blood-spotted green shorts laundry-marked "JW," and an old felt hat, size 7¼, with a label on the sweat band, "Loudy's Smart Shop, Bellevue." There was such a shop in Bellevue, Ohio, and a Bellevue housewife, about two weeks before the murder, had given the hat to a tramp who came to her door. His description matched the dead man's—five feet ten, 145, twenty-five to thirty years, medium-brown hair. But if he was the victim, the police never learned where he had come from before he reached her door or where he had spent the two weeks of life remaining to him.

This body, No. 6, prodded public officials. They met on the night of September 14 in the police laboratory at Central Station—Coroner Gerber, Safety Director Eliot Ness, Police Chief George Matowitz, Detective Inspector Joseph Sweeney, Sergeant James Hogan of Homicide, D. L. Cowles of the Bureau of Ballistics, and three outside medical consultants. They agreed on several conclusions about the Butcher (prefacing each with "probably")—that he was a hunter or a butcher with some knowledge of anatomy but without training in surgery, that he used a heavy sharp knife, that he was "large and strong," that he lived in or near Kingsbury Run and performed his butchery in a "workshop" or "laboratory" there, that he associated with his victims for weeks or months before killing them, that he was not recognizably insane, and that he might well lead a normal life when not engaged in murder. The police thought he was a sexual pervert, but a medical consultant disagreed: he could not reconcile the "pattern of perversion" with decapitation and torso sectioning.

The citizens of Cleveland were uneasy. Six of the Butcher's victims had turned up in less than nine months. The police received hundreds of phone calls, worthless tips of spiteful neighbors, alarms of nervous citizens, baseless theories of the unbalanced—a woman who said an elderly West side doctor was "acting queer," some railroaders who saw a man "putting something in a sewer," boys who found a woman's skeleton near the Nickel Plate (it was a family keepsake), a man who found a human skull and intestines on a city dump (medical school specimens). Railroad workers in Kingsbury Run were frightened. Car inspectors of the Erie worked in teams. A railroad detective remembers, "If you'd go up behind one and touch him on the shoulder, he'd jump three feet."

City detectives consulted with Captain Van Buren and other officers of the Nickel Plate police. Van Buren, a big man with a cigar, remembers, "Many a night I would lay out under the willow trees by Jackass Hill while my partner was off a short distance with a gun. One night I thought I had the damn thing. A man started toward me and just then a big rat got up on my belly and I had to lay there and pretend I was asleep. But the man walked right by me." The detectives often took two or three hundred hobos off a big freight train; each was a suspect, each a potential victim. Anthony Kotowski, another Nickel Plate detective, says, "They lay around in the jungles, drink that smoke, then pass out petrified. It'd be easy for anybody to grab one if he wanted one." Like every team of detectives Kotowski and his partner, Paul Troutman, had their favorite angle. "There was one guy we never could get a look at. All the bums used to tell us about him. They were all scared of him. He had a nest under the Lorain-Carnegie Bridge," a block from Central Market and the Third Precinct. Kotowski says, "He used to go for women's shoes. He had four, five hundred pairs of them. And we'd find chicken feathers scattered around the sewer manhole. We used to stay down here and lay for him. I guess he'd watch us from somewheres. We'd see his footprint, maybe a size twelve. Sometimes we'd find a new hump in the ground and if you poked around with a stick you'd see it was soft, like it'd been dug up. He always had a go-cart or a baby buggy. He could've used it for hauling stuff." Built into the abutment of the next bridge, the Eagle Ramp across the street from Central Market, was a little cell-like enclosure with two barred windows and a padlocked steel door; Kotowski and his partner thought it would have made a perfect abattoir (hobos slept beside it unsuspecting), and for months they checked the padlock, but it never was opened. City authorities told them entry might also be gained to it through an underground sewer, but they couldn't neglect their own work for the railroad to pursue the Butcher, and they never told the city detective about it.

The city detectives turned up hundreds of queer characters. One was an Oriental who lived in a ruined building near the pool, carried a long-bladed knife, and was described thus: "Stocky, full round face, black shaggy hair, stooped over, feet turned out, dark coat black shoes greasy cap." Another: ". . . escaped from Athens state hospital . . . violent type . . . hallucinations . . . picked up in 1934 in Akron with bloody razor. Wife said he had idea some one was trying to kill him. Ran around with knife in his hand. Slept in fields near Trumbull St. bridge. . . ." Another: "Saw man in jungles in rear of Calvary Cemetery between Wheeling and Lake Erie and Penn. R. R. tracks vicious man with black shirt black gloves had machete ran away. White 35-40-5-7-170 stocky build, muscular, complexion dark, beard, sandy colored hair, cut short with clippers, round face, thick neck, high wrinkled forehead, sunken eyes, bulgy and glossy looked like he had been drunk for couple of days, black shirt, trousers, slovak or russian accent." Another: ". . . associates with mentally unbalanced. Supposed to have skulls in his cellar. . . . Marijuana smoker." Another: "Had butcher shop. . . . Chased people with large knife. Insane. Lived in cave at 75 and Bessemer . . . heavy drinker, lost his business. Released . . . no connection." Another: "Freak shop. Heads. Pictures of beheadings." Sodomists, a female impersonator, marijuana growers, two aged junk peddlers with bloodstained axes and knives, an unkempt cave dweller —the lockup was full of suspects. All were cleared. The detectives dug up basements, searched ruins, investigated scores of tips about conversations "overheard in a beer parlor" and a half dozen old wives' tales of long-ago murders. But everything came to nothing.

When No. 6 was found in the pool, Detective Peter Merylo was assigned to the case full time. He spent six years on it and thus became the foremost authority on it. Merylo, a barrel-chested, short-necked man with round face and bulbous nose and stubby hands and a trace of Central European accent, a man of stubborn tenacity and plodding diligence, had been a courier for the chief of police and a detective on special assignments in the Detective Bureau. At the outset much of Merylo's time and that of his partner, Martin Zalewski, was spent in checking out worthless tips received at City Hall. Soon, however, they were talking to informers in the Third Precinct or, in Kingsbury Run, offering themselves as bait to the Butcher. Merylo studied medical books, worked many hours overtime, abandoned other interests. He wrote detailed daily reports of three or four hundred words. Whenever another body was discovered the entire Homicide Unit would become furiously active; but soon other duties would claim their time, and Merylo and his partner alone would keep plugging away. The queerest fish dredged up by other police were turned over to them. The railroad detective Kotowski recalls, "Everybody we'd get a little off the track we'd send him downtown tagged 'Hold for Merylo.'"

On his own Merylo picked up anyone who looked odd, like the man he found on a hot day wearing two pairs of pants, three suitcoats, two overcoats, and, on his head, three caps over a wet towel and carrying in his pockets three big pocket-knives, three safety razors, some used razor blades, two dog's teeth, a whistle, two silver spoons, a six-inch homemade stiletto, a blackjack wrapped in a woman's stocking, three nail-files, and clippings from a financial newspaper. Merylo found a fraternity pin under the East 55th Street Bridge over Kingsbury Run and traced it to its owner, who had gone there on an innocent mission. He investigated a faith healer. He looked for a man convicted of first degree murder and released in 1934. ("This man is known to have a desire to drink human blood.") He arrested a voodoo doctor. He heard about another doctor, the inventor of a "death ray," who had in his house a vivisection room, a bed wired electrically and covered with bloody bedding, and a room paneled in copper; but the doctor satisfied Merylo he was only working on "the cause of cancer and its cure." Merylo was convinced that the Butcher was a sexual pervert. In the medical literature of perversion he encountered no stranger characters than some he met face to face in Cleveland.

One afternoon he and his partner hid in the apartment of a masseuse and, as they had anticipated, a caller arrived: "This man," Merylo later reported, "brought with him a horse whip, a dog collar and a leash and instructed Mrs. —— that she should start on him with massaging and if he did not get satisfaction she should put on the dog collar around his neck and whip him with the horsewhip, but before the whipping started we interrupted and placed this man under arrest." Since the man said "that he does not wish to injure any person but instead he wants the injury inflicted on him," they released him.

Merylo arrested one man who, he reported, admitted having had sexual intercourse with chickens. For several weeks his reports contained phrases like these: "the sadist seen around 3d Prect" or "We then went to the vicinity of Jackass Hill on the lookout for the supposed sadist" who frequented the neighborhood of "Thackery, Longfellow & E. 55th Street." The "sadist" also was called "the Chicken Freak" and was "seen going into assignation houses with chickens under each arm." Finally a prostitute told them she had seen him at 11 A.M. and had noted down his license number; they arrested him. He was a truck driver, powerfully built.

We brought him to this Office, where we questioned him in reference to being a sadist and also Torso Murderer, but he denied being either. We then booked him and held him for further investigation. . . . And after questioning [him] . . . further, as to being sadistic, he did admit that [when] he was twenty-five years of age . . . he went to the poultry house to purchase a chicken, and ordered the chicken dressed, and when watching the woman cutting the chicken's head off . . . "he received sexual satisfaction," and that from that time on, approximately once a week or once in two weeks, until about two months ago, he was buying a live chicken and taking them to houses of prostitution, and would pay one of the girls from a Dollar to Two Dollars to cut the chicken's head off, at which time he stated "he received sexual satisfaction."

The prostitute had to be naked, but the man remained fully clothed.

He also stated that on one occasion, when he again visited a house of prostitution, at which time he did not have a chicken with him; he told a prostitute there to rub his throat with a butcher knife, as if she were cutting his head off, only that she used the dull side of the blade; and during the course of which "he would receive sexual satisfaction" . . . After further and exhaustive questioning . . . and after showing him various photos of the various torso victims, and he stated that he could not "look at them as it might cause him to faint," and he further stated that he never could watch or permit "any human being hurt" and from these observations, we are satisfied that this man had nothing to do with any of our

Torso Murders. However, we caused his fingerprints and photo be taken, also had him make a statement in which he admitted these various acts, in this sadistic manner. We later released him. Reported off duty at 5:30 P.M.

At about the time Merylo was getting started, the Cleveland police received word from police at New Castle, Pennsylvania, that some thirteen nude headless bodies had been found near there in the past ten years, one very recently, and so on October 30, 1936, Sergeant Hogan and other officers went to New Castle, a town on the railroad across the state line from Youngstown, Ohio, and about one hundred miles from Cleveland. The township constable said the earlier bodies had been found in a swamp by the railroad yards, perhaps dumped there by gangsters. The most recent one, however, had been lying on the floor of an old boxcar. It was discovered July 1, 1936, just a few days after the Tattoed Man was found in Kingsbury Run in Cleveland. This body, however, was badly decomposed, and it lay on newspapers three years old—a Pittsburgh *Press* of July 28, 1933, and a Cleveland *Plain Dealer* of July 30, 1933. The Cleveland police concluded that there was "nothing definite to show" that the New Castle murders were committed by the same person as the Cleveland murders. But this is not the last we shall hear of the New Castle swamp.

Body No. 7 began to turn up in Cleveland February 23, 1937. The upper half of a woman's torso was found on the beach at 156th Street, at almost precisely the same spot as No. 0, also a woman, had been found in September of 1934. The arms had been disarticulated neatly. The neck had been disarticulated between the seventh cervical vertebra and the first thoracic vertebra—a little lower than usual. The torso had been severed through the first lumbar vertebra and multiple hesitation marks were present, also a slight deviation from the usual. As in the case of body No. 0, a major question arose at once: Had the body been deposited here by the murderer or had it floated here from the mouth of the Cuyahoga River, which drains the sewers of Kingsbury Run?

Detectives Merylo and Zalewski found what appeared to be a trail of blood spots running for several blocks through streets and backyards to the beach, and in a home along this trail they located a woman who had been wakened by her dog's barking at 2 A.M. Monday. They also found a witness who had seen two men in a rowboat approaching the beach late Saturday afternoon. (The woman probably was killed Friday.) The two clues contradicted each other—the murderer might have thrown the body out of a rowboat on Saturday afternoon or he might have carried it dripping through the streets on Monday morning, but he hardly would have done both, especially if he had the rowboat at his disposal first. On the other hand, the body had been dead only two to four days, in the water not more than three—would this have been time enough for it to have floated so far from the River mouth? It is impossible to say: the movement of flotsam in a shallow lake like Erie depends almost entirely upon wind and wave action, which is capricious. Perhaps the strongest reason for believing that No. 7 floated there is this: On May 5, more than two months later, the lower half of the lady's torso was found floating in Lake Erie off East 30th Street, that is, much closer to the mouth of the river. It matched the upper portion perfectly. The legs had been cleanly disarticulated at the hips. Two "clean sweeping" knife strokes, one in front and one in back, had sufficed for the abdominal incision. Dirt and weeds were found in the organs, suggesting that the body had lain for a time on the ground (in Kingsbury Run?). The spleen was missing, perhaps from decomposition. The arms, legs and head never were found. All efforts at identifying the dead woman failed, and only these meager facts are known: She was about twenty-five to thirty-five years old, one hundred to 120 pounds, medium brown hair, light complexion; she had at some time been pregnant or borne a child; and she was a city dweller (smoke particles in her lungs proved it). The cause of death could not be determined (her heart contained bloodclots, suggesting decapitation had not caused death). As for detective work, there was none, except checking at cleaning establishments which, as usual after a victim of the Butcher was found, reported considerable bloodstained clothing, all innocently explained.

At this point, in March of 1937, Coroner Gerber prepared a recapitulation of the known facts about the murder cycle. He excluded No. 0 since he had not examined it. Of the others he wrote: "All 7 are white, apparently healthy, ablebodied people, in the prime of life between the ages of 25 and 45 years. Five are males and two are females." All were killed within eighteen months. Six were found within two to eight days after death. One was not found for two months. Arranging the bodies by dates of death, rather than by dates of discovery, Gerber concluded that the Butcher suspended operations when a victim was found quickly, that he was encouraged to proceed when a victim lay long undiscovered. Although some circumstances in No. 7 raised the possibility that a second murderer had killed her, Gerber thought not.

It is particularly the peculiar dissection of the bodies which groups these seven cases together. All cases show that the heads were severed from the bodies through the intervertebral discs . . . by means of a sharp knife. Cases No. 3, 6, and 7 showed further that the bodies were cleanly dismembered at the shoulder and hip joints apparently by a series of cuts around the flexure of the joints and then by a strong twist wrenching the head out of the joint cavity and cutting the capsule. The torsos were further sectioned through the abdomen, the knife being carried in cases No. 3 and 6 through the intervertebral discs. . . . Case No. 3 [Flo Polillo] was further mutilated by disarticulating the knee joints roughly, fracturing the midportion of the bones of the lower legs and slashing the abdomen down through the pubic bones. . . . All the skin edges, muscles, blood vessels and cartilages were cut squarely and cleanly, apparently by a long sharp knife such as a butcher or heavy bread knife. There was relatively little hacking of the tissues and relatively few hesitation marks. . . . The direction of these marks indicate . . . a right handed individual. . . . [knife marks] indicate they were cut through anteriorly down to the vertebral spines and then the section completed from behind in all cases. The procedure followed in these cases suggests to us that the dissection was done either by a lay person, or persons, highly intelligent in recognizing the anatomical landmarks as they were approached, or else, as is more likely, by a person, or persons, with some knowledge of anatomy, such as a doctor, a medical student, a (male) nurse, orderly, prosector butcher, hunter or veterinary surgeon. (. . . the bodies may have been sectioned as they were, to facilitate transportation and disposition.)

Since he found no blood clots in the hearts or large blood vessels of No.'s 2, 3, 4, and 6, Dr. Gerber thought their heads had been cut off before death or almost instantly after; in No.'s 2 and 4 the decapitation and exsanguination apparently caused death. No. 7 evidently had been dead awhile before being cut up. In No. 1 and No. 5 decomposition made it impossible to determine the cause of death.

Dr. Gerber thought the sex factor "difficult to evaluate . . . by no means clearly defined." The sex organs were mutilated in No.'s 1, 2, 3, and 7. Detective Merylo believed the murderer committed the crimes "solely for the sexual satisfaction" he secured. Dr. Gerber disagreed. He wrote, "Were these deaths due to sexual perversion (sadism) there would have been multiple body laceration and other mutilation as described by Dr. H. S. Martland . . . in considering the Whitechapel murders in London." Detective Merylo appeared to argue against his own conclusion when he pointed out: "We also learn from history of wholesale murders in other countries . . . that, in each case, it was confined to one sex alone, either a number of men were murdered or a number of women, but these Torso Murders is the first on record where both sexes have been the victims."

It had been five bodies now since a body was identified. And those first two, Andrassy and Flo Polillo, had been found too early to do much good. If only the police could identify the next one, now that they knew so much more. Well, they did. Or, rather, some of them think they did. Others are not so sure. Body No. 8 was actually nothing but a skeleton. It was found June 6, 1937, beneath the Lorain-Carnegie Bridge (the bridge near Central Market where dwelt the invisible collector of women's shoes). The skeleton was complete except for one rib and the bones of the arms and legs. Most of the bones lay in the decayed remnants of a burlap bag that also contained a piece of the *Plain Dealer*.

The Coroner fixed the time of death at early June, 1936—that is, several months before No. 7 was killed (though found more than four months later) and probably before No. 6 (the body in the pool). The coroner concluded that the skeleton was that of a Negro woman, the only Negro victim.

The head had been taken off as usual. The victim in life had probably been about five feet tall. The delicate bones, narrow hips, and small size indicated a weight of about one hundred pounds. The teeth offered the best chance of identification—five had been removed before death, two were decayed, and two gold crowns and a bridge had been installed. Nobody listed in Missing Persons had teeth like these, nor could Cleveland dentists do more than say the bridgework was "poor." But on June 22 the authorities received a letter (further details are lacking) saying that a missing woman named Rose Wallace had had this work done by a Cincinnati dentist dead fifteen years. Coroner Gerber rejects this identification and the Homicide Unit is dubious; but Merylo and some other detectives accept it.

Rose Wallace was about forty and had lived at 2027 Scovill Avenue S.E., in the Third Precinct. A woman who ran a speakeasy on East 19th Street told them that Rose "was hustling for her for about a year." She had disappeared August 21 (three months after Coroner Gerber thought the woman was killed). That afternoon a woman went to Rose Wallace's home and told her a man wanted to see her in a beer parlor at Scovill and East 19th. She went, leaving her laundry in the tub. People at the tavern told detectives she had left for a party on the West Side with a dark skinned white man named Bob. A woman saw her a little later riding in a car with three white men. No one admitted seeing her after that. The dress she had been wearing had a collar like one found near the skeleton. One informant said that a Negro called One Armed Willie was "the only man who had ever kept company with her." One Armed Willie had been accused of having fought with Flo Polillo a day before she was killed, only seven months before Rose Wallace disappeared. Furthermore, Flo Polillo and Rose Wallace may have disappeared from the same saloon near East 19th and Scovill. And

Rose Wallace had been going to a party on the West Side, presumably across the River where Edward Andrassy had lived. From Merylo's detailed reports it is clear that he felt the pieces were almost matching up. But they never did. He found several people who had known Rose Wallace—one man he reported on casually was Frank Dolezal, a name to remember—but none who gave him a lead on who had killed her (if indeed she was dead).

On July 6, 1937, precisely a month after the skeleton was found, body No. 9 began to float piece by piece down the crooked, oily Cuyahoga below Kingsbury Run. At 5:30 A.M. the bridge-tender at the Third Street Bridge saw the lower half of a man's torso. Police found the upper half of the torso and both thighs floating near by. During the ensuing eight days other chunks of flesh drifted downstream and were retrieved and deposited in the ice-box in the cellar of the Morgue —the lower left leg and upper left arm on July 6, both forearms the next day, the upper right arm July 10, and the lower right leg on July 14. All but the head—it never was found.

The surgery presented certain interesting deviations. Disarticulation was as usual. Also as usual, decapitation apparently was the cause of death, and the surgery was performed by a right-handed person who worked methodically. Some cuts were as neat as any he ever made. But other cuts were "cruder than those in the previous torso cases"; in cutting off the right arm, he had to do "considerably more hacking" than usual; in sectioning the torso he fractured the back irregularly, perhaps tearing it asunder when it proved stubborn, and he badly lacerated the diaphragm and part of one lung. So here for the first time the medical evidence suggests the possibility that two butchers, perhaps the master Butcher and an apprentice, were at work. If he worked alone and as usual why was his work so sloppy? Maybe his knife got dull—on one shoulder he made several incisions that failed to break clear through the skin. Maybe he was hurried, feared interruption. Maybe he was nervous, excited beyond his wont, and there was reason for thinking so: this body, alone among all, was eviscerated. The murderer had gone further in dissection than ever before. He had split the abdomen and removed all the internal abdominal organs, also cutting out the heart with a single clean incision. These organs never were found.

The man upon whom all this dissection was performed never was identified. The autopsy surgeon was able to estimate his height at 67 or 68 inches (the arm span, usually considered equal to body length, was 67 inches; the torso plus legs measured 60 inches which added to an 8-inch head gave 68 inches); he was able, by weighing the portions found and allowing 25 pounds for the viscera and 15 for the head and neck, to estimate the weight at 152 ½ pounds; he noted that the spinal vertebrae showed slight arthritic change, suggesting the man was about forty, that the fingers tapered sharply and the fingernails appeared "fairly well groomed," that the skin of the arms and legs was hairy, the right thumb scarred, and the left leg marked with a "blue pigmented cross [a tattoo?]." The man had been dead only about two days when the first part of his body showed up. This meant he probably was killed July 4. A night watchman said he had heard groans that night, and detectives found a vacant garage the groans might have come from and in it newspapers and brown wrapping paper apparently left by hobos; but there was no blood, nothing.

One section of the body had been wrapped in a burlap bag. It had a blue checkerboard pattern and on it was printed in large red letters "100 Lbs. net—Purina 32%-Chowder for poultry." Inside it was a woman's taupe silk stocking, size 9 ½, of a brand costing 59 cents a pair, cheap even then. (Remember, the victim was a man.) The stocking had one runner but was otherwise in good condition; this may mean it had not been in the sack fortuitously, as a rag might have been. Inside the stocking were several hairs, all short and blond except one, which was black and white, and long and tapering, probably a dog's. The bag was about four years old and couldn't be traced. "Therefore," reported Detective Merylo, "we are at a loss." And there it ended. Nothing more ever was learned about No. 9

The detectives themselves seemed to be getting more and more mysterious. A detective reported: "Made a quiet investigation of some information we received about a Physician whose name we cannot mention at this time." Everybody was checking on physicians. Merylo found an aging, once-prominent doctor who had succumbed to narcotics, lost his license, turned to perversion, and taken up residence in a Third Precinct flophouse. Merylo wrote to England about another doctor. The operator of a rundown Third Precinct beer parlor told Detective May about a well-dressed, prosperous man with "long slender fingers" who drank in his place daily for more than six months, who said he was a doctor but had lost his license, who bought drinks for the bums and "seemed to be very accommodating and if anyone wanted to go anywhere he would take them in his car," and who had bought drinks for Flo Polillo a day or two before she was found murdered. Some well-known doctors were found in compromising positions—drinking in Third Precinct dives, seducing young men at the Exposition into homosexuality, registered at hotels with women they weren't married to.

Detectives searched the rag shops and empty buildings of the Third Precinct. People there were getting nervous. Detectives canvassing Kingsbury Run found the hobo jungles nearly deserted except for new arrivals. Citizens of all kinds were jittery, and Merylo complained of the time wasted in checking well-meant but useless tips.

Only a little of this police activity during the summer of 1937 got into the newspapers. Nonetheless the Butcher ceased operations for several months. This tends to confirm the theory that he frequented the dives of the Third Precinct, where the police were most active, though of course he may have lain low for other reasons. While he was idle, Detective Merylo began rechecking the earlier victims, particularly those who had been identified. A Negro informant told him that a Negro religious cult was responsible for the murders. Edward Andrassy's mother now recalled that Andrassy had attended a Negro church near East 40 and Scovill. This was only a few blocks from Jackass Hill where his body was found; it was the first intimation he had hung around there. Mrs. Andrassy said her son, while in the Workhouse, had become friendly with a Negro inmate. Checking there Merylo obtained the Negro's name, but he was innocent of murder. Among Andrassy's papers Merylo found several photographic negatives. Four were pictures of Andrassy—a rather slender, long-legged young man in a double-breasted suit posing stiffly in an unknown bedroom. The wallpaper was flowered, photographs of nudes and of landscapes hung very low on the wall, a Japanese lantern swung from the ceiling, in a corner stood a water jug, on the floor was a cocktail table made from a heavy vase. The bed was of blond wood and new. Merylo wondered whether this room was the Butcher's workshop. Neither he nor the other detectives remembered having seen it. Nor had the acquaintances of Andrassy whom they knew. The *Press* published the pictures. A reader identified the room as that of a fifty-six-year-old man who had enticed him into perversion. He said the man formerly had lived on the West Side where Andrassy had lived. Merylo had visited the house previously, but the room had been remodeled. The man had since moved. Merylo traced him, and he admitted he was a homosexual, "but," Merylo reported, "denied of any relationship with Edward Andrassy saying that Andrassy did not appeal to him." In the man's new home Merylo found blood spots (not human, laboratory tests proved) and a photograph of a handsome young sailor who startlingly resembled the Tattooed Man found in Kingsbury Run. The suspect didn't remember the sailor's name, and the police never found him. And, though Merylo obtained enough evidence to charge the man with sodomy in another case, he could not connect him with the torso murder cycle.

Merylo interviewed men who had gone to school with Andrassy. One said Andrassy had dealt in obscene literature. Another said he once had gone with Andrassy to a house near East 19th and Central (a crucial location for Flo Polillo and Rose Wallace) where Andrassy had "sex relations with a colored man." Another said he too had visited the Negro homosexual with Andrassy (as well as a bootleg joint and a Mexican marijuana joint). Merylo found a Negro who formerly had lived there, but he denied knowing Andrassy.

And in the midst of all this, on April 8, 1938, the lower left leg of body No. 10 was found floating down the Cuyahoga River directly behind Public Square, a little downriver around the bend from the West 3rd Street Bridge where No. 9 had been retrieved. Although the piece of flesh was only a shank, the autopsy surgeon was able to deduce that the person to whom it belonged had been dead not more than a week and perhaps only three days, had been between twenty-five and thirty years old, about five feet, three and one half inches tall, and probably had been a woman. All this was confirmed on May 2, nearly a month later, when more of her body came floating down the river—the left foot, both thighs, and the two halves of the torso. They were in two burlap bags. The head and hands, arms, and right leg and foot never were found. Disarticulation had been performed at the usual places. The autopsy surgeon noted that although most of the work was done skillfully, not all was—in removing the left arm the murderer had made hesitation marks "more numerous and irregular" than usual; in removing the right arm he made a skin incision "somewhat cruder" than usual; in removing the head he did not carry his incision through the intervertebral disc "with the same care and finesse"; in dividing the thorax and abdomen he made long sweeping hesitation marks and crudely fractured the ribs with his hands, lacerating the diaphragm. For the first time he made, on both thighs, "sharp knife-like lacerations" not necessary to the surgery. The crude incision of the neck suggested a knife thrust that had caused death. The dead woman had been pregnant twice; once she had delivered normally and once by Caesarean section. She had weighed about 120 pounds and been brown-haired. The two burlap bags originally had each contained one hundred pounds of Maine potatoes, one bagged by "H. Martin" of Bangor and the other, "Wheel Brand," bagged by the "American Fruit Growers Inc." of Presque Isle, Maine. Detectives found the sole Cleveland distributor for Wheel Brand potatoes at the wholesale market at East 40th and Woodland, not far from Kingsbury Run, but he said tracing the bag would be impossible, since he annually received from four to five hundred carloads, each containing about four hundred bags which he sold to wholesalers who sold them to retailers who in turn sold the potatoes a few at a time, then discarded the bags. Similar circumstances surrounded the "H. Martin" bag.

The case was beginning to get on the nerves not only of the public but of the authorities. The assistant safety director asked Coroner Gerber to obtain an independent estimate on the time the last victim died; Gerber refused. Several detectives were quarreling among themselves. Even the newspapers were showing the strain. In the hope that a complete description might help identify the latest victim they abandoned their customary delicacy and printed the fact that her breasts were small.

Only four months later, on August 16, 1938, the bodies of No. 11 and No. 12 were found. They lay on the lakefront of downtown Cleveland at the foot of East 9th Street on a dump where workmen were reclaiming land behind the scenic new Lakeshore Drive. One was a woman, one a man. They had been killed at different times, the woman sometime between mid-February and mid-April of this same year, 1938, the man probably not later than mid-February, 1938, and perhaps as early as mid-December, 1937. Therefore the man surely, and possibly the woman too, was killed before No. 10.

The man's body was nothing but a skeleton. Several vertebrae, both hands, both feet, and two ribs were missing. The body probably had been disarticulated at the shoulder, hip, ankle, and wrist joints. The man had been rather slight—five feet six to eight, 135 to 140 pounds—about thirty to forty years old, with long brown coarse hair. The teeth were intact. The forehead sloped sharply. At some time his nose had been fractured and was bent to the left. (One recalls that Andrassy's chauffeur friend "Eddie" had a broken nose.)

The woman's body was badly decomposed. It was all found. It had been cut into nine pieces—disarticulated at the neck, the left knee joint, and the shoulder, elbow, and hip joints. The Butcher had displayed his old skill at dissection with a single curious exception: he had botched the job of cutting off the left forearm at the elbow and, indeed, had left it dangling from the upper arm, incompletely severed. Since this operation was the simplest one, surgically, that he was called upon to make, and since it must have been relatively lacking in power to shock him, one can only conclude that he either was interrupted at his work or lost interest in it. The dead woman was about thirty to forty, five feet four, 120–125 pounds, with silky light brown hair. The nail of the left big toe was cut irregularly and farther back than is customary. Her fingerprints matched none in the police files. The right and left lower first molars, the right upper second molar, and the left upper first molar all were missing; the upper right pre-molar and first molar were silver-filled; and the right upper middle incisor was false, all the dental work being "poor." But the teeth did not identify her.

Other clues, however, were at hand this time; indeed, it appeared that the bodies on the dump offered the detectives their best chance since Andrassy and Flo Polillo. The woman's head was wrapped in dark brown paper. The torso was wrapped in brown paper, a page from the March 5 issue of *Collier's*, a man's torn, blue-striped coat with two buttons missing, and a tattered patchwork quilt. The thighs were wrapped in brown paper fastened with a rubber band. The arms and legs were packed in a cardboard container made from two cardboard boxes. In addition, the man's skull was found in a tin can. The detectives traced all these bits of trash with exhaustive diligence, for they seemed to be getting heartbreakingly close to a solution of the murder cycle, closer than ever before.

The brown paper, of course, was the kind found in every hobo jungle, and the page from *Collier's* and the coat could not be traced either. But the tin can, the two halves of the cardboard box, and the quilt—these offered hope.

Let us follow, as characteristic, the investigation of just one of these items—the quilt, the tattered patchwork quilt that had been one of the wrappings for the woman's torso. The *Press* ran a picture of it and a barber, Charles Damyn, recognized it. About five weeks before—about July 6—he had sold it to a junkman. Damyn described the junkman as five feet six, 150 pounds, forty-five to fifty-five years old, swarthy, wearing a dark suit-coat, dark pants, and a light cap. Detectives Theodore Carlson and Herbert Wachsman went to the neighborhood and watched a dozen scavengers go by, pushing their carts, before they spotted him. He was Elmer Cummings. Damyn identified him. And Cummings readily agreed. He had sold the quilt to the Scovill Rag & Paper Co. The detectives questioned him and his wife and neighbors, they searched his room and the yard where he stored his junk, and they found nothing.

So they went to the Scovill Rag & Paper Co., at 2276 Scovill Avenue. Near here Flo Polillo and Rose Wallace had disappeared and parts of Flo Polillo's body had been found. The detectives searched the warehouse fruitlessly. The owner, William Blusinsky, said that his company had sold no rags for eight or ten months, preferring to hold them for a rising market. They had moved several bales of rags to another warehouse, but these were undisturbed. There had been no burglaries. If the quilt had reached his warehouse it could have gotten out in only two ways: either an employee took it out or a stranger snatched it off the receiving platform.

Blusinsky vouched for his six employees, five Negro workmen and a white salesman. The detectives questioned them and searched their homes. As they finished with each they noted: "He lives a very quiet life, is honest, sober, and a working man. . . . [No] criminal record." All were cleared and released. Strangest of all, not one remembered ever having seen the quilt. The detectives could only conclude it had been stolen off the receiving platform. But why would anyone steal so worthless an object? That the murderer stole it for the express purpose of wrapping the body in it seems incredible; any old rag would have served, so why take a chance on daylight theft? The course of the quilt after it left the junkman's hands until it turned up wrapped around the torso on the dump is a complete mystery, and a key one. The quilt offered no help and an equally careful tracing of the cardboard box and the tin can came, at last, to dead ends, too. Once more all the clues found with a body had petered out.

*

The finding of bodies No. 11 and 12 had caused a great public outcry. No wonder. A dozen (thirteen, if we count No. 0) persons had been butchered over a period of four years, from September, 1934, to August, 1938. The crowds and alarms were greater than ever before. The *Press* editorialized on page one: "Unusual means must be taken to bring the detection of one of the most horrible killers in criminal history . . . it is uncomfortable . . . this shuddering horror . . . must be caught for the peace of mind of the city and its good name abroad." The *Press* suggested the city offer a reward of $10,000. And it might have helped. But the city law director ruled such a move illegal, and the county said it wouldn't offer a reward unless the city did, since after all the bodies were found inside the city.

The police reacted strongly to the public outcry. Six detectives working secretly, each with a firewarden (who needed no warrant), searched every building in a triangular ten-square-mile area bounded by East 55th Street, Prospect Avenue, and the River—the Roaring Third. They were looking for the bloody workshop of the Butcher or for his cache of heads. But all they found were hapless people crammed into tenements. Next they descended at 1 A.M. upon three shantytowns in the Flats and Kingsbury Run. By the glare of fire-truck floodlights and amid an uproar of barking dogs and cursing drunks, they rounded up fifty-nine tramps, searched and wrecked and burned their huts, and took them to Central Station. Other squads beat their way along the railroad embankments and river bottom through tangles of sumac bushes and into crumbling masonry, while hobos scurried ahead of them. All those caught were fingerprinted and questioned, a sad lot of men in caps and baggy pants. Those who could prove they had money, a job, or relatives were released; the rest were sent to the Workhouse. The police had hoped to find the Butcher or, failing that, to drive his next victim from the shantytowns to safety or, at the very least, to fingerprint all the bums in sight so they could be identified later if they were murdered. The *Press* called the raids "misguided zeal" and editorialized: "To most of us the arrest of the mad butcher would seem more important than the completing of arrangements for the identification of a possible corpse. . . . That such Shantytowns exist is a sorrowful reflection upon the state of society. The throwing into jail of men broken by experience and the burning of their wretched places of habitation will not solve the economic problem. Nor is it likely to lead to the solution of the most macabre mystery in Cleveland's history."

This last was true enough. Nothing solved the murders. But whether or not the furor frightened him off, the Butcher killed no more, at least not in Cleveland.

The police and public didn't know the end had come, of course. Detectives went looking for "a hospital orderly who boasted of his prowess in cutting up animals," for an eccentric who collected discarded fishboxes and wore heavy clothing in summer and light in winter, for a WPA worker who claimed to "know all about" the murders. An anonymous telephone call sent police hurrying to a damp cellar where they found a severed leg, but it was artificial. Somebody mailed a papier-mâché torso to Coroner Gerber (oddly, the potato sacks in which it was wrapped were exactly like those that had contained Torso No. 10).

Meanwhile, a private detective, Pat Lyons, and two deputy sheriffs who were working on the case for Sheriff Martin L. O'Donnell found, they said, a tavern that had been frequented by Flo Polillo, Rose Wallace, and Andrassy. This was the first time anyone had been able to link the three definitely. Another habitué was Frank Dolezal, previously questioned by Merylo. Searching a near-by room Dolezal formerly had occupied, the sheriff's men announced later, they found stains on the bathroom floor and on some knives. A brother of Lyons who was a chemist said the stains were human blood. Dolezal, a solidly built, unkempt Slav immigrant of fifty-two, was arrested July 5, 1939, locked up in the County Jail and questioned unrelentingly. Sheriff O'Donnell announced some of the additional "evidence" against him—a neighbor had seen "a tattooed sailor" and "a man who looked like" Andrassy go to Dolezal's room; Dolezal admitted entertaining Flo Polillo in his room the night before her body was found a block away; he once had borrowed a butcher knife; he once had thrown a knife at a woman; he once had worked three months in a slaughterhouse; he had a note-book containing some twenty-five names, including that of a sailor living in California; gossip said Dolezal entertained homosexuals. Dolezal's arrest was precipitated when Detective Merylo began investigating the sheriff's undercover investigators. The arrest angered Merylo who, it will be recalled, had questioned Dolezal previously. Dolezal "confessed," the sheriff announced, that he had killed Flo Polillo. He said they had quarreled drunkenly over money, she tried to cut him with a butcher knife, he hit her and she fell against the bathtub striking her head, and, believing her dead, he cut up her body and carried it out piece by piece because it was too heavy to carry intact. He said this had happened the night before her body was found. But most of the evidence at the time had shown she had been dead not less than two days. Dolezal changed his story to fit this fact. In his first try at describing how he had disposed of the body, he got some details wrong; he corrected them in a subsequent "confession." After he had been locked up five days he tried to hang himself; the noose broke. He refused to confess the other torso murders. When after six days he hadn't been charged with anything, the American Civil Liberties Union complained. The sheriff charged Dolezal with first-degree murder and arraigned him hastily without counsel in the office of a justice of the peace. A lawyer, Fred P. Soukup, finally was able to visit Dolezal in jail. Dolezal retracted his confession and claimed he had been gagged, blindfolded, kicked and beaten senseless. The Sheriff denied it. A chemist at Western Reserve University announced that the stains in Dolezal's bathroom were not human blood. Lawyers thought that, inasmuch as the strongest evidence against Dolezal indicated he'd killed Mrs. Polillo in self-defense, the first degree murder charge could not be sustained. Finally Dolezal was rearraigned on a charge of manslaughter. He hanged himself in a County Jail cell August 24, using a rope made from rags hidden in his clothes. Though he was five feet, eight inches tall, he hanged himself from a clothes hook only five feet, seven inches off the floor. An autopsy showed that four of his ribs and two connective cartilages had been fractured after he was arrested.

Coroner Gerber said it was "unfortunate" that the deputy who found Dolezal hanging had not cut him down immediately since doing so might have saved his life. The *Press* criticized "the negligence which resulted in the prisoner's suicide," said it doubted whether Dolezal could have been convicted even of manslaughter, complained that the sheriff's men, "eager to scoop the city police, had arrested their man prematurely," and concluded: "It may sometimes appear that holding a man without communication and hammering his ribs is a short cut to the truth, but actually this kind of procedure usually leads not to the truth but to confusion, as in this instance." Today almost no one thinks Dolezal was the Butcher.

On November 13, New Castle, Pennsylvania, authorities notified the Cleveland police that another decapitated body had been found. The body, a man's, partially burned, lay near the railroad tracks on some boxcar wrapping paper. A week later the head was found in a coal hopper. He never was identified. The murderer had used a saw, something the Cleveland Butcher had never done. Nonetheless, Merylo believed the same man killed all. The following spring, on May 3, 1940, three bodies were found at McKees Rocks, just outside Pittsburgh. One lay in each of three obsolete boxcars. One was intact except for the head; the other two had been dissected at the neck, shoulders and hips; none of the heads ever was found. All had been dead three to six months, were about thirty to forty, had been killed where they lay, and were scorched. On a Youngstown *Vindicator* dated December 11, 1939, was a footprint made by a bloody rubber-soled overshoe or boot, size twelve. In a dried puddle of blood beside one body was a mark made either by a peg leg or a woman's high heel, and near it the butt of a cigarette that Detective Merylo said had been rolled with marijuana. Beside one dark-haired victim was a handful of dark hair and a single strand of blond hair. The man who had lost only his head was identified through fingerprints; he was a vagrant young burglar from Chicago. Acquaintances said he had been a homosexual. The word "Nazi" was carved in his flesh vertically from breast to stomach; the letters were crude capitals, the "Z" reversed. The detectives traced the movements of the boxcars and concluded that the murders had been committed between December 11 and December 27, 1939, at Youngstown. The medical evidence in these three cases pointed more strongly to the Cleveland Butcher than had the evidence at New Castle. Merylo and a partner, disguised as hobos, spent three weeks mingling with hobos and riding freights between Youngstown and New Castle but learned nothing new. Subsequently a skeleton was found in the New Castle murder swamp and two bodies at Pittsburgh, the last June 21, 1942, but they were never linked with the Cleveland series. On June 29, 1942, the chopped-up body of a Negro woman was found in Cleveland in Kingsbury Run near Jackass Hill, but her lover, Willie Johnson, had killed her and cut up her body crudely in order to cram it into two suitcases and get it out of his flat. No evidence could be found connecting him with the torso murders. (His crime did, however, demonstrate that a man can cut up a body in a room, then clean the room so thoroughly that the most careful examination will disclose only a single tiny spot or two of blood; the investigators understood how they might have overlooked the Butcher's abattoir in their house-to-house canvass, which they had hoped would lead them to a room knee-deep in blood.)

There matters rest. No more victims of the Butcher ever were found in Cleveland—at least, not up to this writing. Let us see what conclusions the authorities reached after so many years' work.

Coroner Gerber wrote: "This mass-murder mystery parallels any of the famous mass-murder cases known to history in interest, gruesomeness and ingenuity on the part of the murderer." Noting that between September, 1935, and August, 1938, twelve dead people were found, five women and seven men, and that only two were positively identified, Andrassy and Flo Polillo, he went on to say, "These facts lead us to conclude that these victims were all of the lower stratum of life with little or no family ties, possibly vagrants, prostitutes, perverts, and the like, living in or frequenting the vicinity of Kingsbury Run. To associate with such a group, without arousing suspicion, the murderer must be of the same physical make up, that is, a white person (most likely a male), probably a known frequenter of the same regions, well developed and strong enough to do the heavy work involved in his type of murder and disposal of the victims, and about the same age group (30–40 years)."

The murderer, he thought, "had a definite knowledge of anatomy." He probably was right-handed and used a heavy butcher knife. The cause of death could be determined "fairly definitely" in only three cases: hemorrhage after the throat was cut. In the other cases, decomposition or missing parts precluded more than guesswork. Probably the victims died without struggle, either while asleep or drugged. Evidence of narcotics was found in only one body, No. 10 (and, of course, she could have been an addict). So unless the murderer had administered "some hypnotic drug, which we have as yet been unable to discover," the victims probably died asleep, with one notable exception: Andrassy's rope burned wrists indicated "he was held prisoner for awhile."

"All these facts," the coroner wrote, "lead us to conclude that the murderer was a person of more than the average intelligence. He probably originated from a higher stratum of society . . . and . . . sank to the stratum from which his victims emanated. He may have been a doctor, a medical student, at some time in the past; a prosector butcher, osteopath, chiropractor, orderly, nurse, or hunter. . . . It appears that he gains the confidence and probably the friendship of his victims before killing them. . . . The murderer was probably motivated by either a true insanity of the schizophrenic type or else a border-line insanity, a constitutional psychopathic state, accompanied by aberrant sexual drives."

When Detective Merylo was taken off the case October 1, 1942, he and his partners had made 350 felony arrests (with 333 convictions) and 665 misdemeanor arrests (with 656 convictions). The charges included abortion, auto stealing, bastardy, blackmail, burglary and larceny, embezzlement, felonious assault (34 arrests), illegal entry into the U.S., incest, murder (1), narcotics, neglecting pregnant woman, pandering, possession of obscene literature (48), sodomy (77, the largest number), violating Selective Service Act, white slavery. Merylo had checked out satisfactorily all suspects except two former mental patients, a peg-legged hobo, and the author of an anonymous letter. He wrote: "I am of the opinion that the murderer is a sex degenerate, suffering from NECROPHILIA,* APHRODISIA† or EROTOMANIA‡ and who may have worked in the pathology department of some hospital, morgue or some college where he had an opportunity to handle a great number of bodies, or may have been employed in some undertaking establishment, and that he had a mania for headless nude bodies. . . . I also believe that the Murderer is working alone, and that he may only [have] finished grammar school. He reads newspapers and detective story magazines, especially murder mysteries. He spends all of his time among transients and hobo camps, also he rides the freight trains between this city and Pittsburgh, Pa., and nearby state possibly Virginia." He concluded: "I believe that this man would not stop the killing as long as he is at large, and alive. . . . I will never give up my work on these Torso Murders." He has worked on them since leaving the force. He considers that the Butcher has made off with thirty-three or thirty-four victims and thinks it possible he perpetrated the "Black Dahlia murders" in California. He believes the murderer was a railroad laborer, a psychopath, a marijuana smoker, and probably blond.

In speculating about this case, one cannot say "no" to any idea, however preposterous. The Butcher is preposterous. His butchery is beyond belief. It has been said that a mass murderer is simply a killer who gets away with it longer than most. And this is true of many—of H. H. Holmes, for example, and of Landru; of all those who have

---

Seldom do detectives footnote reports but Merylo or another detective footnoted this:

*"Sexual attraction to the Dead."

†"Exciting sexual impulses. Drug that arouses sexual instinct."

‡"Morbid exaggeration of sexual behavior or reaction."

preyed upon the lonely-hearts or have poisoned for profit. There is also a second type of mass murderer, the madman, frequently a pervert. But perhaps there is a category of mass murderers who are neither greedy men nor mad ones, but simply men with a rationale of murder for it own sake. Perhaps the Cleveland Butcher occupies this lofty eminence alone. We can be sure he did not kill for profit. And it does not appear either that he was completely mad or a pervert. In the first place, if he had been, the police would have had him. But if he had been almost anything else, they would have missed him (and did), for they were looking for little else. (Of course it is possible they had him and didn't know it and let him go.) In the second place, he had to be fairy sane to succeed as he did. Few men ever have been hunted unsuccessfully as hard as he, and for so long. Was he merely dancing between the raindrops? It is doubtful; his luck would have run out sometime. This suggests great craft, a strict discipline, method, and not lunacy. His accomplishment is all the greater if one realizes fully the character of the region where he dwelt and worked, the Third Precinct and Kingsbury Run. It is territory far more dangerous to a murderer than a respectable residential neighborhood, where people go to bed at normal hours. Here people prowl all night. Yet not one eyewitness to the Butcher's movements ever was found. This is nothing less than astounding. In the third place, whereas your madman kills in a frenzy and leaves his victims where they fall, as Jack the Ripper did, the Butcher brazenly went to some trouble to transfer his bodies from a safe and secret place to a public one. In the fourth place, the Butcher operated upon his cadavers as a surgeon would. Madmen do not; they hack and chop and rip. No, it is almost impossible to believe that the Butcher killed for any other reason than a determination to commit murder for its own sake. Let us say it: he was that almost unknown creature, a master criminal. And he succeeded not in the 1880's but in the second quarter of the twentieth century, despite all the apparatus of scientific crime investigation. It can be argued powerfully that he was the greatest murderer of all time.

Did the Butcher also commit the crimes in Youngstown, New Castle, and elsewhere? Merylo says yes, most others either say no or doubt it. It seems extremely unlikely—it would mean the Butcher began operating in 1922 and kept going till 1942 or later. And the weight of other evidence is against it.

Was Dolezal the Butcher? It is true that there was no more butchery in Cleveland after Dolezal died. But, as Coroner Gerber points out, at the time Dolezal was arrested the Butcher had killed no one for nearly a year and a half. "He'd already quit," says Gerber. "The arrest of Dolezal didn't stop the murders; they had already stopped."

Why did he quit? Those who believe he was insane think he may have regained his sanity and is among us today, a useful, harmless citizen. Some thought this of Jack the Ripper. Of him it also was theorized (weakly) that his last murder, the bloodiest, shocked him back to sanity. But this theory will not fit the Butcher, for it was not his last victim whom he carved the most. Perhaps he quit because he was imprisoned for another crime, or was locked up in an asylum. Or perhaps he is dead. He could have died of natural causes or of an accident, unmourned and unidentified as were his victims. For that matter, he could have been murdered. Maybe news of his crimes inspired a second butcher, who chanced to hit upon the Butcher as his only victim. Is this preposterous? No more so than many of the known facts. But the last victim was a woman. Well, maybe the Butcher was a woman. Merylo thought so once. Again, the weight of evidence is against it. And yet—who better than a woman, and especially a prostitute, would have a whack at the throat of sleepers in a secluded chamber? One can speculate endlessly. If he killed because of a determination to commit murders for their own sake, he might be expected to quit when he had satisfied himself he could do so.

That he killed indoors seems certain. The task of dissecting a body so thoroughly takes at least an hour, much longer if the operator works carefully. He could not have risked discovery for so long in the open. But where indoors? If he had a car—as evidence indicates he had—his laboratory could have been in an outlying district, perhaps the far West Side near Big Creek where No. 5 was found or the near West Side where Andrassy lived and where Rose Wallace was headed when she disappeared. (But since No. 5 lay, uniquely, where he died, the Butcher probably killed him, and him alone, far from his laboratory.) At the time it seemed most likely that his abattoir was in the Third Precinct and it still seems so. Detectives making a blind canvass could easily have missed it. Andrassy, Flo Polillo and Rose Wallace frequented the Third Precinct; so, probably, did other victims. Moreover, the Butcher certainly spent some time there, because it was around the market-places and junkyards there that he found the quilt, the cardboard box, and probably the old newspapers and burlap bags. (Was he a junkman himself?)

How did he kill them? Probably by befriending them, then slashing their throats, letting them bleed to death, and then decapitating and dismembering them (though the first blow evidently decapitated some). This also argues for an indoor rendezvous. We can be pretty sure he did not lure them there with promises of liquor, since little was found in their bodies; that he lured them there to practice perversion is mere speculation. In all probability he lured them there with promises of food and lodging, powerful bait for the homeless; food was in the stomachs of several, all must have died asleep. But asleep in what?

In a bed, if he had promised them one. He must have changed the bedding after each victim, else surely one would have taken alarm. But what did he do with the bloody bedding? (He was too smart to wrap the bodies in it.) It never was found. Did he burn it? Possibly. But this is not easy. One wonders if his workshop is not still intact, crammed with bedding, heads, limbs, and other leftovers. (It must have been fairly elaborate; he pickled several bodies and kept some awhile before dumping them.) Or did he burn the place down when he had done it? There is no record that the detectives ever checked unexplained Third Precinct fires after the murders ceased.

That his victims were outcasts of society does not necessarily mean they were hobos. In fact, at least seven certainly were not—Andrassy, Rose Wallace, Flo Polillo, and the four other women (counting No. 0). Were the six unidentified men hobos? We do not know. There is some reason for believing they were not. Fingerprints of two were obtained, but they were not on file, and hobos' fingerprints usually get into police files by the time they attain the age of these victims (only two of the unidentified men were under thirty). For the same reason, we can argue that these two, at least, and the one unidentified woman whose prints were obtained were not professional criminals. Who, then, were these people? (Captain Van Buren suggests all were migratory workers.) Certainly they were not steadily employed, for no employer missed them. Perhaps they were simply "the unemployed," of whom there were many then. It seems probable these people belonged to what some criminologists call the "victim type," those who, like "accident prone" people, are especially vulnerable. Violent death is immanent in this milieu.

Most people seldom realize how much protection we derive from society simply because it is organized. If we disappear we are missed by relatives, friends, employers, many others. Furthermore, if a series of peculiar events occurs down the street, we will notify the police, perhaps saving our own lives. But hobos and migratory workers who meet in one city, then part to meet in some other, halfway across the continent, can scarcely be aware that one by one people around them are disappearing; and prostitutes take into their chambers strangers, some drunk, some perverted, some demented, and they walk by night. All these people live dangerously. So we can understand how the Butcher was able to trap thirteen strangers. Nonetheless, selecting so many unidentifiable persons seems a considerable feat. He made only three mistakes (two, if we reject Rose Wallace's identification). Perhaps he didn't care, chose at random. (Consider the risky choice of the well-labeled Tattooed Man.) Yet if he did choose at random his luck would have had to be unbelievably good.

Why did he cut them up? Murderers usually dismember their victims for one of four reasons—to foil identification, to facilitate disposal of the body, out of lunacy, out of hatred. We cannot believe the Butcher did so to foil identification, for he was not consistent in destroying the heads and hands and, further, sometimes he severed the heads but left them with the bodies. It is doubtful if he did it to facilitate disposal for a man who could not get a corpse out of his apartment and through the streets whole could not do so by taking off only the head. Had he violently hated all these assorted people, he would have been the link among them and thus would have been discovered. And, as we have shown, he did not dissect his victims in an insane rage. So he must have had another reason, perhaps unknown heretofore in criminal history. And unimaginable—unless we accept the theory that his rationale encompassed nothing more than murder for murder's sake. For if this is so, then dismemberment might well be the next logical step, to shock society, to complete the job. Why did he retain, or destroy, the heads of five? We simply do not know, unless he did it as a trophy collector, which many police believe.

"Every once in a while," says Lieutenant David Kerr, head of Homicide, "we still get a tip on the damn thing. Couple of weeks ago someone called up." The police still talk about the Butcher. Dr. Gerber says mildly, eyeing the deepfreeze in the cool cellar of the Morgue, "You know, all these years, I think we still have some parts of those bodies around. They get tucked away." He has one foot left over but he's pretty sure which body it belongs to. The recapitulated police reports run to more than 3,500 pages. "And there they are," says a Homicide detective, kicking at a filing case, "all that work and there they are, gathering dust." The investigators, using ordinary methods, failed utterly. But it is hard to imagine a method that would have succeeded.

Most police have given up any real hope of finding the Butcher. They have not, however, ceased looking. On a drizzly Sunday night Captain Van Buren and Detective Kotowski are questioning three bedraggled hobos in the Nickel Plate office, and from the pockets of one Kotowski takes great sheafs of closely written manuscript. "What's this?" The hobo says resentfully, "It's mine. I write." Kotowski reads it, demented verbiage that rambles through the vocabularies of astronomy and philosophy, nuclear physics and surgery. Surgery—Kotowski looks at the hobo speculatively. Too young: the Butcher must be at least forty now, probably older. The detectives warn the men never again to set foot on railroad property. Watching them scurry up the wet iron steps to the 55th Street Bridge above, Captain Van Buren muses, "You know, I still keep hoping I'll meet that man some day, the torso murderer." Outside a red fuse flickers fitfully by the rails where an engine is switching, and in the distance the sky glows dully with the lights around Public Square. A Rapid Transit train rattles and rolls, leaning on the curve, its windows a streak against the black cliffs; and for an instant its headlight sweeps the foot of Jackass Hill. But only for an instant: the blackness closes in, the night on Jackass Hill is impenetrable as ever.

Butcher's Dozen & Other Murders, 1950

A. J. LIEBLING

After a brief period as an undergraduate at Dartmouth—from which he was expelled for consistently skipping chapel—and two unenthusiastic years in Columbia University's journalism program (which, he later averred, had "all the intellectual status of a training school for future employees of the A.&P."), Manhattan-born Abbott Joseph Liebling (1904–1963) took a beginner's job in the sports department of *The New York Times*. There his primary task was to compile basketball box scores, complete with the referee's name, a detail he was so indifferent to that he began to give it routinely as Ignoto (Italian for "unknown"). He was summarily fired when his editor discovered the ruse. In 1926, he moved on to the Providence (R.I.) *Journal* and *Evening Bulletin*, where—apart from a hedonistic year in Paris at his father's expense—he spent the next four and a half years, "ooz[ing] prose over every aspect of Rhode Island life" (as he put it). Upon his return to New York, he worked as a newspaper columnist before joining the staff of *The New Yorker*, his home for the next 28 years, where he gained prominence as a war correspondent, critic of the daily press, celebrant of the "sweet science" of boxing, Francophilic food writer, and portraitist of Manhattan street life. Liebling's enduring passion for his native city is palpable in this *New Yorker* piece from 1955, a vivid evocation not only of a lurid (if long forgotten) murder mystery but of the heyday of the yellow press, when, in their pursuit of sensational scoops, rival reporters conducted their own investigations and sometimes proved better detectives than the police.

The Case of the Scattered Dutchman

The afternoon of Saturday, June 26, 1897, was warm and moist in New York City, and it is probable that boys were swimming off every idle dock in the North and East Rivers. James McKenna, thirteen years old, of 219 Avenue C, and John McGuire, fourteen years old, of 722 East Twelfth Street—both addresses within a few steps of the East River—were among those who at three o'clock were swimming in the slip on the south side of what was then a disused dock at the foot of East Eleventh Street.

I will lift the next five paragraphs bodily from a story at the top of the first page of the Sporting Edition of the *Evening Telegram* of that date, because I cannot think of any sound way to amend them:

> They saw an object slip into the line of vision past the edge of the dock, and the cross current gave it the appearance of trying to enter the slip. It looked much like a package of merchandise, but the article in which it was wrapped looked like a bright piece of bunting or a flag, with the sun striking it.
>
> The two boys swam eagerly toward what they thought would prove a prize. The bright covering they found to be oilcloth, and the package was carefully tied up with good strong string.
>
> McKenna got on one side and McGuire on the other and between them the package was brought inside the slip and one of the boys pulled one end of the string from around the oilcloth and dropped it over the edge of the string-piece.
>
> There was a general rush on the part of the dock hangers-on to furnish a knife, and McGuire slipped back over the edge of the dock and dug the knife in the oilcloth covering.
>
> The knife stuck and refused to come out, and the boy gave it a wrench. Then he tried again, and succeeded in working a small hole in the cloth. He saw something white, and the sticky feeling of the knife blade sickened him.

The *Telegram*, which specialized in sporting news, had a later final edition than the city's other afternoon papers, since its readers counted on it to report the winner of the last race at Sheepshead Bay. (The race that day was a steeplechase, won by Mars Chan, at 2–1.) On Saturdays, the *Telegram*'s Sporting Edition was even later than on other days, because there were seven races instead of six. The story of the discovery in the East River was the only important nonsporting item on the first page, and over it were these headlines:

MAN'S TRUNK
FLOATS IN RIVER

HEADLESS AND LEGLESS BODY WRAPPED
IN OILCLOTH GETS INTO EAST
ELEVENTH STREET SLIP

FOUND BY SWIMMING BOYS

THEY THINK THEY HAVE A FIND, BUT
MAKE A GHASTLY DISCOVERY

IS THE WORK OF AN EXPERT

CUTS LOOK LIKE THOSE OF DISSECTING
TABLE—MAN WAS IN PRIME

The other top headlines on the page dealt with a bicycle race at Manhattan Beach, the victory of the New York Giants over the Washington Senators (both in the National League then), and the triumph of a two-year-old named Blueaway in the Zephyr Stakes, twenty-five hundred dollars added. (A well-played second choice, he also paid 2–1.)

After telling of the sickened boy, the unknown *Telegram* writer continued:

It was not until a half hour later that someone reported the matter to the Union Market police station [this was on First Avenue, near Tenth Street], saying merely that something securely wrapped in cloth was knocking against the end of the dock.

Policeman Winter was detailed to take care of the matter. With the assistance of some laborers, he got the package upon the boards.

The policeman cut the cords and rolled back the oilcloth, disclosing to view the trunk of a man, in an almost perfect state of preservation.

The neck had been severed cleanly from the body, almost on a line with the shoulders, and the work was done in such a manner as to lead to the conclusion that it was that of someone accustomed to handling amputating instruments.

The work of amputating the legs had not been done so cleanly. They had been severed from the trunk just below the abdomen, in a rather slovenly fashion, not at all like the work of a dissecting table.

The chest had been marked and scarred in a peculiar manner. The flesh had been lifted from the bones just below the left breast and cut off cleanly all the way across the chest to a point almost on a line with the shoulder. The cut was even and laid open to view several of the ribs.

This, in connection with the clean amputation at the neck, inclines the police to the theory that the trunk was fresh from the dissecting table when found.

The only drawback to this is the unprofessional work on the lower half of the trunk.

The possibility that the dissection had been performed by two persons working in great haste—the more professional member of the team on the neck, the other on the torso—had not occurred to the *Telegram* man.

A district reporter for the *Telegram* may have been in the police station when the tip came in, and accompanied Policeman Winter to the dock, or he may have learned of the find from the station blotter and hurried to the dock while the parcel was being dragged from the water. In either event, he—or a police surgeon he may have talked to—was clearly an excellent observer, and the further development of the case was to confirm not only the details he phoned in to the rewrite man but many of the rewrite man's immediate deductions from them. It may be, of course, that my own deductions about how the *Telegram* story was put together are in error, and that the city editor, apprised by telephone of the interesting nature of the find (he could hardly have been informed of it before four o'clock), dispatched a star reporter straight to the scene in a hack. Even with the prevailing speed limit of twelve miles an hour, the reporter could have got from the *Telegram* office, in Herald Square, to the foot of East Eleventh Street in twenty minutes, made his notes from his own observation, and returned to his desk by five, after which he could have written his story between the fifth and seventh races. This would have been drawing it fine, however, even for the newspaper titans of 1897, when, according to an old journalistic friend of mine named Ned Brown, "what they call a porterhouse now wouldn't have counted as a chuck steak."

The rewrite job, as I therefore judge it to be, continues:

The trunk is that of a man who was evidently in the prime of life. He must have weighed fully 180 pounds, and the arms are big and powerful. The chest is that of a man accustomed to unusual exertion and regular calls for increased lung power.

The flesh is clear and white, and indicates that the man was in perfect health, and the muscles of the body show plainly that their possessor was a giant in strength.

The hands are small when figured in proportion to the evident weight and height of the man. The fingers are small and well shaped and do not resemble in any way the fingers of a man accustomed to manual labor.

On the inside of the left palm is a small blue mark, evidently extending deep into the cuticle. It looks as though it might have been burned in with powder. There are no needle pricks to indicate it is a tattoo mark, nor is there any regular formation to it.

The oilcloth in which the body was enclosed was brand new. It had never been placed on a floor as a covering, the underside bearing no mark. It was of good quality. The pattern was red squares with small gilt stars.

The string was white, very heavy, and after the knots were tied had been cut cleanly with a sharp instrument. Scissors or a small pocket knife would not have been able to cut it so cleanly.

A curious crowd surrounded the object as it lay on the Eleventh Street dock. A messenger was sent to the Coroner's office.

The police are taking an extraordinary amount of interest in the case, owing to a great extent to the signs of refinement and the fact that the body had been but such a short time in the water.

Between the oilcloth and the spine of the trunk was found a sheet of new cheesecloth, a little heavier than the ordinary kind, more like that used in hospitals, but in no way resembling absorbent cloth.

This discovery has served to strengthen the theory of the police that the work is that of a band of medical students from the dissecting table of a hospital.

In substantiation of the rumor of foul play, its adherents point to the peculiar wound on the breast, claiming that the strip of flesh may have been taken off to destroy tattoo marks or other marks that would help toward an identification.

They also claim that the legs may have been marked in some way, and they too were taken off and disposed of in some way.

None of the other afternoon papers—the *Evening World*, the *Evening Journal*, and the *Evening Sun*—had so complete and incisive a story.

Their city desks had been put off by the first reports from the police of the precinct, who, the *Evening World*'s brief story said, "incline to the belief that the body may be that of a medical subject." The police claimed later that they had taken this position in an effort to keep the newspaper sleuths our of their way while they got started on the serious business of investigation, but the *Journal*, having been caught flatfooted, continued for weeks to charge that the police had tried to squelch the story just to save themselves trouble. The *Journal*'s implication was that Lord knew how many other crimes had been shrugged off in this fashion; only the enterprise of newspaper reporters—the *Journal*'s of course—had forced the police to revise their attitude in the torso case.

The next morning's *Sun*, on behalf of its teammate, the *Evening Sun*, attributed the medical-subject theory to pure stupidity on the part of the police, and the *World* of that Sunday morning took the same position. The paper was on to the possibilities of the story and gave it two columns on the first page, under the headline "BOY'S GHASTLY FIND." In the course of its account, the *World* observed, "It does not appear that the police made any attempt at investigation, but jumped at and accepted the theory that the portion of the human being had been cast into the river by the students of some medical college who had been studying anatomy." According to the *World*, the discovery that it was probably a case of murder had been made by doctors at the morgue, after the torso was removed there.

None of the Sunday papers had anything substantial to add to the *Telegram* account, although they padded it out with direct quotations from the coroner, a Dr. Tuthill; the medical examiner, a Dr. Dow; and the Superintendent of Bellevue, a Mr. Murphy. (First names of such well-known civic characters were evidently considered superfluous in news stories of that golden age.) Both the *World* and the *Herald* were skeptical about the likelihood of a solution. "The finding of the upper portion of the headless trunk of a man in the East River yesterday furnishes a mystery that will not easily be solved," the *World* reported, and went on, "All indications point to an atrocious murder. There is, however, no apparent clue by which the identity of the victim may be discovered, or his slayer brought to justice." The *Herald* stated, "There is nothing to tell when or where the crime was committed, whether on land or on sea, and there is not one chance in a million that the identity of the victim will be discovered." The suggestion that the man had been murdered and dismembered aboard a ship evoked the romantic possibility that he had been a Spaniard spying on Cuban gunrunners. The police said he could not have been a sailor, because there were no calluses on his hands.

The morning *World* and the *Evening World* had different staffs but shared the eleventh floor of the proud new Pulitzer Building, on Park Row, and dovetailed their coverage of running stories. The Pulitzer Building, with its sixteen floors, was the tallest building in New York, and from their city rooms the men of both *Worlds* could look over to and beyond the North River or out to sea, as well as at Brooklyn, across the only bridge there was over the East River at that time. All Manhattan lay visibly at their feet, and it accentuated their cockiness. The *World* had a circulation of 370,000, which was almost as much as the four other morning papers had among them. These were the *Herald* and the *Sun*, *ex aequo* with 12,0000; the *Times*, with 75,000; and the *Tribune*, with 76,000. The *World's* predominance had been achieved within a few years after Joseph Pulitzer came to New York from St. Louis and bought the paper from Jay Gould, in 1883. The *Evening World*, founded by Pulitzer four years later, had overshadowed its afternoon contemporaries just as decisively until it was challenged by a newer newcomer—young William Randolph Hearst's *Journal*, which made its appearance in 1895. Hearst was trying to take over Pulitzer's afternoon field by imitating all Pulitzer's circus tricks and then adding an extra elephant for the clowns to jump over. By 1897, despite brilliant retaliatory strokes on the part of Pulitzer, Hearst was beginning to show results. The *Evening World* still led the afternoons, with a circulation of 360,000, but the *Journal* claimed 309,000, and was gaining. The *Evening Sun* and the *Evening Telegram*, with 100,000 each, were out of the hunt; Edwin Godkin's *Evening Post*, with 25,000, had become a symbol of the unpopularity of virtue.

The Hearst-Pulitzer feud made for virulent competition, and in its course reporters became direct rivals of the police. A *World* or a *Journal* man finding a useful clue at the scene of a crime would bring it back to his newspaper, in which it would appear as a chalk-plate illustration over the vainglorious line "Made from a photograph taken in the *World* [or *Journal*] office." Had reporters reached the East Eleventh Street dock before the police on the day the torso was found, the officers would have attached no significance to the chunk missing from the victim's brisket. They would have been sure that a *World* or a *Journal* man had carried it away.

Reporters developed their own leads in solving crimes, outbidding the police for stool pigeons and at times outbidding the detective branch for details observed by uniformed men. Then they would follow through in person, "arresting" suspects, if the latter didn't appear dangerous, and extorting confessions from them. These they would publish as scoops. The practice sometimes proved momentarily awkward when it developed that a reporter had abducted an innocent party, but there were few such mistakes a ten-dollar bill couldn't square. Neither the *World* nor the *Journal* begrudged outlays occasioned by excessive zeal. In making "arrests," the reporters, who had shiny badges and pistol permits, usually represented themselves as detectives, but when printing the story their papers invariably said they had "made the arrest as citizens." Some of the reporters, as one might expect, became better detectives than most city detectives, and when a big case broke, the Police Department would put tails on the leading newspapermen, while the newspapers would put tails on the more resourceful detectives. This was a form of recognition the latter enjoyed to the point of sticking to familiar disguises in order not to throw the journalists off their track. Naturally, there were exchanges of information between friends in the two professions, by which cops helped reporters to discredit rival reporters and reporters helped cops to discredit rival cops.

The *World* and the *Journal* assumed airs of independent sovereignty. In headlines as well as editorials, the rival sheets gave themselves credit for defeating candidates they had opposed, rectifying conditions they had deplored, stopping outbreaks of leprosy they said they had detected, setting fashions, making slang, and, above all, solving crimes. Even the sportswriters conveyed the impression that they were not merely reporting games but coaching both teams and refereeing. "Being a newspaperman gave you stature then," says Ned Brown. "Everywhere except in society. It didn't cut any ice there. But elsewhere a first-string reporter on any recognized paper—especially one of the *Worlds*—had a lot of prestige. *Civis Romanus erat*. He was a citizen of no mean state."

Today, Ned Brown, a small man, is as spare and brisk as a whippet, with a sharp, inquisitive profile and lively blue eyes. He prides himself on his penetrating *coup d'œil*, which makes him a master at rapid chess and crossword puzzles, and at sizing up situations. Mr. Brown has worked for only one newspaper in his life—the *World*. The job lasted thirty-four years, until the paper ceased publication in 1931. During most of his service with the *World*, he was a boxing writer, but he didn't begin as one. When the mysterious torso was fished from the river, Ned was a very junior member of the *World* staff; he was working there during the summer vacation following his first year at Bellevue Hospital Medical School, which was then situated at Twenty-sixth Street and First Avenue, across the street from the hospital, with its wards and morgue. He did small assignments, mostly legwork, at space rates— five dollars a column if he telephoned the stuff to a rewrite man and seven dollars and a half if he wrote it himself. The bits he wrote personally were for the most part humorous items he picked up at night in the Tenderloin—the bright-light district that, by his definition, ran from Thirtieth Street to Forty-second, between Sixth and Eighth Avenues. He liked the Tenderloin beat because it permitted him to spend his nights in saloons—looking at people, listening, and fancying himself a young man about town—without having to disguise the fact from his father, who was Frederick Sherwood Brown, the telegraph editor of the *World*. The elder Brown had established his family in Flatbush, a remote *faubourg* of the independent City of Brooklyn.

Ned found Flatbush slow. His official hours were from two in the afternoon until midnight, but often when he was covering the Tenderloin he worked an extra hour or two, business merging with pleasure. On such occasions, the long journey home to Flatbush—by steam elevated train to Brooklyn Bridge and then by trolley car into the dark interior of Long Island—frequently seemed too dismal to endure, and then he would spend the rest of the night in the Murray Hill Baths, on Forty-second Street. The Murray Hill Baths were not on Murray Hill but between Broadway and Sixth Avenue, and, like all the other Turkish-bath establishments of the region, they stayed open all night. Turkish baths were infinitely more popular and numerous then than they are now; men on the town for the evening regularly wound up in one or another of them. An individual cubicle cost a dollar, a bed in the dormitory fifty cents; the ticket for either one included a scrubbing and use of the steam room and the plunge, universally esteemed specifics for overindulgence; an alcohol rub cost an extra two bits. There was always a tip for the rubber, who would not scorn a dime. The baths all favored a fanciful Oriental décor, like the tiled interior of a mosque. The Murray Hill was one of the largest and most ornate.

In those days, Mr. Brown says, few medical students went to a liberal-arts college; he himself entered medical college straight from Erasmus Hall High School, in Brooklyn, and in 1897 he was still in his teens. He was a hard-liquor drinker, but not when he was working; on those nights, he would buy a beer or two in each establishment he visited, "just to hold the franchise." When he retired to the baths, therefore, his mind would still be clear and his curiosity active; he would engage the rubbers in conversation and sometimes land a boulevardesque anecdote worth a dollar and a half at space rates, or a bit of information that might come in handy someday as background. He was keenly interested in anatomy, which was then, as it is now, the principal subject of the medical first year. At the baths, he had before

his eyes a living exhibit of anatomical and dermatological peculiarities, and he was accustomed to discuss these with the rubbers; at heart
every masseur is a doctor *manqué*.

Ned doesn't recall being in the *World* city room when the torso was
first reported, and he is sure he wasn't sent uptown to the dock. But
when he read the Sunday papers the next morning he was fascinated—
both as a medical student and as a newspaperman. Coroner Tuthill, he
noted, had told reporters at the morgue that the disaggregated man
could not have been dead more than twenty-four hours when his chest
was taken out of the river; Dr. Dow had said "ten hours at the most."
Even if one accepted the longer estimate, and added a few hours for
possible error, the man could not have been killed earlier than Friday.
The conclusions different doctors reached as to his height and heft
varied a bit—one doctor explained that his estimate of five feet ten
inches depended on the premise that a man's height is equal to the
reach of his outstretched arms—but all agreed that he had been taller
than average. Every newspaper account mentioned the solid but un-
workmanlike hands. He had been a man who kept himself in good
physical trim, but not by hard labor. A wealthy sportsman? A college
athlete? An Army officer? Any one of them would make a corking good
victim from a newspaper point of view. Ned had a special family interest in this kind of murder, because his father, while a reporter on the
Cincinnati *Enquirer*, had cleared up the murder of a girl named Pearl
Bryan, whose severed head had been thrown from the suspension
bridge over the Ohio River between Cincinnati and Covington, Kentucky. The guilty wretch may have hoped thus to create a conflict of
jurisdiction; the elder Brown, however, proved that the actual crime
had been committed on the Ohio side of the river. It is a spiritless son
who would not like to outdo his father, but Ned, as he rode the trolley
over the bridge to work that Sunday afternoon (like all young and
single men on seven-day newspapers at that time, he worked Sundays
and had a weekday off), had small hope that he would be assigned to
the Ghastly Find story. The Ghastly Find would be in the competent
hands of Gus Roeder, the *World*'s homicide specialist, and of Bill

Reitmeier, who covered Police Headquarters, on Mulberry Street. They would need no help in keeping the story fresh for a day or two, after which, if it was as hopeless as the morning-paper stories indicated, it would lapse and be forgotten.

When Ned stepped off the elevator on the eleventh floor of the Pulitzer Building, he had no need of his peculiar gift to recognize that something extraordinary had happened. The day staff on Sunday was always light, but on that particular afternoon the city room was perfectly empty except for one early copyreader and the man on the desk —a Sunday substitute for Edward J. Casey, the *World*'s assistant city editor. The man on the desk was telephoning, and as he saw Ned come in he put his hand over the mouthpiece and beckoned him with a sweep of his arm. When other reserves are exhausted, even the summer soldier is welcome. The man on the desk took less than a minute to tell Ned that a second parcel wrapped in oilcloth with a pattern of red squares and small gilt stars had been found, this one on the Bronx side of the Harlem River, at about the latitude of 176th Street, or ten miles from where the torso had turned up. Two boys out berrying with their father had come upon it in a sylvan setting, into which it had apparently been tossed from Undercliff Avenue, a winding carriage drive on the side of a hill. When the parcel was opened at the High Bridge police station, in the Bronx, it had yielded another section of the cadaver. The captain there had dispatched it to the morgue to be matched up with the East River bit. "If the pieces fit, it's the same stiff," the man on the desk said. "If it's part of a different stiff, then the guy with the red oilcloth has murdered them both." He spoke, Ned remembers, with the pleasure of a man who cannot lose. From the moment the first tip about the second bundle came in from Reitmeier, the Sunday city editor had been calling every member of the staff he could reach by telephone—directing those who lived uptown to the region of the find and ordering the downtown fellows to converge on the morgue or Police Headquarters. He had also been sending out the regular Sunday men as they reported for duty. He told Ned to hustle up to the morgue and report to Gus Roeder, who was running the Pulitzer operation there. "Do whatever Gus tells you," he said, unnecessarily. "The *Journal's* probably got forty guys there already." Mr. Brown recalls his emotion on being assigned to his first big story, even though he anticipated only a legman's role (for which he was well fitted, being a tireless runner and weighing precisely a hundred and nineteen pounds). The field of his début could not have been better chosen, for, owing to his year at medical school, he was familiar with the morgue, and if there was one subject on which he would back his own opinion, it was a cadaver. The steam elevated bore him to the vicinity of the morgue in quick time, and he ran the rest of the way at a quarter-miler's pace.

Gus Roeder, the homicide man, was a red-faced German-American, already in his forties and therefore, to Ned, a hoary veteran. He could express himself well in English but spoke the language with a perceptible accent. (He worked from pencilled notes, which he surrounded with rhetoric as he dictated his stories to an office boy who, unlike him, knew how to run a typewriter.) He wore conservative dark clothes and a hard hat, and was not enough of a bohemian to be popular with his fellow-reporters. He was on good terms with a powerful faction of the detective force, however, and exchanged information with his police friends, to their advantage and his. He was also a friend of Frederick Sherwood Brown's, and knew that Ned was a medical student. The Bronx portion of torso had by this time been brought downtown, and the two fragments, put together, matched as neatly as pieces of a jigsaw puzzle; so did the cut edges of the two sheets of oilcloth. The second piece of victim included everything from the abdomen to a point above the knees, where the saw or knife had been employed again to detach the legs. These hadn't turned up yet. Ned found the juxtaposed segments of great interest. "The gaping ends of the blood vessels at the neck, where the head had been severed, and the thighs, where the legs had been cut off, indicated that the man had lost a considerable amount of blood before expiring," he says now, relapsing into his freshman patter. "In other words, the guy had been alive while they were cutting him up. That knocked out the medical-school idea." Ned also had a long look at the highly publicized hands. When he finished, he told Roeder what he suspected, and Roeder instructed him to follow his hunch. Roeder already had a score of men out working on even longer shots.

Some indication of the number of paths Roeder's men explored was to be found in the *World* of Monday, June 28th. A five-column top head on the first page thundered:

THE FRAGMENTS OF A
BODY MAKE A MYSTERY

Under it, in lines three columns wide, was:

A PIECE OF A MANGLED TRUNK FOUND
YESTERDAY IN HARLEM FITS
ANOTHER PIECE FOUND SATURDAY
IN THE EAST RIVER

BOTH WRAPPED IN RED
AND GOLD OILCLOTH

Then, in single column:

A MAN OF THE MIDDLE OR BETTER
CLASS HAS EVIDENTLY BEEN
BRUTALLY KILLED

MANY STABS WOUNDS AND BRUISES

PORTIONS OF THE BODY, WHICH MAY
HAVE CONTAINED MARKS OF IDEN-
TIFICATION, CUT AWAY

THE POLICE ARE AS
YET ENTIRELY AT SEA

CARL WEINECKE, WHO DISAPPEARED
MAY 17, HAD MARKS WHICH
WOULD FIT PLACES CUT
AWAY ON THE DEAD
TRUNK

CORONER TUTHILL HAS
A THEORY OF HIS OWN
Thinks the Victim Was Attacked
and Killed in a Fight After a
Hard Struggle

The text of the lead, set in bold type, was exclamatory and consecrated to the obvious. "Somewhere in Greater New York or near it since late Friday afternoon an awful crime has been committed" is a fair sample.

The layout of pictures on the front page illustrated the peculiar attraction of the great Pulitzer's journalism. Nestling under three columns of the top headline was a chalk-plate reproduction of the "Hand of the Headless Murdered Man—Exact Size (from a flashlight photograph made in the morgue last night by a *World* photographer)." The hands of the victim had been described in various accounts as large, small, and medium-sized. When I first saw the "exact-size" illustration in a bound volume of *World*s, I could not resist an impulse to put my hand over it and compare the two, and I suspect that three of every four readers of the paper in 1897 did the same thing. (From my comparison, I judge that the victim, like me, wore a size-8 ½ glove with a wide palm and short fingers.) The stubby thumb in the *World*'s photograph was superimposed on a map showing "Route headless shoulders would take in floating from spot where other part of body was found." This had been drawn in accordance with a theory, enunciated in an interview granted by a former Chief of the United States Secret Service named Andrew L. Drummond, that the murder had been committed in the Bronx and part of the body thrown from High Bridge into the Harlem, which leads into the East River. "It would be foolish for a man to carry the body from the Battery, say, to High Bridge in order to throw it into the water," Mr. Drummond had told a *World* reporter. Next to the upper, or Bronx, end of the map was a sketch of "where the trunk of the body was found," and, next to the Eleventh Street end, a sketch of "where boys found the headless shoulders." The layout was completed by illustrations of the oilcloth ("reproduced from sample brought to the *World* office") and of the "clumsy knot with which each bundle was tied" (also "photographed in the *World* office").

Inside the paper were a dozen stories on assorted angles of the case. The wife of a Dane named Weinecke—an unemployed lumber inspector, of 82 East 115th Street, who had disappeared on May 17th—thought the installments might be of him. The *World* had to take some account of her views, although it did so with patent unenthusiasm; he would have made an anticlimactic victim, despite a halfhearted effort on the part of the editors to supply him with a mysterious past before his arrival in this country. There was a long story on efforts that were being made to trace the red-and-gold oilcloth pattern through jobbers to retailers, in order to question everyone who might remember selling any recently. Police authorities had wisely refused to theorize about the murder, and in revenge the *World* and the other morning papers said they were incompetent and "all at sea." The medical men had allowed themselves to be drawn more easily, and the reporters had induced Dr. Philip F. O'Hanlon, the coroner's physician who performed the autopsy, to venture a surmise as to how the man had been killed. "From what I can learn from the condition of the body, I should say that this is what occurred," the *World* quoted Dr. O'Hanlon as extrapolating. (It was the decade of Sherlock Holmes, and every physician felt that Dr. Watson had been unfairly dealt with.) "The man, who was a big, powerful fellow, was attacked. He made a strong resistance, but I should say he was overpowered by numbers. That he was knocked down I think is proved by the imprints of the toe and boot-heel on his arm. Some of the other bruises on his body may have come from kicks. I should say that he struggled to his feet and was standing erect when someone, who must have been very muscular, stabbed him in the collarbone with a big knife. This was followed immediately afterward by another wound—that which cut the heart. That caused death immediately. The blood under the thumbnail shows that he struggled hard or else that he clasped his hand to his bosom after he had been stabbed."

A *World* story on the autopsy itself reported:

A close inspection was made of the hands with a view to determining the man's position in life. They were long and broad, the fingers were well formed, and while the palms were not callous, yet they indicated that the man had done some work, not recently, perhaps. The nails were cut down almost to the quick, evenly rounded, as though their owner had taken some care of them.

The fingertips of the left hand were smooth and even; on the forefinger was a scar extending from the nail back to the second joint. It was an old one, and in the opinion of the examining physician, might have been caused by an operation. . . . There was little hair on the body, the arms, or the hands, and the latter showed little of the effect of the sun.

Not a man who could live without work, was the judgment of those who examined the trunk, nor yet a man whose livelihood was earned by hard manual labor; he might have been a policeman, a carpenter, a bartender.

The most romantic reconstruction of the crime was furnished by Drummond:

Andrew L. Drummond, for twenty-two years Chief of the Secret Service of the United States Government, and now head of a great detective agency in this city, with offices at No. 1 Park Row, is greatly interested in the developments in the murder case [the *World* reported].

"I read the account in Sunday's *World*," said Mr. Drummond last night, "and from what you tell me now of the finding of another part of the body near High Bridge and of the result of the autopsy, I believe that this most atrocious murder was committed by a foreigner.

"In the whole history of crime in this country murders which were done with like ferocity as this have always been committed by foreigners, usually those of a warmer climate than ours.

"I should judge, from what I have heard of this case, that the murderer is a Sicilian, or possibly a Spaniard or Cuban. Maybe a Spanish spy has been put out of the way by Cubans.

"But the theory of the murder which strikes me as the most likely one is that it is the result of a family feud among Sicilians. I know the ways of the Mafia so well that this strikes me as the most plausible theory. The red oilcloth points to Sicilians, who love bright colors. . . .

"Probably the murdered man was invited to a friendly game of cards at the home of the murderer, who had sworn a vendetta against him for some wrong to his wife or sweetheart. Then, in an unguarded moment, the man was killed and his body cut up for disposal by one or several men."

The Drummond story was the last on the murder in the *World* (it brought the total space the paper devoted to the case to eight and a quarter columns, not counting pictures), and was followed by this plug, in boldface type: "Further developments in New York's great murder mystery will appear in the editions of the *Evening World*."

Ned Brown, reading the story about the hands in the Monday-morning *World*, may have feared that a couple of the details would set somebody else to thinking along the line he was already following. But if so, there was nothing he could do about it, and he had a full program for the day. Ned was searching for a kind of soap called Cotaspam, or Kotaspam—he is no longer sure of the exact spelling. Not that he looked as though he needed soap; that morning Ned was probably the cleanest man in Greater New York. His naturally pink skin was now positively translucent. He had in a pocket ten dollars that he had drawn from the *World* treasurer, on the authorization of Gus Roeder, to use as expenses. Cotaspam was expensive soap—twenty-five cents a cake. Ned had to walk over to Broadway to find a druggist who stocked it, and when he did, he bought two boxes containing a dozen bars each, for a total of six dollars.

The reason Ned wanted Cotaspam specifically, he says, was that once, before having dinner at the home of a wealthy boy he was tutoring in Brooklyn, he had washed his hands in the bathroom there and had been so impressed with the fragrance of the soap that he asked the name of the brand. "It smelled Elysian to me," Mr. Brown says now. "Sandalwood, verbena, geranium, Sen-Sen, and Ed Pinaud's Eau de Quinine all in one." With the two boxes under his arm, Ned took a Broadway car as far as Herald Square, where he transferred to a westbound Thirty-fourth Street crosstown and rode to Ninth Avenue. Then he walked half a block north and entered a tenement at 441 Ninth Avenue. It was a family neighborhood of working people, mostly respectable and chiefly German or Irish. During the years after the end of the Civil War, brick tenements had replaced frame houses as the city marched north. They were mostly small buildings, three or four stories high, with two families on a floor, and sometimes a store on the street level. A parking lot occupies the west, or odd-numbered, side of the block now, but some even-numbered houses still standing on the east side of the avenue in the next block north give at least an idea of what the neighborhood must have looked like. Ned climbed the stairs to the top floor of No. 441 and worked his way down, knocking at each door in turn. There was a woman in practically every flat, and to each Ned presented a cake of soap and delivered a little spiel. The company he represented was trying to find a larger market for its soap, he said, and so was making a special introductory offer. Each recipient was to use the soap for a day, just to experience how good it was. If she liked it, she could give him a nickel for it when he returned in the evening; if not, she was privileged to return the soap without any obligation. "One smell and they fell for it," Mr. Brown says. "They could tell it was expensive soap. Some of them wanted to give me a nickel right then, but I said no dice. 'The company wants to get your opinion of its product after you have used it,' I would say. 'I will be back at six o'clock.'" Such door-to-door canvassing was more common then than it is now; Ned had heard the routine scores of times in his own home. His appearance was plausible; he was young and thin, and wore a cap and a shiny second-best suit. He got rid of half a box of soap in No. 441 and then went through the same performance in Nos. 439 and 437, omitting only one apartment. This was on the second floor, above a drugstore, in No. 439, and a nameplate on its door bore the legend "Mrs. Augusta Nack, Licensed Midwife." When Ned had finished with No. 437, he had only a couple of cakes left, and he stuck them in his pockets. It was nearly noon, and he walked out of the neighborhood to a café near Herald Square to eat lunch and look over the afternoon papers as they came out. Talk about the elegant soap would spread through the three tenements, he knew; the women visited across the halls or from their fire escapes in warm weather, and in the afternoon there would be knots of them on the sidewalk getting a breath of cool air.

"There is nothing like a sweet smell to catch a woman," Mr. Brown says. "I know it from experience now, but at the time I had to figure it out for myself. I was what you might call precocious." Ned read the afternoon papers with apprehension, which turned to smugness as he found more and more signs that they were off what he felt was the right track. Monday morning's papers had had a big new development to report—the discovery of the second segment. All the afternoons could do was ramify speculation.

RIVER'S MURDER MYSTERY
GROWS STRANGER AND DEEPER

the three-o-clock edition of the *Evening World* proclaimed, listing Clues (no new ones) and Theories (same) in its lead. It had on its front page a portrait of the missing Weinecke (which it spelled Weincke), three columns wide, with question marks at either side of his head, but he bore an unexciting resemblance to a testimonial writer in a patent-medicine ad. "Is he the murdered man?" the caption writer asked, and most readers' reaction to Mr. Weinecke's photograph must have been "Who cares?" The *Evening World* had balanced its front page with an equal display of a story headed "JOHN L. SPARS WITH WORLD MAN," written and illustrated by the *World* man, W. O. Inglis; his account of this terrifying experience took the form of a letter addressed to Bob Fitzsimmons, the heavyweight champion, to fight whom the thirty-eight-year-old John L. Sullivan had announced his emergence from retirement. (Sullivan's advertised comeback had a patriotic motive. On losing his championship to James J. Corbett, in 1892, he had said, "I am glad I was beaten by an American." On March 17, 1897, Corbett had lost the title to Fitzsimmons, a New Zealander born in Cornwall.) "Friends tied on our four-ounce gloves," Inglis wrote. "I could not have tied a knot in a two-inch hawser, much less in the laces of a boxing glove. You will feel that way, Mr. Fitzsimmons, when you are getting ready to go into the ring with Sullivan." It was the true *World* tone, and it amused Ned, who correctly suspected that the comeback would go no further than the first time Sullivan raised a thirst.

In the *Evening World*, the exact-size picture of the victim's hand had been moved back to page 2 and reinforced with a diagram of the body, in which the recovered portions were printed in black and missing areas in gray. "The inhuman, fiendish manner in which the butcher cut up the remains of his victim seems to suggest that it was the work of a maniac," a hard-pressed rewrite man had ventured, and there were a couple of sidelight stories on the Jack-the-Ripper murders in London and other unsolved mysteries. "The superb handling of this interesting case in the *World* this morning, both as regards writing and illustration, made all other morning papers look like second-rate provincial sheets," a house plug at the bottom of the page announced. "If there is anything left to tell about the mystery when today's *Evening World* is done with it, the *World* tomorrow morning will again show the little imitation morning papers how to handle a big local story. From the *Evening World*'s last night extra the thread of the strange crime will be taken up and carried on by the morning edition. The *World* is a continuous performance of newsgiving—morning, noon, and night. It never stops. It has no rival. Remember that." Despite this advertised unity, there was hot rivalry between the staffs of the *World* and the *Evening World*.

The *Evening Sun*, which had lost the dash of its Dana days, took a thoroughly dim view of the case and assailed the police. "Indications in Mulberry Street this morning pointed to the conclusion that the police had not yet waked up to the serious import of the case," it grumbled. "Chief Conlin wasn't there. . . . Chief Conlin is a man who has no taste for murder mysteries. . . . Capt. O'Brien [the chief of detectives] has even less than Conlin. Like every other policeman not possessed of distinct detective genius, his one wish is to get rid of a case of that kind, and, consciously or unconsciously, the wish will take the form of pooh-poohing it at first and letting it slip out of sight and out of mind as soon as the excitement about it dies out."

The *Telegram*, its field forces outnumbered by the hordes of *World* and *Journal* reporters, tried to sell papers with the headline:

DR WESTON
SAYS BODY
WAS BOILED

"Coroner's Physician Weston has advanced a most important theory in regard to the great murder mystery," a *Telegram* reporter had written. "He was at the morgue this afternoon on another case, and while he was there he examined the mutilated, headless, and legless trunk. He said to me afterward: 'It appears to me that an attempt has been made to dispose of this body by boiling it. The flesh of the stump of the legs appears to have been dipped in boiling water. It is probable that the murderers thrust the legs into a kettle, hoping to boil the flesh off, but found they could not do it quickly or easily enough, and that they then cut up the remains.'" The doctors made decidedly better copy than the detectives.

Ned moved along to other bars as the afternoon wore on, avoiding those most frequented by newspapermen. Had he been one of the *World*'s stars, he would have had to take precautions against being trailed, but he knew he was too inconspicuous for that. All he had to avoid was a chance encounter. The dark interiors, cooled by electric fans, offered escape from the afternoon sun, and each time he changed saloons he bought a later batch of papers to read over his next nickel beer. The Late Edition of the *Evening World*, which went to press at four o'clock in the afternoon, headlined a typical Pulitzer stroke—a five-hundred-dollar reward. "The *World* will pay $500 in gold for the correct solution of the mystery concerning the fragments of a man's body discovered Saturday and Sunday in the East River and in Harlem," an announcement read. "All theories and suggestions must be sent to the City Editor of the *World*, in envelopes marked 'Murder Mystery,' and must be exclusively for the *World*. Appearance of the solution in any other paper will cancel this offer of reward." There followed a "suggestion" of what the solution should include: motive, identity of the criminal or criminals, time, place, and method of the crime, actions of the criminal or criminals after commission of the crime, and, last but not least, identification of the murdered man.

This was the final regular edition of the *Evening World*, and it ordinarily coincided with the *Journal*'s final, but within minutes of its appearance the latter paper hit the street with an extra run of its Night Edition, in which a three-column head on the right-hand side of the first page read:

$1,000 REWARD

THE NEW YORK JOURNAL WILL PAY
$1,000 FOR INFORMATION OR
CLEWS, THEORIES OR SUG-
GESTIONS WHICH WILL
SOLVE THE UNIQUE
MURDER MYSTERY
OF THE EAST
RIVER

IF NONE OF THE THEORIES OR
SUGGESTIONS IS PERFECTLY EX-
ACT THE $1,000 WILL BE DIVIDED
AMONG THE TEN THAT COME
NEAREST TO SOLVING
THE MYSTERY

It was the familiar Hearst technique, infuriating to *World* men, of waiting for Pulitzer to think of something and then raising his bid.

The *Journal*, Ned noted with distaste, had followed the *World*'s example in its play of the striking hand picture. The first page of the *Journal* bore detailed illustrations of the unknown's right hand, his left hand, his injured finger, and his broken fingernail. "The *Evening Journal* has the Most News, Latest News, Best News," the left ear of the paper's masthead boasted, and the right ear stated, "The *Evening Journal* Prints the Best Local, Telegraph, Cable News." It was enough to raise the hair of Ned's blond, James J. Corbett pompadour haircut.

The *Journal* was also playing up its own favorite candidate of the moment for corpus delicti, with a slashing first-page head:

LOUIS A. LUTZ THE VICTIM?

NEPHEW ALMOST SURE HE RECOGNIZES
THE REMAINS AT THE MORGUE

The missing Mr. Lutz, a carpenter in a piano factory, had not been home for five days, the *Journal* said, and while he had no known enemies, and no money on his person when he left his house, his nephew was sure he had been killed, because he didn't think he would have committed suicide. (No other possible explanations of his absence were considered.) The *Journal* presented a boxed, signed, and undoubtedly paid-for statement by the nephew, who was named Louis E. Lutz, in which, as a clincher, he remembered that his uncle had once hit himself on the left hand with a hammer, injuring a finger. Stephen O'Brien, the Chief of Detectives, had furnished a signed statement to the editor of the *Journal* to the effect that until they found the missing sections of the body, his detectives had little to work on. "LITTLE TO WORK ON" was the headline. Dr. Nelson A. Conroy, of Bellevue, still another medico out to vindicate Dr. Watson, had given the *Journal* a personal statement, in which he declared irrefutably: "It is hard to say just what the man's face looked like." Apparently something of a palmist, Dr. Conroy added, "The conical hand of the man indicates a practical temperament. This man must have been engaged in some useful art—an artist of some sort—for it is evident he had not done any hard work for some time." All references to the dead man's hands had a special interest for Ned, and he was relieved to see that Dr. Conroy was as far off the track as the rest.

If the *Journal* ventured gingerly into palmistry via Dr. Conroy, the *Evening World*, in a Night Extra that shortly followed the *Journal*'s, went all the way.

$500 REWARD TO ANYBODY WHO
UNRAVELS THE MURDER MYSTERY

a headline across the first six columns bellowed, and then:

THEORY OF WOMAN
AND A PALMIST

A four-column cut under the reward line showed the "Hands of the

Murdered Man," and under this was a two-column cut of "The Broken Nail."

"An analysis of the hand of the dead man of the river mystery was made this morning for the *Evening World* by Queen Stella Gonzales," the first-page story began. (The paper's editors brushed off the *Journal*'s Mr. Lutz with a one-paragraph sneer under the lower-case line "Alleged Identification." "The morgue people take no stock in the identification," the item ended.) "Queen Stella and Cheiro are the two most famous palmists of America, Queen Stella's drawing-room reputation excelling that of Cheiro." Queen Stella, the story went on, admitted that she was handicapped by having only a photograph of the back of the hand to work from. "She said it impressed her at once as a tragic hand," the *Evening World* reported. "'. . . Having square nails, that denotes ruling power. His little finger, pointed and reaching above the third phalange, denotes business capacity in a higher degree. . . . Through his domineering disposition and rashness in speech he must have made one or more deadly enemies.'"

Queen Stella's analysis was the beginning of a complete coverage by the *World* of the occult aspects of the case, which included appeals to another palmist (a man, who was smuggled into the morgue), a phrenologist (slightly handicapped by the absence of the head), a clairvoyant, a physiognomist (working from a photograph of the supposed victim after his identity became fairly certain), a handwriting expert, and, finally, a spirit medium.

The woman's-angle theory mentioned in the *Evening World*'s head got equal play with Stella's. It was written by a Mrs. McGuirk, not otherwise identified and possibly invented. It wasn't a woman's work, Mrs. McGuirk ruled, and continued, "There is just one thing in the whole business that might suggest a woman's hand. The knots with which the parcels were fastened are the clumsy, uneven ones which women are prone to make." Mrs. McGuirk thought the victim might have been a peddler and the oilcloth part of his stock in trade. "Women poison," she concluded. "It is easier. They seldom use knives, unless very hot blood runs in their veins." The *Evening World*'s Night Extra had a total of thirteen masterly columns on the case, which make good reading even after fifty-eight years. They included a remarkable collection of mystery-solution letters, which the editors claimed had been written by readers and delivered by hand between four o'clock, when its reward offer appeared, and about five, when the Night Extra went to press. A biting bit next to the reiterated reward offer contrasted honest and dishonest journalism and accused the *Journal* of snitching the letter-contest idea.

By the time Ned had finished with the evening papers, it was nearly six o'clock, and he accordingly made his way back to the west side of Ninth Avenue between Thirty-fourth and Thirty-fifth Streets. One reason Ned chose the time he did to return was that in such a neighborhood it was an hour when the man of the house was almost sure to be at home, except on Saturday night or unless something had happened to him. The women with whom Ned had left soap that morning and who had their nickels ready to clinch their bargain must have been doubly delighted, because he never came back to collect. Instead, he went directly to No. 439, climbed to the floor above the drugstore, and rang the bell at the door—slightly more pretentious than the others—of Mrs. Augusta Nack, Licensed Midwife, which he had skipped a few hours earlier. He waited in hot-and-cold anxiety. It was possible, of course, that Mrs. Nack wasn't at home, or that if she was, she wouldn't come to the door. These were the longest days of the year; it was full daylight, and he hadn't been able to tell by a lighted or unlighted window whether anyone was in. The greatest blow to his hopes would have been the heavy tread of a man coming to answer the doorbell, but, instead, he heard the slupping sound of the advance of a woman in house slippers. Then the door was ajar and Mrs. Nack stood in the aperture. She was just about Ned's height—five feet six—but she must have weighed at least two hundred pounds. Her face was wide and flat and lardy white, with small eyes, not much of a nose, and what Mr. Brown still remembers as an extremely sullen mouth. She was wearing an apron over her house dress, and there was a smell of cooking sauerkraut that has left Mr. Brown with a permanent distaste for the stuff. Ned would have given anything to see into the room behind her, but she was a hard woman to see around.

Before Mrs. Nack could ask what he wanted, Ned began, "Good evening, Madam. Have you enjoyed your trial bar of Cotaspam soap? Hasn't its fragrant lather left your hands feeling as if freshly kissed?"

"You didn't giff me any!" Mrs. Nack replied angrily, and Ned understood immediately why she had looked sore from the moment she laid eyes on him. The other women had decribed him while telling her about the wonderful soap, and Mrs. Nack felt she had been slighted, as usual. (Feeling slighted is a characteristic of especially high incidence among Germans and unattractive women, and Mrs. Nack was both.)

"I would have sworn I'd been to every flat in the house," Ned said. "But I guess I wasn't, or I would have remembered you sure."

It was coquetry lost on Mrs. Nack, who said merely, "Giff me the soap now."

"I'm sorry, Madam, but I'm afraid I can't," Ned said. "You see, I have to get a report for my company on what each lady thought of the soap. That was the purpose of our special offer."

"Leaf it and come back tomorrow," Mrs. Nack commanded.

"I'm sorry, Ma'am, but I can't do that, either," Ned said. "Tomorrow I'll be working up in Yonkers." Then he tried to look as if he had just had a bright thought, and went on, "But I happen to have a couple of bars left over. If you could give the soap a trial now, while I wait, I'd be glad to let you have one."

After thinking this over for a minute, Mrs. Nack said, "All right. Giff me the soap." Ned moved toward her, fumbling in a pocket and being careful not to give her the soap until he was inside the apartment. He knew she wouldn't shut the door in his face before he came through with the special introductory sample. As she pulled back from the door, he went through it as if in the suction set up by her big body.

"Here it is, Ma'am," he said after he was safely inside. Mrs. Nack took the soap in her pale, shovel-like paws, raised it to her nose, and sniffed it. She looked mollified. "As a matter of fact," Ned continued, "I've got just two left, and since I'm putting you to all this trouble, I'm going to let you have both of them, if you like the first one. But I get awfully thirsty, climbing stairs all day in this heat, and I wonder if I might ask you for a glass of water before you start washing your hands."

"I guess so," Mrs. Nack said. "Sit down on the chair there while I get you the water."

Ned sat down in a black leather upholstered chair and looked around him while the woman went to the kitchen, in the rear of the flat, to get his drink. Within a few days, the newspapers were to describe the contents of Mrs. Nack's apartment in much more detail than Ned was in a position to take in, but his eyes fell on one item that subsequent newspapermen were destined never to see. "Leaning against a lamp, on a kind of a knickknack stand, there was a studio photograph of a big blond guy with little turned-up mustaches under his nose—a kind of Dutch version of a sport," Mr. Brown recalls. "The minute I saw it, I was sure I had seen him around, without ever knowing his name." The floor was bare, and Ned noticed that the rug was rolled up and tied, as if Mrs. Nack were getting ready to move. When Mrs. Nack brought the water, he downed it thirstily, just as if he hadn't been drinking beer all afternoon.

"Now, Madam," Ned said after thanking her, "you will have the rare pleasure of making the acquaintance of the world's most luxurious hand soap. Do not hurry it, but run a basin of warm water and then work up a creamy lather. Let your hands soak in it! You will feel each finger separately caressed. When you withdraw your hands, hold them to your nose! The fragrance is a secret formula, copyrighted by the makers of Cotaspam. You have beautiful hands, Madam. They deserve Cotaspam!" The midwife slupped away again, and as soon as Ned heard water running in the rear of the apartment, he grabbed the photograph and slipped it under his jacket. He now passionately desired to leave at once, but he knew that to do so, if his suspicions were correct, would be likely to frighten Mrs. Nack into immediate flight. He also had a hunch that the longer he waited, the more he would learn. All

Mrs. Nack's actions indicated that she was alone in the apartment, but the apparently substantial nature of the meal she was preparing hinted that she expected company for dinner. If it was the man in the photograph, all Ned's theories would come tumbling down and he would probably feel obliged to invite the fellow out to the nearest saloon and buy him a seidel of beer. But if it wasn't the man in the photograph, it might be Mrs. Nack's accomplice in his murder. Ned had formed a most unfavorable impression of Mrs. Nack; she looked capable of murdering an infant—and probably had, for midwives often doubled as abortionists. But he was not physically afraid of her, despite her lardy bulk. He was an athletic young fellow, who, with his brother, had rigged a trapeze and flying rings in the attic at home in Flatbush; Ned could chin himself innumerable times with one arm, and fancied himself as an amateur boxer. The dinner guest, however, would almost certainly prove to be a large adult male, armed and with a nasty taste for fragmentation. While Ned was pondering this prospect, Mrs. Nack returned, a smile for once suffusing her desk blotter of a face. "It is nice soap as possible," she said. "Very elegant."

Ned whipped out his reporter's notebook and started writing in it. "May I quote you, Madam?" he asked. "We intend to publish testimonials in the newspapers, and a testimonial from a midwife would have double value. It would be a good ad for you, too."

"I don't need ads," Mrs. Nack replied. "I am going soon anyway back to Germany." For a moment, she seemed sorry she had said so much, but Ned's look of bland innocence evidently reasured her. "Now you give me the other soap also," she said. "Here is a dime." Ned felt sure she had been told by other women that the soap regularly sold for twenty-five cents—that they knew it did because they had priced it in the drugstore downstairs. "It is wonderful how with any woman the idea of a bargain will obscure larger issues entirely," Mr. Brown says. "She was looking at me and talking about the soap, and it never occurred to her to look around the room and notice that the picture was missing."

Ned gave Mrs. Nack the second bar of soap, took her dime, said goodbye, and walked through the doorway. Then he stopped, because a man was coming up the narrow stairs. "He was a husky man—no giant, but a full-sized middleweight," Mr. Brown says. "About thirty years old, I should guess. He was wearing a derby hat, although it was summer—only the dudes wore straw kellies—and he had long black mustaches. I remember them as black, although the papers said afterward they were light brown. Maybe he had dyed them. Still later, he shaved them off. What I particularly remember about him, though, was his eyes. They were deep-set and glaring, and they shone like a cat's. At his trial, the artists had a field day drawing those eyes. He was furious at seeing me there—the door to the apartment was still open— and he grabbed me by the shoulder. '*Wer ist's?*' he yelled in German— 'Who is it?'—and then he started giving the woman hell. I could see she was frightened—he had her buffaloed. I had learned enough German at Erasmus to understand that he was bawling her out for not keeping the door closed. He said he had told her not to let anybody in. She started explaining who I was, and telling him if he made so much noise the neighbors would come to see what was the matter. Finally, he took his hand off my shoulder—I certainly didn't look dangerous— and went inside. 'Donkey-head!' I heard him call the woman, in German, and then the door slammed, and I heard a slap you could hear right through it. I ran down the stairs and kept going. From the way those two had acted, I was sure that I had the right man's picture and that they were the ones who had killed him."

The reason Ned's skin had appeared translucent that Monday morning was that during the previous evening it had been buffed to gauzy thinness by successive pairs of large, powerful, clean, untanned, uncallused, well-kept hands with nails trimmed extremely short in order not to scratch customers. He had spent a good part of that night, after leaving the morgue, in a series of Turkish baths, making discreet inquiries about rubbers who might be missing from work.

"The minute I saw the hands on the mystery stiff at the morgue, I noticed that the skin on the tips of the fingers was crinkled, like a

baby's sometimes after a hot bath," Mr. Brown says. "I remembered I'd
seen the same thing recently on an adult's fingers, and then I remembered where it was—on a fellow named Bill McPhee, who was giving
me an alcohol rub at the Murray Hill Baths. And I'd asked McPhee,
'Do your hands get that way permanently from the hot water and soap,
or do the crinkles go away when you go home?'

"'Oh, they stay that way for a couple of days, maybe a week, if you
aren't working,' he said. 'But then they go away and the skin looks just
like anybody else's.'

"I sized the stiff up. Good muscular development—massaging
twenty or thirty customers a day is hard work, and some of those fellows used to pride themselves on how hard they could grip. Clean,
white skin—where could you keep cleaner than working in a bath, and
where would you get less sun on you? Carefully trimmed fingernails,
but too short for a dude or a society fellow. The big fuss about the 'extraordinary refinement' of the hands was cleared up in a minute. I told
Gus Roeder that Sunday afternoon in the morgue, 'This guy was a rubber in a Turkish bath,' I said, 'and he must have worked not long before
he was killed, or the crinkles on his hands would have smoothed out.'
Then I explained what McPhee had told me about the crinkles' lasting
only a few days. 'If we check the Turkish baths in the city and find one
that has had a rubber missing for less than a week and more than a day,
we've got our man,' I said. Gus was a hard fellow to get excited. He
pointed out that there were hundreds of baths in the city; they were
popular on the East Side and in Harlem as well as in the Tenderloin,
and you'd have to check those in Brooklyn, too, and anyway the man
might have been lured or shanghaied from out of town. The *World*
didn't have enough men to spare for that kind of quick check, Gus
said. We had a dozen hot crime men—real sleuths—but they all wanted
to try out theories of their own. If we passed my idea on to the police
and they thought much of it, some detective would be sure to spill it
to the *Journal* and we would get no credit for it. 'But if you want to
work your hunch yourself, kiddo, go ahead,' Gus said. 'I assign you to
it. All the baths you take you can put on the swindle sheet, but more

than a quarter tip the auditor won't believe, so don't try to get away with it.'"

Thus admonished, Ned hit out straight for his favorite district, the Tenderloin—first, because the biggest establishments were there, and, second, because he thought the rubbers in that area were more worldly types, and so more likely to get in trouble, than their confreres elsewhere. He did not begin with the Murray Hill, his habitual retreat—probably because we never expect the strange and mysterious in surroundings that are familiar to us. He began, instead, at the Everard, on West Twenty-eighth Street, and tried three more before he arrived at the Murray Hill, at about nine Sunday evening. By that time, he had been scrubbed until all his surfaces felt like Jimmy Valentine's sandpapered fingertips. In each place, he had asked the attendants to put him through fast because he had a heavy date and wanted to get rid of a hangover before he picked her up. He began his quest at each bath by asking where the big fellow was who didn't seem to be on the floor that night. In each, he was told that the staff was at full strength, and upon hearing this he mumbled that he must have been thinking of some other Turkish bath. At the Murray Hill, since he was known there, he varied the approach slightly by remarking to the rubber, McPhee, that the place looked kind of shorthanded, and asking him if anyone was missing. McPhee, an irascible type, said there damn sure was. Bill, the big Dutchman, who always had Sundays off, had taken Friday that week, trading days off with a man who normally would have been working Sunday. The other man had worked Friday and Saturday and then stayed home, but the big Dutchman had failed to show, leaving them one man short. Naturally, there had been more of a rush than they expected. The previous night had produced an unusually heavy crop of bad heads; it always happened that way when you were short a man. "He took Friday off because he was going to look at a house in the country with his girl—or so he said," McPhee snarled. "Saturday, some Dutchman called up to say Guldensuppe wouldn't be in to work Sunday because he was sick. Guldensuppe is his name," McPhee added in a tone of distaste. "Drunk someplace, of course. Today, when he didn't show, the boss said he was fired." Ned submitted to his fifth scrubbing in five hours without feeling any discomfort. He was anesthetized by preoccupation. "About how big is this big Dutchman?" he asked. "I must have seen him around here, but I can't place him in my mind."

"Oh, probably around five eleven," McPhee replied. (That was taller for a man in those days than it is now.) "And he's built big—big shoulders and a fine big chest on him. He's just built like a big Dutchman. You must have noticed him. He has the upper half of a woman tattooed all over his chest—used to be a sailor on one of them Heinie windjammers when he was a kid. He has one of those trick mustaches like two half-moons on his lip. Not a bad Dutchman," McPhee conceded, "but skirt-crazy."

When McPhee mentioned the tattoo, Ned's heart jumped. "I remembered the torso I had looked at that afternoon, with a slab of integument—of whole skin—removed from the chest, apparently to get rid of some distinguishing mark," Mr. Brown says.

Stopping at the cashier's desk on the way out to pay for his massage, Ned asked the cashier where Bill Guldensuppe lived. "I borrowed a dollar from him last time I was in here, and now I hear he's not coming in any more, so I want to send it to him," he explained. The cashier looked at a list and said that he didn't know where Guldensuppe lived but that he got his mail at a saloon on Ninth Avenue, near Thirty-sixth Street—not an unusual arrangement. "And if you're going to write to him, you might add that he's fired," he said. "That'll save us a stamp." When Ned got out of the Murray Hill Baths, he didn't write. He grabbed a hack and told the driver to get down to Thirty-sixth and Ninth and not to spare the horse on the way. He felt like Richard Harding Davis, who at that moment was covering a war between Greece and Turkey, after attending the coronation of Czar Nicholas II in St. Petersburg.

The saloon on Ninth Avenue was quiet that summer evening. It was a Raines Law hotel, with the ten bedrooms upstairs and the petrified sandwich on every table that entitled it to remain open on Sundays, under the statute passed not long before to appease the Sabbatarians upstate. (The bedrooms established its status as a hotel; the sandwiches represented the food that was legally required to be served with every drink.) The Irish bartender had the cowlick center part in his hair and the handle-bar mustaches that were tonsorial caste marks. The sandwich man, on hand in case anybody wanted one that could really be eaten, was an old German. Ned sized the saloon up as a neighborhood headquarters—the most pretentious place for a hundred yards in any direction. He ordered a schooner of beer and knocked it off with unaffected enthusiasm; the baths had dehydrated him until his shoes felt large. He ordered another and bought one for the bartender, at the same time ordering a ham-and-cheese on rye, for he had not eaten since noon. Having established relations, he asked the bartender if he knew big Bill Guldensuppe, the Dutchman who worked at the Murray Hill Baths. Acquaintance with a masseur in a flashy Turkish bath was a social reference over on Ninth Avenue. The bartender said he knew the big Dutchman who worked in the baths, but the last name didn't sound right. He thought it was Nack. The sandwich man, arriving with the ham-and-cheese, said the name was Guldensuppe, all right; he and the rubber belonged to the same Low German death-benefit society. "He even gets mail here under the name Guldensuppe," he said. "He goes by Nack in the neighborhood because he lives with his sweetheart—Mrs. Augusta Nack, the midwife, right over Werner's drugstore." The sandwich man winked. "She got plenty of cash," he said. "She treats him good."

Ned, trying to seem casual, said that he'd happened to be in the neighborhood, so he'd stopped by, hoping to meet Guldensuppe and have a beer with him, since he knew Sunday was the rubber's night off. "He always talks about this place," he said. "He's a hot sketch!"

The bartender said he hadn't seen the big Dutchman for a couple of nights. "Maybe they've went to Coney for the day—him and his lady friend," he suggested. Come to think of it, he added, he hadn't seen him around since late Thursday night. "He usually be in for a few beers after he gets through at the baths," he said. "The work takes the moisture out of them. I hope he isn't deserting us, because he's a good customer." Ned felt like a poker player who, peeking at the second card dealt him, sees it is another ace. If Guldensuppe had been on a protracted drunk, as McPhee had supposed, it was inconceivable that he wouldn't have once poked his nose into his favorite barroom in seventy-two hours.

"He's a hot sketch!" Ned said again, to dissemble the depth of his interest in Guldensuppe's absence. "Always after dames."

"You bet!" the sandwich man said. "You should see some of the letters he gets here. Pink envelopes! No wonder he don't want Mrs. Nack should know."

Ned said, "He's got a hell of a build. If he had been born in this country, he might be fighting Fitzsimmons."

The bartender said he had heard the big Dutchman could handle himself pretty good, at that. "There was a fellow trying to beat his time with some dame, I heard, and the Dutchman give him a good going over," he said. "The fellow pulled a gun and the Dutchman took it away and kept it."

Walking down Ninth Avenue, after a valedictory beer, Ned had a good look at the building that housed Werner's drugstore—No. 439. There were no lights in the windows on the second floor. Back in the *World* office, he found Roeder just finishing off his lead story on the mystery—the one declaring that an awful crime had been committed. After Roeder had dictated and sent away the last take of his two-and-a-half-column story, which would earn him $18.75, he consented to listen to Ned. Roeder was still not overly impressed by Ned's theory. "The fifth place you visit, you find a man missing," he said. "Maybe if you went to all of them you would find two dozen. The tattoo sounds good, all right, and the jealous dame and the fellow with the gun he took away from him. What you got to do tomorrow is have a talk with this Mrs. Nack and get a good look inside the flat. Maybe there are signs of a struggle—bloodstains. Maybe the head is still in the apartment. And get a picture of Guldensuppe."

Ned thought up the soap scheme on his long journey home to Flatbush.

*

With Guldensuppe's picture under his jacket and the other man's glare still vivid in his memory, Ned made his way down to the *World* again on Monday evening. He was now dead certain he had the solution of the mystery. The sequel was inglorious. Colleagues of greater prestige had turned up what the city desk thought was a better bet. When the Early Edition of the next day's *World* came off the presses Monday night, the frontpage headline on the murder read, promisingly enough:

WORLD MEN

FIND A CLUE

But the story under it was a letdown for Ned.

The most interesting discovery of the day was made by reporters for the *World* [it read]. It was that a wagon, in which were two men and which contained two packages, crossed to New York on the ferry from Greenpoint, L.I., on Saturday afternoon, a short time before the finding of the headless shoulders in the East River at Eleventh Street.

The Greenpoint ferry landing on the New York side is at Tenth Street, and a bundle thrown from an incoming boat would have been carried towards the Eleventh Street pier, with the tide running as it was that afternoon. . . .

That a saloonkeeper from that very section was reported missing last night, having left home on June 2 with a considerable amount of money, makes this phase of the case especially interesting.

All day Monday, while Ned was making the rounds with his soap, the *World*'s torso campaign was being run by Casey, the assistant city editor, under constant inspirational prodding from the front office. Roeder, Reitmeier, and a platoon of other reporters were working with the police, and Ike White, the *World*'s famous lone-wolf star reporter, was working against them, with a squad of special undercover agents. Fred Sturtevant, a celebrated rewrite man, was welding the gross crude output into an artistic whole, and the circulation department was having such a picnic that there must have been a substantial psychological resistance to Ned's story, with its possibility of putting an abrupt end to the frenzy. Roeder, however, was beginning to think well of it, and that Monday night he told Ned to hand over his precious photograph to the art department, so that it could have an engraving ready. "It was a good day's work, kiddo," he said. "Thanks."

Ned was so full of his story that even though it was after midnight, when he got home to Flatbush, he awakened his father and told him about it. "Why didn't you grab the fellow and bring him in?" Frederick Sherwood Brown said. "That's what I would have done." He then went back to sleep.

The mystery continued to sell unparalleled multitudes of newspapers all the next day—Tuesday, June 29th. A *World* editorial that morning stated that in offering a reward the paper was acting simply as a minister of justice, without ulterior object. The *Journal* editorialized in the afternoon, "The only reason why every crime is not detected is that society does not employ the best order of brains in its work. . . . The *Journal*'s offer should bring to the investigation of this mystery intellects and intentions not usually given to this kind of work." To offset the *World*'s two-men-on-a-ferry story, Tuesday's *Journal* splashed a report by one Charles Anderson, of No. 7 Bowery, that he had seen two men on a Mount Vernon trolley car on Sunday afternoon loaded down with bundles wrapped in the fateful red oilcloth with gold stars. The resourceful *Telegram*, ever on the lookout for a sporting angle, promoted the candidacy of "a heavy bettor named McManus, who has not been at the track for five or six days," under a headline that read:

RACING MEN
WILL VISIT
THE MORGUE

The *Evening World*, in its Night Extra, which was relatively safe from Hearst plagiarism, offered a stimulating speculation by still another medical man, under the headline

WAS IT CANNIBALISM?

Dr. Frank Ferguson, the Pathologist,
Is Inclined Strongly
to That Belief

The same paper also presented an exclusive interview with former Police Inspector Alexander S. Williams, who said, *inter alia*: "The motive was revenge. . . . More than one person committed the crime. . . . It was probably done by a German."

Ned felt that the former Inspector was getting warm. But there was nothing more he could do about the case himself. Ike White and Roeder had vetoed the idea of going straight to 439 Ninth Avenue and "arresting" Mrs. Nack and the man with the black mustaches before somebody had positively identified the torso as Guldensuppe's. It would have been easy to visit the Murray Hill Baths, collect a couple of the big Dutchman's colleagues, and take them to the Morgue, but this would have been hard to keep quiet from the competition. Roeder therefore waited until Tuesday night and then got a man named Joseph Kavenagh, a Murray Hill rubber who was off duty, to accompany him to the "storehouse," as the gay police reporters called the morgue. In consequence, the Late Edition of Wednesday's *World* had a technical scoop—a brief story on the second page with the headline

ANOTHER IDENTIFICATION

Dead Man Said to Be William
Gildensupper, a Turkish
Bath Attendant

The story under this reported that two detectives had left Police Headquarters at one-thirty that morning looking for a suspect; they were "acting on information given by Joseph Kavenagh, of 229 Madison Street, Hoboken." At the Murray Hill Baths, some cautious person in charge had informed the *World* that Gildensupper (the name was spelled a half dozen ways in the newspapers when the story first broke) had not worked there in three months.

The *World* of Thursday, July 1st, proudly claimed credit for this first revelation of the torso's identity, which it had printed with little display and less conviction. The reason for its original lack of enthusiasm was that on Tuesday night, while Roeder was squiring Kavenagh to the morgue, another identification of the torso had been made, this one seemingly more plausible and circumstantial, and the directors of the *World*'s board of strategy had fallen for it. A cabinetmaker named Theodore Cyklam, who, like the already forgotten Mr. Lutz, had injured the index finger of his left hand (an occupational disfigurement, since a cabinetmaker uses it to hold every nail he drives), had disappeared from his home in College Point. (The locals jibed beautifully with the *World*'s pet exclusive story about the two men and the wagon on the Greenpoint ferry, which carried traffic to and from College Point.) Louis Zimm, the superintendent of the factory employing Cyklam, and three fellow-workmen had appeared at the morgue and sworn, after looking at the torso and its scarred forefinger, that it was Cyklam, or part of him. It was therefore Cyklam's picture, sketched by a *World* artist "from full and detailed description given to the *World* by Louis Zimm," that appeared on the first page of Wednesday morning's paper, instead of Guldensuppe's, reproduced from the photograph snatched by Neil Brown.

Wednesday morning's *Herald*, although it didn't have the murdered man's name, profited by a quick tip from its man at Mulberry Street to head its main story:

MURDERED BY JEALOUS HUSBAND

"It was reported early this morning that the victim of the murder had been identified . . . and suspicion pointed to a jealous husband," the text below this stated. "It was said that the man was a shampooer in an uptown Turkish bath house, who has been missing for a few days. This man, it is said, had been living with a baker's wife."

Mrs. Nack's legal Spouse, Herman Nack, was, in fact, the driver of a bakery delivery wagon, but he had not particularly resented it when his wife left him, and after the identification of Guldensuppe he considered himself lucky to be all in one piece. He nevertheless enjoyed the eminence of a putative master criminal for at least one day.

MURDER MYSTERY SOLVED
BY THE JOURNAL

an eight-column streamer across the front page of that newspaper bragged on Wednesday, and more headlines dropped away beneath it:

Mrs. Nack Identified;
Her Husband Held
by the Police

MRS. MAX RIGER RECOGNIZES THE
MIDWIFE AS THE WOMAN WHO
BOUGHT THE OILCLOTH IN ASTORIA
Storekeeper Found by Evening
Journal Reporters and
Taken to Police
Headquarters
Where She
Tells Her
Story

MRS. NACK IS AT ONCE ORDERED
UNDER ARREST BY THE AUTHOR-
ITIES WHEN MRS. RIGER'S
STATEMENT IS
COMPLETED

Herman Nack Is Run Down and
Handed Over to the Police
by Two Journal Report-
ers Who Find Him
on His Bakery
Wagon Near
His Wife's
Home

The *Journal*—by its own account, at least—had unravelled the whole mystery; it had had the body identified by Guldensuppe's colleagues, had interviewed Mrs. Nack and scared the devil out of her, and had put the police wise to the whole solution, all on the previous day, but had refrained from saying anything about it at the time, for reasons it didn't go into. Nearly half of its Wednesday front page was given over to an idealized sketch of Mrs. Nack's head, which made her look rather like Pallas Athena. The caption under it read, with what papers would now consider reckless disregard of the law of libel, "Mrs. Nack, Murderess!"

> After tracing the bakery wagon driven by Herman Nack all night, *Journal* reporters overtook it at 11:15 this morning at the corner of Fortieth Street and Ninth Avenue [part of the *Journal* eulogy of the *Journal* ran].
>
> It bore the sign of the Astoria Model Bakery, owned by Joseph B. Schaps, of Astoria, L.I.
>
> Nack was on the driver's seat. The two *Journal* representatives tried to climb up on the steps of the wagon, but Nack pushed them off.
>
> He then whipped up his horse and dashed through Fortieth Street to Tenth Avenue.
>
> He turned down Tenth Avenue, with the two *Journal* men in close pursuit. They watched for a policeman, but saw none until they reached the corner of Tenth Avenue and Thirty-third Street.
>
> They managed to attract the policeman's attention, and he joined in the pursuit.
>
> The wagon was overtaken in another half block, and then another struggle ensued.
>
> Nack was desperate, and with his whip beat off the two *Journal* men.
>
> He was ghastly white and seemed determined to escape arrest at all hazards. He fought with desperation.
>
> Finally the policeman, who belonged to the West Thirty-seventh Street station squad, climbed up on the opposite side of the wagon and subdued Nack.
>
> The two men from the *Journal* helped the policeman to overpower the desperate driver, and he was at once taken to the West Thirty-seventh Street station in his wagon.

There he proved to know nothing at all about the murder.

The *Evening World*, chronicling "The Arrest of Supposed Murderer of William Guldensuppe (Nack)," gave all the credit to detectives, and didn't even mention the horsewhipped *Journal* reporters. It published a picture of Mrs. Nack and one of Guldensuppe, which, Ned was delighted to see, it had reproduced from his trophy. It also carried a long, if not entirely veracious, story of Mrs. Nack's love life, obtained by detectives from her and from neighbors of hers on Ninth Avenue. She said that she had quarrelled with Guldensuppe and that he had gone away, but that she did not believe he was dead. She had had telegrams from him on Sunday and Monday, she said. The name of a third man, known familiarly as Fred, crept into the stories of both the *Journal* and the *Evening World*. He was the man who had had the fight with Guldensuppe.

Guldensuppe's legs turned up on the same day, Wednesday, floating into a dock at the Brooklyn Navy Yard. And on the following day a notice appeared on the bulletin board in the *World*'s city room announcing an award of $5 to E. G. Brown, for outstanding work on the Guldensuppe murder case.

During the next few days, it became clear that Fred, and not the complaisant husband, was the man in the case. Fred's real name was Martin Thorn, the police learned, "Thorn" being a Germanization of "Torzewski." Thorn was born in Posen, in German Poland, and was a journeyman barber—a silent, moody kind of man, whom other men shunned and who, like Guldensuppe, lived in part off women; the rubber had been a genial *maquereau*, the barber a sombre one. Guldensuppe had driven Thorn away, but the latter had sneaked back to see Mrs. Nack during the rubber's working hours. Once Mrs. Nack's picture had appeared in the newspapers, a woman in Woodside, Long Island, identified her as the stout woman who, with a male companion, had rented a house from her in what was then a sparsely settled neighborhood. The companion matched the description of Thorn. The house had outside drains, which leaked, and the neighbors' children now recalled that for two days the pipes had run "red water," which ducks had drunk with avidity.

Mrs. Nack was under arrest, but she refused to admit anything. Every policeman and every reporter in town, including Ned Brown, was out looking for Thorn, but nobody turned him up, and there was a report that he had got safely away on a ship to Germany. Actually, he was living in a cheap hotel on money he had obtained by pawning Guldensuppe's watch and clothes. He felt that his revenge on Guldensuppe would be incomplete if he kept it to himself, so within a few days of the identification of the fragments he walked into a barbershop where a man he knew was working, and told him the whole story—swearing him to secrecy, of course. The other barber, a man named Gartha, went home in a cold sweat and told his wife, who went straight to the police. Gartha made a date with Thorn at the corner of 125th Street and Eighth Avenue for nine o'clock on the evening of Tuesday, July 6th. Inspector O'Brien, disguised as a farmer, and about a hundred of his detectives, in various other disguises, kept it—each detective, to judge by subsequent newspaper accounts, trailed by a reporter. Thorn was waiting, and O'Brien arrested him.

The *Sun* of July 8th summarized the story Thorn had told to Gartha more or less as follows: Mrs. Nack had got tired of Guldensuppe (in the *Sun*'s version, Gieldsensuppe) and Thorn hated him. It was not long before they decided to get rid of him for keeps, and for that purpose they rented the house in Woodside, because it was a place where nobody knew them. Guldensuppe had been after Mrs. Nack to open a house of prostitution, so when the time came to do him in, she told him that there was just as much money in baby farming, and that, moreover, taking care of illegitimate children was a legitimate business. Then she said she knew of a good spot for a baby farm in Woodside, and lured Guldensuppe over there to look at it. It is a safe bet that Mrs. Nack packed a picnic lunch for the excursion.

Thorn was at the house when the couple got there, but Guldensuppe didn't know it. Thorn had bought a new revolver. He had a razor, too, and on the way over to Woodside he had bought a saw. The lovers had also laid in a supply of plaster of Paris, oilcloth, cheesecloth, cord, and other supplies they thought might come in handy. When Mrs. Nack and Guldensuppe arrived at the Woodside house, Thorn was hiding in a closet near the second-floor stair landing. He had taken off, and neatly hung up, his outer garments, because he didn't want to get blood on them, and he was standing in his undershirt and socks. When he heard the gate outside the house click shut—a pre-arranged signal—he made ready. Mrs. Nack suggested to Guldensuppe that while she went and had a look at the outhouse, he go upstairs and see what he thought of the arrangement of rooms; she was familiar with it already, she said. Guldensuppe went upstairs, and when he looked into a bedroom by the landing, Thorn opened the closet door behind him and shot him in the back of the neck. The rubber fell, almost certainly mortally wounded but still gasping—"snoring" was Thorn's word. Thorn dragged him into the bathroom, put him in the bathtub, and cut his throat with the razor; Ned Brown's deduction that the man in the morgue had been dissected alive was correct. After the butchery, Thorn ran hot water into the bathtub, washing a good deal of blood down the drain and making the puddle for the ducks. Then he encased the head in plaster of Paris, so that it would sink when he threw it in the river, but he failed to do this with the other pieces, an omission he later regretted. He and Mrs. Nack together tied up their neat bundles, lugged them to a trolley line, and took a car to the Long Island slip of the Greenpoint ferry. The head sank beautifully, but when they saw that the parcels containing the legs and the upper torso were floating, they decided to hold on to the one with the lower torso. The day after the murder, they hired a hack from an undertaker near Mrs. Nack's flat and drove to the Bronx, where they got rid of that bundle. They meant to live happily ever after, in a flat Mrs. Nack had rented at 235 East Twenty-fifth Street, but the excitement over the serialization of Guldensuppe disconcerted them.

Thorn and Mrs. Nack were indicted for murder by a New York County grand jury on July 9th, but the indictment was found faulty, because the crime had been committed in Queens County. They were reindicted there, and in November Thorn was found guilty of murder in the first degree. He appealed, and was granted several stays, but in August, 1898, he was electrocuted in Sing Sing. Mrs. Nack, who had turned state's evidence against him, was permitted to plead guilty to manslaughter in the first degree. In January, 1898, she was sentenced to fifteen years in state's prison, which meant, with good conduct, nine years and seven months. The District Attorney defended this leniency on the ground that without her testimony it might have been difficult to establish a corpus delicti, since Guldensuppe's head had not been found; William F. Howe, of Howe & Hummel, who was Thorn's attorney, was prepared to contend to the last ditch that the pieced-together headless body could have been that of anybody at all. Mr. Howe said that Mrs. Nack reminded him of Lady Macbeth and all the Borgias rolled into one, and that she had hypnotized his client. "Martin Thorn is a young man of candor," he said. "From my first interview with him I found him saturated with chivalry—ready, if necessary, to yield his life as a sacrifice to the Delilah who has placed him in his present position."

Mr. Howe said this on November 11, 1897. By then, the Bellevue Hospital Medical School had been in session for a good month. But Edwin Gerald Brown, better known as Ned, had not reported for his sophomore year. In fact, he never has.

The New Yorker, September 24, 1955

ZORA NEALE HURSTON

The killing of Florida physician Clifford LeRoy Adams Jr. by his African-American mistress Ruby McCollum was one of the signal crimes of the late Jim Crow era. McCollum, a well-off housewife whose husband ran a federally licensed numbers game known as "bolita," had already given birth to one child by Dr. Adams, and was pregnant with another when she confronted him in his office on the morning of August 3, 1952. Their ensuing altercation ended when McCollum shot him four times in the back. Despite widespread rumors of scandal, Adams—a powerful figure in the community who had just been elected to the state senate—was eulogized in the local press as a virtual saint, while McCollum was denounced as a vicious "Negress" who had murdered him in a dispute over an unpaid bill for six dollars. The other African-American citizens of Suwannee County, a Ku Klux Klan stronghold, found it prudent to adhere, in public at least, to the official line.

At McCollum's trial in October 1952 the judge disallowed all mitigating testimony that might expose the racist status quo—a system in which, among other holdovers from the days of slavery, powerful white men continued to exert a *droit de seigneur* over black women. Covering the trial for the *Pittsburgh Courier,* a nationally distributed African-American newspaper, was the novelist and anthropologist Zora Neale Hurston (1891–1960), who wrote 20 stories on the case between October 11, 1952, and May 3, 1953. Refused permission to interview McCollum, Hurston enlisted the help of Southern journalist William Bradford Huie, who later incorporated an edited version of her typewritten account of the trial into his 1956 book *Ruby McCollum: Woman in the Suwannee Jail.*

Found guilty by an all-white, all-male jury, McCollum was sentenced to die in the electric chair, but her conviction was overturned by the Florida Supreme Court. In a subsequent trial, she was declared mentally incompetent and committed to a state mental hospital, where she spent the next 20 years. She was released in 1974 and died 18 years later at the age of 82.

The Trial of Ruby McCollum

My comprehensive impression of the trial was one of a smothering blanket of silence. I gained other vivid impacts, but they were subsidiary and grew out of the first. It was as if one listened to a debate in which everything which might lead to and justify the resolution had been waived. Some of the actors attained silence by a murmuration of evasions; others by a bald statement that this was something which it would not be decent to allow the outside world to know about.

It amounted to mass delusion by unanimous agreement. The motive for the slaying had been agreed upon—he dunned her, she got mad, and she killed him; and however bizarre and unlikely this motive might appear either at home or abroad, it was going to be maintained and fought for. Anything which might tend to destroy the illusion must be pushed or wished away.

I found myself groping in this foggy atmosphere even before the sanity hearing. To avoid the suspicion of having told anything to an "outsider," most of the Negroes in Live Oak fled my presence. Others loudly denounced Ruby to make certain that "if the white folks heard anything that they said about the case at all," it would be pleasing to them.

"Ruby," they said (before the murder they would not have spoken of her by her first name), "she done killed the good-heartedest and the best white man in Suwannee County, if not in the whole State of Florida. They won't be doing her right unlessen they gives her the chair."

"Ruby McCollum knowed better than to go messing around with that white man in the first place. She knowed so well that she was a nigger. How come she couldn't stay among her own race?"

"I hope and pray that there ain't no salvation for Ruby at all. Killing up that nice Dr. Adams. You could always go to him when you was in a tight for change and he sure would help you out. And if you couldn't pay when he waited on you, he'd scold at you and say, 'Did I ask you for money? I'm a-tryin' to get you well.' And Ruby had to go and kill a nice man like that."

"Naw, Doc Adams *never* dunned nobody for money at all. You could pay him when you was able. Never heard of him bearing down on nobody."

"But Sam and Ruby wasn't no bad pay neither. That's how come I can't see to my rest how they got to fussin' over her doctor's bill and ended up in this killing scrape. Everybody knows that them McCollums paid what they owed on the dot. They had it to pay with and they paid. Everybody in the county will give 'em that. They never owed nobody."

It was words like that which gave away the code—let you understand that they were play-acting in their savage denunciation of Ruby. The sprig of hyssop was in their hands, and they were sprinkling the blood of the paschal lamb around their doorways so that the Angel of Death would pass over them. This, never you forget, was West Florida.

Inside the courthouse on the December day of the trial, a couple came up the stairs to the galleries reserved for Negro spectators, and took seats next to me. The woman murmured for my benefit, "Don't be surprised what might come off here." They looked down the row of seats and the man said, "I hope no fool don't go and block up that aisle."

"But you wouldn't run off and leave me, honey, if something was to take place, would you?"

"Not if you can keep up, baby."

The whites felt no such timidity about violence. But they were afraid. They were afraid of "outsiders"—what the outside world might learn and say. So the white judge refused to let any reporter talk with Ruby.

"She has killed a white man—the most prominent white man in the county. She ought to die for that, and she's gonna die. We don't want these newspapermen coming in here and printing lies about us. She was just full o' meanness, shooting the doctor rather than pay her honest bill."

"We don't have to believe no word that a nigger woman says who will murder a good man just because he sent her a bill for waiting on her. That baby of hers is not the doctor's. It may be bright-colored, but it's just a throwback."

"Sure, we know the doc stepped around among the ladies, like the girl in Lake City. He was separated from his wife until he put in to run for the senate. But he never had nothing to do with a nigger. She's lying. She just hated to pay him that money she owed him. That's the nigger for you."

It was like chant. The Doctor Bill; the Mad, Mean Nigger Woman. It was dogma. It was a posture, but a posture posed in granite. There was no other circumstance in the case, let alone an extenuating one. This was the story; and the Community was sticking to it. The press was requested to take the Community's story, not to dig up any "confusing" material. And the press took it.

There was no digging. Only the chant of the dogma: The Murder That Grew Out of an Argument over a Doctor Bill.

That the Negroes were using protective coloration was evidenced too by the fact that the closer their association had been with the McCollums the more violent was their denunciation of Ruby. An example was Charles Hall, the undertaker numbers writer. McCollum money had set Hall up in business; and Hall had functioned as a sort of numbers ambassador to Dr. Adams: he often drove the doctor at night to rendezvous. Hall knew that he would be suspected of sympathy for Ruby, so his voice was the loudest raised against her. He was giving himself a cat-bath—washing himself off with his tongue.

Then there was the janitor at the courthouse. He had been the McCollum yardman for twelve years, had enjoyed numerous favors from them. But he recounted loudly how he prayed for Ruby's execution. He waited on the judge every morning, to carry his briefcase. He was so obsequious, so diligent in his efforts to "show the judge how the Colored community felt," that the judge publicly thanked him at the end of the trial.

I bear no resentment for this humble man. Human nature cannot be ignored. The McCollums were wealthy; they lived in a big house and drove big cars. These local Colored people were, for the most part, little people, the kind of people, irrespective of race, who have only the earth as their memorial. They must always resent success. The story in which the poor triumph over the fortunate must be eternal; and Heaven must ever be where the earth's humble become superior to the earth's powerful. So to see Ruby brought low was satisfying to Suwannee County Coloreds.

And there was human satisfaction on the part of Negro men in that Ruby had gotten into "bad trouble" by giving herself to a white man. This is from slavery days, the advantage with women that white men have over Negro men. In a Negro café, with the jookbox playing at the top of its voice, a tall man was pleasuring himself with breaded pork chops and side dishes of collard greens and fried sweet potatoes.

"I ain't got no sympathy for Ruby," he said. "She wouldn't even wipe her feet on nobody like us. If she had to have herself an outside man, she could'a got any kind she wanted right inside her own race. That's one thing about our race, we're just like a flower garden, you can get any color from coal-scuttle blond to pink-toed white." (This is a common boast when Negroes rail against miscegenation. They don't seem to realize that by it they are endorsing the very action which is being denounced, for obviously if there had been no miscegenation, there could be nothing but dark individuals among us.) "Naw, she had to go and have that white man, and when she knows so well how these white men don't allow us no chance at all with *their* women. Colored women ought to be proud to stick to their own men and leave these white men alone.

"And more specially when they ought to know that white men ain't no trouble at all. They can't do nothing in bed but praise the Lord. Nothing to 'em at all."

There was a guffaw of gloating laughter from all the men at this. The thought sort of evened things up.

"We gets all we wants for nothing, but they got to pay for it, and they had better, 'cause they sho' ain't got what it takes to bring sinners to repentance!"

There was even louder laughter. But one drunken woman dared to disagree.

"Talk that you know and testify to that you done seen," she shouted. "Some of these here white men got lightning in their pants. They're in the 'Be' class: be there when you start and be there a long time after you done fell out."

But in the enraged silence the slattern took backwater fast. "That is, it could be," she added. "I wouldn't know my own self."

"You better say 'Joe' 'cause you don't know," a man growled. " 'Tain't a thing to the bear but his curly hair. Don't you stand there and tell that lie that a white man can do with a woman what a Colored man can do. Sho', some of these trashy nigger women who is after money will lay up under 'em, like Ruby done, and moan and squall and cry and make 'em think they're done comin' to Jesus, but that's only because of the spendin' change the white man puts out. But everybody knows that a white man ain't no trouble, not a damn bit, and any old nappy head that tells me they is in my hearing is gonna get a righteous head-stomping."

No female accepted the challenge, so the men beat their breasts in a vimful "reading." They poured out all the resentment of the centuries since 1619, when the first batch of Negro slaves were landed in the English colonies. This old hobbyhorse was flogged from Ginny-Gall to Diddy-Wah-Diddy. (Mythical places of Negro folklore reputedly a long way off. Like Zar, which is on the other side of Far.)

In a way, but in a limited way, these men had a point. But by the measuring stick of history their contention has no standing for the reason that force is lacking to back it up. From the cave man to the instant minute, to the victor has gone the spoils, and the primest spoils are women. We will know that the blessed millennium has arrived when this is no longer so.

No Negro man even hinted that the passage of money between Dr.

Adams and Ruby had been in her favor. But the scab of the old sore was scraped off, and it oozed blood afresh.

I talked several times with Judge Adams. He is a man possessed of many substances marketable in the human bazaar. I found no fault with the broad, black Stetson, the black string tie of the past century, the chewing tobacco, the efforts at wit, or yet the mouthful of Southern idioms. To me these are externals and need not indicate a turn of mind. How he conducted the trial was my yardstick.

I was disappointed when he denied me permission to interview Ruby. But he was not curt or harsh. He said that the nature of the case made it advisable to deny the press access to the defendant. He didn't want the case tried in the newspapers.

I concluded that Judge Adams was contributing the power of his position toward the establishment of the local dogma as to motive. But I pondered this question: Was such action on his part native to the judge's spirit, or was he a captive of geographical emotion and tradition?

All of us who love the South know that there is precedent for this query: the case of Robert E. Lee. The great-souled general hated slavery, had freed his slaves, and reverenced the Union. Yet when struggle came, he had to stand with his "folks." Many latter-day Southerners are caught in this same old web.

Because of this question, Judge Adams, to me, was the most interesting figure at the trial. The slaying had been admitted by the defendant; only the degree of her guilt was left to be decided. So the real drama was in Judge Adams, in how far he would allow Ruby to go in explaining extenuating circumstance. We have a Southern saying: "A man ain't got no business pulling on britches until he's got guts enough to hold 'em up." The judge had on the britches; did he have guts enough to let the truth come out?

From my seat in the balcony on the east side of the building, I had a good view of the courtroom. It was clean and comfortable enough as courtrooms go. Provision had been made for custom and comfort. Tobacco-chewing and snuff-dipping are common enough in the area not to be apologized for, so spittoons were handy, particularly to the judge and jury.

The substantial building had been constructed before drinking fountains became common in such places, so the janitor presently came up the center aisle toting a bucket of ice water which he balanced on the corner of the railing enclosing the court officers. A glance told me that a man had bought the bucket and dipper: the bucket was white enamel with a red rim, while the dipper was white enamel with a blue handle. A women would have seen that they matched. The janitor passed the bucket and the dipper around to the jury, and also to court officers, but white spectators could go up and get a drink. Under the separate-but-equal doctrine there was a similar bucket for the Negro galleries.

The room filled up rapidly, and it was plain that no one doubted the conclusion of the trial. The uprising would be put down. Emotion rose like a fume from the lower floor.

As the hour drew near, Judge Adams passed down the aisle, exchanging pleasantries with friends in the audience and behind the rail. Visiting lawyers, including an ex-governor, occupied seats inside the railing on the right of the bench.

There was State Attorney Keith Black and his assistant, O. O. Edwards. Black is a short, plump man in a rumpled blue suit, with a bald spot on top of his head so perfectly round that it might be the tonsure of a monk. He is not impressive in appearance, but a Negro behind me murmured: "Don't let that sleepy look fool you. He's just playing possum. He's gonna burn Ruby. That Black is a 'getting fool.' I done seen him at it." Edwards did little mixing around. He appeared to be preoccupied, perhaps dedicated; his look was grim.

Frank Cannon made his entrance like a star. He was the homebred boy who had made good in the big city. He is possessed of a challenging head of thick, wavy white hair; he has a handsome profile, a becoming suntan; and tall, graceful, he wears clothes of good quality. Smiling voices called out to Cannon. Hands were extended. He was a one-man procession down the aisle.

Court sat at last, and when Ruby was led in by a state trooper, the place really came alive. She had been given the opportunity to groom herself with some care. Her hair was pressed and hung in a long bob to her shoulders, confined loosely by a net. It was parted neatly on the left side, and since it was December, she wore a coat, a bright green camel's hair over a pale yellow wool dress. Her small feet were in low-heeled black pumps. She is little, and she looked almost childish in her seat.

She walked in briskly with an expressionless face and took her seat beside Cannon. In the course of the sanity hearings, the balked first trial, and the real trial, I have striven to enclose my impression of Ruby McCollum in a sentence, but I have failed. She is attractive but not beautiful. Sort of chestnut-brown in color, with the breadth of face I think of as feline, though I could discern nothing sly or calculating. Even under her terrible strain she appeared to be possessed of dignity. She seemed to set herself in a resolved position. Her right elbow rested on the arm of the chair, her head on her hand lightly inclined to the right. I had the impression that every muscle in her body was consciously set and locked in place lest she betray her inner turmoil. The only sign of nervous strain was an occasional swinging of her crossed feet; she was too small for her feet to reach the floor. She would extend her right hand at full length and examine it in detail, flex and extend the fingers and regard them studiously, turn the hand and regard it palm and back as if it were something new and interesting to her. Since it was the hand that had wielded the gun, I thought she might be regarding it as having a separate existence, a life and will of its own, and having acted without her knowledge or consent.

There was one poignant moment while Ruby was on the stand. She maintained her shut-in, expressionless mask through the questioning by State and her own counsel until one felt that she was a woman without nerves. Then came the moment, as Cannon led her through the story of the actual slaying. Ruby did not break down and weep; she did not scream out in an agony of memory; but there was an abrupt halt in her testimony as emotion gushed up from the deeps of her soul and inhabited her face. I saw it: the quintessence of human agony. I saw the anguish of the hours, perhaps the days and weeks which preceded the slaying. I saw the awful emotions of the resolve to slay, to blot out from the world that which she had come to know. I saw the emotions which tightened the hand upon the gun. And I saw memories of it all, which lived down deep in barred cavities in the cellar of her soul.

What I saw in the eyes of Ruby McCollum in that instant when she balked into silence, when the agony of her memories robbed her of the power of speech, may God never permit me to behold again. In that instant I beheld the infinity of the human mind, mother of monsters and angels, and I comprehended the ineffable glory and horror of its creations.

That illuminated moment was the life of the trial for me. Now I could see that what was transpiring in the courtroom was nothing more than a mask; that the real action existed on the other side of silence. The defendant had admitted the slaying; she was in the hands of the law; thus there was no reason for the legal machinery of the State of Florida to be operating except to fix the degree of guilt. This could be done, in justice, only by hearing and weighing the defendant's own explanation of her motives.

Ruby was allowed to describe how, about 1948, during an extended absence of her husband, she had, in her home, submitted to the doctor. She was allowed to state that her youngest child was his. Yet thirty-eight times Frank Cannon attempted to proceed from this point; thirty-eight times he attempted to create the opportunity for Ruby to tell her whole story and thus explain what to her were her motives; thirty-eight times the State objected; and thirty-eight times Judge Adams sustained these objections.

"In your long sexual relationship with Dr. Adams, Ruby, was he cruel to you?" "Did he ever strike you?" "Did you have any reason to fear for your life?" "Did you love him?" "Did he love you?" "Did he acknowledge his child?" "Was he proud of it?" "How much of the bolita money was he extracting from you and Sam, Ruby?" "Why did you decide to kill him?" These were questions which Ruby could have answered. But there were the objections of the State, recited, as if by rote, by Black or Edwards:

"We object to that because it is shown that the question was asked for the purpose of obtaining testimony as to a preposterous act and matter which can constitute no defense to this charge. It is seeking testimony which is entirely irrelevant and immaterial, and it is seeking testimony back at an uncertain time which could have bearing on the issue of the case. It is shown that the question is propounded for the purpose of obtaining testimony to confuse the issue that is now being tried in this case, and it is clearly shown that such a question is seeking testimony that is improper and inadmissible in this trial."

"Objection sustained!"

I had begun the trial with some faith in Judge Adams, and I kept looking at him confidently and saying, almost audibly, "No, Judge Adams will never allow this. He will never send a human being to her death without permitting the jury to hear her side of the story. He won't!" But then I watched the judge grow angry and threaten Cannon with contempt of court if he persisted with his questions, and I wilted, first in my soul and then in my chair. My disillusionment was complete. I heard Cannon's words, uttered with resignation: "May God forgive you, Judge Adams, for robbing a human being of life in such a fashion. I would not want it on my conscience."

Race had nothing to do with my disillusionment. Had Judge Adams been as black as Marcus Garvey and Ruby McCollum as fair as the Maid of Astolat, I would have felt the same. My discomfort increased when I recalled that Black and Dr. Adams had been on the most intimate terms, so it seemed hardly possible that he did not know all that Ruby had to tell. Yet Black, for the State of Florida, even denied at the top of his voice that a sexual relationship exsited between Ruby and the doctor. "It is preposterous! It is unthinkable!" he shouted.

One tiny incident let the whole cat out of the State's bag. A colored nurse for Dr. Adams, Thelma Curry, was called by the State. She described the office procedure for sending out bills—as she had obviously been called and coached to do. But she ventured further: she tried to tell about a quarrel she had overheard between the doctor and Ruby a few days before the murder. Summarily, she was jerked from the stand by the State, and Judge Adams growled at her: "Get down and go back where you came from!"

I was tired and embittered by the time Ruby was asked if she had anything to say. She replied simply: "I do not know whether I did right or not when I killed Dr. Adams."

And it was as if I walked in a dream as I listened to Judge Adams intone: "A jury having found you, Ruby McCollum, guilty of murder in the first degree . . . and that at the time so designated the said superintendent of State prison or one of his authorized deputies shall cause to pass through your body a current of electricity of sufficient intensity to cause your immediate death and shall continue application of such current until you are dead. And may God have mercy upon your soul!"

The trial was ended. A Negro woman had become infuriated over a doctor bill, and she had killed the good doctor . . . the friend of the poor . . . a man whose only rule had been the Golden Rule. And now the poor men would have their justice: their eye for an eye and tooth for a tooth.

The Community will had been done.

William Bradford Huie, Ruby McCollum: Woman in the Suwannee Jail, 1956

JACK WEBB

Raised in a poor section of downtown Los Angeles, Jack Webb (1920–1982) began his radio career in 1945 following his discharge from the U.S. Army Air Forces. After playing a tough detective on a show about waterfront crime, he began working with the LAPD to develop a new police series based on actual police files. The result was the pioneering, documentary-style *Dragnet*, a huge hit on radio (1949–57) and subsequently a staple of early TV. (After going off the air in 1959, *Dragnet* returned in a second incarnation that ran from 1967 to 1970.) With his clipped delivery, stony affect, and trademark request for "just the facts," Webb's detective hero, Sgt. Joe Friday, became one of the iconic figures of mid-20th-century American popular culture.

Webb became so completely identified with his character that he merged, in the public's mind, with his role. It is Friday's laconic voice that seems to be speaking in this selection from Webb's 1958 book *The Badge: True and Terrifying Crime Stories That Could Not Be Presented on TV, from the Creator and Star of Dragnet*. His account of the infamous "Black Dahlia" case had a life-changing impact on the celebrated crime writer James Ellroy, who received a copy of the book for his 11th birthday, not long after the murder of Ellroy's mother. As Ellroy declares in the introduction he contributed to the 2005 reissue of the book: "*The Badge* got me hooked. I just followed Jack Webb's lead."

The Black Dahlia

She was a lazy girl and irresponsible; and, when she chose to work, she drifted obscurely from one menial job to another, in New England, south to Florida, westward to the Coast.

No matter how they die, most drifters leave nothing behind, and many of the 25,000 graves dug yearly in Los Angeles are marked by blank stones, for their occupants didn't even leave a name. Yet today, more than a decade after her strange and awful death, this girl remains hauntingly, pathetically alive to many persons.

To the sociologist, she is the typical, unfortunate depression child who matured too suddenly in her teens into the easy money, easy living, easy loving of wartime America. To the criminologist, though the case is almost too melodramatic in its twists, her tortured, severed body is an eerie blend of Poe and Freud. To millions of plain Americans, fascinated by the combined savagery and cool intellect that went into her murder, she is "The Black Dahlia."

The other side of the shield.

Right from the first erroneous report to the police at 10:35 A.M. that gray mid-January day in 1947, the investigation was askew through no fault of the police. In the days, months, years of sleuthing that followed, it never quite got back into balance, again through no fault of the detectives. More than any other crime, murder is sometimes like that.

In the University section, along a dreary, weedy block without a house on either side, a housewife was walking to the store with her five-year-old daughter, scolding her a little because she wanted to play in the dew-wet lots.

Halfway up the block, the mother stopped in horror at something she saw in one of the lots. "What's that?" the child asked. The mother didn't answer. Grabbing her hand, she ran with her to the nearest neighbor's house to call the police.

And the first, wrong alarm went out: "Man down, 39th and Norton."

Within ten minutes, about 10:45 A.M., the first patrol car had reached the scene. Quickly a team of detectives from Central Division, a full crew from the Crime Lab, newspaper legmen, and photographers followed. The street was blocked off to keep back the curious, and the investigation got underway.

Sergeant Finis Arthur Brown of the Homicide Division, who was going to live with this ugly thing for months and years, hadn't yet arrived.

At 9 A.M. that day, he had been in court to testify in another case. After that, he went to Sixth and Rampart Streets to check out a dead-body report. An elderly man had died of natural causes, but Brown followed through with routine questioning of the rooming house operator.

Then there was a phone call for him. Captain Jack Donahoe told him to get over quick to the 3900 block on South Norton. "Looks like we got a bad one, Brownie," he warned.

At 11:05 A.M., just half an hour after the discovery of the body, Brown was there. He saw what he was up against, and, in another twenty-five minutes, additional manpower was at the scene. Nobody could say later that LAPD hadn't rolled hard and fast on this one.

Efficiently, detectives fanned out through the neighborhood. They wanted to find the woman who had made the first call. They hoped to locate some resident who had perhaps heard or seen something, *anything*, though the chances were one-hundred-to-one against them. The lot was a good hundred yards from the nearest house, and the body had probably been dumped at three or four o'clock in the morning.

They got nowhere. Neither did the "hard facts" men who sifted patiently through the weeds, turning up broken glass, rusted cans and other rubbish; but not a clue. The only bit of physical evidence was a set of tire marks on the pavement; and, if they came from the killer's car, they were never to prove useful.

But there was the body.

Old homicide hand though he was, Sergeant Brown had to make a conscious effort to study it.

It was nude. It showed evidence of slow, deliberate torture. There were neat, deep slashes around the breasts and on them. Rope burns on the wrists and ankles indicated the victim had been spread-eagled to heighten her agony. Her mouth had been deeply gashed from ear to ear so that her face was fixed in a grotesque and leering death smile. Finally, the body had been cleanly, surgically cut in two at the waist.

Brown was glad to turn away and check with Lee Jones of the Crime Lab. There were two interesting things to note. A sprinkling of bristles on the body indicated that it had been scrubbed. And, despite the lavish mutilation, there was only one drop of blood in the field.

Scientists, especially hard-bitten police scientists, usually don't give in to emotion. Lee Jones couldn't restrain himself. "This is the worst crime upon a woman I've ever seen," he blurted.

Sergeant Brown's pressing job was identification. But the body had been stripped, and there was only the long shot that maybe the girl had got into trouble and maybe her fingerprints were on file. Brown had copies of them rushed to the FBI in Washington by means of newspaper telephoto equipment.

Then he used the press another way, asking them to publish an artist's recreation of the girl's face (without the awful death smile). And, though not for publication, he had every inch of the weedy lot photographed, right down to three-dimensional shots of the severed corpse.

No one came forward to identify the victim, and though the forlorn files in Missing Persons were checked and rechecked, not a single description resembled the butchered remains at 39th and Norton.

But even before they knew whom they were looking for, LAPD launched the biggest crime hunt in modern Los Angeles history.

Every one of the city's dozen police divisions was subdivided down to each radio car beat. House to house, door to door in the apartment buildings, more than 250 policemen rang bells and asked questions.

Did you hear any unusual noises or screams last night or yesterday or the night before?

Have you noticed anything unusual around the neighborhood? Anybody acting peculiarly? Anybody digging in a yard, maybe burying a pile of woman's clothing? Or burning anything?

Very possibly, one of the 250 officers talked to the killer that day, or to someone who had a terrible suspicion about his (or her) identity. Yet all 250 drew a blank. Where the girl had been murdered was as much a mystery as the why of it, and the who, for that matter.

Next day the FBI kick-back supplied the who. Her name: Elizabeth Short, age 22; height, five feet five inches; weight, 120 pounds; race, Caucasian; sex, female; description, black hair (dyed) and blue eyes.

The FBI had her because just once, four years earlier in Santa Barbara, Elizabeth had been picked up. She was a minor then, and a policewoman caught her drinking in a bar with a girl friend and two soldiers.

In a sense, it was ironic. The wrong way of life that was to lead her to death at least had left behind a clue to her identity, and she would escape the drifter's nameless grave.

Now that Brown had something to go on, the pace of the investigation accelerated. Who was Elizabeth Short? Where did she come from? What did she do? Boy friends? Associates? Habits? When was she last seen alive?

For seventy-two hours, Brown and many of the original twenty detectives assigned to the mystery worked day and night without letup. In fact, during the next thirty days, Brown was to cram in an additional thirty-three days of overtime. During one three-day period, he never got around to changing his shirt.

At the end of the first, furious three days of investigation, Brown knew a great deal about Betty Short or "The Black Dahlia," as an imaginative police reporter had re-christened her for all time. Those seventy-two hours had yielded the secret of The Dahlia's past right down to the date of her disappearance. Another seventy-two hours of such detective work, at most a week, and by all the normal odds LAPD would be putting the collar on a suspect.

Four years later, Sergeant Brown was down in Texas, chasing still another lead that led nowhere.

The girl who was to bloom into a night flower was one of four sisters reared by their mother in Salem, Massachusetts. About the time the war broke out, when she was in her middle teens, Betty Short went to work. She ushered in theaters, she slung plates as a waitress. It was the kind of work where a girl too young and attractive would meet too many men.

For a time, her father reappeared in Salem, and then left again for northern California. Maybe there was something romantic about this man who came and went; maybe he told her stories about sunny California, so different from cold little Salem. At any rate, at eighteen, Betty went West and joined him briefly.

Then she struck out on her own for Los Angeles, the city of opportunity where many another waitress, poor but beautiful, had made it in the movies. She settled near the campus of the University of Southern California, and she may even have walked past the lot at 39th and Norton. It wasn't far away.

Los Angeles, like every other city, was at war. On a tip from a soldier, Betty went to Camp Cook, north Los Angeles, and got a sales job in the PX.

Then the first ominous thing happened. Betty suddenly threw up the job. There were barracks room whispers that some soldier had beaten her up badly. Why? Nobody seemed to know.

Betty drifted on to Santa Barbara; and, after the policewoman caught her in the bar with the two soldiers, she returned to New England. For almost two years, she sort of settled down, working as a waitress and cashier in a Boston restaurant.

Restlessness seized her again, and she took a bus all the way to Miami, working there for a winter. Then she came back to Boston and got a job across the Charles River in Cambridge in a café near the Harvard University campus.

There was a brief romance with a Harvard undergrad. All spring they dated; they even exchanged photographs. But when the school year ended in June, he went home; and Betty was on the move again. For a time, she lived in Indianapolis, and then in Chicago in the bright and noisy hotels that cluster round the Loop.

Something happened there that never has been fully established. Apparently, she met a handsome young Air Force flier. Maybe she even married him. No one has been able to check it out definitely, one way or the other.

At any rate, she loved him enough to go halfway across the country when he pleaded with her by wire to join him in Long Beach, California. There he met her at the train and took her to a hotel room he had arranged. From there, they journeyed on to Hollywood.

And then one day he told her he had to fly East to be separated from the service. He was like her college student; she never saw him again.

The war was over, the men were going home. At twenty-one, when she should have been starting married life or maybe a modest career, she was already obsolescent.

For three months, The Dahlia moved in with a girl friend; then went to a small home for would-be actresses; moved again to a private home; then to a hotel for girls in Hollywood.

She had no job. She killed time hanging around the radio studios and attending the radio shows. She sponged off friends and even got money from her mother back home. She lost her clothes to the landlady in lieu of rent. She mooched at the night spots and the bars where a pretty girl could easily cadge a drink. She was careless about the company she kept.

Two or three times, friends later remembered, Betty had hitched rides to the Sixth Street area when she was out of funds. After a day or so, she would reappear, mysteriously replenished. Where she got the money never was known.

Some six weeks before the end, The Dahlia met a salesman in Hollywood. The salesman rented a room for her in a hotel, but he signed the register "Mr. and Mrs." Later, he took her to a bus depot, bought her a ticket for San Diego and said good-bye.

In San Diego, aimless, drifting, The Dahlia happened into an all-night theater. She got into a conversation with the cashier. Little by little, The Dahlia let drop her affecting story of misfortune and unhappiness.

Generously, the cashier brought her home with her that night and then let her stay for the next month. But something seemed to be driving The Dahlia toward her fate. She met another young salesman and begged him to drive her to Los Angeles the following day.

Perhaps with romantic hopes in mind, he did so, but as soon as they arrived, The Dahlia skillfully avoided a dinner date with him. She had some other plan in mind. Her sister, she explained, was down from Berkeley and stopping at the Hotel Biltmore. Regretfully, the salesman waited while she checked her bag at the bus depot and then dropped her off at the hotel.

It was 7 P.M., January 10.

For three more hours, The Dahlia moved freely. Three hours in which chance, a friend happening by, or an attractive well-dressed stranger might have diverted her from her plan, whatever it was.

Dozens of men must have observed her, for she spent the time waiting near the phone booths and she was, in her black cardigan jacket and skirt, white blouse, red shoes, red purse, and beige sport coat, the kind of girl that men observe. Yet none offered a merciful, life-saving flirtation.

Once The Dahlia changed a dollar bill at the hotel cigar stand and made a phone call, maybe two. Then she waited, as though expecting a call back. When none came, she walked out the front door, smiling to the doorman as he tipped his cap. He observed her trim form swinging south on Olive Street toward Sixth, the slim legs striding easily, the red heels tapping purposefully on the sidewalk.

It was 10 P.M.

And thus Sergeant Brown traced The Dahlia back to childhood, forward to the brink of eternity. And there the investigation stood still. Five days, from the doorman's last salute to the living, up to the discovery of the mutilated thing, remained a blank.

Medical evidence could say what must have happened during part of that time, but not why or by whom, nor could it locate the abattoir.

The Dahlia had been roped and spread-eagled and then hour after hour, for possibly two or three days, slowly tortured with the little knife thrusts that hurt terribly but wouldn't kill. She had made the rope burns on her wrists and ankles as she writhed in agony.

Finally, in hot rage or *coup de grâce*, there had come the slash across the face from ear to ear, and The Dahlia choked to death on her own blood.

But the killer had not done with her body.

Afterwards, he (or she) drained the system of blood, scrubbed the body clean and even shampooed the hair. Then it was neatly cut in two and deposited at 39th and Norton.

*

Five days after the first report of "man down," the twenty original investigators were increased to fifty. Now the newspapers were playing the case as no crime had ever been played in Los Angeles, and the publicity was both a blessing and a burden to LAPD.

Every hour seemed to turn up a new "lead" that had to be checked out; and suddenly dozens of persons who had not recognized The Black Dahlia's sketch in the papers four days earlier volunteered bits and pieces of information about her life. Nothing, however trivial, could be ignored. Everything was run down, saved or discarded.

Some fifteen times, the Crime Lab and men from the Detective Bureau went over houses, from cellar to attic, where the slow torture killing might have been played out. They found nothing. Having been lost en route, The Dahlia's trunk at last arrived from Chicago. Again, nothing.

There had to be a touch of lunacy in a killing like that, and madness communicates with madness. Now the "confessions" began pouring in to irritate and distract Finis Brown. One man telephoned that he was coming in to surrender, and he did—three or four times when the detectives wouldn't believe him the first time. "Confessin' Tom," they finally called the nuisance.

At Fort Dix, New Jersey, a soldier sobbed out the story of the murder he hadn't committed. Four times at his own expense, a man traveled west from Utah and sat, drenched with sweat in the interrogation room, while he begged detectives to believe his preposterous admission of the killing.

At times it seemed the case needed a division psychiatrist more than a Homicide man, but with remarkable restraint, LAPD booked only one of the confessors for insanity.

In all, thirty-eight confessions had to be double-checked, and the waste of time was deplorable. Scores more had to be at least listened to before detectives knew they weren't worth even a rundown. Now and then, fighting to unclutter his few hard facts from all the fancies being pressed on him, Finis Brown wondered if he wouldn't tip over himself.

But if a madman had killed The Dahlia, he might be among those psychos, and the loony bin had to be emptied, one poor deluded mind at a time, just to make sure.

Then there were the stacks of mail that came in daily, mostly abusive, obscene or plain crazy but now and then intelligently written notes that were even more annoying. These contained pompous advice from amateur detectives telling the police how to go about their business.

Everything had to be read because The Dahlia's butcher might just be the egocentric who would delight in needling the police. At first, Sergeant Brown kept a ledger to catalogue the mail, but the volume overwhelmed him. So names and addresses of the writers were filed on cards to be checked out gradually when there was time for it.

In ten days, the hysteria seemed to have run its course. For the first time, the newspapers took The Dahlia off page one, and LAPD enjoyed a moment of quiet. The quiet before the storm, as it turned out.

That very same evening, a mail truck emptied a box near the Hotel Biltmore, and among other pieces picked up a simple carton, wrapped in brown paper and addressed to the police. Next morning, when they unwrapped the package, Finis Brown and his detectives relieved themselves with words that would have made an old Army sergeant shake his head in envy.

Inside were The Black Dahlia's purse, her Social Security card, her birth certificate, a batch of miscellaneous cards and papers, scraps with numbers and names on them, even an address book. The killer was laughing at Homicide, telling the detectives contemptuously to go ahead and make something of it.

But he (or she) had been careful to leave no traces. Postmark and printing, carton and brown paper, yielded no clues. There was a faint odor to the contents, and scientific tests confirmed the suspicions of the detectives. Everything had been carefully washed in gasoline to remove any trace of where it had been or who had touched it. Tantalizingly, about a hundred pages had been ripped out of the address book. Some two hundred names remained, and Finis Brown had each one checked out, in vain.

With this mocking gesture, the killer bowed out; and, though the papers hastily brought The Dahlia back to page one, though the humiliated detectives bird-dogged even harder, this was really the end of the line.

There is no statute of limitations on murder, and LAPD will not admit defeat.

Two years later, Finis Brown thought he had a lead on the mysterious soldier who had given Betty the bad beating at Camp Cook. The lead ran dry.

Three years later, he was able to make a complete check on the salesman who had signed the register "Mr. and Mrs." in Hollywood and then put her on the bus to San Diego.

Four years later, he was down in Austin and Dallas, Texas, and after that up in Boston interviewing the Harvard man who had dated her one spring.

Nothing, nothing, except to close out false scents and then try to get back to the right one.

Sometimes police know their man and yet cannot pin the evidence on him. Sometimes they sense with the hunter's intuition that they are close, very close, and lose him only because he has suddenly died or managed to flee into obscurity. Usually, almost always, they can reconstruct the motive and sex of the killer. Murder is their business, and these things are not surprising.

But with the monster who slowly, delectably tortured The Black Dahlia to death, they have never felt that they were anywhere near close. They have never known the motive, nor whether the slayer was man or woman, nor where the agony was perpetrated.

Was the killer The Dahlia's lover or husband who felt he had been betrayed? But what betrayal, even unfaithfulness or a mocking laugh, merited revenge like this?

Was it perhaps a woman who had taken The Dahlia as wife in Lesbian marriage? Was that why the body had to be bisected, so that she could carry out the parts to her car?

Was the killer, man or woman, a sadist with a blood fetish who slashed for no comprehensible reason at all?

All LAPD can say is that its detectives have exonerated every man and woman whom they've talked to, including the scores who insist to this day that they are guilty.

Beyond that, you are free to speculate. But do him a favor—don't press your deductions on Finis Brown.

The Badge, 1958

ELIZABETH HARDWICK

The case of Caryl Chessman was, in its time, an international *cause célèbre.* A petty crook and self-described "grinning, brooding, young criminal psychopath," Chessman had already spent years behind bars before being arrested in 1948 as the "Red Light Bandit," a police-impersonating predator who committed a string of robberies and two sexual assaults on lovers' lanes in San Francisco. Coerced into a confession he later recanted and charged with kidnapping because one of his female victims had been dragged a short distance from her car, he was sentenced to death after a trial at which, with characteristic swagger, he insisted on representing himself. While awaiting execution in San Quentin—a period that stretched into an unprecedented 12 years as he managed to win one delay after another—Chessman became a self-taught expert in the law and produced three best-selling memoirs that brought him worldwide attention and sympathy: *Cell 2455, Death Row* (1954), *Trial by Ordeal* (1955), and *The Face of Justice* (1957). Despite appeals for clemency from the likes of Albert Schweitzer, Aldous Huxley, Robert Frost, and Eleanor Roosevelt, he was sent to the gas chamber on May 2, 1960.

The following piece by Elizabeth Hardwick (1916–2007) first appeared in *Partisan Review,* a journal she started writing for in 1945, a few years after moving from Kentucky to Manhattan with the aim, as she once put it, of becoming a New York Jewish intellectual. Novelist, biographer, reviewer, and co-founder of *The New York Review of Books,* Hardwick received her greatest acclaim as a literary essayist. Here she offers a powerful meditation on the dark forces that drove the young Chessman, the extraordinary personal effort by which he achieved "salvation of the self," and the hidden fears and desires of the society that demanded his death.

The Life and Death of Caryl Chessman

> They rode together in harmony, Abraham and Isaac, until they came to
> Mount Moriah. But Abraham prepared everything for the sacrifice, calmly
> and quietly; but when he turned and drew the knife, Isaac saw that his left
> hand was clenched in despair, that a tremor passed through his body—but
> Abraham drew the knife. Then they returned again home, and Sarah has-
> tened to meet them, but Isaac had lost his faith. No word of this had even
> been spoken in the world, and Isaac never talked to anyone about what he
> had seen, and Abraham did not suspect that anyone had seen it.
>
> Kierkegaard, *Fear and Trembling*

The "abominable and voluptuous act known as *reading the paper*," Proust called it. In a bleary, addicted daze I followed the last years in the life of Caryl Chessman and, with increasing interest—or *consumption*, perhaps one should call the taking in of the flesh and blood of a person through the daily press—his last months. After the shock of his pointless execution, after his exit from the front pages, Chessman still did not entirely remove himself from public contemplation to make room for the young criminals who seemed to spring from the earth just as his bones were lowered into it. Even during the triumphal procession, soon after his death, of Tony and Margaret—the short, little couple, their hands raised as if in a benediction—the ghostly, beaky, droopy, heart-shaped face remained, creating one of those accidental juxtapositions whose significance is everything or nothing.

I wondered how Chessman had appeared in the newspapers during his arrest and trial as "the red light bandit." I went back to the files of the *New York Herald Tribune* and looked up the dates of his tragic history. January 23, 1948, when Chessman was arrested in a stolen car and identified as the man who made assaults on two women—there was nothing in the paper; May 18th, 1948, when he was convicted on seventeen of eighteen charges—nothing; June 25, 1948, when he was given two death sentences—no mention of the case; July 3, 1948, when, at the age of twenty-seven, he entered Death Row in San Quentin prison—blankness in the *Herald Tribune* on this matter. To the East at least, Chessman had been nonexistent as a criminal, as a case, as a doomed young man. He had to bring himself forth from the void of prison, from nothingness, from nonexistence. This condition of his nothingness, his nonexistence, makes his remarkable articulation, his tireless creation of himself as a fact, his nearly miraculous resurrection or birth—which it was we do not know—a powerfully moving human drama. With extraordinary energy, Chessman made, on the very edge of extinction, one of those startling efforts of personal rehabilitation, salvation of the self. It was this energy that brought him out of darkness to the notice of the Pope, Albert Schweitzer, Mauriac, Dean Pike, Marlon Brando, Steve Allen, rioting students in Lisbon (Lisbon!)— and, perhaps by creating his life, Chessman had to lose it. The vigor of his creation aroused fear, bewilderment, suspicion. As he tells us in his accounts of his fellow convicts on Death Row, it is usually the lost, the cringing, the deteriorated who are finally reprieved. A man needs a measure of true life in order to be worth execution.

People on the street, talking about the case, found Chessman's energy, his articulation of his own tragic trap, his stubborn efforts on his own behalf, truly alarming. These efforts were not mitigating; indeed they were condemning. He had trained himself to sleep only a few hours a night so that he could write his books, study law, work on his case. But suppose another condemned man wanted his sleep, couldn't bother to work on his own destiny, hadn't the strength or the talent to bring himself from darkness to light—what then? Lest his very gifts save him, some people wanted him executed in order to show the insignificance of personal vigor before the impersonal law. And, true, his energy is very uncommon among habitual criminals. "Flabby, bald, lobotomized" Lepke; dreamy, paretic gangsters; depressed, deteriorated murderers; goofs putting bombs on planes. Chessman was a young hoodlum who was able, in the last decade of his life, to call upon strange reserves of strength. His early violence and his late effort at personal integration seem to have come from the same mysterious source. Life is haunted by one so peculiarly instructive, a history so full of fearful symbolism.

Cell 2455, Death Row, Chessman's autobiography, is a work of genuine and poignant interest. (Its faults as literature are those almost inevitably found in naturalistic first novels by young men who are writing from harsh experience: occasional sentimentality, strained efforts at rhetorical decoration, cultural pretentiousness. Its virtues are of the same genre—power, natural expressiveness, authenticity.) This is an oddly American book. The need to confess violent thoughts is softened by the cream of despairing sentiment, remembered hopes, perfect loves, and the incongruent beauties of the jungle. I had not thought of reading it until after the execution. It had not seemed likely that Chessman would have sufficient objectivity to tell us what we wanted to know about him; or that, if he had the intention to give a serious picture, he would have the words at hand. Almost unwillingly one discovers that he really had, as he said, a great deal to tell. The life of a chronic offender, existence reduced to chaos or ruled by tides of compulsion, reform school, jail, parole, jail once more, and death at the end of it—that history he is abundantly able to record.

The aim of this aching revelation was to save the author from the gas chamber and that it did not do. Its other aim—to picture the life of a young criminal—is accomplished with exceptional truth. Careening cars, gun fights, arrests, escapes, loyalties and betrayals, horror, confusion, defiance, manic decision, hopeless cruelties: there it is. But it is not a collage. In the center is a person, young, monstrously careless, living in hell, acting out these sordid images and twisted yearnings. Chessman is himself and also a national and international phenomenon of our period. Someone like him will be in the news tomorrow in New York, in Paris, in Moscow. History has an uncanny application at a hundred points. You never doubt his existence or that of his companions, desperate boys named Tuffy or Skinny, and coarse girls, defiantly self-debasing. These are harsh portraits, very unlike the social worker's case history, the TV delinquents, who cannot avoid a false tidiness and handsomeness as they sweat to render an image not their own. The kindly, manly interviewer, the restless kid, the nagging, hysterical parents—the truth is so much worse than the "problem." We know convicts and condemned men are people, but we are always certain they are not the people in the movies. Their restless, self-devouring emptiness, so like our own, has an unbearably great importance because of their crimes against others and their torture to themselves. Chessman's books, particularly *Cell 2455*, and many passages from his other books about his case, could not possibly be negligible because of the information he was peculiarly able to impart. And beyond that, the fact that he, from whom nothing could have been expected, was able to write them at all is a circumstance of compelling interest. It seems to suggest that only through "art," through some difficult and utterly personal expression is reclamation and prevention possible. This is a world beyond the therapy of the basketball court, the recreation center, the social worker's hopeful sympathy. Its energy alone could only be used up in some violent dedication.

The Story: Chessman's family, his early years, are not what one would expect. He was an only child who loved his parents and was loved by them. Perhaps this love lends itself to interpretation because of his tendency to idealize his parents and his failure to make them real. About his mother: "Hallie was a dreamer, at heart a poetess with both feet firmly planted on the ground and her soft, searching blue eyes in the heavens." In any case, the affection on both sides was real and lasting. Chessman was spared the blight of neglect, abandonment, beatings, drunkenness; his severe delinquency does not easily yield its secret and the family situation is a clue to his strength rather than his weaknesses. His parents urged him to "do the right thing," to return to reform school when he had escaped and so on, but he does not record any pressure more coercive than their mere hopes and pleas. They were feeble trusting people. They believed whatever excuse their son gave for staying out all night and were always surprised and dismayed to learn he had been "getting into trouble." Chessman's schemes, his plans, his hopes, all expressed in the vigorous distortions of his own personality, were of a degree of vitality and daring beyond anything the parents could call upon. They were frail, harmless branches blown about by a genuine tornado. To the tornado, they are the idealized calm, pitiful and innocent. He defends and destroys them at the same time. After he was grown, Chessman learned that his mother was a foundling. She did not know who she was. He set out to find her. With the money he got holding up brothels, he hired a detective to trace his mother's origins. Nothing was discovered.

Early, he contracted bronchial asthma. He was nursed and protected by his parents, but in his own mind the asthma was a profound indication of weakness and shame. "The need to be strong became more demanding with each passing attack." A few years later, an attack of encephalitis left Chessman tone deaf. "The disease ravaged [his] personality as well as his physical self." This was followed by tantrums at school, cruelty, and hatred of himself because of aggressive feelings. His mother was injured in an automobile accident and became permanently paralyzed. Disasters multiplied. All the family resources were spent on the mother's illness. When Chessman was fifteen, his father attempted suicide, "with a prayer for forgiveness." The family went on the dole. With the humiliation of food packages, Chessman began his criminal activity. He told his credulous parents that he had a paper route and got up early in the morning to rob stores of provisions left outside. The dole, the food packages, the search for new doctors and new operations for the mother are pretexts for crime; he does not pretend they were more than that.

All pretexts are gradually discarded. Motivation is hidden and justification is not even attempted beyond the hunger of vanity and the compulsion of destructiveness. "He committed nine burglaries, he purchased food with forged personal checks and got, in addition to the food, a dollar or two back in cash." Because of his childhood illnesses and physical weaknesses, Chessman convinced himself that he wouldn't live long and that his thefts and forgeries would be punished by God. His guilt was relieved and, waiting as he was upon his final and eternal judgment, he could hope his parents would not discover his misdeeds. Not long after, he went to a doctor for a simple stomach ache and had his illusion of imminent death destroyed. He was told he was sound and healthy. "These words had an almost paralyzing effect. . . . They meant he wouldn't die!" His parents, after all, would have the sorrow of his disgrace. "God had no right to punish his parents for what he had done! Already they had been made to suffer too much. Already they had made too many sacrifices for him. He, alone, deserved punishment." (These are youthful sentiments, recalled later. Chessman died an atheist, rejecting religious rites and burial and saying that for him to call upon God would be hypocrisy. One of his lawyers thought this his worst trait of character.)

It is hard to avoid the thought that Chessman's conscious feelings about his parents masked other feelings of great distress to himself. Shortly after his discovery that he would have to live, he began to risk everything. And the story of his life, at the point of its greatest recklessness and violence, becomes more truthful. Self-knowledge increases, as nostalgia, adolescent notions, acceptable fears and longings withdraw.

Cars: "That night he stole two cars and committed three burglaries." The young offender's dreams are alive with the embraces of warm, fat, forbidden cars. The car is freedom, power, exhilaration, madness. "Driving was a joyous form of creative expression. Driving made him free. Driving was his personal, triumphant accomplishment." Yet, the pleasure of driving is no greater than the joy in wrecking. ". . . he practiced driving or 'tooling' these hot heaps. He learned to corner, to broadside, to speed and snap-shift them. He purposely rolled and crashed them. He sent them hurtling through traffic at high speeds. He sought out patrol cars and motorcycle cops and taunted them into chasing him, just for the thrill of ditching them, just for the hell of it, and for practice." The car is escape—and capture. No sooner are Chessman and the other reform boys out of jail than they are in a stolen car, running through a stop light, alerting the police, who start after them and put them back in jail. The car is not stolen, altered, driven, to provide accommodation for the criminal on the run. It is wrecked just when it would be most useful. It is driven conspicuously, not stealthily.

Capture: Capture is courted with all the passionate energy that just a few weeks previously went into escape. "I stepped into a stolen car the Glendale police had staked out and was promptly arrested by two detectives with drawn guns." Or "I wanted peace and I unhesitatingly declared war to find it. I wanted to get even, to have one last defiant fling, and to go out in a blaze of ironically stolen glory." There is no meaning, no purpose, no gain. "Repeatedly we had had it impressed upon us that the road we followed led not to riches but to prison or the grave. Soon we reached the point where we were unable to justify the continuation of our collective effort without frankly admitting that our goal was merely to raise as much violent, dramatic, suicidal hell as possible. . . ."

He was put in reform school, released in April, 1937. He came home to his weak, lenient, kind parents. "The next day he was home and his homecoming was a happy one. . . . Not a word of censure did he hear. His parents' sole concern was for his future and how it could be made a success. And they were immensely pleased at how sturdy and healthy he appeared." Freedom is brief. The need to get back in conflict with the law begins almost at the prison gate, after the handshake with the paroling officer, after the lecture. Paroled in April, in May he had stolen a car and more armed robberies began. All of this culminated years later in his arrest and identification as the "red light bandit," an armed robber who flashed a red light into cars parked on "lovers' lanes," robbed the couple, and twice sexually assaulted the women. "After nine years of criminal violence and penal servitude following his release from reform school, he had come to the condemned row at San Quentin prison, twice condemned to death."

San Quentin at last. Prison is a part of the cycle; escape and capture, alternate back and forth, "naturally." Capture is rest from the manic push. The glum, exhausted face of the young outlaw is as revealing as his arrogant, excited mask during the chase. There is no sensible plan, no criminal organization; it is crime and punishment, escape and capture, parole and violation. San Quentin, the ultimate, the final, appears early in this grim dialogue. With Chessman, the exhilaration of violence gives way to extraordinary exertion in handling the fact of imprisonment.

Cruelty and threats have no meaning to men who live by cruelty and threats. They merely provide self-justification. The desire to be strong, not to bend under punishment, keeps criminal defiance alive. "I preferred to stand on my own feet, even if it was in hell." Independence, fearlessness, distorted into horrors, have a monstrous power over the convict. Chessman certainly died with "dignity," and that was the best he could do for himself, even if his kind of fearlessness is a tragic example of strength. Even his last words make much of the crippling "courage" he had lived by. "When you read this, they will have killed me. I will have exchanged oblivion for an unprecedented twelve year nightmare. And you will have witnessed the final, lethal, ritualistic act. It is my hope and my belief that you will be able to report that I died with dignity, without animal fear and without bravado. I owe that much to myself."

The woe of his crimes and the waste of his life lay upon Chessman's soul. He feels that society does not understand the young criminal. It is his mission to explain. "It is the story of a grinning, brooding, young criminal psychopath in definitely willing bondage to his psychopathy." The fate is personal, mysterious. "My father had failed to grasp the real reason for my many clashes with authority. He would never understand what drove me. He never would be fully aware of the jungle."

And what drove him? What was the jungle? "I ventured the thought that perhaps after one spends a while in a jungle world he gets so he cannot or does not want to believe there is anything better, or that it is attainable in any case. Maybe hate has a lot to do with it. Hate for everybody, for himself."

"But there are periods of self-doubt when you know yourself for what you really are—an angry, hating, fighting *failure*. Usually then you curse your doubts and blaspheme the imagery [*sic*] of the self you see."

His history is appalling. "Yes, I have been in reform schools, jails, and prisons most of my life. Yes, I had committed many, many crimes and had ample warning of what to expect if I kept on. Yes, I had kept on nevertheless. No, I was not guilty of the crimes for which I was sentenced to death. I was not the red light bandit. . . . Yes, I would say I was not the red light bandit even if I were."

The Thing is describable but inexplicable. "I was one of the trees in this dark and forbidding forest. I knew what it meant to live beyond the reach of other men or God. I had 'proved' everything I had felt the need to prove: that I couldn't be scared or broken or driven to my knees, that I didn't give a damn. But here is where the tragedy lies: this felt need is compulsive and negative only. It is a need to prove one can do without—without love, without faith, without belief, without warmth, without friends, without freedom. This negative need to prove becomes progressively greater and greater . . . the ultimate (conscious or unconscious) need is to prove that one can do without even life itself."

How is society to heal such a desperate sickness? Chessman puts himself in the position of a leper who is also a physician. He studies his own pains and deformations; he does not find the answer. Each offender is different from every other. The salvation of the meanest or the mildest is as complicated and difficult as the life of every non-criminal man. It is tedious, discouraging, even hopeless. Society is too dull, too rigid, too tired to make the effort. We do not even want to reform the criminal because of our anger that we have sometimes tried and failed. Every account of jails, of guards and matrons seems to show that reform is not believed in or encouraged. If a man might be saved by eight hours at the piano, the warden is sure to put him in the jute mill to teach him his lesson. The senseless determination of the prison officials to keep poor Chessman from writing is one of time most depressing and telling aspects of this sad case. One of the wardens at San Quentin, admitting that Chessman was not a difficult disciplinary problem, said, "So far as I'm concerned, our only problems with him have been literary."

The case: There was a large element of the sacrificial in Chessman's execution. Even if he was absolutely guilty, the way of stating the charge and the decision to give the death penalty were severe beyond anything we are accustomed to. Further, the fact that the unusual severity of the sentence, in a case where murder was not involved or kidnapping either in any sense in which the world understands the term, could not be modified after exhaustive litigation suggests again the sacrificial and symbolic nature of the case. In Mark Davidson's study in *The Californian* he says, ". . . Chessman was not convicted of rape, because in both of the robbery-attack offenses for which he was condemned, the victims persuaded the bandit not to pursue coitus. The bandit instead had them perform *fellatio*. . . ." It has been widely suggested that Chessman's execution was society's punishment of its own perverse sexual wishes or deeds.

The mystery and force of Chessman's character were probably more outraging than the sordid crime itself. This older juvenile posed the question for which we have no answer. Why had he been a hoodlum at all? His cockiness, his loquaciousness, his cleverness, his energy, his talents only made his life more mysterious and more repulsive. His command of the word repelled the jurors. One of them twelve years later told a reporter that Chessman was just "as vicious as ever." When asked how she could know this, she replied, "After all, I seen his picture in the papers and he still has that same mean look, don't he?" He went on talking, defying, acting as his own lawyer, writing books, trying society's patience more and more. His life represents our defeat, our dread of the clear fact that we do not know how to deal with the senseless violence of the young. It is not too hard to understand organized crime, but how can you understand two young boys who kill an old couple in their candy store for a few dollars? In our rich society, the smallness of the sums for which people are killed shows a contempt for money as well as for human life. The nihilism at the bottom of Chessman's fate, his brains, what the newspapers called his "evil genius," made him a fearful and dreadful example. His cleverness undid him. His fight for his life was stubborn, cocky, pugnacious—and defiant.

In a sacrificial death, the circumstances that the mass fears and dreads and violently condemns may arouse involuntary feelings of wonder and grief in others. There was something almost noble in the steely, unyielding effort Chessman had made to define and save himself. He was a real person. He had breathed life into himself. One could only say that when he died this poor criminal was *at his best*. It was dismal to think his struggle counted for nothing. His ordeal was a tangle of paradoxes. He had spent twelve years in the death house because the law hesitated to deny him every possibility for reversal of the sentence. Those were horrible years, awaiting the answer. Would it have been better if he had been executed six months after his sentence? No, it would not have been better. And yet twelve years are twelve years, a unique suffering that cannot be denied. Somehow a justice complicated enough to delay twelve years to study the "technicalities" should have been complicated enough to refuse death simply because so many delays were legally possible. A part of the protest was a cry against rigidity and against the element of meanness in the law's refusal to place the case in a human context. And there was the *feeling* that Chessman might be innocent.

The claims for innocence: 1. The transcript of the trial was deeply impugned by the death of the court stenographer before he had transcribed more than a third of his private notes. The transcription and the enlargement were done, without Chessman's approval, by a relative of the prosecutor. 2. The description of the red light bandit, given before the arrest, did not entirely fit Chessman. 3. He was identified not in the line-up, but in handcuffs. 4. He had committed a wide variety of crimes, none of them involving attacks on women before this arrest. 5. He said he was innocent of the crimes for which he was sentenced to death.

After Chessman died in the death chamber, Governor Brown said he was sorry he had had no power to stay the execution and claimed he said this even though he was fully satisfied of Chessman's guilt. It was reported he then went for a lonely, sorrowing ride in the country.

A detective who worked on Chessman's case and later married one of the victims attended the execution at San Quentin and said, when the death was at last accomplished, "I'm satisfied."

The end was reported with prodigal fullness. As I gluttonously read a dozen newspapers—a dozen newspapers all telling the same story of the gas pellets, the winks, the final lip-read goodbyes, the last struggles of the body—I remembered a hanging that had taken place in my youth. On the morning a Negro was to be hanged in the courthouse yard, other Negroes stayed at home from their work for fear of the way the wind might blow. That same morning a relation of mine went downtown to shop in a department store. The Negro who would ordinarily have been operating the elevator was at home, quietly waiting for the dangerous day to pass. My relation fell down the elevator shaft and suffered ghastly damage to her body and mind.

Partisan Review, Summer 1960

ROBERT BLOCH

If, as Ernest Hemingway declared, all modern American literature comes from *Adventures of Huckleberry Finn*, then it may be said with equal assurance that all modern American horror comes from the outrages of Edward Gein. A mild-mannered psychotic living in bitter isolation in the tiny farming community of Plainfield, Wisconsin, Gein embarked on a 12-year spree of grave-robbing following the death of his mother in 1945. Making midnight raids on local graveyards, he dug up the corpses of middle-aged women and brought them back to his ramshackle farmhouse, where he converted their body parts into various appalling artifacts. On at least two occasions, Gein also resorted to murder. Shortly after the disappearance of his final victim, a 58-year-old grandmother named Bernice Worden, her dressed-out and decapitated corpse was found hanging in his summer kitchen. The discovery of her body, along with the other contents of Gein's ghoulish "house of horrors," set off shock waves whose ripples can still be felt today.

Residing in Wisconsin at the time of Gein's arrest was Robert Bloch (1917–1994). A prolific writer of pulp horror and fantasy who began his career as a teenage devotee and correspondent of H. P. Lovecraft, Bloch immediately saw in the case the raw material for a first-rate tale of terror. The result was his 1959 novel *Psycho*, which Alfred Hitchcock transformed into a landmark of cinematic horror. The schizoid mama's boy Norman Bates became the first mythic avatar of Gein, whose fictional alter egos also include "Leatherface" in Tobe Hooper's *The Texas Chainsaw Massacre*, "Buffalo Bill" in Thomas Harris's *The Silence of the Lambs*, and—in a larger sense—every blood-crazed psycho to rampage across the screen in the last 40 years.

The Shambles of Ed Gein

"**S**earchers after horror haunt strange, far places," wrote H. P. Lovecraft in the opening of his story, "The Picture in the House." "For them are the catacombs of Ptolemais, and the carven mausolea of the nightmare countries. They climb to the moonlit towers of ruined Rhine castles, and falter down black cobwebbed steps beneath the scattered stones of forgotten cities in Asia. The haunted wood and the desolate mountain are their shrines, and they linger around the sinister monoliths on uninhabited islands. But the true epicure in the terrible, to whom a new thrill of unutterable ghastliness is the chief end and justification of existence, esteems most of all the ancient, lonely farmhouse of backwoods New England; for there the dark elements of strength, solitude, grotesqueness and ignorance combine to form the perfection of the hideous."

Lovecraft's tale then goes on to describe a visit to one of these "silent, sleepy, staring houses in the backwoods" inhabited by a weird eccentric whose speech and dress suggest origins in a bygone day. An increasingly horrible series of hints culminates in the revelation that the inhabitant of the house has preserved an unnatural existence for several centuries, sustaining life and vigor through the practice of cannibalism.

Of course it's "only a story."

Or—is it?

On the evening of November 16, 1957, visitors entered an ancient, lonely farmhouse—not in backwoods New England but in rural Wisconsin. Hanging in an adjacent shed was the nude, butchered body of a woman. She had been suspended by the heels and decapitated, then disemboweled like a steer. In the kitchen next to the shed, fire flickered in an old-fashioned potbellied stove. A pan set on top of it contained a human heart.

The visitors—Sheriff Art Schley and Captain Lloyd Schoephoester —were joined by other officers. There was no electricity in the darkened house and they conducted their inspection with oil lamps, lanterns, and flashlights.

The place was a shambles, in every sense of the word. The kitchen, shed, and bedroom were littered with old papers, books, magazines, tin cans, tools, utensils, musical instruments, wrapping paper cartons, containers, and a miscellany of junk. Another bedroom and living room beyond had been nailed off; these five rooms upstairs were nailed off and deserted.

But amidst the accumulated debris of years in the three tenanted rooms, the searchers found:

two shin bones;

a pair of human lips;

four human noses;

bracelets of human skin;

four chairs, their woven cane seats replaced by strips of human skin;

a quart can, converted into a tom-tom by skin stretched over both top and bottom;

a bowl made from the inverted half of a human skull;

a purse with a handle made of skin;

four "death masks"—the well-pressed skin from the faces of women —mounted at eye level on the walls;

five more such "masks" in plastic bags, stowed in a closet;

ten female human heads, the tops of which had been sawed off above the eyebrows;

a pair of leggings, fashioned from skin from human legs;

a vest made from the skin stripped from a woman's torso.

The bodies of 15 different women had been mutilated to provide these trophies. The number of hearts and other organs which had been cooked on the stove or stored in the refrigerator will never be known. Apocryphal tales of how the owner of the house brought gifts of "fresh liver" to certain friends and neighbors have never been publicly substantiated, nor is there any way of definitely establishing his own anthropophagism.

But H. P. Lovecraft's "true epicure of the terrible" could find his new thrill of unutterable ghastliness in the real, revealed horrors of the Gein case.

Edward Gein, the gray-haired, soft-voiced little man who may or may not have been a cannibal and a necrophile, was—by his own admission—a ghoul, a murderer, and a transvestite. Due process of law has also adjudged him to be criminally insane.

Yet for decades he roamed free and unhindered, a well-known figure in a little community of 700 people. Now small towns everywhere are notoriously hotbeds of gossip, conjecture, and rumor, and Gein himself joked about his "collection of shrunken heads" and laughingly admitted that he'd been responsible for the disappearance of many women in the area. He was known to be a recluse and never entertained visitors; children believed his house to be "haunted." But somehow the gossip never developed beyond the point of idle, frivolous speculation, and nobody took Ed Gein seriously. The man who robbed fresh graves, who murdered, decapitated, and eviscerated women when the moon was full, who capered about his lonely farmhouse bedecked in corpse-hair, the castor-oil-treated human skin masks made from the faces of his victims, a vest of female breast and puttees of skin stripped from women's legs—this man was just plain old Eddie Gein, a fellow one hired to do errands and odd jobs. To his friends and neighbors he was only a handyman, and a most dependable and trustworthy babysitter.

"Good old Ed, kind of a loner and maybe a little bit odd with that sense of humor of his, but just the guy to call in to sit with the kiddies when me and the old lady want to go to the show . . ."

Yes, good old Ed, slipping off his mask of human skin, stowing the warm, fresh entrails in the refrigerator, and coming over to spend the evening with the youngsters; he always brought them bubble gum. . . .

A pity Grace Metalious wasn't aware of our graying, shy little-town handyman when she wrote *Peyton Place!* But, of course, nobody would have believed her. New England or Wisconsin are hardly the proper settings for such characters; we might accept them in Transylvania, but Pennsylvania—never!

And yet, he lived. And women died.

As near as can be determined, on the basis of investigation and his own somewhat disordered recollections, Gein led a "normal" childhood as the son of a widowed mother. He and his brother, Henry, assisted in the operation of their 160-acre farm.

Mrs. Gein was a devout, religious woman with a protective attitude toward her boys and a definite conviction of sin. She discouraged them from marrying and kept them busy with farm work; Ed was already a middle-aged man when his mother suffered her first stroke in 1944. Shortly thereafter, brother Henry died, trapped while fighting a forest fire. Mrs. Gein had a second stroke from which she never recovered; she went to her grave in 1945 and Ed was left alone.

It was then that he sealed off the upstairs, the parlor, and his mother's bedroom and set up his own quarters in the remaining bedroom, kitchen, and shed of the big farmhouse. He stopped working the farm, too; a government soil-conservation program offered him subsidy, which he augmented by his work as a handyman in the area.

In his spare time he studied anatomy. First books, and then—

Then he enlisted the aid of an old friend named Gus. Gus was kind of a loner, too, and quite definitely odd—he went to the asylum a few years later. But he was Ed Gein's trusted buddy, and when Ed asked for assistance in opening a grave to secure a corpse for "medical experiments," Gus lent a hand, with a shovel in it.

That first cadaver came from a grave less than a dozen feet away from the last resting place of Gein's mother.

Gein dissected it. Wisconsin farm folk are handy at dressing-out beef, pork, and venison.

What Ed Gein didn't reveal to Gus was his own growing desire to become a woman himself; it was for this reason he'd studied anatomy, brooded about the possibilities of an "operation" which would result in the change of sex, desired to dissect a female corpse and familiarize himself with its anatomical structure.

Nor did he tell Gus about the peculiar thrill he experienced when he donned the grisly accoutrement of human skin stripped from the cadaver. At least, there's no evidence he did.

He burned the flesh bit by bit in the stove, buried the bones. And with Gus's assistance, repeated his ghoulish depredations. Sometimes he merely opened the graves and took certain parts of the bodies—perhaps just the heads and some strips of skin. Then he carefully covered up traces of his work. His collection of trophies grew, and so did the range of his experimentation and obsession.

Then Gus was taken away, and Gein turned to murder.

The first victim, in 1954, was Mary Hogan, a buxom 51-year-old divorcée who operated a tavern at Pine Grove, six miles from home. She was alone when he came to her one cold winter's evening; he shot her in the head with his .32-caliber revolver, placed her body in his pickup truck, and took her to the shed where he'd butchered pigs, dressed-out deer.

There may have been other victims in the years that followed. But nothing definite is known about Gein's murderous activities until that day in November 1957, when he shot and killed Mrs. Bernice Worden in her hardware store on Plainfield's Main Street. He used a .22 rifle from a display rack in the store itself, inserting his own bullet which he carried with him in his pocket. Locking the store on that Saturday morning, he'd taken the body home in the store truck. Gein also removed the cash register, which contained $41 in cash—not with the intention of committing robbery, he later explained in righteous indignation, but merely because he wished to study the mechanism. He wanted to see how a cash register worked, and fully intended to return it later.

Mrs. Worden's son Frank often assisted her in the store, but on this particular Saturday morning he'd gone deer hunting. On his return in late afternoon he discovered the establishment closed, his mother missing, the cash register gone. There was blood on the floor. Frank Worden served as a deputy sheriff in the area and knew what to do. He immediately alerted his superior officer, reported the circumstances, and began to check for clues. He established that the store had been closed since early that morning, but noted a record of the two sales transactions made before closing. One of them was for a half gallon of antifreeze.

Worden remembered that Ed Gein, the previous evening at closing time, had stopped by the store and said he'd be back the next morning for antifreeze. He'd also asked Worden if he intended to go hunting the next day. Worden further recalled that Gein had been in and out of the store quite frequently during the previous week.

Since the cash register was missing, it appeared as if Gein had planned a robbery after determining a time when the coast was clear.

Worden conveyed his suspicions to the sheriff, who sent officers to the farm, seven miles outside Plainfield. The house was dark and the handyman absent; acting on a hunch, they drove to a store in West Plainfield where Gein usually purchased groceries. He was there—had been visiting casually with the proprietor and his wife. In fact, he'd just eaten dinner with them.

The officers spoke of Mrs. Worden's disappearance. The 51-year-old, 140-pound little handyman joked about it in his usual offhand fashion; he was just leaving for home in his truck and was quite surprised that anyone wanted to question him. "I didn't have anything to do with it," he told them. "I just heard about it while I was eating supper." It seems someone had come in with the news.

Meanwhile, back at the farmhouse, the sheriff and the captain had driven up, entered the shed, and made their gruesome discovery.

Gein was taken into custody, and he talked.

Unfortunately for the "searchers after horror," his talk shed little illumination on the dark corners of his mind. He appeared to have only a dim recollection of his activities; he was "in a daze" much of the time during the murders. He did recall that he'd visited about 40 graves through the years, though he insisted he hadn't opened all of them, and denied he'd committed more than two murders. He named only nine women whose bodies he'd molested, but revealed he selected them after careful inspections of the death notices in the local newspapers.

There was a lie-detector test, a murder charge, an arraignment, a series of examinations at the Central State Hospital for the Criminally Insane. He remains there to this day.

The case created a sensation in the Midwest. Thousands of "epicures of the terrible"—and their snotty-nosed brats—made the devout pilgrimage to Plainfield, driving bumper-to-bumper on wintry Sunday afternoons as they gawked at the "murder farm." Until one night the residence of the "mad butcher" went up in smoke.

I was not among the epicures. At that time I resided less than fifty miles away, but had no automobile to add to the bumper crop; nor did I subscribe to a daily newspaper. Inevitably, however, I heard the mumbled mixture of gossip and rumor concerning the "fiend" and his activities. Curiously enough, there was no mention of his relationship with his mother, nor of his transvestism; the accent was entirely on proven murder and presumed cannibalism.

What interested me was this notion that a ghoulish killer with perverted appetites could flourish almost openly in a small rural community where everyone prides himself on knowing everyone else's business.

The concept proved so intriguing that I immediately set about planning a novel dealing with such a character. In order to provide him with a supply of potential victims, I decided to make him a motel operator. Then came the ticklish question of what made him tick—the matter of motivation. The Oedipus motif seemed to offer a valid answer, and the transvestite theme appeared to be a logical extension. The novel which evolved was called *Psycho*.

Both the book and a subsequent motion picture version called forth comments which are the common lot of the writer in the mystery-suspense genre. "Where do you get those perfectly dreadful ideas for your stories?"

I can only shrug and point to the map—not just a map of Wisconsin, but any map. For men like Edward Gein can be found anywhere in the world—quiet little men leading quiet little lives, smiling their quiet little smiles and dreaming their quiet little dreams.

Lovecraft's "searches after horror" do not need to haunt strange, far places or descend into catacombs or ransack mausolea. They have only to realize that the true descent into dread, the journey into realms of nightmare, is all too easy—once one understands where terror dwells.

The real chamber of horrors is the gray, twisted, pulsating, blood-flecked interior of the human mind.

The Quality of Murder, 1962

MIRIAM ALLEN deFORD

While the 1920s produced some of the most sensational murder cases of the century, only one has stood the test of time. Mention Snyder-Gray or Hall-Mills to most people and they'll respond with blank stares. By contrast, the case of the young Jazz Age "thrill killers" Leopold and Loeb has never lost its fascination, inspiring works as varied as Patrick Hamilton's play *Rope* (1929), filmed by Alfred Hitchcock in 1948, Meyer Levin's barely fictionalized 1956 best-seller *Compulsion* and its subsequent theatrical and movie adaptations, and the 1991 film *Swoon*.

Miriam Allen deFord (1888–1975) worked at various jobs—editor of commercial house organs in Baltimore and Boston, public stenographer in San Diego and Los Angeles, insurance claims adjuster in Chicago and San Francisco—before becoming a full-time freelance writer in 1925. During her long and prolific career, she wrote science fiction and mystery stories, histories and biographies, poems and periodical articles, but by her own admission her favorite genre was true crime. "I'm interested in the psychology of the criminal," she observed, "and if he's a real person, naturally, it's more interesting." Though she won an Edgar Award for her 1960 book *The Overbury Affair: The Murder That Rocked the Court of King James I,* her shorter pieces—much admired by many writers in the field—remained uncollected until 1965 when a British publisher brought out *Murderers Sane and Mad: Case Histories in the Motivation and Rationale of Murder,* the source of this selection.

Superman's Crime: Loeb and Leopold

*W*ith these two celebrated murderers, and particularly with Rich- ard Loeb, we meet with the true psychopathic configuration: a profound emotional (rather than mental) disorder, which in Loeb's case at least was probably incurable.*

Murder without motive is very rare. Murder by a near-genius, whose act can be traced not to any demonstrable insanity, but to a profound physical and emotional abnormality, is rarer still. In 1924 such a murder struck Chicago and became a world-wide sensation.

This celebrated case had still further anomalies. It was the deed of two young boys, acting together; and in view of all the evidence it can be said categorically that the crime would never have been committed by either of them acting independently; it was the combination of their peculiar personalities and their reaction on each other that brought it about. It is known as the Loeb-Leopold case.

In 1900 the youngest child of Nathan F. Leopold, a millionaire business man, was born in Chicago and named for his father—though to his family he was always known as "Babe."

The boy was not very old before any competent physician could have seen that there was something very wrong with his physical make-up. In every way he was precocious—but precocious as a forced plant is, which grows awry, develops brilliant premature blossoms, and from root to leaf-tip is subtly malformed. Nathan Leopold's adrenal, pineal, and thymus glands were all diseased—either insufficiently developed or too early involuted; while his thyroid gland was overactive. He grew up an undersized, round-shouldered boy, with coarse hair and skin and bulging eyes. Sexually he was fully developed at an age when most boys are just beginning to feel the first stirrings of puberty. Like any other intelligent child, he realized very well his deficiencies and peculiarities, compared himself painfully to others, and suffered. Human beings thus forced into an inferiority complex may succumb to it and end in shrinking abjectness; or they may react by what is called over-compensation. Young Leopold's was the latter way. He became touchy, sensitive, easily offended, a permanent chip attached to his drooping shoulder. And he built up a comforting picture of himself as superior to all of humankind—a Superman who could do no wrong. His extraordinary mind helped him to put over the picture; for Nathan Leopold was far more than just a brilliant student. He was widely read in literature and philosophy—Friedrich Nietzsche and his theory of the Superman became his guiding principle; he was an inspired amateur ornithologist and botanist whose work was taken seriously by professionals; he spoke nine languages fluently. In his ordinary studies he did so well that at eighteen he received his B.Ph. degree from the University of Chicago—the youngest graduate in its history—and then went on to its law school, where he equally distinguished himself.

All this might have built up a not altogether unknown figure—the child prodigy who makes up for weaknesses and defects by exaggerated distinctions and abilities, and who probably ends as an honored and a bit out-dated professor. This boy ended as a convicted murderer.

Why? There are many answers; but one which is glaringly obvious is the idiotic nature of his upbringing. If his well-meaning parents had deliberately set out to make a monster of their child, they could not have succeeded better.

Here was a boy who needed above all things to be made to feel one with the rest of humanity—different, perhaps, but still essentially akin to his fellow beings. Instead, he learned from his earliest childhood that his family's possession of great wealth gave him special privileges and immunities; the laws that govern others did not govern him. Did he want to kill birds in the park or fish out of season? Very well: his father would secure a special permit for him or pay his fines and get him off. Was there anything at all he wanted? Here it was: $125 a month allowance; a car of his own; $3000 for a trip to Europe before he entered the Harvard Law School. The one thing never told him was that he owed any duties or obligations to anyone.

All this might only have turned him into a hard and selfish creature; but far worse developments occurred. From the beginning, Leopold's disordered glandular system doomed him to sexual aberration. He was shy, he was afraid of girls, his daydreams were all of someone stronger and bigger whom he could worship, whose cruelty would be his joy. As Irving Stone put it, this boy who boasted of being a Nietzschean Superman actually yearned to become "a superwoman, a female slave . . . to some big, handsome, powerful king." He was to find his king, but not until he had been thoroughly warped into an unchangeable pattern.

In early childhood he was put completely under the charge of a governess straight out of horror fiction. She obsessed him, she fostered the rank growth of his Uranian tendency, and being herself a pervert, she took delight in practicing on the child, and in teaching him to practice on her, forms of abnormal sex play that only Kinsey can describe in print.

Then, when at last his parents noticed that Babe did not seem to have the normal boy's attitude towards girls, they devised a marvellous scheme to cure him. They deliberately sent him—under the care of this same governess—as the only boy pupil in a school for girls!

Finally, as if to make sure that nothing was lacking for his ruin, his mother died when he was an adolescent. She had been the one exception to his horror of the female—she was a "saint," a "Madonna." Her death "proved" that there was no God.

Somehow this boy—who had become almost a classic case history of the growth of a psychopathic personality—might still have adjusted himself superficially to the demands of normal society, except for one thing. At the age of fourteen he met the personification of his dream of the god-king to whom he could be a worshipping slave.

This other boy, a year younger, was Richard A. Loeb, known as "Dickie," son of Albert H. Loeb, vice-president of Sears, Roebuck and Company. In his own way, Dickie was as abnormal as Babe, but on the surface they were very different. Where Leopold's intellect was of the first order, Loeb was merely a clever lad who learned easily without trying; he in turn became the youngest graduate of the University of Michigan, and was ready to enter law school at seventeen. He too had been reared to think of himself as outside the restrictions that bound those of lesser wealth, and he had been even more pampered, if that were possible—his allowance was twice the size of Leopold's, for example. But where Leopold worked his rearing into a fantasy of the Superman and the Superman's only god, the god of pure strength, Loeb had become merely callous and arrogant.

In two other aspects he was very different from Leopold, and these differences were the seed of the evil plant that grew from their association. Loeb was tall, handsome, a good athlete, with a ready smile and charming manners. To be sure, he also had his physical abnormalities —a stutter, a tic, a tendency to sudden fainting which resembled the *petit mal* of epilepsy, a suicidal trend. But these were not apparent, as were Leopold's shortness and ugliness. Outwardly he was exactly the master of Leopold's swooning dreams.

The other differences between them were even more fatal. For Dickie Loeb was, if such a thing exists, a congenital criminal. Subconsciously he sought the catharsis of indirect participation by reading of crime and playing the detective—even as you and I, the readers and writer of this book. But there was too much of it in him, and it overflowed. Where Leopold dreamed of a god to worship, Loeb dreamed of a perfect crime to commit. As Dr. William J. Healy said at their trial, "each supplemented the other's abnormal needs in a most unique way." And as Dr. William Alanson White put it, Leopold would never have committed the crime alone; he had no basic criminal tendencies as Loeb had: but Loeb "would never have gone as far as he did without Leopold to give him the final push."

When these two potential monsters met, at thirteen and fourteen, Leopold instantly fell in love with Loeb, and begged him for a pederastic relation. Loeb was rather repelled by the idea (though his ending proved that he was at least bisexual if not exclusively homosexual), but he agreed—on one condition. This was that Leopold should sign with him a formal compact, agreeing, in exchange for sexual favors, to enter into a career of crime with his lover.

For four years both sides of the compact were kept—interrupted, however, by violent quarrels, by threats of murder on both sides and threats of suicide on Loeb's. Loeb was obsessed by the glories of crime; he who seemed so frank, honest, and lovable was actually an incorrigible thief, who lied and cheated as if by instinct. Kleptomania has a deep underground connection with sexual aberrance, and it was the form that Loeb's sexual disturbance naturally took. So he and Leopold, under Dickie's leadership always, committed petty thefts, devised a system of cheating at bridge, set small fires and turned in false alarms, perpetrated acts of vandalism. They were caught sometimes, but they were never taken seriously, never punished or stopped.

In Loeb's mind all this was the merest apprenticeship. He longed to commit, and get away with, the perfect crime. Leopold, no criminal at heart, nevertheless found the commission of such a crime quite consonant with his Nietzschean philosophy. "The Superman," he wrote to Loeb, "is not liable for anything he may do, except for the one crime that it is possible for him to commit—to make a mistake."

In 1924 the four-year relationship was about to be broken up. Leopold was going to Europe on a vacation trip, and from there to Harvard. Loeb began to cast about in his mind for a "new pal" who would be his accomplice when he and Babe parted. But first, here was the final opportunity for them to reach the criminal heights together—to carry away with them the memory of having accomplished the ultimate, the supreme, the never suspected felony.

The whole thing was considered and planned like a scientific experiment—which, indeed, in some sort they felt it to be. No hatred, no revenge, was involved—even profit was not the motive, though they certainly intended to profit financially by it. After long discussion they decided that the apex in crime was kidnapping, murder, and the collection of ransom. An essential feature was that the ransom was to be collected *after* the murder, while the victim's family was still being assured that he was alive. Carefully, they worked out every detail. They made their arrangements for weeks in advance. In fact, they may be said to have begun them the previous November, when they attended a football game at Ann Arbor, and Loeb stole a portable Underwood typewriter from his fraternity house—together with some gold pins, watches, and money, just to keep his hand in. This was the typewriter on which the ransom notes were written. The police stupidity in insisting at first that these notes had been written on a Corona—the only possible explanation being that they thought all portables had the same type—is matched only by some of the other official antics before

Leopold and Loeb confessed, such as reliance on the visions of a clairvoyant and the frantic hunt for a mythical red-haired woman.

They did not want to use Leopold's own car, for obvious reasons. Deviously they set about renting one. First they took a room at the Hotel Morrison under the name of Morton D. Ballard. Then Leopold, as Ballard, "a salesman from Peoria," went to the Rent-A-Car agency and applied to its president, a man named Jacobs, for the hire of a sedan. As reference he gave one Louis Mason, with an address and a telephone number. Mason was Dickie Loeb. He was waiting at the number and gave "Ballard" a fine recommendation. Leopold then paid a $50 deposit, took the car out for two or three hours to establish credit, and was all set to pick it up when it was needed.

Meanwhile they had provided also for the disposition of the proposed ransom. They opened bank accounts, not in their own banks, under the names of Ballard and Mason. The money was to be paid in currency and would probably have been deposited gradually in these accounts.

Next, every afternoon at three o'clock, from April to the week of May 15th, the two of them boarded a Michigan Central train, buying tickets to Michigan City. Standing in the observation car Loeb, the athlete, practiced throwing off packages of the right dimensions and weight at the spot selected by Leopold (who knew this territory well from his ornithological and botanical trips).

By May 20th the boys were almost ready. They took out the rented car and after lunch they went to a near-by hardware store, at 43rd Street and Cottage Avenue, and bought a chisel, some rope, and hydrochloric acid. (There had been some discussion whether hydrochloric or sulphuric acid was better for destroying the identity of their victim, and they finally agreed on hydrochloric.) The first plan was to garrote the chosen victim, each of them holding one end of the rope so that each would be equally guilty. The chisel was a second choice, but proved to be the correct one.

From a medicine chest in Leopold's house, the next afternoon, May

21st, they got adhesive tape with which to bind the chisel to make it easier to hold. At Leopold's home they also collected a lap-robe, some cloth rags to use as a gag, and hip boots, since the place selected to hide the corpse was in a swamp. Each boy carried a loaded pistol in case of emergency. Now everything was prepared. The ransom notes were already written—all but the name on them.

The one thing they had *not* arranged in advance was the victim.

The only important requisite was that he must be a boy, small and weak enough for them to overpower easily, since neither Leopold nor Loeb had much physical courage. The victim must also possess a wealthy father, able and willing to pay out $10,000, the sum the boys had fixed upon as proper ransom.

They talked over possibilities but could find nobody who exactly fitted their qualifications. The two discussed Loeb's young brother Tommy but decided it would be difficult for Dickie to collect ransom from his own family without being caught. Next they thought of Billy Deutsch, a grandson of the famous philanthropist Julius Rosenwald, president of Sears, Roebuck; but they dropped him because Loeb's father was vice-president of the firm, and it "would hurt the business." Then they played with the idea of taking on their close friend Dick Rubel, with whom they had lunch three times a week, but vetoed him because his father was a notorious tightwad.

Finally they decided to cruise around the Harvard Preparatory School (Loeb's own former school), across the street from Leopold's home, and see what could be found. Some boys were playing outside and they quickly settled on one of the right size whom they knew by sight, Johnnie Levison. But the pair were not sure of his address, so they drove away to look it up in the phone book. When they returned they couldn't find him. They got Leopold's spyglasses, continued hunting for Johnnie, located him, and started to follow him home, but he went up an alley and disappeared.

Both got out of the car and scouted around. Leopold reported some boys near by on Ellis Avenue, so they drove there. The first one sighted was Bobbie Franks, just fourteen, a distant relative of Loeb's. Leopold scarcely knew him by sight but Loeb had often played tennis with Bobbie. Later Babe called him "a nice little boy," but apparently Dickie didn't like him much. When, in the early days of the police hunt, he was excitedly "helping" detectives and reporters to search for Bobbie's murderer, he blurted out: "If I were going to pick out a boy to kidnap or murder, that's just the kind of cocky little son-of-a-bitch I would pick." But Bobbie wasn't picked because Dickie disliked him; any other boy who met the specifications would have done just as well. Robert Franks was small, his father was a millionaire retired box manufacturer, Jacob Franks; so he fitted excellently.

When they spotted Bobbie, Loeb called him over to the car and invited him for a ride. Bobbie declined; he was about to go home, and he didn't know Leopold. Dickie asked him to get in for a minute to talk about a new tennis racket. Unsuspecting, Bobbie climbed in.

After Leopold and Loeb had confessed, there was at first but one discrepancy in their stories. Loeb insisted that he had been driving the car; that Leopold had sat behind and had hit Bobbie Franks over the head with the chisel. He refused to demonstrate the murder method unless he could sit in the driver's seat of their rented car, parked in the yard of the police station. Leopold, disgusted, called Loeb "only a weakling, after all," and said (which was the truth, as Loeb himself acknowledged later) that it had been he who had driven the car and Loeb who had done the actual killing.

In broad daylight, on a crowded street, the rope strangulation had been out of the question. Loeb struck Bobbie from behind four times and the boy fell to the floor of the car, streaming with blood from the gashes in his head. The murderers stuffed his mouth with the rags they had brought—it was a needless gesture as he became unconscious immediately—and let him lie there and slowly bleed to death.

Meanwhile they were driving around aimlessly, waiting for it to grow dark enough to hide the body. Once they stopped for a slight snack, leaving the corpse in the auto. So that his family wouldn't worry about him, Leopold also phoned his home, saying he would be back late. Later they went to a restaurant and ate a hearty dinner.

When darkness came at last, the two killers drove to 118th Street and the Panhandle tracks, where a concrete culvert, or drain pipe, opened from a swamp not far from the highway. At one time they had thought of throwing the body into Lake Michigan, and had brought along some bricks from a building going up near the Harvard Preparatory School with which to weight it. Now the bricks weren't needed so they threw them away. Bobbie's shoes, stockings, and trousers were removed in the car, he was wrapped in the lap-robe, and carried out to the edge of the swamp. There they stripped him completely and Loeb poured the acid on his face and body. Loeb carried the clothes back to the car while Leopold changed into hip boots, after taking off his coat to give himself more freedom of movement, and stuffed the body into the drain pipe with his foot. They had been carrying it around so long that *rigor mortis* had set in, so it was a hard job. Their belief was that the corpse would not be discovered for a long time, probably not until after it had been reduced to an unidentifiable skeleton. In the darkness neither noticed that one naked foot protruded.

The job done, they drove to Leopold's house, leaving the car parked next door to a large apartment house. Bobbie's blood had seeped through the lap-robe and the upholstery was spotted with blood. They hid the lap-robe temporarily in the yard, burned some of the clothing in the furnace, and addressed the already typed ransom letter.

Then they started out again. They drove to a country spot in nearby northern Indiana, and buried Bobbie's shoes, belt-buckle and class-pin—everything which had metal in it. When they got back to the city, Leopold telephoned the Franks home. He asked for the father, but got Bobbie's worried mother instead; the family had been trying to learn where Bobbie was ever since he had failed to return in time for dinner at half-past six.

"Your boy has been kidnapped," the strange voice told her calmly. "He is safe and unharmed." He added the usual threat that if the police were informed the boy would be killed at once, and told the parents they would receive a ransom letter the next day.

The distracted father, when he arrived to hear this news, communicated at once with his attorney. By his advice, Mr. Franks did tell the police, but secured their promise to avoid any publicity for the present. The next morning the ransom note came by special delivery. It was signed "George Johnson." It directed Mr. Franks to prepare $10,000—$2,000 in $20 bills, $8,000 in 50's, all old, unmarked money— and to put it in a small cigar box or a heavy cardboard box, wrapped in white paper sealed with sealing wax. The kidnapper would phone further instruction after one p.m.

In the meantime, Leopold and Loeb had been very busy. There was still much to do. They had concluded the previous evening at Leopold's house, playing cards till midnight, when Babe drove Dickie home. Now, this morning, they drove the rented car into Leopold's garage and set to work trying to wash the blood spots off the upholstery. The chauffeur, a man named Englund, noticed them, and was told they had spilled red wine in the car. They took the hidden lap-robe to a vacant lot in the outskirts of the city and burned it. Next, they drove to Jackson Park and Loeb twisted the keys off the typewriter. They threw the keys in one lagoon, the rest of the machine in another.

Next, they went to the Illinois Central station and Loeb boarded the Michigan Central train they had taken so often in the past few weeks. In the telegram slot of the stationery desk of the observation car he placed another letter, written long beforehand as the ransom note had been, but now addressed in ink to Jacob Franks. On the outside was written: "Should anyone else find this note, please leave it alone. The letter is very important."

It contained Franks's instructions for delivering the ransom money. He was to wait until the train passed "the first LARGE red brick factory on the east side of the track, with a black water tower with CHAM-PION printed on it. Wait till you have completely passed the south end of the factory, count five, and then immediately throw the package as far east as you can." This letter was found, when the train had reached New Haven, by Andy Russo, a yard electrician.

Loeb got off the train at 63rd Street, where he rejoined Leopold. Leopold then telephoned Jacob Franks, saying he was "George Johnson," and told Franks to take a taxi that was being sent to his house and to go to a drugstore on East 63rd Street, where he would be told by telephone what to do next. Franks was told that if he had already disobeyed orders and informed the police, then he must keep these further developments from them or his son would be killed. He must be alone, have the money with him, and see to it that the public phone was kept clear.

Leopold then called the Yellow Cab Company and ordered a taxi sent to the Franks home. The two youths drove about until they felt Franks had had time to reach the drugstore, then Leopold phoned there and asked for Franks. He had not arrived. Leopold phoned three times without results. That worried them, for there was now barely time for Franks to catch the train.

It was at this moment that they saw newspaper extras announcing that Bobbie's body had been found and identified.

A railroad maintenance man had seen the protruding foot. He notified the police, who got in touch with Jacob Franks. Franks, with a pathetic belief in the word of the kidnapper who had phoned and written him, refused to agree that this might be Bobbie's corpse but he did send his brother-in-law to view the body. Five minutes before the taxi arrived at the Franks's door, the brother-in-law had reported his identification.

The city, which was inured to gang massacres but not to atrocious murders of children, was in an uproar. Jacob Franks was a rich and prominent business man, one of a group of millionaires of German Jewish descent—many of them related by blood or marriage—living in the exclusive Kenwood district. These people had much influence, and they spurred the hunt. Arrests were made wholesale. The usual psychopaths "confessed." The clairvoyant came forward and her tips were followed. Some of the innocent people picked up and questioned (including two teachers at the Harvard Preparatory School) were ruined for life by the notoriety.

Leopold sat tight and said nothing, but Loeb became feverishly active. He carried around clippings about the case, he could talk of nothing else. Franks, in his bewilderment and grief, had forgotten the address of the drugstore to which he had been directed to go; it was Dickie who suggested questioning all drugstores on 63rd Street until they found the one—as they did—that had received a phone call asking for Jacob Franks.

There were few useful clues. Somebody found the bricks, somebody else found the bloodstained taped chisel. The police made the absurd error of deciding the notes were typed on a Corona and arrested a typewriter repair man who had been carrying one around near the school. Bobbie's clothing had disappeared. There was no success in tracing the phone calls, which had all been made from public booths. The officials continued to arrest people almost at random.

And then, near the culvert where the body had been found, a pair of horn-rimmed glasses was picked up. By May 30th they had been traced to Almer Coe and Company. Mr. Coe and his associate, Jacob Weinstein, said that they had sold only three pairs with these unusual rims. One had gone to a lawyer who was now in Europe. A second had been sold to a woman who, when interviewed by the police, was wearing them. The third had been purchased by Nathan F. Leopold, Jr.

Leopold readily admitted that the glasses were his—or that they could be his, if he wasn't sure his own were at his home. He seldom wore or carried them, he said. At the request of Police Captain Wolff, he searched his room for them but found only the case. Then Leopold said he must have dropped them from his coat-pocket during one of his ornithological trips, many of which had been made in that general neighborhood. He recalled having stumbled once or twice and the loss must have happened then. But when by request he put his glasses in his pocket and then stumbled deliberately, they did not fall from his coat pocket. When he took off his coat and lifted it by the tail, they did. What really must have happened was that when he called to Loeb to carry his coat back to the car, while he was changing back from his boots to shoes, the glasses fell without either of them noticing.

Asked what he had been doing on Wednesday, May 21st, Leopold said he had been driving with Loeb in his own car and that in the evening they had taken two girls for a ride in Lincoln Park. Loeb, questioned a day later, said he couldn't remember what he had done. This was by previous arrangement; if they were questioned within a week or so of the crime, they were to give the prepared alibi; if later, they were to say they had forgotten Wednesday's events.

Rather apologetically, State's Attorney Robert E. Crowe took both youths into custody and held them for further questioning. Crowe said this was being done "merely out of prudence," and the boys' fathers agreed, confident that their sons could easily clear themselves of any suspicion. Crowe held them as his personal prisoners in the Hotel LaSalle, instead of taking them to the Cook County jail.

Soon each became snarled in contradictions. The chauffeur, Englund, revealed that Leopold's car had been in the garage for repairs all day of the twenty-first. Other discrepancies piled up until first Loeb and then Leopold made full confessions.

The news that the boys had confessed came as a terrific shock to their families. Loeb's father, already an invalid, died two months after his son was sentenced. Very probably his death was largely caused by his grief and shame. So long as he lived he never again spoke Dickie's name or allowed it to be mentioned in his presence. Loeb's mother refused to visit him in jail until Clarence Darrow persuaded her to come for one unsatisfactory interview. Leopold's father was equally shaken and horrified. These parents had reared their sons to feel that their immense wealth gave them immunity from the obligations and standards of society, yet saw no connection between such an upbringing and the crime.

Both families did rally to the defense so far as legal help was concerned. While the two were only being held "out of prudence" for questioning, the services of Loeb's first cousins, Walter and Benjamin C. Bachrach, both well-known attorneys, were thought sufficient. But when they confessed and were indicted on two charges of kidnapping and murder, there was only one man who could possibly save them from execution. That man was Clarence Darrow.

Darrow was probably the most famous and the best criminal defense lawyer in America. He was the champion of the underdog and he had saved 102 accused murderers from the gallows. He was a convinced oppponent of the death penalty, and his avowed object was "while the state was trying Loeb and Leopold, to try capital punishment." Leopold himself wrote that Darrow's advocacy was "more than bravery; it is heroism."

For the news that Darrow was to be the chief defense attorney loosed a tremendous wave of popular fury. Darrow was accused of having sold out—he who had always defended the poor and defenseless. It was prophesied that he would have the boys declared insane; then, after a few comfortable years in some luxurious private asylum, their families would secure their freedom by bribery. The rumor was that Darrow was to receive $1,000,000 for his defense. As a matter of fact, no sum was agreed upon in advance; Darrow waited seven months after the trial for his fee, with all reminders unanswered. Finally he was paid $30,000, with the remark that "the world is full of eminent lawyers who would have paid a fortune for the chance to distinguish themselves in this case." This from the same man who had literally thrown himself on his knees to beg Darrow to undertake the defense!

There was only one bright aspect to this sorry story. There was no opportunity (as would have been only too easy, in the inflamed state of popular opinion) to inject the issue of anti-Semitism into the case. The victim as well as everybody else concerned in it (except Loeb's mother) was Jewish.

Darrow decided to plead his clients guilty to both charges. He knew he had no chance whatever before a jury; he was also preventing bringing up of the charges separately and so risking a capital sentence on one charge if not on the other.

The judge on whom rested the whole of this dreadful responsibility was John R. Caverly, Chief Justice of the Criminal Court of Cook County, who had long been a judge of the circuit and municipal courts and had helped to establish the juvenile court in Chicago. The defendants pleaded guilty on July 21, 1924. Two days later the trial began, with the prosecution in the hands of Crowe and his assistants, Thomas Marshall and Joseph B. Savage. Darrow's chief associates were the Bachrach brothers.

The trial lasted thirty-three days. Darrow's concluding speech and the final speech of the chief prosecutor took up three days apiece. Crowe had to ask for frequent recesses, in the Chicago summer weather, to change his sweat-soaked clothing and have an alcohol rub.

The Chicago papers and those of the whole nation—and outside it—ran thousands of columns on the case. The courtroom was packed daily, and crowds were turned away. Judge Caverly was the recipient of hundreds of threatening letters (as was Darrow), in which Leopold and Loeb were called unspeakable names, the mildest of which were "rattlesnakes" and "mad dogs." Charges that Darrow had made sure of a "friendly judge" infuriated Caverly, who called them "a cowardly and dastardly assault upon the integrity of this court."

Against all this, Clarence Darrow stood alone, pleading for reason and justice and mercy against the unthinking rage of a public bent on vengeance.

The judge agreed to listen to evidence in mitigation of the crime. The defense tried hard to prevent the presentation of evidence on details of the killing, but the prosecution got around that by claiming that these details demonstrated the "state of mind" of the defendants. Darrow and his associates did not cross-examine any of the state's witnesses and the only lay witnesses they called were a dozen or so of the boys' schoolmates, to testify to their abnormality of mind. The defendants were not, Darrow alleged, technically "insane," but they were demonstrably "mentally diseased."

Both sides brought in a battery of psychiatric aces; of these, the real stars were those who testified for the defense. Darrow's experts included an endrocrinologist, and it was easy for him to show how much both of the defendants, and Leopold especially, were suffering from abnormalities of the endocrine glands. It was not the minds of the pair, it was their bodies and their "moral sense" that were corrupted. Loeb and Leopold were moral imbeciles—what is called nowadays psychopathic personalities.

The fact shown most clearly by the painstaking researches of the psychiatrists called by Darrow was that, inherently, Leopold had no criminal bent. He followed blindly wherever his lord and master led him, but he had little of Loeb's cold cruelty. When little Bobbie Franks slumped down in the car, it was Leopold who cried: "Oh, God, I didn't know it would be like this!" But Loeb, when he chanced to pass the Franks home as his victim's coffin was being borne out of the house by "small white-faced boys," merely felt, for a brief moment, "a little bit uncomfortable."

But in the eyes of the prosecution there could be no mitigation. Crowe exclaimed that if Darrow won, "a greater blow had been struck to our institutions than by a hundred, aye, a thousand murders! . . . There is nothing wrong with them mentally. The only fault is the trouble with their moral sense, and *that is not a defence in a criminal case.*" (Italics mine.)

To Darrow, it took "something more than brains to make a human being who can adjust himself to life." He was fighting, not for the lives of two miserable, maladjusted boys, but for the triumph of reason and mercy over the barbarity of "a life for a life." In his great concluding speech, a classic of legal pleading, he said:

"I know the future is with me, and what I stand for here; not merely for the lives of these two unfortunate lads, but for all boys and all girls; for all the young; as far as possible, for all the old. I am pleading for life, understanding, charity, kindness, and the infinite mercy that considers all."

If Judge Caverly ordered Leopold and Loeb to hang, Darrow cried, he would be turning his face toward the past, "making it harder for every other boy who in ignorance and darkness must grope his way through the mazes which only childhood knows. . . . I am pleading for the future; I am pleading for a time when hatred and cruelty will not control the hearts of men, when we can learn by reason and judgment and understanding and faith that all life is worth living and that mercy is the highest attribute of man. . . . If I can succeed, my greatest reward and my greatest hope will be that I have done something for the tens of thousands of other boys, for the countless unfortunates who must tread the same road in blind childhood . . . something to help human understanding, to temper justice with mercy, to overcome hate with love."

Judge Caverly took until October 10th to pronounce sentence. Then he condemned both defendants to life imprisonment on the murder charge, and to ninety-nine years on the kidnapping charge, "not because they are abnormal or because they pleaded guilty, but solely because they are under age." He recommended that neither of them should ever be paroled. And he added: "To the offenders, particularly for the type they are, the prolonged suffering of years of confinement may well be the severer form of retribution and expiation."

The judge made it plain that he did not consider this case a test for others involving psychopaths, and that he felt himself bound only by the legal precedent that boys in their teens were not ordinarily sentenced to execution. He did say that the psychiatric evidence presented by the defense was "a contribution to the study of criminology." He was eminently fair. Apparently he was uninfluened by Darrow's arguments. He was not lenient and he did not recommend leniency. His insistence on lifelong imprisonment for both defendants was sufficient demonstration of his viewpoint.

Loeb and Leopold were both sent to the Northern Illinois Penitentiary, at Stateville (usually called Joliet because it is near that city). Little was heard of them until February, 1936. Then Loeb was killed by another convict, James Day.

Leopold and Loeb had not been kept apart in prison. Leopold had been a teacher in the prison school and a nurse in the prison hospital. In 1933 he and Loeb were allowed together to inaugurate a correspondence school for inmates. Day, a bantamweight prizefighter in for larceny, was given a clerical job in this school, of which Loeb was registrar. Loeb made homosexual advances to him; Day spurned him and

Loeb was persistent. The prison wing was being remodeled, and in the confusion some inmates were using an officers' shower-room in violation of rules. Loeb, armed with a razor he had stolen from the barber shop, cornered Day in this room. Desperate, Day kicked Loeb in the groin, then grabbed the razor from him and in a frenzy slashed him fifty-six times. Loeb, as blood-covered as had been little Bobbie Franks on that day nearly twelve years before, managed to get the door opened and staggered naked into the corridor, where he collapsed.

His mother, by permission of Warden James Ragen, rushed the family physician to the prison. Leopold stood by Loeb's bed in the prison hospital, and heard him whisper, "I think I'm going to make it." But his jugular vein had been severed, and he died soon after. A hearse with its plates covered was sent for his body, and police kept out the curious crowds at the funeral parlor and the cemetery. There were wild rumors that the whole thing was a fake; that the killing had been an invention and that the Loeb family had plotted a successful escape. But that was nonsense; Dickie Loeb was dead. Day was tried for murder and acquitted on the ground of self-defense.

So now only Nathan Leopold was left. He had been a model prisoner. He kept up his studies in half a dozen fields, eventually securing a Ph.D. for a thesis on ornithology. He continued to carry on the prison correspondence school after Loeb's death. In 1924 Darrow had said that both boys should be "permanently isolated from society." But later in his defense he remarked that he was not without hope that "when life and age have changed their bodies and emotions . . . at the next stage of life, at forty-five or so," they might be fit to be free. Leopold at forty-six, in his own words, had been "an irresponsible youth, but [was] now a new man."

By Illinois law, a life prisoner is eligible for parole after twenty years. A prisoner sentenced to a specific term of years is eligible after a third of his sentence has expired. According to this, on the 99-year kidnapping sentence, Leopold could not apply for parole until 1957. In 1949 he petitioned for a reduction of this sentence. The Parole Board turned him down.

But during World War II, Leopold was one of the volunteers at Joliet who permitted themselves to be inoculated with experimental sera in studies of the treatment of malaria, and he became seriously ill as a result. These volunteers had all been promised reduction of their sentences. So on September 22, 1949 the board reduced his kidnapping sentence to 85 years, making him eligible for parole at the end of 1952. Adlai Stevenson, then governor of Illinois, approved the ruling. Darrow had died in 1938 and could not be consulted.

From 1953 on, the board kept refusing his application. Early in 1958 his autobiography, *Life Plus 99 Years*, was published and became almost a best seller. Royalties from it went to support a foundation to aid emotionally disturbed, retarded, and delinquent children, under the direction of his new lawyer, Elmer Gertz.

Finally, after five years, his fourth application for parole was granted. "I am a broken old man," he said. (He was fifty-two; he had diabetes and a bad heart.) "I want a chance to find redemption for myself and to help others."

He was released on March 13, 1958, and went to Puerto Rico, where he became a laboratory technician at the Church of the Brethren Hospital in Castaner, and enrolled in the department of social work at the University of Puerto Rico.

In January 1961 Leopold asked that he be discharged from parole to enable him to become a teacher, and also to make it possible for him to marry. The board refused him a full discharge (they finally granted it in March 1963), but they did give permission for his marriage to a widow, Trudi Feldman Garcia deQuevedo, who ran a flower shop in Santurce. They also agreed that he might teach if the Puerto Rico authorities approved. A month after his marriage in February he was appointed a lecturer at the university, under a special dispensation by Governor Luis Munoz Marin.

He taught mathematics in night school while he worked for his M.A. in social work; his thesis was on alcoholism and its relation to criminality. Now he is director of a research project for the Puerto Rican Department of Health, which is studying parasites. In 1963 he came back to Chicago for the first time since 1924, to attend a national convention on tropical diseases and hygiene. At the same time he is working on a book which will deal with "the relation between penal methods and parole administration as they affect readjustment of the paroled prisoner."

The whole course of Nathan Leopold's later life goes to verify the judgment that his extremely high mental endowment was accompanied by an equally extreme psychic disturbance which was finally outgrown. Whether Richard Loeb, with a rather less brilliant mind and a still more marked emotional disorder, would ever have been able to rehabilitate himself as Leopold has done, is exceedingly doubtful.

Murders Sane and Mad, 1965

W. T. BRANNON

That the enormity perpetrated by Richard Speck became the basis for a world-famous painting—the 1966 group portrait *Eight Student Nurses* by German artist Gerhard Richter—is indicative not only of the international shockwaves set off by the crime but of its resonance as a cultural symbol. In its sheer nihilistic savagery, it seemed to epitomize a decade in the throes of a violent social breakdown.

The following gripping account of the Speck murders and their aftermath is the work of William Tibbetts Brannon (1906–1981), one of the most prolific true-crime writers of his time. Under various pseudonyms he turned out thousands of stories and articles for pulp mystery and detective magazines in the course of his 50-year career. To his peers, who recognized his achievements with multiple Edgar Awards, he was known as "The Dean of American Crime Writers"—the "grandest of Grand Old Pros in fact-crime," as Anthony Boucher called him.

As for Richard Speck, the jury at his April 1967 trial found him guilty after deliberating for less than an hour. He escaped the death penalty when it was declared unconstitutional by the U.S. Supreme Court in 1972 and died in prison of a heart attack in December 1991, one day before his 50th birthday.

Eight Girls, All Pretty, All Nurses, All Slain

Shortly before 10 a.m., Thursday, July 14, 1966, the Chicago newspaper truck darted northward on Clark Street and jolted to a stop at the Belmont Avenue intersection just ahead of a bus. The bus driver grumbled a little, but halted behind the truck.

A bundle of papers was dropped off and the newsie hurried to open it. The headline was tall and black, visible even to the bus driver. He couldn't believe what he saw and he opened the door and got out for a better look.

Now, the bus riders were beginning to grumble. The driver, visibly shaken, held up a copy of the paper so that the passengers could see what had taken him away from his post behind the wheel.

Now the passengers, their gripes forgotten, streamed off the bus. They snatched up papers fast as the newsboy could pass them out. It was there in cold print, but they found it hard to believe. It was something they just couldn't take in.

Standing there on the street, before the open door of the bus, they read the sparse details. It had happened more than 20 miles away on the far southeast side in the 2300 block of East 100th Street. And the lone killer had escaped.

Somewhere on the streets of Chicago, he was at large, a menace to every woman who still lived. The men shuddered, some of the women wept as they filed back on the bus. They were like most other Chicagoans; they had become inured to the atmosphere of crime that had cloaked the city ever since the days of Capone.

They were blasé about gang killings and they had even learned to shrug off multiple slayings. But this was neither. It was mass murder—it was massacre. . . .

Harried Chicago police had their troubles. On Tuesday evening, July 12th, a fire hydrant was opened at Roosevelt Road and Throop Street, in a predominantly Negro district. As required by law, some policemen shut it off. A teenager opened it up again and he was arrested.

A minor riot erupted, some store fronts were kicked in and there was looting until police reinforcements restored order. The next night the weather had cooled—but tempers hadn't. The rioting flared anew, with bands of young hoodlums roving westside streets, breaking windows and looting.

After a hurried conference among top police officials, Deputy Superintendent James B. Conlisk ordered Plan 3 to go into effect at 6 p.m., Thursday. This meant that every man on the force would be working a 12-hour day, that the police department itself would operate on two 12-hour shifts instead of the usual three watches of eight hours.

Plans were quickly made for shifting 1,000 policemen to the riot-torn west side. In many areas, where the crime rate was low, one man would be withdrawn from every two-man squad. In most of the districts, this would make no difference.

Such a section was the neighborhood known as Jeffrey Manor, part of the larger area of the city called South Chicago. In Jeffrey Manor there are many single residences, homes of one and two stories.

It is a quiet area of friendly people where crime is unusual and violence is a virtual stranger. This was particularly true of the 2300 block of East 100th Street. On the south side of this block is a complex of town houses, six two-story units in one connected building.

Three of these—the one at the east end and the two adjoining it on the west—have been rented by South Chicago Community Hospital to house 24 student nurses, eight in each unit, because there was not enough room in the regular nurses' residence at the hospital. All 24 of the nurses were senior students or registered nurses taking graduate studies. In the third unit from the end lived a housemother, whose duty it was to supervise the coming and going of the young nurses, all in their early twenties.

Of all the streets in quiet Jeffrey Manor, this block probably was the most trouble-free, a section that seldom required police attention.

It was, that is, until Thursday, July 14th.

About six o'clock that morning, Commander Francis Flanagan, chief of Chicago homicide detectives, was getting ready to go to his office in the main police building on South State Street when the call came.

There was a lot of excitement in the town houses in the 2300 block of East 100th Street. At least one student nurse had been murdered. There had been several calls from residents of the area.

"What about the coroner?" Flanagan asked.

"He's been notified."

"And the crime lab?"

"They're on the way."

"Better call Dragel—he lives down this way," Flanagan said, referring to Director Daniel T. Dragel of the police crime lab. "I'm on my way."

Commander Flanagan himself lives in Jeffrey Manor and his home is only three blocks from the town houses. He knew the location well and he walked to the scene in about five minutes.

Already, two police cars were there and many residents, attracted by the unusual activity, had surrounded the end town house. As Flanagan started in the front door, he met Patrolman Daniel Kelly of the South Chicago, District Station.

Kelly and Patrolman Leonard Ponne recognized Flanagan. Kelly pointed to a couch against the west wall of what was the downstairs living room. Face down lay the nude body of a young girl, a strip torn from a bedsheet tightly knotted about her neck.

"There are seven more upstairs," Kelly said.

"*Seven more girls?*"

"I know it's hard to believe," Kelly replied, struggling to keep his composure. "Maybe you'd better take a look for yourself."

Flanagan did look. In the second floor hall outside the bathroom he found one body. The girl was in night clothes that now were crimson. She apparently had been stabbed repeatedly and lay in a pool of her own blood.

Now in his twentieth year as a homicide detective, Flanagan is a veteran of 4,000 murder investigations in the city that has been called the crime capital of the world. After disputing that label for two decades, Flanagan wasn't so sure now.

Lines began creasing is normally good-natured features as he turned to his right and entered the bedroom at the end of the hall. Here he found three girls, stacked one upon another in the narrow floor space between the bunk bed and the door.

All these girls had been stabbed and a wide, irregular pool of blood surrounded them. Flanagan, who had been an Air Force pilot during World War II with 55 missions over Germany, was reminded of the gory slaughter in Nazi concentration camps.

The lines of his face deepening so that he was beginning to look much more than his 48 years, Flanagan backed out into the hall and turned left into the adjoining bedroom. Three more bodies of young women lay before his disbelieving eyes.

One was on a bed against the wall. Two others, piled one upon the other, were on the floor between the bed and the dresser. The girl on the bed had been strangled with a strip from a bedsheet and had been stabbed in the left breast.

One of the other girls had been strangled. The other had been strangled, stabbed in the back, in the left eye and in the back of the neck.

Despite his wide experience, Commander Flanagan found this almost beyond belief. He turned away from the corpses, back to Patrolman Kelly. "Tell me all you know about it," he said.

Kelly gave this account:

Several persons in the neighborhood were up early that morning. In addition to the complex of six town houses in one building, there was a building at each end of the block containing three town house units. In one of these lived Mrs. Alfred Windmiller, who awoke about an hour earlier than usual that morning—around six o'clock.

She heard what she thought was a woman screaming, and told her husband. He thought it was one of the neighborhood kids. But Mrs. Windmiller didn't agree and quickly dressed.

From the other end of the block, a nurse, Judy Dykton, who was acquainted with the students, heard the screaming, too. She ran to the end unit, looked in and saw the nude body on the couch in the living room and ran back to phone police and tell the house mother, Mrs. Laura Bisone.

When Mrs. Windmiller went downstairs, she encountered Robert Hall, 52, a supervisor at a steel mill and a resident of one of the town-house units. He was out early walking his dog. Now, both heard the screaming and they hurried to the end unit of the six-unit complex.

A dark-haired girl in night clothes stood on the second floor balcony-like ledge just outside a window from which the screen had been kicked out. She was screaming:

"Help me! Help me! They're all dead. Oh, God! I'm the last one alive on the sampan!" She kept repeating variations of this, sometimes in accented English, sometimes in English so broken it was difficult to understand. Only Miss Dykton knew that the girl was a Filipino and that some of what she was screaming was in her native dialect. Miss Dykton knew she was Corazón Amurao, 23.

"Don't jump!" Mrs. Windmiller cried. "Go back inside and take the stairs and come out the back door."

In addition to Miss Dykton, others in the neighborhood, hearing the girl's hysterical plea for help, had telephoned POlice 5-1313 and the alarm had gone out from the communications center.

Both Mrs. Windmiller and Mr. Hall ran back onto 100th Street and flagged down Patrolman Kelly, who happened to be passing. They quickly told him what little they knew and he, too, saw the girl cringing on the balcony. He shouted for her not to jump and told her he would come inside.

Pausing only to radio the South Chicago police station and ask for help, Kelly tried the front door and found it locked. As he hurried around to the rear, another police car, hailed by Hall, skidded to a stop. Patrolman Leonard Ponne got out.

Kelly had noticed that a screen had been removed from a rear window, but when he tried the back door, he found it unlocked. He entered a kitchen, where he noticed nothing unusual except a sink full of dirty dishes.

He went on through another door into the living room. His glance quickly took it in. Across on the other side was the front door he had tried earlier. To the far right was the stairway leading to the second floor. To the right near the wall was a U-shaped writing desk. In one corner was a TV set.

But what caught Kelly's eye was against the left wall—a two-cushion, reddish orange davenport. Sprawled across it face down was the nude body of a girl. For a moment, Kelly just stood and stared in stunned silence.

Then he strode to the couch, checked to see if there was any chance of saving the girl's life. There was no pulse, the flesh was clammy, but he couldn't tell how long the girl had been dead.

Kelly's wife is a nurse at South Chicago Community Hospital. She was acquainted with all the students and Kelly himself knew some of them. Now, he lifted the head and suffered more shock. He recognized the dead girl as Gloria Jean Davy, 23. Before his marriage, he had dated her as well as her sister; he was acquainted with the family, whose home was in Dyer, Indiana, a small city a few miles across the state line and in the Chicago metropolitan area.

Was the killer still in the building? Was that why the girl was out on the balcony screaming? Patrolman Kelly drew his gun, then called to Patrolman Ponne whose voice he could hear outside.

"Get in here, Lennie," he shouted. "A girl's been killed. Maybe the guy's still in the building."

Ponne hurried into the room, took one look at the dead girl and his mouth dropped open. He, too, quickly drew his service revolver.

"I'll go upstairs, you take the basement," Kelly said.

Both men moved cautiously in opposite directions. But when Kelly had discovered the other seven slain girls, he shouted in a hoarse voice for Ponne, who had found nothing in the basement.

The girl who had cried out the alarm now was framed in the window of one of the bedrooms. Kelly helped her inside.

"Do you know who did this?" he asked.

"One man," she replied in her accented English. She said he was a man she didn't know. But he had killed all her friends.

"Can you describe him? Tell me what he looks like?" Kelly pressed desperately, realizing that the girl was in shock, that she was near hysteria and might crack up at any moment.

She obviously tried hard and she came up with a description: The man was about 25, he weighed about 170 pounds and he had a crew cut. She wasn't sure about the color of his hair—it could have been brown to black. He wore a dark waist-length jacket and dark pants and a white T-shirt. She couldn't remember anything else. And she wanted to get away from this house of horror.

Patrolman Ponne escorted her to the town house unit two doors to the west, where she was turned over to the housemother, Mrs. Bisone. Kelly radioed the description to the communications center.

"I'll want to talk to her," said Commander Flanagan, "but first I'd better call in."

He went outside, where the gathering crowd was growing with each passing moment. The street now was jammed with police cars from which uniformed patrolmen and plainclothes detectives were hurrying toward the town house unit.

In the forefront was Lieutenant John Griffith, commander of the homicide and sex crime unit at Area 2 Detective Headquarters at 92nd and Cottage Grove Avenue, only a short distance away. With him were veteran homicide Detectives Byron Carlisle and Jack Wallenda.

The detectives and patrolmen gently but firmly urged the crowd back and quickly barricaded the area from the sidewalk in front, around the east side of the building to the driveway in the rear. Here, fresh skid marks were visible. Had the killer parked directly behind the town house unit he invaded, then made a fast getaway in a car?

Lieutenant Griffith quickly paired off detectives in teams and sent them to question people in the crowd and anybody who hadn't left his home in the immediate vicinity.

Meanwhile, from the nearest car radio, Commander Flanagan contacted Central Headquarters. He was told that Superintendent of Police Orlando W. Wilson had been notified at his home, as had Chief of Detectives Otto Kreuzer and Dr. Andrew J. Toman, Cook County coroner. Portable crime labs with 10 technicians were on the way.

As he broke the connection, Flanagan turned to Patrolman Kelly and said: "Let's talk to the girl."

She was in the town house two doors away, being comforted by the house mother, Mrs. Bisone. Realizing that she held a possible key to the killer's identity, the attractive, dark-haired, dark-eyed Filipino girl composed herself with some effort and gave Flanagan this account of what had happened:

Late Wednesday evening—she didn't know the exact time, but it was around 11 o'clock—she had changed into her night clothes and was ready for bed. She sat in the smallest bedroom with her friend and roommate, Merlita Gargullo, 23, who had just come from the hospital. There was a rap on the door and Miss Amurao got up to open it.

A tall young man stood there, a knife in one hand, a revolver in the other. "I'm not going to hurt you," he said. "I need your money to get to New Orleans."

Miss Amurao backed away as he stepped across the threshold.

"I'm not going to hurt you," he repeated. "I just want your money."

Gesturing with the gun and knife, he ordered the girls out into the hall and directed them to go into the next bedroom, where there were four other girls. All six were told to lie face down on the floor.

Faced with the gun and knife the girls complied. He pulled a sheet off one of the beds and expertly tore it into strips, which were used to bind the girls' wrists. In addition to Miss Amurao and Miss Gargullo, the others tied up were Patricia Matusek, 20, whose home was in Chicago; Pamela Wilkening, 20, of suburban Lansing; Nina Schmale, 24, of Wheaton, a suburb to the west; and Valentina Pasion, 23, of the Philippines.

The intruder had barely finished tying up the six girls when there was a noise downstairs as the front door opened and closed. Then the captive girls could hear the voice of Gloria Jean Davy, 23, a brunette beauty who was president of the Student Nurses' Association of Illinois, as she talked on the house phone in the kitchen and told the house mother that she was home safe from a date.

She came upstairs, only to be greeted by the man with the knife and gun. He ordered her to lie down with the other girls. She did and he bound her wrists.

He talked to the girls in a slow, pleasant voice, again assuring them that he did not intend to harm them. While he was talking the front door opened and two more girls came in. One was Suzanne Farris, 22, who lived in the town house. The other was Mary Ann Jordan, also 22, a student nurse who was visiting.

There was more than the usual bond of friendship between the two girls. Mary Ann's brother was engaged to be married to Suzanne. Mary Ann normally slept in the nurses' residence near the hospital, but she had obtained permission to visit tonight with Suzanne in the town house. She would spend the night.

The girls went into the kitchen, phoned the house mother and told her they were in for the night. They went upstairs to their bedrooms and changed to night clothes. Then the man with his knife and gun appeared and herded them in with the other girls—nine in all, now.

The young man seemed in no hurry. He told the girls again that he was not going to harm them, that he merely had tied them up until he could get their money, which he needed to make his way to New Orleans.

Whether they believed him or not, they kept quiet and didn't scream. Miss Amurao didn't believe him; she was terrified and kept thinking of what she might do to escape.

The young man stood up, gestured to one of the girls, and led her out of the room. He was gone a few minutes, then came back and escorted a second girl out of the room. By this time, Miss Amurao was convinced that their lives were in danger. She managed to roll under the bunk bed, out of sight. She huddled there against the wall, scarcely daring to breathe. She was aware of the man as he made other trips out of the room, each time leading one of the girls.

She wondered when he would miss her and start looking. But miraculously, he didn't. She lay quiet, still too terrified to make a move, and the night passed. Was the man still in the house? What had happened to her friends?

In one of the rooms, an alarm clock went off. She knew it was five o'clock. It went off every morning at that time to awaken some of the students who had to report at the hospital early.

Miss Amurao thought if the man was still in the house that he surely would be frightened by the alarm clock. She listened as it ran down and stopped and she stayed under the bed for another half hour trying to detect some sound of movement.

But there was none and she decided now that it was safe to try to get out and find out what had happened. She struggled with her bonds and finally her wrists were free. She crawled out from under the bed and walked soundlessly out into the hall. The body of a nurse lay half in, half out of the bathroom door.

She looked into a bedroom and saw three more bodies. In the front bedroom were three more. She stepped over them, kicked out the screen and stepped out onto the balcony where she began crying for help.

She bit back the tears as she concluded her account, forcing herself to remain composed until Flanagan had finished writing his notes.

"Do you think you'll know this man if you ever see him again?" the homicide chief asked.

She said she was sure she would.

"Is there anything else you can think of?" Flanagan asked.

Yes, she said; she was sure that the man had been drinking heavily before he invaded the town house. The stale odor of alcohol created a stench every time the man talked.

She repeated the description she already had given Patrolman Kelly. There still was confusion about the color of the stranger's hair, perhaps because of the survivor's overwrought condition.

Meanwhile, hospital authorities had been notified of the savage slaughter and an official hurried to the scene. He said he thought Miss Amurao should be in a room in the hospital and that he would arrange for it.

"Okay, we'll get her over there," the homicide chief replied. "But since she is the only known witness, her life may be in danger. The killer may try to get at her, even in a hospital room. We must see that she's fully protected."

The hospital official explained why the girls had been in the town house, some seven blocks north of the hospital. He said that the nurses' residence was full and that some outside quarters had to be found. It had been decided to put only girls in their senior year or graduate students in the town houses, because they were more mature and they would be in less danger than younger girls.

However, because of the character of the neighborhood and its low crime rate, none of the hospital officials had suspected the girls were in danger. A house mother supervised the three units in each of which were eight students.

Among those living in the end unit, he said, were three Filipino girls. Each was a graduate of a nursing school in the Philippine Republic and each had come to Chicago for graduate study under the State Department's exchange program. Miss Amurao and the two others—both slain—in the end unit had begun their duties at the South Chicago Hospital on June 5th. He said there were many other Filipino nurses in Chicago, over 100 distributed among 10 hospitals.

When Commander Flanagan went back outside, he discovered that the area was crawling with policemen. Director Dan Dragel of the crime lab was there with 10 of his technicians and they already had started dusting likely surfaces for fingerprints.

From the evidence, said Dragel, it appeared that the killer had come in the back by removing a screen and had left via the rear door which Patrolman Kelly had found unlocked.

From the start, the technicians began to develop prints. They were all over the place and undoubtedly many had been made by the victims.

Their prints would be taken for later comparison and elimination, but first, the hapless girls received the attention of Dr. Toman and his battery of six pathologists—Drs. David Petty, John Belmonte, Edwin Hirsch, James W. Henry, Walter John Miller and Eugene H. Tapia.

They entered the building with Dr. Toman, a hospital employe, and homicide Detectives Carlisle and Wallenda. They began a careful, professional preliminary examination after each girl had been identified by the hospital employe.

Meanwhile, Deputy Chief of Detectives Michael Spiotto, who would have overall direction, with Flanagan, of the entire investigation, had arrived. First, he took a look at the carnage. Then he went back outside to talk to Flanagan and plan the investigation.

Now, after a quick conference with Flanagan, it was decided that all leaves in the detective division would be canceled. Sixty men reporting for duty at Area 2 Detective Headquarters at eight o'clock that morning would be assigned to the case. They would be backed up by 80 other detectives to be detailed to Area 2 Headquarters from various other detective headquarters throughout the city.

It was also agreed that Spiotto and Flanagan would set up a command post in the Area 2 building. Here, on the sprawling second floor, additional telephones would be installed in the offices to be used by Spiotto and Flanagan as well as in other offices and the big assembly room that occupied a large part of the floor.

Already, reporters and photographers from five Chicago daily papers and from four television and radio networks were swelling the crowd outside the town house and the two veteran officials knew that more would be at the command post.

The place would be crowded, but they would make room. Both Flanagan and Spiotto, along with their boss, Superintendent Wilson, believe that a certain amount of publicity—bringing possible help from the public—is desirable. Wilson has proved this in his Crime-Stop program through which thousands of arrests have been made and as many crimes prevented with the help of alert citizens.

Perhaps publicity would help to solve this case, the worst slaughter in the modern-day history of Chicago, so they were prepared to release as much information as they could without jeopardizing their case.

Flanagan's order canceling leaves and Spiotto's order for 80 additional men to be sent to Area 2 were implemented in an incredibly short time.

When detectives appeared for morning roll call at eight o'clock—just two hours after the first news of the murders—20 of them were selected to canvass the immediate area.

Spiotto told them he believed that the killer was someone who knew there were eight girls in each town house unit.

"That's right," Flanagan agreed. "He was expecting eight—he didn't know an extra girl was going to come visiting and that's how he lost count. That's how one girl was able to survive."

Detectives Carlisle and Wallenda had talked to residents of the town house units and had been told that the walls were "paper thin." One woman had told them the walls were so thin she could hear her neighbor's TV as well as if it had been in her own room.

"The eight nurses who live in the second unit are on vacation and nobody's there," Carlisle added. "This fellow must have known that and picked the end unit deliberately. If there was any unusual noise, it wouldn't carry through the vacant unit to the third one where the house mother was."

"That means," said Spiotto, "that he probably has been watching the place. He might be a resident of the neighborhood, he might be a hobo who got off a train"—he pointed to the railroad tracks only five minutes' walk across a field—"or a bum who hangs around the taverns and happened to notice this place."

He suggested that some of the detectives begin their canvass at the city limits, 100th and Torrence Avenue, and that others concentrate on taverns and rooming houses in the area.

Armed with Miss Amurao's description of the killer, the detectives started out.

Inside the town house, Detective Carlisle, Wallenda and others methodically checked the bedrooms. Each was in a state of wild disarray. Some of this could have been caused by last minute struggles by the girl victims. But most of it undoubtedly had been caused by the killer as he ransacked drawers and searched every place where he thought he was likely to find money. Examination of the purses belonging to the nine nurses showed there was no money in any of them. Between them, Miss Amurao and her roommate had $31 and that was missing. How much was taken from the other purses was not known and probably never will be.

Detectives Carlisle and Wallenda had watched the pathologists as they removed the bindings from the wrists of each of the slain girls.

"The way he tied those girls up he had to know how to tie knots," Carlisle told Chief Spiotto. "They were good, square knots. Nobody could open them and he had their hands tied behind them the right way, with the front of the wrists against each other and the palms facing the sides."

"That's the way we handcuff prisoners," Wallenda added. "If you tie the hands with the palms straight down, they can work them around and twist their fingers enough to get at the rope."

"Not the way this guy did it," said Carlisle. "He must have been arrested in his time. A convict, probably. And he surely has been around rope."

"A seaman, maybe," Spiotto suggested.

Down the street, just across the next intersection to the east, less than half a block from the murder scene, was the hiring hall of a seaman's union. It would be a place for the canvassing detectives to ask a few questions.

One team of those detectives—Eugene Ivano, Edward A. Wielosinski, Edward A. Boyle and John T. Mitchell—already had picked up a lead that seemed worth following. At a filling station at 100th and Torrence, near the Indiana line, they had described the killer to the owner.

Yes, he told the detectives, a man who matched that description had come to the station Tuesday afternoon, carrying a brown plaid flight bag and a small brown overnight case. He explained that he had gone to Indiana when he heard of a job opening, but it had been filled.

The talkative young man, who spoke in a soft voice with a southern accent, said he now was looking for a place to stay. He said he had slept on the beach Sunday night and had stayed in a rooming house Monday night. But his room was taken when he got back from Indiana.

He asked permission to leave his bags at the filling station and the owner readily agreed. The young man showed up the next morning, Wednesday, claimed his bags and said he was going to check in at the Ship Yard Inn.

The detectives hurried to the Ship Yard Inn, whose clientele is mostly transients and seamen. The clerk said a man matching the description had checked in and paid $9 for a week's rent. Then he had made a call to a sister who lived in Chicago.

For some reason, unknown to the hotel personnel, the man had checked out Thursday, taking his bags. They had no idea where he had gone. He had used a name, but the detectives were reasonably sure it was fictitious.

Nevertheless, it was called in by radio to the Criminal Records section at central headquarters, where recently installed electronic devices make it possible to check out a record in moments. Word came back that there was no record for that name.

It was agreed among the detectives that the man might have gone back to the rooming house or that he might be in some tavern in the area. A radio call went out to the other canvassing teams to meet the first group.

The other teams were Lieutenant William McCarthy, Detectives Carl R. Edenfield, Peter S. Valesaresand, Joseph M. Dawson; Sergeant Victor A. Vrdyolak, Detectives William McHugh, Thomas Doyle and Arthur Robinson; Sergeant Michael E. Cleary, Detectives Thomas Kelleher, John Griffin and Joseph Nolan; Detectives James Madison, Robert R. Reynolds, James McDonough and William Tolliver.

They all went into a huddle to consider what the first team had discovered. It was agreed that a canvass of rooming houses and barrooms should be productive, so while the first group went on to the seamen's hiring hall near the nurses' town house, Lieutenant McCarthy led the group of 15 detectives on the canvass and the original four officers started for the hiring hall.

Before they went into the hall, they checked with Deputy Chief Spiotto, who told them of the square knots used by the killer to tie up the girls. The hiring hall seemed the logical place to look next.

Meanwhile, the surviving nurse had been escorted to South Chicago Community in a state of shock. She was heavily guarded in the convoy that took her. Two rooms had been made available, one for Miss Amurao and one for the police. She was put to bed and given heavy sedation, while a uniformed policeman took a seat in front of her door. Others waited in the room next door and detectives prowled the floors of the 300-bed hospital.

Detectives also were assigned to check the hospital's 600 employees, any one of whom could have known about the town house arrangement for student nurses and one of whom might have had some reason for invading the nurses' residence. Checking of employees began, but it had to be handled carefully. The hospital's routine must not be disrupted more than it already had been by the tragic news that now had most of the nurses, especially the students, in a state of nervous tension.

In other parts of Chicago, people were looking for a tall man who wanted to go to New Orleans. At the Delta Airlines ticket office in the Loop, a man was making reservations for New Orleans when the clerk noticed bloodstains on his shirt.

When he saw her staring at the stains, he fled. But police quickly nabbed him at nearby State and Madison Streets. He was questioned and satisfied the officers that he had not been near the murder scene. He also satisfactorily accounted for the bloodstain on his shirt. He said he panicked when he realized that he was the same general size as the killer, that he was going to New Orleans and that he had blood on his shirt.

He was cleared and released.

At the union hiring hall, the detectives made inquiries. They were told that a man matching the description had come in Monday and asked about a job as a seaman, saying he would like to get on a ship for New Orleans.

The only opening was on an ore boat operating out of Indiana Harbor. He went to see about that, but was too late. He returned to the union hall Tuesday and Wednesday. There was nothing for him, but he had made an application and it was kept on file. It showed that he had worked on Great Lakes ore ships as a laborer, but that he was learning to be a seaman.

His name was Richard F. Speck and clipped to his application was a passport type photo of the kind produced by a 25-cent coin machine. Nevertheless, it was a good picture.

The union official, William O'Neill, said that Speck had come again Wednesday, but there still was nothing. He had left the phone number of his sister, who could be called if a job opening occurred.

Questioning others, the detectives were told that Speck had strolled over to Luella Park, directly behind the town houses, and loafed during the afternoon. The witnesses said it was not unusual for one or more of the student nurses to sunbathe in the yard behind the town houses. One speculated that this could have attracted Speck to the park, where he would have a good view of the girls if they did appear to sunbathe.

Since then, nobody had seen Speck.

Excited and believing they might be on the trail of the killer, the detectives reported to Deputy Chief Spiotto and Commander Flanagan. Both agreed it was a good lead. But the detectives were instructed that nothing was to be mentioned about it yet.

Plans for trapping Speck were carefully made. Spiotto ordered additional copies of the picture made so that one would be available to each of the 20 detectives assigned to this phase of the investigation. Then Spiotto checked the files at central headquarters; there was nothing on Speck.

But union officials said a more complete dossier, including fingerprints, could be obtained from the National Maritime Commission in Washington. Spiotto took this up with Marlin W. Johnson, special agent in charge of the FBI office in Chicago.

"How's the fastest and best way to get that record?" the deputy chief asked.

Marlin said he would send a special agent to Washington by plane to pick up the dossier and prints. However, there was an airline strike on and the earliest reservation the agent could get was Friday morning, with a return Friday evening.

Meanwhile, at the hiring hall, a detective phoned Speck's sister and posing as a union official, told her to have her brother come to the hall as soon as she could get in touch with him.

At 3:10 that afternoon, a man phoned and identified himself as Richard Speck. The detective, still posing as a union official, told him there was a job for him and asked how soon he could get to the hall. Speck said he would be there within the hour.

Commander Flanagan was notified and the long wait for the goods began.

On a widespread front, other phases of the investigation were going on. The crime lab technicians had found more than 100 fingerprints and all but 36 had been matched up with those of the nine nurses. The remainder, some fragmentary, could not be identified.

Director Dragel and his men impatiently awaited Friday evening and the prints of Richard Speck from Washington. But they had much other work. From the town house, they had taken more than 125 items of possible evidence, in addition to bloodstained night garments removed from the slain girls, as well as many bloodsoaked uniforms, apparently stained when they were tossed out of closets and drawers by the ransacking killer.

At the Cook County morgue, relatives made tearful identifications of six of the student nurses. Friends had identified the Filipino girls. Then the pathologists had made their post mortem examinations and made their preliminary report:

Evidence indicated that none of the girls had been raped or sexually molested. The girls had died in this manner:

Miss Davy had been strangled. Miss Farris had died of stab wounds, as had Miss Jordan and Miss Gargullo. Miss Matusek had been strangled. Miss Farris, Miss Wilkening, Miss Schmale and Miss Pasion all had been stabbed and strangled.

Preliminary examination also indicated, the pathologists said, that none of the girls had been drugged. However, tissue tests would be made to determine this more definitely.

Scrapings were taken from under the fingernails of each of the victims. These would be examined by crime lab technicians to determine if any of the girls scratched the killer. This seemed unlikely, however, since all were bound.

When he talked to reporters after the eight murders, Dr. Toman called it "the crime of the century." He said it was the worst mass murder in Chicago since the St. Valentine's Day Massacre. On February 14, 1929, seven members of the Bugs Moran gang were lined up against the wall inside a garage on North Clark Street and shot to death. The massacre was attributed to the Al Capone gang, though this was never proved in court.

Commander Flanagan, haggard from the worry of the investigation and the fear that the killer, still at large, might strike again, was asked to comment for TV cameras. "What kind of a human being would do a thing like this? He's a sub-animal. I don't know who he is or where he is or how soon we'll get him. *But get him we will!*"

About 250 miles downstate, a truck driver reported that he had given a ride to a tall, blond young man who was hitchhiking his way to Louisiana. Roadblocks were set up by the state police and the young man was soon picked up.

But he was able to prove that he had not been in Chicago at the time the student nurses were murdered and he was released.

At the union hall, an hour passed and Richard Speck didn't show up. The detectives stayed there until the hall closed and he still had not put in an appearance. It was improbable that he would.

But the detectives under Lieutenant McCarthy had better luck. They found the rooming house where Speck had rented a room on Monday night. He had returned on Tuesday and the room was rented. But he had come back Tuesday night and had been permitted to sleep on a couch in the living room.

He hadn't been back for a room, but the manager said that he had spent a lot of time at a nearby tavern. The detectives went there and picked up Speck's trail. Armed with the pictures, they learned he had been at several taverns.

Finally, they came to one where he had been that day. He had left, but a man who had worked with him on an ore boat and who had drunk with him was found. He said Speck had tried to get him to go up on the north side where there was "some action," but refused.

He said this happened shortly after Speck had made two telephone calls. He thought one was to his sister, he didn't know what the other was. They had parted when Speck had taken a cab. Fortunately, he recalled the cab.

The detectives began the long, tedious search for the cabbie.

Even though this was the most spectacular case in their history, the Chicago police could not give it their undivided attention. For as night fell, the rioting flared again on the west side. Despite the presence of more than 1,000 cops, vandalism spread.

Scores of display windows were broken and looters invaded the stores, carting away nearly everything that wasn't nailed down. Gangs of young hoodlums, some armed with rocks, some with guns, attacked the police and frustrated them in their attempts to halt the vandalism and restore order.

In some sections, fires were started and as firemen fought the blazes the hoodlum gangs pelted them with rocks. It was not until the police moved in with riot guns that the firemen were able to bring the fires under control.

It was a wild, chaotic night for the Chicago police. Even with Plan 3 in operation with all police officers assigned to 12-hour shifts and many working around the clock, the force of some 12,000 officers was not enough.

Early Friday, Mayor Daley asked Governor Otto Kerner for help. The governor promptly sent out a call for 3,000 National Guardsmen to report to the turbulent west side. Almost immediately, units began to mobilize and trucks rolled toward Chicago.

Friday was destined to be an eventful, unforgettable day for the Chicago police. Early that morning, the detectives under Lieutenant McCarthy—none had slept and all 20 had worked through the night—found the cabbie who had picked up Richard Speck. He said he had taken Speck to the 1300 block of North Sedgwick Street. He hadn't gone to any particular address and had been put out on the street with his bags. The fare was $5.90.

Since this was a neighborhood whose residents were predominantly Negro, Lieutenant McCarthy hoped that Speck's presence would have been noticed by someone. Commander Flanagan was notified of the latest development and Lieutenant McCarthy and his 19 men sped to the north side.

The 1200 block of North Sedgwick did not offer much hope. On the west side is a parking lot, on the east side a high school. But there were apartment buildings in both the 100 and 1300 blocks. It was a tedious job, but Lieutenant McCarthy split the group and they began canvassing both blocks.

About that time, an FBI special agent left for Washington to pick up the dossier on Richard Speck.

Also about that time, Deputy Chief Spiotto was notified that Corazón Amurao had slept through the night, that she had awakened refreshed and that she could be questioned. Spiotto contacted Flanagan, Otis Rathel, a police artist assigned to the crime lab, and Detective Joseph Gonzales, who speaks Spanish and is attached to the crime lab.

Before he left central headquarters, Spiotto had picked up 180 mug shots of men in their twenties who had been suspected of crimes against women or who had served time and been released. Each matched the general description given by the survivor. Included in these 180 mug shots was one of Richard Speck, a copy of the picture obtained from the union hiring official.

Spiotto confined his questioning of Miss Amurao to the man's appearance. The girl was remarkably perceptive and was able to describe the killer's features as Rathel made quick strokes with his pencil. He determined the size of the face in the sketch by comparison with his own face—by asking if the face was larger or smaller than his, if it was longer or shorter, wider or narrower.

The facial expression was important, he told her. She said he looked like a man who wouldn't harm anybody; she said he had a very gentle appearance.

When the first sketch had been completed, Miss Amurao said the eyes looked too mean and she had him soften their expression. Then she suggested other changes. He used an eraser to wipe out the part to be changed, then drew it again. One change was in the mouth. Another was in the hair. She was vague about the color of what appeared to be a long crewcut, but with the help of Detective Gonzales, she conveyed the impression that the hair could best be described as "dishwater blond," a shade of light brown.

Finally, the sketch was completed and Miss Amurao said it looked like the killer. Rathel left and took the sketch to central headquarters, where Superintendent Wilson ordered it reproduced in 40,000 copies of the daily Police Bulletin. Of these, 20,000 would be for the use of police officers in the Chicago area, the others would be distributed to law enforcement agencies throughout the country.

Other copies were made for immediate distribution to newspapers, wire services, television stations and networks.

After the artist had left, Deputy Chief Spiotto produced the mug shots and Miss Amurao began studying them.

On Sedgwick Street, meanwhile, Lieutenant McCarthy's detectives struck pay dirt in the first building they canvassed in the 1100 block. A woman living on the 12th floor of a highrise apartment building said she had been looking out the window with binoculars when she saw a cab stop in the 1300 block late Thursday afternoon. A tall, blond young man with two bags got out, paid the cabbie and the taxi left.

She watched as the young man strolled back to Division Street, which is 1200 north, then turned east. She was able to see him until he turned south in Dearborn Street. And, she told the officers, a tattoo "Born to Raise Hell" was plainly visible on his arm.

With this lead, the detectives began canvassing southward on Dearborn Street, where there are many small hotels and rooming houses and on Clark Street, which has many small hotels as well as an abundance of barrooms. This is the section that is best known as Chicago's vice strip.

Using the police sketch the detectives began asking for Speck. In a tavern on North Clark Street, they encountered a man suspected of being a narcotics pusher. When they told him they were not looking for him on a narcotics charge, he seemed so relieved that he eagerly looked at the picture.

"Sure, I seen that guy in here, but he didn't stay long. I think he was looking for broads."

The man said he believed Speck had gone on to the next tavern. The detectives went there and encountered two more men with records of narcotics arrests. Both agreed that he had stayed there for some time, drinking and dancing and finally left with a prostitute they knew only as Mary.

But Mary wasn't there. She might be in any of the taverns along the street or she might be in a room in some hotel with a customer.

The detectives decided to try the Clark Street hotels.

At the hospital, Miss Amurao continued to look at mug shots, discarding one after another. She looked at 177 and there were only three left. Then Deputy Chief Spiotto slipped the three in front of her. Without hesitation, she pointed to the picture in the center.

It was the photo of Richard Speck.

"This is similar," she said. "Everything except the hair."

In the picture the hair was long. Miss Amurao remembered it as a long crewcut. But she was positive in her identification.

Deputy Chief Spiotto left and hurried to central headquarters, where he huddled with Superintendent Wilson, Chief of Detectives Kreuzer and Commander Flanagan.

The resemblance between the picture of Speck and Rathel's drawing was remarkable. Already, phones at central headquarters and in numerous other police stations in Chicago were jangling. Many people thought they recognized the man in the sketch, which had been shown on TV and was now appearing in the afternoon papers.

All these calls were carefully checked out. But they didn't lead to Richard Speck.

The top brass debated whether to reveal the identity of the wanted man and decided against it for the time being. They would wait for the FBI agent to return from Washington. He was due back at seven o'clock.

The canvassing detectives came to a hotel on North Clark Street where the picture of Speck was recognized. He had come in Thursday evening with a prostitute known as Mary. The girl had left about midnight, Speck about 3 a.m. He apparently had a sleeping room somewhere else.

So the detectives started looking again, for Speck and for the girl named Mary. They finally found her and she cooperated. She admitted having gone to the hotel with Speck, said she had left about midnight, after paying her $3. She didn't know where he lived, but she thought it was at another place, because he'd had to register when they entered the hotel where she had entertained him.

The detectives kept inquiring and they found a habitué of a saloon with a four o'clock closing license who said he had seen the man in the picture. He had shown up a little after 3 a.m., and had left with a 40-year-old Negro prostitute, whose price was $5. He didn't know where they had gone.

The weary detectives kept trying.

On the west side, the National Guard arrived in force. There were a few incidents of looting, but the presence of the armed men, whose orders were to shoot to kill if anyone shot at them, had its effect. Most of the troublemakers stayed under cover.

The FBI special agent phoned from Washington to say that he had Speck's dossier. It showed that he was an ex-convict, that he had been in trouble with the law when he was 18 and that he had a long record in Dallas, Texas. He was a native of Monmouth, Illinois. The agent said he expected to arrive on schedule.

But long before that time, the Chicago police were checking on the man who now had become their prime suspect. Records in Dallas showed that Speck had been convicted of forgery in 1963 and had been sent to prison for three years. He had been released on parole in January, 1965, and in a few months was in trouble again.

He had put a knife to the neck of a young woman as she parked her car late one night in the garage behind her home. She had screamed and a man living across the alley had shouted at Speck. He fled but was caught. He still had the weapon, a carving knife with a blade more than 17 inches long. He admitted threatening the woman and was convicted on a charge of aggravated assault. He was sentenced to serve 490 days in the county jail in Dallas.

However, he was sent back to the state prison at Huntsville as a parole violator, on June 16, 1965. But he was released again 16 days later and didn't bother to return to serve his county jail sentence, though he did return to Dallas briefly for a visit to the home of his mother.

He held many laboring type jobs, though none of them for very long. He wandered about the country and worked on ore boats on the Great Lakes. He had been married, but his wife had divorced him. He went back to Dallas for a visit in March, 1966, but soon left.

Next he showed up in Monmouth, Illinois, where he was born and attended the first grade. After the death of his father, his mother moved to Dallas and took him with her. He attended Dallas schools through the ninth grade.

An older brother had remained in Monmouth, where he has become a respected citizen. Dick Speck went to visit his brother, who got him a job as an apprentice carpenter and arranged for a place for him to live. But he didn't live there long, moving instead into a Monmouth hotel.

His principal pastime appeared to be hanging around Monmouth taverns where, according to his drinking companions, he was known as a woman chaser.

"He bragged about all the women he could get, but he never got a date with one," said one man. "He'd stare at a girl and then tell me: 'I'd like to meet her.' Girls would talk to him, dance with him, but he never got a date with one."

The last week he was in Monmouth was eventful. On April 10th, Mrs. Mary Pierce, a divorcee who was a barmaid at a tavern where Speck drank, disappeared. Three days later, her nude, beaten body was found in a hogpen on a lot behind the tavern.

Five days later, a 65-year-old woman was raped and robbed. Police Chief Harold Tinder wanted to question Speck, but when he went to the hotel, Speck had left suddenly. Chief Tinder said he still wanted to question Speck about the Monmouth rape and murder.

Maritime records showed that Speck had gone to work on a Great Lakes ore boat shortly afterward. He had been fired from one job and had obtained another. While at work on this boat on May 3rd, Speck had become violently sick and had been rushed to St. Joseph Hospital in Hancock, Michigan.

He had an appendix that was about to rupture and quick surgery saved his life. During his recuperation he became acquainted with and dated one of the nurses. When he was well enough, he left and took another ore boat job. The nurse said he wrote her many letters from Sault Sainte Marie and Chicago.

A month later, he came to visit her and she noticed a change. "He was still gentle, but he had a hatred in him," she said. Once, she said, he told her about two people in Texas he didn't like and if he ever got the chance, he would kill them.

She said she had last seen him on June 27th. "For some reason, I thought of him when I heard about the girls," she said. "Then I felt bad for even thinking it."

The records showed that Speck had been fired from his job on the ore boat when it was at Indiana Harbor on July 2nd. Only a short distance away that same day, three girls who had gone to the Indiana Dunes Park for an outing mysteriously disappeared. They were in swim suits and left behind were their purses, their personal belongings and a car belonging to one of them. A week-long widespread search failed to turn up the missing girls. They are still missing.

In Benton Harbor, Michigan, less than 50 miles away, four females were murdered. They were of four generations: One was seven, one was 19, another was 37, the other was 60. One was found in an abandoned building in February, 1966. The others all were found on the same day in April, their bodies within 200 feet of each other. Some had been strangled, one had been slashed from breastbone to pelvis, another had been decapitated.

The killer is still at large, but when the Benton Harbor police learned of the murders of the eight girls, they suspected that the same man could be responsible.

By the time the Chicago police had learned all this, it was decided to set the entire department to looking for the fugitive. That was after the FBI agent had returned and handed the dossier on Richard Speck to Crime Lab Director Dan Dragel.

Dragel immediately assigned Lieutenant Emil G. Giese and Sergeant Hugh Granahan to begin their comparisons—Speck's prints against the unidentified prints found at the town house where the eight girls were slain. Dragel told them to notify him if they learned anything.

Meanwhile, the order to look for Speck was received at the Chicago Avenue police station. Somebody recalled a report that had been turned in that morning, as the result of a call from a small hotel on Dearborn Street. A prostitute had left a man's room about seven that morning and had stopped at the deck. She had told the manager the man she had been with had a gun. The manager reported this to the Chicago Avenue police station and two patrolmen were sent to the man's room.

He gave his name as Richard Speck and readily produced a .22 caliber revolver and six cartridges. He said the gun was not his, that it belonged to the woman who had just left. The officers took the gun and ammunition, which were inventoried at the station about nine o'clock Friday morning.

At the time, they had not heard the name Speck and they didn't connect it with the slaughter of the eight nurses. Now they did. Lieutenant McCarthy and his men, still canvassing the area—they were only a short distance from the hotel—were notified.

They immediately surrounded the hotel and one detective went in. The manager said Speck was registered there and his rent had been paid up for a week. But he had left about 30 minutes before, carrying a bundle and saying casually that he was going out to a laundromat.

The hotel was staked out and hours passed. Speck didn't return. His room was searched and the clothing Miss Amurao had described—a black jacket, black pants and a T-shirt—were there. They were on hangers and they had been freshly laundered.

The stakeout was maintained through the night and continued Saturday morning. But Speck did not appear.

Meanwhile, the Philippine consul in Chicago had visited Miss Amurao and she had cleared up a point that had puzzled investigators ever since the eight bodies were found: Why hadn't the girls screamed? Why hadn't they ganged up on him and tried to fight him off?

Miss Amurao said that after the first girl had been led from the room—to be killed, as it later developed—the eight who remained had discussed this. The three Filipino girls wanted to scream and fight. But the American girls didn't.

"Maybe if we are quiet and calm, he will be quiet and calm," Miss Amurao quoted one of the American girls.

"But they were wrong," she said. "They were too trusting." Then she added: "But the other girls said they were sure that he would not harm anyone. They said: 'We more or less have to trust him. If we keep quiet, maybe he won't do something crazy.'"

Miss Amurao hadn't agreed with this and after the second girl had been led away, she rolled under the bunk bed and hid, saving her own life.

The fingerprint technicians worked until early morning and they found four prints that matched those of Speck on at least 12 points—the legal requirement. When they were sure, Director Dragel was notified. That was about 4:30 a.m. Saturday.

Dragel contacted Commander Flanagan who was out on the street, directing the manhunt. He hadn't slept since the crime broke and he was haggard and weary, but his spirit was undaunted.

As soon as he had the news, he called Lieutenant Griese and said: "You boys have done it again! Great work."

Some of the identified prints had come from the door to the bedroom where the girls had been held captive. Dragel and some of his men immediately drove to the town house, which had been sealed and guarded by the police. The door was removed and preserved as evidence.

During that Saturday morning, there was a lot of discussion among the top brass as to whether the identity of the suspect should be publicly disclosed. They all had in mind recent Supreme Court decisions about publicity and its effect on a fair trial.

Finally, when Speck hadn't returned to his room by early afternoon and it became clear that he didn't intend to, Superintendent Wilson decided to ask the help of the public. At 2:40 p.m., he went before the television network cameras and announced that Richard Speck had been identified by the police as the killer. He said the police had enough evidence to convict him and that the survivor had identified his picture.

In the dossier brought from Washington was the information that there were tattoos on both of Speck's arms. The outstanding one was an inscription on the left arm: BORN TO RAISE HELL.

Then Superintendent Wilson held up a picture of Speck. He said he was sure this was the right man.

The picture was published in all Chicago papers and in newspapers throughout the country. But hours passed and there was no trace of Richard Speck. Had he left the city or the state?

U.S. Attorney Edward Hanrahan went before a federal judge and obtained a fugitive warrant on the theory that the suspect had left the state. This provided federal jurisdiction and the FBI immediately entered the case.

Even so, Speck might have escaped attention had it not been for the publicity given the hunt for him. A young man in a skid row hotel on West Madison Street apparently attempted suicide by cutting a vein on his left arm and on his right wrist. This happens so often in skid row hotels that it has become routine. Two patrolmen took the man to County Hospital, where he was wheeled to the trauma ward to be treated by Dr. Leroy Smith, a resident. Only a short time before, Dr. Smith had read of the identification of Speck and the search for him. He had noted the photograph and had read about the tattoos.

Now, as he looked down at his new patient, he thought the face was familiar. He looked at the right arm and saw a tattoo. But the left arm was covered with blood.

"Bring me a copy of a newspaper," he told Nurse Kathy O'Connor.

While she was away, he moistened a finger and rubbed some of the blood away. The letter "B" emerged. Then Dr. Smith rubbed off more blood and the whole tattoo—BORN TO RAISE HELL—was visible.

Nurse O'Connor returned with the paper and they compared the picture with the face of the patient, who had been listed as B. Brian, the name of the skid row hotel register.

"What's your name?" Dr. Smith asked.

"Richard," the man replied and as Dr. Smith waited: "Richard Speck." Then, after a pause: "Are you going to get the $10,000 reward?"

Dr. Smith didn't answer this and he didn't question Speck further. "Get the police," he told nurse O'Connor.

There was a policeman in the hospital and he made the arrest. Then headquarters was notified.

From that moment on, the authorities literally walked on eggs to be sure they didn't violate any of the guidelines laid down by the Supreme Court's June decision about interrogation of prisoners.

Speck was heavily guarded and as soon as he had been given emergency treatment, he was moved to the Bridewell Hospital adjacent to the county jail. It was then early Sunday morning. Prosecutor Ward planned to take Speck into court on Monday morning on a charge of murdering one girl.

But doctors at the hospital said Speck was too weak and the hearing was postponed. Nevertheless, the murder warrant was issued. Miss Amurao was taken to the hospital and remained outside for 2 ½ hours, but she wasn't permitted to see Speck. She was returned to South Chicago Hospital under heavy guard.

Later, doctors said Speck had suffered a minor heart attack and it might be three weeks before he could appear in court. Meanwhile, as his condition improved, Miss Amurao was taken into his room. She left after five minutes and said: "That is the man."

At the request of Speck's relatives, Public Defender Gerald Getty was appointed to defend him. Getty has hinted that he will enter an insanity plea.

As this is written, Richard Speck is still in the closely guarded Bridewell Hospital and further legal action against him is pending. Meanwhile, the Chicago police have been widely acclaimed for the heads-up police work.

Homicide Commander Frank Flanagan and a lot of his buddies who had worked 72 hours without rest finally got a good night's sleep. So did thousands of jittery residents of Jeffrey Manor.

True Detective, October 1966

DON MOSER

Heinous as they were, the crimes of Charles Schmid might have remained a strictly local affair had it not been for veteran *Life* magazine reporter Don Moser (b. 1932), who not only gave the bizarre young serial murderer nationwide exposure but tagged him with the kind of nickname that endows such psychopaths with a disturbing mystique. Moser's invocation of the legendary child-seducer imbued Schmid's story with the haunting atmosphere of a supernatural horror tale. It was this quality that impressed writer Joyce Carol Oates when she encountered Moser's article in the March 4, 1966, issue of *Life* and that she conveys so powerfully in her short story "Where Are You Going, Where Have You Been?" The story relates how an adolescent girl named Connie is lured from her suburban home by Arnold Friend, a malevolent figure who shares Charles Schmid's taste for pancake makeup and leather boots stuffed with rags and crushed tin cans. In Oates' version a vicious self-aggrandizing sociopath takes on the quality of an ageless demon lover, decked out as a hotrodding juvenile delinquent.

Sentenced to death for the murders of sisters Gretchen and Wendy Fritz, Charles Schmid was saved from the gas chamber when Arizona abolished the death penalty in 1971. (He had pled guilty to second-degree murder in the death of Alleen Rowe.) Four years later, he was stabbed to death by two fellow inmates.

The Pied Piper of Tucson

Hey, c'mon babe, follow me,
I'm the Pied Piper, follow me,
I'm the Pied Piper,
And I'll show you where it's at.
—Popular song,
Tucson, winter 1965

At dusk in Tucson, as the stark, yellow-flared mountains begin to blur against the sky, the golden car slowly cruises Speedway. Smoothly it rolls down the long, divided avenue, past the supermarkets, the gas stations and the motels; past the twist joints, the sprawling drive-in restaurants. The car slows for an intersection, stops, then pulls away again. The exhaust mutters against the pavement as the young man driving takes the machine swiftly, expertly through the gears. A car pulls even with him; the teen-age girls in the front seat laugh, wave and call his name. The young man glances toward the rearview mirror, turned always so that he can look at his own reflection, and he appraises himself.

The face is his own creation: the hair dyed raven black, the skin darkened to a deep tan with pancake make-up, the lips whitened, the whole effect heightened by a mole he has painted on one cheek. But the deep-set blue eyes are all his own. Beautiful eyes, the girls say.

Approaching the Hi-Ho, the teen-agers' nightclub, he backs off on the accelerator, then slowly cruises on past Johnie's Drive-in. There the cars are beginning to orbit and accumulate in the parking lot—neat sharp cars with deep-throated mufflers and Maltese-cross decals on the windows. But it's early yet. Not much going on. The driver shifts up again through the gears, and the golden car slides away along the glitter and gim-crack of Speedway. Smitty keeps looking for the action.

Whether the juries in the two trials decide that Charles Howard Schmid Jr. did or did not brutally murder Alleen Rowe, Gretchen Fritz and Wendy Fritz has from the beginning seemed of almost secondary importance to the people of Tucson. They are not indifferent. But what disturbs them far beyond the question of Smitty's guilt or innocence are the revelations about Tucson itself that have followed on the disclosure of the crimes. Starting with the bizarre circumstances of the killings and on through the ugly fragments of the plot—which in turn hint at other murders as yet undiscovered, at teen-age sex, blackmail, even connections with the Cosa Nostra—they have had to view their city in a new and unpleasant light. The fact is that Charles Schmid— who cannot be dismissed as a freak, an aberrant of no consequence— had for years functioned successfully as a member, even a leader, of the yeastiest stratum of Tucson's teen-age society.

As a high school student Smitty had been, as classmates remember, an outsider—but not that far outside. He was small but he was a fine athlete, and in his last year—1960—he was a state gymnastics champion. His grades were poor, but he was in no trouble to speak of until his senior year, when he was suspended for stealing tools from a welding class.

But Smitty never really left the school. After his suspension he hung around waiting to pick up kids in a succession of sharp cars which he drove fast and well. He haunted all the teen-age hangouts along Speedway, including the bowling alleys and the public swimming pool—and he put on spectacular diving exhibitions for girls far younger than he.

At the time of his arrest last November, Charles Schmid was 23 years old. He wore face make-up and dyed his hair. He habitually stuffed three or four inches of old rags and tin cans into the bottoms of his high-topped boots to make himself taller than his five-foot-three and stumbled about so awkwardly while walking that some people thought he had wooden feet. He pursed his lips and let his eyelids droop in order to emulate his idol, Elvis Presley. He bragged to girls that he knew 100 ways to make love, that he ran dope, that he was a Hell's Angel. He talked about being a rough customer in a fight (he was, though he was rarely in one), and he always carried in his pocket tiny bottles of salt and pepper, which he said he used to blind his opponents. He liked to use highfalutin language and had a favorite saying, "I can manifest my neurotical emotions, emancipate an epicureal instinct, and elaborate on my heterosexual tendencies."

He occasionally shocked even those who thought they knew him well. A friend says he once saw Smitty tie a string to the tail of his pet cat, swing it around his head and beat it bloody against a wall. Then he turned calmly and asked, "You feel compassion—why?"

Yet even while Smitty tried to create an exalted, heroic image of himself, he had worked on a pitiable one. "He thrived on feeling sorry for himself," recalls a friend, "and making others feel sorry for him." At various times Smitty told intimates that he had leukemia and didn't have long to live. He claimed that he was adopted, that his real name was Angel Rodriguez, that his father was a "bean" (local slang for Mexican, an inferior race in Smitty's view), and that his mother was a famous lawyer who would have nothing to do with him.

What made Smitty a hero to Tucson's youth?

Isn't Tucson—out there in the Golden West, in the grand setting where the skies are not cloudy all day—supposed to be a flowering of the American Dream? One envisions teen-agers who drink milk, wear crewcuts, go to bed at half past 9, say "Sir" and "Ma'am," and like to go fishing with Dad. Part of Tucson is like this—but the city is not yet Utopia. It is glass and chrome and well-weathered stucco; it is also gimcrack, ersatz and urban sprawl at its worst. Its suburbs stretch for mild after mile—a level sea of bungalows, broken only by mammoth shopping centers, that ultimately peters out among the cholla and saguaro. The city has grown from 85,000 to 300,000 since World War II. Few who live there were born there, and a lot are just passing through. Its superb climate attracts the old and the infirm, many of whom, as one citizen put it, "have come here to retire from their responsibilities to life." Jobs are hard to find and there is little industry to stabilize employment. ("What do people do in Tucson?" the visitor asks. Answer: "They do each others' laundry.")

As for the youngsters, they must compete with the army of semi-retired who are willing to take on part-time work for the minimum wage. Schools are beautiful but overcrowded; and at those with split sessions, the kids are on the loose from noon on, or from 6 p.m. till noon the next day. When they get into trouble, Tucson teen-agers are capable of getting into trouble in style: a couple of years ago they shocked the city fathers by throwing a series of beer-drinking parties in the desert, attended by scores of kids. The fests were called "boondockers" and if they were no more sinful than any other kids' drinking parties, they were at least on a magnificent scale. One statistic seems relevant: 50 runaways are reported to the Tucson police department each month.

Of an evening kids with nothing to do wind up on Speedway, looking for action. There is the teen-age nightclub ("Pickup Palace," the kids call it). There are the rock 'n' roll beer joints (the owners check ages meticulously, but young girls can enter if they don't drink; besides, anyone can buy a phony I.D. card for $2.50 around the high schools) where they can Jerk, Swim and Frug away the evening to the room-shaking electronic blare of *Hang On Sloopy*, *The Pied Piper* and a number called *The Bo Diddley Rock*. At the drive-in hamburger and pizza stands their cars circle endlessly, mufflers rumbling, as they check each other over.

Here on Speedway you find Richie and Ronny, out of work and bored and with nothing to do. Here you find Debby and Jabron, from the wrong side of the tracks, aimlessly cruising in their battered old car looking for something—anything—to relieve the tedium of their lives, looking for somebody neat. ("Well if the boys look bitchin', you pull up next to them in your car and you roll down the window and say, 'Hey, how about a dollar for gas?' and if they give you the dollar then maybe you let them take you to Johnie's for a Coke.") Here you find Gretchen, pretty and rich and with problems, bad problems. Of a Saturday night, all of them cruising the long, bright street that seems endlessly in motion with the young. Smitty's people.

He had a nice car. He had plenty of money from his parents, who ran a nursing home, and he was always glad to spend it on anyone who'd listen to him. He had a pad of his own where he threw parties and he had impeccable manners. He was always willing to help a friend and he would send flowers to girls who were ill. He was older and more mature than most of his friends. He knew where the action was, and if he wore make-up—well, at least he was *different*.

Some of the older kids—those who worked, who had something else to do—thought Smitty was a creep. But to the youngsters—to the bored and the lonely, to the dropout and the delinquent, to the young girls with beehive hairdos and tight pants they didn't quite fill out, and to the boys with acne and no jobs—to these people, Smitty was a kind of folk hero. Nutty maybe, but at least more dramatic, more theatrical, more *interesting* than anyone else in their lives: a semi-ludicrous, sexy-eyed pied piper who, stumbling along in his rag-stuffed boots, led them up and down Speedway.

On the evening of May 31, 1964, Alleen Rowe prepared to go to bed early. She had to be in class by 6 a.m., and she had an examination the next day. Alleen was a pretty girl of 15, a better-than-average student who talked about going to college and becoming an oceanographer. She was also a sensitive child—given to reading romantic novels and taking long walks in the desert at night. Recently she had been going through a period of adolescent melancholia, often talking with her mother, a nurse, about death. She would, she hoped, be some day re-incarnated as a cat.

On this evening, dressed in a black bathing suit and thongs, her usual costume around the house, she had watched the Beatles on TV and had tried to teach her mother to dance the Frug. Then she took her bath, washed her hair and came out to kiss her mother good night. Norma Rowe, an attractive, womanly divorcee, was somehow moved by the girl's clean fragrance and said, "You smell so good—are you wearing perfume?"

"No, Mom," the girl answered, laughing, "it's just me."

A little later Mrs. Rowe looked in on her daughter, found her apparently sleeping peacefully, and then left for her job as a night nurse in a Tucson hospital. She had no premonition of danger, but she had lately been concerned about Alleen's friendship with a neighbor girl named Mary French.

Mary and Alleen had been spending a good deal of time together, smoking and giggling and talking girl talk in the Rowe backyard. Norma Rowe did not approve. She particularly did not approve of Mary French's friends, a tall, gangling boy of 19 named John Saunders and another named Charles Schmid. She had seen Smitty racing up and down the street in his car and once, when he came to call on Alleen and found her not at home, he had looked at Norma so menacingly with his "pinpoint eyes" that she had been frightened.

Her daughter, on the other hand, seemed to have mixed feelings about Smitty. "He's creepy," she once told her mother, "he just makes me crawl. But he can be nice when he wants to."

At any rate, later that night—according to Mary French's sworn testimony—three friends arrived at Alleen Rowe's house: Smitty, Mary French and Saunders. Smitty had frequently talked with Mary French about killing the Rowe girl by hitting her over the head with a rock. Mary French tapped on Alleen's window and asked her to come out and drink beer with them. Wearing a shift over her bathing suit, she came willingly enough.

Schmid's two accomplices were strange and pitiable creatures. Each of them was afraid of Smitty, yet each was drawn to him. As a baby, John Saunders had been so afflicted with allergies that scabs encrusted his entire body. To keep him from scratching himself his parents had tied his hands and feet to the crib each night, and when eventually he was cured he was so conditioned that he could not go to sleep without being bound hand and foot.

Later, a scrawny boy with poor eyesight ("Just a skinny little body with a big head on it"), he was taunted and bullied by larger children; in turn he bullied those who were smaller. He also suffered badly from asthma and he had few friends. In high school he was a poor student and constantly in minor trouble.

Mary French, 19, was—to put it straight—a frump. Her face, which might have been pretty, seemed somehow lumpy, her body shapeless. She was not dull but she was always a poor student, and she finally had simply stopped going to high school. She was, a friend remembers, "fantastically in love with Smitty. She just sat home and waited while he went out with other girls."

Now, with Smitty at the wheel, the four teen-agers headed for the desert, which begins out Golf Links Road. It is spooky country, dry and empty, the yellow sand clotted with cholla and mesquite and stunted, strangely green palo verde trees, and the great humanoid saguaro that hulk against the sky. Out there at night you can hear the yip and ki-yi of coyotes, the piercing screams of wild creatures—cats, perhaps.

According to Mary French, they got out of the car and walked down into a wash, where they sat on the sand and talked for a while, the four of them. Schmid and Mary then started back to the car. Before they got there, they heard a cry and Schmid turned back toward the wash. Mary went on to the car and sat in it alone. After 45 minutes, Saunders appeared and said Smitty wanted her to come back down. She refused, and Saunders went away. Five or 10 minutes later, Smitty showed up. "He got into the car," says Mary, "and he said, 'We killed her. I love you very much.' He kissed me. He was breathing real hard and seemed excited." Then Schmid got a shovel from the trunk of the car and they returned to the wash. "She was lying on her back and there was blood on her face and head," Mary French testified. Then the three of them dug a shallow grave and put the body in it and covered it up. Afterwards, they wiped Schmid's car clean of Alleen's fingerprints.

More than a year passed. Norma Rowe had reported her daughter missing and the police searched for her—after a fashion. At Mrs. Rowe's insistence they picked up Schmid, but they had no reason to hold him. The police, in fact, assumed that Alleen was just one more of Tucson's runaways.

Norma Rowe, however, had become convinced that Alleen had been killed by Schmid, although she left her kitchen light on every night just in case Alleen did come home. She badgered the police and she badgered the sheriff until the authorities began to dismiss her as a crank. She began to imagine a high-level conspiracy against her. She wrote the state attorney general, the FBI, the U.S. Department of Health, Education and Welfare. She even contacted a New Jersey mystic, who said she could see Alleen's body out in the desert under a big tree.

Ultimately Norma Rowe started her own investigation, questioning Alleen's friends, poking around, dictating her findings to a tape recorder; she even tailed Smitty at night, following him in her car, scared stiff that he might spot her.

Schmid, during this time, acquired a little house of his own. There he held frequent parties, where people sat around amid his stacks of *Playboy* magazines, playing Elvis Presley records and drinking beer.

He read Jules Feiffer's novel, *Harry, the Rat with Women*, and said that his ambition was to be like Harry and have a girl commit suicide over him. Once, according to a friend, he went to see a minister, who gave him a Bible and told him to read the first three chapters of John. Instead Schmid tore the pages out and burned them in the street. "Religion is a farce," he announced. He started an upholstery business with some friends, called himself "founder and president," but then failed to put up the money he'd promised and the venture was short-lived.

He decided he liked blondes best, and took to dyeing the hair of various teen-age girls he went around with. He went out and bought two imitation diamond rings for about $13 apiece and then engaged himself, on the same day, both to Mary French and to a 15-year-old girl named Kathy Morath. His plan, he confided to a friend, was to put each of the girls to work and have them deposit their salaries in a bank account held jointly with him. Mary French did indeed go to work in the convalescent home Smitty's parents operated. When their bank account was fat enough, Smitty withdrew the money and bought a tape recorder.

By this time Smitty also had a girl from a higher social stratum than he usually was involved with. She was Gretchen Fritz, daughter of a prominent Tucson heart surgeon. Gretchen was a pretty, thin, nervous girl of 17 with a knack for trouble. A teacher described her as "erratic, subversive, a psychopathic liar."

At the horsy private school she attended for a time she was a misfit. She not only didn't care about horses, but she shocked her classmates by telling them they were foolish for going out with boys without getting paid for it. Once she even committed the unpardonable social sin of turning up at a formal dance accompanied by boys wearing what was described as beatnik dress. She cut classes, she was suspected of stealing and when, in the summer before her senior year, she got into trouble with juvenile authorities for her role in an attempted theft at a liquor store, the headmaster suggested she not return and then recommended she get psychiatric treatment.

Charles Schmid saw Gretchen for the first time at a public swimming pool in the summer of 1964. He met her by the simple expedient of following her home, knocking on the door and, when she answered, saying, "Don't I know you?" They talked for an hour. Thus began a fierce and stormy relationship. A good deal of what authorities know of the development of this relationship comes from the statements of a spindly scarecrow of a young man who wears pipestem trousers and Beatle boots: Richard Bruns. At the time Smitty was becoming involved with Gretchen, Bruns was 18 years old. He had served two terms in the reformatory at Fort Grant. He had been in and out of trouble all his life, had never fit in anywhere. Yet, although he never went beyond the tenth grade in school and his credibility on many counts is suspect, he is clearly intelligent and even sensitive. He was, for a time, Smitty's closest friend and confidant, and he is today one of the mainstays of the state's case against Smitty. His story:

"He and Gretchen were always fighting," says Bruns. "She didn't want him to drink or go out with the guys or go out with other girls. She wanted him to stay home, call her on the phone, be punctual. First she would get suspicious of him, then he'd get suspicious of her. They were made for each other."

Their mutual jealousy led to sharp and continual arguments. Once she infuriated him by throwing a bottle of shoe polish on his car. Another time she was driving past Smitty's house and saw him there with some other girls. She jumped out of her car and began screaming. Smitty took off into the house, out the back and climbed a tree in his backyard.

His feelings for her were an odd mixture of hate and adoration. He said he was madly in love with her, but he called her a whore. She would let Smitty in her bedroom window at night. Yet he wrote an anonymous letter to the Tucson Health Department accusing her of having venereal disease and spreading it about town. But Smitty also went to enormous lengths to impress Gretchen, once shooting holes through the windows of his car and telling her that thugs, from whom he was protecting her, had fired at him. So Bruns described the relationship.

On the evening of Aug. 16, 1965 Gretchen Fritz left the house with her little sister Wendy, a friendly, lively 13-year-old, to go to a drive-in movie. Neither girl ever came home again. Gretchen's father, like Alleen Rowe's mother, felt sure that Charles Schmid had something to do with his daughters' disappearance, and eventually he hired Bill Heilig, a private detective, to handle the case. One of Heilig's men soon found Gretchen's red compact car parked behind a motel, but the police continued to assume that the girls had joined the ranks of Tucson's runaways.

About a week after Gretchen disappeared, Bruns was at Smitty's home. "We were sitting in the living room," Bruns recalls. "He was sitting on the sofa and I was in the chair by the window and we got on the subject of Gretchen. He said, 'You know I killed her?' I said I didn't, and he said, 'You know where?' I said no. He said, 'I did it here in the living room. First I killed Gretchen, then Wendy was still going *"huh, huh, huh,"* so I . . . [Here Bruns showed how Smitty made a garroting gesture.] Then I took the bodies and put them in the trunk of the car. 1 put the bodies in the most obvious place I could think of because I just didn't care any more. Then I ditched the car and wiped it clean.'"

Bruns was not particularly upset by Smitty's story. Months before, Smitty had told him of the murder of Alleen Rowe, and nothing had come of that. So he was not certain Smitty was telling the truth about the Fritz girls. Besides, Bruns detested Gretchen himself. But what happened next, still according to Bruns's story, did shake him up.

One night not long after, a couple of tough-looking characters, wearing sharp suits and smoking cigars, came by with Smitty and picked up Bruns. Smitty said they were Mafia, and that someone had hired them to look for Gretchen. Smitty and Bruns were taken to an apartment where several men were present whom Smitty later claimed to have recognized as local Cosa Nostra figures.

They wanted to know what had happened to the girls. They made no threats, but the message, Bruns remembers, came across loud and clear. These were no street-corner punks: these were the real boys. In spite of the intimidating company, Schmid lost none of his insouciance. He said he didn't know where Gretchen was, but if she turned up hurt he wanted these men to help him get whoever was responsible. He added that he thought she might have gone to California.

By the time Smitty and Bruns got back to Smitty's house, they were both a little shaky. Later that night, says Bruns, Smitty did the most unlikely thing imaginable: he called the FBI. First he tried the Tucson office and couldn't raise anyone. Then he called Phoenix and couldn't get an agent there either. Finally he put in a person-to-person call to J. Edgar Hoover in Washington. He didn't get Hoover, of course, but he got someone and told him that the Mafia was harassing him over the disappearance of a girl. The FBI promised to have someone in touch with him soon.

Bruns was scared and said so. It occurred to him now that if Smitty really had killed the Fritz girls and left their bodies in an obvious place, they were in very bad trouble indeed—with the Mafia on the one hand and the FBI on the other. "Let's go bury them," Bruns said.

"Smitty stole the keys to his old man's station wagon," says Bruns, "and then we got a flat shovel—the only one we could find. We went to Johnie's and got a hamburger, and then we drove out to the old drinking spot [in the desert]—that's what Smitty meant when he said the most obvious place. It's where we used to drink beer and make out with girls.

"So we parked the car and got the shovel and walked down there, and we couldn't find anything. Then Smitty said, 'Wait, I smell something.' We went in opposite directions looking, and then I heard Smitty say, 'Come here.' I found him kneeling over Gretchen. There was a white rag tied around her legs. Her blouse was pulled up and she was wearing a white bra and Capris.

"Then he said, 'Wendy's up this way.' I sat there for a minute. Then I followed Smitty to where Wendy was. He'd had the decency to cover her—except for one leg, which was sticking up out of the ground.

"We tried to dig with the flat shovel. We each took turns. He'd dig for a while and then I'd dig for a while, but the ground was hard and we couldn't get anywhere with that flat shovel. We dug for 20 minutes and finally Smitty said we'd better do something because it's going to get light. So he grabbed the rag that was around Gretchen's legs and dragged her down in the wash. It made a noise like dragging a hollow shell. It stunk like hell. Then Smitty said wipe off her shoes, there might be fingerprints, so I wiped them off with my handkerchief and threw it away.

"We went back to Wendy. Her leg was sticking up with a shoe on it. He said take off her tennis shoe and throw it over there. I did, I threw it. Then he said, 'Now you're in this as deep as I am.'" By then, the sisters had been missing for about two weeks.

Early next morning Smitty did see the FBI. Nevertheless—here Bruns's story grows even wilder—that same day Smitty left for California, accompanied by a couple of Mafia types, to look for Gretchen Fritz. While there, he was picked up by the San Diego police on a complaint that he was impersonating an FBI officer. He was detained briefly, released and then returned to Tucson.

But now, it seemed to Richard Bruns, Smitty began acting very strangely. He startled Bruns by saying, "I've killed—not three times, but four. Now it's your turn, Richie." He went berserk in his little house, smashing his fist through a wall, slamming doors, then rushing out into the backyard in nothing but his undershorts, where he ran through the night screaming, "God is going to punish me!" He also decided, suddenly, to get married—to a 15-year-old girl who was a stranger to most of his friends.

*

If Smitty seemed to Bruns to be losing his grip, Richie Bruns himself was not in much better shape. His particular quirk revolved around Kathy Morath, the thin, pretty, 16-year-old daughter of a Tucson postman. Kathy had once been attracted to Smitty. He had given her one of his two cut-glass engagement rings. But Smitty never really took her seriously, and one day, in a fit of pique and jealousy, she threw the ring back in his face. Richie Bruns comforted her and then started dating her himself. He was soon utterly and irrevocably smitten with goofy adoration.

Kathy accepted Bruns as a suitor, but halfheartedly. She thought him weird (oddly enough, she did not think Smitty in the least weird) and their romance was short-lived. After she broke up with him last July, Bruns went into a blue funk, a nosedive into romantic melancholy, and then, like some love-swacked Elizabethan poet, he started pouring out his heart to her on paper. He sent her poems, short stories, letters 24 pages long. ("My God, you should have read the stuff," says her perplexed father. "His letters were so romantic it was like 'Next week, East Lynne.'") Bruns even began writing a novel dedicated to "My Darling Kathy."

If Bruns had confined himself to literary catharsis, the murders of the Rowe and Fritz girls might never have been disclosed. But Richie went a little bit around the bend. He became obsessed with the notion that Kathy Morath was the next victim on Smitty's list. Someone had cut the Moraths' screen door, there had been a prowler around her house, and Bruns was sure that is was Smitty. (Kathy and her father, meantime, were sure it was Bruns.)

"I started having this dream," Bruns says. "It was the same dream every night. Smitty would have Kathy out in the desert and he'd be doing all those things to her, and strangling her, and I'd be running across the desert with a gun in my hand, but I could never get there."

If Bruns couldn't save Kathy in his dreams, he could, he figured, stop a walking, breathing Smitty. His scheme for doing so was so wild and so simple that it put the whole Morath family into a state of panic and very nearly landed Bruns in jail.

Bruns undertook to stand guard over Kathy Morath. He kept watch in front of her house, in the alley, and in the street. He patrolled the sidewalk from early in the morning till late at night, seven days a week. If Kathy was home he would be there. If she went out, he would follow her. Kathy's father called the police, and when they told Bruns he couldn't loiter around like that, Bruns fetched his dog and walked the animal up and down the block, hour after hour.

Bruns by now was wallowing in feelings of sacrifice and nobility— all of it unappreciated by Kathy Morath and her parents. At the end of October, he was finally arrested for harassing the Morath family. The judge, facing the obviously woebegone and smitten young man, told Bruns that he wouldn't be jailed if he'd agree to get out of town until he got over his infatuation.

Bruns agreed and a few days later went to Ohio to stay with his grandmother and to try to get a job. It was hopeless. He couldn't sleep at night, and if he did doze off he had his old nightmare again.

One night he blurted out the whole story to his grandmother in their kitchen. She thought he had had too many beers and didn't believe him. "I hear beer does strange things to a person," she said comfortingly. At her words Bruns exploded, knocked over a chair and shouted, "The one time in my life when 1 need advice and what do I get?" A few minutes later he was on the phone to the Tucson police.

Things happened swiftly. At Bruns's frantic insistence, the police picked up Kathy Morath and put her in protective custody. They went into the desert and discovered—precisely as Bruns had described them —the grisly, skeletal remains of Gretchen and Wendy Fritz. They started the machinery that resulted in the arrest a week later of John Saunders and Mary French. They found Charles Schmid working in the yard of his little house, his face layered with make-up, his nose covered by a patch of adhesive plaster which he had worn for five months, boasting that his nose was broken in a fight, and his boots packed full of old rags and tin cans. He put up no resistance.

*

John Saunders and Mary French confessed immediately to their roles in the slaying of Alleen Rowe and were quickly sentenced, Mary French to four to five years, Saunders to life. When Smitty goes on trial for this crime, on March 15, they will be principal witnesses against him.

Meanwhile Richie Bruns, the perpetual misfit, waits apprehensively for the end of the Fritz trial, desperately afraid that Schmid will go free. "If he does," Bruns says glumly, "I'll be the first one he'll kill."

As for Charles Schmid, he has adjusted well to his period of waiting. He is polite and agreeable with all, though at the preliminary hearings he glared menacingly at Richie Bruns. Dressed tastefully, tie neatly knotted, hair carefully combed, his face scrubbed clean of make-up, he is a short, compact, darkly handsome young man with a wide, engaging smile and those deepset eyes.

The people of Tucson wait uneasily for what fresh scandal the two trials may develop. Civic leaders publicly cry that a slur has been cast on their community by an isolated crime. High school students have held rallies and written vehement editorials in the school papers, protesting that they all are being judged by the actions of a few odd-balls and misfits. But the city reverberates with stories of organized teen-age crime and vice, in which Smitty is cast in the role of a minor-league underworld boss. None of these later stories has been substantiated.

One disclosure, however, has most disturbing implications: Smitty's boasts may have been heard not just by Bruns and his other intimates, but by other teen-agers as well. How many—and precisely how much they knew—it remains impossible to say. One authoritative source, however, having listened to the admissions of six high school students, says they unquestionably knew enough so that they should have gone to the police—but were either afraid to talk, or didn't want to rock the boat. As for Smitty's friends, the thought of telling the police never entered their minds.

"I didn't know he killed her," said one, "and even if I had, I wouldn't have said anything. I wouldn't want to be a fink."

Out in the respectable Tucson suburbs parents have started to crack down on the youngsters and have declared Speedway hangouts off limits. "I thought my folks were bad before," laments one grounded 16-year-old, "but now they're just impossible."

As for the others—Smitty's people—most don't care very much. Things are duller without Smitty around, but things have always been dull.

"There's nothing to do in this town," says one of his girls, shaking her dyed blond hair. "The only other town I know is Las Vegas and there's nothing to do there either." For her, and for her friends, there's nothing to do in any town.

They are down on Speedway again tonight, cruising, orbiting the drive-ins, stopping by the joints, where the words of *The Bo Diddley Rock* cut through the smoke and the electronic dissonance like some macabre reminder of their fallen hero:

> *All you women stand in line,*
> *And I'll love you all in an hour's time. . . .*
> *I got a cobra snake for a necktie,*
> *I got a brand-new house on the roadside*
> *Covered with rattlesnake hide,*
> *I got a brand-new chimney made on top,*
> *Made out of human skulls.*
> *Come on baby, take a walk with me,*
> *And tell me, who do you love?*
> *Who do you love?*
> *Who do you love?*
> *Who do you love?*

Life, March 4, 1966

CALVIN TRILLIN

Though best known for his witty paeans to regional American cuisine, journalist Calvin Trillin (b. 1935) has confessed to a lifelong attraction to "stories of sudden death" that nearly matches his interest in Kansas City barbecue and Chicago-style pizza. His accounts of small-town murder, collected in his 1984 book *Killings*, originally appeared as part of his regular "U.S. Journal" series for *The New Yorker*: reports from the road about the everyday events that make up the lives of his countrymen. Like the unpretentious fare he favors, the crimes that Trillin writes about have nothing extraordinary about them, no headline-grabbing glamour or deep sociological significance. They reflect, as he puts it, no "national trends." On the contrary, he is drawn to them precisely because they involve the kind of "unimportant" people whose lives and deaths attract little attention beyond their immediate communities. "If the old newspaper phrase didn't bring to mind an item about a motherly cocker spaniel adopting orphaned ducklings, I would be comfortable with calling them human-interest stories," he says of his true-crime accounts. "Their appeal was that they were about specific humans, and I chose them, of course, because they sounded interesting."

A Stranger with a Camera

Jeremiah, Kentucky
April 1969

On a bright afternoon in September, in 1967, a five-man film crew working in the mountains of Eastern Kentucky stopped to take pictures of some people near a place called Jeremiah. In a narrow valley, a half-dozen dilapidated shacks—each one a tiny square box with one corner cut away to provide a cluttered front porch—stood alongside the county blacktop. Across the road from the shacks, a mountain rose abruptly. In the field that separated them from the mountain behind them, there were a couple of ramshackle privies and some clotheslines tied to trees and a railroad track and a rusted automobile body and a dirty river called Rockhouse Creek. The leader of the film crew was a Canadian named Hugh O'Connor. Widely acclaimed as the co-producer of the Labyrinth show at Expo 67 in Montreal, O'Connor had been hired by Francis Thompson, an American filmmaker, to work on a film Thompson was producing for the American pavilion at HemisFair in San Antonio. O'Connor went up to three of the shacks and asked the head of each household for permission to take pictures. When each one agreed, O'Connor had him sign the customary release forms and gave him a token payment of ten dollars—a token that, in this case, happened to represent a month's rent. The light was perfect in the valley, and the shooting went well. Theodore Holcomb, the associate producer of the film, was particularly struck by the looks of a miner, still in his work clothes and still covered with coal dust, sitting in a rocking chair on one of the porches. "He was just sitting there scratching his arm in a listless way," Holcomb said later. "He had an expression of total despair. It was an extraordinary shot—so evocative of the despair of that region."

The shot of the coal miner was good enough to be included in the final version of the film, and so was a shot of a half-dozen children who, somehow, lived with their parents in one of the tiny shacks. After about an hour and a half, the crew was ready to leave, but someone had noticed a woman come out of one of the shacks and go to the common well to draw some water, and she was asked to repeat the action for filming. As that last shot was being completed, a woman drove up and told the filmmakers that the man who owned the property was coming to throw them off of it. Then she drove away. A couple of minutes later, another car arrived, and a man—a thin, bald man—leaped out. He was holding a pistol. "Get off my property!" he shouted again and again. Then he shot twice. No one was hit. The filmmakers kept moving their equipment toward their cars across the road while trying to tell the man that they were leaving. One of them said that the man must be shooting blanks. "Get off my property!" he kept screaming. Hugh O'Connor, who was lugging a heavy battery across the highway, turned to say that they were going. The man held the pistol in both hands and pulled the trigger again. "Mr. O'Connor briefly looked down in amazement, and I saw a hole in his chest," Holcomb later testified in court. "He saw it and he looked up in despair and said, 'Why did you have to do that?' and, with blood coming from his mouth, he fell to the ground."

Whitesburg, a town about twelve miles from Jeremiah, is the county seat of Letcher County—headquarters for the county court, the sheriff, and assorted coal companies and anti-poverty agencies. Word that someone had been killed reached Whitesburg quickly, but for a couple of hours there was some confusion about just who the victim was. According to various stories, the dead man had been a representative of the Army Corps of Engineers, a Vista volunteer, or a C.B.S. cameraman—any of whom might qualify as a candidate for shooting in Letcher County. The Corps of Engineers had proposed building the Kingdom Come Dam across Rockhouse Creek, thereby flooding an area that included Jeremiah, and some opponents of the dam had been saying that the first government man who came near their property had better come armed. Throughout Eastern Kentucky, local political organizations and coal-mining interests had warned that community organizers who called themselves Vistas or Appalachian Volunteers or anything else were nothing but another variety of Communists—three of them had been arrested on charges of attempting to overthrow the government of Pike County—and even some of the impoverished people whom the volunteers were supposedly in Kentucky to help viewed them with fear and suspicion. A number of television crews had been to Letcher County to record the despair that Holcomb saw in the face of the miner sitting on the front porch. Whitesburg happens to be the home of Harry M. Caudill, a lawyer who drew attention to the plight of the mountain people in 1963 with an eloquent book called *Night Comes to the Cumberlands*. Television crews and reporters on a tour of Appalachia are tempted to start with Letcher County in order to get the benefit of Caudill's counsel, which is ordinarily expressed in a tone of sustained rage—rage at the profit ratio of out-of-state companies that take the region's natural resources while paying virtually no taxes, rage at the strip mines that are gouged across the mountains and at the mud slides and floods and pollution and ugliness they cause, rage at the local merchants and politicians who make a good living from the trade of welfare recipients or the retainers of coal companies and insist that there is nothing wrong with the economy, and, most of all, rage at the country that could permit it all to happen. "Look what man hath wrought on *that* purple mountain's majesty," he will say as he points out the coal waste on the side of a mountain that had once been beautiful. "A country that treats its land and people this way deserves to perish from the earth."

In the view of Caudill and of Tom Gish, the liberal editor of the *Mountain Eagle*, a Letcher County weekly, the reactions of people in Jeremiah to the presence of O'Connor's film crew—coöperation by the poor people being photographed in their squalid shacks, rage by the man who owned the shacks—were characteristic of Letcher County: a lot of people who are still in Eastern Kentucky after years of welfare or subsistence employment have lost the will to treat their situation as an embarrassment, but outside journalists are particularly resented by the people who have managed to make a living—running a country store or a filling station or a small truck mine, working for the county administration, managing some rental property. They resent the impression that everyone in Eastern Kentucky is like the people who are desperately poor—people whose condition they tend to blame on "just sorriness, mostly." In Letcher County, fear of outsiders by people who are guarding reputations or economic interests blends easily into a deep-rooted suspicion of outsiders by all Eastern Kentucky mountain people, who have always had a fierce instinct to protect their property and a distrust of strangers that has often proved to have been justified. All of the people in Letcher County—people who live in the shacks up remote hollows or people who run stores on Main Street in Whitesburg—consider themselves mountain people, and, despite an accurate story in the *Mountain Eagle*, many of them instinctively believed that the mountaineer who killed Hugh O'Connor was protecting his property from smart-aleck outsiders who wouldn't leave when they were told.

The mountaineer's name was Hobart Ison. There have always been Isons in Letcher County, and many of them have managed somewhat better than their neighbors. Hobart Ison had inherited a rather large piece of land in Jeremiah—he raised chickens and rented out shacks he himself had built and at one time ran a small sawmill—but he was known mainly as an eccentric, mean-tempered old man. Everyone in Letcher County knew that Hobart Ison had once built and furnished a house for his future bride and—having been rejected or having been afraid to ask or having had no particular future bride in mind—had let the house remain as it was for thirty years, the grass growing up around it and the furniture still in the packing crates. He had occasionally painted large signs attacking the people he thought had wronged him. He was easily enraged by people hunting on his property, and he despised all of the local Democrats, whom he blamed for injustices that included dismissing him from a post-office job. A psychiatrist who examined him after the shooting said, "Any reference to 'game warden' or 'Democrat' will provoke him tremendously." Once, when some local youths were taunting him, he took a shot at them, hitting one in the shoulder. "A lot of people around here would have welcomed them," Caudill said of the filmmakers. "They just happened to pick the wrong place."

Streams of people came to visit Ison in the Letcher County jail before he was released on bail. Women from around Jeremiah baked him cakes. When his trial came up, it proved impossible to find a jury. The Letcher County commonwealth's attorney and Caudill, who had been retained by Francis Thompson, Inc., secured a change of venue. They argued that Ison's family relationship in Letcher County was "so extensive as to comprise a large segment of the population," and, through an affidavit signed by three citizens in position to know public opinion, they stated that "the overwhelming expression of sentiment has been to the effect that the defendant did right in the slaying of Hugh O'Connor and that he ought to be acquitted of the offense of murder."

Harlan County is a mountain or two away from Letcher County. In the town of Harlan, benches advertising Bunny Enriched Bread stand outside the front door of the county courthouse, flanking the First World War monument and the Revolutionary War monument and the plaque recalling how many Kentucky courthouses were burned down by each side during the Civil War. On the ground floor of the courthouse, the men who habitually gather on the plain wooden benches to pass the time use old No. 5 cans for ashtrays or spittoons and a large container that once held Oscar Mayer's Pure Lard as a wastebasket. In the courtroom, a plain room with all of its furnishings painted black, the only decoration other than pictures of the men who have served as circuit judge is a framed poster in praise of the country lawyer—and also in praise, it turns out upon close reading, of the Dun & Bradstreet Corporation. The front door of the courthouse is almost always plastered with election stickers. In the vestibule just inside, an old man sits on the floor behind a display of old pocketknives and watchbands and billfolds and eyeglass cases offered for sale or trade.

The commonwealth's attorney of Harlan County is Daniel Boone Smith. Eight or nine years ago, Smith got curious about how many people he had prosecuted or defended for murder, and counted up seven hundred and fifty. He was able to amass that total partly because of longevity (except for a few years in the service during the Second World War, he has been commonwealth's attorney continuously since 1933), partly because he has worked in an area that gives anyone interested in trying murder cases plenty of opportunity (the wars between the unions and the coal operators in Harlan County during the thirties were almost as bloody as the mountain feuds earlier in the century), and partly because he happens to be a quick worker ("Some people will take three days to try a murder case," he has said. "I usually get my case on in a day"). During his first week as commonwealth's attorney of Harlan and an adjoining county, Smith tried five murder cases.

These days, Harlan County may have about that many a year, but it remains a violent place. The murders that do occur in mountain counties like Harlan and Letcher often seem to occur while someone is in a drunken rage, and often among members of the same family—a father shooting a son over something trivial, one member of a family mowing down another who is breaking down the door trying to get at a third. "We got people in this county today who would kill you as quick as look at you," Smith has said. "But most of 'em are the type that don't bother you if you leave them alone." Smith is known throughout Eastern Kentucky for his ability to select jurors—to remember which prospective juror's uncle may have had a boundary dispute with which witness's grandfather twenty years ago—and for his ability to sum up the case for them in their own language once the evidence has been heard. He is an informal, colloquial, storytelling man who happens to be a graduate of the Harvard Law School.

A lack of fervor about convicting Hobart Ison was assumed in Harlan County when he came up for trial there in May 1968. "Before the case, people were coming up and saying, 'He *should've* killed the son of a bitch,'" Smith said later. "People would say, 'They oughtn't to make fun of mountain people. They've made enough fun of mountain people. Let me on the jury, Boone, and I'll turn him loose.'" Smith saw his task as persuading the citizens and the jurors that the case was not what it appeared to be—that the filmmakers were not "a bunch of privateers and pirates" but respectable people who had been commissioned by the United States government, that the film was not another study of how poor and ignorant people were in Eastern Kentucky but a film about the whole United States in which the shots of Eastern Kentucky would take up only a few seconds, that the filmmakers had behaved properly and politely to those they were photographing. "Why, if they had been smart alecks come to hold us up to ridicule, I'd be the last man to try him," Smith assured everyone. It took Smith only a day or so to present his case against Hobart Ison, although it took three days to pick the jury. On the witness stand, the surviving filmmakers managed to avoid admitting to Ison's lawyers that it was the appalling poverty of his tenants that had interested them; they talked about being attracted by expressive family groups and by the convenience of not having to move their equipment far from the road. The defense asked if they were planning to take pictures of the Bluegrass as well as Appalachia. Were they going to make a lot of money from the film? How many millions of viewers would see the pictures of poor Eastern Kentucky people? Had they refused to move? Had they taunted Ison by saying he was shooting blanks? Did the people who signed the release forms really know what they were signing? (At least one of the signers was, like one out of four of his neighbors, unable to read.)

Except for the underlying issue of Eastern Kentucky v. Outsiders, the only issue seriously in contention was Ison's sanity. The director of a nearby mental-health clinic, testifying for the defense, said that Ison was a paranoid schizophrenic. He told of Ison showing up for one interview with long socks worn on the outside of his trouser legs and of his altercations with his neighbors and of his lack of remorse. The prosecution's psychiatrist—an impressive woman from the University of Kentucky who had been retained by Francis Thompson, Inc.—said that Ison had grown up at a time when it was common practice to run people off of property with a gun, and, because he had lived with aging parents or alone ever since childhood, he still followed that practice. Some of Ison's ideas did have "paranoid coloring," she said, but that could be traced to his being a mountaineer, since people in isolated mountain pockets normally had a suspicion of strangers and even of each other. "Socio-cultural circumstances," she concluded, "lead to the diagnosis of an individual who is normal for his culture, the shooting and the paranoid color both being present in other individuals in this culture who are considered normal." In the trial and in the insanity hearing that had earlier found Ison competent to stand trial, Smith insisted that Ison was merely peculiar, not crazy. "I said, 'Now, I happen to like mayonnaise on my beans. Does that make *me* crazy?'" Smith later recalled. "I turned to one of the jurors, a man named Mahan Fields, and I said, 'Mahan, you remember Uncle Bob Woolford, who used to work up at Evarts? Did you ever see Uncle Bob in the winter when he didn't have his socks pulled up over his pants legs to keep out the cold? Now, was Uncle Bob crazy? Why, Mahan, I bet on many a winter morning *you* wore *your* socks over your pants legs.'"

In his summation, Smith saved his harshest words not for the defendant but for the person who was responsible for bringing Hobart Ison, a mountaineer who was not quite typical of mountaineers, and Hugh O'Connor, a stranger with a camera who was not quite typical of strangers with cameras, into violent conflict. Judy Breeding—the operator of a small furniture store near Ison's shacks, and the wife of Ison's cousin—had testified that she was not only the woman who told the film crew that Ison was coming but also the woman who had told Ison that the film crew was on his property. "Hobart," she recalled saying, "there is some men over there taking pictures of your houses, with out-of-state license." Smith looked out toward the courtroom spectators and suddenly pointed his finger at Judy Breeding. He told her that he would like to be prosecuting her, that if it hadn't been for her mouth Hugh O'Connor would not be in his grave and Hobart Ison would be back home where he belonged. Later, Smith caught a glimpse of Mrs. Breeding in the hall, and he thought he saw her shake her fist at him, smiling. "You know," he said, "I believe the idea that she had anything to do with bringing that about had never occurred to her till I mentioned it."

The jury was eleven to one for conviction, but the one held out. Some people were surprised that Ison had come that close to being convicted, although it was generally agreed that the prosecution's psychiatrist had out-talked the psychiatrist who testified for the defense. Smith believed that his case had been greatly strengthened by the fact that the filmmakers had been respectful, soft-spoken witnesses—not at all smart-alecky. "If there was anything bigheaded about them," he said, "it didn't show."

*

The retrial was postponed once, and then was stopped suddenly during jury selection when Smith became ill. On March 24th, Hobart Ison came to trial again. The filmmakers, who had been dreading another trip to Kentucky, were at the county courthouse in Harlan at nine in the morning, ready to repeat their testimony. Although Smith had anticipated even more trouble finding a jury, he was prepared to go to trial. But Ison's lawyers indicated to Smith and Caudill that their client, now seventy, would be willing to plead guilty to voluntary manslaughter, and they finally met Smith's insistence on a ten-year sentence. Ison—wearing a baggy brown suit, his face pinched and red— appeared only briefly before the judge to plead guilty. A couple of hours after everyone arrived, Caudill was on his way back to Whitesburg, where he was working on the case of a Vietnam veteran accused of killing two men during an argument in the street, and the filmmakers were driving to Knoxville to catch the first plane to New York.

The following day, the clerk of the court, a strong-looking woman with a strong Kentucky accent, happened to get into a discussion about the filmmakers with another citizen who had come to know them in the year and a half since Hugh O'Connor's death—a woman with a softer accent and a less certain tone to her voice.

"You know, I asked those men yesterday morning if they were happy with the outcome," the clerk said. "And they said, 'Yes.' And I said, 'Well, you know, us hillbillies is a queer breed. We are. I'm not offering any apologies when I say that. Us hillbillies *are* a queer breed, and I'm just as proud as punch to be one.'"

"Not all of us are like that," the other woman said. "Mean like that."

"Well, I wouldn't say that man is mean," the clerk said. "I don't guess he ever harmed anybody in his life. They were very nice people. I think it was strictly a case of misunderstanding. I think that the old man thought they were laughing and making fun of him, and it was more than he could take. I know this: a person isolated in these hills, they often grow old and eccentric, which I think they have a right to do."

"But he didn't have a right to kill," the other woman said.

"Well, no," the clerk said. "But us hillbillies, we don't bother nobody.

We go out of our way to help people. But we don't want nobody pushin' us around. Now, that's the code of the hills. And he felt like—that old man felt like—he was being pushed around. You know, it's like I told those men: 'I wouldn't have gone on that old man's land to pick me a mess of wild greens without I'd asked him.' They said, 'We didn't know all this.' I said, 'I bet you know it now. I bet you know it now.'"

The New Yorker, April 29, 1969

GAY TALESE

An ex-jailbird with a glib tongue, Charles Manson became guru to a coterie of drug-addled dropouts during the fabled "Summer of Love." In the spring of 1968 Manson's ragtag commune settled in a dusty, disused ranch outside Los Angeles, where they enjoyed a squalid, orgiastic existence overseen by their increasingly demented messiah. Obsessed with the Beatles' song "Helter Skelter," which he interpreted as a bizarre doomsday allegory, Manson concocted a scheme to provoke an apocalyptic race war by slaying white people in a way that would supposedly implicate black revolutionaries. On August 9, 1969, Manson sent four of his disciples to invade the home of film director Roman Polanski, who was away on a shoot. They butchered his pregnant wife, Sharon Tate, along with four other people, and scrawled cryptic graffiti in their victims' blood. The following night, Manson himself led a party of his "creepy crawlers" to the home of Leno and Rosemary LaBianca, who were slaughtered in a similar fashion.

Public fascination with Manson and his "Family" was reflected in an outpouring of writing about every facet of the case, including this 1970 *Esquire* magazine piece by Gay Talese (b. 1932). One of the pioneers of the "New Journalism," Talese started out at *The New York Times*, eventually taking over Meyer Berger's "About New York" column after Berger's death in 1959. It was his work for *Esquire*, however, that helped introduce something radically new into American journalism, a style of reporting that exploited novelistic techniques and that made Talese's deeply researched accounts read like literary fiction.

Charlie Manson's Home on the Range

The horse wrangler, tall and ruggedly handsome, placed his hands on the hips of a pretty girl wearing white bell-bottomed trousers and casually lifted her onto a hitching post near the stable; then, voluntarily, almost automatically, she spread her legs and he stood between her, moving slowly from side to side and up and down, stroking her long blonde hair while her arms and fingers caressed his back, not quickly or eagerly but quite passively, indolently, a mood harmonious with his own.

They continued their slow erotic slumber for several moments under the mid-morning sun, swaying silently and looking without expression into one another's eyes, seeming totally unaware of their own lack of privacy and the smell of horse manure near their feet and the thousands of flies buzzing around them and the automobile that had just come down the dusty road and was now parked, motor idling, with a man inside calling through an open window to where the wrangler stood between the girl.

He slowly turned his head toward the car but did not withdraw from the girl. He was about six feet four and wore a bone-like ornament around his neck, and he had a long angular face with a sandy beard and pale sharply focused blue eyes. He did not seem perturbed by the stranger in the automobile; he assumed that he was probably a reporter or detective, both having come in great numbers recently to this ranch in Southern California to speak with the proprietor, an old man named George Spahn, about a group of violent hippies that had lived on the ranch for a year but were now believed to have all moved away.

Spahn was not reluctant to talk about them, the wrangler knew, even though Spahn had never seen them, the old man being blind; and so when the man in the car asked for George Spahn, a little smile formed on the wrangler's face, knowing but enigmatic, and he pointed toward a shack at the end of a row of dilapidated empty wooden buildings. Then, as the car pulled away, he again began his slow movements with the girl delicately balanced on the hitching post.

Spahn's ranch is lost in desert brush and rocky hills, but it is not so much a ranch as it is the old Western movie set it once was. The row of empty buildings extending along the dirt road toward Spahn's shack—decaying structures with faded signs marking them as a saloon, a barbershop, a café, a jail, and a carriage house—all were constructed many years ago as Hollywood settings for cowboy brawls and Indian ambushes, and among the many actors who performed in them, or in front of them, were Tom Mix and Johnny Mack Brown, Hoot Gibson, Wallace Beery, and The Cisco Kid. In the carriage house is a coach that supposedly was used by Grace Kelly in *High Noon*, and scattered here and there, and slept in by the stray dogs and cats that run wild on this land, are old wagons and other props used in scenes in *Duel in the Sun*, *The Lone Ranger* television series and *Bonanza*. Around the street set, on the edge of the clearing near the trees, are smaller broken-down shacks lived in by wranglers or itinerants who drift to this place periodically and work briefly at some odd job and then disappear. There is an atmosphere of impermanence and neglect about the place, the unwashed windows, the rotting wood, the hauling trucks parked on inclines because their batteries are low and need the momentum of a downhill start; and yet there is much that is natural and appealing about the place, not the ranch area itself but the land in back of where the old man lives, it being thick with trees and berry bushes and dipping toward a small creek and rising again toward the rocky foothills of the Santa Susanna Mountains. There are a few caves in the mountains that have been used from time to time as shelters by shy vagrants, and in the last few years hippies have sometimes been seen along the rocky ridges strumming guitars and singing songs. Now the whole area is quiet and still and, though it is only twenty miles northwest of downtown Beverly Hills, it is possible from certain heights to look for miles in any direction without seeing any sign of modern life.

Spahn came to this region in the Nineteen-Thirties in the first great migration of the automobile age, a time when it was said to be the dream of every Midwestern Model T salesman to move to sunny Southern California and live in a bungalow with a banana plant in the front yard. Except George Spahn had no such dream, nor was he a Midwestern Model T salesman. He was a fairly successful dairy farmer from Pennsylvania with a passion for horses, preferring them to cars and to most of the people that he knew. The fact that his father had been kicked to death by a horse, an accident that occurred in 1891 when the elder Spahn was delivering slaughtered livestock in a horse-drawn wagon near Philadelphia, did not instill in the son any fear of that animal; in fact, Spahn quit school after the third grade to work behind a horse on a milk wagon, and his close association with horses was to continue through the rest of his life, being interrupted by choice only once.

That was during his sixteenth year when, temporarily tired of rising at three a.m. for his daily milk route, he accepted a job as a carpenter's apprentice, living in the carpenter's home and becoming in time seduced by the carpenter's lusty nineteen-year-old daughter. She would entice him into the woods beyond the house on afternoons when her father was away, or into her bedroom at night after her father had gone to sleep; and even, one day, observing through her window two dogs copulating in the yard, she was suddenly overcome with desire and pulled Spahn to the floor on top of her—all this happening when he was sixteen, in 1906, a first sexual relationship that he can remember vividly and wistfully even now at the age of eighty-one.

Though never handsome, Spahn was a strong solidly built man in his youth with a plain yet personable manner. He had a hot temper at times, but he was never lazy. When he was in his middle twenties his milk business in Willow Grove, Pennsylvania, was large enough for him to operate five wagons and seven horses; and one of the men whom he employed, more out of kindness than anything else, was his stepfather, Tom Reah, whom he had once despised. Spahn could never understand what his strict German-Irish mother had ever seen in Reah, a rawboned man with a large belly who, when drunk, could be vicious. When in this condition, Reah would sometimes assault young Spahn, beating him badly; although later Spahn fought back, once swearing at Reah: "You son of a bitch, I'm gonna kill you some day!" On another occasion he threw an ice ax at Reah's head, missing by inches.

Before Spahn was thirty he had obtained an eighty-six-acre farm near Lansdale, Pennsylvania, on which he kept thirty-five cows, several horses, and a lady housekeeper he had hired after placing an advertisement in a local newspaper. She had previously been married to a racing-car driver who had been killed, leaving her with one child. Spahn found her congenial and able, if not reminiscent of the carpenter's daughter; and at some later date that Spahn cannot remember, they were married. While it would not be an entirely happy or lasting marriage, they would remain together long enough to have ten children, nearly all of whom would be named after Spahn's horses. He named his first daughter, Alice, after a yellow-white pinto he had once owned; and his second daughter, Georgianna, was named in honor of a gelding called George. His third daughter, Mary, was named after a big bay mare; and when Spahn had a son, he named him George after himself *and* the aforementioned gelding. Next came Dolly, after a big sorrel mare; and Paul, after a freckled pinto; and so on down the line.

During the early Thirties, in the Depression, Spahn contemplated moving West. Animal feed was scarce in Pennsylvania, the milk was frequently spoiled by the inadequate refrigeration system on his farm, and he was becoming disenchanted with life in general. In an advertisement circulated by the Union Pacific Railroad, he had read about the virtues of Southern California, its predictable and mild climate, its lack of rain in summertime, its abundant feed for animals, and he was tempted. He first came alone by train to see Southern California for himself; then, satisfied, he returned home. He sold his farm and packed his family, his furniture, and his horse collars in a Packard sedan and a truck, and shipped his best horses separately by rail. He began the long voyage across the continent. He would not regret his decision.

Within a few years, giving up the milk business to concentrate on raising horses and operating a riding stable, he prospered. Within a decade, moving from Long Beach to South Los Angeles, and then to North Hollywood, he expanded his business to include children's pony rides, the rental of horses for parades and fairs, and the supplying of horses and wranglers for use in cowboy films. In one movie that featured a desert battle between Arabs and Ethiopians, Spahn himself became part of the cast, playing an Arab horseman and wearing a desert robe and white bloomers. In 1948, when one of the ranches used by the moviemakers was offered for sale, a ranch once owned by William S. Hart, a cowboy star of the silent screen, Spahn bought it. Spahn and his wife parted company at about this time, but there soon appeared at Spahn's side a new leading lady of the ranch, a onetime dog trainer and circus performer named Ruby Pearl.

She was a perky redhead of about thirty with lively blue eyes, a petite figure, and lots of nerve. She had been born on a farm in Sandstone, Minnesota, and had a desire to get into show business somehow, an ambition that was as confusing as it was shocking to her mother, a Christian preacher's daughter, and her father, a conscientious routine-oriented railroad man. After graduating from high school, where she had acted in school plays and had won first prize in the girls' hundred-yard dash and broad-jump competition in a county-wide track meet, she traveled to Minneapolis on her father's railroad pass, presumably to attend secretarial school and embark on a respectable career in that city. But one day, scanning the classified ads in *The Minneapolis Tribune*, she saw a job opportunity that appealed to her. She applied and got the job, that of being a cocktail waitress at Lindy's, a local club patronized by, among other distinguished figures, Al Capone.

When Capone and his men were in town they were invariably accompanied by very attractive girls in ermine or mink, and they were always given the large table at Lindy's in the back room where the drinks were served all night. Ruby Pearl liked serving the big table, not only because of the generous tips she received but because of the sense of excitement she felt in the Capone party's presence. But she had neither the desire nor the time to become further involved, devoting all her free hours and earnings to the dancing school she attended every day, learning ballet and adagio, tap-dancing, the rumba, and the tango. After Lindy's was raided by the police and closed down, Ruby Pearl supported herself as a bus girl in a cafeteria, pouring coffee and clearing dishes. Soon she caught the eye of the assistant manager, an engineering student at the University of Minnesota. He became her first lover and husband, and after his graduation he was hired by Lockheed in Burbank, California, and the newly married couple set up housekeeping in a motor court on the fringe of Hollywood.

On certain evenings, together with other young engineers from Lockheed and their wives, Ruby and her husband would go to The Brown Derby and Ciro's and various night spots where there was live entertainment and dancing. Ruby invariably became restless and tense on these occasions, seated around the table with the others, sipping her drink, and wishing that she was not with the dull wives of engineers but rather that she was in the spotlight on the stage, kicking up her heels.

Her marriage did not produce children, nor did she want any. She wanted to resume with her dancing, and she did, attending classes conducted by a sleek French-Indian adagio dancer who later gave Ruby a part in his touring trio that featured himself and his jealous girl friend. Ruby also danced in a chorus of a Hollywood club for a while, as her marriage deteriorated and finally ended in divorce.

At about this time, approaching an age when she could no longer maintain a dancer's pace, she was introduced, by a man she had met, to a new career of training dogs to dance, sit, jump through hoops, and ride atop ponies. She had a natural facility for animal training, and within a few years she had perfected an act with three dogs and a pony that was booked at several community fairs in Southern California, in addition to a number of schools, circuses, and local television shows. At one community fair, in Thousand Oaks, Ruby met a man, a wrestler, who would become her next husband. He was a burly, strong, and tender man who had done quite well financially, and he also owned a restaurant on the side, a subject of interest to Ruby because of her days as a waitress. Not long afterward, Ruby met another man with whom she had much in common, a proprietor of a pony-riding ring for children and a movie ranch—George Spahn.

She had seen Spahn at a few of the parades for which he had provided horses, and on a few occasions she had helped with the handling of the horses, displaying her skill as a wrangler. After Spahn had obtained the movie ranch, Ruby applied for a job there and was hired. Spahn was happy to have her. His eyesight was not yet so poor that he was unaware of her fine figure and appeal, and he also welcomed the return of a woman's touch around the place, for it had been absent since the recent departure of his wife. There was not only the film business but also the riding stable that required extra help, particularly on weekends when there would sometimes be a long line of cars with people wanting to rent a horse and go riding through the woods for an hour or two. Ruby knew the horses well, knew the frisky ones from the slower ones, and she could tell pretty much by the way people walked up to the riding stable whether or not they possessed the coordination to safely mount and ride Spahn's better horses. Ruby Pearl was also important to Spahn because she could keep an eye on the young wranglers' manners with regard to the schoolgirls and other young women who often rented horses, although he had to admit that some of the women seemed deliberately dressed for a seduction scene when they came to the ranch—skintight chinos and no bras, their long hair loose and legs wide and bumping up and down as they capered through the woods—it was a risky business.

But Ruby Pearl kept order, and the more responsibility she took the more Spahn relied upon her. His children were now grown and married. Occasionally, Ruby would spend the night on the ranch, and as Spahn's sight worsened in the next few years she accompanied him on shopping trips off the ranch, held him close as they climbed steps, guided his hand as he signed checks, dialed telephone numbers for him, helped to prepare his meals. There were rumors in the nearby town, and among the ranch hands, that associated the pair romantically, and once her husband, the wrestler, complained about the time she was devoting to the ranch. But she quickly dismissed the subject, saying sharply, "I'm *needed* there."

In the last few years, however, Spahn gradually began to notice changes in Ruby Pearl. Slowly, as his sight failed completely and his imagination sharpened, he began to think that she was drifting away from the ranch and himself. He began to notice a difference in the way she held his arm as they walked—she seemed to be holding on more to the cloth of his sleeve than to his arm, and eventually it seemed that she was leading him around while holding *only* to the cloth. He began to miss, or to imagine he was missing, many of the things he once had, among them the presence of female voices on the ranch at night. Perhaps that is why, when the hippie girls arrived, even though they were often noisy and sang songs all night, he felt more alive than he had felt in a very long time.

He does not remember exactly when they first moved onto the ranch. He believes one group of hippie girls and boys arrived sometime in 1967, possibly having come down from San Francisco, and settled briefly in a roadside church several miles north of his ranch; and eventually, in their wanderings down the hill searching for food, they discovered the many empty shacks along the riding path in the woods. They lived in the shacks briefly, and Spahn did not object; but one morning there was a police raid in search of marijuana, and many of the young people were taken into custody. The police asked if Spahn wished to press charges, but he said he did not. The police nonetheless warned the hippies against trespassing, and for a long time it was again very quiet on the ranch at night.

Then one day a school bus carrying hippies arrived at the ranch and parked in the woods, and young girls approached Spahn's doorway, tapping lightly on the screen, and asked if they could stay for a few days. He was reluctant, but when they assured him that it would be only for a few days, adding that they had had automobile trouble, he acquiesced. The next morning Spahn became aware of the sound of weeds being clipped not far from his house, and he was told by one of the wranglers that the work was being done by a few long-haired girls and boys. Later, one of the girls offered to make the old man's lunch, to clean out the shack, to wash the windows. She had a sweet, gentle voice, and she was obviously an educated and very considerate young lady. Spahn was pleased.

In the days that followed, extending into weeks and months, Spahn became familiar with the sounds of the other girls' voices, equally gentle and eager to do whatever had to be done; he did not have to ask them for anything, they saw what had to be done, and they did it. Spahn also came to know the young man who seemed to be in charge of the group, another gentle voice who explained that he was a musician, a singer and poet, and that his name was Charlie Manson. Spahn liked Manson, too. Manson would visit his shack on quiet afternoons and talk for hours about deep philosophical questions, subjects that bewildered the old man but interested him, relieving the loneliness. Sometimes after Spahn had heard Manson walk out the door, and after he had sat in silence for a while, the old man might mutter something to himself—and Manson would reply. Manson seemed to breathe soundlessly, to walk with unbelievable silence over creaky floors. Spahn had heard the wranglers tell of how they would see Charlie Manson sitting quietly by himself in one part of the ranch, and then suddenly they would discover him somewhere else. He seemed to be here, there, everywhere, sitting under a tree softly strumming his guitar. The wranglers had described Manson as a rather small, dark-haired man in his middle thirties, and they could not understand the strong attraction that the six or eight women had for him. Obviously, they adored him. They made his clothes, sat at his feet while he ate, made love to him whenever he wished, did whatever he asked. He had asked that the girls look after the old man's needs, and a few of them would sometimes spend the night in his shack, rising early to make his breakfast. During the day they would paint portraits of Spahn, using oil paint on small canvases that they had brought. Manson brought Spahn many presents, one of them being a large tapestry of a horse.

He also gave presents to Ruby Pearl—a camera, a silver serving set, tapestries—and once, when he said he was short of money, he sold her a $200 television set for $50. It was rare, however, that Manson admitted to needing money, although nobody on the ranch knew where he got the money that he had, having to speculate that he had been given it by his girls out of their checks from home, or had earned it from his music. Manson claimed to have written music for rock-and-roll recording artists, and sometimes he was visited at the ranch by members of The Beach Boys and also by Doris Day's son, Terry Melcher. All sorts of new people had been visiting the ranch since Manson's arrival, and one wrangler even claimed to have seen the pregnant movie actress, Sharon Tate, riding through the ranch one evening on a horse. But Spahn could not be sure.

Spahn could not be certain of anything after Manson had been there for a few months. Many new people, new sounds and elements, had intruded so quickly upon what had been familiar to the old blind man on the ranch that he could not distinguish the voices, the footsteps, the mannerisms as he once had; and without Ruby Pearl on the ranch each night, Spahn's view of reality was largely through the eyes of the hippies or the wranglers, and he did not know which of the two groups was the more bizarre, harebrained, hallucinatory. He knew that the wranglers were now associating with the hippies; he could hear them talking together during the day near the horse corral, and at night he thought he recognized wranglers' voices in the crowd that had gathered to hear Manson's music in the café of the old Western movie set. The hippies were wearing Western clothes and boots and were riding the horses, he had heard; and perhaps the motorcycle sounds he heard in the morning were being made by wranglers, he did not know. The atmosphere was now a blend of horse manure and marijuana, and most of the people seemed to speak in soft voices, wranglers as well as hippies, and this greatly irritated the old man. He yelled toward them: "Speak up, *speak up*, I want to hear too!" They would speak up, but in tones still soft and placid; and Spahn often overheard them describing him as a "beautiful person."

None of Spahn's experience in life had prepared him for this; he was thoroughly confused by Manson and his followers, yet was pleasantly distracted by their presence and particularly fascinated by Manson's girls. They would do anything that Manson asked, anything, and their submissiveness was in sharp contrast to all the women that Spahn had ever known, beginning with his stern mother in Pennsylvania and extending through the carpenter's aggressive daughter, and the untimid housekeeper who became his wife, and the independent woman who was Ruby Pearl. Manson's girls, intellectually superior to all the women that George Spahn had known, were also more domestic: they liked to cook, to clean, to sew, to make love to Manson or to whomever he designated.

On occasions when Manson was in Spahn's shack, the old man tried to learn the secret of Manson's handling of women, but the latter would mostly laugh—"All you gotta do, George, is grab 'em by the hair, and kick 'em you know where"—and then Manson would be gone, his secret unexplained, and the girls would arrive, docile, delightful.

Abruptly, it ended.

Manson and his followers left the ranch in their bus one day, going as mysteriously as they had come, and for a while the old man's life reverted to what it had been. But then the police and detectives began to visit the ranch, inspecting the movie shacks where the hippies had lived, taking fingerprints and even digging large holes in the woodlands beyond the clearing in search of bodies. Then the reporters and television cameramen arrived, flashing light into Spahn's face that was so bright he could see it, and asking him questions about Charlie Manson and his "family" who were now charged with murdering Sharon Tate and several others. Spahn was stunned, disbelieving, but he told them what he knew. He sat in his shack for several hours with the press, slumped in a chair, holding a cane in one hand and a small dog in the other, wearing a soiled tan Stetson and dark sunglasses to protect his head and eyes from the flies and the light and the dirt and the flicking tails of his horses, and he answered the reporters' questions and posed for photographs. Hanging from the wall behind him, or resting on the mantel, were psychedelic portraits of him done by the girls, and on a nearby table was a guitar, and on another wall was the tapestry of a horse that Manson had given him.

For the next several days, with the television cameras on trucks focusing on the ranch, lighting up the rickety Hollywood sets, it was like old times for Spahn. Ruby Pearl was there to lead him around, although still holding him by the cloth of his sleeve, and his picture appeared on television and his words were quoted in the national press. He said that it was hard for him to believe that the girls had participated in the murders; if they had, he continued, they were undoubtedly under the influence of drugs.

As for Manson, Spahn said, there was no explanation—he had a hypnotic spell over the girls, they were his slaves. But Spahn was reluctant to say too much against Manson; and when the reporters asked why this was so, Spahn confessed that he was somewhat fearful of Manson, even though the latter was in jail. Manson might get out, Spahn suggested, or there might still be people on the ranch who were loyal to him.

The reporters did not press Spahn further. After they had finished with their questions, they wandered around the ranch taking photographs of the movie set and the soft-spoken wranglers and the girl who stood near the hitching post.

Esquire, March 1970

TRUMAN CAPOTE

A preternaturally charming man who moved easily among the rich and famous, Truman Capote (1924–1984) made a sensational debut at the age of 24 with the publication of his first novel, *Other Voices, Other Rooms*, a coming-of-age story that caused a stir as much for its notorious author's photo—an epicene Capote languidly sprawled on a divan—as for its evocative story and poetic style. Over the next decade, when he wasn't hobnobbing with socialites and movie stars, Capote worked in a variety of genres, from screenplays and Broadway shows to journalism and fiction, achieving major success with his 1958 novella *Breakfast at Tiffany's*. The book that put him in the forefront of American writers, however, was his "nonfiction novel" *In Cold Blood* (1966), which traced the intersecting lives of a midwestern farm family and the two dead-end drifters who murdered them. The book became a cultural and commercial phenomenon, but its six-year composition—and the intimate bond Capote established with one of its subjects, the condemned killer Perry Smith— took a heavy psychological toll. Capote spiraled into drug use and alcoholism and produced nothing to match the achievements of his earlier work. Occasionally, however, he was still capable of effective writing, as in this jailhouse interview with Manson associate Robert Beausoleil, from the 1980 collection *Music for Chameleons*.

Then It All Came Down

*S*cene: A cell in a maximum-security cell block at San Quentin prison in California. The cell is furnished with a single cot, and its permanent occupant, Robert Beausoleil, and his visitor are required to sit on it in rather cramped positions. The cell is neat, uncluttered; a well-waxed guitar stands in one corner. But it is late on a winter afternoon, and in the air lingers a chill, even a hint of mist, as though fog from San Francisco Bay had infiltrated the prison itself.

Despite the chill, Beausoleil is shirtless, wearing only a pair of prison-issue denim trousers, and it is clear that he is satisfied with his appearance, his body particularly, which is lithe, feline, in well-toned shape considering that he has been incarcerated more than a decade. His chest and arms are a panorama of tattooed emblems: feisty dragons, coiled chrysanthemums, uncoiled serpents. He is thought by some to be exceptionally good-looking; he is, but in a rather hustlerish camp-macho style. Not surprisingly, he worked as an actor as a child and appeared in several Hollywood films; later, as a very young man, he was for a while the protégé of Kenneth Anger, the experimental film-maker (*Scorpio Rising*) and author (*Hollywood Babylon*); indeed, Anger cast him in the title role of *Lucifer Rising*, an unfinished film.

Robert Beausoleil, who is now thirty-one, is the real mystery figure of the Charles Manson cult; more to the point—and it's a point that has never been clearly brought forth in accounts of that tribe—he is the key to the mystery of the homicidal escapades of the so-called Manson family, notably the Sharon Tate–Lo Bianco murders.

It all began with the murder of Gary Hinman, a middle-aged professional musician who had befriended various members of the Manson brethren and who, unfortunately for him, lived alone in a small isolated house in Topanga Canyon, Los Angeles County. Hinman had been tied up and tortured for several days (among other indignities, one of his ears had been severed) before his throat had been mercifully and lastingly slashed. When Hinman's body, bloated and abuzz with August flies, was discovered, police found bloody graffiti on the walls of his modest house ("Death to Pigs!")—graffiti similar to the sort soon to be found in the households of Miss Tate and Mr. and Mrs. Lo Bianco.

However, just a few days prior to the Tate–Lo Bianco slayings, Robert Beausoleil, caught driving a car that had been the property of the victim, was under arrest and in jail, accused of having murdered the helpless Mr. Hinman. It was then that Manson and his chums, in the hopes of freeing Beausoleil, conceived the notion of committing a series of homicides similar to the Hinman affair; if Beausoleil was still incarcerated at the time of these killings, then how could he be guilty of the Hinman atrocity? Or so the Manson brood reasoned. That is to say, it was out of devotion to "Bobby" Beausoleil that Tex Watson and those cutthroat young ladies, Susan Atkins, Patricia Krenwinkel, Leslie Van Hooten, sallied forth on their satanic errands.

RB: Strange. Beausoleil. That's French, My name is French. It means Beautiful Sun. Fuck. Nobody sees much sun inside this resort. Listen to the foghorns. Like train whistles. Moan, moan. And they're worse in the summer. Maybe it must be there's more fog in summer than in winter. Weather. Fuck it, I'm not going anywhere. But just listen. Moan, moan. So what've you been up to today?

TC: Just around. Had a little talk with Sirhan.

RB (laughs): Sirhan B. Sirhan. I knew him when they had me up on the Row. He's a sick guy. He don't belong here. He ought to be in Atascadero. Want some gum? Yeah, well, you seem to know your way around here pretty good. I was watching you out on the yard. I was surprised the warden lets you walk around the yard by yourself. Somebody might cut you.

TC: Why?

RB: For the hell of it. But you've been here a lot, huh? Some of the guys were telling me.

TC: Maybe half a dozen times on different research projects.

RB: There's just one thing here I've never seen. But I'd like to see that little apple-green room. When they railroaded me on that Hinman deal and I got the death sentence, well, they had me up on the Row a good spell. Right up to when the court abolished the death penalty. So I used to wonder about the little green room.

TC: Actually, it's more like three rooms.

RB: I thought it was a little round room with a sort of glass-sealed igloo hut set in the center. With windows in the igloo so the witnesses standing outside can see the guys choking to death on that peach perfume.

TC: Yes, that's the gas-chamber room. But when the prisoner is brought down from Death Row he steps from the elevator directly into a "holding" room that adjoins the witness room. There are two cells in this "holding" room, two, in case it's a double execution. They're ordinary cells, just like this one, and the prisoner spends his last night there before his execution in the morning, reading, listening to the radio, playing cards with the guards. But the interesting thing I discovered was that there's a *third* room in this little suite. It's behind a closed door right next to the "holding" cell. I just opened the door and walked in and none of the guards that were with me tried to stop me. And it was the most haunting room I've ever seen. Because you know what's in it? All the leftovers, all the paraphernalia that the different condemned men had had with them in the "holding" cells. Books. Bibles and Western paperbacks and Erle Stanley Gardner, James Bond. Old brown newspapers. Some of them twenty years old. Unfinished crossword puzzles. Unfinished letters. Sweetheart snapshots. Dim, crumbling little Kodak children. Pathetic.

RB: You ever seen a guy gassed?

TC: Once. But he made it look like a lark. He was happy to go, he wanted to get it over with; he sat down in that chair like he was going to the dentist to have his teeth cleaned. But in Kansas, I saw two men hanged.

RB: Perry Smith? And what's his name—Dick Hickock? Well, once they hit the end of the rope, I guess they don't feel anything.

TC: So we're told. But after the drop, they go on living—fifteen, twenty minutes. Struggling. Gasping for breath, the body still battling for life. I couldn't help it, I vomited.

RB: Maybe you're not so cool, huh? You seem cool. So, did Sirhan beef about being kept in Special Security?

TC: Sort of. He's lonesome. He wants to mix with the other prisoners, join the general population.

RB: He don't know what's good for him. Outside, somebody'd snuff him for sure.

TC: Why?

RB: For the same reason he snuffed Kennedy. Recognition. Half the people who snuff people, that's what they want: recognition. Get their picture in the paper.

TC: That's not why you killed Gary Hinman.

RB: (Silence)

TC: That was because you and Manson wanted Hinman to give you money and his car, and when he wouldn't—well . . .

RB: (Silence)

TC: I was thinking. I know Sirhan, and I knew Robert Kennedy. I knew Lee Harvey Oswald, and I knew Jack Kennedy. The odds against that —one person knowing all four of those men—must be astounding.

RB: Oswald? You knew Oswald? Really?

TC: I met him in Moscow just after he defected. One night I was having dinner with a friend, an Italian newspaper correspondent, and when he came by to pick me up he asked me if I'd mind going with him first to talk to a young American defector, one Lee Harvey Oswald. Oswald was staying at the Metropole, an old Czarist hotel just off Kremlin Square. The Metropole has a big gloomy lobby full of shadows and dead palm trees. And there he was, sitting in the dark under a dead palm tree. Thin and pale, thin-lipped, starved-looking. He was wearing chinos and tennis shoes and a lumberjack shirt. And right away he was angry—he was grinding his teeth, and his eyes were jumping every which way. He was boiling over about everything: the American ambassador; the Russians—he was mad at them because they wouldn't let him stay in Moscow. We talked to him for about half an hour, and my Italian friend didn't think the guy was worth filing a story about. Just another paranoid hysteric; the Moscow woods were rampant with those. I never thought about him again, not until many years later. Not until after the assassination when I saw his picture flashed on television.

RB: Does that make you the only one that knew both of them, Oswald and Kennedy?

TC: No. There was an American girl, Priscilla Johnson. She worked for U.P. in Moscow. She knew Kennedy, and she met Oswald around the same time I did. But I can tell you something else almost as curious. About some of those people your friends murdered.

RB: (Silence)

TC: I knew them. At least, out of the five people killed in the Tate house that night, I knew four of them. I'd met Sharon Tate at the Cannes Film Festival. Jay Sebring cut my hair a couple of times. I'd had lunch once in San Francisco with Abigail Folger and her boyfriend, Frykowski. In other words, I'd known them independently of each other. And yet one night there they were, all gathered together in the same house waiting for your friends to arrive. Quite a coincidence.

RB (lights a cigarette; smiles): Know what I'd say? I'd say you're not such a lucky guy to know. Shit. Listen to that. Moan, moan. I'm cold. You cold?

TC: Why don't you put on your shirt?

RB: (Silence)

TC: It's odd about tattoos. I've talked to several hundred men convicted of homicide—multiple homicide, in most cases. The only common denominator I could find among them was tattoos. A good eighty percent of them were heavily tattooed. Richard Speck. York and Latham. Smith and Hickock.

RB: I'll put on my sweater.

TC: If you weren't here, if you could be anywhere you wanted to be, doing anything you wanted to do, where would you be and what would you be doing?

RB: Tripping. Out on my Honda chugging along the Coast road, the fast curves, the waves and the water, plenty of sun. Out of San Fran, headed Mendocino way, riding through the redwoods. I'd be making love. I'd be on the beach by a bonfire making love. I'd be making music and balling and sucking some great Acapulco weed and watching the sun go down. Throw some driftwood on the fire. Good gash, good hash, just tripping right along.

TC: You can get hash in here.

RB: And everything else. Any kind of dope—for a price. There are dudes in here on everything but roller skates.

TC: Is that what your life was like before you were arrested? Just tripping? Didn't you ever have a job?

RB: Once in a while. I played guitar in a couple of bars.

TC: I understand you were quite a cocksman. The ruler of a virtual seraglio. How many children have you fathered?

RB: (Silence—but shrugs, grins, smokes)

TC: I'm surprised you have a guitar. Some prisons don't allow it because the strings can be detached and used as weapons. A garrote. How long have you been playing?

RB: Oh, since I was a kid. I was one of those Hollywood kids. I was in a couple of movies. But my folks were against it. They're real straight people. Anyway, I never cared about the acting part. I just wanted to write music and play it and sing.

TC: But what about the film you made with Kenneth Anger—*Lucifer Rising*?

RB: Yeah.

TC: How did you get along with Anger?

RB: Okay.

TC: Then why does Kenneth Anger wear a picture locket on a chain around his neck? On one side of the locket there is a picture of you; on the other there is an image of a frog with an inscription: "Bobby Beausoleil changed into a frog by Kenneth Anger." A voodoo amulet, so to say. A curse he put on you because you're supposed to have ripped him off. Left in the middle of the night with his car—and a few other things.

RB (narrowed eyes): Did he tell you that?

TC: No, I've never met him. But I was told it by a number of other people.

RB (reaches for guitar, tunes it, strums it, sings): "This is my song, this is my song, this is my dark song, my dark song . . ." Everybody always wants to know how I got together with Manson. It was through our music. He plays some, too. One night I was driving around with a bunch of my ladies. Well, we came to this old roadhouse, beer place, with a lot of cars outside. So we went inside, and there was Charlie with some of his ladies. We all got to talking, played some together; the next day Charlie came to see me in my van, and we all, his people and my people, ended up camping out together. Brothers and sisters. A family.

TC: Did you see Manson as a leader? Did you feel influenced by him right away?

RB: Hell, no. He had his people, I had mine. If anybody was influenced, it was him. By me.

TC: Yes, he was attracted to you. Infatuated. Or so he says. You seem to have had that effect on a lot of people, men and women.

RB: Whatever happens, happens. It's all good.

TC: Do you consider killing innocent people a good thing?

RB: Who said they were innocent?

TC: Well, we'll return to that. But for now: What is your own sense of morality? How do you differentiate between good and bad?

RB: Good and bad? It's *all* good. If it happens, it's got to be good. Otherwise, it wouldn't be *happening*. It's just the way life flows. Moves together. I move with it. I don't question it.

TC: In other words, you don't question the act of murder. You consider it "good" because it "happens." Justifiable.

RB: I have my own justice. I live by my own law, you know. I don't respect the laws of this society. Because society doesn't respect its own laws. I make my own laws and live by them. I have my own sense of justice.

TC: And what is your sense of justice?

RB: I believe that what goes around comes around. What goes up comes down. That's how life flows, and I flow with it.

TC: You're not making much sense—at least to me. And I don't think you're stupid. Let's try again. In your opinion, it's all right that Manson sent Tex Watson and those girls into that house to slaughter total strangers, innocent people—

RB: I said: Who says they were innocent? They burned people on dope deals. Sharon Tate and that gang. They picked up kids on the Strip and took them home and whipped them. Made movies of it. Ask the cops; they found the movies. Not that they'd tell you the truth.

TC: The truth is, the Lo Biancos and Sharon Tate and her friends were killed to protect you. Their deaths were directly linked to the Gary Hinman murder.

RB: I hear you. I hear where you're coming from.

TC: Those were all imitations of the Hinman murder—to prove that you couldn't have killed Hinman. And thereby get you out of jail.

RB: To get me out of jail. (He nods, smiles, sighs—complimented) None of that came out at any of the trials. The girls got on the stand and tried to really tell how it all came down, but nobody would listen. People couldn't believe anything except what the media said. The media had them programmed to believe it all happened because we were out to start a race war. That it was mean niggers going around hurting all these good white folk. Only—it was like you say. The media, they called us a "family." And it was the only true thing they said. We *were* a family. We were mother, father, brother, sister, daughter, son. If a member of our family was in jeopardy, we didn't abandon that person. And so for the love of a brother, a brother who was in jail on a murder rap, all those killings came down.

TC: And you don't regret that?

RB: No. If my brothers and sisters did it, then it's good. Everything in life is good. It all flows. It's all good. It's all music.

TC: When you were up on Death Row, if you'd been forced to flow down to the gas chamber and whiff the peaches, would you have given that your stamp of approval?

RB: If that's how it came down. Everything that happens is good.

TC: War. Starving children. Pain. Cruelty. Blindness. Prisons. Desperation. Indifference. All good?

RB: What's that look you're giving me?

TC: Nothing. I was noticing how your face changes. One moment, with just the slightest shift of angle, you look so boyish, entirely innocent, a charmer. And then—well, one can see you as a sort of Forty-second

Street Lucifer. Have you ever seen *Night Must Fall?* An old movie with Robert Montgomery? No? Well, it's about an impish, innocent-looking delightful young man who travels about the English country-side charming old ladies, then cutting off their heads and carrying the heads around with him in leather hat-boxes.

RB: So what's that got to do with me?

TC: I was thinking—if it was ever remade, if someone Americanized it, turned the Montgomery character into a young drifter with hazel eyes and a smoky voice, you'd be very good in the part.

RB: Are you trying to say I'm a psychopath? I'm not a nut. If I have to use violence, I'll use it, but I don't believe in killing.

TC: Then I must be deaf. Am I mistaken, or didn't you just tell me that it didn't matter what atrocity one person committed against another, it was good, all good?

RB: (Silence)

TC: Tell me, Bobby, how do you view yourself?

RB: As a convict.

TC: But beyond that.

RB: As a man. A *white* man. And everything a white man stands for.

TC: Yes, one of the guards told me you were the ringleader of the Aryan Brotherhood.

RB (hostile): What do *you* know about the Brotherhood?

TC: That it's composed of a bunch of hard-nosed white guys. That it's a somewhat fascist-minded fraternity. That it started in California, and has spread throughout the American prison system, north, south, east, and west. That the prison authorities consider it a dangerous, troublemaking cult.

RB: A man has to defend himself. We're outnumbered. You got no idea how rough it is. We're all more scared of each other than we are of the pigs in here. You got to be on your toes every second if you don't want a shiv in your back. The blacks and Chicanos, they got their own gangs. The Indians, too; or I should say the "Native Americans"— that's how these redskins call themselves: what a laugh! Yessir, *rough*. With all the racial tensions, politics, dope, gambling, and sex. The blacks really go for the young white kids. They like to shove those big black dicks up those tight white asses.

TC: Have you ever thought what you would do with your life if and when you were paroled out of here?

RB: That's a tunnel I don't see no end to. They'll never let Charlie go.

TC: I hope you're right, and I think you are. But it's very likely that you'll be paroled some day. Perhaps sooner than you imagine. Then what?

RB (strums guitar): I'd like to record some of my music. Get it played on the air.

TC: That was Perry Smith's dream. And Charlie Manson's, too. Maybe you fellows have more in common than mere tattoos.

RB: Just between us, Charlie doesn't have a whole lot of talent. (Strumming chords) "This is my song, my dark song, my dark song." I got my first guitar when I was eleven; I found it in my grandma's attic and taught myself to play it, and I've been nuts about music ever since. My grandma was a sweet woman, and her attic was my favorite place. I liked to lie up there and listen to the rain. Or hide up there when my dad came looking for me with his belt. Shit. You hear that? Moan, moan. It's enough to drive you crazy.

TC: Listen to me, Bobby. And answer carefully. Suppose, when you get out of here, somebody came to you—let's say Charlie—and asked you to commit an act of violence, kill a man, would you do it?

RB (after lighting another cigarette, after smoking it half through): I might. It depends. I never meant to . . . to . . . hurt Gary Hinman. But one thing happened. And another. And then it all came down.

TC: And it was all good.

RB: It was all good.

Music for Chameleons, 1980

JIMMY BRESLIN

Concealing his considerable erudition behind the guise of a tough-talking working stiff, journalist and best-selling novelist Jimmy Breslin (b. 1930) spent a dozen years as a sportswriter before becoming a columnist for the *New York Herald Tribune* in 1963. A pioneering practitioner of the "New Journalism," he made himself an omnipresent character in his columns: the streetwise reporter with a wide range of Runyonesque acquaintances, a bone-deep sympathy for the common man, and a boundless zest for taking on city hall. In 1969 he joined Norman Mailer's quixotic campaign for mayor by running for city council president in the Democratic primary on the Mailer ticket. Eight years later, Breslin's unique status among New York City journalists was confirmed when he received an admiring letter from a serial killer then terrorizing the metropolis, the shadowy gunman who called himself "Son of Sam."

The murder spree had begun the previous summer with the shooting death of a young woman and the wounding of her female friend as they sat in a parked car in the Bronx. Similar attacks followed in the subsequent months. Because of his weapon of choice, the tabloids initially dubbed the unknown shooter the ".44-Caliber Killer." In April 1977, however, police found a chilling note at the scene of the latest shooting, a double murder, declaring "I am the 'Son of Sam.' I am a little brat." In the end, "Son of Sam" turned out to be a pudgy-faced postal worker named David Berkowitz who was finally captured in August of that year.

"Son of Sam"

We put the letter on the table and read it again. In his opening paragraph he wrote:

> *Hello from the gutters of N. Y. C which are filled with dog manure, vomit, stale wine, urine, and blood. Hello from the sewers of N. Y. C which swallow up these delicacies when they are*

washed away by the sweeper trucks. Hello from the cracks in the sidewalks of N. Y. C. and from the ants that dwell in these cracks and feed on the dried blood of the dead that has settled into the cracks.

'He's a pretty good writer,' somebody at the table said.

'Yes, he is,' I said.

The letter was from the person who called himself 'Son of Sam.' He prowled the night streets of New York neighborhoods and shot at young girls and sometimes their boyfriends too, and he had killed five and wounded four. He crept up on victims with a .44-caliber pistol. Most of the young women had shoulder-length brown hair.

One of the victims was Donna Lauria, who was eighteen when the killer shot at her as she sat in a car with her girlfriend outside the Laurias' apartment house on Buhre Avenue in the Bronx. Donna Lauria was the only victim mentioned by the killer in his letter, which was sent to me at my newspaper in New York, the *Daily News.* So I took the letter up to the fourth-floor apartment of Donna Lauria's parents, and I sat over coffee and read the letter again and talked to the Laurias about it.

The killer had sent one communication before this one. He left a note to police after murdering a girl and boy as they sat in a parked car at a place only five blocks from where Donna Lauria had been killed. Both notes were hand-printed. In the sadness and tension of the Laurias' dining room, I read the letter again. After the first paragraph, it said:

J. B., I'm just dropping you a line to let you know that I appreciate your interest in those recent and horrendous .44 killings. I also want to tell you that I read your column daily and find it quite informative.

Tell me, Jim, what will you have for July Twenty-Ninth? You can forget about me if you like because I don't care for publicity. However, you must not forget Donna Lauria and you cannot let the people forget her, either. She was a very sweet girl but Sam's a thirsty lad and he won't stop me killing until he gets his fill of blood.

Mr. Breslin, sir, don't you think that because you haven't heard from [me] for a while that I went to sleep. No, rather, I am still here. Like a spirit roaming the night. Thirsty, hungry, seldom stopping to rest, anxious to please Sam. I love my work. Now, the void had been filled.

Perhaps we shall meet face to face someday or perhaps I will be blown away by the cops with smoking .38s. Whatever, if I shall be fortunate enough to meet you I will tell you all about Sam if you like, and I will introduce you to him. His name is 'Sam the Terrible.'

Not knowing what the future holds I shall say farewell, and I will see you at the next job. Or, should I say you will see my handiwork at the next job? Remember Ms. Lauria. Thank you.

In their blood
and
From the gutter
'Sam's Creation' .44

P.S.: J.B., please inform all the detectives working on the slayings to remain.

P.S.: J.B., please inform all the detectives working on the case that I wish them the best of luck. 'Keep Em digging, drive on, think positive, get off your butts, knock on coffins, etc.'
Upon my capture I promise to buy all the guys working on the case a new pair of shoes if I can get up the money.

'Son of Sam'

Directly under the signature was a symbol the killer drew. It appeared to be an X-shaped mark with the biological symbols for male and female, and also a cross and the letter S.

When I finished reading the letter, Mike Lauria, the father, said to me, 'What do you think?'

'Want to see for yourself?'

He pushed the letter away from him: 'I don't want to see it.'

'Let me,' his wife, Rose, said.

'You don't want to see it,' the husband said.

'Yes, I do. I have a lot of the cards she used to get. Maybe the printing is the same.'

The husband shrugged. 'Go ahead then.'

We took out the first page that mentioned her daughter and gave Rose Lauria the rest. Her large, expressive brown eyes became cold as she looked at the printing. On the wall behind her was a picture of her daughter, a lovely brown-haired girl with the mother's features. The mother put the pages down and looked up. 'He's probably a very brilliant man, boy, whatever he is,' she said. 'His brain functions the opposite way.'

She looked up at the picture of her daughter. 'She was a dancer and a half. Every place you went, people used to praise her. Is it possible he saw her someplace and she didn't speak to him or something?'

Nobody knew. The .44 killer appeared to be saying that he was controlled by Sam, who lived inside him and sent him onto the streets to find young people to shoot. He did this at close range: one young woman, walking home from college, held a textbook over her face, and he put the gun up to the book and killed her. The detectives, whose shoes he would buy, walked the streets at night and hoped for a match with the man with the .44. 'He's mine,' one of them, a friend of mine, said. 'The man is Jack the Ripper, and I'm making a personal appointment with him.'

The hope was that the killer would realize he was controlled by Sam, who not only forced him into acts of horror but would ultimately walk him to his death. I felt that the only way for the killer to leave this special torment was to give himself up to me, if he trusted me, or to the police, and receive both help and safety. If he wanted any further contact, all he had to do was call or write me at the *Daily News*. It's simple to get to me. The only people I don't answer are bill collectors. The time to do it was right then, however. We were too close to the July 29 that the killer mentioned in his letter. It was the first anniversary of the death of Donna Lauria.

'She was sitting in the car with her girlfriend Jody Valenti,' Rose Lauria was saying. Jody Valenti was wounded but recovered. 'Mike and I came walking up. We'd been to a wake. I went up to the car and I said, "Tell me, Jody, what happened tonight?" "Donna'll tell you when she gets upstairs." Now my husband says to Donna, "What are you doing here at 1.00 a.m., you got to work tomorrow." I said to him, "What is she doing that's wrong?"

'So we went upstairs. My husband says, "I'm going to walk the dog." He goes with the dog to the elevator, and I hear Jody's horn blowing downstairs. I called out in the hall to my husband. He says to me, "Well, go look out the window and see." I look out and here's Jody screaming that Donna's been shot.'

Rose Lauria, nervous now, got up from the table. 'You know the last month when he killed the two more around here? My husband and I were at a wedding. We were supposed to meet some people after it. We left the wedding, and I said to my husband, "I don't want to meet anybody. Something's the matter. I want to go home." And we just got inside at the same time the two got killed.'

'She was pacing around here like a cat,' Mike Lauria said.

He walked me downstairs to the street. He stood in an undershirt, with the sun glaring on his wide shoulders, and he pointed to the spot where his daughter had been shot.

'She was starting to get out of the car when she saw this guy on the curb. Right where we are. Donna said to Jody, "Who's this guy now?" Then the guy did what he did. Jody, she can't get herself to come near my wife. Forget about it. I saw her a couple of weeks ago. She spoke to me from the car. Told me she got engaged. She couldn't even look at me. I told her, "All right, Jody, go ahead, I'll see you." I let her go home.'

He turned and walked back into his building. I took my letter from his daughter's killer and went back to the street and out of his wounded life.

Everyone was waiting for the July 29 anniversary of the Lauria killing, but Son of Sam didn't strike until two days later, when he killed Stacy

Moskowitz and wounded Robert Violante, both twenty, in a car in Brooklyn. It was the first time the killer had struck outside the Bronx and Queens, and terror gripped all New York City.

NO ONE IS SAFE FROM SON OF SAM

the *New York Post* blared on August 1. But the killer had made a mistake. While stalking the Brooklyn victims, he had left his car in front of a fire hydrant, and the police ticketed it. They traced the licence number——561 XBL—to David Berkowitz, 24, of Yonkers, a postal worker and former auxiliary policeman.

Suspicious about what a Jew from Yonkers would be doing in a quiet Italian neighborhood in Brooklyn at that time of night, detectives went to his apartment on August 10. They found the car in front and, peering through the window, saw the butt of a submachine gun and a letter addressed to the police.

Berkowitz was arrested when he came out to start the car. 'I'm Son of Sam. O.K., you've got me,' he said. The letter in the car indicated that he had planned a machinegun raid that night on a Hampton's discotheque and that the authorities 'would be all summer counting the bodies.' In the car, police also found a loaded, .44-caliber Bulldog revolver, which turned out to be the weapon that had killed and wounded all those people.

Later, in taped interviews with a psychiatrist, Berkowitz said that 'howling and crying demons demanding blood' had ordered him to kill. 'I'm the Son of Sam, but it's not me,' he said. 'It's Sam who works through me. I'm David Berkowitz. That's all I want to be. They use my body.' In April, 1978, Brooklyn Supreme Court Justice Joseph Corso ruled that Berkowitz was competent to stand trial for the murder of Stacy Moskowitz.

Berkowitz pleaded guilty to six murders, and he was sentenced to 315 years in prison.

New York *Daily News*, June 5, 1977; reprinted in *The Mammoth Book of Murder*, 1989

JAY ROBERT NASH

The centuries-old genre of the true-crime anthology is best represented in the current era by the work of Indianapolis-born author Jay Robert Nash (b. 1937). Like such early-American specimens as *The Record of Crimes in the United States* and *Celebrated Criminal Cases of America*, Nash's highly popular collections—especially his 1973 *Bloodletters and Badmen: A Narrative Encyclopedia of American Criminals from the Pilgrims to the Present*—fulfilled the major function of the form, serving up true-crime tidbits for the delectation of a sensation-craving public. The following account, from Nash's 1983 collection *Murder Among the Mighty*, relates one of the most sensational Hollywood murder cases, a scandal concocted of such lurid ingredients that no screenwriter would have dared to invent it.

The Turner-Stompanato Killing

A Family Affair

Abandonment, sadism, and murder made up the legacy of Lana Turner's childhood. The auburn-haired girl was born February 8, 1920, into poverty in Wallace, Idaho, a small mining town where her father, John Virgil Turner, labored as an itinerant copper miner but spent most of his time gambling away his meager salary. Julia Jean Mildred Frances Turner was seven when her mother, Mildred, left her father. Destitute, Mrs. Turner sent her child to Modesto, California, to a foster home where, according to Lana's later statements, she was "treated like a scullery maid," making the family's breakfast before leaving for school, and washing and ironing. For household chores she was too tired to complete she was beaten with a stick until "my back was bruised and bleeding." When the child was ten, her father, on December 15, 1930, left a crap game in San Francisco a heavy winner, and one of the other players, police later guessed, followed him and blackjacked him to death in a dark alley. Police were unable to solve the murder.

Following the death of her father Lana was reunited with her mother, moving to San Francisco, where Mildred Turner found work as a hairdresser. Their income was so scant in those Depression years that Mrs. Turner pawned most of the family's possessions merely to stay alive. By 1936, Mrs. Turner and her blossoming teen-age daughter were living in Los Angeles, where Lana attended Hollywood High. One day in January of that year the girl skipped her classes and spent some time in a drugstore, sipping a strawberry malt. And on that day, in that hour, fate in the form of a dapper man with a black mustache stepped forth to "discover" a Hollywood sex goddess.

William Wilkerson, editor and publisher of the powerful *Hollywood Reporter*, was having coffee in the drugstore. (The exact store, still in debate, was either the Top Hat Malt Shop at Sunset Boulevard and Highland Avenue, or Schwab's.) Wilkerson could not take his eyes off the curvaceous, large-eyed girl. He finally put down his coffee cup and walked up to her uttering a line that would later become the most often used cliché in Hollywood: "How would you like to be in pictures?" She nodded a vacant yes, and Wilkerson handed her his card, telling her to call him.

A short time later, after Wilkerson established contacts for her, the teen-ager was led by agent Henry Wilson to director Mervyn LeRoy at Warner Bros. LeRoy was about to begin filming an antilynching movie entitled *They Won't Forget*; he took one look at the well-developed Turner girl and signed her to a $50-a-week contract, changing her name to Lana. She appeared briefly in the 1937 film's first reel almost as Wilkerson had discovered her: sipping a soda in a drugstore, wearing a tight sweater and an even tighter skirt that sharply outlined her sensual figure. She then sauntered down the street and across the town square to be raped and murdered. Her brief appearance electrified audiences nationwide, particularly males. Lana Turner was on her way to stardom, even though she recoiled in embarrassment when she first viewed herself in the film, crying: "I look so *cheap!*" (This was not actually her first motion picure appearance; she had been a crowd extra in *A Star Is Born*, released earlier that year.) Later, the woman who would be among the ten top female film stars in the nation would look back upon her first solo appearance and remark: "I was one of those photogenic accidents. I was a fifteen-year-old kid [she had just turned seventeen] with a bosom and a backside strolling across the screen for less than a minute." It was a minute no one ever forgot, except, of course, Jack Warner, the dictatorial head of Warner Bros., who was never known for his commercial or artistic vision. After Lana appeared in a few more small roles, Warner took LeRoy aside, scolding him: "She hasn't got it! She's just a kid." LeRoy felt otherwise, and when he left Warners to go to Metro-Goldwyn-Mayer, the director took his "discovery" with him. For the next eighteen years Lana Turner would call MGM (the "family" studio, as that benevolent monarch Louis B. Mayer was fond of saying) not only her home but the source of fabulous wealth, prestige, power, and more glamour than it was possible for any one human being to bear.

"The Sweater Girl," as Lana Turner was first aptly known, appeared in several B pictures, including *Love Finds Andy Hardy* opposite Mickey Rooney and Judy Garland; Lana was the love that found Andy. In 1941, MGM decided to make luscious Lana a superstar, casting her in a lead role in *Ziegfeld Girl* opposite Hedy Lamarr and Judy Garland. She played the role of a girl who became a theatrical success but whose life was ruined by personal tragedy, a role Lana again played effectively eleven years later in *The Bad and the Beautiful*; her real life reflected these roles with devastating accuracy.

MGM lavished upon Lana big-budget pictures and a $4,000-a-week salary by the mid-1940s. Her male leads were Hollywood superstars John Garfield, Spencer Tracy, Robert Taylor, and Clark Gable. She made four movies with Gable: *Honky Tonk, Somewhere I'll Find You, Homecoming,* and *Betrayed*. That Lana was attracted to Gable there was no doubt in anyone's mind, especially in the mind of Gable's fiery wife, comedienne Carole Lombard. Knowing her husband was attracted to blondes—Lana was by then a platinum bombshell—before the first

Turner-Gable film was shot, Lombard went to MGM studio boss Louis B. Mayer. She told the mogul in her usual blunt manner that if there was any hanky-panky between Lana and Gable, she would make sure her husband would never appear again on the set. As a result the Gable-Turner relationship was cordial but cool.

Lombard's apprehensions about Lana were normal. Lana Turner at the time had the reputation of seducing her leading men. Her love life, on and off the screen, was rampant and wide-ranging. Her life, like her screen image, was devoted to romance, to men. Groomed and cultured as a Hollywood hothouse plant, Lana Turner was, in the estimate of one observer, the "most complete studio product." And as such she pursued men created for fame and glamour—Robert Hutton, Rory Calhoun, Turhan Bey, Frank Sinatra, Howard Hughes, John Dall, Fernando Lamas, Tommy Dorsey, Tyrone Power, and others.

Immature, naive, and flagrantly fickle, Lana married almost on whim, selecting and discarding husbands with alarming alacrity. She blamed it on curiosity, once saying: "Let's be honest, the physical attracts me first. Then, if you get to know the man's mind and soul and heart, that's icing on the cake."

Artie Shaw was the first "cake," baked and served in record time. Lana had been dating Hollywood attorney Gregson Bautzer. The lawyer made the mistake of breaking an appointment with his fiancée one night. Angrily, Lana took her revenge as only she could. "I had a date with Greg," the star later gushed to gossip columnist Louella Parsons, "and he called to say that he couldn't keep it. Some kind of legal business. I got mad and decided that I'd go out anyway, and I thought of someone who'd make Greg mad and jealous." She phoned the much-marrying bandleader Artie Shaw. Before midnight on their first date, "Artie said it would be nice if we got married. I said it would be nice, too. The next thing I knew we were on our way to Las Vegas." The marriage lasted four months.

Stephen Crane, an unknown actor, dated Lana for less than a month in 1943 before wedding her. An annulment quickly followed when Lana learned that Crane's divorce from a previous spouse was not final. Discovering herself pregnant, Lana married Crane again. In 1944, Cheryl Crane, Lana's only child, was born. A year after that Lana divorced Crane.

Next came Henry J. "Bob" Topping, millionaire playboy, a two-fisted drinker and fighter who shared his love of pornographic films with Lana and guests attending parties at their luxurious mansion. The Turner-Topping marriage, which ended after four and a half years in Nevada, was regularly puncuated with accusations, drunken revels, and violence. On one occasion Lana brought home singer Billy Daniels whose private warbling to her was interrupted by a drunken, indignant Topping, who slugged Lana and ordered Daniels from his home.

Lana, forever being marked up by her lovers, employed dark glasses to hide black eyes. "I find men terribly exciting," Lana was quoted at this time, "and any girl who says she doesn't is an anemic old maid, a streetwalker or a saint."

The star, who continued to appear in box-office if not critical successes, such as *The Postman Always Rings Twice* (which many consider Lana's best performance in a wholly lackluster career), realized that her marital adventures were impulsive at best. "How does it happen," she inquired of Louella Parsons, "that something that makes so much sense in the moonlight doesn't make any sense in the sunlight?" Later she would muse: "Whenever I do something, it seems so right. And turns out so wrong."

More wrong turns in marriage were made with actor Lex Barker, Fred May, and Robert Eaton; her seventh marriage was to Ronald Dante. Throughout her shaky unions Lana lived like an empress, spending her enormous salary on a huge Beverly Hills home, servants, jewels, furs, cars, a wardrobe, spending at a rate that alarmed at least one of her husbands, Lex Barker. When Barker pointed out that she was throwing money away, Lana agreed to curb her spendthrift ways, promising to limit her weekly purchases. Some weeks later Barker accused her of going on a shopping spree. Lana admitted that she had purchased hundreds of dollars' worth of items but that she hadn't "spent a dime." How was that possible, Barker wanted to know. "I charged it," replied Lana.

The marriage to Barker, some later claimed, was broken up by Lana's daughter, Cheryl; in fact the girl was charged with destroying three marriages altogether, whispering her suspicions of her mother's mates into Lana's ear, accusing the husbands of being unfaithful and, in one instance, too attentive to Cheryl herself. "Possibly it was a case of jealousy," wrote Charles Nuetzel in *Whodunit? Hollywood Style*. "Possibly Cheryl felt that her mother was away too much on motion picture locations and she didn't want to share any of her mother's time with strange men." That both Lana and her daughter were overly possessive of each other became evident with the surfacing of the shady Hollywood gigolo and sometime mobster, Johnny Stompanato.

Stompanato was a rugged-looking ex-Marine born in Woodstock, Illinois, in 1925. He attended Kemper Military School in Boonville, Missouri, graduating in 1943 and entering Notre Dame for a brief period until joining the Marine Corps in 1944, being discharged three years later. By 1948, Stompanato had been married and divorced twice, and was in Hollywood. The darkly handsome drifter was taken under his wing by gangster Mickey Cohen, successor to West Coast rackets king, Benjamin "Bugsy" Siegel. Cohen used Stompanato as his bodyguard and chauffeur, later promoting him to his bagman, collecting money extorted from movie officials. Soon Stompanato sidelined in blackmail, a racket that became so lucrative it made him independent. His prey consisted of wealthy females, usually divorced or separated from Hollywood husbands.

Stompanato's technique followed traditional blackmail methods. He would ingratiate himself with a victim, romancing her into a bedchamber where hidden cameras recorded their sexual encounter. The photos were then sold, along with the negatives, to the victim for large amounts. Years after Stompanato's violent end a wooden box belonging to the gigolo was delivered to Beverly Hills Police Chief Clinton H. Anderson, who later reported: "Inside the box, along with a revolver [.32-caliber snub-nosed], bankbooks and personal papers, officers found a roll [of] film negatives. Printed and enlarged, the negatives revealed pictures of nude women in compromising situations. Some of the pictures had apparently been taken while the victims were unaware they were being photographed, and they were recognizable. The pictures would have been a gold mine for a blackmailer." Writing in *Beverly Hills Is My Beat*, Anderson added: "Stompanato's unusual picture collection verified information we already had, but we made no serious attempt to pursue our investigation further. It would have been cruel embarrassment to the victims, and would have served no legal purpose since the principal was now dead." It was no secret to the police, Anderson also insisted, that Stompanato "had accepted money from a number of his women friends," ostensibly in the role of a gigolo, but more likely as a lover-turned-blackmailer.

How this unsavory fellow came to know and woo superstar Lana Turner is not clear. Some reports had it that Stompanato, who kept close checks on available Hollywood women of means, learned of Lana's break-up with Lex Barker (in 1957) and, only a few days after the dissolution of that marriage, boldly called the lovesick woman, asking for a date, his smooth request answered with a desperate yes. Yet others claim that Lana met Stompanato through mobster Mickey Cohen. "Movie stars have long been suckers for gangsters," wrote William H. A. Carr in *Hollywood Tragedy*, "and Lana appears to have been attracted to them, like so many others."

Johnny Stompanato, with his short dark curly hair, sharp jaw and profile, projected little more than the predictable beach athlete. Addicted to shiny shirts that he wore open almost to the navel to exhibit his chest, ostentatious, gauche, even crude, he was completely unlike the male stars with whom Lana had acted, and just the opposite of most of her husbands. Yet Stompanato held for her a fatal charm, captivating her, almost enslaving her. Lana undoubtedly had the mean-streaked, passionate, almost lethal Stompanato in mind when she later complained that she "usually wound up with delinquent adults." She also told journalist Jim Bacon: "I really am stupid about men."

At first it was all charm, with Stompanato playing the perfect gentleman. He paid a great deal of attention to Cheryl, swimming and horseback riding with the teen-ager, writing her long letters when she was traveling with Lana. Mickey Cohen, when later asked about the relationship between his underworld protégé and Lana's daughter, held up crossed fingers, commenting in his usual snarl: "Johnny and the kid was like that. She was crazy about him."

Lana's dependency upon Stompanato, which had grown to an obsession, may have been caused by her recent release from MGM after eighteen years of stardom. The thirty-five-year-old actress, suddenly adrift, became desperate not only for work in films but for a continuation of the kind of attention showered upon her during her MGM heyday. Her handsome Johnny filled that need. Even when Lana finally landed another leading part, opposite Sean Connery, in *Another Time, Another Place*, which was filmed on location in England, she begged for Stompanato's understanding, support, and, slavishly, his love, writing him imploring letters that gushed schoolgirl devotion.

Some samples:

My Beloved Love, just this morning your precious exciting letter arrived. . . . Every line warms me and makes me ache and miss you each tiny moment—it's true—it's beautiful, yet terrible. But, just so, is deep love . . .

I'm your woman and I need you, my man! To love and be loved by—don't ever doubt or forget that. . . .

Sweetheart, please keep well, because I need you so—and so you will always be strong and able to caress me, hold me, tenderly at first, and crush me into your very own being. . . .

There's so much to say—but it's easier when you're holding me all through the night. And we can either whisper, or shout, or scream our love for each other to each other. . . . And oh, so many, many kisses—so fierce that they hurt me.

The "aches" apparently overwhelmed Lana to the point where she asked Johnny to join her and Cheryl in London. The actress generously paid for his plane fare and covered his expenses, a gesture that had developed by this time into an unthinking habit. Lana set up Stompanato in a luxurious London house, and during the early stages of the filming the couple seemed rapturously happy. Then Stompanato began making increasing financial demands upon the actress; she had already given him $10,000, a "loan" that of course was never repaid. Johnny told his blond paramour that he required an additional $50,000. He explained that the funds were needed to buy a screenplay for a movie in which he, Johnny Stompanato, would star. Stunned, Lana explained that she did not have that kind of money. What may have been most shocking to the actress was Stompanato's sudden and desperate desire to become an actor, a secret ambition the gigolo had nurtured since he began to drift in the Hollywood backwaters. Stompanato insisted she advance the money. Lana said that her financial advisers would not tolerate the expenditure. All right, soothed Johnny, and asked for only $1,000, which would be enough "earnest money" to secure the rights to the story. Again, Lana turned him down.

Stompanato had overplayed his hand. He knew it. His blatant trading on love in return for hard cash had been obvious even to the emotionally muddled actress. Instead of developing another ploy, Stompanato erupted, first with indignation, then seething anger, opting for intimidation, threats, and outright violence. He appeared without warning on the set of *Another Time, Another Place*, marching up to the actress's costar, Sean Connery, and bellowing: "Stay away from Lana!" When Connery appeared to ignore him, Stompanato yanked out a pistol, waving it in the actor's face. With a single punch Connery sent the mobster to the floor. Despite this blow to his tough-guy image, Johnny still treated Lana as his gun moll: "When I say hop, you'll hop!" he once yelled at her. "When I say jump, you'll jump!"

He also persisted in his money demands. Lana continued to refuse until one night Stompanato exploded in a rage. "I'll mutilate you!" he screamed. "I'll hurt you so you'll be so repulsive you'll have to hide forever!" He leaped for her throat.

The terrorized actress would never forget the scene:

After he had choked me and thrown me down, he went into the bathroom and he got a razor and he came and grabbed my head, all the time screaming at me violent things. Then he said that it may only start with a little one now, just give me a taste of it, and even so, he would do worse.

I pleaded. I said I would do anything, anything, just please don't hurt me. "If you claim to love me, how can you hurt me? Please don't." As he let go of me, he said: "That's just to let you know I am not kidding. Don't think you can ever get away!"

Lana did manage to escape, but only after going to her director, who contacted Scotland Yard. Police quietly escorted Johnny Stompanato to the airport and sent him back to America. Many believed that the actress had successfully removed the hustler from her life, yet Lana Turner's dependency upon Stompanato was deeper than she would admit. No sooner did she finish shooting her picture and return to her California home than she contacted the man who had threatened to mutilate her for life. Before long, Stompanato was once again enjoying Lana's pleasure palace, an imposing mansion with twenty-some rooms, including a private beauty parlor, soda fountain (in honor, no doubt, of the site of her discovery and the scene in her first important film appearance), and private projection room where she watched not only the latest Hollywood releases but films of a racier nature. The gigolo swam in Lana's king-size pool and lounged next to a cabana the size of a small apartment house, where hot and cold showers and sunray rooms and massage rooms were made available to Johnny and guests. Completely air-conditioned, the entire estate, down to the last guest room, was wired with a loudspeaker system. Dozens of phones were available to guests who, along with lover-boy Stompanato, ate off a $25,000 silver service (for sixty guests). Stompanato sank easily and unashamedly into such luxury, thinking Lana's comforts to be his right.

The actress never let him think otherwise as she continued to lavish gifts upon Johnny. To strengthen their relationship, or perhaps to obviate hidden bitterness over their London horrors, Lana and Johnny decided in the spring of 1958 to take a seven-week vacation in

Acapulco. They stayed at the Vía Vera Hotel, where guests in adjacent rooms "complained of their noisy love-making," according to Kenneth Anger writing in *Hollywood Babylon*. The couple spent half of their vacation aboard the yacht *Rose Maria*, and whether the ship was sailing or at anchor, Lana was observed by the crew to be constantly at Stompanato's side. "I couldn't understand," the captain later commented, "why a movie queen would keep on chasing after him. But no matter what he was doing on board, she was at his side. He would sit in a deck chair and she would come along and all of a sudden sit right down in his lap without being asked."

The Mexican fling ended at the Los Angeles airport, where news photographers and Cheryl Crane had assembled to greet the returning movie star. Cheryl, by now a tall girl who almost towered over Johnny, exchanged happy smiles with her mother's boyfriend. Two weeks later she became his killer.

The couple began battling again, Stompanato coming close to violence again and again over Lana's refusal to allow him to escort her to the Academy Awards. (She was nominated for an Oscar for her role in *Peyton Place*, that great and, for that era, scandalous soaper. She did not win.) It was obvious to Stompanato that Lana did not wish to be seen in his company. A further source of argument were the large gambling debts Johnny had run up through his friend Mickey Cohen. Stompanato demanded that Lana cover these IOU's. When she refused, he went berserk.

As the two argued in an upstairs bedroom of the mansion in the early evening of April 4, 1958, Stompanato's voice rose to a roar. Cheryl ran upstairs and listened at the door to his obscenities and threats. The teen-ager heard Stompanato (as was later claimed at the coroner's inquest) tell her mother that he would beat her up, disfigure her for life with a razor. "If a man makes a living with his hands, I would destroy his hands. You make your living with your face, so I will destroy your face. I'll get you where it hurts the most. . . . I'll cut you up and I'll get your mother and your daughter, too . . . that's my business!"

Stompanato grabbed Lana by the arms. She broke away, opening the bedroom door and seeing her daughter. "Please Cheryl, please don't listen to any of this," Lana said, according to her later testimony. "I beg you to go back to your room." She closed the door and turned to Johnny. "That's just great, my child had to hear all that. . . . I can't go through this anymore."

Stompanato went to a closet, took out a jacket on a hanger, and then stood facing Lana, swearing at her. "[He] was holding the jacket on the hanger in a way that he was going to strike me with it."

Lana stood up to him. "Don't—don't ever touch me again. I am—I am absolutely finished. This is the end. And I want you to get out!" She walked to the bedroom door, Stompanato moving fast behind her. As Lana again threw open the door Cheryl rushed forward. Lana later claimed that she never saw the butcher knife with a nine-inch blade that Cheryl had retrieved from the kitchen. "I swear it was so fast, I—I truthfully thought she had hit him in the stomach. The best I can remember, they came together and they parted. I still never saw a blade."

Stompanato grabbed his abdomen, wordlessly gasping, taking a few wobbly steps forward. Then he turned slightly and fell backward onto the thick pink carpet, his arms clutching his stomach, then flying outward. Lana, at first petrified in shock, suddenly ran to her stricken lover, bending over him, lifting his sweater. "I saw the blood. . . . He made a horrible noise in his throat. . . . It's like a great nightmare. I can't believe it happened."

The actress next ran to her bathroom to snatch a towel and return to the fallen Stompanato, pressing the towel to the bloody wound. Cheryl stood nearby, sobbing. Lana's efforts to save her paramour were useless. She knelt next to Stompanato, listening to the "very dreadful sounds in his throat of gasping—terrible sounds. I tried to breathe air into his semi-open lips . . . my mouth against his. . . . He was dying." There was nothing more to do. Lana went to the phone and called her mother, "because I had been out of the country so long and I could not remember my doctor's number." Next, Lana called the famous Hollywood lawyer Jerry Geisler, who picked up his phone a few minutes before 9 P.M. that Good Friday. "This is Lana Turner," he heard the actress say. "Could you please come to my house? Something terrible has happened." Geisler was on his way within minutes.

Cheryl was also on the phone, calling her father, Stephen Crane, at his restaurant, the Luau. "Daddy, Daddy, come quick!" the girl shouted. "Something terrible has happened."

"What's the matter?"

"Don't ask questions, Daddy. Just hurry, please!"

Crane, who was without a car, asked one of his patrons to drive him to Lana's mansion in Beverly Hills. He arrived before anyone else, leaping from the car and sprinting up the walkway. Cheryl was at the door, shouting: "Daddy, Daddy!"

"I'm coming." Half-running, he followed his daughter into the house and up the stairs, two at a time, to the second floor.

Lana met her ex-husband in the hall and said in a calm voice: "Something terrible has happened."

Crane peered into the bedroom, to see Stompanato lying on the carpet, bleeding. He turned to his daughter: "What happened, Cherie?"

"I did it, Daddy," sobbed Cheryl, "but I didn't mean to. He was going to hurt Mommy." She wept uncontrollably. "I didn't mean to, I didn't mean to."

Lana pulled the girl close to her. "I know you didn't."

"I just wanted to protect you."

In response to phone calls, two physicians arrived to work over the fatally wounded Stompanato. An ambulance was called. A beat cop, eyes wide with wonder, answered a "disturbance" call. He phoned his boss, Clinton H. Anderson, chief of the Beverly Hills Police Department. Jerry Geisler appeared, assuring Lana Turner that she would receive all his legal expertise. (This was the first meeting between the criminal lawyer and the movie queen.) Reporter Jim Bacon showed up and gained entrance to the mansion by telling policemen—by then cops were all over the estate—that he was from the "coroner's office." The house was filling up fast. By the time Chief Anderson arrived, Lana and Cheryl were weeping hysterically.

Lana pleaded with Anderson to put the blame on her. "Cheryl has killed Johnny," she sobbed. "He threatened to kill me and poor Cherie got frightened. My poor baby. Please say that I did it. I don't want her involved. Poor baby. Please say that I did it."

Geisler put his arm gently and protectively about the actress's shoulders, telling her: "Your daughter has done a courageous thing. It's too bad that a man's life is gone [Stompanato by this time had been pronounced dead] but under the circumstances the child did the only thing she could do to protect her mother from harm." He looked at Anderson and then, obviously more for the policeman's benefit and his client's strange position, said: "I understand your concern for the child's welfare. But you won't get anyplace by hiding the truth. Will she, Chief?" Anderson gave the lawyer a solemn nod.

Lana began to recite to Anderson the abuses Stompanato had heaped upon her in recent months, describing in detail how he had almost choked her to death in London. But the sympathetic police chief already knew of Johnny's unsavory past and his violent ways with women. Anderson was later to remark: "We had considerable information on him [Stompanato]. We knew he had obtained large sums of money from individuals who were afraid to complain to the police, and we were aware that he had accepted money from a number of his women friends."

As Anderson watched medical aides cover the gigolo's body and move it slowly from the Beverly Hills mansion—Lana, Cheryl, Crane, Geisler, and a host of others staring after the stretcher—the policeman remembered the last time he had seen Johnny Stompanato. "I had assisted him out the rear door of a prominent Beverly Hills hotel," he later recalled, "holding him by the collar and the seat of his well tailored slacks, after he had become abusive during a police investigation. Had we known positively that he was there for the purpose of extorting money from a hotel guest, we could have saved his victim thousands of dollars, and Stompanato might have been alive today—and in prison."

Gently, Anderson interrogated Cheryl. She was "still shocked and unable to believe that Johnny Stompanato was dead."

"I didn't mean to kill him," Cheryl told Anderson woodenly. "I just meant to frighten him."

Anderson patiently listened to the girl's story, then informed Lana that her daughter would be locked up in the Juvenile Section of the city jail. The actress broke into tears once again, begging Anderson to take her, not Cheryl.

"Can't you arrest me instead?" pleaded Lana. "It was my fault. Poor baby's not to blame for all this mess."

Hours later the fourteen-year-old was locked up, charged with murder. A short time later the press had the story and the storm broke. It was wildly speculated that Lana had really committed the killing after finding Stompanato in bed with her daughter. The columnists and gossip hounds enjoyed a field day of rumors and conjectures. Some, while appearing to be sympathetic to Lana's dilemma, used the killing as a way of indicting the actress's life-style. Wrote George Sokolsky in the *New York Journal-American*: "Cheryl Crane, the little girl of too many fathers, is a sad girl who could have had everything but who had nothing; a girl who spent her childhood and girlhood watching a procession of lovers and husbands wander in and out of her mother's bedroom and to whom the sight of her mother being physically abused by men became an everyday occurrence. She is a girl who learned about life long before she understood what she was learning." Louella Parsons dredged up every interview she had had with Lana, selected the juiciest parts, those that applied to the actress's tempestuous love life, and put the material to work again in print. Hedda Hopper, Louella's rival Hollywood sob sister, wrote: "My heart bleeds for Cheryl."

Another bombshell exploded after Mickey Cohen suddenly appeared in the editorial offices of the *Los Angeles Herald Examiner*, a Hearst newspaper, where he released the torrid love letters from Lana to Johnny. He had obtained them by sending some of his goons to Stompanato's lodgings as soon as he heard of the killing. (His thick-fingered thugs overlooked the box that contained Stompanato's blackmail photos, later given to the police.) It was Cohen who paid for Stompanato's funeral. He had expected Lana Turner to pay, and when he got the bill he became enraged and turned over her letters to the press in revenge.

The publication of the letters caused the newspaper opinion-shapers to turn against the actress. Only Walter Winchell, king of the gossipmongers, thought to champion Lana Turner, a move he knew would create controversy and sell newspapers carrying his syndicated column. "She is made of rays of the sun," waxed Winchell about Lana,

woven of blue eyes, honey-colored hair and flowing curves. She is Lana Turner, goddess of the screen. . . . She is lashed by vicious reporting, flogged by editorials, and threatened with being deprived of her child. And of course, it is outraged virtue which screams the loudest. It seems sadistic to me to subject Lana to any more torment. No punishment that could be imagined could hurt her more than the memory of this nightmarish event. And she is condemned to live with this memory to the end of her days. In short, give your heart to the girl with a broken heart.

For the most part the Hollywood community, which has always carried its heart in its pocketbook, remained silent, fearing that the industry would be hurt if Lana was shown any sort of public support from members. Feisty Gloria Swanson did speak up, however, but not in support of Lana Turner. She attacked the actress *and* Winchell for coming to Lana's aid, telling the columnist that what he had written was "disgusting . . . you are trying to whitewash Lana. You are not a loyal American. . . . As far as that poor Lana Turner is concerned, the only true thing you said is that she sleeps in a woolen night-gown . . . she is not even an actress . . . she is only a trollop."

Cheryl was brought before the juvenile Court, the charge against her reduced to manslaughter. Jerry Geisler, in a deft move, put Lana on the witness stand. She told the story of the killing with tearful passion and choking words, defending her daughter's actions. It was, as Geisler knew it would be, the finest performance the actress ever gave. Photographers ran out of film as they snapped Lana weeping and mopping her brow, appearing close to a faint as she struggled through her testimony. Cheryl repeated the story her mother gave, and the coroner's jury, having only the identical testimony of the two females upon which to base its conclusion, ruled that Cheryl committed justifiable homicide in defense of her mother.

Another emotion-packed scene took place a short time later in the courtroom of Superior Court Judge Allen T. Lynch of Santa Monica, where Cheryl was made a ward of the state and placed in the custody of her grandmother, Mildred Turner. Photographers were again rewarded with weepy scenes of Lana kneeling before her mother, eyes closed, hands clutching her mother's, a thoroughly penitent pose.

The police and courts were inundated with mail, the public accusing the police of "covering up" the real facts in the case. Oddly, syndicate gangsters like Mickey Cohen grumbled openly about the court decision. This attitude Chief Anderson found "most ironic," in that "the underworld [refused] to believe that this 'tough' ex-Marine could have been killed so easily by a fourteen-year-old girl. [Stompanato] had been considered one of their best bodyguards, and it was a damaging blow to their ego."

The case did not end with the freeing of Cheryl Crane. Mildred Turner found it too difficult to care for her granddaughter, and Cheryl was sent by court order to the El Retiro School for Girls in the San Fernando Valley. After running away twice from the school, Cheryl was allowed by the court to reunite with her mother. The girl later went to work as a hostess in the restaurant owned by her father, Stephen Crane.

Lana Turner weathered this fiercest storm of her life without loss of money or prestige. In fact, the killing and its scandalous aftermath seemed to strengthen her career; eventually the American public, as it is generally wont to do, supported the highly publicized underdog. The Stompanato affair worked favorably not only for Lana but for Hollywood. A movie based on the killing, *Where Love Has Gone*, proved to be a box-office success, as was Lana's next movie, *Imitation of Life*.

Many more films followed, including *Madame X*. Lana's appearance in this film moved critic Pauline Kael to write: "She's not *Madame*

X; she's brand X; she's not an actress, she's a commodity." Countered Hollywood historian Adela Rogers St. Johns: "Look, let's not get mixed up about the *real* Lana Turner. The *real* Lana Turner is Lana Turner. She was always a movie star and loved it. Her personal life and her movie life *are one.*"

And as an actress and a person Lana Turner went on meeting and marrying men who made her unhappy. In 1976, Lana Turner vowed to live alone. "I have matured with the realization that I can live without a man!" she then exclaimed. "I can get through a day without being emotionally involved with another human being." The fifty-six-year-old star was exuberant about her decision to cut men out of her life: "Oh, how I treasure this freedom. I really do. It's a glorious, wonderful experience. I am off marriage—for life!"

Murder Among the Mighty, 1983

ALBERT BOROWITZ

Whether Alice Crimmins was guilty of the crimes for which she stood trial remains an open question. As Ann Jones and other feminist scholars have pointed out, she may have been convicted more for her freewheeling sexual behavior than for the conflicting evidence against her. This judicious account of the case is by Albert Borowitz (b. 1930), a lifelong aficionado of crime literature who began producing his own articles on the subject while practicing corporate law in the Midwest. Following his retirement in 1995, he created a major reference work, *Blood & Ink: The International Guide to Fact-Based Crime Literature*, published in 2002 by Kent State University, which also houses his extensive collection of crime books and memorabilia. In his various essays, Borowitz often focuses on the relationship between artists and crime. As he told an interviewer for *Legal Studies Forum*: "I study with particular interest writers, intellectuals, musicians, and artists who have directly confronted crime in their own lives or were inspired by actual criminal cases to create significant works of the imagination." While the Alice Crimmins case has not generated any literary masterpieces on the order of Dreiser's *An American Tragedy*, it did serve as the basis for the 1975 thriller *Where Are the Children?*, the book that launched the career of best-selling mystery writer Mary Higgins Clark. The playwright John Guare, best known as the author of *Six Degrees of Separation* and *The House of Blue Leaves*, also drew on the Crimmins case for his 1977 black comedy *Landscape of the Body*.

The Medea of Kew Gardens Hills

On the morning of 14 July 1965, Eddie Crimmins received a telephone call from his estranged wife Alice, accusing him of having taken the children. When she had opened their bedroom door, which she kept locked by a hook-and-eye on the outside, she had seen that the beds had been slept in but Eddie Jr, aged five, and his four-year-old sister Alice (nicknamed Missy) were gone. The casement window was cranked open about 75 degrees; Alice remembered having closed it the night before because there was a hole in the screen and she wanted to keep the bugs out. The screen was later found outside, leaning against the wall beneath the window, and nearby was a 'porter's stroller'—a converted baby-carriage with a box on it.

Alice's husband, an aeroplane mechanic who worked nights, protested that he knew nothing of the children's whereabouts and, alarmed by the message, said he would come right over to see her. Alice and the children lived in a dispiriting redbrick apartment complex flatteringly named Regal Gardens, located near the campus of Queens College in the Kew Gardens Hills section of the New York City borough of Queens. Shortly after joining his wife, Eddie called the police, and the first contingent of patrolmen were on the scene in a matter of minutes. By 11 a.m. precinct cars were parked all around the grassy mall adjoining Alice's apartment building at 150–22 72nd Drive.

Jerry Piering, who was the first detective to arrive, quickly made the case his own. Hoping for a promotion to second grade on the Queens' detective command, he immediately sensed that he had stepped into an important investigation. It took only one glance at Alice for him to decide that she did not look the picture of the anxious mother, this striking redhead in her twenties, with thick make-up, hip-hugging toreador slacks, flowered blouse and white high-heeled shoes. Patrolman Michael Clifford had already filled Piering in on the background—the Crimminses were separated and in the middle of a custody fight, but the role that the vanished children might have played in their skirmishing was still obscure.

The first fruits of Piering's look around the premises confirmed the unfavourable impression Alice had made. In the garbage cans there were about a dozen empty liquor bottles that Alice later attributed to good housekeeping rather than over-indulgence, explaining that she had been cleaning the apartment in anticipation of an inspection visit from a city agency in connection with the custody suit. Still more revealing to Piering was a proverbial 'little black book' that Alice had dropped outside; the men listed outnumbered women four to one.

While Piering was making his rounds, Detective George Martin found trophies of Alice's active social life in a pastel-coloured overnight bag stowed under her bed. The greetings and dinner programmes that filled the bag documented her relationship with Anthony (Tony) Grace, a fifty-two-year-old highway contractor with ties to important Democratic politicians. Alice's souvenirs showed that Tony Grace had introduced her to such party stalwarts as Mayor Robert Wagner and Senator Robert Kennedy; messages from Grace and important city officials addressed her as 'Rusty'.

Piering took Alice into her bedroom and questioned her about her activities on 13 July. Between 2.30 and 4.30 in the afternoon she and the children had picnicked in Kissena Park, six blocks from the apartment. They came home after stopping to pick up some food for dinner; at Sever's delicatessen in the neighbourhood she had bought a package of frozen veal, a can of string beans and a bottle of soda. When she arrived home she called her attorney, Michael LaPenna (recommended to her by Grace), to discuss the custody case which was scheduled for a hearing in a week. She was concerned about a former maid, Evelyn Linder Atkins, who claimed that Alice owed her $600 and, according to Alice, had hinted that if she were paid she would not testify against her in the proceedings. Evelyn had a worrisome story to tell the judge if she decided to do so, for Alice had without warning abandoned the children one weekend while she took a boat trip to the Bahamas with Tony Grace and his friends. Alice told Piering that it was not her fault; she had thought she was aboard only for a *bon voyage* party but the men had playfully locked her and a girlfriend in a washroom and carried them off to sea. Perhaps LaPenna shared her concern about the maid, because the lawyer did not seem as optimistic about her chances of retaining custody as he usually did.

After dinner, Alice took the children for a ride in the direction of Main Street, wanting to find out the location of a furnished apartment to which her husband had recently moved. Knowing that Eddie had planted a crude 'bug' on her telephone, she was hoping to retaliate by finding him to be living with a woman. She drove around for more than an hour until it was almost dark and then gave up the search.

Upon returning home, Alice prepared the children for bed about 9 p.m. (Theresa Costello, aged fourteen, Alice's former babysitter, later told the police that it was at this very moment that, passing below the bedroom window on her way to a babysitting job, she heard the Crimmins children saying their prayers.) Alice brought a replacement screen from her room to the children's bedroom but noticed that it had been fouled by her dog, Brandy. She therefore reset the children's punctured screen in the window without bothering to bolt it into place. Mindful of the coming agency visit, she disposed of wine and liquor bottles and made a pile of old clothing; by 10.30 p.m. she was tired, and collapsed on the living-room couch to watch *The Defenders* on TV. The programme did not make her forget that Tony Grace had not returned the call she had made earlier in the day. She reached him at a Bronx bar and to her jealous questions he responded that he was alone. After she hung up, Alice received a call from a man Grace had apparently replaced in her favour, a house renovator named Joe Rorech. Alice had met Rorech in January 1964 when she was working as a cocktail waitress at the Bourbon House in Syosset, Long Island. After Eddie had moved out of the Crimmins apartment, another Bourbon House waitress, Anita ('Tiger') Ellis, had come to live with Alice. For a while they had shared the favours of Joe Rorech, but 'Tiger' had soon moved on to new attachments. In their conversation last night, Joe Rorech asked Alice to join him at a bar in Huntington, Long Island, but she evaded the invitation, pleading the unavailability of a babysitter.

After talking to Joe, Alice returned to her television set. At midnight she took little Eddie to the bathroom but could not wake Missy; she thought she had re-latched the bedroom door. (The door was kept locked, she explained, to keep Eddie from raiding the refrigerator.) Afterwards, Alice took the dog Brandy for a walk, then sat on the front stoop for a while. She told Piering that she may not have bolted the front door at the time. When at last she was getting ready for bed, her husband called and angered her by repeating the maid's claim that Alice owed her money. Alice calmed down by taking the dog out again and, after a bath, went to sleep between 3.30 and 4 a.m.

Alice and Eddie, childhood sweethearts, had been married seven years. They were reasonably happy for a while but, soon after the birth of their son, they quarrelled frequently about Eddie's staying out late working or drinking with friends. After Missy was born, Alice decided to have no more children and Eddie, brought up a good Catholic (as was she) never forgave her after he found birth control devices in her purse. Their relationship went from bad to worse until, on 22 June 1965, he went to the Family Court to seek custody of the two children. By then, the couple were already separated, the children living on with Alice at the Regal Gardens. The custody petition charged that, immediately after the separation, Alice 'began to indulge herself openly and brazenly in sex as she had done furtively before the separation'. It was further detailed in the petition that Alice 'entertains, one at a time, a stream of men sharing herself and her bedroom, until she and her paramour of the evening are completely spent. The following morning, the children awake to see a strange man in the house.'

Combining a high degree of jealousy with a flair for the technology of snooping, Eddie had devoted many of his leisure hours to surveillance of her relations with men. He had much to observe, for when Alice gave up her secretarial work to become a waitress at a series of Long Island restaurants and bars, her opportunities for male acquaintance multiplied. To keep his compulsive watch, Eddie bugged her telephone and installed a microphone in her bedroom which he could monitor from a listening-post he had established in the basement below. Once he had burst in on Alice and a usually overdressed waiter named Carl Andrade, who had fled naked out of the window to his car.

Eddie liked to think that the purpose of his spying was to gather evidence for the custody case, but he ultimately admitted that he had often invaded Alice's apartment when she was out just to be near her 'personal things'. During their separation, so Alice said, Eddie told her that he had exposed himself to little girls in a park, but Alice disbelieved him, thinking that he was trying to play on her sympathy for his loneliness and distress.

Eddie's preoccupation with his wife's love life dominated his activities on 13 July, as he recounted them to the police. At 7 a.m. he had played a poor round of golf at a public course at Bethpage in Nassau County. Afterwards he drank three beers in the clubhouse with a friend and watched the New York Mets baseball game on television, leaving around 2 p.m. before the game ended. He then drove to Huntington to see whether Alice was visiting Joe Rorech but was disappointed to find no sign of her four-year-old Mercury convertible there. He arrived home at 5 p.m. and spent the evening watching television. Then, about 11 p.m., he drove along Union Turnpike to a small fast food stand near St John's University, bought a pizza and a large bottle of Pepsi Cola, and returned home. Alice, though, was still very much on his mind. After driving back to the Union Turnpike and drinking gin and tonic at a bar until 2.45 a.m., he drove into the parking lot behind his wife's bedroom window; he thought he saw a light there and in her living-room. He went home and called up Alice to talk about the maid. When Alice hung up, he watched a movie on television, read briefly and fell asleep by 4 a.m. A detective who checked out Eddie's story found that the movie he claimed to have seen on the CBS channel had actually been on much earlier.

In addition to questioning Alice, Jerry Piering, a fledgling in his job, directed the police inspection and photographing of the apartment, apparently with more enthusiasm than expertise. Piering later claimed that when he first came into the children's room, he observed a thin layer of dust on the bureau-top, which in his mind eliminated the possibility that the children had left the room through the window since they would have had to cross over the bureau. However, technicians had covered the top of the bureau with powder for detecting fingerprints before the bureau could be photographed in its original condition. It was Piering's further recollection that when he had moved a lamp on the bureau, it had left a circle in the layer of dust. This story was later disputed by Alice's brother, John Burke, and others, who agreed that the lamp on the bureau had tripod legs. Also, many people had come into the room before Piering arrived; Eddie Crimmins had leaned out of the window to look for the missing children, and, of course, Alice on the previous evening had removed and replaced the screen; it seemed unlikely that Piering's dust-film would have remained undisturbed amid all this activity. In any event, neither the layer of dust nor the impression left by the lamp base was noted in Piering's first reports.

In the early afternoon of 14 July 1965, the Crimmins case was transformed from mysterious disappearance into homicide. A nine-year-old boy, Jay Silverman, found Missy's body in an open lot on 162nd Street, about eight blocks from the Regal Gardens. A pyjama-top, knotted into two ligatures, was loosely tied around her bruised neck. An autopsy, performed with the participation of Dr Milton Helpern, New York City's distinguished Chief Medical Examiner, found no evidence of sexual assault; haemorrhages in the mucous membranes in the throat and vocal cords confirmed that Missy had been asphyxiated. The contents of the stomach were sent to an expert, who reported finding, among other things, a macaroni-like substance. This discovery rang a bell with Detective Piering, who recalled that on the morning of 14 July he had seen in Alice's trash can a package that had held frozen manicotti and had also noticed a plate of leftover manicotti in her refrigerator. However, none of this evidence had been preserved— nor had Piering's discoveries been referred to in his contemporaneous reports.

Following the discovery of Missy's body, the search for young Eddie intensified. A false alarm was raised in Cunningham Park when what looked like a blond-headed body turned out to be a discarded doll. On Monday morning, 19 July, Vernon Warnecke and his son, walking together to look at a treehouse used by the children in the neighbourhood, found Eddie Crimmins on an embankment overlooking the Van Wyck Expressway. The boy's body was eaten away by rats and insects and in an advanced state of decay. The site was about a mile from Alice Crimmins's apartment and close to the grounds of the New York World's Fair that was then in progress.

After the children were buried, Alice and her husband, reunited by their tragedy, faced a relentless police investigation which explored many trails, always only to return to Alice. Detectives pursued reports of strange intruders in the Crimmins neighbourhood, including a so-called 'pants burglar' who broke into homes only to steal men's trousers. A closer look was taken at the boyfriends whose names filled Alice's black book. Anthony Grace admitted in a second interview that he had lied when he told the police he had never left the Bronx on the night of 13/14 July. He now stated that he had driven over the Whitestone Bridge to a restaurant called Ripples on the Water with a group of 'bowling girls', young married women who partied around town under the pretext that they were going bowling. Grace maintained that he had stayed away from Alice during the period of the custody battle and had not seen her much recently. She had called him several times on 13 July but he was preoccupied with business and had taken his wife to dinner without remembering to call Alice back. At 11 p.m. she phoned him again at the Capri Bar, telling him that she wanted to join him for a drink. He had put her off by telling her that he was about to leave and had denied her well-founded suspicion that he was with the bowling girls.

Joe Rorech told Detective Phil Brady that he had called Alice twice on the night of the disappearance, first after 10 p.m., when she declined his invitation to the Bourbon House bar, and then at 2 a.m., when there had been no answer. Rorech had been drinking all night and admitted he might have misdialled the number. On 6 December 1965 the police administered the first of two sodium pentothal 'truth tests' to Rorech. Satisfied with the results, and finding Rorech's self-confidence weakened by business reverses, they conscripted him as a spy. Joe took Alice to motel rooms where recorders had been planted, but their conversations contained nothing of interest.

At first Eddie Crimmins had been more inclined to cooperate with the police than Alice. He submitted to a session with the lie detector, and persuaded Alice to take the test. However, after she agreed and the preliminary questions were completed, she refused to continue. With the exception of Detective Brady, the police now decided to forget about Eddie and concentrate on Alice. Before the Crimminses moved into a new three-room apartment in Queens to avoid the eyes of their unwanted public, the police, succeeding to the role long played by Alice's jealous husband, planted ultrasensitive microphones and tapped the telephone wires. Detectives monitored the apartment around the clock from the third floor pharmacy of a neighbouring hospital, but could not pick up a single incriminating statement. Their failure was not remarkable since Alice seemed well aware of the police presence, beginning many of her conversations, 'Drop dead, you guys!' Unable to overhear a confession, the secret listeners were tuned into the sounds of Alice's sexual encounters, which resumed shortly after she took up her new residence. As their high-tech recording devices picked up Alice's cries of physical need, her pursuers became more certain of her guilt, convinced as they were that grief for the dead children would demand an adjournment of the flesh.

According to reporter Kenneth Gross, who has written the principal account of the case, police investigators vented their hostility against Alice by interfering with the love affairs that they were recording so assiduously. When the tireless eavesdroppers overheard Joe Rorech and Alice making love, they informed Eddie Crimmins, who promptly called and was assured by Alice that she was alone. The police, hoping for a confrontation between lover and outraged husband, flattened Rorech's tyres, but he managed to have his car towed safely out of the neighbourhood before Eddie got home. When Alice moved out of the apartment to live with an Atlanta man for whom she was working as a secretary, the police thoughtfully advised the man's wife, and when she came to New York, helped her destroy Alice's clothing. Undaunted by this harassment, Alice reappeared in her familiar nightspots, now as a customer instead of cocktail waitress.

The investigation dragged on for a year and a half without result, and meanwhile there was a growing public clamour for action. At this point New York politics intervened to step up the pace of events: Nat Hentel, an interim Republican appointment as Queens District Attorney, was soundly defeated for re-election and decided to convene a grand jury before his term of office expired. The grand jury failed to return an indictment, and a second grand jury impanelled under Hentel's Democratic successor 'Tough Tommy' Mackell also disbanded without indictment in May of the following year. Then, on 1 September 1967, Assistant District Attorney James Mosley went before still another grand jury to present the testimony of a 'mystery witness', who was soon identified as Sophie Earomirski.

Sophie's original entrance into the case had been anonymous. On 30 November 1966, she had written to then District Attorney Hentel telling him how happy she was to read that he was bringing the Crimmins case to a grand jury. She reported an 'incident' she had witnessed while looking out of her living-room window on the early morning of 14 July 1965. Shortly after 2 a.m., a man and woman came walking down the street towards 72nd Road in Queens. The woman, who was lagging about five feet behind the man, was holding what appeared to be a bundle of blankets shining white under her left arm, and with her right hand led a little boy walking at her side. The man shouted at her to hurry up and she told him 'to be quiet or someone will see us'. The man took the blanket-like white bundle and heaved it onto the back seat of the nondescript automobile. The woman picked up the little boy and sat with him on the back seat; she had dark hair, and her companion was tall, not heavy, with dark hair and a large nose. Sophie apologised for signing merely as 'A Reader'.

Shortly after he was entrusted with the Crimmins case by Mackell, Mosley came across Sophie's letter, and the hunt for her began. The police obtained samples of the handwriting of tenants living in garden apartments from which the scene described in the letter could have been viewed, and they identified Sophie, who recognised Alice's photograph as resembling the woman she had seen. Sophie's testimony before the third grand jury was decisive, and Queens County finally had its long-coveted indictment, charging Alice Crimmins with the murder of Missy. The prosecution had persuaded the grand jury that there was reasonable cause to believe that the bundle of blankets Sophie had seen contained the little girl's dead body.

On 9 May 1968, the trial began in the ground floor courtroom of the Queens County Criminal Court Building amid widely varying perceptions of the defendant. To the sensationalist press, Alice was a 'modern-day Medea' who had sacrificed her children to a deadly hatred for her husband, and the pulp magazine *Front Page Detective*, invoking another witch from antiquity, called her an 'erring wife, a Circe, an amoral woman whose many affairs appeared symptomatic of America's Sex Revolution'. A group of radical feminists offered to identify Alice's cause with their own, but she declined their help. Between these two wings of public opinion there was a dominant vision of Alice as a manhunting cocktail waitress, and her longer years as housewife, mother and secretary receded into the background.

The prosecution case was presented for the most part by James Mosley's aspiring young assistant, Anthony Lombardino, but Mosley himself scored the first important point while questioning Dr Milton Helpern. The forensic expert testified that the discovery of as much food as was found in Missy's stomach was consistent with a post-ingestion period of less than two hours. If Helpern was right, then assuming that Alice had been the last to feed the children, she could not have seen them alive at midnight, as she claimed.

Lombardino insisted that the prize job of examining the prosecution's star witness was his—his alone. Since the police had first enlisted Joe Rorech's aid, Joe's difficulties had continued to mount; his marriage was in trouble and he had been upset by a brief period of arrest as a material witness. In his testimony he made it plain that he had lost any vestige of loyalty to his former mistress.

The defence, led by Harold Harrison, was unmoved when Rorech indirectly quoted Alice, 'She did not want Eddie to have the children. She would rather see the children dead than Eddie have them.' Harrison had not heard this before, but he did not regard the statement as damaging; surely the jury would understand that it was just the kind of thing that a divorcing spouse was likely to say in the heat of a custody battle. Rorech, though, had something more to disclose that would change the course of the trial. Though the police had learned nothing incriminating from electronic eavesdropping, Joe testified to a long conversation with Alice at a motel in Nassau County. After weeping inconsolably, she had said again and again that the children 'will understand, they know it was for the best'. At last she had added, 'Joseph, please forgive me, I killed her.'

Stung by the witness's words, Alice jumped out of her chair and banged her fists on the defence table, crying, 'Joseph! How could you do this? This is not true! Joseph . . . you, of all people! Oh, my God!' Harrison was unable to follow Alice's outburst with telling cross-examination for he had no effective means of rebutting Rorech's quotes. In fact, he may have been preoccupied by a dilemma of his own: the next morning he went before judge Peter Farrell and unsuccessfully sought to withdraw from the case on the grounds that prior to the trial he had represented Joe Rorech as well as Alice, to whom Joe had introduced him.

After Rorech's damning testimony, the appearance of Sophie Earomirski, The Woman in the Window, came as an anticlimax. Sophie elaborated the scene she had recalled in her anonymous letter by adding a pregnant dog. She told the jury that the woman had responded to her male companion's order to hurry by explaining that she was waiting for the dog. She had said, 'The dog is pregnant,' and the man had grumbled, 'Did you have to bring it?' In fact, Brandy *was* pregnant that night, but several witnesses swore that nobody had recognised the pregnancy—that when the dog produced a single puppy the week after the killing, Alice and the neighbours were surprised.

The defence tried to destroy Sophie's credibility, but the scope of the attack was narrowly limited by Judge Farrell. The judge excluded an affidavit of Dr Louis Berg to the effect that a head injury suffered by Mrs Earomirski at the World's Fair had resulted in 'permanent brain damage'. Defence lawyer Marty Baron questioned her about two suicide attempts, but to no avail: the courtroom spectators cheered her recital that she had placed her head in an oven to see how dinner was coming along. A press photograph records Sophie's exit from the courthouse, her hand raised in triumph like a triumphant boxer, still champion, on whom the challenger could not lay a glove.

The principal strategy of the defence was to put Alice on the stand to deny the murder charge and to show that she was not made of granite, as portrayed by certain sections of the media. When Baron's questioning turned to the children, Alice began to tremble and whispered to Judge Farrell that she could not continue. Farrell declared a recess. When the trial resumed, Alice concluded her testimony with a strong denial of Rorech's account of her confession.

The decision to permit Alice to testify gave prosecutor Lombardino the opportunity he had been waiting for: to question her closely about her love life. All the most titillating incidents were brought out: the night Eddie had caught her in bed with the amorous waiter Carl Andrade, an afternoon tryst with a buyer at the World's Fair, a 1964 cruise with Tony Grace to the Democratic National Convention in Atlantic City, and nude swimming at Joe Rorech's home when, Lombardino was careful to stress, the children were dead. To reporter Kenneth Gross it seemed that Lombardino had torn away the last shred of Alice's dignity when he enquired whether she remembered making love with her children's barber in the back of a car behind the barbershop; Alice admitted having had ten dates with the barber, but, straining at a gnat, couldn't recall the incident in the car. Lombardino continued the catalogue of Alice's conquests with obvious relish until the judge ordered him to conclude.

The trial ended after thirteen days on Monday 27 May, and early the next morning the jury returned a verdict of guilty of manslaughter in the first degree; one of the jurors said that a large majority had voted for conviction on the first ballot, but that he had doubts about the proof and did not regard her as a danger to society. At her sentencing hearing, Alice protested her innocence and angrily told Judge Farrell, 'You don't care who killed my children, you want to close your books.

You don't give a damn who killed my kids.' The judge sentenced her to be confined in the New York State prison for women at Westfield State Farms, Bedford Hills, New York, for a term of not less than five nor more than twenty years.

Alice's conviction was far from the last chapter of the case. In December 1969 the Appellate Division of the New York Supreme Court, an intermediate appeals court, ordered a new trial because three of the jurors had secretly visited the scene of Sophie Earomirski's identification of Alice. One of the jurors had made his visit alone at about two in the morning, hoping to verify what Sophie could have seen at that hour. The court reasoned that 'the net effect of the jurors' visits was that they made themselves secret, untested witnesses not subject to any cross-examination'. The State's highest court, the Court of Appeals, agreed, ruling in April 1970 that the unauthorised visits were inherently prejudicial to the defendant, and adding, in a significant aside, that the evidence of guilt 'was not so overwhelming that we can say, as a matter of law, that the error could not have influenced the verdict'. The Court noted that only two witnesses, Sophie Earomirski and Joe Rorech, had directly implicated Alice, and that Rorech's testimony 'was seriously challenged, and the witness was subjected to searching cross-examination'.

When the case was retried in 1971, a change in counsel and the presiding judge and the cooling of community passions resulted in a more restrained courtroom atmosphere. Gone from the prosecution team was Tony Lombardino, replaced by Thomas Demakos, the experienced chief of the District Attorney's trial bureau. The judge to whom the second trial was assigned, George Balbach, planted court attendants in the courtroom and adjacent corridors to assure better order. Perhaps the most significant change was at the defence table, where Herbert Lyon, a leader of the Queens trial bar, now sat in the first chair. Lyon had devised a more conservative defence plan, intended to place greater stress on Alice's grief and loss, and to keep her off the witness stand so that the prejudicial parade of her love affairs could not be repeated.

The stakes had been raised in the second trial, which began on Monday, 15 March 1971. As Alice's first jury had found her guilty of manslaughter in the death of Missy, principles of double jeopardy prohibited her from being charged with a greater offence against her daughter, but the prosecution had compensated for that limitation by obtaining an additional indictment for the murder of young Eddie. Though the state of his remains ruled out proof of cause of death, Demakos offered the evidence of Dr Milton Helpern that murder could be 'inferred' because of the circumstances of his sister's death. Joe Rorech, obliging as ever, adapted his testimony to the new prosecution design; according to his revised story, Alice had told him that she had killed Missy and 'consented' to the murder of her son.

The presentation of defence evidence was already in progress when Demakos, over vigorous objection by Lyon, was permitted to bring a surprise witness to the stand. Mrs Tina DeVita, a resident of the Kew Gardens Hills development at the time of the crime, testified that on the night of 13/14 July, while driving home with her husband, she had looked out of the driver's window from the passenger's side and seen 'people walking, a man carrying a bundle, a woman, a dog, and a boy'. The angry Lyon could not shake Mrs DeVita's story but did much to neutralise its impact by introducing an unheralded witness of his own, Marvin Weinstein, a young salesman from Massapequa, Long Island. Weinstein swore that on the morning of 14 July he, together with his wife, son and daughter, had passed below Sophie Earomirski's window on the way to his car; he had carried his daughter under his arm 'like a sack' and they were accompanied by their dog—who might well have looked pregnant for she had long ago lost her figure. As a final jab at the State's case, Lyon called Vincent Colabella, a jailed gangster who had reportedly admitted to a fellow prisoner that he had been Eddie's executioner, only to deny that report when questioned by the police. On the stand Colabella chuckled as he disowned any knowledge of the crime; he said that he had never seen Alice Crimmins before.

In his closing argument, Lyon cited Sophie Earomirski's testimony that she had been led to tell her story by the voices of the children crying from the grave; if they were crying, Alice's defence lawyer suggested, they were saying, 'Let my mother go; you have had her long enough!' Demakos had harsher words, reminding the jury of Alice's failure to take the stand, 'She doesn't have the courage to stand up here and tell the world she killed her daughter.' Alice interrupted to protest, 'Because I didn't!' but the prosecutor went on without being put off his stroke, 'And the shame and pity of it is that this little boy had to die too.'

The jury deliberations began after lunch on Thursday 23 April and ended at 5.45 p.m. on the following day. Alice was found guilty of murder in the first degree in the death of her son and of manslaughter in the strangling of Missy.

On 13 May 1971 Alice Crimmins was remanded to Bedford Hills prison, and there she stayed for two years while her lawyers continued the battle for her freedom in the appellate courts. In May 1973 the Appellate Division ruled for a second time in her favour. The court threw out the murder conviction on the grounds that the State had not proved beyond reasonable doubt that young Eddie's death had resulted from a criminal act. With respect to the manslaughter count relating to Missy, the court ordered a new trial on the basis of a number of errors and improprieties, including the prosecutor's comment that Alice lacked the courage to admit the killing of Missy: this argument amounted to an improper assertion that the prosecutor knew her to be guilty and, in addition, was an improper attack on her refusal to testify. Alice was freed from prison following this ruling, but the rejoicing in her camp was premature. The tortuous path of the judicial proceedings had two more dangerous corners.

The first setback was suffered when the Court of Appeals in February 1975 announced its final decision in the appeals relating to the verdicts in the second trial. The court sustained the decision of the Appellate Division only in part: it agreed with the dismissal of the murder charge but reversed the grant of a new trial in the manslaughter conviction for the killing of Missy, returning that issue to the Appellate Division for reconsideration. Explaining the latter ruling, the Court of

Appeals conceded that Demakos's comment on Alice's refusal to testify violated her constitutional privilege against self-incrimination. However, in seeming contradiction of its sceptical view of the prosecution case in the first trial, the court decided that the constitutional error was harmless in view of the weighty evidence of Alice's guilt.

The Appellate Division confirmed the manslaughter conviction in May 1975, and Alice was once again sent back to prison to continue serving her sentence of from five to twenty years. Persevering in his efforts for her vindication, Lyon still had one card to play, an appeal from the denial of his motion for retrial, based on newly discovered evidence. A would-be witness, an electronics scientist named F. Sutherland Macklem, had given the defence an affidavit to the effect that, shortly after one o'clock on the morning of 14 July 1965, he had picked up two small children, a boy and a girl, hitchhiking in Queens County. The boy had told him he knew where his home was, and Macklem had let them out, safe and sound, at the corner of 162nd Street and 71st Avenue. The affiant did not learn the children's names, but stated that the boy could well have identified his companion as 'Missy' instead of 'my sister', as he had first thought. He admitted that he had identified his passengers as the Crimmins children only after reading newspaper accounts of the first trial, three years after the incident.

On 22 December 1975, the New York Court of Appeals affirmed the trial court's rejection of this defence initiative. The court was influenced by the affiant's seven year delay in coming forward, and commented scathingly that the affidavit 'offers an imaginative alternative hypothetical explanation [of the crime], worthy of concoction by an A. Conan Doyle'.

In January 1976 Alice Crimmins became eligible for a work-release programme and was permitted to leave prison on week days to work as a secretary. In August 1977 the New York *Post* reported that Alice had spent the previous Sunday 'as she has spent many balmy summer Sundays of her prison-term—on a luxury cruiser at City Island'. (Under the work-release programme, participants were allowed every other weekend at liberty.) In July 1977, Alice married the proprietor of the luxury cruiser, her contractor boyfriend, Anthony Grace. The *Post* was indignant over the nuptials, furnishing telephoto shots of Alice in a bikini and T-shirt, and headlining a follow-up story with a comment of the Queens District Attorney, 'Alice should be behind bars!'

On 7 September 1977, Alice Crimmins was granted parole, after thirty months in prison and nine months in the work-release programme. When a new petition for retrial was denied in November, she slipped into what must have been welcome obscurity; she had become that stalest of all commodities, old news.

The Crimmins case remains an intractable puzzle. In his opening argument in the second trial, Herbert Lyon invited the jury to regard the case as a troubling mystery that had not been solved. It is always difficult to persuade the community to live at ease with an unknown murderer, but never more so than when a child or spouse has been killed and the evidence suggests that the household was the scene of the crime or of the victim's disappearance. As in the Lindbergh kidnapping or the murder of Julia Wallace, there is a strong tendency to suspect an 'inside job'. Alice Crimmins, who slept close by but claimed to have heard nothing out of the ordinary during the murder night, naturally came under suspicion. She was a mother (perhaps harbouring the nameless daily hostilities familiar to the annals of family murder) and the only adult living in the Kew Gardens Hills apartment, and she had the opportunity to commit the crime—but can anything more be said to justify the certainty the investigators showed from the start that she was guilty? If we reject the equation that the State of New York made between sexuality and murderousness, it appears that Alice displayed only one suspicious trait: despite her avowed grief over her lost children, she does not seem to have shown much interest in helping the authorities to identify the killer. Even this curious passivity may have been due to the defensive posture into which she was immediately thrust by police antagonism and surveillance, and she may also have genuinely believed that the murderer was not to be found in her circle of acquaintances, however wide and casual.

The prosecution never attributed a plausible motive to Alice. The presence of Missy and young Eddie in the apartment does not seem to have inhibited Alice's amorous adventures, but if she found the children to be under foot, she could easily have surrendered custody to her husband. It was rumoured that she had never liked Missy much, that she had killed her in anger and then called for underworld help to dispose of her son as an inconvenient witness. Under those circumstances it is hard to visualise the boy going willingly to his doom, a docile figure in the peaceful domestic procession belatedly recalled by Sophie Earomirski in which the murderers and their future victim were accompanied by a pregnant dog. If the theory of sudden anger did not sell, the police investigators were likely to fall back on Alice's own words, that she would rather see her children dead than lose them to Eddie in the pending custody battle. Alice enjoyed a tactical advantage as a mother in possession of the children, and there is no reason to conclude that, despite the lessened optimism she detected in her lawyer's voice during their conversation before the children's disappearance, the prospect was hopeless, or that she thought so. If the uncertainty of the divorce court's ruling provided a viable motive, the police had as good a reason to charge Eddie with the crime, but they never took him seriously as a suspect.

In the mind of Joe Rorech, the theory of underworld involvement in the murder of Alice's son took on an even more sinister tone. After the second trial he told New York *Post* reporter George Carpozi Jr that Alice 'had to have those children out of the way to avoid the custody proceedings' that were to have been held on 21 July 1965. He spelled out his belief that Alice had arranged for three of her girlfriends to sleep with a prominent New York politician, who was afraid that the details of his indiscretion would come out at the custody hearing. Therefore, the man, who was 'deeply involved in New York politics and relied almost solely on the Democratic organisation for his bread and butter', had called on his gangland connections to eliminate the children, thereby averting the hearing. Rorech had no satisfactory answer when Carpozi asked him why the same objective could not have been accomplished with less pain to Alice by the murder of her estranged husband. Rorech's theory also fails to explain why the politician's scandal was deemed more likely to be publicised in a custody hearing than in the course of a murder investigation that was bound to focus on Alice Crimmins and her florid love life.

If Alice was in fact guilty, the reason for her crime must, despite the best surmises of the police and Joe Rorech, remain wrapped in mystery. Even more puzzling, though, is the autopsy evidence regarding Missy's last meal, which raises doubts concerning the time and place of the child's murder. This strange facet of the case was prominently featured in the dissenting opinion rendered by Justice Fuchsberg when the New York State Court of Appeals rejected Alice's motion for a new trial in 1975. Justice Fuchsberg noted that the testimony of the Queens medical examiner, Dr Richard Grimes, indicated that Missy had died shortly after ingesting a meal including a macaroni-like substance that differed substantially from the last dinner that Alice had told the police she served the children. This evidence suggested to the judge that 'the child might have had another meal at some unknown time and unknown place considerably after the one taken at home'.

Could Alice Crimmins have been so cunning a criminal planner as to have created this enigma by lying to the police about the food she had served on the night of the crime? Apart from the difficulty of finding traits of calculation and foresight in her character, many circumstances militate against the inference that the veal dinner was a fabrication intended by Alice to mislead the investigation. When she first mentioned the purchase of the frozen veal to Detective Piering, neither of the children's bodies had been found. If she was the murderer and had hidden the corpses, she had reason to hope that they would long remain undiscovered. Even if she feared the worst—that the victims would soon be found—it seems doubtful that she was so familiar with the capabilities of forensic medicine that she decided to turn to her own account the possibility that an autopsy might be performed in time to analyse the contents of the last meal.

There would have been a powerful deterrent to Alice's lying about the veal dinner. She told Piering that she had purchased the veal on the afternoon of 13 July in a neighbourhood delicatessen; she was presumably well known there, and the grocer who had waited on her could very likely have contradicted her story. As events turned out, the grocer did not remember what she had purchased, but she could not have counted on that in advance.

If the Crimmins case is viewed with the hindsight of the 1980s—when a young mother with a strong sexual appetite is less likely to be pronounced a Medea—it seems that Alice is entitled to the benefit of the Scottish verdict: Not Proven.

The Lady Killers, 1991

JAMES ELLROY

Few crime writers have come to their calling out of a background as dark and troubled as James Ellroy's. The only child of a "great looking and cheap couple," Ellroy, a native Angeleno, was six when his parents divorced. Four years later his mother's garroted corpse was found dumped near a high school athletic field. Her unsolved killing soon became linked in his imagination with the infamous Black Dahlia murder, a case (see page 524) that he first read about in Jack Webb's *The Badge*, a gift from his father on his 11th birthday.

To supplement the reading matter supplied by his father, Ellroy began shoplifting from the local bookstore. By his teens, he had become a heavy-drinking, swastika-sporting dropout and small-time thief. After an aborted stint in the army, he lived a down-and-out existence for the next dozen years, abusing alcohol and drugs and racking up roughly 30 arrests, 12 convictions, and eight months of jail time for various petty crimes. He began to turn his life around in 1977 when he joined Alcoholics Anonymous and took a caddying job at the Bel-Air Country Club. In 1981, he published the noir thriller *Brown's Requiem*, set in a seedy L.A. landscape Ellroy knew firsthand. Eleven more hard-boiled crime novels followed over the next 14 years, including his acclaimed "L.A. Quartet," consisting of *The Black Dahlia* (1978), *The Big Nowhere* (1988), *L.A. Confidential* (1990), and *White Jazz* (1992)—books whose violence and ferocity justified his self-proclaimed status as the "Demon Dog of American literature." In 1994, as described in this piece from *GQ* magazine, he set out to find his mother's murderer, a quest that became the subject of his widely admired 1996 memoir *My Dark Places*.

My Mother's Killer

I thought the pictures would wound me.

I thought they would grant my old nightmare form.

I thought I could touch the literal horror and somehow commute my life sentence.

I was mistaken. The woman refused to grant me a reprieve. Her grounds were simple: My death gave you a voice, and I need you to recognize me past your exploitation of it.

Her headstone reads GENEVA HILLIKER ELLROY, 1915–1958. A cross denotes her Calvinist youth in a Wisconsin hick town. The file is marked "JEAN (HILLIKER) ELLROY, 187PC (UNSOLVED), DOD 6/22/58."

I begged out of the funeral. I was 10 years old and sensed that I could manipulate adults to my advantage. I told no one that my tears were at best cosmetic and at worst an expression of hysterical relief. I told no one that I hated my mother at the time of her murder.

She died at 43. I'm 46 now. I flew out to Los Angeles to view the file because I resemble her more every day.

The L.A. County Sheriff handled the case. I set up file logistics with Sergeant Bill Stoner and Sergeant Bill McComas of the Unsolved Unit. Their divisional mandate is to periodically review open files with an eye toward solving the crimes outright or assessing the original investigating officers' failure to do so.

Both men were gracious. Both stressed that unsolved homicides tend to remain unsolved—thirty-six-year-old riddles deepen with the passage of time and blurring of consciousness. I told them I had no expectations of discovering a solution. I only wanted to touch the accumulated details and see where they took me.

Stoner said the photographs were grisly. I told him I could handle it.

The flight out was a blur. I ignored the meal service and the book I had brought to kill time with. Reminiscence consumed five hours—a whirl of memory and extrapolatable data.

My mother said she saw the Feds gun down John Dillinger. She was 19 and a nursing-school student fresh off the farm. My father said he had an affair with Rita Hayworth.

They loved to tell stories. They rarely let the truth impinge on a good anecdote. Their one child grew up to write horrible crime tales.

They met in '39 and divorced in '54. Their "irreconcilable differences" amounted to a love of the flesh. She majored in booze and minored in men. He guzzled Alka-Seltzer for his ulcer and chased women with an equal lack of discernment.

I found my mother in bed with strange men. My father hid his liaisons from me. I loved him more from the gate.

She had red hair. She drank Early Times bourbon and got mawkish or hellaciously pissed off. She sent me to church and stayed home to nurse Saturday-night hangovers.

The divorce settlement stipulated split custody: weekdays with my mother, three weekends a month with my father. He rented a cheap pad close to my weekday home. Sometimes he'd stand across the street and hold down surveillance.

At night, I'd douse the living-room lights and look out the window. That red glowing cigarette tip? Proof that he loved me.

In 1956, my mother moved us from West Hollywood to Santa Monica. I enrolled in a cut-rate private school called Children's Paradise. The place was a dump site for disturbed kids of divorce. My confinement stretched from 7:30 A.M. to 5 P.M. A giant dirt playground and a swimming pool faced Wilshire Boulevard. Every kid was guaranteed passing grades and a poolside tan. A flurry of single moms hit the gate at 5:10. I developed a yen for women in their late thirties.

My mother worked as a nurse at the Packard Bell electronics plant. She had a boyfriend named Hank, a fat lowlife missing one thumb. Once a week she'd take me to a drive-in double feature. She'd sip from a flask and let me gorge myself on hot dogs.

I coveted the weekends with my father. No church, sleepover studs, or liquored-up mood swings. The man embraced the lazy life, half by design, half by the default of the weak.

Early in 1958, my mother began assembling a big lie. This is not a revisionist memory—I recall detecting mendacity in the moment. She said we needed a change of scenery. She said I needed to live in a house, not an apartment. She said she knew about a place in El Monte, a San Gabriel Valley town twelve miles east of L.A. proper.

We drove out there. El Monte was a downscale suburb populated by white shitkickers and pachucos with duck's-ass haircuts.

Most streets were unpaved. Most people parked on their lawns. Our prospective house: a redwood job surrounded by half-dead banana trees.

I said I didn't like El Monte. My mother told me to give it time. We hauled our belongings out early in February.

I traded up academically: Children's Paradise to Anne Le Gore Elementary School. The move baffled and infuriated my father. Why would a (tenuously) middle-class white woman with a good job thirty-odd miles away relocate to a town like El Monte? The rush-hour commute: at least ninety minutes each way. "I want my son to live in a house": pure nonsense. My father thought my mother was running. From a man or to a man. He said he was going to hire detectives to find out.

I settled into El Monte. My mother upgraded the custody agreement: I could see my father all four weekends a month. He picked me up every Friday night. It took a cab ride and three bus transfers to get us to his pad, just south of Hollywood.

I tried to enjoy El Monte. I smoked a reefer with a Mexican kid and ate myself sick on ice cream. My stint at Children's Paradise left me deficient in arithmetic. My teacher called my mother up to comment. They hit it off and went out on several dates.

I turned 10. My mother told me I could choose who I wanted to live with. I told her I wanted to live with my father.

She slapped me. I called her a drunk and a whore. She slapped me again and raged against my father's hold on me.

I became a sounding board.

My father called my mother a lush and a tramp. My mother called my father a weakling and a parasite. She threatened to slap injunctions on him and push him out of my life.

School adjourned for summer vacation on Friday, June 20. My father whisked me off for a visit.

That weekend is etched in hyper-focus. I remember seeing *The Vikings* at the Fox-Wilshire Theatre. I remember a spaghetti dinner at

Yaconelli's Restaurant. I remember a TV fight card. I remember the bus ride back to El Monte as long and hot.

My father put me in a cab at the depot and waited for a bus back to L.A. The cab dropped me at my house.

I saw three black-and-white police cars. I saw my neighbor Mrs. Kryzcki on the sidewalk. I saw four plainclothes cops—and instinctively recognized them as such.

Mrs. Kryzcki said, "That's the boy."

A cop took me aside. "Son, your mother's been killed."

I didn't cry. A press photographer hustled me to Mr. Kryzcki's toolshed and posed me with an awl in my hand.

My wife found a copy of that photograph last year. It's been published several times, in conjunction with my work. The second picture the man took has previously never seen print.

I'm at the workbench, sawing at a piece of wood. I'm grimacing ear to ear, showing off for the cops and reporters.

They most likely chalked my clowning up to shock. They couldn't know that that shock was instantly compromised.

The police reconstructed the crime.

My mother went out drinking Saturday night. She was seen at the Desert Inn bar in El Monte with a dark-haired white man and a blonde woman. My mother and the man left the bar around 10 P.M.

A group of Little Leaguers discovered the body. My mother had been strangled at an unknown location and dumped into some bushes next to the athletic field at Arroyo High School, a mile and a half from the Desert Inn.

She clawed her assailant's face bloody. The killer had pulled off one of her stockings and tied it loosely around her neck post-mortem.

I went to live with my father. I forced some tears out that Sunday—and none since.

My flight landed early. L.A. looked surreal, and inimical to the myth town of my books.

I checked in at the hotel and called Sergeant Stoner. We made plans to meet the following day. He gave me directions to the Homicide Bureau; earthquake tremors had ravaged the old facility and necessitated a move.

Sergeant McComas wouldn't be there. He was recuperating from open-heart surgery, a classic police-work by-product.

I told Stoner I'd pop for lunch. He warned me that the file might kill my appetite.

I ate a big room-service dinner. Dusk hit—I looked out my window and imagined it was 1950-something.

I set my novel *Clandestine* in 1951. It's a chronologically altered, heavily fictionalized account of my mother's murder. The story details a young cop's obsession: linking the death of a woman he had a one-night stand with to the killing of a redheaded nurse in El Monte. The supporting cast includes a 9-year-old boy very much like I was at that age.

I gave the killer my father's superficial attributes and juxtaposed them against a psychopathic bent. I have never understood my motive for doing this.

I called the dead nurse Marcella De Vries. She hailed from my mother's hometown: Tunnel City, Wisconsin.

I did not research that book. Fear kept me from haunting archives and historical sites. I wanted to contain what I knew and felt about my mother. I wanted to acknowledge my blood debt and prove my imperviousness to her power by portraying her with coldhearted lucidity.

Several year later, I wrote *The Black Dahlia*. The title character was a murder victim as celebrated as Jean Ellroy was ignored. She died the year before my birth, and I understood the symbiotic cohesion the moment I first heard of her.

The Black Dahlia was a young woman named Elizabeth Short. She came west with fatuous hopes of becoming a movie star. She was undisciplined, immature, and promiscuous. She drank to excess and told whopping lies.

Someone picked her up and tortured her for two days. Her death was as hellishly protracted as my mother's was gasping and quick. The killer cut her in half and deposited her in a vacant lot twenty miles west of Arroyo High School.

The killing is still unsolved. The Black Dahlia case remains a media cause célèbre.

I read about it in 1959. It hit me with unmitigated force. The horror rendered my mother's death both more outré and more prosaic. I seized on Elizabeth Short and hoarded the details of her life. Every bit of minutiae was mortar with which to build walls to block out Geneva Hilliker Ellroy.

This stratagem ruled my unconscious. The suppression exacted a price: years of nightmares and fear of the dark. Writing the book was only mildly cathartic; transmogrifying Jean to Betty left one woman still unrecognized.

And exploited by a master self-promoter with a tight grip on pop-psych show-and-tell.

I wanted her to fight back. I wanted her to rule my nightmares in plain view.

The Homicide Bureau was temporarily housed in an East L.A. office complex. The squad room was spanking clean and cop-antithetical.

Sergeant Stoner met me. He was tall and thin, with big eyes and a walrus mustache. His suit was a notch more upscale than his colleagues'.

We had a cup of coffee. Stoner discussed his most celebrated assignment, the Cotton Club murder case.

The man impressed me. His perceptions were astute and devoid of commonly held police ideology. He listened, carefully phrased his responses, and drew information out of me with smiles and throwaway gestures. He *made me* want to tell him things.

I caught his intelligence full-on. He knew I caught it.

Talk flowed nicely. One cup of coffee became three. The file rested on Stoner's desk—a small accordion folder secured by rubber bands.

I knew I was stalling. I knew I was postponing my first look at the pictures.

Stoner read my mind. He said he'd pull the worst of the shots if I wanted him to.

I said no.

The file was a mishmash: envelopes, Teletype slips, handwritten notes and two copies of the Detective Division Blue Book, an accumulation of reports and verbatim interviews. My first impression: This was the chaos of Jean Ellroy's life.

I put the photograph envelope aside. Penal-code numbers and birth dates jumped off the Teletypes.

The DOBs ran from 1912 to 1919. The codes designated arrests for aggravated assault and rape.

My mother left the bar with a "fortyish" man. The Teletypes deciphered: requests for information on men with sex-crime priors.

I read some odd notes. Minutiae grabbed me.

The Desert Inn bar: 11721 East Valley Boulevard. My mother's '57 Buick: license KFE 778. Our old house: 756 Maple Avenue.

I read the names on the front of the Blue Book. The investigating officers: sergeants John Lawton and Ward Hallinen.

The squad room lapsed into slow motion. I heard Stoner telling people that Bill McComas had aced his surgery. I spotted two full-size sheets of stationery with memo slips attached.

Early in 1970, two women wrote Homicide and informed "To Whom It May Concern" that they believed their respective ex-husbands murdered Geneva Hilliker Ellroy. Woman Number One stated that her ex worked at Packard Bell and had had affairs with my mother and two other women there. The man "behaved in a suspicious fashion" in the weeks following the killing and hit her when she pressed him about his whereabouts on the night of June 21. Woman Number Two said that her ex-husband harbored a "long-standing grudge" against Jean Ellroy. My mother refused to process a workers' compensation claim that the man had proffered, and his resentment sent him "off the deep end."

Woman Number Two included a postscript: Her ex-husband

torched a furniture warehouse in 1968 to avenge a dinette-set repossession.

Both letters read vindictively sincere. Both were respectful of police authority. Memorandums indicated that the leads were checked out.

One detective interviewed both ex-husbands. He concluded that the allegations were groundless and that the women did not know each other and thus could not have colluded.

A relatively obscure homicide. Two disturbingly similar accusations —*unrelated* accusations—eleven and a half years after the crime.

I examined the Blue Book. The reports and interview transcripts lacked a continuous narrative line. I scanned a few pages and realized that my basic knowledge of the case was sufficient to make odd bits of data cohere.

The crime-scene report was logged in mid-book. The first El Monte cop to respond reported that "the victim was lying on her back at the side of the road. There was dry blood on her lips and nose. The lower part of the victim's body was covered with a woman's coat. The victim was wearing a multi-colored (blue and black) dress. A brassiere appeared to be around the victim's neck."

Further examination reveals:

The brassiere is really a stocking.

A necklace strand rests under the body.

Forty-seven individual pearls are scattered nearby.

The coroner arrives. He views the body and points out bruises on the neck. He thinks the woman was strangled with a window-sash cord or clothesline. Drag marks on the woman's hips indicate that she was killed elsewhere and brought to this location.

The investigation commenced. My memory filled in Blue Book continuity gaps.

No identification was found on the body. The El Monte Police Department called in the Los Angeles County Sheriff's Detective Bureau.

Radio bulletins went out. The dead woman's description was flashed Valley-wide.

Our neighbor Mrs. Kryzcki responded. She was brought to the county morgue and identified the body. She said Jean Ellroy was a fine lady, who did not drink or date men.

My mother's car was discovered parked behind the Desert Inn. Bar employees were detained at El Monte police headquarters.

They identified my mother from a snapshot that Mrs. Kryzcki provided. Yes, the woman came in last night. She arrived alone about eight o'clock and later joined a man and a woman. Said man and woman were not regular patrons. None of the staff had ever seen them before.

The man was a swarthy Caucasian or a Mexican. He was about 40 years old, thin, between five feet nine and six feet tall. The woman was white, blonde, and in her late twenties. She wore her hair tied back in a ponytail.

No one heard them exchange names. A waitress recalled that a regular named Michael Whitaker had several drinks with the dead woman and two unknowns.

A waitress supplied more names: every *known* patron in the bar Saturday night. Sergeants Hallinen and Lawton checked the El Monte PD arrest docket and learned that Michael Whitaker was picked up for plain drunk at 4 A.M.

The man, 24, was spotted on foot near Stan's Drive-In. He sobered up in the El Monte drunk tank and was released at 9 A.M.

The known patrons were brought in and questioned. Several remembered seeing my mother with the Swarthy Man and the Blonde. None of them had ever seen my mother before. None of them had ever seen the Swarthy Man or the Blonde.

Michael Whitaker was brought in. Hallinen and Lawton questioned him. A police stenographer recorded the interrogation.

Whitaker's memory was booze-addled. He couldn't recall the name of the woman he was currently shacked up with. He said he danced with my mother and hit her up for a Sunday-night date. She declined, because her son was coming back from a weekend with his father.

Whitaker said the Swarthy Man told him his name. He couldn't remember it.

He said my 43-year-old mother looked "about 22." He said he got "pretty high" and fell off his chair once.

He said he saw the Swarthy Man and my mother leave together at about 10 P.M.

The Swarthy Man told Whitaker his name. This supported my long-held instinct that the murder was not premeditated.

A waitress confirmed Whitaker's account. Yes, Michael fell off his chair. Yes, the redhead left with the Swarthy Man.

Hallinen and Lawton retained a sketch artist. Desert Inn patrons and employees described the Swarthy Man. The artist drew up a likeness.

The drawing was circulated to newspapers and every police agency in Los Angeles County. The Desert Inn crew examined thousands of mug shots and failed to identify the Swarthy Man.

Officers canvassed the area around Arroyo High School. No one had noticed suspicious activity late Saturday night or Sunday morning. Hallinen and Lawton interrogated a score of local cranks, perverts, and career misogynists.

No leads accumulated. No hard suspects emerged.

On Wednesday, June 25, a witness came forth—a Stan's Drive-In carhop named Lavonne Chambers. Hallinen and Lawton interviewed her. Her testimony—recorded verbatim—was precise, articulate, and perceptive. Everything she said was new to me. Her statement radically altered my take on the crime.

She served the Swarthy Man and my mother—*on two different occasions*—late Saturday night and early Sunday morning. She described my mother's dress and mock-pearl ring. She described the Swarthy Man's car: a '55 or '56 dark-green Olds. She said the sketch was accurate and ID'd the man as white, not Latin.

They arrived at 10:20, shortly after their Desert Inn departure. They "talked vivaciously" and "seemed to have been drinking." The man had coffee. My mother had a grilled cheese sandwich. They ate in the car and left a half hour later.

Miss Chambers worked late that night. My mother and the Swarthy Man returned at 2 A.M.

He ordered coffee. He seemed "quiet and sullen." My mother was "quite high and chatting gaily." The man "acted bored with her."

Miss Chambers said my mother looked "slightly disheveled." The top of her dress was unbuttoned, and one breast was spilling out.

Sergeant Hallinen: "Do you think they might have had a petting party?"

Miss Chambers: "Maybe."

They left at 2:45. Jean Ellroy's body was discovered eight hours later.

I turned to the autopsy report. The coroner noted signs of recent intercourse. My mother's lungs were severely congested, presumably from years of heavy smoking.

She died of ligature asphyxiation. She sustained several blows to the head. Her fingernails were caked with blood, skin, and beard fragments.

She fought back.

I opened the photo envelope. The first stack of pictures: detained and exonerated suspects.

Cruel-looking men. Rough trade. White trash with a vengeance. Hard eyes, tattoos, psychopathic rectitude.

I recognized Harvey Glatman, a sex killer executed in 1959. A note said he passed a polygraph test.

The second stack: miscellaneous photos and wide-angles of the crime scene.

My father, circa 1946. A notation on the back: "Vict's ex-husband." A faded snapshot: my mother in her teens. The man beside her? Probably my German-immigrant grandfather.

Arroyo High School, 6/22/58. Santa Anita Road and King's Road— a football field with jerry-built goalposts. Those right-hand-corner X marks: the curbside bushes where they found her. The topography lacked perspective. Every detail hit my eyes as too small, and unequal to the central myth of my life.

I looked at the pictures of my dead mother. I saw the stocking around her neck and the insect bites on her breasts.

Lividity had thickened her features. She did not look like anyone I had ever known.

I knew it wasn't over. I knew my hours with the file constituted an ambiguous new start.

I left the squad room and drove to El Monte. The years then to now had been cruel.

I clenched up. It felt like something had to hit me at any second. I kept expecting a migraine or a bad case of the shakes.

New prefab houses had aged and split at the joints. Smog obscured the San Gabriel peaks.

The Desert Inn was gone. A taco hut replaced it. The El Monte PD building had been razed and rebuilt.

Anne Le Gore School remained intact. Gang graffiti on the walls provided an update.

Stan's Drive-In was gone. My old house had been face-lifted past recognition.

Arroyo High School needed a paint job. The playing field needed a trim. Weeds grew thick all around the X-marked spot.

The town had compressed. Its old secrets had subsided into the memories of strangers.

Stoner told me Sergeant Lawton was dead. Sergeant Ward Hallinen: 82 years old and living outside San Diego.

I called him and explained who I was. He apologized for his failing memory and said he couldn't recall the case. I thanked him for his efforts thirty-six years ago. I remembered a cop who gave me a candy bar, and wondered if it was him.

It wasn't over. The resolution felt incomplete.

*

I canceled a dinner date and willed myself to sleep. I woke up at 3 A.M. —unclenched and sick with it.

Conscious thoughts wouldn't process. I went down to the hotel gym and slammed weights until it hurt.

Steam and a shower helped. I went back to my room and let it hammer me.

New facts contradicted old assumptions. I had always thought my mother was killed because she wouldn't have sex with a man. It was a child's coda to horror: A woman dies fending off violation.

My mother made love with her killer. A witness viewed postcoital moments.

They left the drive-in. He wanted to ditch this desperate woman he fucked and get on with his life. The combustion occurred because she wanted more.

More liquor. More distance from the Dutch Reformed Church. More self-abasing honky-tonk thrills.

More love 16,000 times removed in desiccation.

I inherited those urges from my mother. Gender bias favored me: Men can indiscriminately fuck women with far greater sanction than women can indiscriminately fuck men. I drank, used drugs, and whored with the bravado of the winked-at and condoned. Luck and a coward's circumspection kept me short of the abyss.

Her pain was greater than mine. It defines the gulf between us. Her death taught me to look inward and hold myself separate. That gift of knowledge saved my life.

It wasn't over. My investigation will continue.

I took a new gift away from El Monte. I feel proud that I carry her features.

Geneva Hilliker Ellroy: 1915–1958.

My debt grows. Your final terror is the flame I touch my hand to.

I will not diminish your power by saying I love you.

August 1994

ANN RULE

Hailed by her legion of readers as America's "Queen of True Crime," Ann Rule (b. 1935) was exposed to the world of law enforcement at an early age. Her grandfather and an uncle served as sheriffs, another uncle was a medical examiner, and a cousin was a district attorney. During summer visits to her grandparents in Stanton, Michigan, she got a close-up look at small-town police work and spent time around the county jail, helping her grandmother serve meals to inmates. After graduating from the University of Washington, where she studied creative writing and criminology, she worked for 18 months as a provisional police officer with the Seattle Police Department before failing her eye exam. She later began contributing pseudonymous articles to true detective magazines, writing as the masculine "Andy Stack," while taking classes in forensic science to increase her expertise. Her commercial break-through came about through an eerie circumstance: in the early 1970s Rule worked at a suicide hotline at the Seattle Crisis Center, where she manned a phone next to a clean-cut student volunteer named Ted Bundy. Her personal knowledge of the man who turned out to be one of the most infamous serial killers of the 20th century helped make her first true-crime book, *The Stranger Beside Me* (1980), into a particularly gripping narrative. Since then, she has produced a steady stream of non-fiction best sellers, some of them book-length studies, others collections of short case histories. Like the selection reprinted here, taken from her 2001 book *Empty Promises*, Rule's true crime accounts are characterized by taut, suspenseful narratives, sympathetic attention to the victims, and admiring portrayals of the dedicated and selfless agents of the law.

Young Love

Unrequited love can be as painful as an abscessed tooth. The pain is throbbing, searing, and anyone who has suffered from it remembers the wakeful nights when sleep would not come. But there is nothing more agonizing than the loss of first love. Those

of us who survive that initial heartbreak learn that love can—
and will—come again, but try to tell that to a teenager who has
lost that first, flawless love. Young people believe that there will
be no tomorrow, and all you will get is an incredulous look if
you try to tell them otherwise. When you are eighteen, you can
visualize only endless years of aching loss. Most of us do get over
it, and live to enjoy mature relationships. Some of us do not.

A lifetime relationship was never going to happen for eighteen-
year-old John Stickney and Leigh Hayden, but John refused to
accept reality. He stubbornly believed that he and Leigh be-
longed together forever; and he was determined to do whatever
he had to do to see that they would never part.

Mercer Island, Washington, is to Seattle what Grosse Pointe is to Detroit, what River Oaks is to Houston, and what Beverly Hills is to Los Angeles. Located near the south end of Lake Washington, Mercer Island is among the more expensive and desirable suburbs for those who can afford the good life. The lushly vegetated island was once almost inaccessible, but the construction of the first floating bridge across Lake Washington sixty years ago made Mercer Island ripe for a building boom. The first homes, naturally, were built along the waterfront and have their own docks to moor sleek cabin cruisers or high-masted sailboats. Many of the homes here have swimming pools and tennis courts. Even as construction moved farther inland, a sense of forest remains. Row houses have no place on Mercer Island. Homes here are built to accommodate the trees and native vegetation and are painted in earth tones. There are bicycle paths and jogging trails, and the residents, many of them doctors, lawyers, computer entrepreneurs, and CEOs, use the floating bridge to escape the city to this suburban paradise in only fifteen minutes.

Most Mercer Island kids grow up in affluent families. High school parking lots are filled with late-model cars belonging to students. There are the usual police problems caused by teenagers who are bored because they don't have to work after school, kids who sample drugs, kids who get drunk and drive too fast. But if one could choose a place to raise children, Mercer Island would be it. No ghettos. No high crime neighborhoods. Only parks and discreet shopping areas.

John Stickney grew up in a rural region on the southern end of Mercer Island. At eighteen, he was 6 feet 1, a handsome blond boy who excelled in athletics. The neighbors liked him; his friends liked him. He and his family were solid members of the Mercer Island Covenant Church, a Fundamentalist church that promoted the tenets outlined in the Old Testament and whose members eschewed alcohol and tobacco.

John seemed to be the kind of boyfriend that all parents would want for their daughter. But it was pretty Leigh Hayden he fell in love with. The attraction was mutual, and people smiled to see them together. They started going steady when they were fourteen years old; indeed, neither had ever known another love. Had it been another time, another place—perhaps back in the days of the pioneer settlers who homesteaded in Washington—they might have married when they were only sixteen and grown old together. But it wasn't 1850; it was 1979. John wanted to marry Leigh. He had no plans for college. In fact, he had dropped out of high school. But Leigh had plans and was nowhere near ready to get married. She was a good student and had been accepted at Washington State University in Pullman. "Wazzu," as Washington State was called, was 300 miles east of Mercer Island and a world away from John.

He couldn't bear the idea of Leigh going away. They had been attached at the hip for four years. Sure, they had broken up for short periods, but he'd always been able to persuade Leigh to come back. He couldn't really believe that she would actually pack up and move clear across the state from him. And he was afraid she would meet someone else or that she would change and they would no longer have anything in common.

John was a bright young man, but he suffered from learning disabilities. His schoolwork had never mirrored what he really knew, what his IQ really was. He was one of thousands of kids hampered by dyslexia and therefore unable to read well; words appeared backward or upside down or jumbled to him. As a result, there was no question of John's going to college with Leigh. The experience would have been frustrating for him. He thought about getting a job in Pullman so he could be close to her, but he sensed that might be even more painful. He would be on the fringe of her life, and he already had a good job at home, which he didn't want to risk leaving. His family cared deeply for John, as did his church congregation. They tried to help him, prayed for him, hoped that his life would straighten out, and that he would fulfill the promise he had shown.

John's job was with the Industrial Rock Products Company, a firm that specialized in rock blasting. Freeways were being widened, and it was necessary to literally blast away sections of mountain rock to accommodate them. There would be ongoing demand for skills in this area, so John's community felt that his future was off to a good start.

Blasting with explosives is precise and terribly dangerous work, but John proved adept at it, even when he was in his mid-teens. Many of the men he worked with in this hazardous occupation had known him since he was only twelve years old. They liked the kid who was always cheerful, who never seemed to lose his temper, no matter how difficult a task. By December 1979, Stickney had worked in the rock quarry for a few years, and his boss considered him "one of the old-timers."

But John Stickney's fascination with explosives continued after he left his eight hours on the job. A friend who attended school with John recalled, "He liked to blow things up. He was always blowing something up—a tree, or whatever. He'd blow things up just for the hell of it."

The fall of 1979 was bitterly lonely for John Stickney. Leigh was so far away, caught up in the excitement of college life, going to football games, participating in dorm activities. She had told him that she planned on dating other men. That was the most agonizing part for him to accept. John was handsome, and he had a job that paid well; plenty of Mercer Island girls would gladly have dated him. But he wasn't interested. He wanted only Leigh. Every night he was on the phone calling her, trying to persuade her to come back to him. His constant calls only made her pull away more. What he had feared most was coming true: Leigh was interested in another man.

John's calls continued. Finally, Leigh's roommate complained to the dorm adviser that she couldn't use the phone because John called so much. The phone rang constantly whether Leigh was in her dorm room or not. When John did catch her in, he dragged out the conversations as if he could bind her to him with a telephone cord.

Several times during the fall, John drove to the Washington State campus, deliberately arriving unexpectedly. Each time, he convinced himself that everything would be all right again. And sometimes Leigh seemed glad to see him. But there were also times when she tried to tell him that it was really over between them and that he had to stop coming to Pullman. It was a twelve-hour drive round-trip, which gave him time to obsess about what he had lost.

John was on an emotional yo-yo. Of course the more he tried to hold on to Leigh, the more she pulled away. She felt suffocated. One can only imagine his thoughts as he made the grueling trip—up over Snoqualmie Pass, where the blizzards piled up drifts of snow from November to May, and then across the endless rolling wheat fields of the Palouse country. There weren't many towns along the way to take John's mind off his mission.

As Christmas neared, John began to realize that Leigh really *was* leaving him. He had tried pleading and cajoling. Worse, he'd even tried physically forcing her into his car when he saw her walking on campus. Her reaction was to pull even further away from him. Any love she'd had for him was now gone. Leigh was only eighteen; she wanted to be free. At first, she thought John would give up peaceably. She was as deluded as every other woman who realizes too late that she has become the focal point of a man's obsessive love.

Leigh Hayden began to be frightened. She no longer wanted to see John at all. Leigh tried to focus on her new world. She told Janet McKay, a senior who served as a resident adviser in her dorm, that John had been bothering her. She wanted to make it official that he was not a welcome visitor. If he came around to surprise her, she didn't want to have to talk to him.

Lovesick boyfriends aren't that unusual in college dorms. Leigh's friends and counselors realized that John always seemed to be shadowing her, but they all assumed he'd give up sooner or later. Leigh and her roommate lived on the fifth floor of the Streit-Perham Dormitory in the middle of the Wazzu campus, near the Performing Arts Coliseum. The dormitory, which was built in 1962, consisted of two six-story towers connected by a common lounge and dining room. Approximately 550 students were housed in the towers, and 46 of them lived on the fifth floor of Perham Hall where Leigh Hayden lived. It was a coeducational dorm, a circumstance which would have horrified the parents of college students two decades earlier, and John Stickney hated the arrangement.

It was the week before Christmas 1979. Residents of the Streit-Perham towers were preparing to pack up and go home for the holidays. Washington State was on a semester system, so Christmas festivities were not marred by the tension of final exams. Those would come later, at the end of January. This was a time for fun and celebration, and many groups of students crossed the state line into Moscow, Idaho, less than fifteen miles away, where the legal drinking age was eighteen. The county and state cops kept a permanent watch on the roads between Pullman and Moscow, trying to keep accidents and DUI tickets among the student drivers to a minimum.

The towers of Streit-Perham were decorated for the holidays, and most of the residents had adorned their rooms with holly, fir boughs, and miniature Christmas trees. Winter snow was the rule rather than the exception in Pullman, and the frigid winds that swept across the hilltop campus did nothing to dampen the spirit of the season.

Leigh Hayden knew that she would have to talk with John when she got home; there was no way he would not try to see her when they were both on Mercer Island. They had shared wonderful Christmases together, but those were in the past, and she would have to let him know that. He had to follow the same rules at home that he did when he came to the campus. They were not going steady anymore. As far as she was concerned, they were no longer even dating.

For the time being, during this last week before the Christmas holidays began, Leigh decided not to worry about it. She didn't think John would attempt to make the drive over the snow-clogged mountain passes, especially when he knew she'd be home on December 22.

On Monday, December 17, John Stickney put in a full eight hours on his job, blasting rock out of a quarry with dynamite. His foreman and his co-workers didn't notice that he behaved any differently than he always did. He didn't seem upset or angry. He was just the same open-faced dependable kid they'd always known.

When John left the job that night, it was already dark. He shouted that he'd see his co-workers the next morning. But John didn't go home that night. He didn't call Leigh either. Instead, he got in his car and headed east. Up through Issaquah and North Bend, then up over the summit of Snoqualmie Pass. It was icy at the top, with snow drifting across the road as he neared the summit. Even the skiers had given up for the night, and the lighted slopes were deserted.

John Stickney had 300 miles to go. He had confided to a friend that he was going to talk to Leigh one more time and that this time it would be decided "one way or another."

His words were so cryptic and so unlike him that his friend was concerned. Just to be on the safe side, John's friend called the head resident adviser in the dorm where Leigh lived. "John Stickney is on his way over there again. He said he's going to see Leigh."

Later, there were rumors that the phone call included the warning that John had a gun. Except for the few times he had grabbed Leigh in frustration and pulled her into his car, he had never been a violent man. The warning that John Stickney was headed toward the Washington State campus was taken seriously, probably because the dorm adviser wanted to spare Leigh any embarrassment that John might cause her. Nobody was really worried that he would be violent. John's demeanor with the staff at Perham Hall had always been courteous and quiet. When he showed up there, he only asked to see Leigh; he had never caused a scene.

Leigh and her roommate were quietly moved to a room on the sixth floor of the dorm. If and when John actually showed up, he wouldn't be able to find her.

The night wore on. At 10:00 P.M., the outer doors to the dorm were locked. Leigh and her roommate tried to fall asleep in the temporary room on the sixth floor. If John was really headed for Pullman, which was still only a rumor, he would probably check into a motel and call Leigh's room from there.

John Stickney *was* on his way. A little before 11:30 his car reached the top of the hill approaching Pullman. He could see the campus lights across the valley, twinkling on the next hill. He knew Leigh was there, snug and warm inside one of the red-brick buildings. He was sure that this time she wouldn't be expecting him. She would really be surprised to see him this late on a weeknight. It was desperately important to him that this visit be a happy surprise.

The campus police had been alerted that John might show up at Perham Hall. Officers on the night shift patrol were asked to keep an eye out for him. Somehow—and no one knows how—John Stickney managed to get into the locked dormitory at 11:30 P.M. Without hesitating, he headed for Leigh's room on the fifth floor. He knocked. There was no answer. He knocked again and waited. He couldn't hear a radio or television or the girls' voices. He opened the unlocked door, and found the room unoccupied.

Where was she? She should have been there.

John turned swiftly and walked down to Adviser Janet McKay's room. She gasped when he opened her door. She wondered how he had managed to get into the Perham tower. Still, he was as polite and cordial as ever. He wore blue jeans and a parka, and he looked tired, but he didn't appear manic or dangerous.

"Where's Leigh?" he asked. "She's not in her room."

"I haven't seen her all evening," Janet answered. "You really shouldn't be here now. It's after lockup time."

For the first time, John showed irritation. He said he had no intention of leaving until he saw Leigh. Janet McKay managed to call the campus police, and they persuaded him to leave. He was not combative and he left quietly. The police kept an eye on him, but all he did was drive aimlessly around the campus during the early morning hours. He made no attempt to get back into Perham Hall.

It was Tuesday afternoon before John finally got Leigh on the phone. He said he needed to talk to her face-to-face, and he insisted that he would not go back to Mercer Island until she agreed to talk to him. That was all he was asking. It was finally arranged that the ex-sweethearts would meet on neutral ground—in Adviser McKay's room.

The meeting lasted only ten minutes. Exactly what Leigh told John was never made public, but it was clear that she was adamant this time. Finally and forever it was all over between them. There would be no more pleading, no more promises, nothing would change her mind.

John Stickney left. The romance seemed to be over, and everyone heaved a sigh of relief.

Less than fifteen minutes later, however, Head Adviser Mary Beth Johnson entered an elevator on the ground floor and was startled to find John Stickney inside. She recognized him and introduced herself. She told him that she was aware of his problem, and he replied that he had to see Leigh just one more time. There was an odd urgency about him that alarmed Mary Beth Johnson.

John Stickney had taken nothing to the meeting in Janet McKay's office, but Ms. Johnson didn't know that. Now she noted that he had a book bag over his arm and that it appeared to be quite heavy.

"I understand that you want to see Leigh," she said carefully, "but I'd like to talk with her for a few minutes first. Would you agree to that?"

Stickney nodded. But when the elevator arrived on the fifth floor he got off right behind her and she could hear his footsteps keeping pace with hers down the long hallway. Thinking fast, she reached Leigh's room, stepped inside, and quickly locked the door behind her. Now Leigh Hayden, her roommate, Janet McKay, and Mary Beth Johnson were inside a small dorm room with nothing but a thin door between them and John Stickney.

Before Ms. Johnson had a chance to say anything, there was a crashing, splintering sound at the door. John was trying to kick it in. Again and again, he slammed his boot into the door. It shuddered and held. The women huddled together, frightened. There was nowhere to hide, and they were five floors up, so they couldn't escape out the window. John's voice was very calm, but he gave orders in a forceful way. "Open the door," he said stubbornly. "I want you to open the door." While they huddled against the opposite wall, he kicked it again, and bric-a-brac fell off a shelf and shattered.

Mary Beth Johnson grabbed the phone and alerted the campus police that John Stickney was back, that there was trouble, and that they needed help.

Suddenly the crashing against the door stopped. There was dead silence for a moment or so. And then John began speaking again in a flat voice with no emotion. Leigh had never heard him speak in this matter-of-fact way and it was far more frightening than when he raised his voice.

"I have a bomb," he said in that same awful voice. "Someone's going to get hurt if you don't let me in."

He wasn't shouting; he didn't even sound angry, but Leigh knew that he meant what he said. She knew that he was an expert in explosive devices. He could have walked away from his job with everything he needed to make a bomb. He worked with dynamite, and he knew how to set a charge and detonate a device with enough power to blow away half of a rocky hill. It had been his craft for several years, and he was good at it. She knew he was capable of blowing the whole dorm to kingdom come. "He probably does have a bomb," she said. "He means it. He knows how to make one."

The women looked at one another and silently agreed to make a run for it. They had nothing to lose, and if they didn't try, they might all die—and so would the other residents in rooms along the fifth-floor hall. Mary Beth Johnson flung open the door, and the four women took John Stickney by surprise as they tumbled out of the room and ran screaming down the hall. "Run! Run!" they cried out to the other three dozen residents on the floor. "He has a bomb!"

It was chaos as frightened coeds raced down the hall, most of them so intent on getting away that they didn't even see the tall blond man in the parka. The fifth floor was soon deserted. The only person left was John Stickney. He hadn't tried to stop the fleeing women. He had watched them run, his face as calm as if everything was completely normal. He hadn't tried to follow them. Oddly, he didn't even reach out for his beloved Leigh one last time.

Anyone who thinks a campus cop has an easy job might consider the task facing the Washington State campus officers who raced to the fifth floor of Perham Hall, as the coeds fled. Lieutenant Mike Kenny, age thirty-five, and Officer David Trimble, twenty-six, reached the floor first, followed by Officer Roger Irwin.

They stopped when they saw John Stickney, standing almost motionless in the hallway. He had a bomb all right; he must have carried it in the innocuous-looking book bag. Now they could see that it was a metallic cylinder three or four inches in diameter and a foot long— just the right size to hold sticks of dynamite. He held two wires that led to a battery. If it was like most simple bombs, that battery would detonate blasting caps and dynamite. Kenny and Trimble held their hands in the air as John ordered; they were desperately fighting for time, and they didn't want to irritate the tall blond youth. They knew that other officers were frantically trying to clear the dormitory of the hundreds of students who occupied all the other floors. The crisis could have been worse; it was two in the afternoon by now and many of the residents were in class. But this was bad enough.

All working police officers take a class in dealing with bombs, and all of them fervently hope they will never come in contact with one. Compared to seeing a bomb in the hands of a deranged subject, facing a .357 Magnum is a picnic.

The two officers moved toward Stickney, talking quietly, fighting to keep the tremor from their voices. "Come on, John . . . we can talk,"

Mike Kenny said. "This isn't the answer. Think about what you're doing. Let's put the bomb down. Let's talk about it. Things aren't as bad as you think."

Stickney shook his head.

"Put it down, John. Put it down. You don't really want to hurt anyone. You're mixed up." Moving so slowly that the inches they covered were almost imperceptible, the two officers advanced down the hall toward John, their hands still high over their heads. From the end of the hall, Officer Roger Irwin watched, barely breathing.

"We'll help you work it out," Officer Trimble said. "You can talk to Leigh. She'll understand. What are you? Eighteen? Nineteen? Hell, there's a whole life ahead of you. Put [the bomb] down, and we'll see that you get some help. You don't want to hurt anybody. We don't want you to get hurt." Trimble was close enough to touch Stickney now. The bomb was within arm's reach. It looked deadly. It looked as if it could level the whole dorm. Trimble no longer thought about himself; he prayed that all the students had made it safely outside. "Come on, John. Give it to me . . . gently," Trimble said in as calm a voice as he could manage. "Just hand it over, and you won't be sorry. I promise you, you won't be sorry."

Trimble and Kenny felt as if they were moving through quicksand. The whole scene had a psychedelic quality. They were caught in a slow-motion horror film, red and green and silver Christmas decorations sliding past them in their peripheral vision.

One step.

Two steps.

Trimble reached out. And suddenly he had the bomb in his two hands. He concentrated on standing upright and maintaining minimum movement. But then suddenly John Stickney fought back. He and Trimble fell to the floor, wrestling, the bomb between them. A few steps down the hall, Roger Irwin held his breath. Surely it was going to blow now and take all of them with it.

But no. Stickney and Trimble were back on their feet, but now John Stickney was holding the bomb again. Suddenly, he turned away from the two officers and moved down the hallway, the bomb held tight against his stomach. David Trimble and Mike Kenny could see only his back.

And then there was a roar the likes of which Irwin had never heard in his life. Smoke and dust obscured his vision when he peered down the hall. He had a sense that the whole tower was coming apart at the seams. For the moment there was a floor beneath him, but surely it was going to crumble. Plaster and glass showered the whole area. Every window on the fifth floor was blown outward by the force of the blast. Four or five of the rooms closest to where John Stickney had stood forty-five seconds ago were simply gone.

Down below, shivering in the frigid winter afternoon, the evacuated students heard the explosion and saw the tower vibrate. They began to scream and sob.

Fighting his way through the debris, Roger Irwin fully expected to find his fellow officers dead. They could not have survived. They had been within ten feet of the blast. He braced himself for what he would find.

John Stickney was dead. No one would ever know if he blew himself up deliberately or by accident. He would no longer suffer the anguish of unrequited love.

At first glance, Irwin thought Mike Kenny and David Trimble were dead, too. They lay still, their uniforms ripped into strips and tatters, their skin blackened. Irwin shouted into his radio, asking for paramedics and an ambulance, although he had precious little hope that anyone could help his colleagues.

As Irwin drew closer, he saw Kenny stir and heard Trimble moan. Miraculously, they were alive. John Stickney's body had taken the full force of the blast, and that alone had saved them. Had he been facing toward them when the dynamite detonated, the cops would surely have died too.

David Trimble, only twenty-six, was in critical condition. He had sustained puncture wounds in his chest, abdomen, and hands, and he had first- and second-degree burns all over his body. Both of his eardrums were ruptured. Mike Kenny had been a little farther away from the center of the blast, but his eardrums had been ruptured, too.

An ambulance rushed Trimble to Sacred Heart Hospital in Spokane where he underwent hours of surgery. Doctors stated cautiously that he would live but that his hearing would be permanently damaged. Lieutenant Kenny was treated at Pullman Memorial Hospital where physicians held out hope that his hearing would be only minimally affected. They were police officers and keen hearing is essential to their profession.

The two officers had come very close to sacrificing their lives for the students of Perham Hall. It could have been so much worse. Only three students were injured, and their injuries were only minor cuts and shock.

Leigh Hayden's new boyfriend hadn't been too concerned when he received threats from John Stickney, but now police checked his car carefully to be sure there wasn't a bomb hidden there. They found nothing. Nor was there a bomb in John Stickney's car. He had carried only the one bomb with him. Perhaps he had hoped that Leigh would agree to go for a ride with him. If she said she still loved him, the bomb would have stayed in the book bag. If she truly said it was the end for them, then he could have set off the bomb and they would have died together.

But in the end, nothing had worked for John and he had died alone.

Campus cops are often derided by students who delight in calling them pigs, but the students of Washington State University realized that Mike Kenny, Roger Irwin, and David Trimble had risked their lives to save them.

To show their appreciation, the residents of Streit-Perham immediately established a fund to help the families of Lieutenant Kenny and Officer Trimble. They started the fund by donating the money they had allocated for their social functions for the school year, and then solicited funds from other students and Pullman townspeople. It would be a bleak Christmas for the injured policemen, but the students were determined to do what they could to help.

In the meantime, sororities, fraternities, and the citizens of Pullman rushed to help the forty-six students who had lost all their clothing, books, and possessions when the fifth floor was leveled. University insurance eventually reimbursed them for some of their losses. As for the dormitory itself, a policy was in place that covered explosions. It had a $10,000 deductible but that was a bargain, considering the awesome damage John Stickney's bomb had done.

Back on Mercer Island, John Stickney's boss and his fellow workers were "absolutely flabbergasted" when they learned of the tragedy. "We're almost speechless here," his boss said. "There was no indication he was having any kind of problems. There are people in our organization who have known him since he was twelve years old. He was a pretty popular guy and everybody seemed to like him. We never even knew he had a temper."

If John Stickney had been able to show a temper, if he had not kept his pain and frustration bottled up inside, his story might have had a happier ending. But no one knew he needed help.

Perhaps someone should have paid attention when John Stickney blew up things "for the hell of it." When his world crashed around him, he turned to the one method he had of showing anger.

In the wake of the Washington State bombing, the Bellevue Police Department reopened its investigation into a mysterious explosion that had occurred near the Mercer Island Slough two months before the fatal bombing in Pullman. In the predawn hours of a Sunday morning, someone had tried to blow up a section of the 1-90 freeway. One of the concrete piers under the freeway structure that runs over the slough was damaged by a blast of tremendous proportions. It may have been only a coincidence that this bridge pier—within a few miles of John Stickney's home—was bombed. Or it might have been a test run to see how much dynamite it might take to blast through concrete and iron rebars.

Ironically, when it was far too late for John Stickney, a UPI feature story appeared in newspapers all across America: "Love Affairs on Campus Can Produce Signs of Stress." The text of the article noted that the top stressors, in order of importance, were "ending the hometown relationship," "staying free," and "breaking up."

Empty Promises, 2000

DOMINICK DUNNE

Dominick Dunne (b. 1925) came to true-crime writing through the most devastating circumstance imaginable. After his glitzy life as a television and movie producer ended in divorce, bankruptcy, and the humiliation of a very public arrest for drug possession, he retreated to a one-room cabin in Oregon and, at the age of 50, reinvented himself as a novelist, drawing on his insider's knowledge of high-society scandal for his plots. The very year that his first novel was published, his 22-year-old daughter, Dominique, a television and movie actress, was strangled to death by her former boyfriend, John Sweeney, head chef at the trendy West Hollywood restaurant Ma Maison. Dunne's powerful account of Sweeney's trial—which resulted in his receiving a six-and-a-half-year sentence for manslaughter—was published in *Vanity Fair* and launched his career as a crime journalist, specializing in corruption and murder among (in his phrase) "the upper echelons." This close-up, behind-the-scenes look at the Menendez case, one of the most sensational American murders of the 1990s, was written just prior to the first trial of the two defendants, which ended with a hung jury. Tried for a second time, Erik and Lyle Menendez were each found guilty of two counts of first-degree murder with special circumstances, plus another count of conspiracy to commit murder. Spared the death penalty, they were sentenced to life without parole.

Nightmare on Elm Drive

On a recent New York–to–Los Angeles trip on MGM Grand Air, the most luxurious of all coast-to-coast flights, I was chilled to the bone marrow during a brief encounter with a fellow passenger, a boy of perhaps fourteen, or fifteen, or maybe even sixteen, who lounged restlessly in a sprawled-out fashion, arms and legs akimbo, avidly reading racing-car magazines, chewing gum, and beating time to the music on his Walkman. Although I rarely engage in conversations with strangers on airplanes, I always have a certain curiosity to know who everyone is on MGM Grand Air, which I imagine is a bit like the Orient Express in its heyday. The young traveler in the swivel chair was returning to California after a sojourn in Europe. There were signals of affluence in his chat; the Concorde was mentioned. His carry-on luggage was expensive, filled with audiotapes, playing cards, and more magazines. During the meal, we talked. A week before, two rich and privileged young men named Lyle and Erik Menendez had been arrested for the brutal slaying of their parents in the family's $5 million mansion on Elm Drive, a sedate tree-lined street that is considered one of the most prestigious addresses in Beverly Hills. The tale in all its gory grimness was the cover story that week in *People* magazine, many copies of which were being read on the plane.

"Do you live in Beverly Hills?" I asked.

"Yes."

"Where?"

He told me the name of his street, which was every bit as prestigious as Elm Drive. I once lived in Beverly Hills and knew the terrain well. His home was in the same general area as the house where Kitty and Jose Menendez had been gunned down several months earlier in a fusillade of fourteen twelve-gauge shotgun blasts—five to the head and body of the father, nine to the face and body of the mother—that left them virtually unrecognizable as human beings, according to eyewitness reports. The slaying was so violent that it was assumed at first to have been of Mafia origins—a hit, or Mob rubout, as it was called, even in the *Wall Street Journal.* The arrest of the two handsome, athletic Menendez sons after so many months of investigation had shocked an unshockable community.

"Did you ever know the Menendez brothers?" I asked the teenager.

"No," he replied. They had gone to different schools. They were older. Lyle was twenty-two, Erik nineteen. In that age group, a few years makes an enormous difference.

"A terrible thing," I said.

"Yeah," he replied, "but I heard the father was pretty rough on those kids."

With that, our conversation was concluded.

Patricide is not an altogether new crime in the second echelon of Southland society. Nor is matricide. On March 24, 1983, twenty-year-old Michael Miller, the son of President Reagan's personal lawyer, Roy Miller, raped and clubbed to death his mother, Marguerite. In a minimally publicized trial, from which the media was barred, Miller was found guilty of first-degree murder but was acquitted of the rape charge, presumably on the technicality that the rape had occurred after his mother was dead. The judge then ruled that young Miller, who had been diagnosed as schizophrenic, was legally innocent of murder by reason of insanity. "Hallelujah," muttered Michael Miller after the verdict. He was sent to Patton State Hospital, a mental institution in California.

On July 22, 1983, in a Sunset Boulevard mansion in Bel Air, twenty-year-old Ricky Kyle shot his father, millionaire Henry Harrison Kyle, the president of Four Star International, a television-and-movie-production firm, in the back after awakening him in the middle of the night to tell him there was a prowler in the house. Several witnesses testified that Ricky had confided in them about a longstanding desire to kill his father, who was alleged to have been physically and mentally abusive to his son. The prosecution argued that Ricky was consumed with hatred for his father and greed for his fortune, and that, fearing that he was about to be disinherited, he plotted the ruse of the prowler. With the extraordinary leniency of the Southern California courts for first-time murderers, young Kyle was sentenced to five years for the slaying. Expressing dismay with the verdict, Ricky's mother told reporters she had hoped her son would be spared a prison term. "I think he has suffered enough," she said. Ricky agreed. "I feel like I don't deserve to go to prison," he said.

And then there were the Woodman brothers, Stewart and Neil, accused of hiring two assassins to gun down their rich parents in Brentwood. Tried separately, Stewart was convicted of first-degree murder. To escape the death penalty, he incriminated his brother. Neil's trial is about to start.

Further elaboration is not necessary: the point has been made. One other case, however, on a lesser social stratum but of equal importance, under the circumstances, should be mentioned: the Salvatierra murder, which received international attention. In 1986, Oscar Salvatierra, the Los Angeles–based executive of a newspaper called *Philippine News*, was shot while he was asleep in bed, after having received a death threat that was at first believed to be tied to the newspaper's opposition to former Philippine president Ferdinand Marcos. Later, Arnel Salvatierra, his seventeen-year-old son, admitted sending the letter and killing his father. In court, Arnel Salvatierra's lawyer convinced the jury that Arnel was the victim of a lifetime of physical and psychological abuse by his father. The lawyer, Leslie Abramson, who is considered to be the most brilliant Los Angeles defense lawyer for death-row cases, compared Arnel Salvatierra to the tragic Lisa Steinberg of New York, whose father, Joel Steinberg, had been convicted of murdering her after relentlessly abusing her. "What happens if the Lisa Steinbergs don't die?" Abramson asked the jury. "What happens if they get older, and if the cumulative effect of all these years of abuse finally drives them over the edge, and Lisa Steinberg pulls out a gun and kills Joel Steinberg?" Arnel Salvatierra, who had been charged with first-degree murder, was convicted of voluntary manslaughter and placed on probation.

This story is relevant to the Menendez case in that the same Leslie Abramson is one-half the team defending the affluent Menendez brothers. Her client is Erik Menendez, the younger brother. Gerald Chaleff, with whom she frequently teams, is representing Lyle. On an earlier burglary case involving the brothers, Chaleff, who gained prominence in criminal law as the defender of the Hillside Strangler, represented Erik. It is rumored that Abramson and Chaleff are each being paid $700,000. Psychological abuse is a constant theme in articles written about the brothers, and will probably be the basis of the defense strategy when the case comes to trial. There are even whispers—shocker of shockers—of sexual abuse in the Menendez family.

*

Jose Enrique Menendez was an American success story. A Cuban émi-gré, he was sent to the United States by his parents in 1960 at age fif-teen to escape from Castro's Cuba. His father, a onetime soccer star, and his mother, a former champion swimmer, stayed behind until their last properties were seized by Castro. Young Jose, who excelled in swimming, basketball, and soccer, won a swimming scholarship to Southern Illinois University, but he gave it up when he married Mary Louise Andersen, known as Kitty, at the age of nineteen and moved to New York. He earned a degree in accounting at Queens College in Flushing, New York, while working part-time as a dishwasher at the swank '21' Club in Manhattan, where, later, successful and prosperous, he would often dine. Then began a career of astonishing ascendancy which took him through Hertz, where he was in charge of car and commercial leasing, to the record division of RCA, where he signed such high-earning acts as Menudo, the Eurythmics, and Duran Duran. By this time he and Kitty had had two sons and settled down to a graceful life on a million-dollar estate in Princeton, New Jersey. The boys attended the exclusive Princeton Day School and, urged on by their father, began developing into first-rate tennis and soccer players. Their mother attended every match and game they played. When Jose clashed with a senior executive at RCA in 1986, after having been passed over for the executive vice presidency of RCA Records, he up-rooted his family, much to the distress of Kitty, who loved her life and house in Princeton, and moved to Los Angeles. There he leapfrogged to I.V.E., International Video Entertainment, a video distributor which eventually became Live Entertainment, a division of the hugely suc-cessful Carolco Pictures, the company that produced the Rambo films of Sylvester Stallone as well as some of Arnold Schwarzenegger's ac-tion films. Jose Menendez's success at Live Entertainment was daz-zling. In 1986 the company lost $20 million; a year later, under Menen-dez, Live earned $8 million and in 1988 doubled that. "He was the perfect corporate executive," I was told by one of his lieutenants. "He had an incredible dedication to business. He was focused, specific about what he wanted from the business, very much in control. He believed that whatever had to be done should be done—with no heart, if necessary."

The family lived at first in Calabasas, an upper-middle-class suburb of Los Angeles, inland beyond Malibu, where they occupied one house while building a more spectacular one on thirteen acres with mountaintop views. Then unexpectedly, almost overnight, the family abandoned Calabasas and moved to Beverly Hills, where Jose bought the house on Elm Drive, a six-bedroom Mediterranean-style house with a red tile roof, a courtyard, a swimming pool, a tennis court, and a guesthouse. Built in 1927, rebuilt in 1974, the house had good credentials. It had previously been rented to Elton John. And Prince. And Hal Prince. And a Saudi prince, for $35,000 a month. Erik Menendez, the younger son, transferred from Calabasas High to Beverly Hills High, probably the most snobbish public school in America. Lyle was a student at Princeton University, fulfilling one of the many American dreams of his immigrant father.

They were the ideal family; everyone said so. "They were extraordinarily close-knit," an executive of Live Entertainment told me. "It was one big happy family," said John E. Mason, a friend and Live Entertainment director. They did things together. They almost always had dinner together, which, in a community where most parents go to parties or screenings every night and leave their children to their own devices, is a rare thing. They talked about world events, as well as about what was happening in Jose's business. On the day before the catastrophic event, a Saturday, they chartered a boat called *Motion Picture Marine* in Marina del Rey and spent the day together shark-fishing, just the four of them.

On the evening of the following day, August 20, 1989, the seemingly idyllic world that Jose Menendez had created was shattered. With their kids at the movies in Century City, Jose and Kitty settled in for a comfortable evening of television and videos in the television room at the rear of their house. Jose was in shorts and a sweatshirt; Kitty was in a sweatshirt, jogging pants, and sneakers. They had dishes of strawberries and ice cream on the table in front of the sofa where they were sitting. Later, after everything happened, a neighbor would report hearing sounds like firecrackers coming from the house at about ten o'clock, but he took no notice. It wasn't until a hysterical 911 call came in to the Beverly Hills police station around midnight that there was any indication that the sounds had not been made by firecrackers. The sons of the house, Lyle and Erik, having returned from the movies, where they said they saw *Batman* again after they couldn't get into *License to Kill* because of the lines, drove in the gate at 722 North Elm Drive, parked their car in the courtyard, entered the house by the front door, and found their parents dead, sprawled on the floor and couch in the television room. In shock at the grisly sight, Lyle telephoned for help. "They shot and killed my parents!" he shrieked into the instrument. "I don't know . . . I didn't hear anything . . . I just came home. Erik! Shut up! Get away from them!"

Another neighbor said on television that she had seen one of the Menendez boys curled up in a ball on the lawn in front of their house and screaming in grief. "I have heard of very few murders that were more savage," said Beverly Hills police chief Marvin Iannone. Dan Stewart, a retired police detective hired by the family to investigate the murders, gave the most graphic description of the sight in the television room. "I've seen a lot of homicides, but nothing quite that brutal. Blood, flesh, skulls. It would be hard to describe, especially Jose, as resembling a human that you would recognize. That's how bad it was." According to the autopsy report, one blast caused "explosive decapitation with evisceration of the brain" and "deformity of the face" to Jose Menendez. The first round of shots apparently struck Kitty in her chest, right arm, left hip, and left leg. Her murderers then reloaded and fired into her face, causing "multiple lacerations of the brain." Her face was an unrecognizable pulp.

The prevalent theory in the days following the murders was that it had been a Mob hit. Erik Menendez went so far as to point the finger at Noel Bloom, a distributor of pornographic films and a former associate of the Bonanno organized-crime family, as a possible suspect.

Erik told police and early reporters on the story that Bloom and his father had despised each other after a business deal turned sour. (When questioned, Bloom denied any involvement whatsoever.) Expressing fear that the Mob might be after them as well, the brothers moved from hotel to hotel in the aftermath of the murders. Marlene Mizzy, the front-desk supervisor at the Beverly Hills Hotel, said that Lyle arrived at the hotel without a reservation two days after the murders and asked for a two-bedroom suite. Not liking the suites that were available on such short notice, he went to another hotel.

Seven months later, after the boys were arrested, I visited the house on Elm Drive. It is deceptive in size, far larger than one would imagine from the outside. You enter a spacious hallway with a white marble floor and a skylight above. Ahead, to the right, is a stairway carpeted in pale green. Off the hallway on one side is an immense drawing room, forty feet in length. The lone piece of sheet music on the grand piano was "American Pie," by Don McLean. On the other side are a small paneled sitting room and a large dining room. At the far end of the hallway, in full view of the front door, is the television room, where Kitty and Jose spent their last evening together. On the back wall is a floor-to-ceiling bookcase, filled with books, many of them paperbacks, including all the American-history novels of Gore Vidal, Jose's favorite author. On the top shelf of the bookcase were sixty tennis trophies—all first place—that had been won over the years by Lyle and Erik.

Like a lot of houses of the movie nouveaux riches still in their social and business rise, the grand exterior is not matched by a grand interior. When the Menendez family bought the house, it was handsomely furnished, and they could have bought the furniture from the former owner for an extra $350,000, but they declined. With the exception of some reproduction Chippendale chairs in the dining room, the house is appallingly furnished with second-rate pieces; either the purchase price left nothing for interior decoration or there was just a lack of interest. In any case, your attention, once you are in the house, is not on the furniture. You are drawn, like a magnet, to the television room.

Trying to imagine what happened that night, I found it unlikely that the boys—if indeed it was the boys, and there is a very vocal contingent who believe it was not—would have come down the stairs with the guns, turned right, and entered the television room, facing their parents. Since Jose was hit point-blank in the back of the head, it seems far more likely that the killers entered the television room through the terrace doors behind the sofa on which Kitty and Jose were sitting, their backs to the doors, facing the television set. The killers would probably have unlocked the doors in advance. In every account of the murders, Kitty was said to have run toward the kitchen. This would suggest, assuming she was running away from her assailants, that they had entered from behind.

Every person who saw the death scene has described the blood, the guts, and the carnage in sick-making detail. The furniture I saw in that room was replacement furniture, rented after the murders from Antiquarian Traders in West Hollywood. The original blood-drenched furniture and Oriental carpet had been hauled away, never to be sat on or walked on again. It is not farfetched to imagine that splatterings of blood and guts found their way onto the clothes and shoes of the killers, which would have necessitated a change of clothing and possibly a shower. There is no way the killers could have gone up the stairs, however; the blood on their shoes would have left tracks on the pale green stair carpet. The lavatory beneath the stairs and adjacent to the television room does not have a shower. What probably happened is that the killers retreated out the same terrace doors they had entered, and went back to the guesthouse to shower and change into clothes they had left there. The guesthouse is a separate, two-story unit beyond the swimming pool and adjacent to the tennis court, with a sitting room, a bedroom, a full bath, and a two-car garage opening onto an alley.

There is also the possibility that the killers, knowing the carnage twelve-gauge-shotgun blasts would cause, wore boots, gloves, and overalls. In that event, they would have only had to discard the clothes and boots into a large garbage bag and make a dash for it. One of the most interesting aspects of the case is that the fourteen shell casings were picked up and removed. I have been told that such fastidiousness is out of character in a Mafia hit, where a speedy getaway is essential. There is a sense of leisurely time here, of people not in a hurry, not expecting anyone, when they delay their departure from a massacre to pick the shell casings out of the bloody remains of their victims' bodies. They almost certainly wore rubber gloves to do it.

Then they had to get rid of the guns. The guns, as of this writing, have still not been found. We will come back to the guns. The car the killers left in was probably parked in the guesthouse garage; from there they could make their exit unobserved down the alley behind the house. Had they left out the front gate on Elm Drive, they would have risked being observed by neighbors or passersby. Between the time the killers left the house and the time the boys made the call to the police, the bloody clothes were probably disposed of.

On the day before the fishing trip on the *Motion Picture Marine*, Erik Menendez allegedly drove south to San Diego and purchased two Mossberg twelve-gauge shotguns in a Big 5 sporting-goods store, using for identification the stolen driver's license of a young man named Donovan Goodreau. Under federal law, to purchase a weapon, an individual must fill out a 4473 form, which requires the buyer to provide his name, address, and signature, as well as an identification card with picture. Donovan Goodreau had subsequently said on television that he can prove he was in New York at the time of the gun purchase in San Diego. Goodreau had once roomed with Jamie Pisarcik, who was, and still is, Lyle Menendez's girlfriend and stalwart supporter, visiting him daily in jail and attending his every court session. When Goodreau stopped rooming with Jamie, he moved into Lyle's room at Princeton, which was against the rules, since he was not a student at the university. But then, Lyle had once kept a puppy in his room at Princeton, and having animals in the rooms was against the rules too.

What has emerged most significantly in the year since the murders is that all was not what it seemed in the seemingly perfect Menendez household. There are people who will tell you that Jose was well liked. There are more people by far who will tell you that he was greatly disliked. Even despised. He had made enemies all along the way in his rise to the high middle of the entertainment industry, but everyone agrees that had he lived he would have gone right to the top. He did not have many personal friends, and he and Kitty were not involved in the party circuit of Beverly Hills. His life was family and business. I was told that at the memorial service in Los Angeles, which preceded the funeral in Princeton, most of the two hundred people who attended had a business rather than a personal relationship with him. Stung by the allegations that Jose had Mob connections in his business dealings at Live Entertainment, allegations that surfaced immediately after the murders, the company hired Warren Cowan, the famed public-relations man, to arrange the memorial service. His idea was to present Menendez as Jose the family man. He suggested starting a Jose Menendez scholarship fund, a suggestion that never came to fruition. It was also his idea to hold the memorial service in an auditorium at the Directors Guild in Hollywood, in order to show that Jose was a member of the entertainment community, although it is doubtful that Jose had ever been there. Two people from Live Entertainment gave flowing eulogies. Brian Andersen, Kitty's brother, spoke lovingly about Kitty, and each son spoke reverently about his parents. One person leaving the service was heard to say, "The only word not used to describe Jose was 'prick.'"

Although Jose spoke with a very slight accent, a business cohort described him to me as "very non-Hispanic." He was once offended when he received a letter of congratulations for having achieved such a high place in the business world "for a Hispanic." "He hated anyone who knew anything about his heritage," the colleague said. On the other hand, there was a part of Jose Menendez that secretly wanted to run for the U.S. Senate from Florida in order to free Cuba from the tyranny of Fidel Castro and make it a U.S. territory.

Kitty Menendez was another matter. You never hear a bad word about Kitty. Back in Princeton, people remember her on the tennis courts with affection. Those who knew her in the later years of her life felt affection too, but they also felt sorry for her. She was a deeply unhappy woman, and was becoming a pathetic one. Her husband was flagrantly unfaithful to her, and she was devastated by his infidelity. There has been much talk since the killings of Jose's having had a mistress, but that mistress was by no means his first, although he was said to have had "fidelity in his infidelity" in that particular relationship. Kitty fought hard to hold her marriage together, but it is unlikely that Jose would ever have divorced her. An employee of Live Entertainment said, "Kitty called Jose at his office every thirty minutes, sometimes just to tell him what kind of pizza to bring home for supper. She was a dependent person. She wanted to go on his business trips with him. She had June Allyson looks. Very warm. She also had a history of drinking and pills." Another business associate of Jose's at Live said, "I knew Kitty at company dinners and cocktail parties. They used to say about Kitty that she was Jose with a wig. She was always very much at his side, part of his vision, dedicated to the cause, whatever the cause was."

A more intimate picture of Kitty comes from Karen Lamm, one of the most highly publicized secondary characters in the Menendez saga. A beautiful former actress and model who was once wed to the late Dennis Wilson of the Beach Boys, Lamm is now a television producer, and she and her partner, Zev Braun, are developing a miniseries based on the Menendez case. Lamm is often presented as Kitty's closest friend and confidante. However, friends of Erik and Lyle decry her claims of friendship with Kitty, asserting that the boys did not know her, and asking how she could have been such a great friend of Kitty's if she was totally unknown to the sons.

Most newspaper accounts say that Karen Lamm and Kitty Menendez met in an aerobics class, but Lamm, who says she dislikes exercise classes, gave a different account of the beginning of their friendship. About a year before the murders, she was living with a film executive named Stuart Benjamin, who was a business acquaintance of Jose Menendez. Benjamin was a partner of the film director Taylor Hackford in a production company called New Visions Pictures, which Menendez was interested in acquiring as a subsidiary for Live Entertainment. During the negotiation period, Benjamin, with Lamm as his date, attended a dinner party at the Menendez house on Elm Drive. Lamm, who is an effusive and witty conversationalist, and Kitty spent much of the evening talking together. It was the beginning of a friendship that would blossom. Lamm described Kitty to me as being deeply unhappy over her husband's philandering. She claims that Kitty had tried suicide on three occasions, the kind of at-home suicide attempts that are more cries for help than a longing for death. Kitty had once won a beauty contest and could still be pretty on occasion, but she had let her looks go, grown fat (her autopsy report described her as "fairly well-nourished" and gave her weight as 165), and dyed her hair an unbecoming blond color that did not suit her. Lamm suggested that she get back into shape, and took her to aerobics classes, as well as offering her advice on a darker hair color. During the year that followed, the two women became intimate friends, and Kitty confided in Lamm, not only about Jose's infidelity but also about the many problems they were having with their sons.

Lamm said she met the boys three times, but never talked to them in the house on Elm Drive. She told me, "Those kids watched their mother become a doormat for their father. Jose lived through Lyle. Jose made Lyle white bread. He sent him to Princeton. He gave him all the things that were not available to him as an immigrant." Lamm finally talked with Kitty's sons at the memorial service at the Directors Guild. She was introduced to Lyle, who, in turn, introduced her to Erik as "Mom's friend." She said that Lyle had become Jose overnight. He radiated confidence and showed no emotion, "unless it was a convenient moment." Erik, on the other hand, fell apart.

Over the previous two years, the handsome, athletic, and gifted Menendez sons had been getting into trouble. Although a great friend of the boys dismissed their scrapes as merely "rich kids' sick jokes," two events occurred in Calabasas, where the family lived before the move to Beverly Hills, that were to have momentous consequences for all the members of the family. The brothers got involved in two very serious criminal offenses, a burglary at the home of Michael Warren Ginsberg in Calabasas and grand theft at the home of John Richard List in Hidden Hills. In total, more than $100,000 in money and jewels was taken from the two houses—not an insignificant sum.

Jose dealt with his sons' transgressions the way he would deal with any prickly business problem, said a business associate, by "minimizing the damage and going forward, fixing something that was broken without actually dealing with the problem." He simply took over and solved it. The money and jewels were returned, and $11,000 in damages was paid. Since Erik was underage, it was decided that he would take the fall for both brothers, thereby safeguarding Jose's dream of having Lyle study at Princeton. Jose hired the criminal lawyer Gerald Chaleff to represent Erik—the same Gerald Chaleff who is now representing Lyle on the charge of murdering the man who once hired him to represent Erik on the burglary charge. Everything was solved to perfection. Erik got probation, no more. And compulsory counseling. And for that, Kitty asked her psychologist, Les Summerfield, to recommend someone her son could go to for the required number of hours ordered by the judge. Les Summerfield recommended a Beverly Hills psychologist named Jerome Oziel, who, like Gerald Chaleff, continues his role in the Menendez saga right up to the present.

Prior to the thefts, Erik had made a friend at Calabasas High School who would also play a continuing part in the story. Craig Cignarelli, the son of a prominent executive in the television industry, is a Tom Cruise look-alike currently studying at the University of California in Santa Barbara. Craig was the captain of the Calabasas High School tennis team, and Erik, who had recently transferred from Princeton Day, was the number-one singles player on the team. One day, while playing a match together, they were taunted by two students from El Camino High School, a rival school in a less affluent neighborhood. Menendez and Cignarelli went out to the street to face their adversaries, and a fight started. Suddenly, a whole group of El Camino boys jumped out of cars and joined the fray. Erik and Craig were both badly beaten up. Erik's jaw was broken, and Craig received severe damage to his ribs. The incident sparked a close friendship between the two, which would culminate in the cowriting of a movie script called *Friends*, in which a young man named Hamilton Cromwell murders his extremely rich parents for his inheritance. One of the most quoted passages from this screenplay comes from the mouth of Hamilton Cromwell, speaking about his father: "Sometimes he would tell me that I was not worthy to be his son. When he did that, it would make me strive harder . . . just so I could hear the words 'I love you, son.' . . . And I never heard those words." To add to the awful irony, Kitty, the loving mother who could not do enough for her sons, typed the screenplay in which her own demise seems to have been predicted. In the embarrassing aftermath of the burglaries, the family moved to the house on Elm Drive in Beverly Hills. Jose told people at Live Entertainment that he was upset by the drug activity in Calabasas and that the tires of his car had been slashed, but it is quite possible that these stories were a diversionary tactic, or smoke screen, created to cover the disgrace of his son's criminal record.

A further setback for the family, also partly covered up, had occurred the previous winter, when Lyle was suspended from Princeton after one semester for cheating in Psychology 101. Taken before a disciplinary committee, he was told he could leave the university voluntarily or be expelled. He chose to leave. This was a grave blow to Jose, who loved to tell people that he had a son at Princeton. Again taking over, he tried to talk the authorities at Princeton into reinstating his son, but this time the pressure he applied did not work. The suspension lasted a year. In a typical reaction, Jose became more angry at the school than he was at his son. He urged Lyle to stay on in Princeton rather than return to Beverly Hills, so that he would not have to admit to anyone that Lyle had been kicked out.

But Lyle did return, and worked briefly at Live Entertainment, where he showed all the worst qualities of the spoiled rich boy holding down a grace-and-favor job in his father's company. He was consistently late for work. His attention span was brief. He worked short hours, leaving in the afternoon to play tennis. He was unpopular with the career-oriented staff. "The kids had a sense of being young royalty," said an employee of the company. "They could be nasty, arrogant, and self-centered." But, the same person said, Jose had a blind spot about his sons. And tennis held the family together. Once, Jose took the Concorde to Europe just to watch Lyle play in a tennis tournament, and then came right back. However, for all the seeming closeness of the family, the sons were proving to be disappointments, even failures, in the eyes of their perfection-demanding father. Jose had apparently come to the end of financing his recalcitrant sons' rebellion, and there are indications that he planned to revise his will.

After the Calabasas debacle, Erik transferred to Beverly Hills High School for his senior year. His classmates remember him chiefly as a loner, walking around in tennis shorts, always carrying his tennis racket.

"A girl I was going out with lusted after him," a student told me. "She said he had good legs."

"Was he spoiled?"

"Everyone at Beverly High is spoiled."

Like his father, Lyle is said to have been a great ladies' man, which pleased Jose, but several of Lyle's girlfriends, mostly older than he, were not considered to be suitable by his parents, and clashes occurred. When Jose forbade Lyle to go to Europe with an older girlfriend, Lyle went anyway. A person extremely close to the family told me that another of Lyle's girlfriends—not Jamie Pisarcik, who has been so loyal to him during his incarceration—was "manipulating him," which I took to mean manipulating him into marriage. This girl became pregnant. Jose, in his usual method of dealing with his sons' problems, moved in and paid off the girl to abort the child. The manner of Jose's interference in so personal a matter—not allowing Lyle to deal with his own problem—is said to have infuriated Lyle and caused a deep rift between father and son. Lyle moved out of the main house into the guesthouse at the back of the property. He was still living there at the time of the murders, although Erik continued to live in the main house.

Karen Lamm told me that in her final conversation with Kitty, three days before the killing and one day before the purchase of the guns in San Diego, Kitty told her that Lyle had been verbally abusive to her in a long, late-night call from the guesthouse to the main house.

From the beginning, the police were disinclined to buy the highly publicized Mafia-hit story, on the grounds that Mafia hits are rarely done in the home, that the victim is usually executed with a single shot to the back of the head, and that the wife is not usually killed also. The hit, if hit it was, looked more like a Colombian drug-lord hit, like the bloody massacre carried out by Al Pacino in the film *Scarface*, which, incidentally, was one of Lyle's favorite movies.

Months later, after the arrests, the Beverly Hills police claimed to have been suspicious of the Menendez brothers from the beginning, even from the first night. One detective at the scene asked the boys if they had the ticket stubs from the film they said they had just seen in Century City. "When both parents are hit, our feeling is usually that the kids did it," said a Beverly Hills police officer. Another officer declared, two days after the event, "These kids fried their parents. They cooked them." But there was no proof, nothing to go on, merely gut reactions.

Inadvertently, the boys brought suspicion upon themselves. In the aftermath of the terrible event, close observers noted the extraordinary calm the boys exhibited, almost as if the murders had happened to another family. They were seen renting furniture at Antiquarian Traders to replace the furniture that had been removed from the television room. And, as new heirs, they embarked on a spending spree that even the merriest widow, who had married for money, would have refrained from going on—for propriety's sake, if nothing else—in the first flush of her mourning period. They bought and bought and bought. Estimates of their spending have gone as high as $700,000. Lyle bought a $60,000 Porsche 911 Carrera to replace the Alfa Romeo his father had given him. Erik turned in his Ford Mustang 5.0 hardtop and bought a tan Jeep Wrangler, which his girlfriend, Noelle Terelsky, is now driving. Lyle bought $40,000 worth of clothes and a $15,000

Rolex watch. Erik hired a $50,000-a-year tennis coach. Lyle decided to go into the restaurant business, and paid a reported $550,000 for a cafeteria-style eatery in Princeton, which he renamed Mr. Buffalo's, flying back and forth coast to coast on MGM Grand Air. "It was one of my mother's delights that I pursue a small restaurant chain and serve healthy food with friendly service," he said in an interview with *The Daily Princetonian*, the campus newspaper. Erik, less successful as an entrepreneur than Lyle, put up $40,000 for a rock concert at the Palladium, but got ripped off by a conman partner and lost the entire amount. Erik decided not to attend U.C.L.A., which had been his father's plan for him, but to pursue a career in tennis instead. After moving from hotel to hotel to elude the Mafia, who they claimed were watching them, the brothers leased adjoining condos in the tony Marina City Club Towers. "They liked high-tech surrounds, and they wanted to get out of the house," one of their friends said to me. Then there was the ghoulish sense of humor another of their friends spoke about: Sitting with a gang of pals one night, deciding what videos to rent for the evening, Erik suggested *Dad* and *Parenthood*. Even as close a friend as Glenn Stevens, who was in the car with Lyle when he was arrested, later told the *Los Angeles Times* that two days after the murders, when he asked Lyle how he was holding up emotionally, his friend replied, "I've been waiting so long to be in this position that the transition came easy." The police were also aware that Lyle Menendez had hired a computer expert who eradicated from the hard disk of the family computer a revised will that Jose had been working on. Most remarkable of all was that, unlike the families of most homicide victims, the sons of Jose and Kitty Menendez did not have the obsessive interest in the police search for the killers of their parents that usually supersedes all else in the wake of such a tragedy.

As the C.E.O. of Live Entertainment, Jose Menendez earned a base pay of $500,000 a year, with a maximum bonus of $850,000 based on the company's yearly earnings. On top of that, there were life-insurance policies. An interesting sidebar to the story concerns two policies that were thought to have been taken out on Menendez by Live Entertainment. The bigger of the two was a $15 million keyman policy, $10 million of which was with Bankers Trust and $5 million with Crédit Lyonnais. Taking out a keyman life-insurance policy on a top executive is common practice in business, with the company being named as beneficiary. Live Entertainment was also required to maintain a second policy on Menendez in the amount of $5 million, with the beneficiary to be named by him. Given the family's much-talked-about closeness, it is not unlikely that Kitty and the boys were aware of this policy. Presumably, the beneficiary of the insurance policy would have been the same as the beneficiary of Jose's will. In the will, it was stated that if Kitty died first everything would go to Jose, and if Jose died first everything would go to Kitty. In the event that both died, everything would go to the boys.

The murders happened on a Sunday night. On the afternoon of the following Tuesday, Lyle and Erik, accompanied by two uncles, Kitty's brother Brian Andersen and Jose's brother-in-law Carlos Baralt, who was the executor of Jose's will, met with officials of Live Entertainment at the company's headquarters to go over Jose's financial situation. At that meeting, it became the difficult duty of Jose's successor to inform the heirs that the $5 million policy with beneficiaries named by Jose had not gone into effect, because Jose had failed to take the required physical examination, believing that the one he had taken for the $15 million policy applied to both policies. It did not. A person present at that meeting told me of the resounding silence that followed the reception of that information. To expect $5 million, payable upon death, and to find that it was not forthcoming, would be a crushing disappointment. Finally, Erik Menendez spoke. His voice was cold. "And the $15 million policy in favor of the company? Was that in order?" he asked. It was. Jose had apparently been told that he would have to take another physical for the second policy, but he had postponed it. As an officer of the company said to me, "That anything could ever happen to Jose never occurred to Jose."

The news that the policy was invalid caused bad blood between the family and the company, especially since the immediate payment of the $15 million keyman policy gave Carolco one of its biggest quarters since the inception of the company. One of Jose's former employees in New York, who was close enough to the family to warrant having a limousine sent to take him from a suburb of New York to the funeral in Princeton, said to me, "The grandmother? Did you talk to her? Did she tell you her theory? Did she tell you the company had Jose taken care of for the $15 million insurance policy?" The grandmother had not told me this, but it is a theory that the dwindling group of people who believe in the innocence of the Menendez boys cling to with passion. The same former employee continued, "Jose must have made a lot of money in California. I don't know where all that money came from that I've been hearing about and reading about."

Further bad feelings between the family and Live Entertainment have arisen over the house on Elm Drive, which, like the house in Calabasas, is heavily mortgaged: Approximately $2 million is still owed on the Elm Drive house, with estimated payments of $225,000 a year, plus $40,000 a year in taxes and approximately $40,000 in maintenance. In addition, the house in Calabasas has been on the market for some time and remains unsold; $1.5 million is still owed on it. So, in effect, the expenses on the two houses are approximately $500,000 a year, a staggering amount for the two sons to have dealt with before their arrest. During the meeting on the Tuesday after the murders, when the boys were told that the $5 million life insurance policy had not gone into effect, it was suggested that Live Entertainment might buy the house on Elm Drive from the estate, thereby removing the financial burden from the boys while the house was waiting to be resold. Furthermore, Live Entertainment was prepared to take less for the house than Jose had paid for it, knowing that houses where murders have taken place are hard sells, even in as inflated a real estate market as Beverly Hills.

Ads have run in the real estate section of the *Los Angeles Times* for the Elm Drive house. The asking price is $5.95 million. Surprisingly, a buyer did come along. The unidentified person offered only $4.5 million, a bargain for a house on that street, and the offer was hastily accepted. Later, however, the deal fell through. The purchaser was said to have been intimidated by the event that occurred there, and worried about the reaction neighborhood children would have to his own children for living in the house.

The arrangement for Live Entertainment to purchase the property from the estate failed to go into effect, once the police investigation pointed more and more toward the boys, and so the estate has had to assume the immense cost of maintaining the properties. Recently, the Elm Drive house has been leased to a member of the Saudi royal family—not the same prince who rented it before—for $50,000 a month to allay expenses.

Carolco, wishing to stifle rumors that Live Entertainment had Mob connections because of its acquisition of companies like Strawberries, an audio-video retailing chain, from Morris Levy, who allegedly has Genovese crime-family connections, and its bitter battle with Noel Bloom, hired the prestigious New York firm of Kaye, Scholer, Fierman, Hays & Handler to investigate the company for underworld ties. The 220-page report, which cynics in the industry mock as a whitewash, exonerated the company of any such involvement. The report was read at a board meeting on March 8, and the conclusion made clear that the Beverly Hills police, in their investigation of the Menendez murders, were increasingly focusing on their sons, not the Mob. An ironic bit of drama came at precisely that moment, when a vice president of the company burst in on the meeting with the news that Lyle Menendez had just been arrested.

Concurrently, in another, less fashionable area of the city known as Carthay Circle, an attractive thirty-seven-year-old woman named Judalon Rose Smyth, pronounced Smith, was living out her own drama in a complicated love affair. Judalon Smyth's lover was a Beverly Hills psychologist named Jerome Oziel, whom she called Jerry. Dr. Oziel was the same Dr. Oziel whom Kitty Menendez's psychologist, Les Summerfield, had recommended to her a year earlier as the doctor for her troubled son, after the judge in the burglary case in Calabasas had ruled that Erik must have counseling while he was on probation. During that brief period of court-ordered therapy, Jerome Oziel had met the entire Menendez family. Judalon Smyth, however, was as unknown to Lyle and Erik as they were to her, and yet, seven months from the time of the double murder, she would be responsible for their arrest on the charge of killing their parents.

On March 8, Lyle Menendez was flagged down by more than a dozen heavily armed Beverly Hills policemen as he was leaving the house on Elm Drive in his brother's Jeep Wrangler, accompanied by his former Princeton classmate Glenn Stevens. Lyle was made to lie on the street, in full view of his neighbors, while the police, with drawn guns, manacled his hands behind his back before taking him to the police station to book him for suspicion of murder. The arrest came as a complete surprise to Lyle, who had been playing chess, a game at which he excelled, until two the night before at the home of a friend in Beverly Hills.

Three days earlier, Judalon Smyth had contacted the police in Beverly Hills and told them of the existence of audiotapes in the Bedford Drive office of Dr. Oziel on which the Menendez brothers had allegedly confessed to the murders of their parents. She also told police that the brothers had threatened to kill Oziel if he reported them. Lastly, she told them that the two twelve-gauge shotguns had been purchased at a sporting-goods store in San Diego. All of this information was unknown to the Beverly Hills police, after seven months of investigation. They obtained a subpoena to search all of Oziel's locations. The tapes were found in a safe-deposit box in a bank on Ventura Boulevard.

Lyle's arrest was reported almost immediately on the local Los Angeles newscasts. Among those who heard the news was Noel Nedli, a tennis-team friend from Beverly Hills High who was Erik Menendez's roommate in a condominium that Erik was leasing for six months at the Marina City Club Towers, next to the condominium that his brother had leased with his girlfriend, Jamie Pisarcik. Erik was playing in a tennis tournament in Israel, where he had been for two weeks, accompanied by Mark Heffernan, his $50,000-a-year tennis coach. By a curious coincidence, Erik happened to telephone Nedli at almost the same moment Nedli was listening to the report of Lyle's arrest on the radio. It was merely a routine checking-up-on-everything call, and Nedli realized at once that Erik did not know about Lyle's arrest. He is reported to have said to Erik, "I hope you're sitting down." Then he said, "Lyle was just arrested."

"Erik became hysterical. He was crying, the whole nine yards," said a friend of Nedli's who had heard the story from him. This friend went on to say that the immediate problem for Erik was to get out of Israel before he was arrested there. Accompanied by Heffernan, who was not aware of the seriousness of the situation, the two got on a plane without incident, bound for London. There they split up. Heffernan returned to Los Angeles. Erik flew to Miami, where several members of the Menendez side of the family reside. An aunt advised him to return to Los Angeles and turn himself in. Erik notified police of his travel plans and gave himself up at Los Angeles International Airport, where he was taken into custody by four detectives. He was later booked at the Los Angeles County Men's Central Jail on suspicion of murder and held without bond.

According to Judalon Smyth, and the California Court of Appeals decision, she had stood outside the door of Dr. Oziel's office and, unbeknownst to the Menendez brothers, listened to their confession and threats. Dr. Oziel has denied this.

Approximately a year before any of the above happened, Judalon Smyth told me, she telephoned Jerome Oziel's clinic, the Phobia Institute of Beverly Hills, after having heard a series of tapes called *Through the Briar Patch*, which had impressed her. She was then thirty-six, had been married twice, and was desirous of having a relationship and a family, but she tended to choose the wrong kind of men, men who were controlling. The *Briar Patch* tapes told her she could break the pattern of picking the wrong kind of men in five minutes.

She says Oziel began telephoning her, and she found him very nice on the phone. She felt he seemed genuinely interested in her. After

Oziel's third call, she sent him a tape of love poems she had written and called *Love Tears*. She also told him she was in the tape-duplicating business. She found his calls were like therapy, and she began to tell him intimate things about herself, like the fact that she had been going to a professional matchmaker she had seen on television. "I was falling in love over the phone," she said. "You don't think someone's married when he calls you from home at night."

Eventually, he came to her house with two enormous bouquets.

"The minute I opened the door I was relieved," she said. "I wasn't attracted to him. He was shorter than me, blond, balding, with a round face." She told me she was attracted to men who looked like the actor Ken Wahl or Tom Cruise. Oziel was forty-two at the time. "He kept trying to get physical right away. I said 'Look, you're not my type. I'm not attracted to you.' He said he just wanted a hug. I said, 'Just because you know all this intimate stuff about me doesn't mean . . .'

"Finally I gave in. It was the worst sex I ever had in my life. To have good sex you either have to be in love or in lust. I wasn't either. It was also awful the second time. The third time was better. I broke off with him four or five times between September and October. Then Erik Menendez came."

Although Dr. Oziel had not seen any members of the Menendez family since Erik's counseling had ended, when news of the murders was announced in August 1989, according to Smyth, he became consumed with excitement at his proximity to the tragedy. "Right away, he called the boys and offered his help." At the time, the boys were hiding out in hotels, saying they thought the Mafia was after them. "Jerry would go to where the boys were. He was advising them about attorneys for the will, etc. He had an I'll-be-your-father attitude."

At the end of October, Smyth told me, Oziel got a call from Erik, who said he needed to talk with him. Erik came at four in the afternoon of Halloween, October 31, to the office at 435 North Bedford Drive. There is a small waiting room outside the office, with a table for magazines and several places to sit, but there is no receptionist. An arriving patient pushes a button with the name of the doctor he is there to see, and a light goes on in the inner office to let the doctor know that his next patient has arrived. Off the waiting room is a doorway that opens into a small inner hallway off which are three small offices. Oziel shares the space with several other doctors, one of them his wife, Dr. Laurel Oziel, the mother of his two daughters.

Once there, Erik did not want to talk in the office, so he and Oziel went for a walk. On the walk, according to Smyth, Erik confessed that he and his brother had killed their parents. Lyle, who was at the Elm Drive house at the time, did not know that Erik was seeing Oziel for that purpose. Lyle did not know either that Erik had apparently also confessed to his good friend Craig Cignarelli, with whom he had written the screenplay called *Friends*.

When Smyth arrived at the office, Erik and Oziel had returned from their walk and were in the inner office. According to Smyth, Oziel wanted Erik to tell Lyle that he had confessed to him. Erik did not want to do that. He said that he and Lyle were soon going to the Caribbean to get rid of the guns and that he would tell him then. The plan, according to Erik, Judalon Smyth told me, was to break down the guns, put them into suitcases, and dump the bags in the Caribbean. On the night of the murders, the boys had hidden the two shotguns in the trunk of one of their parents' cars in the garage. The police had searched only the cars in the courtyard in front of the house, not the cars in the garage. Subsequently, the boys had buried the guns on Mulholland Drive. Smyth says Dr. Oziel convinced Erik that the boys would certainly be caught if they were carrying guns in their luggage. He also persuaded him to call Lyle and ask him to come to the office immediately.

It took ten minutes for Lyle to get to the office from the house on Elm Drive. Smyth says he did not know before he got there that Erik had confessed. When he walked into the waiting room, he picked up a magazine and chatted briefly with Smyth, assuming that she was another patient. "Been waiting long?" he asked her. He also pushed the button to indicate to Oziel that he had arrived. Oziel came out and asked Lyle to come in.

According to the California Court of Appeals decision, Smyth says she listened through the door to the doctor's meeting with the boys and heard Lyle become furious with Erik for having confessed. She told me he made threats to Oziel that they were going to kill him. "I never thought I believed in evil, but when I heard those boys speak, I did," she said.

The particulars of the murders she is not allowed to discuss, because of an agreement with the Beverly Hills police, but occasionally, in our conversation, things would creep in. "They did go to the theater to buy the tickets," she said one time. Or, "The mother kept moving, which is why she was hit more." Or, "If they just killed the father, the mother would have inherited the money. So they had to kill her too." Or, "Lyle said he thought he committed the perfect murder, that his father would have had to congratulate him—for once, he couldn't put him down."

Judalon went on to say, and it is in the opinion of the California Court of Appeals, that she was frightened that she might be caught listening if the boys came out of the office. She went back to the waiting room. Almost immediately, the door opened. "Erik came running out, crying. Then Lyle and Jerry came out. At the elevator, I heard Jerry ask if Lyle was threatening him. Erik had already gone down. Lyle and Jerry followed." From a window in the office, Smyth could see Lyle and Oziel talking to Erik, who was in his Jeep on Bedford Drive.

According to Smyth, Erik knew, from his period of therapy with Oziel after the burglaries, where the doctor lived in Sherman Oaks, a suburb of Los Angeles in the San Fernando Valley. Fearing the boys might come after him, Oziel called his wife and told her to get the children and move out of the house. "Laurel and the kids went to stay with friends," said Smyth. Oziel then moved into Smyth's apartment, the ground floor of a two-family house in the Carthay Circle area of Los Angeles.

In the days that followed, Smyth told several people what she had heard. She has her own business, an audio-video duplicating service called Judalon Sound and Light, in the Fairfax section of Los Angeles. Behind her shop, in which she also sells crystals, quartz, and greeting cards, there is a small office which she rents to two friends, Bruce and Grant, who also have a video-duplicating service. As self-protection, she told them that the Menendez boys had killed their parents. She also told her mother and father and her best friend, Donna.

Then Oziel set up another meeting with the boys. He told them on the second visit that everything they had told him was taped. According to Smyth, the original confession, on October 31, was not taped. What was taped was Oziel's documentation of everything that happened in that session and subsequent sessions with the boys, giving times and dates, telling about the confession and the threat on his life, "a log of what was happening during the time his life was in danger." Smyth further contends that, as time went on, the relationship between the doctor and the boys grew more stable, and the doctor no longer felt threatened.

She said that Oziel convinced the boys "he was their only ally—that if they were arrested he would be their only ally. He was the only one who knew they were abused children, who knew how horrible their home life was, who knew that Jose was a monster father, who knew that Kitty was an abused wife. He convinced them that if they had any hope of ever getting off, they needed him."

Meanwhile, the personal relationship between Smyth and Oziel deteriorated. In a lawsuit filed in the Superior Court of the State of California by Judalon Rose Smyth against L. Jerome Oziel, Ph.D., on May 31, three months after the arrest of the Menendez brothers, it is charged that while Smyth was receiving psychiatric and psychological counseling from defendant Oziel he "improperly maintained Smyth on large doses of drugs and, during said time periods, manipulated and took advantage of Smyth, controlled Smyth, and limited Smyth's ability to care for herself . . . creating a belief in Smyth that she could not handle her affairs without the guidance of Oziel, and convincing

Smyth that no other therapist could provide the insight and benefit to her life that Oziel could." In the second cause of action in the suit, Smyth charges that on or about February 16, 1990, defendant Oziel "placed his hands around her throat attempting to choke her, and pulled her hair with great force. Subsequently, on the same day, Defendant Oziel forced Smyth to engage in an act of forcible and unconsented sexual intercourse." According to the California Court of Appeals decision, approximately three weeks after the alleged attack, Smyth contacted the police in Beverly Hills to inform them about the confession she said the Menendez brothers had made to Oziel.

Oziel's lawyer, Bradley Brunon, called Smyth's allegations "completely untrue," and characterized her behavior as "an unfortunate real-life enactment of the scenario in *Fatal Attraction*. . . . She has twisted reality to the point where it is unrecognizable."

"The boys are *adorable*. They're like two foundlings. You want to take them home with you," said the defense attorney Leslie Abramson, who has saved a dozen people from death row. She was talking about the Menendez brothers. Leslie Abramson is Erik's lawyer. Gerald Chaleff is Lyle's.

"Leslie will fight to the grave for her clients," I heard from reporters in Los Angeles who have followed her career. "When there is a murder rap, Leslie is the best in town."

Abramson and Chaleff have worked together before. "We're fifty-fifty, but she's in charge," Chaleff said in an interview. They like each other, and are friends in private life. Abramson met her present husband, Tim Rutten, an editorial writer for the *Los Angeles Times*, at a dinner party at Chaleff's home.

During the arraignment in the Beverly Hills courthouse, I was struck by the glamour of the young Menendez brothers, whom I was seeing face-to-face for the first time. They entered the courtroom, heads held high, like leading actors in a television series. They walked like colts. Their clothes, if not by Armani himself, were by a designer heavily influenced by Armani, probably purchased in the brief period of their independent affluence, between the murders and their arrest. Their demeanor seemed remarkably lighthearted for people in the kind of trouble they were in, as they smiled dimpled smiles and laughed at the steady stream of Abramson's jocular banter. Their two girlfriends, Jamie Pisarcik and Noelle Terelsky, were in the front row next to Erik's tennis coach, Mark Heffernan. Everyone waved. Maria Menendez, the loyal grandmother, was also in the front row, and aunts and uncles and a probate lawyer were in the same section of the courtroom. Several times the boys turned around and flashed smiles at their pretty girlfriends.

They were told to rise. The judge, Judith Stein, spoke in a lugubrious, knell-like voice. The brothers smiled, almost smirked, as she read the charges. "You have been charged with multiple murder for financial gain, while lying in wait, with a loaded firearm, for which, if convicted, you could receive the death penalty. How do you plead?"

"Not guilty, Your Honor," said Erik.

"Not guilty," said Lyle.

Later I asked a friend of theirs who believes in their innocence why they were smiling.

"At the judge's voice," she replied.

Leslie Abramson's curly blond hair bounces, Orphan Annie style, when she walks and talks. She is funny. She is fearless. And she is tough. Oh, is she tough. She walked down the entire corridor of the Beverly Hills courthouse giving the middle finger to an NBC cameraman. "This what you want? You want that?" she said with an angry sneer into the camera, thrusting the finger at the lens, a shot that appeared on the NBC special *Exposé*, narrated by Tom Brokaw. Her passion for the welfare of the accused murderers she defends is legendary. She is considered one of the most merciless cross-examiners in the legal business, with a remarkable ability to degrade and confuse prosecution witnesses. "She loves to intimidate people," I was told. "She thrives on it. She knows when she has you. She can twist and turn a witness's memory like no one else can." John Gregory Dunne, in his 1987 novel *The Red White and Blue*, based the character Leah Kaye, a left-leaning criminal-defense attorney, on Leslie Abramson.

"Why did you give the finger to the cameraman?" I asked her.

"I'll tell you why," she answered, bristling at the memory. "Because I was talking privately to a member of the Menendez family, and NBC turned the camera on, one inch from my face. I said, 'Take that fucker out of my face.' These people think they own the courthouse. They will go to any sleazoid end these days. So I said, 'Is this what you want?' That's when I gave them the finger. Imagine, Tom Brokaw on a show like that.

"I do not understand the publicity of the case," she continued, although of course she understood perfectly. "I mean, the president of the United States wasn't shot."

Before I could reply with such words as "patricide," "matricide," "wealth," "Beverly Hills," she had thought over what she had said. "Well, I rate murder cases different from the public." Most of her cases are from less swell circumstances. In the Bob's Big Boy case, the only death-penalty case she has ever lost, her clients herded nine employees and two customers into the restaurant's walk-in freezer and fired shotguns into their bodies at close range. Three died and four were maimed. One of those who lived had part of her brain removed. Another lost an eye.

"What's the mood of the boys?" I asked.

"I can't comment on my clients," she said. "All I can say is, they're among the very best clients I've ever had, as far as relating. Both of them. It's nonsense, all this talk that there's a good brother and a bad brother. Lyle is wonderful. They're both adorable."

In the avalanche of media blitz that followed the arrest of the Menendez brothers, no one close to Lyle and Erik was the object of more intense fascination and scrutiny than Craig Cignarelli, Erik's tennis partner, with whom he had written the screenplay *Friends*. A family spokesperson told me that in one day alone Craig Cignarelli received thirty-two calls from the media, including "one from Dan Rather, *A Current Affair, Hard Copy*, etc., etc. I can't remember them all. We had to hire an attorney to field calls." The spokesperson said that "from the beginning it was presumed that Craig knew something."

Craig, clearly enjoying his moments of stardom following the arrests of his best friend and best friend's brother, talked freely to the press and was, by all accounts of other friends of the brothers, too talkative by far. In articles by Ron Soble and John Johnson in the *Los Angeles Times*, Craig said he was attracted to Erik by a shared sense that they were special. He recalled how they would drive out to Malibu late at night, park on a hilltop overlooking the ocean, and talk about their hopes for the future, about how much smarter they were than everyone else, and about how to commit the perfect crime. They had nicknames for each other: Craig was "King," and Erik was "Shepherd." "People really looked up to us. We have an aura of superiority," he said.

As the months passed, it was whispered that Erik had confessed the murders to Craig. This was borne out to me by Judalon Smyth. But he confessed them in an elliptical manner, according to Smyth, in a suppose-it-happened-like-this way, as if planning another screenplay. It was further said that Craig told the police about the confession, but there were not the hard facts on which to make an arrest, such as came later from Judalon Smyth.

Craig's loquaciousness gave rise to many rumors about the two boys, as well as about the possibility that a second screenplay by them exists, one that parallels the murders even more closely. Craig has since been requested by the police not to speak to the press.

At one point, Cignarelli was presumed to be in danger because of what he knew, and was sent away by his family to a place known only to them. An ongoing story is that a relation of the Menendez brothers threatened Craig after hearing that he had gone to the police. The spokesperson for Craig wanted me to make it clear that, contrary to rumors, Craig "never approached the police. The police approached Craig. At a point Craig decided to tell them what he knew." When I asked this same spokesperson about the possibility of a second screenplay written by Craig and Erik, he said he had never seen one. He also said that the deputy district attorney, Elliott Alhadeff, was satisfied that all the information on the confession tapes was known to Craig, so in the event that the tapes were ruled inadmissible by the court he would be able to supply the information on the stand.

Sometime last January, two months before the arrests, the friendship between the two boys cooled. That may have been because Erik suspected that Craig had talked to the police.

Earlier that month, during a New Year's skiing vacation at Lake Tahoe, Erik had met and fallen in love with Noelle Terelsky, a pretty blond student at the University of California in Santa Barbara from Cincinnati. The romance was instantaneous. "Erik's not a hard guy to fall for," said a friend of Noelle. "He's very sweet, very sexy, has a great body, and is an all-around great guy." Noelle, together with Jamie Pisarcik, Lyle's girlfriend, visits the brothers in jail every day, and has been present at every court appearance of the brothers since their arrest. Until recently, when the house on Elm Drive was rented to the member of the Saudi royal family, the two girls lived in the guesthouse, as the guests of Maria Menendez, the proud and passionate grandmother of Lyle and Erik, who believes completely in the innocence of her grandsons. Maria Menendez, Noelle, and Jamie are now living in the Menendezes' Calabasas house, which has still not been sold.

Five months had passed since the arrest. Five months of hearings and deliberations to see whether the audiotapes of Dr. Jerome Oziel were admissible in the murder trial of Lyle and Erik Menendez. Police seizure of therapy tapes is rare, because ordinarily conversations between patients and therapists are secret. But there are occasional exceptions to the secrecy rule, one being that the therapist believes the patient is a serious threat to himself or others. Only the defense attorneys, who did not want the tapes to be heard, had been allowed to participate in the hearings. The prosecution, which did want them to be heard, was barred. Oziel had been on the stand in private hearings from which the family, the media, and the public were barred. Judalon Smyth had also been on the stand for two days in private sessions, being grilled by Leslie Abramson. The day of the decision had arrived.

There was great tension in the courtroom. Noelle and Jamie, the girlfriends, were there. And Maria, the grandmother. And an aunt from Miami. And a cousin. And the probate lawyer. And others.

Then the Menendez brothers walked in. The swagger, the smirks, the smiles were all gone. And the glamour. So were the Armani-type suits. Their ever-loyal grandmother had arrived with their clothes in suit bags, but the bags were returned to her by the bailiff. They appeared in V-necked, short-sleeved jailhouse blues with T-shirts underneath. Their tennis tans had long since faded. It was impossible not to notice the deterioration in the appearance of the boys, especially Erik. His eyes looked tormented, tortured, haunted. At his neck was a tiny gold cross. He nodded to Noelle Terelsky. He nodded to his grandmother. There were no smiles that day.

Leslie Abramson and Gerald Chaleff went to Judge James Albracht's chambers to hear his ruling on the admissibility of the tapes before it was read to the court. The brothers sat alone at the defense table, stripped of their support system. "Everybody's staring at us," said Erik to the bailiff in a pleading voice, as if the bailiff could do something about it, but there was nothing the bailiff could do. Everybody did stare at them. Lyle leaned forward and whispered something to his brother.

The fierce demeanor of Leslie Abramson when she returned to the courtroom left no doubt that the judge's ruling had not gone in favor of the defense. As the judge read his ruling to the crowded courtroom, Abramson, with her back to the judge, kept up a nonstop commentary in Erik Menendez's ear.

"I have ruled that none of the communications are privileged," said the judge. There was an audible sound of dismay from the Menendez family members. The tapes would be admissible. The judge found that psychologist Jerome Oziel had reasonable cause to believe that Lyle and Erik Menendez "constituted a threat, and it was necessary to disclose the communications to prevent a danger." There was no doubt that this was a serious setback to the defense.

Abramson and Chaleff immediately announced at a news conference that they would appeal the judge's ruling. Abramson called Oziel "a gossip, a liar, and less than credible." Neither Judalon Smyth's name nor her role in the proceedings was ever mentioned.

A mere eight days later, in a stunning reversal of Judge Albracht's ruling, the 2nd District Court of Appeals blocked the release of the tapes, to the undisguised delight of Abramson and Chaleff. Prosecutors were then given a date by which to file opposing arguments. Another complication occurred when Erik Menendez, from jail, refused to provide the prosecution with a handwriting sample to compare with the handwriting found on forms for the purchase of two shotguns in San Diego, despite a warning by the court that his refusal to do so could be used as evidence against him. In a further surprise, Deputy District Attorney Elliott Alhadeff, who won the original court ruling that the tapes would be admissible, was abruptly replaced on the notorious case by Deputy District Attorney Pamela Ferrero.

Since their arrest in March, Lyle and Erik Menendez have dwelt in the Los Angeles County Men's Central Jail, in the section reserved for prisoners awaiting trial in heavily publicized cases. The brothers' cells are not side by side. They order reading material from Book Soup, the trendy Sunset Strip bookshop. Erik has been sent *The Dead Zone*, by Stephen King, and a book on chess. They have frequent visits from family members, and talk with one friend almost daily by telephone. That friend told me that they have to pay for protection in jail. "Other prisoners, who are tough, hate them—who they are, what they've been accused of. They've been threatened." He also told me they feel they have lost every one of their friends. Late in August, when three razor blades were reportedly found in Erik's possession, he was put in solitary confinement, deprived of visitors, books except for the Bible, telephone calls, and exercise. That same week, Lyle suddenly shaved his head.

*

Los Angeles District Attorney Ira Reiner stated on television that one motive for the murders was greed. Certainly it is possible for a child to kill his parents for money, to wish to continue the easy life on easy street without the encumbrance of parental restrictions. But is it really possible for a child to kill, for merely financial gain, in the manner Kitty and Jose Menendez were killed? To blast holes into one's parents? To deface them? To obliterate them? In the fatal, *coup de grâce* shot, the barrel of one shotgun touched the cheek of Kitty Menendez. You wonder if her eyes met the eyes of her killer in the last second of her life. In this case, we have two children who allegedly participated in the killing of each parent, not in the heat of rage but in a carefully orchestrated scenario after a long gestation period. There is more than money involved here. There is a deep, deep hatred, a hatred that goes beyond hate.

The closest friend of the Menendez brothers, with whom I talked at length on the condition of anonymity, kept saying to me over and over, "It's only the tip of the iceberg." No amount of persuasion on my part could make him explain what the iceberg was. Months earlier, however, a person close to the situation mouthed but did not speak the word "incest" to me. Subsequently, a rich woman in Los Angeles told me that her bodyguard, a former cop, had heard from a friend of his on the Beverly Hills police force that Kitty Menendez had been shot in the vagina. At a Malibu barbecue, a film star said to me, "I heard the mother was shot up the wazoo." There is, however, no indication of such a penetration in the autopsy report, which carefully delineates each of the ten wounds from the nine shots fired into Kitty Menendez's body. But the subject continues to surface. Could it be possible that these boys were puppets of their father's dark side? "They had sexual hatred for their parents," one of the friends told me. This same person went on to say, "The tapes will show that Jose molested Lyle at a very young age."

Is this true? Only the boys know. If it is, it could be the defense argument that will return them to their tennis court, swimming pool, and chess set, as inheritors of a $14 million estate that they could not have inherited if they had been found guilty. Karen Lamm, however, does not believe such a story, although it is unlikely that Kitty would have revealed to her a secret of that dimension. Judalon Smyth was also skeptical of this information when I brought up the subject of sexual abuse. She said she had heard nothing of the kind on the Halloween afternoon when, according to the California Court of Appeals decision, she listened outside Dr. Oziel's office door as Lyle and Erik talked about the murders. She said that last December, almost two months after the October 31 confession to Oziel, which was not taped, the boys, feeling that the police were beginning to suspect them, voluntarily made a tape in which they confessed to the crime. In it, they spoke of their remorse. In it, apparently, they told of psychological abuse. But sexual abuse? Judalon Smyth did not hear this tape, and by that time Dr. Oziel was no longer confiding in her.

———

I became deeply and personally involved in this story. The trial went on for months. Erik and Lyle Menendez, the young killers, became romantic figures in the televised proceedings. In cases of high crime, I've never made any attempt to present a balanced picture. This was no exception. I was appalled by the lies I heard defense attorneys tell in the courtroom. I became despised by Leslie Abramson, the lead defense attorney. I couldn't have cared less. The trial ended in a hung jury, which was considered a victory for the defense. Their luck did not hold for the second trial. They are both doing life without the possibility of parole in separate prisons in California.

Justice, 2001

SOURCES AND ACKNOWLEDGMENTS

·

INDEX

Sources and Acknowledgments

Great care has been taken to locate and acknowledge all owners of copyrighted material included in this book. If any such owner has inadvertently been omitted, acknowledgment will gladly be made in future printings.

Anonymous, "An Account of the Murder Committed by Mr. J— Y—, Upon His Family": *The New York Weekly Magazine*, July 20, 1796, p. 20, and July 27, 1796, p. 28.

Anonymous, "Jesse Strang": *The Record of Crimes in the United States* (Buffalo: H. Faxon, 1834), pp. 202–13.

Anonymous, "Jesse Harding Pomeroy, the Boy Fiend": *Jesse Harding Pomeroy, the Boy Fiend* (Taunton, Massachusetts: Taunton Publishing Company, 1875).

Herbert Asbury, from *The Gangs of New York: The Gangs of New York* (New York: Knopf, 1928), pp. 272–87. Copyright © 1928 by Alfred A. Knopf, Inc. and renewed © 1956 by Herbert Asbury. Used by permission of Alfred A. Knopf, a division of Random House, Inc.

Alexander Beard, *see* Murder Ballads.

James Gordon Bennett, "The Recent Tragedy": *The New York Herald*, April 11, 1836.

Meyer Berger, "Veteran Kills 12 in Mad Rampage on Camden Street": *The New York Times*, September 7, 1949, p. 1. Copyright © 1949 The New York Times. All rights reserved. Used by permission and protected by the Copyright Laws of the United States. The printing, copying, redistribution, or retransmission of the Material without express written permission is prohibited.

Ambrose Bierce "Crime News from California": *The Ambrose Bierce Satanic Reader* (Garden City, New York: Doubleday & Company, Inc., 1968), pp. 51, 54, 55, 56, 59, 60, 62, 121, 125. Originally published separately in *San Francisco News Letter and California Advertiser*, December 26, 1868; February 13, 1869; June 4, 1870; December 3, 1870; August 6, 1870; January 20, 1872; *Argonaut*, April 28, 1877; July 20, 1878; January 26, 1878; December 21, 1878.

Robert Bloch, "The Shambles of Ed Gein": *The Quality of Murder*, Anthony Boucher, ed., (New York: E.P. Dutton & Co., 1962), pp. 13–19. Copyright © Robert Bloch. Published by permission of The Estate of Robert Bloch c/o Ralph M. Vicinanza, Ltd.

Albert Borowitz, "The Medea of Kew Gardens Hills": *The Lady Killers*, Jonathan Goodman, ed., (London: Piatkus, 1990), pp. 55–73. Copyright © 1991 by Albert Borowitz. Reprinted with permission of the author.

William Bradford, "The Hanging of John Billington": *History of the Plymouth Plantation* (Boston: Massachusetts Historical Society, 1856), pp. 276–77.

W. T. Brannon, "Eight Girls, All Pretty, All Nurses, All Slain": *True Detective Magazine*, October 1966, pp. 14–19, 62–66. Copyright © 1966 by W. T. Brannon.

Jimmy Breslin, "Son of Sam": *The Mammoth Book of Murder* (New York: Carroll & Graf, 1989), pp. 553–58. Originally published in a different form in *The New York Daily News*, June 5, 1977. Reprinted by permission of Sll/Sterling Lord Literistic, Inc. Copyright © 1977 by James Breslin.

Thomas Byrnes, "The Murder of Annie Downey": *Professional Criminals of America* (New York: Cassell, 1886), pp. 360–62.

Truman Capote, "Then It All Came Down": *Music for Chameleons* (New York: Random House, 1980), pp. 211–23. Copyright © 1975, 1977, 1979, 1980 by Truman Capote. Used by permission of Random House, Inc.

Miriam Allen deFord, "Superman's Crime: Loeb and Leopold": *Murderers Sane and Mad* (New York: Abelard-Schuman, 1965), pp. 149–68. Copyright © 1965 by Miriam Allen deFord.

Theodore Dreiser, "Dreiser Sees Error in Edwards Defense": *New York Post*, October 5, 1934. Copyright © 1934. Reprinted by permission of the Dreiser Trust.

Dominick Dunne, "Nightmare on Elm Drive": *Justice* (New York: Random House, 2001), pp. 83–113. Copyright © 2001 by Dominick Dunne. Used by permission of Crown Publishers, a division of Random House, Inc.

Thomas S. Duke, "Mrs. Cordelia Botkin, Murderess": *Celebrated Criminal Cases of America* (San Francisco: J. H. Barry, 1910), pp. 133–38.

Timothy Dwight, "A crime more atrocious and horrible than any other": *Travels in New-England and New-York* (New Haven: Timothy Dwight, 1821), Vol. 1, pp. 227–32.

James Ellroy, "My Mother's Killer": *Crime Wave* (New York: Vintage, 1999), pp. 49–62. Copyright © 1999 by James Ellroy. Used by permission of Vintage Books, a division of Random House, Inc.

Edna Ferber, "Miss Ferber Views 'Vultures' at Trial": *The New York Times*, January 28, 1935, p. 4. Copyright © 1935 The New York Times. All rights reserved. Used by permission and protected by the Copyright Laws of the United States. The printing, copying, redistribution, or retransmission of the Material without express written permission is prohibited.

Benjamin Franklin, "The Murder of a Daughter": *Silence Dogood, The Busy-Body, and Early Writings*, J. A. Leo Lemay, ed. (New York: The Library of America, 1987), pp. 233–34.

Susan Glaspell, "The Hossack Murder": *Des Moines Daily News*, December 3, 1900–April 19, 1901.

Elizabeth Hardwick, "The Life and Death of Caryl Chessman": *A View of My Own* (New York: Farrar, Straus & Cudahy, 1962), pp. 69–83. Originally published in *Partisan Review*, Summer 1960. Copyright © 1962 by The Elizabeth Hardwick Estate, reprinted with permission of The Wylie Agency, Inc.

Nathaniel Hawthorne, "A show of wax-figures": *The American Notebooks* (Columbus: Ohio State University Press, 1972), pp. 176–78. Copyright © 1932, 1960, 1972 by the Ohio State University Press. All Rights Reserved. Reprinted by permission of the publisher.

Lafcadio Hearn, "Gibbeted": *Cincinnati Commercial*, August 26, 1876.

Zora Neale Hurston, "The Trial of Ruby McCollum": William Bradford Huie, *Ruby McCollum: Woman in the Suwannee Jail* (New York: Dutton, 1956), pp. 89–101. Used with the permission of the Estate of Zora Neale Hurston.

Dorothy Kilgallen, "Sex and the All-American Boy": *Murder One* (New York: Random House, 1967), pp. 153–87. Copyright © 1967. Reprinted by permission.

A. J. Liebling, "The Case of the Scattered Dutchman": *The New Yorker*, September 24, 1955, pp. 50–111. Copyright © 1955 by A. J. Liebling, renewed in 1983 by Norma Liebling Stonehill. Originally published in *The New Yorker*. Reprinted by the permission of Russell & Volkening as agents for the author.

Abraham Lincoln, "Remarkable Case of Arrest for Murder": *Speeches and Writings 1832–1858*, Don E. Fehrenbacher, ed. (New York: Library of America, 1989), pp. 130–37. Reprinted from *The Collected Works of Abraham Lincoln*, Roy P. Basler, ed. (Brunswick, N.J.: Rutgers University Press, 1953–55). Copyright © 1953 by the Abraham Lincoln Association. Copyright © 1974 by Roy P. Basler. Reprinted by permission of Rutgers University Press.

José Martí, "The Trial of Guiteau": *José Martí: Selected Writings*, Esther Allen, ed. and trans. (New York: Penguin Classics, 2002), pp. 94–106. Spanish text originally published in *La Opinion Nacional* (Caracas), December 26, 1881. Edited and Translated by Esther Allen. Copyright © 2002. Used by permission of Viking Penguin, a division of Penguin Group (USA) Inc.

John Bartlow Martin, "Butcher's Dozen": *Butcher's Dozen & Other Murders* (New York: Harper & Bros., 1950), pp. 9–48. Copyright © 1949, 1976 John Bartlow Martin. Reprinted by permission of Harold Ober Associates Incorporated. First published in *Harper's*, November 1949.

Cotton Mather, "Pillars of Salt": *Pillars of Salt* (Boston: B. Green and J. Allen, 1699), pp. 59–110.

H. L. Mencken, "More and Better Psychopaths": *Baltimore Evening Sun,* December 3, 1934. Copyright © 1994 by the Estate of H. L. Mencken. Used by permission of Alfred A. Knopf, a division of Random House, Inc.

Joseph Mitchell, "Execution": *My Ears Are Bent* (New York: Pantheon Books, 2001), pp. 205–11. Originally published ca. 1934. Copyright © 1938, 2001, renewed 1966 by the estate of Joseph Mitchell. Reprinted by permission of the estate of Joseph Mitchell.

Don Moser, "The Pied Piper of Tucson": *Life*, March 4, 1966, pp. 18–24, 80–90. Copyright © 1967 by Donald B. Moser. Reprinted by permission of the author.

[Murder Ballads] Anonymous, "The Murder of Grace Brown"; "Belle Gunness"; "Trail's End": *American Murder Ballads and Their Stories*, Olive Woolley Burt, ed., (New York: Oxford University Press, 1958), pp. 32–4, 74, 212–14. Anonymous, "Poor Naomi"; "Stackalee": *American Poetry: The Nineteenth Century, Volume Two*, John Hollander, ed. (New York: Library of America), pp. 800–1, 809–12. "Poor Naomi" originally published in *The Patriot*, Greensboro, North Carolina, April 1874; "Stackalee" originally published in Sigmund Spaeth, *Weep Some More, My Lady* (New York: Doubleday, Page, 1927). Alexander B. Beard, "The Murder at Fall River": Broadside (West Manchester, New Hampshire: [Alexander B. Beard], n.d.).

Jay Robert Nash, "The Turner–Stampanato Killing: A Family Affair": *Murder Among the Mighty: Celebrity Slayings that Shocked America* (New York: Delacorte, 1983), pp. 136–54. Copyright © 1983 by Jay Robert Nash. Used by permission of Dell Publishing, a division of Random House, Inc.

Frank Norris, "Hunting Human Game": *Frank Norris of "The Wave"* (San Francisco: The Westgate Press, 1931), pp. 118–22. Originally published in *The Wave*, January 23, 1897.

Edmund Pearson, "Hell Benders, or The Story of a Wayside Tavern": *Murder at Smutty Nose and Other Murders* (New York: Doubleday, Doran & Co., 1926), pp. 263–90. Copyright © 1926 by Edmund Lester Pearson. Used by permission of Doubleday, a division of Random House, Inc.

Ann Rule, "Young Love": *Empty Promises* (New York: Pocket Books, 2000), pp. 245–64. Copyright © 2001 by Ann Rule. Reprinted with the permission of Pocket Books, a division of Simon & Schuster Adult Publishing Group.

Damon Runyon, "The Eternal Blonde": *Trials and Other Tribulations* (Philadelphia: J.B. Lippincott, 1947), pp.115–84. Reproduced by permission of American Rights Management Company, LLC. Damon Runyon (1884–1946) was a correspondent for the Hearst chain of papers in New York City. He complemented his journalism with plays, short stories, and poetry, and became one of the most recognizable voices of the Depression era. Penguin Classics published a collection of writings by Damon Runyon entitled *Guys and Dolls and Other Writings* with an Introduction by Pete Hamill and Notes by Daniel R. Schwarz in May 2008.

Gay Talese, "Charlie Manson's Home on the Range": *Esquire*, March 1970, pp. 101–02, 193–95. Copyright © 1970 by Gay Talese. Originally published in *Esquire* Magazine. Reprinted with permission of the author.

Celia Thaxter, "A Memorable Murder": *Atlantic Monthly*, May, 1875, pp. 602–15

Jim Thompson, "Ditch of Doom": *Master Detective*, April 1936, pp. 23–27, 78–81. Copyright © Jim Thompson. Reprinted by permission of the Richard Curtis Agency.

James Thurber, "A Sort of Genius": *My World—and Welcome To It* (New York: Harper & Bros., 1942), pp. 172–95. Originally published in *The New Yorker*, January 23, 1937. Copyright © 1957 by James Thurber, renewed © 1985 by Rosemary A. Thurber. Used by permission of Rosemary A. Thurber and the Barbara Hogenson Agency, Inc.

Calvin Trillin, "A Stranger with a Camera": *Killings* (New York: Ticknor & Fields, 1984), pp. 1–14. Copyright © 1969, 1984 by Calvin Trillin. Originally appeared in *The New Yorker*. Reprinted by permission of Lescher & Lescher, Ltd. All rights reserved.

Mark Twain, from *Roughing It: The Innocents Abroad & Roughing It*, Guy Cardwell, ed. (New York: Library of America, 1984), pp. 781–91. Originally published in 1872.

Jack Webb, "The Black Dahlia": *The Badge* (New York: Thunder's Mouth Press, 2005), pp. 22–35. Copyright © 1958 by Mark VII Ltd. Reprinted by permission of Da Capo/ Thunder's Mouth, a member of Perseus Books Group.

Alexander Woollcott, "The Mystery of the Hansom Cab": *While Rome Burns* (New York: Viking Press, 1934), pp. 243–50. Copyright © 1943 by Alexander Woollcott, renewed © 1962 by Joseph P. Hennessey. Used by permission of Viking Penguin, a division of Penguin Group (USA) Inc.

Index

050032086